Real Estate Finance

Real Estate Finance

HENRY E. HOAGLAND, Ph.D.
Professor Emeritus of Business Finance
College of Administrative Science
The Ohio State University
Former Member, Federal Home Loan Bank Board

LEO D. STONE, J.D., M.B.A.
University of South Florida, St. Petersburg
Professor Emeritus of Business Finance
The Ohio State University
Member of the Ohio Bar

Fifth Edition
1973

RICHARD D. IRWIN, INC.
Homewood, Illinois   60430
Irwin-Dorsey International, London, England   WC2H 9NJ
Irwin-Dorsey Limited, Georgetown, Ontario   L7G 4B3

© RICHARD D. IRWIN, INC., 1954, 1961, 1965, 1969, and 1973

All rights reserved. No part of this publication may be reproduced, stored in a retrieval system, or transmitted, in any form or by any means, electronic, mechanical, photocopying, recording, or otherwise, without the prior written permission of the publisher.

Fifth Edition

First Printing, January 1973
Second Printing, July 1973
Third Printing, December 1973
Fourth Printing, April 1974
Fifth Printing, November 1974
Sixth Printing, May 1975

ISBN 0-256-01391-8
Library of Congress Catalog Card No. 72-86626

Printed in the United States of America

Preface

The dynamic changes in policies, techniques, and institutional patterns in real estate finance during the late 1960s and early 1970s have made another revision of this book necessary. The recent historically high interest rates sent shock waves throughout the institutional structures and management, causing new attitudes toward old policies. This was particularly noteworthy in the areas of interest rates and equity participations, development of secondary markets, and deeper involvement of the federal government in subsidized housing, particularly for persons with low and moderate incomes. These trends have occasioned new consideration of variable interest rates, arrangements whereby equity participations are granted institutional providers of funds, privatization of the Federal National Mortgage Association and its move toward establishing a secondary market for conventional mortgages, establishment of tandem relationships between the Federal National Mortgage Association and the Government National Mortgage Association, and the launching of the Federal Home Loan Mortgage Corporation as an auxiliary agency in the secondary market. Scarcities of funds in thrift institutions, brought on by extensive disintermediation by the public, encouraged extensive growth of real estate investment trusts and new forms of syndications as additional means of public participation in real estate finance. These trends are taken into account, and the development and characteristics of the new business forms are discussed in this edition.

The organization of the book has not been changed from previous editions. After several early chapters devoted to basic legal concepts, each of the major institutional sources of funds is considered in turn. The procedures and problems of originating and servicing loans, including appraisal and title analysis, are then discussed. Special chapters are devoted to subdivision and development projects and recent trends in the secondary mortgage markets. The final chapters describe and seek to put in order the expanding roles of the federal government in its various approaches to assistance in the financing of real estate.

This edition is designed for both students and professionals. Its goal is to provide not only a basic orientation in commonly used instruments and institutional structures and policies, but also a deeper understanding of the many interrelationships involved in accomplishing the real estate financing functions.

December 1972 HENRY E. HOAGLAND
LEO D. STONE

Contents

1. Introduction 1
2. Legal Nature of Real Estate Mortgages 16
3. Kinds of Mortgages 34
4. Mortgage Default and Its Consequences 55
5. Mortgage Adjustments 74
6. Junior Liens 90
7. Real Estate Bonds, Investment Trusts, and Cooperatives 109
8. Land Contracts 129
9. Financing Long-Term Leases 145
10. Purchase and Leaseback 161
11. Savings and Loan Associations 178
12. Savings and Loan Associations (continued) 199
13. Financing of Real Estate by Banks 217
14. Financing of Real Estate by Life Insurance Companies 240
15. Mortgage Banking 257
16. Miscellaneous Sources of Real Estate Finance 282
17. Loan Applications 310
18. Appraisal for Financing Purposes 330
19. Title Analysis for Financing Purposes 349
20. Mortgage Loan Servicing 371

viii   Contents

21. Financing Subdivisions and Development Projects 393
22. Financing Farms and Rural Development 420
23. Federal Home Loan Bank System 438
24. Affiliates of Federal Home Loan Bank System 456
25. Federal Housing Administration 475
26. Financing Homes for Veterans 503
27. Secondary Mortgage Markets 520
28. The Federal National Mortgage Association and the Government National Mortgage Association 534
29. Government Financing of Real Estate 552
Selected References 581
Index 591

1

Introduction

Place of Real Estate in Our Economy Various terms are used to describe our economic system in comparing it with contemporary systems throughout the world. We speak of our "capitalistic system," "free enterprise," "economic democracy," "machine age," and so forth. It would not be inappropriate to call ours a "real estate" economy, since the uses of real estate are so pervasive as to play a major role in most of our economic plans. "Real estate" has different meanings under different kinds of governmental control. In this text we shall be concerned with American real estate and its connotations. Primarily we shall confine our discussions to the methods commonly used to finance the variety of real estate uses required to maintain the kind of economy we have chosen to foster. As the pattern of our economy is modified, so also must our methods of financing real property be changed. For reasons that will be evident as the material of this text unfolds, the rigidities of real estate finance resist innovations. Nevertheless, these rigidities eventually respond to pressures, and changes are brought about.

Real estate finance looms large in the pattern of our economy. We have reached the astounding total of over $450 billion in real estate mortgages in this country. This means that the savings of millions of people have made possible the use of these accumulated funds for the purchase and construction of the many kinds of real estate needed for an expanding economy. The millions of users of these funds are enabled to enjoy standards of living higher than would have been possible without this assistance. Our accomplishments to date are noteworthy. Future progress demands that encouragement both to thrift and to the economical use of its fruits should be continued.

Real Estate and Private Enterprise Ownership of real estate has always been one of the strongest bulwarks of private enterprise. It is significant that, in the countries which have fallen under Communist rule, communization of farms and owner-occupied homes has been among the last changes made by those in political and economic control. Ownership of homes and other real estate is a natural concomitant of political democracy. Individual freedom, private enterprise, and home-ownership are parts of the same whole. Where one is lost, the other two are likely to disappear soon afterward.

That is why in America, where we still believe in the virtue of the freedom of the individual to make his own choices, and where we still adhere to the doctrine that private enterprise is better than collective control of all economic decisions, belief in homeownership, including farm ownership by those who manage and work our farms, is still strong. Collective farms and government ownership of housing facilities would weaken our faith in individual freedom and sap the vitality of our private enterprise system.

Influence of Government This does not mean that the government has played no part in our plans concerning real estate ownership. A volume could be written on the influence of government upon real estate ownership and finance in this country. In the early days the cost of government was saddled largely upon those who owned real estate. At that time ownership of land and its improvements was the one common denominator of the ability to pay taxes. Wealth was measured in acres. Today we pass laws and constitutional amendments limiting the amount of taxes that can be levied against real estate. We substitute a whole series of taxes on income, purchases, luxuries, excises, and so forth, thereby lifting some of the burden from real estate.

Much of early police protection was provided to prevent damage to property—real property. While a part of the time of law enforcement officers is now devoted to the protection of persons, this is in the nature of an addition to, rather than a substitute for, the earlier protection of property. In the early days governmental agencies took the desirability of real estate ownership for granted but, true to the laissez-faire origin of our public attitude toward private affairs, did little directly to foster it. They never did anything to discourage such ownership, however. Today we have a whole series of bureaus and agencies organized for the express purpose of assisting our citizens to own real estate. Some of these are discussed in later chapters of this text. It should be pointed out, however, that not all of the recent legislation in this field was written to foster private ownership. Some of it places the emphasis upon government contributions instead of upon individual responsibility. All legislation of this sort in recent years does have as one of its objectives greater stability of real estate values, even though the paths followed do not always lead in that direction.

Roots in the Soil A few generations ago most Americans were dependent upon the tilling of the soil for a livelihood. Its response in the form of bountiful harvests seems to have endeared us to the land in a manner hard to alter. This inherently favorable attitude toward land and its productivity is easily carried over into a belief in the productivity of urban land—productive, that is, in profits from its ownership. Even persons without experience in land ownership or without successful investment experience of any kind have less hesitancy in making a commitment for the purchase of real estate than for any other comparable venture. We may recognize our inability to judge the investment quality of stocks and bonds. This does not stop us from passing judgment upon the value of a parcel of real estate. We feel closer to the land than to less familiar competitive investment opportunities.

Search for Security The tangible nature of real estate has always had a strong appeal for many people. Some go so far as to say that real estate is the only safe kind of investment, because it possesses the quality of tangibility. The number of such people is decreasing, although recent fears for stability in our monetary unit have caused a resurgence of this attitude. Uncertainties tend to increase the number of people who search for security. The concept of home has generally been associated in our thinking with proper regard for family welfare because, in the home, each member is interested in protecting the welfare of the others. Since we associate family solidarity with the real estate that houses it, we come to think of real estate and home as more or less synonymous.

Pay While You Use One of the beckoning causes of our faith in real estate ownership, particularly of residential property, is the not too well-analyzed belief that real estate will pay for itself. "Why buy rent receipts when the same money will pay for a home?" has been a slogan that has helped to induce the purchase of many houses. This carries an implication that many landlords would like to see realized. Investment in rental property, and particularly in single houses, is not always the source of great profit that is sometimes pictured. Nevertheless, the common feeling that the landlord takes an undue share of the tenant's income has resulted in a great many shifts from tenant status to owner status.

Even though there is not always a clear understanding about the comparative costs of tenancy versus ownership, this does not mean that the change of status is undesirable. In addition to the nonfinancial advantages of home ownership, the purchase of a home is one means of inducing savings where none might be present otherwise. Once a purchaser has made a commitment to buy a home, he will sacrifice some luxuries and even some conveniences, if necessary, to keep up his payments on his mortgage. As a result, the argument of rent receipts versus home purchase becomes more or less academic. A frugal and industrious family can pay for a home while it is being used.

Long-Term Value Trends Every period of depression leaves in its wake broken hopes and wrecked fortunes. Real estate commitments do not escape such catastrophes. At such times we question such slogans as "Buy land in a growing city and it will make you wealthy." In spite of the evidence to the contrary, those who really own the land and are able to carry it, come what may, will find that, disregarding temporary market fluctuations, long-term value trends tend to slant upward for many parcels of real estate.

The real estate inflation that followed the close of World War II carried prices of many individual properties to a level at least twice as high as a decade earlier. This is the comparison most of us remember. How did the prices of 1940 compare with those of a generation earlier? And with those of a generation before that? Compare the values of modest single houses of a century ago with those of any prolonged period since, and be prepared to marvel at the general upward trend.

Visitors to the street of magnificent old homes in Salem, Massachusetts, built many years ago for the sea captains of the day, wonder at the evidence of great wealth possessed by those who owned such substantial and beautiful homes. As a matter of fact, the owners of those homes were not wealthy if measured by today's standards. The reason they could afford to own houses that would cost, if reproduced today, $75,000 to $100,000 or more each was that the cost of them was only a few thousand dollars—a fraction of today's prices. In general, values in terms of dollars have trended upward since the early days of our republic. This fact helps to account for the interest of today's generation in real estate ownership.

Outlet for Savings In the purchase of residential property the owner-occupant accomplishes a double purpose. In the first place, he acquires a home for his family. The financing presumably will be arranged in such a manner that the purchaser can pay off the mortgage from income. With the liquidation of his mortgage as a goal, he now has a second purpose—an outlet for his savings that will be safe and will afford a reasonable return. If the mortgage is modern in its terms, it will probably permit prepayments at the option of the mortgagor. By taking advantage of this option, the mortgagor will have an outlet for his savings that is safe and that will pay more than a competitive investment return. Under the most favorable circumstances, barring a substantial windfall, the mortgagor will find need for all his savings for several years to pay off his mortgage.

Rapid Growth of Cities As soon as urbanization of America started, pressure came for housing accommodations to provide for the needs of rapidly growing cities. Pioneers had literally hewn their homes out of virgin forest trees, with the help of neighbors at house-raising time. Urban dwellers who made their living from pursuits which city life fostered had neither the time, the skill, nor the facilities to enable them to follow in the footsteps of their rural cousins. Neither had they accumulated the capital required to buy a home unencumbered with a mortgage. They needed assistance from those with money to invest.

While real estate owners in rural areas are also users of borrowed money, the concentration of real estate finance in urban areas is well recognized. The ownership of farms combines real estate finance and business finance in a manner not paralleled in manufacturing and merchandising enterprises. While it is true that real estate is used in the latter categories, its financing is frequently separated from the financing of general business operations. In farming, real estate is almost synonymous with land utilization. While a chapter of this text will be devoted to farm finance, for the most part this book deals with the problems of financing urban real estate.

Shifting Urban Population As a result of reports of the 1970 federal census of population, in city after city, protests have been made that the enumeration was incomplete or defective. It failed to show expected gains in population during the past decade. In some cases it showed a loss instead of any gain. Hence, the disappointment of the city fathers was followed by a demand for a recount. Such demands are not new. They have followed every report of a population census in recent decades. The protests are becoming louder and more numerous. More cities are feeling the effects of shifting urban populations.

What is happening is not very mysterious. Populations of corporate cities are overflowing into the fringe areas surrounding them. To get away from the disagreeableness of congested central cities, the urban sprawl is taking families into the suburbs. Trade follows the shift of residential uses, with even department stores and financial institutions establishing branches in the new population centers. The population census of metropolitan cities—including the satellite suburbs—shows substantial increases in some cases where the corporate cities record decreases.

The real estate implications of this shifting urban population are serious and far reaching. Since it is man's interest in land that gives it value, his loss of or decline in interest will inevitably be followed by a decline in the values of property in the area that is being deserted. In the meantime, values will increase in the areas where more people are showing added interest. While shifting populations cannot take their real estate into the suburbs, they can take much of its value with them and add it to that of the area that benefits from the shift.

Managers of institutions that finance real estate must be alert to shifts in population within their lending areas. Unless proper forecasts are made, both for the area that is suffering from such shifts and for the one that benefits, loans in the older areas may become more hazardous. Meanwhile, opportunities for better loans in the newer areas may be bypassed. If the management is sufficiently aware of what is happening, it can act in such a manner as to protect itself on both counts. Population shifts normally take place gradually. They are not rapid enough to jeopardize good loans already on the books. New loans should be made with greater caution in the declining areas and with greater boldness in those enjoying sound growth. It is necessary for the lending institution to make the right forecasts. This is not always easy.

If recoveries in values of real estate occur in declining areas, they are likely to be brought about under only two sets of circumstances: (1) The decline must run its course to the point where the values of obsolete buildings approach the vanishing point, so that there is an inducement for land speculators to demolish them in order to make way for a higher and better use of the land. (2) The recovery must be on a broad scale. Piecemeal rebuilding of an obsolete section involves too great a risk to invite the type of investment needed for a successful face-lifting operation. Stuyvesant Town and Peter Cooper Village in mid-Manhattan, New York, and Lake Meadows in Chicago are examples of what can be done privately on a broad scale. For the last two decades, of course, federal assistance through urban renewal has implemented broad scale recovery of values in declining areas in many cities.

What Constitutes Real Property In spite of the care that has been exercised to distinguish real property from chattels, there is still a foggy twilight zone separating the two. Because of this, some mortgages specifically mention those items about which there may be dispute. For example, a commonly used mortgage form provides that, in addition to the legal description of the real property as taken from the records, it shall include "all heating, plumbing, and lighting fixtures and equipment now or hereafter attached to or used in connection with the said premises." Whether the phrase "or used in connection with" would always be interpreted by courts to describe a real estate interest is not at issue in this discussion. The fact that the mortgage form includes it is evidence of the uncertain character of the law of fixtures. Instead of mentioning fixtures as such, the mortgagee undertakes to spell out just what fixtures he has in mind.

Confusion of Physical and Economic Qualities of Land In much of our thinking about real estate finance, we are inclined to confuse the physical with the economic characteristics of land. We think of the immobility and the indestructibility of land and draw conclusions that are frequently unwarranted. For example, land and the improvements thereon have relatively long lives. Translating this fact into economic terms, are we justified in concluding that the value of land and its improvements will necessarily continue throughout their physical lives? Deep-seated longings tend to color our concepts about economic affairs. Most Americans have a desire to own land—to acquire a possessive relationship with Mother Earth.

Then, too, we are acquainted with instances of real estate values that, over the years, have risen to fantastic heights. While it is true that monopolistic sites command very high prices, we are inclined to overlook the fact that it is not the physical characteristics of the site that give it value. Other sites within a stone's throw of the one commanding the highest price possess the same physical qualities. Yet, in the absence of essential nonphysical relationships, their prices amount to only a fraction of that paid for the one at the top of the list. Occasionally a site increases very rapidly in value when a new use is found for it. Yet its physical characteristics have not changed.

Dependence upon Credit Ours is a credit economy. The breadth and depth of business operations that we commonly enjoy would be unthinkable on a cash-and-carry basis. Credit is a prominent member of a whole family of "Cs" which play a major part in our economic progress. It provides capital for those in the best position to use it. If everybody owned outright all of the resources for which there is any need, there would be no occasion for credit. But since the owners are frequently not the users of these resources, credit is the vehicle by which they are transported from those who contribute to the production process through their ownership of capital to those who direct its use.

Credit is based upon confidence. Legal formalities used to establish contractual relationships, including the provision of security for loans, are merely the machinery needed to implement the operation of confidence in established contracts. On occasion the mechanisms are present without modification and still no credit is granted, because there is no confidence in the repayment capacities of the borrower. On other occasions much more informality characterizes the use of credit, because confidence is abundantly evident.

The use of credit requires courage. The borrower must possess the courage of his convictions about his future plans. He not only has thought out a program which requires credit for its execution, but he has the courage required to enable him to assume the obligations which credit instruments place upon him. Credit is used primarily for the purpose of making life more worthwhile for the consumer. The end of all production and distribution processes is the consumption of the products and services of industry by those to whom they are made available.

Dependence upon Borrowed Capital In the financing of real estate there is frequently greater dependence upon borrowed capital than upon equity funds. Railroads make generous use of bonds in their financial plans. Except for equipment trust certificates, most of the fixed charge securities issued by railroad corporations are real estate bonds. The same is true of other business enterprises that are common borrowers of long-term capital funds. At the other end of the line, merchandisers who own no real estate seldom issue bonds. Their borrowings are for short terms and may be classed as inventory loans. If they own the buildings in which they operate, they are commonly issuers of real estate bonds with the land and buildings as security.

Except for borrowed capital available to purchasers of residential property, markets for residential real estate would not be as active as they normally are. Both from the standpoint of demand for mortgage financing and from that of the supply of funds available for this purpose, high percentage loans have become the standard pattern in the construction and sale of residential real estate. This is true in spite of past experiences, still green in the memory of many adults, which were not pleasant for either borrower or lender. How much of real estate finance can be said to be based upon a calculated risk and how much upon less easily measured considerations, no one knows. Both play major parts in mortgage finance.

Nature of Real Estate Credit Real estate credit is used to serve all elements in our economy. Loans to producers are used to buy sites for factory buildings and to create structures thereon. Advances to merchandisers sometimes perform similar functions. Loans on residential property may represent either consumer credit, producer credit, speculative credit, or investment credit, depending upon the circumstances surrounding each particular case. The land developer who uses a mortgage to finance the purchase at wholesale of land which he hopes to sell at retail, and the building contractor who uses a construction loan to finance his operations, are using producer credit. The person who buys an apartment house encumbered by a mortgage, with the expectation that he will be able to trade on his equity and make a correspondingly larger profit when he sells his property, thinks in terms of speculative credit. If, on the other hand, he plans to keep the property indefinitely for its income return, he thinks of credit as an investment instrument.

The owner of a single residence which he occupies as his home is using consumer credit. By the use of a mortgage he is enabled to occupy the property while he is paying for it. Without mortgage financing his ownership would be either postponed indefinitely or denied him altogether. It should be emphasized that the home is a durable consumer good. "Durable" implies long life but not perpetual life. The homeowner who acquires the property through the use of an amortized mortgage absorbs his debt in installments from his future income. While he is absorbing his debt, he is gradually consuming the value of the improvements on his land. Unless he receives satisfaction from the amenities of being a property owner, it is not always clear that he should assume the responsibilities that accompany homeownership. From a purely financial point of view, homeownership may not always be advantageous.

Large Amounts Involved In general, real estate credit, even that involved in the financing of a single residence, requires greater single commitments than any other form of credit. This results in a reversal of trends in certain other business transactions. A merchandiser who owns his business extends credit in relatively small amounts to a large number of his customers. The debtor who obligates himself to finance a real estate purchase requires an amount that usually represents the savings of many people. For that reason the majority of real estate financial arrangements are funneled through financial institutions which, in one form or another, collect the investable surpluses of large numbers of people and disburse them in relatively large amounts to a smaller group of borrowers. Over the years these investors may accumulate sizable credits to their accounts. But at any given time numerous investors are required to contribute the amounts needed to finance in one lump sum the commitment of a single real estate borrower. A discussion of these financial institutions and the services they render to real estate finance is an integral part of this study.

In thinking of such institutions, one basic idea must be kept in mind. There would be no need for them if there were not thrifty people who spend less than they earn. At the foundation of all credit arrangements is the need for accumulation by somebody of the funds required to finance the hopes and ambitions of somebody else. Should all of us completely abandon thrifty habits, credit institutions will no longer be needed, and the services in which they deal will no longer be supplied.

Determinants of Real Estate Prices During the 1950s and through the mid-1960s, the American economy received two important stimuli that caused a major expansion in residential construction. There was the pent-up demand occasioned by the severe housing shortage, negligible production of new housing units during the war years, and the rapid growth of population. Second, and equally important, was the phenomenal ease of credit available at low rates through the new institutional lending patterns. These conditions unleashed an unprecedented purchasing power for new housing.

In spite of complicating factors affecting real estate markets, the law of supply and demand still plays an important part in determining real estate prices. At any given time, the number of units of improved real estate in any locality is relatively fixed. They cannot be increased quickly and are not normally decreased overnight. As a result, any sudden increase in demand—such as that which occurred at the end of World War II—is immediately reflected in an increase in price.

One of the major factors which result in an expansion or contraction in demand for real estate is the level of incomes available for housing purposes. During the depression of the 1930s, without any reduction in the number of families there was a marked decline in the demand for real estate; people could no longer pay the rents demanded or the carrying charges on real estate owned. Again in the late 1960s and early 1970s, with skyrocketing construction costs to builders and prohibitive financing costs to potential buyers, the market languished. Here we have vivid examples of the elastic nature of real estate demand. These conditions have a marked effect on real estate prices, as well as on the supply of new housing units brought into the market.

It must be recognized that in many instances the total price asked is only one of the factors that determine the sale. Equally important and frequently more determining are the amounts of the down payment required and of the monthly carrying charges. Liberal loans and low monthly payments encourage real estate prices to remain high. When a fixed supply, an increase in demand, and liberal financing such as that provided by the GI program are concurrent, the effects upon the price structure are not difficult to forecast.

An additional important development should also be mentioned. Financing sources established by the federal government have added to those funds provided by individual savers, directly or through institutional channels, for use in the mortgage market. Direct Treasury financing, the Federal National Mortgage Association, and the Federal Home Loan Banks are powerful tools. By January 1, 1971, the Federal National Mortgage Association held over $15.5 billion of mortgage debt. At the same time, the Federal Home Loan Banks showed outstanding advances to members of $10.6 billion.

Effects of Mortgage on Price The effect of a mortgage upon price depends upon the term and the rate of interest on the mortgage. For example, a $10,000 loan at 8 percent interest, amortized over a period of 30 years, would cost the borrower as much as a $15,300 loan for the same period of time at only 4 percent interest. In other words, the purchaser of the property could afford to pay $5,300 more for the property financed with the 4 percent loan. If the period of amortization is reduced to 10 years, the cost to the borrower of a $10,000 loan at 8 percent interest would be about the same as that of a $12,100 loan financed at 4 percent interest. From the standpoint of total cost only, the purchaser could afford to pay $2,100 more for the property financed with the 4 percent mortgage.

Traditions of Real Estate Finance The many uses of credit in our economy have become so commonplace that we take them for granted. Historically speaking, most of these uses are of recent origin. All of them stem from the original application of credit to real estate. As the earliest form of wealth which was tangible and presumably fixed in nature, real estate was used as security for loans long before debenture bonds and consumer credit for the purchase of many items were dreamed of. Our earliest records of moneylending practices tell of what we now recognize as mortgage security. From the experiences of borrowers and lenders in this field of activity, other forms of credit have evolved.

Because of the long history of real estate loans, traditions have developed which govern the nature of business and legal forms surrounding transactions in this area. For the most part these traditions are merely crystallized experiences. So long as governing conditions remained static or approximately so, this pragmatic approach proved quite satisfactory. But under a new and different set of circumstances, it may become hard to live with traditions. Breaking such traditions is not easy, but it sometimes becomes necessary. Throughout this text we shall encounter illustrations of attempts to do so and shall try to evaluate the results.

Compensation for Risk During the 1930s and through the mid-1940s there was a distinct decline in the level of interest rates on real estate mortgages. Up to the depression of the 1930s, interest rates were at a high level and were governed in part by geography. In the newer, less stable sections of the country, mortgage interest rates were much higher than in the older sections. Although each loan was expected to stand on its own feet, the influence of geography was distinctly felt. The rate on any particular loan was governed in part by the estimate of the amount of risk involved and in part by the locality in which the property was situated.

Over the period from the early 1930s to the end of World War II, interest rates of mortgage loans became national in scope and attained a high degree of standardization at a much lower level than formerly prevailed. The general decline in the level of interest rates was due to several causes, among which were the decline in the value of the dollar and the shifting of much of the risk from the lender to a governmental agency. The standardization of interest rates regardless of geography was due largely to the influence of various governmental activities which will be discussed in this text.

The standardization of interest rates and their general decline were reflected not only in loans for which a governmental agency assumed a part of the risk, but in other loans as well. Insured and guaranteed loans were in competition with those not enjoying this advantage. If the latter were to be made, their lenders had to keep one eye upon the nature of the competition offered in the same market for the same type of loan and possessing the element of guarantee or insurance.

Financing Trends since World War II The restoration of vitality to the economy after the termination of World War II had a salutary effect on interest rates. Investment demand for funds ran ahead of savings supply, and, except for brief remissions in 1954 and 1958, interest rates rose consistently. Repeatedly during the last few years the byword of builders and home buyers alike has been "tight money." The trend of effective interest rates in the money markets has often placed those rates above the maxima allowed by federal mortgage insurance and guarantee programs, and hence has limited the effectiveness of federal financial aids.

Along with higher money costs, the strong demand has brought about higher site and building costs. Land costs have doubled and tripled. Residential construction costs have risen more sharply than either wholesale or consumers' price indexes since the 1947–49 base period through 1971.

During the early 1960s, the very magnitude of the real estate mortgage market focused the attention of institutions on problems inherent in its size and distribution.[1] Above all, geographical restrictions on mortgage lending began to distort sound growth of financial institutions subject to such restrictions. The institutions reacted to this condition by seeking broader authority and better facilities for making extraterritorial loans. FHA and VA financing became relatively less important as conventional mortgages were used with increasingly liberal terms, particularly in loan-to-value ratios. There was a concomitant increase in foreclosures, although it has not been considered dangerous by normal standards. A huge volume of mortgage credit is being extended for financing and refinancing existing real estate to derive funds for other uses, suggesting greater permanency to the present mortgage debt than was previously supposed. The implications of this nullification of the benefits of amortization must be taken into account.

Changing Patterns of Real Estate Finance Some patterns of real estate finance have stood the test of time for generations. They change but little over the years. Others maintain the basic character with which they started, but their details are modified from time to time. Still others ebb and flow with changing economic and financial conditions. In the latter group, a few interesting illustrations come to mind. Real estate bonds, as generally used during the 1920s, have almost disappeared as a means of financing new buildings. One good reason for their disappearance was the absence of new office and apartment buildings to be financed. As construction of new office buildings and apartment developments again became important in the late 1950s, direct institutional mortgage financing was available, particularly from life insurance companies. Should this source fail to meet the need, the former pattern of use of real estate bonds may experience a revival.

---

[1] Edward S. Edwards, "Changing Character of the Real Estate Mortgage Markets," *The Journal of Finance*, Vol. XIX, No. 2 (May 1964), Part I, pp. 313–20.

Second mortgages on residential properties always represented a hidden dagger ready to be thrust into the back of an unwary purchaser of a modest home as soon as he failed to meet the requirements of his contract. With high percentage loans common during recent years, there has been little need for second mortgages. Inflated prices in the postwar years invited the first common use of second mortgages in a couple of decades. Recently, even third liens have been used to some extent, and their sale to investors has been a matter of considerable concern to both the state securities commissions and the U.S. Securities and Exchange Commission.

Within the last two or three years some very fundamental changes have taken place. Notably, there have been the development of the Federal National Mortgage Association auction system, the rise of mortgage-backed securities guaranteed by the Government National Mortgage Association, progress in the design of a standard mortgage instrument to facilitate the operation of a true secondary market for mortgages conventionally originated, and the emergence of the real estate investment trusts. These and other changes in methods of financing real estate will be discussed in succeeding chapters.

Real Estate Financial Ills We are so accustomed to thinking of real estate as very different from other articles of value that we place it in a class by itself when we consider business problems. We even go further and consider that each parcel of real estate is unique—different from every other parcel in one or more important particulars. Finally, we are prone to endow real estate with a personality that more or less cuts it off from its owner and from his financial problems. Perhaps we would progress more rapidly in our understanding of real estate finance if we would look for those elements which it enjoys in common with other business operations. At least we can admit that the disagreeable word "failure" which plagues business managers in other lines of economic activity is unfortunately not unknown in real estate finance.

Some of the conditions which result in real estate financial ills are as follows: (1) Overoptimism may entice commitments not warranted by sober second thought. This afflicts not only mortgagors but mortgagees as well. (2) A poor financial plan may demand interest rates that are too high, an amortization program that is too exacting, and so forth. (3) There is a lack of the financial reserves needed to tide the borrower over a temporary period when expected income is not realized. (4) Shoestring financing, comparable to thin margins on stock speculation, has been used. Even a slight shock may cause the financial structure to collapse. (5) Inexperience, dishonesty, and carelessness on the part of the management are causes of failure.

In attempting to diagnose real estate financial ills, several possibilities come to mind. Some of these ills exhibit the characteristics of a sudden attack of indigestion that may be corrected easily. If these attacks become chronic, however, the simple remedy that cures a single attack may cease to relieve subsequent recurrences. In many instances nothing short of a major operation will be effective. Moratoriums, getting the property into stronger hands, new management, and refinancing to squeeze the water out of inflated values and overfinanced properties are all remedies that may be applied as occasion requires.

Pattern of This Text This text deals first with the instruments of real estate finance. Here are discussed in order the various facets of mortgages in which students of real estate finance have an interest.

Next are presented chapters dealing with real estate bonds, investment trusts, land contracts, the financing of long-term leases, and the practice by financial institutions of purchasing investment property, then leasing it back to its former owners.

Next this text deals with the sources of funds for financing real estate. Separate chapters are devoted to the parts played by savings and loan associations, banks (savings and commercial), life insurance companies, and mortgage banks. Other sources of funds for financing real estate are discussed more briefly in a single chapter.

Then follows a discussion of the procedure most commonly followed in originating and in servicing real estate loans. The specific subjects discussed include loan applications, appraisal for financing purposes, title analysis, and mortgage loan servicing. This is followed by presentations of some special problems of mortgage lending. These include chapters on the financing of subdivisions and development projects and the financing of farms.

Had this text been written before 1932, the remaining chapters would certainly have been omitted. But because of changes that have taken place in the intervening years, the subjects treated in these chapters of the text are among the extremely significant ones to which all students of real estate finance must pay close attention. The general subject of this part of the text is the participation of the federal government in the financing of real estate.

The individual chapters deal with the Federal Home Loan Bank system and its affiliates, the Federal Housing Administration, the financing of homes for veterans with the aid of governmental guarantees, the assistance of the federal government in the development of the secondary mortgage market, and the direct financing of real estate by the federal government.

QUESTIONS AND PROBLEMS

1. Ownership of real estate is considered a major support of the private enterprise system. Is this condition less true today than it has been in the past? Why or why not?

2. Review the long-term value trends of real estate in this country. Can you draw any conclusions from these trends which might indicate the potential of investments in real estate as price level hedges?

3. Compare and contrast the factors creating problems in financing ownership of urban and rural real property.

4. In general, what problems are created by the necessity of distinguishing between real and personal property?

5. In times of economic stress, some persons buy land to gain the sense of security attributable to its indestructibility. Can you reconcile this logic with the economic factors determining land value?

6. How can geographical factors affect decision making in the field of real estate finance? Give examples.

7. What kinds of data might you seek to evaluate the local real estate market in the following respects?
   a) The demand-supply relationship for residential housing.
   b) The demand-supply relationship for rental housing.
   c) The demand-supply relationship for commercial buildings.
   d) Real estate activity.

8. Real estate credit may be producer credit, consumer credit, speculative credit, or investment credit. How might the nature of the credit affect the lender's credit terms?

9. How would you expect a transition from a "buyer's" market to a "seller's" market in a locality to affect financing terms?

10. Real estate values are dependent upon the economic life of the locality. Take two cities near you, one industrial and one commercial, and distinguish the effects of the economic activities on real estate prices. Where will the prices be higher? Why?

11. Select a city with which you are well acquainted. From a point near the center of the city, can you draw concentric circles which show a common pattern of uses within the bands created by the circles? Can you explain deviations from the pattern?

12. How are new concepts of suburban living and shopping center development affecting traditional notions of how a city grows, and what adjustments are real estate financing institutions making to this change?

13. What have been the principal factors contributing to the rising cost of home construction in recent years? Do you foresee any change in the relative importance of these factors in the near future?

2

Legal Nature of Real Estate Mortgages

Definition of Mortgage A standard law treatise on mortgages says: "A real estate mortgage is a lien on an interest in the land, created by a formal agreement, by a transfer of such interest, to secure the payment of money or the performance of some other act."[1] In the model "Power of Sale Mortgage Foreclosure Act," promulgated by the National Conference on Uniform State Laws in 1940, a mortgage is defined as "any form of instrument whereby a lien is created upon real estate or whereby title to real estate is reserved or conveyed as security for the payment of a debt or other obligation." As will be noted from both of the above definitions, the essential point is their application to an interest in real estate in the form of an agreement which establishes a lien against the particular interest in question.

Interests Covered Because "interest in real estate" covers a wide variety of possibilities, "mortgage" must be considered equally broad in its applications. In general we are accustomed to think of the mortgage in relation to fee ownership. In addition it may cover any interest in real estate that is a proper subject of sale, grant, or assignment. This means that rents, dower interests, an estate for years, the rights of a remainderman, reversion rights, life estates, the interest of an heir or devisee (subject to the debts of the decedent), an option in a lease, improvements apart from the land, and so forth, are all proper bases for mortgages so far as legal theory is concerned. Whether, as a matter of sound business judgment, mortgagees would be willing to lend money against each of the above-named interests is quite another question.

---

[1] H. T. Tiffany, *A Treatise on the Modern Law of Real Property* (Chicago: Callaghan & Co., 1940), p. 912.

In addition, mortgages are used to protect obligations that are more or less independent of the property mortgaged. For example, a mortgage on a home may be used to protect a line of credit to be used for business purposes; to assure the payment of an annuity; to guarantee an agreement by A to support B during the latter's lifetime; to make sure that some contract will be fulfilled; and so forth.

Rural Origins of Real Property Law Impatient laymen find the law of real property unsuited to the complicated and complex society in which we live because it fails to take into account changing consumer habits and revolutionary technological changes. Social reformers are equally impatient with its adherence to a heritage of plans and objectives that do not take sufficiently into account the shift in objectives of a planned economy, which undertakes to make for the individual many decisions that his forefathers made for themselves. Both overlook the rural origins of the common law of real property.

Here the philosophy that dominated social thinking was aptly phrased laissez-faire. This much overworked phrase is frequently used by people who fail to understand its meaning. It does not characterize a system of government charged with the duty of keeping hands off, as is commonly supposed. Instead laissez-faire assigns to the government a very important role. Under this system, individuals first make contracts. Then the government steps in to see that such contracts are lived up to. The government does not keep hands off. Neither does it make the decisions in terms of what is best for the parties to the contract. It assumes their complete competency to consummate such contracts as they see fit and then supports either party to enforce the contract against the other.

Background of Legal Theory Legal theories frequently represent the accumulation of experiences—some of which are in conflict with one another—which may start by accident rather than by intent. One accidental experience produces results which are sufficiently satisfactory to warrant its repetition by intent. Continued repetition crystallizes the practices into what we come to recognize as law. Because the law is never final in its implications until it has been accepted by the courts, we are accustomed to place much emphasis upon court interpretations. Those situations which have been adjudicated tend to give color to future thinking, even after new conditions seem to dictate entirely new approaches in our processes of analysis. Because of this, much of our legal theory is based upon a process of accretion. We are much more prone to add to what we already have than to substitute the new for the old.

Nowhere in our body of law does the past intrude into the present and threaten to influence our future thinking more than in the field of real estate law. This is an inevitable result of the manner in which real estate law has evolved. While progress is being made toward clarification of real estate legal theory and simplification of business practices governed by it, the wheels of legal machinery grind exceedingly slowly—or so thinks the layman.

Even experts interested in clarification and simplification are not always successful in securing approval of their recommendations. For example, in 1927 the National Conference on Uniform State Laws proposed to the various state legislatures the adoption of a uniform mortgage law. Since this offer had no takers, in 1938 the same group selected one item from their proposed law and recommended the enactment of a model power of sale mortgage foreclosure act. This proposal was no more successful than the previous recommendation. Recently, the group has had under consideration a proposal for a Uniform Real Estate Financing Code. In the interest of expanding the secondary market for conventionally originated mortgages, the Federal National Mortgage Association has mustered a major effort to obtain a standard mortgage form.

Objectives of Uniform Mortgage Law Few subjects which come before the courts frequently have been discussed as generally as the great divergence of mortgage practices in this country. As early as 1911, the National Conference of Commissioners on Uniform State Laws wrestled with this question, but gave up the quest for a uniform law as too complicated for an agreement among the conflicting interests to be hoped for. Leniency for deserving mortgagors does not easily fit into the pattern of the desire of the mortgagee for a simple, quick, and inexpensive method of laying hands upon the security for a defaulted loan.

The objectives sought in most attempts to draft a uniform mortgage law include the following: (1) to prevent unconscionable deficiency judgments; (2) to encourage high percentage loans, thus spreading the advantages of homeownership; (3) to extend leniency to unfortunate mortgagors without jeopardizing too severely the legitimate interests of the mortgagee; (4) to find ways of reducing the cost of mortgage money by making mortgages more marketable; (5) to reduce foreclosure costs, which are really a part of the cost of mortgage money; and (6) to reduce the costs of drafting and recording mortgages.

Every mortgagee, under whatever theory in operation, is concerned with the following: (1) He wants to be assured that he has a proper lien and that he will retain it until the obligation to him has been met. (2) He wants to be able to realize as much as possible in the disposal of the security which protects his claim, should a default occur. (3) He wants to have the right to elect the time of asking that the security be disposed of, subject to confirmation by a court of equity. (4) In order to protect his rights, he wants the privilege of bidding at the foreclosure sale. (5) Finally, he would like to get control of the property if default occurs to prevent waste and to make sure that its income-producing capacities will be used to best advantage to apply against his claims.

Title Theory The title theory of mortgages is one of our heritages from England. Under it, the title to the land rests with the mortgagee. Those who adhere to it take the mortgage deed seriously enough to conclude that title and the right of possession actually pass from the mortgagor to the mortgagee at the time the mortgage is executed. Even if the mortgagor retains physical possession of the land, he does so at the sufferance of the mortgagee, who can dispossess the mortgagor at any time. Since the mortgagor is not admitted to own any estate in the land so long as it is mortgaged to another, he can be dispossessed by that other even without notice. Since the real owner is the mortgagee, he is obligated to observe and to be held liable for all covenants that run with the land.

Under this theory, the mortgagor, by virtue of the terms of the mortgage, particularly the defeasance clause, retains the right to revest title in himself and thereby regain the right of possession if he should meet his obligations to the mortgagee on the due day. Thanks to the equity of redemption, this right of revesting title and of securing lawful possession is extended beyond the due date of the mortgage to the time of foreclosure sale of the land which secured it.

In the United States this theory, in the states where it still prevails, has been subjected to several modifications. From the standpoint of the mortgagee, his liability to observe the covenants that run with the land has been largely abandoned. The mortgagor, meantime, has been given more protection by the provision that so long as he abides by the terms of the mortgage he cannot be dispossessed. It is only when he defaults in his obligations that possession of the land may be passed to the mortgagee.

Lien Theory This theory developed somewhat later than the title theory. Its use has now become the prevalent one in this country. It prevails in all states west of the Mississippi except Arkansas and Missouri. In addition, some of the older states east of the Mississippi have adopted it. The lien theory adheres more directly than the title theory to the idea that the mortgage merely provides security to protect the obligations that are due the mortgagee. It grants neither title nor the right of possession to the mortgagee. Indeed, even after a default by the mortgagor, the latter can retain possession of the land unless he voluntarily surrenders it in accordance with the terms of the mortgage.

The exceptions to the above rule apply in those cases where a court may decree that the mortgagor shall turn possession over to a receiver, pending the completion of arrangements for a foreclosure sale of the security behind the mortgage. Since not all states recognize the need or desirability of receivers for this purpose, the mortgagor may retain possession until dispossessed as a result of the sale.

The differences between these two theories may be material, even though they finally lead to the same destination. The right of the mortgagee in title-theory states to take possession of his property upon default by the one who has been using it seems logical enough and is so recognized in some state laws. Likewise, the denial of the right of possession except with the consent of the mortgagor in lien-theory states is also consistent with the basic idea that the mortgagee is not yet the owner of the real property and therefore should be denied possession of it until its ownership is determined as the result of a foreclosure sale.

Defeasance Clause The clause in the mortgage which gives the mortgagor the right to redeem his property upon the payment of his obligations to the mortgagee is known as the defeasance clause. This clause is a double-edged instrument. On the one hand it says "Pay and you get your property back." But it also says "Fail to pay and you lose your property and any rights therein."

This clause is usually made a part of the mortgage, even though it frequently takes the form of an afterthought added at the end of a document which reads quite differently. It may assume the character of a separate instrument, with no mention of it within the body of the mortgage. If a separate instrument is used for this purpose, the protection of all concerned is best served if mortgage and defeasance instrument are treated as one document, even to the extent of having them recorded at the same time. To serve purposes which are not always in the best interest of all concerned, they are sometimes kept separate.

To avoid possible confusion, some state statutes require the defeasance clause to be included in the mortgage or, if separately written, to accompany the mortgage. Pennsylvania goes so far as to require that a separately written clause be acknowledged and recorded along with the mortgage.

Equity of Redemption At common law, the defeasible fee of a mortgagee became absolute if payment was not made by the law day. The necessity for strict compliance with the exact terms of the defeasance clause frequently worked hardship upon hard-pressed mortgagors. In response to complaints about the inequity of rigid requirements of this clause, equity courts came to view the subject from the point of view of fairness to all concerned. Out of this grew the equity of redemption, which says that equitable principles rather than technical rules should govern whenever the mortgagor is unable to live up to the letter of the contract.

The result of the substitution of equity for rigid rules was an extension of time for redemption, this extension to be fixed by chancery. Hence the name "equity of redemption." Early decrees for this purpose fixed the time to which the equity of redemption must conform. Only after this time extension expired and the mortgagor failed to meet his obligations did the mortgagee obtain an unqualified title. In fact, courts of equity became overzealous in recognizing the equity of redemption. This position radically limited the effectiveness of the mortgage as a security instrument until the courts developed the decree of foreclosure, whereby a forfeiture of the equity of redemption could be declared under appropriate conditions.

In the exercise of this equity of redemption, the mortgagor possesses the absolute right to recover the property mortgaged upon the payment of all obligations due the mortgagee, plus all costs and expenses incurred in connection with the foreclosure suit and sale. This right may be exercised at any time before the actual confirmation of sale. It applies regardless of the form of foreclosure action.

The mortgagee is given the right to foreclose upon a breach of contract by the mortgagor. As a reciprocal right, the mortgagor may redeem his property upon meeting his obligations. The equity of redemption constitutes an estate in the land. The mortgagor may not be estopped from exercising it; nor may he be bargained out of it except upon fair terms. By agreement, the parties at interest may extend the time for redemption. This will not affect the rights of intervening interests who also possess the right of redemption—for example, those of a junior mortgagee. Any purchaser of the equity of redemption has the same rights under it as the mortgagor.

Who Share in Equity of Redemption Not only the mortgagor but others possess rights to the equity of redemption. Those who share in these rights include holders of dower and curtesy interests and all junior lienors. This is another reason for joining all of these interests in foreclosure suits. If they or any of them are not joined, any foreclosure decree does not affect their interests. If they are joined, they must be given their day in court. Failure to protect their interests on such occasion will result in having such interests cut off by the foreclosure decree. Since the interests of all such claimants are of the same nature as that of the mortgagor, they must be protected in the same way—pay up or lose. Any party who shares in the equity of redemption with the mortgagor may protect his interests by meeting the obligations of those whose claims are superior to his own. On occasion this can be accomplished by compromise or by agreement to keep the prior claim alive.

Statutory Redemption The equity of redemption is a right confirmed by a court of equity. It ceases when the property is sold at foreclosure sale. In about half of the states there is, in addition, a legal right to redeem, granted mortgagors by statute, which becomes effective at the time of foreclosure sale and runs for varying periods of time thereafter. The longest period permitted is two years. Statutory redemption is a right granted to the owner having an equity of redemption before foreclosure and to all junior lienholders, including judgment creditors. Usually the law provides one period of time for the mortgagor, with a succeeding period for junior lienors. The amount required for redemption covers the sale price, interest to the date of redemption, and expenses. At the expiration of the time permitted for statutory redemption, this right too is cut off.

Meantime the purchaser possesses what may be termed only nascent title. He may not even receive a deed as evidence of his interest, but only a certificate of purchase. His chances of losing his title by redemption by a claimant protected by statutory redemption depend upon a combination of circumstances. Near the top of the list of such circumstances is the price he paid for the property at foreclosure sale. If he paid approximately all the property is worth, his chances of losing the property are certainly less than if he paid much less than it is worth on the open market or than it may become worth during the period when the statutory redemption is effective.

Mortgage Forms The best assurance that a mortgage conforms to the laws of the state to which it applies, and that it represents the type of lien it purports to be, is to have it drafted or at least inspected by a competent attorney thoroughly familiar with the laws and court decisions of the state on the subject of real estate encumbrances. This may become expensive. Such a mortgage may easily contain three to four thousand words. As an alternative, printed mortgage forms are available which can be used to establish real estate liens. The short form is sometimes opposed because it omits some of the covenants which are considered essential for the protection of the mortgagee. The long form spells out these covenants in terms that are more or less common to all such mortgages. Why not have these covenants incorporated into the statutes? Then let each mortgage, by the use of the word or phrase, include each of such statutory covenants as are agreed upon by the mortgagor and the mortgagee. Such a practice would not eliminate the need for a legal counsel. But it would reduce his duties and, presumably, his charges, without causing undue risk to those whom he serves.

Minimum Contents of Mortgage Whether a printed form of mortgage instrument is used or an attorney draws up a special form, certain subjects must always be included. The proper names of both mortgagor and mortgagee should be used with great care. If possible, the mortgagor should use the same form of name by which he is known as the lawful owner of the property. In case there has been a change of name since the property was acquired, either through marriage or otherwise, this fact should be shown in the records to avoid future confusion. Likewise, the proper and correct name of the mortgagee is important, whether an individual or a corporation is involved.

In like manner the description of the property which serves as security for the loan should be the legal description as recorded in the public records. While this is not an absolute requirement, it can save future confusion. In any event, the property must be described in such terms that there can be no reasonable doubt about its identification. The mortgagee is usually given the right to transfer his interests to his heirs and assigns (successors and assigns in the event that the mortgagee is a corporation).

As a practical matter, the covenant of seizin and warranty may give the mortgagee paper protection against the mortgagor, but no substantial protection in case the mortgagee depends too much upon this clause. For example, such a clause commonly reads as follows: "The mortgagor covenants that he is lawfully seized of the above described premises in fee simple, and has good right to bargain and sell the same; and that the same are free from all encumbrances whatsoever; and that he will warrant and defend said premises, with all the appurtenances thereto belonging, against all lawful claims or demands." A breach of this covenant by a financially irresponsible mortgagor might result in a worthless judgment in favor of the mortgagee and against the mortgagor. Nevertheless, it is well to include this clause and then to determine the seizin part of it by an independent check of the records. If this is done, the warranty part assumes less importance. However, an occasion in which the covenant of seizin and warranty may become important arises when the mortgagor later acquires a title of which he was not seized when he executed the mortgage on the property. By his covenant he is estopped from denying the full effect of his mortgage grant as a conveyance, and the subsequently acquired title inures to the benefit of the mortgagee.

The dower clause should be observed if the mortgagor is married. If not, the mortgage should show his unmarried status. This too should be checked for the protection of the mortgagee. Execution and acknowledgment should carefully follow the established practices in the state in which the property is located.

Acceleration Clause Most modern mortgages contain an acceleration clause. In effect this permits the mortgagee, in case of default by the mortgagor, to declare the full amount of the obligation due and payable immediately. In other words, even though the terms of the mortgage give the mortgagor 20 years within which to amortize the principal amount of a loan, in monthly installments or otherwise, the acceleration clause in the mortgage gives the mortgagee the right to demand payment of the full amount of the debt should the mortgagor fail to meet a specified small number of payments. Although legally any default will authorize the holder to make use of the acceleration clause, this is rarely done on default in a single payment. Most holders seek to avoid foreclosure and a forbearance of 60 to 90 days is common.

Also, it should be remembered that the acceleration clause merely represents an option available to the mortgagee. He may use it or not as he sees fit. Whether or not he exercises his rights under it usually depends upon a combination of factors, including his estimate of the amount of cushion of value left in the property to protect his lien, the circumstances which resulted in the default, the attitude and intentions of the mortgagor, the state of the real estate market, the presence and amount of junior liens, and a variety of other conditions. As a general rule, the mortgagee would prefer to help the mortgagor solve his financial problems rather than to take advantage of the first opportunity to exercise his option under an acceleration clause.

There is another type of acceleration clause, no longer in common use, that has been given the not too complimentary name of "sleeper" clause. This is a clause that permits acceleration at the expiration of some period of time, say three years, even though the mortgagor is not in default. Since the average mortgagor does not read the fine print carefully, or does not grasp its significance, he is not aware of the authority of the holder to accelerate the debt and demand payment in full. Later, at a most inconvenient time, he may awake in dismay to the acceleration of the full debt when he has promptly met all of his obligations. Such a clause is outlawed by the regulations of the Federal Housing Administration and the Veterans Administration, but it may still be found in conventional loan mortgages.

This type of acceleration clause is wholly unrelated to the paying habits of the mortgagor. He may meet every payment on an installment mortgage on the due date or even in advance. Resting in the confidence that so long as he keeps up this record he will have 20 years in which to amortize his debt, he may be rudely shocked at the expiration of only 3 years to find in his mail a demand from the mortgagee to pay the balance due under the mortgage within 30 days.

Such shocks usually come in pairs. The first one tells him that he has obligated himself, in signing the mortgage, to permit the mortgagee—at his option—to declare the full amount of the unpaid balance of the debt due and payable at any time after two years from the date of execution of the mortgage, regardless of the payment record of the mortgagor. The second shock hits the mortgagor when he learns that his ability to refinance his loan is greatly restricted at the time the mortgagee sees fit to exercise his option under an acceleration clause of this type. Such an option would be used only in a tight money market, when the mortgagee can use the money to better advantage than to leave it tied up in the mortgage.

Nor does it always follow that only Shylocks take advantage of the sleeper type of acceleration clause. Sometimes a hard-pressed mortgagee turns reluctantly to such a clause as a means of extricating himself from a tight spot; he, too, is being pressed by those who have a right to call upon him for liquid funds when he is short of cash. Generally speaking, however, it appears clear that the inexperienced mortgagor needs freedom from this type of acceleration clause more often than the experienced mortgagee needs its protection. It is not difficult to find valid reasons why this type of mortgage is looked upon with distinct disfavor by progressive mortgage lenders as well as by experienced and informed borrowers.

One use of the sleeper type of acceleration clause is perhaps less defensible than the desire for liquidity in a tight money market. If the mortgage is executed at a time when competition favors the borrower, a sleeper acceleration clause may operate to his disadvantage when the wheel of fortune turns in favor of lenders who are willing to recast the loan on much less favorable terms. For example, the mortgagee may exercise his option under this clause, call the loan, and then make a new loan at a higher interest rate, for a shorter period of time, and with other features less favorable to the mortgagor. This assumes that the borrower has no alternative source of funds—an assumption that would frequently hold good in a tight money market—more or less without regard to his equity in the property and his credit standing.

Still another type of acceleration clause included in some mortgages gives the mortgagee the right to declare the unpaid balance of the debt due and payable in case the mortgagor sells his property to someone not acceptable to the mortgagee. Even the FHA at one time included in one mortgage form the following clause: "If there shall be any change in the ownership of the premises covered hereby without the consent of the Grantee, the entire principal and all accrued interest shall become due and payable at the election of the Grantee, and foreclosure proceedings may be instituted thereon." The justification for such a clause is that since the mortgagee takes pains to measure the moral hazard of the borrower before he makes the loan originally, he should have the same opportunity to examine and evaluate the moral hazard of any person who assumes the mortgage.

Absence of Acceleration Clause Failure to include any acceleration clause in a mortgage means that a default occurs only in the part of the debt that is matured and unpaid. The remainder of the debt cannot be said to be in default, because it is not yet due. Consequently the mortgagee may find that he is permitted to sue only for the matured and unpaid part of the debt. This would suggest a succession of suits as additional installments of the debt fall due, if they remain unpaid. Under these circumstances an appeal to a court of equity would probably result in a decree of foreclosure and sale, subject to the unmatured part of the debt.

Some statutes come to the rescue of the mortgagee at this point, permitting him to bring foreclosure suit, involving the entire amount of the debt to date but omitting any consideration of unmatured interest. Public policy as represented in such statutes assumes that the mortgagee would rather realize his principal and accrued interest at the time of foreclosure sale than to wait until unmatured interest has accrued.

Escalator Clauses and Variable Rate Mortgage Plans A mortgage provision that has been little used in this country until its recent revival with the rapidly rising interest rates is called an escalator clause. This provision gives the mortgagee, at his option, the right to raise the interest rate on the loan at any time after a specified interval, or upon the occurring of a certain condition, regardless of the debt-paying experience of the mortgagor.

When the mortgage interest rate may be raised or lowered over the life of the loan in accord with the variation of some other financial rate, the borrower has what is known as a variable interest rate mortgage. Commonly used reference series are the Federal Reserve discount rate, the prime rate for bank borrowers, the Federal Home Loan Bank Board series of effective mortgage rates, a bond rate, or some other indicator of current money costs. Often upper and lower limits are also established by the rate variation formula.

From the lender's point of view, variable rate mortgages add considerable attractiveness to long-term lending at times of rapid shifts in capital market money rates. By this plan, the mortgagee achieves increased flexibility in portfolio earnings. Furthermore, with interest rates subject to adjustment the mortgage more nearly retains its par value in the secondary market in times of rising money costs.

Along with these advantages, the lender must accept certain drawbacks. The flexible interest rate injects an element of uncertainty into cash flow projections that affect the valuation process and marketability of the mortgage. If the mortgage interest rate is changed, it should be clear whether the monthly debt-service payments will be raised or lowered without changing the maturity date, or the monthly payments held constant and the maturity date altered. A second problem for the lender created by variable interest rates arises out of increased uncertainty of gross earnings on his loan portfolio. In a period of declining interest rates, coverage of dividends or interest costs on savings accounts or time deposits may be jeopardized. There are also obvious problems in loan servicing and customer relations associated with every change in rate.

So long as both fixed and variable rate options are open, the borrower will avoid variable plans in periods of low interest rates and surplus available funds, but will seek them out when the opposite condition of high interest rates and tight money exists. The lender will move in the opposite direction. The only way to avoid this counteractive expression of preferences would be for variable mortgage plans to become universally adopted to the exclusion of fixed rate plans.

A recent American Bankers Association study has revealed a slight, cautious institutional interest in variable rate plans [2] Of bankers replying to a questionnaire sent to members of the Mortgage Finance Commitee and the Mortgage Advisory Council of the American Bankers Association, 82 percent did not offer variable rate mortgages. Those offered were concentrated in commercial and industrial property mortgages. Only in five states did banks offer variable rate mortgages on single-family homes.

A 1969 survey of the United States Savings and Loan League found that at that time only about 1 out of 10 associations used interest adjustment clauses in its mortgages. A similar number, in addition, said that they intended to use such clauses in the future.

At the present time, these studies show three main reasons advanced against adoption of variable rate mortgage plans These reasons relate to legal problems, public relations, and marketing of the institution's services.

Escalation in Event of Default One of the paradoxes of real estate finance is the use of the escalator clause against mortgagors in default. For example, the mortgage may be written to provide for 7 percent interest but with a proviso that, in case of default in two successive installment payments, the rate shall be increased, at the option of the mortgagee, to 8 percent. While it is recognized that this is a penalty clause to prevent default, nevertheless it seems a bit odd to tell the mortgagor, "If you can't pay 7 percent we shall charge you 8 percent."

The opposite policy is sometimes written into a mortgage in order to reach the same goal as does the escalator clause. The mortgage may be written at a rate of 8 percent. Then the borrower is told, "So long as you make regular payments without default, we will charge you only 7 percent. In other words, we will allow you a bonus of 1 percent for living up to your contract." Or this kind of a clause may provide in addition that, while the mortgagee reserves the right to charge the contract rate of 8 percent at some future time, he will not make the change during the first two (or three) years and then only after notice of the change of 30 to 90 days. The psychological effect upon the borrower of starting with a bonus which may later be eliminated, instead of assessing a penalty, seems to favor the substitute plan.

---

[2] Wray O. Candilis, *Variable Rate Mortgage Plans* (Washington, D.C.: American Bankers Association, 1971), p. 27.

Note or Bond A mortgage is usually accompanied by a note or "bond" which deals with the features of the debt secured by the mortgage. This note may be written separately or may be made a part of the mortgage. If written separately, it may be copied into the mortgage. In either event the note is the primary obligation of the mortgagor. The mortgage merely represents the security to protect the noteholder in case of default. If the lender were sufficiently confident that the borrower would always be able to meet his obligations, no mortgage would be necessary. The note constitutes all the evidence of the debt that is needed.

In fact, in case of default the mortgagee may elect to disregard the mortgage and sue on the note. The judgment awarded him as the result of the suit on the note may be attached to other property owned by the mortgagor which, through sale, may enable the mortgagee to recover the amount of his claims more readily than if he foreclosed his mortgage. Should the mortgagee elect to do so, he may take double-barreled action against the mortgagor simultaneously. He may bring suit in a court of law praying for relief on the note and at the same time enforce his foreclosure rights in a court of equity. Unless one of these suits results in a decision which completely satisfies his claim, the other is not affected. Since, however, such simultaneous suits are not likely to produce either more speedy or more complete results than one of them, simultaneous suits are seldom resorted to.

In some states the note given may be a judgment, or cognovit, note. It is a promissory note containing a power of attorney authorizing the holder of the note, or an attorney or any other person, after maturity of the note or default, to appear in any court of competent jurisdiction and confess judgment against the maker for amounts due thereon without prior notice to the maker. Such summary proceedings are recognized in Colorado, Delaware, Illinois, Maryland, Ohio, Pennsylvania, Virginia, Wisconsin, and Wyoming.

Just as a debt could be evidenced without a mortgage, so is it possible to have a mortgage without a note. The mortgagee could agree to leave the mortgagor free from any form of personal liability. Such an arrangement would not affect the validity of the mortgage. If the mortgagor undertakes no personal liability, the mortgagee must look to the security alone to provide the means of satisfying his claims. In such case, he would be in no different position than if he failed to ask for a deficiency judgment or if he failed to pursue his rights under it if a judgment were rendered in his favor.

Because of recent practices, it is recommended that the note not only be a separate instrument from the mortgage but that its terms be omitted from the mortgage. Reference to the note in such terms as to identify it without stating its terms is sufficient to fix the mortgage as its security. By this means the rate of interest, the terms of repayment, and so forth, are not made matters of record. A common form of reference to the note in the mortgage mentions a "certain promissory note of even date herewith in the principal sum of (amount here filled in) with interest from date at the rate therein specified." Consequently, competitors of the mortgagee who might take advantage of the knowledge they could gain from the record for raiding purposes are denied this privilege.

Meaning of "Raiding" By "raiding" we mean this: Financial institutions which find the demand for loans insufficient for their capacity to lend sometimes look for opportunities to refinance mortgages held by their competitors. First they search the records for mortgages that appear to be well seasoned and that carry a rate of interest higher than the searcher would be willing to accept or repayment terms that bear more heavily upon the purse of the mortgagor than the searcher feels would be necessary for his protection. Then a representative contacts the mortgagor and undertakes to convince him of the advantages of shifting his financing to the new institution. While this practice is legal and represents an application of the good old American spirit of competition, nevertheless it is characterized by the somewhat uncomplimentary term "raiding" and probably merits this appellation.

One particularly bad feature of raiding practices is the secrecy with which such practices are surrounded. Frequently the existing mortgagee has no notice that he is about to lose a mortgage that he would prefer to keep until he is notified that a commitment has been made to refinance the property. After it is too late, the mortgagor may find that the mortgagee would have been glad to recast the loan on terms as favorable as those offered by the new mortgagee. One possible protection for the mortgagee against raiding practices is the inclusion in the mortgage contract of prepayment penalties. Another answer to this problem would be to have mortgagees examine their seasoned loans from time to time and voluntarily grant better terms to those who merit them. This is being done by some financial institutions. It is not usually a complete answer to the raiding problem. Raiders frequently do not even consider favorably the nature of the risk carried by the mortgagee who made the first loan. This is particularly true if it is a construction loan. The institution which makes it carries it through its period of greater risk and then may lose it to an institution that refuses to carry heavy risks but is willing to compensate for low risk loans by easier terms than are normally granted in the mortgage market.

Discharge of Debt Cancels Lien Since the mortgage lien is currently considered to be merely security for an obligation, it necessarily follows that any discharge of the debt will cancel the lien of the mortgage. Whether the debt be paid in cash, by a valid check, by accumulation of rents collected by the mortgagee in possession, by the proceeds of an insurance policy, by an offset of counterclaims, or in any other lawful manner, the effect is the same. Even forgiveness of the obligation by the mortgagee or any part of it in consideration for meeting the remainder will constitute a termination of the lien. Acceptance of less than the full amount obligated will not necessarily result in a cancellation of the lien unless the mortgagee is willing voluntarily to grant a release to the mortgagor. Obviously the latter should always insist upon a release in such form that it may be used to cancel the lien of record. In exceptional cases it may be necessary for the mortgagor to resort to court action to obtain a release of the mortgage.

In lien states a satisfaction piece is sufficient to clear the record. This merely directs the county clerk or registrar to indicate on the record of the mortgage that the lien no longer applies against the property. It should be drawn with sufficient care to make sure that the description of the property, the amount of the loan, the names of the mortgagor and the mortgagee, and the date and place of the recorded mortgage are all properly included. Meanwhile, if there has been an assignment of the mortgage, this fact should be recited in the satisfaction piece. Whether the satisfaction piece is tendered voluntarily by the mortgagee or is issued by a court of equity, the effect is the same. In title states, the cancellation of a mortgage lien is usually dependent upon whether the debt secured by the mortgage was paid before or after default. Payment of the debt in accordance with the terms of the note terminates the right of the mortgagee and an unencumbered title remains in the mortgagor, when entry is made of record, without a reconveyance or other act on the part of the mortgagee. Payment of the debt after maturity or other default, on the other hand, has generally been held not to restore title in the mortgagor, since an absolute title passed to the mortgagee upon default. In such cases, the mortgagor must secure a reconveyance of title—from the mortgagee if voluntarily given or from a court of equity if not voluntarily given. In some title states, however, payment has the effect of continuing title in the name of the mortgagor whether made before or after default.

Canceled Mortgage Dead A mortgage which has been canceled, followed by the recording of a satisfaction piece or a reconveyance of title, cannot be revived. As long as the mortgage is kept alive its lien may be extended beyond its stated maturity by agreement between the mortgagor and the mortgagee. In such case it is not necessary for the extension agreement to be spread upon the record. As long as the original mortgage remains on the record it serves notice to all and sundry that it is there to protect the unpaid claims of the mortgagee. But once the lien of the mortgage is discharged, a new instrument is required to protect new or different claims of the mortgagee. This is a frequent reason why a mortgagee has a nominee purchase his mortgage. He may thereby employ the subterfuge of keeping the mortgage alive after actual payment of the obligation instead of having its cancellation tell the true story of what has happened.

Recording of Mortgages Public records provide opportunities for the protection of holders of estates in real property and, at the same time, place upon them obligations to make use of them. By recording a mortgage we simply mean having it copied by a public official into a public record kept for that purpose. Indexes and cross-indexes are used for convenience in the use of the records and are usually considered to be a part of the record. The first recording act in the United States was passed in Massachusetts Bay Colony in 1634. Other colonies soon followed the example of Massachusetts.

Records are usually kept in the county (or township in some states) where the property is located. If the property is located in more than one county, a record should be made in the proper public office in each county concerned. Before the mortgage is made a part of the record it must be "admitted to record." By this is meant that all formalities peculiar to the locality must be observed. These peculiarities attain significance for anyone who is required to search the records to discover the quality of title to a piece of real estate. Unless the searcher knows what to look for and where to find it, he may waste much time and still fail to reach his goal.

A mortgage record is expected to speak for itself. If errors appear in it, they can be corrected. If the errors result from the carelessness of the recording agents, they can be corrected without too much trouble. But if the errors appearing in the record are also in the documents recorded, changes can be made only as the result of a suit to reform the record.

Because time is of the essence in settling disputes where priorities of liens are concerned, it becomes a matter of very great importance to have the time of acceptance for record show not only the day but the exact hour and minute. It should be noted that the time that governs is not the time of spreading the mortgage upon the records. Instead it is the day, hour, and minute that shows the act of accepting the mortgage for record. This means that anyone searching the records should include in his search mortgages accepted for record but not yet recorded.

When a property is transferred from one party to another with new financing involved in the transaction, the new deed is usually filed as of one instant of time, a senior mortgage as of a couple of minutes later, and a second mortgage, if any, as still later, in order to show the proper order of claims. For purchase-money mortgages, however, the deed and the mortgage should be filed for record simultaneously. The record should show no gap between them.

Purpose of Recording As between the mortgagor and the mortgagee, recording is usually not necessary. Recording is not essential to the validity of a mortgage unless the statutes of the state require it. For example, in Maryland a mortgage must be filed within six months of its execution or it is not a valid lien.

The act of recording creates no rights that did not exist before. But it does give notice of their existence. And it does put all other parties in a position where they are obligated to search the record or take the consequences of their negligence. In other words, a recorded mortgage protects its holder by giving him priority over the subsequent acts of the mortgagor. In general the priority of successive liens is determined by the time of accepting them for record.

Since records are available for those entitled to make use of them, failure to take advantage of the opportunities offered may result in loss to the mortgagee. In most states junior lienors of record without notice of the existence of a senior mortgage may acquire priority of lien over an unrecorded senior mortgage. Likewise, judgments, which are statutory liens upon property that the debtor presently owns or may later acquire title to, may take precedence over unrecorded mortgages. Even subsequent recordation of an antecedent mortgage lien will not affect the order of priority.

Not all equitable mortgages are recorded. In some cases they are not intended to be recorded as mortgages, because they appear to be something else. Even what is presumed to be a regular mortgage may lose the effect of the mortgage as such. Suppose that a regular mortgage deed is spread upon the record, omitting the defeasance clause which takes the form of a separate instrument and is not recorded. An unscrupulous mortgagee could sell the property to a bona fide purchaser for value without notice of the defeasance clause, since it is not a part of the record. In this case the purchaser would have unencumbered title to the property, leaving the mortgagor with an unsecured claim against the mortgagee.

Other Form of Notice Since the purpose of recording a mortgage is essentially to put on notice all those having a possible interest in the property that it already has a lien against it, other forms of notice may accomplish the same purpose. This means that an unrecorded mortgage would maintain its priority over all subsequent lienors if they knew of its existence and effect. Whenever the mortgagee knows of possible complications arising from his failure to have his mortgage recorded, he can counteract this failure by letting others know about his lien.

Even though the mortgagee takes no positive action to warn others of his lien, one form of notice is usually considered adequate where it obtains. Interested parties are usually put on notice to ascertain the nature of the interest held by the party in possession of the property. The mortgagee would seldom be in possession. Since the mortgagor would usually possess the property and even occupy it, he could easily deceive others about the absence of an unrecorded mortgage, should he care to do so. In inducing another party to grant a loan with mortgage security, he might become involved in later trouble even though a much needed loan would serve a present purpose.

QUESTIONS AND PROBLEMS

1. What theory of mortgages do you favor—the title theory, the lien theory, or a modified position?

2. What are the relative advantages and disadvantages of borrowing on a real estate mortgage in a state where the mortgagor has a right to redeem for a statutory period after foreclosure?

3. What is the effect of recording a mortgage on notice requirements to third parties?

4. A holds the legal title to Brownacre. B holds A's note and an unrecorded mortgage on Brownacre. Under his mortgage rights, B has gained possession of Brownacre upon default in payments due on the note. A assigns his title to C, who lives in Texas and has never seen the land. What are C's rights?

5. How important is the covenant of seizin and warranty in a mortgage instrument?

6. What purpose is served by an acceleration clause in a note?

7. What is a "sleeper" clause as related to acceleration provisions in a mortgage note? Is this type of clause defensible? Why or why not?

8. What parties share in the equity of redemption and what rights does it give them?

9. Compare the early mortgages with those generally in use today. In what principal respects do they differ?

10. What are the holder's alternative courses of action available in event of default on a mortgage note?

11. What is "raiding" and what measures may financial institutions take in defense against this practice?

12. What are the advantages and disadvantages of variable mortgage rate plans from the point of view of (1) the lender; (2) the borrower; and (3) the public interest?

3

Kinds of Mortgages

Three Kinds of Mortgages There are essentially three kinds of mortgages in common use. First, there are those that are recognized as such. When the term "mortgage" is used it is generally assumed that it means the kind of financial instrument discussed in the preceding chapter. As such it is presumed to constitute the first private lien against the real estate which is used to secure it. Public claims—such as tax liens—take precedence over first or prior lien mortgages. By statutory exception, federal income tax liens are only effective against subsequent lienors after notice has been filed by the District Director of Internal Revenue. Whenever mortgages are not given first private lien status they are usually designated in such manner as to indicate their junior position. Such mortgages are discussed in Chapter 6. Some characteristics of ordinary mortgages will be discussed in this chapter.

Second, there are equitable mortgages, frequently given too little attention even by those whose business interests involve first mortgages. For this reason they are defined with some care in this chapter.

Third, what may be classed as "collective" mortgages are commonly known as mortgage bonds. They are collective in the sense that instead of a single mortgagee there may be many beneficial owners of one mortgage. Since bonds play major parts in the financing of many types of real estate, particularly those involving relatively large sums, they will be described in Chapter 7.

Equitable Mortgages In addition to regular mortgages which are readily identifiable as such, common practice sanctions the use of a variety of financial arrangements which are really mortgages even though they carry some other label. These are called equitable mortgages. A few examples will suffice to indicate possibilities in this direction.

What appears to be an outright conveyance of title to a property by the use of a deed may be construed to be a mortgage if the parties to the deed intended it to be merely security for a debt. Even though no written evidence of the debt exists, parol evidence, if it be clear, convincing and unequivocal, will be sufficient to determine the true character of the transaction. Even presumedly innocent purchasers of the property in question may not rely solely upon the record of sale rather than the mortgage against the property if they have notice of the facts. This apparent transfer of title is usually construed to be an equitable mortgage instead.

Likewise, a sale of property with an option to repurchase may be construed to be an equitable mortgage. If it is a bona fide sale, the option must be exercised according to the terms of the option, including its date of expiration Otherwise, the rights of the seller to repurchase cease to exist. On the other hand, if the option to repurchase can be held to be a mortgage in fact if not in form, the seller can exercise the option any time before foreclosure sale becomes effective. In case of doubt, a court of equity may resolve a dispute concerning the facts in favor of the seller of the property and construe the sale as a mortgage.

A third example is provided by the circumstances which result in an advance of funds to purchase property which is to become the security for a regular mortgage. While this is not a common practice, it occurs occasionally. For some reason it may not be feasible for the cancellation of one mortgage to take place simultaneously with the placing of a new one. Hence, a friend of the purchaser may advance the money, knowing that his loan will soon be secured by a regular mortgage, the terms of which have no doubt been subject to previous discussion and agreement. Until this regular mortgage becomes effective, the creditor has an equitable mortgage against the property.

Vendor's Lien Another form of equitable mortgage is the vendor's (or grantor's) lien. When a trusting vendor transfers title to property in return for only part of the payment agreed upon, the property in question is considered to be an implied security for the payment of the remainder of the purchase price. At best, this is an unsatisfactory method of transferring title, since an innocent third party who may not know of the unpaid balance, if it does not show on the record, may acquire title to the property free of the vendor's lien.

For his own protection the vendor may do one of two things: (1) He may take back a purchase-money mortgage even though it is to remain in effect only a short time. (2) He may recite in the deed that there is an unpaid remainder which the vendor proposes to protect. Such a recital will be notice to all of the presence of an equitable mortgage. The purchase-money mortgage and, where recognized by statute at least, the second form of protection will give the vendor priority over both dower interests and judgment liens.

Vendee's Lien Whenever a purchaser of real estate advances any part of the purchase money before he receives title to the property, he does so on his faith in the integrity of the seller. Should the seller or vendor violate this confidence and fail to convey title according to the terms of the sale contract, the vendee would have an equitable mortgage against the property. The right is enforceable in equity in the same manner that vendors' liens are enforceable. This situation may arise when a purchaser of real estate signs a preliminary contract and shows his good faith by the tender of a binder check for a part of the purchase price. In case the vendor keeps the binder payment but fails to consummate the deal according to its terms, the vendee would have an equitable mortgage claim against the property.

Land contracts upon which payments have been made may also be construed to be in the nature of equitable mortgages. They are discussed in Chapter 8.

Debts of Decedent Debts of a decedent constitute a lien against whatever property he may possess at the time of his death. These are again in the nature of equitable mortgages. They follow the property, but the purchaser of such property is not bound to assume personal responsibility for their payment if he does not care to do so. He may be asked to assume them as a part of the bargain when the purchase of the property is arranged. The purchaser usually cannot claim that he did not have notice of such debts, since the records of the estate will be a necessary part of public records which should be searched before purchase is consummated. Difficulties may arise, however, where additional estate tax assessments are made by governmental authorities upon audit of tax returns long after the property has passed to a new purchaser. The purchaser's examination of the records of the estate should take contingent liabilities fully into account.

Priority of Equitable Mortgage Depending upon the circumstances in each particular case, an equitable mortgage may or may not enjoy high priority. Liens of record at the time an equitable mortgage is established would normally take precedence. Generally speaking, however, an equitable mortgage will enjoy priority over unsecured creditors. Vendors' liens and long-term land contracts are now commonly accepted for record.

Deed of Trust One of the differences in detail mentioned in the preceding chapter makes use of a deed of trust instead of the regular mortgage. For example, in several states the borrower ordinarily conveys title to a trustee to be held in trust so long as his rights are alive. The conveyance is by a deed absolute, but the transfer is accompanied by a trust agreement, either as a part of the deed or in addition to it, setting forth the terms of the security arrangement and giving the trustee a power of sale in event of default. The deed of trust is commonly used in California, Colorado, District of Columbia, Delaware, Mississippi, Missouri, Tennessee, Texas, Virginia, and West Virginia. Deeds of trust are not extensively used in other states because their courts have held that any conveyance of real estate given to secure a debt is a mortgage, irrespective of the form of the instrument used. In some jurisdictions, like California, both the mortgage and the deed of trust are used.

Where the deed of trust is used, the trustee is authorized, in case of default, to foreclose the mortgagor's equity by a sale of the property at public auction, after proper advertisement. He must account to both parties for the proceeds of the sale. Each is entitled to his share as his interest may appear, after expenses of the sale, including compensation of the trustee, have been met. Since the mortgagor has never actually relinquished his title, but only the power of sale in case of his default, the purchaser must look to the mortgagor for title.

The deed of trust is such a mixture of trust and mortgage law in concept that anyone using it should act under the counsel of a local real estate lawyer. In general, however, the legal rules surrounding the creation and evidence of the debt in the form of a note, rights of the borrower left in possession, legal description of the property, creation of a valid lien on after-acquired property, and recording are the same for both mortgages and deeds of trust. Similarly, a property subject to a deed of trust may be sold subject to the deed of trust either with or without an assumption of the debt by the purchaser. The assignment of the lender's rights is similar to assignment of a mortgagee's interest except that an assignment under a deed of trust need never be recorded. The original recording of the trust deed gives notice of the lien on the real estate, and only the trustee can release this lien by an appropriate act of reconveyance. In event of failure or refusal of a trustee to execute a reconveyance when the borrower repays his debt, the trustee may be forced to act by legal process. In fact, the trustee can be removed and a successor appointed by the noteholder without recourse to court or execution of a conveyance if the trust deed provides for such action.

In California, where deeds of trust and mortgages are used side by side, several distinctions are made between the two instruments. Whereas a mortgage may be discharged by a simple acknowledgement of satisfaction on the record, a reconveyance of title is considered necessary to extinguish a deed of trust. Under a deed of trust, an assignee of a creditor cannot sell the security property because his assignor did not have the power of sale to transfer; only the trustee has this power. Where a mortgage is used, however, if it contains a power of sale, the assignee of the note can himself exercise the power of sale if he has the assignment acknowledged and recorded.

Deeds of trust are necessarily used in connection with corporate mortgages. They have been so used in this country since the corporate mortgage first came into use more than a century ago.

Mortgage for Future Advances Since a mortgage provides security to protect an obligation, this obligation may take the form of an executory contract as well as a debt already in existence. While it is expected that a mortgage will always state the total amount of the debt it is expected to secure, this amount may be in the nature of a forecast of total debt incurred in installments. In other words, a mortgage may cover future as well as current advances. For example, a mortgage may be so written that it will protect several successive loans under a general line of credit extended by the mortgagee to the mortgagor. In case the total amount cannot be forecasted with accuracy, at least the general nature of the advances or loans must be apparent from the wording of the mortgage.

From one of the mortgagor covenants of a mortgage form in common use, the following quotation indicates the intent of the mortgagor and the mortgagee on this subject:

> That the mortgagee or legal holder of this mortgage may make future advancements for the repair, restoration and improvement of said buildings, and that the amount of funds so advanced may be added to the then unpaid balance on said loan and bear interest as provided by the terms of the original note, and shall be secured by and subject to all of the terms of this mortgage deed.

One excellent illustration of a mortgage for future advances (sometimes called an open or open-end mortgage) takes the form of construction loans. Here the borrower arranges in advance with a mortgagee for a total amount—usually definitely stated in the mortgage—which will be advanced under the mortgage to meet the part of the costs of construction which the owner of the property does not expect to meet from his own capital funds. As the structure progresses, the mortgagor has the right to call upon the mortgagee for successive advances on the loan.

The timing and amounts of these advances follow various patterns. If a residence is being financed, one pattern follows a rule of thumb plan which reads somewhat as follows: One third is advanced when the house is under roof. Presumably the builder's capital or his credit or unsecured short-term loans will take care of his bills up to this point. He may use the proceeds of the first advance to meet his obligations to short-term creditors presently owed. A second third may be advanced when the house is plastered. This does not imply that the plastering cost alone will justify this second advance. Rather, other work has been in progress, including plumbing, painting, and so on. The final third is advanced when the house is completed and ready for occupancy.

Sometimes a small portion of this final advance is held back for a time to meet the obligations of materialmen, laborers, or others who have not been paid by the builder.

Some lenders on construction loans hold back a portion of the loan commitment when the mortgagor is a speculative builder. The amount held back may be as much as 20 percent. It may be released only when the loan has been assumed by an owner-occupant. The occupancy of the property by the owner is presumed to add security to the loan.

A variation of this plan calls for four payments instead of three: (1) the first payment when the building is enclosed; (2) the second when the interior rough work is completed and the building is ready for plastering; (3) a third when wood trim has been applied; and (4) the fourth and final payment when the building is completed and ready for occupancy.

Still other variations follow a variety of practices. One calls for advances at such stages as: installation of the foundation; construction of superstructure floor by floor; completion of roof; plastering; installation of trim; and so forth. In more informal disbursements, the practice is to avoid a fixed pattern but to make advances to the builder as he needs cash, provided the inspector knows the builder well and feels that the lender is well protected by the progress of the building plus the lot value. This kind of disbursement procedure is not recommended, because it is too personal in character.

A second kind of pattern of advances requires the builder to submit all bills for material, from subcontractors in particular, to the mortgagee. These bills may be paid directly by the latter and charged against the construction loan. This plan is most often resorted to in periods of economic uncertainty or in cases where the mortgagee is not too sure of the financial status of the mortgagor.

A third pattern, applicable particularly to more pretentious structures, sets up a definite schedule of advances which is related to the progress of the work. While the mortgagee should make frequent enough inspections to keep himself informed of the progress of construction—under either plan of advances—he is likely to be best informed when a definite schedule of advances is stipulated.

The use of construction loans is restricted to certain types of financial institutions that have found them advantageous. Insurance companies generally, and many commercial banks, have made little use of them in the past. There is some evidence that they are becoming more interested in them. Savings and loan associations, on the other hand, frequently supply construction loan funds. The ordinary individual lenders make little use of construction loans. Their lack of experience with such types of financing causes them to avoid complications which may surround their use.

Nature of Construction Loan Mortgage The mortgage used to evidence a debt incurred to provide funds needed for construction purposes may follow one of several patterns. In one, commonly used for home construction in particular, the mortgage may read just like any other such instrument with all the details needed to anticipate a maturity in 20 years. In other words, there is nothing to identify such a mortgage in terms of a construction loan. If it permits unrestricted prepayments it may be superseded by a different mortgage, probably with a different mortgagee, as soon as the construction is completed. This is usually designated as the permanent mortgage. As stated above, the original mortgage may be the permanent one.

In a second case, the lender may be willing to accept the debt-paying capacity of the original borrower but may hesitate to agree in advance to permit the substitution of a subsequent purchaser of the completed property unless and until he is satisfied with the ability of such a purchaser to meet his obligations on the loan. The mortgage in such case is drawn in a manner that permits the lender to continue the loan with a subsequent purchaser or to refuse to permit the assumption of the mortgage without the consent of the lender. Such an arrangement also leaves the purchaser free to do his own financing, using the proceeds to pay off the original mortgage.

In the third place, some lenders are restricted either by the law under which they operate or by their policies from making construction loans. They will gladly do the permanent financing once the building is completed. In such cases it is necessary to use the facilities of another lender for construction financing. The mortgage used for this purpose will be a term mortgage, to be superseded by the permanent loan after construction is completed. In fact, when a definite takeout commitment is made by the prospective holder of the permanent mortgage, the interim financing partakes of the nature of ordinary business credit, backed by the financial ability and reputation of the borrower.

Procedure for Construction Loans Because so many real estate mortgage institutions have been hesitant about making construction loans, a representative of a federal savings and loan association that was an early lender in the field set forth the procedure followed by his association.[1] The steps recommended were as follows: (1) Promote construction loan services by contacting particularly architects, builders, and building supply dealers. (2) Have plans and specifications accompany the application for a loan. This will enable the lender to check the capacity of the builder and, if necessary, to recommend changes in plans and specifications. (3) Have a definite agreement upon stage payments based upon work progress. (4) Make adequate periodic inspec-

---

[1] Julian R. Fleischmann, "Why Make Construction Loans?" *National Savings and Loan Journal,* April 1950, pp. 8–9.

tions (not less than the number of stage payments in addition to footer inspection) to check the quality of construction against the plans and specifications and to make sure that the borrower is entitled to his next advance on the loan. (5) Use a definite written agreement to accompany the execution of the mortgage, to provide not only for a schedule of payments but for other matters such as failure to comply with plans and specifications. (6) Arrange for continuation searches to protect against intervening liens. (7) Provide for retention of a sufficient part of a loan to protect against unfinished items which might cause embarrassment to the owner-occupant.

Construction Loan Fees Fees charged for construction loans are presumed to cover extra costs incurred by the mortgagee, particularly for inspections of the building as it progresses. In practice, several patterns are used: (1) In highly competitive markets, with several bidders for construction loans, the costs, or most of them, may be absorbed by the lender. Where this is done the lender may lose money if the mortgage is prepared within a year or two. (2) Fees sufficient to meet the additional out-of-pocket costs incurred by the lender, as determined by his past experience, may be charged. (3) The lender may charge what the traffic will bear under the guise of construction loan fees, with the expectation that he will realize a profit therefrom. If this induces him to make construction loans because of their profit possibilities, he may make loans with too high an element of risk.

One note of caution should be observed in drafting agreements for the payment of construction loan fees. The attorney for the mortgagee should make sure that the agreement is so drawn that the payments made by the mortgagor are for the protection of the mortgagee only. Otherwise the latter may find that he is undertaking to protect the mortgagor against the failure of the contractor or others to live up to the terms of the plans and specifications. Since this is not ordinarily the intent of construction loan fees, the contract should be so drawn that there is no doubt about this limitation.

Policies in Granting Construction Loans Lending institutions follow one of four policies on the subject of construction loans: (1) Some know what problems are involved and stay away from them because of their complications. (2) Some make no construction loans because they fear the presence of problems of which they know too little. (3) A third group makes construction loans without seriously investigating the presence of problems which may cause trouble. (4) Some make construction loans only after careful safeguards of the interests of the lender have been provided. Probably only the first and last of these policies can be defended.

Many complications in making construction loans are not normally present in making loans against properties already constructed. Some of them are legal. Others are not. Contingencies of all sorts may interfere with the plans of the borrower. Among them are delays caused by bad weather, material shortages, labor stoppages, and so on. Whatever the cause, the failure of the builder to make a success of his venture may catapult the lender into the construction business. Occasionally, if the lender is forced to take over an incomplete structure, he may be able to dispose of it as is. More often he is obligated to complete the building, for sale if possible and for renting if necessary.

In spite of the hazards of construction loans, someone must provide needed financial support for builders in most markets. For the institution which knows the nature of these hazards and provides for protection against them, this is a good source of business. If the institution knows the hazards and still decides that it is not equipped to handle construction loans, it is better to avoid possible trouble rather than court it by doing the job poorly.

Intervening Liens One problem that is always faced by a mortgagee when the mortgage provides for future advances has to do with the priority of intervening liens. Suppose, for example, that a construction mortgage has been duly executed and recorded, and a first advance has been made. Suppose also that, before a second advance is due, a junior lien of some kind is filed against the property. If now a second advance is made under the original mortgage, does it take precedence over the intervening junior lien? Here again there is considerable confusion, because of a variety of court decisions, some of which conflict with others made under similar conditions.

A general rule seems to sanction the idea that if the mortgage contract makes the future advances obligatory if stipulated conditions are met by the mortgagor, then the mortgagee may make the future advances regardless of the existence of intervening liens. This rule seems to govern even though the obligatory nature of the advances is not spelled out in the mortgage but is dependent upon a definite oral agreement. When the mortgage mentions future advances, however, junior lienors are at least on notice of the probable superior lien of the senior mortgagee. The junior lienor may still wish to pursue the subject further to try to determine if a contract for future advances actually exists.

Maryland follows a practice different from the one generally accepted. Here a contract for future advances must be definite to the point of stating specifically the exact amount of each advance and the time it is to be made. Otherwise, intervening liens may acquire priority over the part of the mortgage on which advances have not been made.

Where there is no definite contract requiring the mortgagee to make future advances, court decisions may follow at least two paths. One leads to the conclusion that the mortgagee is protected in the priority of his future advances, even though he does not take the trouble to search the record for intervening liens. However, if he has notice outside of the record that such junior liens exist, he is bound by their priority over his future advances. This seems to be the prevailing rule. The other path leads to a different conclusion. In a minority of cases, the courts hold that, before discretionary future advances are made by the mortgagee, he must search the record and be bound by any intervening liens that he finds there. The unsatisfactory nature of the answers available in considering the question at issue places both mortgagee and mortgagor at a distinct disadvantage. For example, suppose that a mortgagor borrows $8,000 and gives a first mortgage to secure his debt. Suppose that by regular and uninterrupted payments he has reduced the amount of his indebtedness to $5,000. Suppose that he now needs to borrow $1,000 for repairs to his house or for any other purpose. Can the mortgagee make this advance safely without a search of the records for intervening liens? Because of his past satisfactory experience with the borrower, he might like very much to make the advance and add it to the unpaid balance of the loan. But if he must first search the record for intervening liens, he can hardly afford to render this service without charging the borrower for it.

Then, if he finds intervening liens which he must observe, he may be compelled to refuse the request of the borrower, thereby possibly reducing the value of his security because the owner cannot finance needed repairs. Nor can the lender recast the loan, adding to a new mortgage the amount needed by the mortgagor. In this case he has incurred an expense which he must pass along to the borrower without rendering him an acceptable service.

Some mortgagees rely primarily upon their past experience with the mortgagor, obtain from him an affidavit to the effect that there are no intervening liens, and disregard the record. They testify that the risk they run under such conditions is not great. Meantime, if his past experience with the mortgagor has been unsatisfactory, the mortgagee would probably not wish to make an additional advance, regardless of the existence or absence of intervening liens.

Other Uses of Open-End Mortgage The open-end mortgage is generally desirable from the standpoint of both borrowers and lenders. Under present payment plans, a mortgage is commonly amortized over an extended period of time. Under an open-end mortgage, the mortgagor can maintain or improve his mortgaged property, often his home, by borrowing from his original lender within the terms of his original mortgage. Repayment of the additional borrowing can be amortized by a relatively small addition, if any, to the monthly payments required under the mortgage. Compared with personal loans or even FHA loans for modernization, which must be repaid in a relatively short time, borrowing under an original open-end mortgage is often decidedly advantageous. The borrowing costs where repairs and improvements are financed by a loan secured by a second mortgage are also relatively high. The advantage of the open-end mortgage to the lender is readily appreciated if a comparison is made of the relative security values of a property which is well maintained or improved and one which is allowed to deteriorate.

Use of the open-end mortgage is not limited to application of the newly borrowed funds to improving the mortgaged property. Increasing the lien under such a mortgage can also provide economical financing of other unusual family obligations, such as purchase of a new car, medical care, or education for the children.

What is particularly desired in an open-end mortgage is to secure future advances without running the risk of making such advances junior to intervening liens. In recent years several states have passed legislation pointing in this direction. Among these states are Connecticut, Louisiana, Maryland, Massachusetts, Missouri, New Jersey, New Hampshire, North Dakota, and Vermont.

In the absence of such legislation, numerous questions are left unanswered. One answer given to financial institutions by conservative lawyers is the use of second mortgages to evidence future advances. For example, suppose that a mortgagor executed an original mortgage for $8,000. Suppose also that this mortgage has been amortized down to $4,500. An additional advance of $2,000 is desired, for any purpose that may suit the needs of the borrower. The mortgagee secures from the borrower and his spouse signatures to a second mortgage for the added advance. If a short check of the record—covering the period since the original loan was granted—finds no intervening liens, the money is disbursed to the borrower. Should there be an intervening lien—say, for $250—the second mortgage could then be rewritten for $2,250, and $250 could be held in escrow by the lending institutions until this intervening lien has been canceled.

Where such a plan is followed, the amount of the advance will be added to the balance on the books of the lender. The monthly payments may or may not be increased. The period of amortization will probably be extended to take care of the additional repayments. The sum of the first mortgage balance and the second mortgage will probably not exceed the original amount of the first mortgage. Since a second mortgage is being used, this total might be larger than the original amount. The time necessary to amortize the two mortgages will not be longer than the period for which the lender is authorized to make real estate loans. This is necessarily so, since the new payment program will amortize the remainder of the first loan balance as well as the second mortgage over the remaining time necessary to pay off both loans.

This plan meets the needs of many borrowers and is a source of new business for lending institutions. The short check of the record may be inexpensive except for very small advances desired. For example, such a record check would cost as much for a $100 advance as for one for $3,000. The interest rate may or may not be increased. That will depend upon the cost of money at the time of the new advance. Indeed, costs might differ for the two loans. The original loan might continue to carry a 6 percent rate while the second mortgage might be written for 8 percent.

Participation Mortgage One plan of real estate finance which formerly had considerable favor in the eastern section of the country, particularly during the decade of the 1920s, is the participation mortgage. In effect, this was a form of trust. The *res*, or trust property, consisted of one large mortgage or a collection of smaller mortgages. If the latter, considerable leeway was given the trustee in permitting substitutions of collateral as the small individual mortgages were paid off. The money needed to finance the collateral held by the trustee was obtained by selling what amounted to certificates of beneficial interest in the total collateral. These participation certificates possessed some, but not all, of the characteristics of mortgage bonds issued by a corporation.

Both lack of capital and lack of experience recommend the use of mortgage-participation certificates as an alternative to the direct purchase of mortgages. The investor may have only a limited amount of money that he can use for this purpose. He can buy a participation certificate for $100 or $1,000, whereas he probably could not invest this amount either directly or indirectly in a single mortgage. Even though his investable surplus is sufficient to cover the amount of a single mortgage, his lack of experience might cause him to hesitate to take the risk involved. By buying a certificate of beneficial interest in a block of mortgages, his risk is spread instead of concentrated. In addition, he should have the benefit of expert and experienced management to manage his investment for him.

In recent years, institutional lenders have been acquiring interests in mortgage participations as a convenient means of expanding loan portfolios, particularly on an extraterritorial basis. The new Government National Mortgage Association (GNMA) will guarantee securities backed by pools of federally underwritten mortgages in order to tap the public market for funds to finance more real estate acquisition and development.

Because of a recent change in the federal income tax law creating tax benefits for investors in real estate investment trusts meeting certain requirements, this form has experienced a revival. This new type of investment trust is discussed in detail in Chapter 7.

Purchase-Money Mortgage Any mortgage given by the vendee to secure the payment of all or a part of the purchase price of the land is called a purchase-money mortgage. As such it must be differentiated from mortgages given to secure a loan from a third party for the purchase of the land. It has been said that a purchase-money mortgage carries the highest priority that an equity court can consider. If it is executed simultaneously with the deed which conveys title to the property, it takes precedence over judgments, other mortgages, liens, and all other debts of the mortgagor. If the mortgagor should anticipate a purchase of land by placing a mortgage against it before the deed and purchase-money mortgage are executed, the latter would take precedence over the former even though the former were made a matter of record first. The recorded mortgage could have no effect until the mortgagor obtained title to the land. By the time he did so, it would be encumbered by the purchase-money mortgage.

While the purchase-money mortgage need not be designated as such to give it priority, its time of execution is governing. If, for example, a deed were executed some time before the purchase-money mortgage, intervening liens could take priority over such a mortgage if they were filed after the deed was executed but before the mortgage was placed upon the record. The purchase-money mortgage should be filed simultaneously with the deed to avoid any question about intervening liens.

Purchase-money mortgages retain their priority even when written in the name of a third party at the request of the vendor of the real estate. It is not necessary for the spouse of the mortgagor to sign the mortgage. This is true even when the mortgagee becomes a third person. This third person may even provide the funds with which to purchase the property. For the protection of the mortgagee, it is well to state in the mortgage that the mortgage is accepted as a part of the purchase price of the property. A purchase-money mortgage can represent either a senior or a junior lien against the property used as security.

Subordination Clause In the disposal of unimproved land, a variety of practices are followed. In one that is frequently used, the seller transfers title, taking back a purchase-money first mortgage as part payment for the land. Since such a sale is likely to be to a builder who needs a construction loan to finance the improvements which he plans to place on the land, it follows that such a loan must be given priority over the purchase-money mortgage. The well-informed subdivider is not likely to accept a second mortgage which permits just any first lien to take precedence over it. In such a case, an unscrupulous purchaser might take advantage of the seller and simply borrow money with the land as security for a first mortgage which would have priority over the purchase-money second mortgage.

The more common practice would be to make the purchase-money mortgage a first mortgage in form but include a subordination clause which agrees that it shall become a junior lien if and when a construction loan is obtained for the purpose of financing the structure to be built upon the land. As a result, the original first lien purchase-money mortgage becomes a junior lien. This the subdivision company seller willingly agrees to because it will be to its advantage in selling additional building sites to encourage all the construction possible in its locality. The average individual who owns a building site for sale can ill afford to run the risk of selling it in the manner indicated here.

Maturity Dates of Mortgages The maturity dates of mortgages represent a most interesting process of evolution. The earliest concept of maturity date left the determination of the time the mortgage should fall due largely to the discretion of the mortgagee. In other words, the mortgage was a demand instrument. This form of mortgage was common in the northeastern part of the United States until fairly recently. The next step was to write the mortgage for a nominal term of one year. This was later extended to become an actual term mortgage with a definite term of one year or more. When the principle of amortization was introduced into real estate finance, the concept of maturity at a fixed future date faded into obscurity. The payment experience of the borrower, rather than the calendar, fixed the maturity date of the mortgage. This was particularly true when prepayment privileges were added to the principle of amortization.

Demand and One-Year Mortgages Mortgages written to be paid on demand of the mortgagee or for a nominal period of one year are likely to continue in effect indefinitely. As long as the mortgagor meets his interest obligations and pays the taxes on the property, the principal amount of the debt is not likely to be demanded of him. The result is a long-term mortgage without any reduction of principal required. Due to transfers of title or to the desires of the mortgagor, the mortgage may be redeemed at any time and hence may actually be a short-term mortgage. On the other hand, there are cases where demand or one-year mortgages have been in effect for as long as half a century or more.

This form of mortgage results in a curious paradox. As long as the interest is being paid when due and as long as tax payments are kept current, the mortgagee is content to retain his investment. If economic conditions make it necessary for the debtor to default in his taxes or interest, such default will occur in a depressed real estate market. Consequently, a foreclosure suit would probably result in passing title to the mortgagee at a time when he has no use for the property and might have difficulty in disposing of it to his advantage. Hence he may not act quickly in case of default, but will temporize with the situation in the hope that the mortgagor will recover his debt-paying capacity. The net result is a paradox: the mortgagee does not desire to demand the repayment of the principal when interest payments are being met; and he is reluctant to make such a demand when they are in default.

Term Mortgages Some mortgages mature at a stipulated future date with no amortization of the principal. Interest payments on term loans are usually required semiannually. The most common terms for which such mortgages run are two, three, or five years. Since there is no provision for amortization of the principal, the percentage of loan to appraised value of the security is likely to be somewhat lower than in the case of amortized mortgages. Where the term mortgage is used, in contrast with the demand mortgage or one written for a nominal term of one year, it is expected that the mortgage will be repaid at the maturity date. It may be extended, or a new mortgage for another term of years may succeed it.

Sometimes provision for partial amortization is written into the mortgage. For example, suppose that the maturity date of the mortgage is five years hence. At each semiannual interest-paying period perhaps $2\frac{1}{2}$ percent will be required to be paid on the original amount of the loan principal. At the maturity date of the mortgage 25 percent of the amount of the loan will have been paid off. If the mortgage is renewed, the amount owed at the beginning of the next period will therefore be only 75 percent as large as the original loan.

Amortized Mortgages The latest pattern to develop in the evolution of the mortgage repayment program is the amortized mortgage. Recognizing that values of real estate may decline over the years, plans have been developed for the progressive improvement in the status of the mortgagee by writing the mortgage in such terms that, as the property depreciates in value, the amount of the debt is reduced correspondingly. This gradual but persistent reduction in the amount of the debt is known as amortization. In practice it follows several variations.

One of the earliest, and still commonly used, plans of mortgage amortization pays homage to the sanctity of mortgage repayments based upon 1 percent of the original amount of the debt per month. Regardless of the percentage of debt to security value, there has developed a kind of theological preference for a payment representing 1 percent of the original debt per month. In earlier days principal adjustments were made only at the end of each six months. One result of this practice was to make the effective interest rate higher than the nominal rate, since the mortgagee had free use of the excess of payments over interest accruals. The use of 1 percent per month is not as common as formerly, particularly in view of the higher interest rates of recent years.

It is not necessary to have monthly payments in order to apply the principle of amortization. Quarterly, semiannual, or annual payments might serve equally well. Or even irregular payments conceivably might result in amortization of the debt. The important consideration is to make sure that the payments include not only interest accruals but something to be applied against the principal as well.

Reduction of principal follows either of two patterns. In one, the periodic decrease in the amount of the outstanding indebtedness is predetermined. For example, on a $6,000 loan it may be agreed that $35 shall be paid on the principal each month. Interest for the month is added to this amount to determine the amount due. If the interest rate is 7 percent, the amount due at the end of the first month would be $70—$35 to be applied to the principal and $35 as interest. For the second month the principal would be only $5,965, so the interest would be only $34.80; total payment, $69.80. In other words, the monthly payment would decrease month by month, reflecting the decreasing interest charged.

Under the alternative plan, a level payment per month for the entire life of the loan, to include interest and principal installments, would be agreed upon at the time the mortgage is executed. In the above case, let us assume that $70 per month is the amount agreed upon. At the end of the first month, $35 would be deducted for interest and $35 would be used to reduce the principal balance. At the end of the second month, $34.80 would be deducted for interest and $35.20 would be credited to the balance of the loan. In other words, each month the interest charges would decrease and the principal installment would increase correspondingly. The level payment plan is more commonly used than the variable payment plan. It is usually designated as the standard amortization plan. The other plan is called the Springfield plan.

Monthly Payment Direct Reduction Mortgages The youngest member of the amortization family is the monthly payment direct reduction loan. While not confined entirely to residential real estate, it is most commonly used there. While the 1 percent per month payment pattern can be used here, it receives less emphasis than formerly. First, the mortgagee and the mortgagor agree upon the essential features of the loan plan. These include the amount of the loan, the number of years allowed for repayment, and the rate of interest. These are dependent rather than independent variables. For example, a high percentage loan, in relation to the appraised value of the security, might call for a higher rate of interest and a shorter period of amortization, whereas a low percentage loan would merit a lower interest rate and a longer period of amortization.

The interrelation of the three factors mentioned above determines the amount of the monthly payment. From each payment is first deducted the amount of interest accrued on the unpaid principal of the debt. Second, the mortgagee reimburses itself for any taxes, insurance premiums, or other expenses, if any, incurred by it for the preservation and protection of its security. The balance is applied against the principal, thereby establishing a new and smaller principal upon which interest for the succeeding month is calculated. This process continues until the entire debt is amortized. Should the debtor fail to meet a regular payment, the interest is still computed on a monthly basis. With a level monthly payment throughout the life of the mortgage and with a decreasing amount of this credited to interest payments, the amounts used to reduce the principal balance increase correspondingly month by month.

The monthly payment direct reduction loan plan helps both mortgagor and mortgagee. It enables the owner of the property to absorb his debt from his income. It never falls due at an inconvenient time. Sometimes it is said to have no maturity date because, so long as the debtor meets his obligations, the creditor has no right to demand the full amount due on the debt. As a matter of fact, however, a portion of the debt matures each month. Failure to pay this portion when it is due may cause the acceleration clause in the mortgage to be invoked, thereby precipitating the maturity of the unpaid principal.

As a further means of helping the mortgagor, the monthly payment direct reduction loan plan frequently provides that, with each monthly payment of interest and principal installment, there shall be included a pro rata proportion of annual real estate taxes (estimated if necessary) and perhaps of insurance premiums as well. Since most borrowers upon residential real estate security can budget their income and expenses on a monthly basis more readily than upon a semiannual basis, this monthly payment of taxes avoids the complications that arise twice a year when both tax and mortgage payments are due in the same month. The mortgagee holds tax and insurance payments as trustee and pays them out as they fall due.

Meantime, the monthly payment direct reduction loan plan helps the lender by increasing the security behind his loan as each monthly installment on the principal amount of the debt is credited. Month by month the indebtedness decreases, in most cases more rapidly than the value of the property declines. Another factor of strength for the mortgagee is that prepayment privileges are usually included in monthly payment direct reduction mortgages. Mortgagors who take advantage of this type of privilege increase the margin of safety for the mortgagee and build for themselves a better basis for adjustment in their obligations in times of crisis.

Advance payments may be handled in one of two ways by the mortgagee. The one selected usually follows the wishes of the mortgagor. Under one—less commonly used—the mortgagor may build up a credit equivalent to a few monthly payments. This credit is held in a separate account and may be drawn upon to liquidate the obligations of future monthly payments that otherwise might be in default. One disadvantage of this method is that the mortgagor receives no return upon this amount unless he has it credited to a savings account. Otherwise, the mortgagee is simply a trustee holding funds at the command of the mortgagor.

Under the other plan the advance payments are used immediately to reduce the principal balance of the loan. This improves the position of the mortgagee so that he can afford to be lenient in helping the mortgagor to make adjustments, should they be necessary at some future time, without jeopardizing his own security. It sometimes happens that, after the principal balance has been reduced substantially, the mortgagee would prefer to collect only interest for a considerable time thereafter, thus maintaining a larger income-producing potential in the mortgage.

At such time the amount of the monthly payments may be substantially reduced, either at the request of the mortgagor or at the suggestion of the mortgagee. Or the amount of the loan may later be increased, for the purpose of making repairs or improvements to the property or for any other purpose, without any increase in the amount of the monthly payments. Subject to the limitations of future advances on mortgage security, discussed earlier in this chapter, this may be a very fruitful source of satisfactory business for the mortgagee.

Packaged Mortgage The growing popularity of practices of selling in one package not only the land and the structure erected thereupon, but all the fixtures needed for comfortable living, makes necessary a reexamination of what is meant by "fixtures." Tradition has included in the meaning of this term three concepts, each of which is capable of flexibility of definition: (1) A fixture must be annexed to and made a part of the real estate. (2) It must be appropriate to the part of the real estate to which it is attached. (3) It must be intended by the party making the annexation that it shall become and remain a part of the real estate. All that remains is to determine the meaning of "annexation," "appropriate," and "intention."

In times past our ancestors heated water in a kettle on a stove in order that members of the family could take their Saturday night bath in the family tub. No one considered either kettle or tub as real estate. They were not annexed to the real estate. Therefore, the other two concepts mentioned above can be disregarded. Modern practice does annex the bathtub as a part of the bathroom fixtures and annexes the automatic water heater as a part of the permanent plumbing fixtures of the house. We find both of these fixtures appropriate to their uses. We also find that the person responsible for their installation intended them to serve the purposes for which they are now used.

Currently we are wondering why kitchen ranges, refrigerators, garbage disposal units, kitchen cabinets (not necessarily built in), ventilating fans, and even air-conditioning units, television sets, and home-freezer units should not be considered as attached to the real estate. To be sure, the method of attachment may be by a pipe coupling, an electric plug, or a few screws instead of by nails or bolts and nuts, but they are, nevertheless, attached. They are certainly appropriate to the uses to which they are being put. And their sale as a part of the house that is being sold indicates the intent of the person who installed them. In one combination or another they are needed for comfortable living.

Yet we hesitate to include some of the facilities mentioned above when we mortgage real estate for fear that they will be adjudged to be chattels instead of real estate fixtures. If the court finds them to be the former, the mortgagee may discover that his security is worth somewhat less than he thought it was. About a century ago a judge found that "the law of fixtures is in a somewhat chaotic state."[2] The learned jurist would find familiar surroundings if he were to reexamine the law of fixtures today.

Some brave souls undertake to sanction the financing of these articles needed for comfortable living as a part of the security for the real estate mortgage by enumerating, immediately following the land description in the mortgage, the things that are sought to be included, but about which there may be some doubt as to legal coverage. This enumeration is then followed by a declaration that such articles "are and shall be deemed to be fixtures" and are to be considered in all respects as a part of the real estate which serves as security for the mortgage. This is a brave declaration which attempts to settle legal difficulties by a sort of manifesto. However, the courts may still decide that all or some of the articles enumerated are still chattels and therefore not a proper subject for inclusion in a real estate mortgage. Therefore, their removal and sale would not affect the interests of the real estate mortgagee.

Prior to the Uniform Commercial Code, a great many mortgagees took the precaution of double-filing. That is, the real estate mortgage was placed on record as such, and the property described in the mortgage that was capable of being considered personal property was covered by a chattel mortgage that was filed among personal property records. In some cases, the original real estate mortgage describing items that might be considered personal property was recorded as a real estate lien and filed as a lien on chattels simultaneously.

This situation has been ameliorated by the adoption in all states, except Louisiana, of the Uniform Commercial Code. This law has been generally adopted to provide that when the collateral is goods which at the time the security attaches are, or are to become, fixtures, the security instrument (no longer called a "chattel mortgage") should be filed in the office where a real estate mortgage would be filed. Fortunately there is general agreement that one place for filing is sufficient and that the proper place is where a real estate mortgage would be

---

[2] *State Savings Bank* v. *Kercheral,* 65 Mo. 682 (1877).

filed or recorded. Thus, under the new law there is no additional filing required with the chattel records.

Arguments in Favor of Packaged Mortgages At least six arguments are advanced in favor of the use of packaged mortgages. These are in addition to the selling argument of the builder who presents a house equipped with those appliances needed for comfortable living. From the purely financing point of view, the arguments in favor of packaged mortgages are: (1) The homeowner deals with one lender only. He need not worry about a variety of monthly payments to cover parts of the same property. (2) Payments for the home equipment are distributed over a longer repayment period. Instead of allowing a few months or, at most, a few years for purchasing the refrigerator and other household equipment, their financing covers essentially the same period of time as the financing of the house. (3) The interest rate on the mortgage loan, which in this case covers equipment also, is always lower than the carrying charges on installment sales. (4) The payments may be made uniform throughout the life of the loan. As an alternative, where several items of household equipment are purchased on the installment plan, the monthly payments required will be very heavy for several months or a few years. In some cases a middle position is agreed upon, with the monthly payments on the packaged mortgage somewhat larger for the first 10 years of the mortgage term. Even then they would be less than under installment purchases. (5) Since the cost of the equipment is merged with the cost of the house, the amount of the down payment attributable to equipment alone is less than if the equipment were purchased separately. (3) The mortgagee can better control the total amount of monthly payments by the mortgagor.

Blanket Mortgages As the name suggests, a blanket mortgage covers several pieces of real estate as security. Several sets of circumstances give rise to its use. Subdividers sometimes give a blanket mortgage as part payment for acreage. As each lot is sold it is released from this mortgage by agreement with the mortgagee according to a schedule of release credits. Normally, the amount of cash required to be paid to the mortgagee would be considerably more than the ratio of the number of lots to the amount of the mortgage. For example, if 500 lots are covered by a $100,000 mortgage, it might require a payment of $400 instead of $200, to obtain a release of 1 lot from the mortgage.

Sometimes an owner of various pieces of real estate needs to borrow more than any one property can produce by the use of a mortgage. Several properties are included as security for a blanket mortgage. As lump-sum payments, agreed upon in advance or at the time of the payments, are made on the unpaid balance of the debt, one by one the properties are released from the mortgage.

A third practice commonly used by some mortgagees follows a pattern like this. A wishes to purchase B's unencumbered property for $20,000. A hopes to dispose of his own property, presently mortgaged for $5,000 and priced at $15,000. Instead of making sure of the sale of his own property first, he contracts to buy B's property, putting up $5,000 in cash and offering both properties as security for a blanket loan of $20,000. The new mortgagee pays off the mortgage on A's property and has a first lien on both. The proceeds from the sale of A's property are applied to the blanket mortgage, securing a release of A's property so that it may be sold to C. The remainder of the debt is then owed by A against the property formerly owned by B as security.

Corporate mortgages are frequently of a blanket character. In addition to specific property named in the mortgage as security, arrangements such as "after-acquired" property clauses and "general" mortgages carry the blanket connotation.

QUESTIONS AND PROBLEMS

1. What are the three principal kinds of mortgages and how are they basically different in derivation?
2. Would you recognize an equitable mortgage by the form of the instrument on which it is based? Why or why not?
3. What is a vendor's lien? How may a vendor protect it?
4. How does a deed of trust differ from a mortgage?
5. What problems do subsequent lienholders create for first mortgagees holding open-end mortgages permitting future advances? What precautions may be taken to maintain the highest priority?
6. What are the common practices for making advances under construction loans and for policing the loans after advances have been made?
7. What is a purchase-money mortgage and how is it different in effect from a mortgage given to secure a loan from a third party for the purchase of land?
8. Is it essential that a mortgagor's wife sign a release of dower on a purchase-money mortgage? Why or why not?
9. If mortgages usually establish priority by the time at which they are recorded, what purpose is fulfilled by the use of subordination clauses in the mortgage instrument?
10. Indicate the present status of each of the following forms of mortgages: (a) demand, (b) term, and (c) amortized.
11. What is a packaged mortgage? Do you consider this form of financing sound?
12. What is a blanket mortgage and how is it used?

4

Mortgage Default and Its Consequences

What Constitutes Default An ordinary dictionary definition of a "default" is "a failure to fulfill a contract, agreement, or duty, especially a financial obligation." From this it follows that a default in a mortgage contract can result from any breach of the contract. The most common is the failure to meet an installment of the interest or principal payments. But failure to pay taxes or insurance premiums when due may also result in a default which may precipitate a foreclosure action. Indeed, some mortgages make specific stipulations to this effect. Even a failure to keep the security in repair may constitute a technical default. We speak of this as a technical default because it would seldom result in an actual foreclosure sale. It might be difficult for the mortgagee to prove that the repair clause in the mortgage had been broken unless the property showed definite evidence of the effects of waste.

From another point of view, default is defined first in the breach of the letter of the contract and then in the attitude of the mortgagee. By this is meant that, even though there is a breach of contract, the mortgagee may see fit to ignore it or to postpone action in doing something about it. In case of default accompanied by abandonment, the probabilities are that the mortgagee will act quickly to protect his interests against vandalism, neglect, and waste. If, on the other hand, the mortgagor is a man of good character, has generally met his obligations promptly in the past, wishes to retain his interest in the property, and is only temporarily unable to meet his obligations, a default is not likely to be declared by the mortgagee for an indefinite period.

A form of default definition currently used reads as follows:

It is agreed that time is of the essence of this contract and that in the event of default in payment of any monthly installment or any part thereof for a period of sixty days after the same is due and payable as herein provided, or in the event of failure to pay when due all the premiums and renewals on the insurance policies on said real estate, and to pay when due all the taxes, assessments or other charges that may be levied, assessed or charged by any public authority on said real estate or the interest of this Association in said real estate or the interest of this Association in this note, or in the event of a breach of any covenant or condition in the mortgage given to secure this note, then the whole of the principal and accrued interest on this note, shall at the option of the holder hereof become immediately due and payable without demand or notice, and the undersigned do hereby specifically waive such demand or notice, and the filing of any action on this note shall be deemed to be an exercise of said option. Any failure to exercise said option shall not constitute a waiver of the right to exercise the same at any other time.

Foreclosure When we speak commonly of "mortgage foreclosure" we are using language loosely. What is really foreclosed is the mortgagor's equity of redemption. When the equity of redemption merely takes the position that a mortgagor in default should have more time in which to meet his obligations, this could become unfair to the mortgagee unless some provision is made to limit the amount of time at the disposal of the mortgagor. Hence, as an offset to the equity of redemption, the mortgagee was given the right to foreclose it or cut it off.

In practice, most mortgagees are not anxious to take property from mortgagors. They prefer to collect the amounts owed them and are likely to be lenient and patient when circumstances warrant it. Seldom does the mortgagee insist upon the exact letter of his contract. Nor does he rush into court to insist upon his full pound of flesh. But after patience and leniency have been extended to delinquent mortgagors, eventually a settlement seems necessary. Then foreclosure proceedings are started. Incidentally, it is interesting to see how frequently a delinquent mortgagor gets off the delinquent list by paying up past-due obligations as soon as foreclosure proceedings are started.

Strict Foreclosure It is still possible in some instances to follow the rule of strict foreclosure. In other words, in such cases the mortgagee may ask that the mortgagor's right of redemption be completely cut off and that unqualified title be vested in the mortgagee. If this is done the mortgagor loses all rights in the property if he does not redeem it before foreclosure becomes effective. After the equity court gives the mortgagor one last chance to meet his obligations, he is thereafter barred from troubling the mortgagee about the property mortgaged—if he fails to make good. However, the court may not relieve him of his obligations. He may still be held for any part of his obligations that cannot be satisfied by the forfeiture of his claims against the property.

In general, however, the strict foreclosure rule is not favored. In most states, legislation has eliminated it, at least in theory. In specific cases, an equity court may permit its application if it finds that undue injury will not result.

Where strict foreclosure is permitted, after the mortgagee obtains title to and possession of the property, he may then proceed to bring suit for a deficiency judgment against the mortgagor, if any applies. The amount of such judgment would be determined by the court by the process of a proper valuation of the property to determine its relation to the amount claimed by the mortgagee. In the state of Maine, it is still possible to use the strict rule of foreclosure without resorting to the formality of a sale of the property.

Strict foreclosure is sometimes used where a junior lienor is inadvertently left out of the list of those joined in a suit against the mortgagor obligated on the senior lien. Subsequent to the foreclosure suit against the one obligated on the first mortgage, the plaintiff may see fit to bring a strict foreclosure suit against the holder of the junior lien. By this action the plaintiff puts the junior lienholder on notice that he must either act to protect his interests or be frozen out at the time the foreclosure sale of the property takes place.

Alternatives to Strict Foreclosure In the absence of the right of strict foreclosure, the mortgagee possesses two types of remedies to protect his interests in case of default by the mortgagor: (1) He may sue in a law court on the debt, obtain judgment, and execute the judgment against the property of the mortgagor. (2) He may bring foreclosure suit in a court of equity, following the form of strict foreclosure, but ending in a decree of foreclosure and sale. Since these choices are open to the mortgagee in some states, he must determine from the facts in the case which route to follow.

If he elects to sue on the debt, any intervening liens entered between the date of execution of the mortgage and the date of judgment on the debt must be taken into account. They cannot be frozen out, as they could be under foreclosure sale. On the other hand, a judgment against the debtor can be executed against any property owned by him. For this reason it may be advantageous in some cases for the mortgagee to sue on the debt rather than foreclose if he is given a choice.

The prevailing procedure in this country is a resort to a court of equity looking toward a decree of foreclosure and sale of the security. In many states this method of procedure is mandatory in all cases where the plaintiff resorts to a court of equity. While these are really two separate steps—foreclosure and sale—they are commonly treated as one.

Sale of Property Even though the mortgagor who defaults in his obligations and thereby faces foreclosure of his equity of redemption is unable to take advantage of his time extension, he is currently considered to have rights which should be protected in ways never contemplated in early mortgages. He is presumed to have an equity which can be realized only in the marketplace. Hence, currently, equity courts called upon to grant the mortgagee the right of foreclosure accompany their decision with a decree of sale to determine whether or not there is anything left for the mortgagor. Where a sale is decided upon, this of course represents a departure from the strict foreclosure rule.

If such sale realizes a price high enough to meet the expenses of the sale and the claims of the mortgagee and still leave a balance, this balance goes to the mortgagor. The demands of other claimants will be considered later. While foreclosure of the mortgagor's equity of redemption and sale of the property may be undertaken in two separate actions, at the present time they usually go together in practice.

In determining the amounts to be accounted for at a foreclosure sale, it must be remembered that the mortgage secures not only the principal amount of the debt but all lawful interest as well. The interest to be accounted for includes not only all amounts unpaid up to the time of foreclosure but all amounts accruing after default up to the date of the decree of sale.

The advertising of the sale, the place where it takes place, and the method of sale by a county sheriff, a referee, an auctioneer, or a master are all matters that are governed by local practice. While details differ, the results are approximately the same in all localities.

Taxes in Default Payment of taxes is an obligation of the mortgagor. As such, taxes constitute a prior lien against the security. Transfers of title always take into account accrued but unpaid taxes. Mortgages commonly contain tax clauses giving the mortgagee the right to pay taxes not paid regularly by the mortgagor. The amounts so paid are then added to the claims of the mortgagee. While the lien of taxes gives tax-collecting authorities the right to foreclose in case of default, such right is seldom exercised on first or even second default. Instead, the taxing authority may pursue an alternative policy of selling tax liens from time to time. Since they constitute superior liens prior to the claims of mortgagees if the taxing authorities have observed statutory procedure, and since they customarily carry high effective rates of interest, the mortgagee may prefer to save the accumulation of high interest as a prior claim by paying delinquent taxes and adding them to his claims.

If foreclosure becomes necessary, the mortgagee includes all taxes paid by him. Usually at the time of a foreclosure sale the purchaser is expected to pay all delinquent taxes, thus making the tax status of the property current. While this is common practice, on occasion the purchaser may take title subject to the lien of accumulated taxes instead. This is not likely to afford him an added advantage, since it would be seldom indeed that the property would not be worth the amount of accumulated taxes if it has had a mortgage against it.

Tax Sales In the preceding section we discussed the relation of delinquent taxes and mortgages. Where there is no mortgage against the property or where the mortgagee does not act to protect his interests against tax liens, it is expected that, sooner or later, pressure will be brought by taxing authorities to collect delinquent taxes. In effect, if not in form, the procedure followed is intended to parallel that in the foreclosure of mortgages. The time interval between the date of delinquency and the sale date varies from 20 days to 18 months. At the time of sale the purchaser receives a tax certificate, which is then subject to redemption in nearly all states. The period of redemption is usually two or three years. If the property is not redeemed by the delinquent taxpayer within this period, the purchaser at the tax sale is then entitled to receive a deed to the property. In Ohio, no period of redemption is provided, but the tax sale is postponed for three years and eight months after the date of delinquency. Meantime, the property may be redeemed at any time before the tax sale takes place but may not be subject to redemption thereafter.

In the absence of bidders at a tax sale—as might occur in periods of depression or in the sale of inexpensive vacant land—the property usually reverts to the state, the county, or some other local governmental unit. Such reversions do not in all cases enrich the new owner or provide the means of meeting delinquent tax obligations. Either the property may be practically worthless, as the complete absence of private bidders suggests, or the governmental unit may neglect to take steps to realize the best price that can be obtained from its disposition. States and local units are notoriously careless in their housekeeping habits in this area.

Tax Titles Tax titles are usually looked upon as weak evidences of ownership. The interest of the tax collector is to find someone willing and able to pay taxes for someone else in return for a claim against the property. The collector is not greatly concerned about passing good title. There is no suggestion of warranty. In addition to any defects in title irrespective of delinquent taxes, the unconcern of the tax collector may in turn result in added clouds on the title. Among the latter the following may occur: (1) Because of inaccurate description of the property or incorrect records of ownership, the notice of sale may be defective. (2) The property owner may have been denied his day in court. (3) The line of authority for the sale may not be clear. (4) Irregularities and carelessness, even in minor procedural matters, may give rise to an invalidation of the tax sale.

All of these depend in part upon the recuperative powers of the delinquent taxpayer. If he has lost interest in the property, or if he lacks the financial resources to protect his interests, he may interpose no objections that will interfere with the plans of the purchaser at the tax sale. Nevertheless, the risk is great enough to suggest caution and due attention even to minor details before purchasing tax liens.

Sale of property which has reverted to the state or some other governmental unit involves fewer complications than sale of tax liens with a tax deed to follow. Because of this, it appears that much confusion could be avoided if the governmental unit would follow a procedure which includes these steps: (1) retain tax liens until the end of the redemption period; (2) foreclose unredeemed liens; (3) sell titles to lands so acquired, giving good title therefor.

Fixing a Price Mortgage foreclosure sale proceeds from the assumption that a public auction is a satisfactory way to realize the best possible price in selling property. Hence, in some jurisdictions, the highest bidder gets the property irrespective of its cost, the amount of liens against it, or any other consideration. The mortgagee is usually the successful bidder. He can use his claims as a medium of exchange in the purchase—except for costs which must be paid in cash. Others must pay cash for their purchases, unless the successful bidder can arrange with the mortgagee to keep his lien alive. As a consequence, frequently only the mortgagee makes any serious bid for the property. In some states his right to bid is protected by statute, while in others the court of equity recognizes this method of protecting the mortgagee's interests. In the absence of either statutory permission or approval by the equity court, a mortgagee who buys the security for his claims may run some risk. However, this issue is academic, since it is inconceivable that a court of equity would refuse to grant the mortgagee the right to protect his interests in this manner.

In a few states an upset price is fixed in advance of the sale. By this is meant that an appraisal by agents of the court fixes a value for the property that must be reached in the bidding or the court will refuse to confirm the sale. This is not a common practice. In any event, the court of equity is expected to determine that the price realized at the foreclosure sale is adequate before it is confirmed. But adequacy is a flexible concept. Even though the court may have some doubt about it, it may question whether a subsequent sale would produce a price as high as the highest one offered at the first sale.

Nevertheless, a judicial sale may be a poor method of realizing the true value of the property. Recognizing this, the court must exercise its best judgment in viewing the offers made for the property at the foreclosure sale. Hence, while every offer made by a prospective purchaser is irrevocable and may not be withdrawn, the court is not bound to accept any offer made. At the outset the court may condition its confirmation by providing, for example, that the price paid must be sufficient to pay all expenses of the sale and the debts of the mortgagor.

It would be quite difficult for the court to fix the price which the property must bring at the foreclosure sale. On the one hand, the court is interested in doing justice to the mortgagor. Since a deficiency judgment may be decreed in case the mortgagee is not completely satisfied from the proceeds of the sale, the lower the price, the larger the deficiency judgment. On the other hand, the mortgagee's rights must be protected also. If the court should attempt to insist upon too high a price, no sale would be effected, and hence the mortgagee would receive no satisfaction of his claims.

Nature of Title at Foreclosure Sale The purchaser of property at a foreclosure sale is, in effect, the purchaser of the rights of the mortgagor whose interests are cut off by the sale. Even though the sale is conducted under court procedure, the court makes no representation concerning the nature of the title. Certainly there is no implication that a title passed by a court carries any suggestion of full warranty. Any defects that may have been applicable to the title as it was held by the mortgagor will continue with the title as it passes to the purchaser at foreclosure sale. If a junior lienor's interests have been omitted in the suit for foreclosure, his claims will not be cut off by such suit. As long as lienor claims are not satisfied, the purchaser, instead of acquiring a fee simple unencumbered, stands in the position of a mortgagee in possession of his security.

The obvious conclusion to be drawn from this analysis is that any prospective purchaser at a foreclosure sale should have the record of the title to the property thoroughly searched before he bids for it. He should know exactly the nature of the title which he may be able to secure. Relying on the assumption that the title was properly searched before the mortgagee accepted a lien upon the property may not be a safe practice.

Parties to Foreclosure Suit When the holder of a senior mortgage brings suit to foreclose the equity of redemption, he must join in the suit all who share the mortgagor's interest. These include not only junior mortgage holders but judgment creditors, a purchaser at an execution sale, and a trustee in bankruptcy, if any. Failure to include all of these might improve their position with the foreclosure of the senior lien. For example, should the senior mortgagee become the successful bidder at the foreclosure sale, and should a junior lienor of record be not joined in the suit, it is possible that, when the senior mortgagee takes title to the land, the junior mortgagee may acquire the position of a senior lienor. To make sure of the avoidance of this possibility, every foreclosure action should be preceded by a careful search of the record to discover all junior lien claimants who should be joined in the foreclosure suit.

Should any junior lienor think that he has an equity to protect, he has the right to purchase the property at a foreclosure sale, paying off or otherwise providing for the interests of the claimants whose liens are superior to his. It is not uncommon for a senior claimant to agree in advance upon the method of settlement of his claims. This may include an agreement to renew the senior mortgagee's claims, either with or without a reduction in their amount.

The purchaser at the foreclosure sales takes over the property free of the lien of the mortgage being foreclosed, but also free of all holders of junior liens who have been joined in the foreclosure action. If the senior mortgage holder or a third party purchases the property at a foreclosure sale, all such junior liens are of no further force or effect. If, however, the mortgagor purchases the property at such sale, all liens against it will remain alive; except, of course, such liens as may have been satisfied from the proceeds of the sale. There is one exception to this rule. If the mortgagor borrowed the money with which to purchase the property, the lender comes in ahead of the liens wiped out by the sale.

If a junior lienholder brings suit for foreclosure, he should not join the senior lienholder in the suit. Instead, he should sue subject to the senior lien. By this means he is not obligated to pay off the senior lienholder. He may prefer to keep the senior mortgage alive. The holder of the senior lien may join the action voluntarily, and sometimes does so to make sure that his interests are fully protected. He may wish to have determined by the court the amount due him to be assumed by the purchaser. Or, should there be any question about the order of priority of his lien, he may join the foreclosure action to have this question answered. Again he may have a side agreement with the junior lienor to continue his mortgage unchanged in amount. In case the junior mortgage holder plans to buy the property at the foreclosure sale, he may prefer to pay off the senior lien as well. This must be done with the consent of the lienholder if he is not a party to the suit. This practice represents a redemption of the senior mortgage and follows the English maxim of "Redeem up, but foreclose down." In other words, redeem claims superior to your own, but wipe out, by the process of foreclosure, those that are inferior.

When separate suits are brought contemporaneously by both a senior and a junior lienor, they should be joined in a single action. The consequences of separate suits would be the same as those following a single suit.

Holders of junior liens which are destroyed in a foreclosure action are entitled to have the surplus of sale price over senior mortgage claims applied to their claims. If there is no surplus, then they are entitled to a judgment for the full amount of their claims. From that time on, they are merely general, unsecured creditors of the mortgagor, unless the latter should own other real estate to which such judgments would attach.

Effect of Foreclosure on Junior Lienors If a senior mortgage holder brings foreclosure suit and joins junior claimants in the suit, the question arises, "What happens to the claims of those cut off by the foreclosure sale?" As indicated above, any surplus remaining, after satisfying the costs of foreclosure and the claims of the senior lienor, is distributed according to the priority rights of junior claims. Sometimes the distribution of this surplus is not as simple as it sounds. Frequent disputes concerning the order of priority require action by a court of equity to establish the order of settlement.

Where there is no surplus, or where it is insufficient to meet all claims, the holders thereof still maintain their rights to pursue the mortgagor on whatever personal obligation he has incurred in establishing their interests. This legal right may or may not result in satisfaction of claims to their holders. It may acquire only nuisance value to rise up and plague the mortgagor at some future time should he ever recover his economic status sufficiently to make pursuit of claims against him worthwhile.

Unrecorded Liens on Foreclosure It has been pointed out that the mortgagor's interest in mortgaged property is essentially limited to his equity of redemption. While the purchaser at a foreclosure sale is expected to acquire only the mortgagor's interest, he may acquire more than this if he makes the purchase without notice of latent equities. He might even acquire the property free of a mortgage if the mortgage is not recorded. In any event, his equity of redemption usually gives him the right to redeem an underlying mortgage, whether or not it is on record and whether or not he assumes it at the time of purchase.

As pointed out above, the purchaser should cause a thorough search of the record to discover the condition of the title. Having done so, he is entitled to rely upon the record to disclose the existence of any liens against the property, unless he has other forms of notice of such liens.

Deficiency Judgment While a sale of the mortgaged property may result in a surplus to which the mortgagor is entitled, it may, on the contrary, be consummated at a price that fails to satisfy the claims of the mortgagee. Since equity courts have arrived at the conclusion that the mortgagor is entitled to the surplus, they have followed this with the correlative decision that any deficit should constitute a continuing claim by the mortgagee against the mortgagor. This is known as a deficiency judgment. Since all mortgages involve one or more specific properties—which must be accurately described in the mortgage—the mortgagee must look to such property to provide primary security for his claim.

Deficiency judgments are unsecured claims—unless the mortgagor owns other real estate—and take their place alongside other debts of the mortgagor. Unlike the mortgage from which such judgment springs, the latter gives the holder no right of preference against any of the non-real estate assets of the debtor. Hence, the value of deficiency judgments is always open to serious question. This is true in part because of the ways by which they can be avoided or defeated.

One paradox of deficiency judgments is that they tend to protect dishonest mortgagors against whom they are filed. By this is meant that while an honest debtor will frequently strive to discharge them, even at the expense of self-denial for himself and those dependent upon him, the presence of a deficiency judgment may not interfere with the spending habits of debtors whose consciences are callous to them. Since such judgments could be attached only to real estate which the debtor holds or may acquire in the future, the dishonest debtor may see to it that he does not acquire any future real estate interests; or if he does so, he will be careful to have the titles recorded in names other than his own.

In some quarters there is considerable sentiment in favor of legislation to abolish deficiency judgments altogether, leaving the mortgagee with only the property to protect his claims. California, North Carolina, and Montana, for example, forbid a deficiency judgment on real estate mortgages or similar instruments given to secure the balance of the purchase price. Nebraska and South Dakota limit the granting of a deficiency judgment to a court determination not necessarily dependent upon the results of a foreclosure sale. The South Dakota law specifically provides that if a foreclosing mortgagee is not willing to bid the full amount of the judgment debt for the real estate covered by his lien, he must introduce competent proof that the fair and reasonable value of the property is less than the sum due on his mortgage note, together with costs and expenses of the sale. Only when the court is satisfied that this condition exists, after the foreclosure sale, may the mortgagee proceed against the mortgagor's other property to recover for the deficiency. In several states, particularly New Jersey and Tennessee, deficiency judgments have been sharply limited in practice without the formality of a statute.

It should be noted that a deficiency judgment is always entered against the person of the mortgagor or his successor. Hence, it cannot be entered unless he is personally served as a part of the proceedings for foreclosure and sale.

Significance of Possession A little thought will show the significance of the right of possession after default, but before a foreclosure sale. If the mortgagor is in lawful possession, he is not accountable to the mortgagee for either the disposition of the proceeds of the mortgage or the income which he may derive from the property while he possesses it. Even where it is evident that the security is inadequate to protect the obligations due the mortgagee, this rule is not relaxed. An honest mortgagor may continue to enjoy normal income until he is dispossessed lawfully as the result of a foreclosure sale. A dishonest or, shall we say, a resourceful mortgagor can find means of increasing normal income substantially, perhaps at the expense of the mortgagee. Such mortgagors are called "milkers."

Hence, the only way for the mortgagee to protect his interest adequately is to obtain possession and, through it, control over the property and its potential income. If he can get possession, he can better protect the property against waste. Even though waste committed by the mortgagor while in possession may decrease the value of the security and correspondingly increase the amount of the deficiency judgment, this may not result in collection by the holder of the judgment of amounts to offset the effects of the waste.

While the mortgagee in possession is in effect a pledgee, he at least has an opportunity to collect whatever income is available and apply it on the obligations owed to him. Or he may use a portion or all of the income to make necessary repairs to the property, thus protecting his security. If he deems it necessary to protect his interests, he may pay taxes as they accrue and redeem prior encumbrances. In both cases, he would enjoy the right of recovery.

Even rent clauses and other types of income clauses in mortgages are not adequate substitutes for possession. If the mortgagor feels that he has little at stake in his equity of redemption, he may lose interest in collecting the income which he has agreed in the mortgage to turn over to the mortgagee. Or income may be so difficult to define that it disappears entirely. It may not be in the nature of rent, but of net income from business operations. If the mortgagor's financial affairs are in such condition that it is impossible for him to keep up the contractual payments on his mortgage, his ability to produce any net income from his business may have reached the vanishing point. To be sure, adverse economic conditions rather than inherent managerial weakness may be at the base of his troubles. Even this explanation fails to produce anything to credit to the amounts due the mortgagee. Or a junior lienor may be more agile than the holder of the senior mortgage and may secure the right to collect rents which he may apply toward the liquidation of his own claims.

For these and other less obvious reasons, the significance of possession becomes quite apparent. In the end the law and court decisions may decree that both title and lien theories reach the same destination. The mortgaged property is sold, and the proceeds are applied to the satisfaction of the obligations owed the mortgagee. If these obligations are not completely liquidated, the mortgagor will be liable under a deficiency judgment. Until actual foreclosure sale is consummated, the mortgage continues to be a security device.

Meantime, unrecoverable wastes may occur, and income may flow into channels which lead away from the mortgagee's interests rather than toward them. Deficiency judgments may be in perfect legal form, but also may be perfectly worthless in the recovery of funds that might have been diverted to the mortgagee had he been in possession pending foreclosure sale of the mortgaged property. In some instances the rent assignment clause in a mortgage is so drawn that, in effect, it virtually gives the mortgagee possession of the property upon default and until the foreclosure sale is confirmed.

While the mortgagee is in possession he may find it necessary or desirable to spend money for repairs or improvements on the property. Subsequently, he may be called upon to demonstrate that these expenditures were needed to protect his interests. Even though he benefits therefrom, there will be little difficulty in adding such costs to the previous claims of the mortgagee. But if the expenditures merely cause the property to look better, he may have difficulty in recovering such expenditures.

However, the mortgagee in possession is required to render an account annually to the equity court, showing the amount of his receipts from the operation of the property and their disposition. In general, these receipts must be applied first to expenses of operation—including necessary repairs, then to interest accruals, and finally to a reduction in the principal balance. This requirement for an annual reduction in the principal balance is called an "annual rest." Its purpose is to prevent the mortgagee from having free use indefinitely of funds collected from the use of the property.

Receivership Frequently a mortgage contains a clause which permits the mortgagee to have a receiver appointed to protect his interests in case of a default. Even though the statute makes no specific provision for the appointment of a receiver, it may result from an agreement written into the mortgage or may be agreed upon at the time of default. The receivership should be looked upon merely as an interim device for temporary control pending the consummation of a foreclosure sale. As such, it takes the place of a mortgagee in possession. While it is preferable to have a disinterested, impartial person appointed as a receiver, the mortgagor may serve in this capacity if the mortgagee consents.

Where a receiver is appointed, he is recognized as the direct representative of the mortgagee. He is not expected to represent all creditors of the mortgagor. Even when the mortgagee has the right to ask for the appointment of a receiver, he may not see fit to exercise it. The most common motives for the use of receivers are the desire to conserve already inadequate security and the fear of waste which may cause the security to depreciate in value before a foreclosure sale can be arranged. "Waste" means any condition which results directly in a diminution in the value of the property. It may be due to intentional destructive tactics or to neglect of needed repairs. A serious hole in the roof may be just as injurious as acts of vandalism. Sometimes, also, the relationship between mortgagor and mortgagee may play its part. If the former should show any indication of resisting the plans of the latter, a receiver may be used to take possession away from the mortgagor.

If the property over which the receiver assumes jurisdiction happens to be the mortgagor's home, the receiver may not ask the mortgagor to vacate the property immediately. Instead, he may determine reasonable rent for it and give the mortgagor the privilege of continuing to occupy the property, pending foreclosure sale, as long as he pays the rent asked of him. In general, there is a tendency to permit the mortgagor in default to occupy his home until the foreclosure sale takes place.

Frequently the right of the mortgagee to have a receiver appointed is written into the mortgage instrument. In such case the mortgagee sees to it that the right is as inclusive as possible. One such clause reads in part as follows:

> In the event of any breach of the terms or conditions of this mortgage or the note which this mortgage secures, the holder of this mortgage shall be entitled to the appointment of a receiver of the rents, issues, and profits of said premises, without regard to the value of the mortgaged premises as security for the amount due, or the solvency of any person or persons liable for the payment of the amount due, and without notice to any party, and in the event of any such default herein described, such rents and profits are hereby assigned to the holder of this mortgage as further security for the payment of said indebtedness.

Power of Sale As a substitute for a foreclosure sale, the statutes of about a third of the states permit the use of the power of sale, provided it is written into the mortgage. Even though the procedure of satisfying a mortgagee's claims is supposed to be faster and more economical where the power of sale is exercised, the use of this practice is not always followed, even in the states that have legislated on the subject. Some state statutes prohibit its use. A few undertake to regulate the manner of its use. Where the deed of trust is in use, the power of sale must be exercised by the trustee. One reason why it is not always used is that whenever questions arise that do not produce the same answers for both mortgagor and mortgagee, resort must be had to a court of equity. Then follows foreclosure sale as described above. One question about which there may be a disagreement is the exact amount of the indebtedness. Questions even may arise concerning the fairness of the manner in which the sale is conducted.

Another complication in the use of the power of sale arises when the mortgagee may wish to buy the property. In the absence of statutory permission, the mortgagee may not purchase the property either directly or indirectly. If the mortgagee prefers to bid on the property at its sale, he should follow the foreclosure route.

While the mortgagee may dispose of his interest in a mortgage at private sale, the power of sale must be exercised only in public, and the successful bidder must pay cash. Proceeds of the sale go first to pay the expenses of the sale, then to apply on the claims of the senior mortgagee. Any surplus is applied successively to the claims of junior lienors, then to the mortgagor. If there is a deficiency instead of a surplus, the mortgagee is entitled to bring suit for a deficiency judgment.

The notice of the sale must state the total amount claimed by the mortgagee. Unless the statute so requires, no special notice need be sent to holders of junior liens. They are supposed to look out for their own interests. The mortgagor, on the other hand, is entitled to special notice of the sale. This is so because a power of sale may not cut off or impair his equity of redemption. This is his right up to the time of the actual sale of the property.

The purchaser under power of sale acquires the same kind of title that would be available to him where foreclosure proceedings are used. He merely succeeds to the type of interest which the mortgagor held. In effect, he receives only a special warranty deed.

Some laws tend to abolish deficiency judgments where power of sale is used. In other cases the statutes place limits upon the amount of deficiency judgments by providing that such judgment may not be greater than the difference between the amount claimed by the mortgagee and the fair value of the property, instead of the amount realized at the sale. The burden of proof for establishing the fair value usually rests upon the mortgagee.

First by emergency statutes during the depression of the 1930s and later by permanent statutes, some states—including New York—have taken the position that a mortgagee may not take advantage of a depressed real estate market, use his power of sale to dispose of the property at a price that represents less than its long-term value, and saddle the mortgagor with a correspondingly large deficiency judgment. The mortgagee may not even anticipate such a situation and use a waiver of this mandatory law which he requires the mortgagor to sign at the time the mortgage is executed.

Whether or not the power of sale (or sale by advertisement as it is sometimes called) is used may depend upon other factors in the legislation governing defaults in real estate mortgages. For example, in Minnesota the power of sale is commonly used because the foreclosure sale does not suit the purposes of the mortgagee. If the sale is made by order of the court, it takes place immediately after the foreclosure judgment is entered. Statutory redemption in Minnesota is determined by the sale price rather than by the amount of the debt. Hence, the mortgagee will normally bid up to the full amount of the debt so that the mortgagor may not redeem the property for less than the debt, thereby leaving the mortgagee with an unsecured deficiency judgment, but no property. Consequently, mortgagees in Minnesota find the power of sale more advantageous than foreclosure sale.

In Wisconsin, on the other hand, foreclosure sale takes place only after the statutory redemption period has expired. The right of redemption is then calculated from the amount of the mortgage debt instead of the price realized at the foreclosure sale. Hence, if the mortgagee thinks he has any chance of recovery on a deficiency judgment, he prefers a foreclosure sale to the use of the power of sale.

Sometimes mortgagees use the foreclosure sale in preference to the power of sale because they fear that questions may be raised about the marketability of the title if the land is sold under power of sale. Such questions are predicated upon the existence of some irregularity in connection with the sale that might result in its nullification. The same doubts are not usually present when title passes as a result of a foreclosure sale.

Foreclosure of Deeds of Trust It has generally been held that when money is raised with a deed of trust given as security the creditor cannot bring a foreclosure action. Instead, he relies upon the trustee to exercise the powers conferred directly by the trust instrument. In California, however, the trustee has a statutory option to foreclose by suit and decree. Foreclosure is also commonly available, without the necessity of a statute, when judicial aid is required to determine parties' rights, as where it is necessary to have an accounting, adjust setoffs, ascertain the amount due in event of dispute, or establish whether the debt is really in default. Sometimes there are junior liens and their relative priorities are unclear. In such cases the trustee may sue to foreclose. Once the matter has been brought within the jurisdiction of the court the property may then be sold by an officer of the court, as in foreclosure proceedings, rather than by the trustee.

A right of redemption exists after a mortgage foreclosure sale, but not after a trustee's sale under a deed of trust. If the holder of the deed, however, elects to foreclose it in the same manner as a mortgage, the debtor has the same rights of redemption as though a mortgage had been executed in the beginning. In the event a receivership becomes necessary, properly drawn trust deeds usually give more protection than mortgages. This is true because under an ordinary mortgage the receiver cannot acquire possession until foreclosure and then he must return the property to the mortgagor after the foreclosure sale until the redemption period runs. On the other hand, where a trust deed is used, the receiver may take possession under its terms and retain it until the property is turned over permanently to the purchaser at the sale.

Foreclosure by Entry In several New England states foreclosure by peaceable entry is permitted, provided all formalities are observed. These include the requirement that the entry must be without the opposition of the mortgagor. If it is opposed, resort must be had to judicial proceedings, which means that it soon develops into a foreclosure sale. The entry must be made in the presence of witnesses who can testify to its peaceable nature. And a certificate of entry reciting the action taken by the mortgagee must be properly recorded. Even where foreclosure by entry is used, the mortgagor is protected by a right of recovery of the difference if the security is more valuable than the debt. In addition, the mortgagor enjoys the statutory right of redemption where foreclosure by entry is used. The statutes allow a period varying from one to three years after entry before the right of redemption is cut off.

Also, in some New England states the mortgagee may foreclose by writ of entry. This kind of action partakes of some of the characteristics of equity proceedings. After the amount of the debt is judicially determined, the mortgagor in default is given a definite period of time within which to meet his obligations. If he fails, or is unable to take advantage of this opportunity, the mortgagee is put in possession of the property. He then occupies the same position as if he had foreclosed by peaceable entry as described in the preceding paragraph.

Under both of these plans of foreclosure the mortgagor is allowed a statutory right of redemption varying from one to three years. A long period of redemption may interfere with the plans of the mortgagee in disposing of the property. For this reason foreclosure sales are frequently resorted to even though foreclosure by peaceable entry or by writ of entry is available to the mortgagee.

Volume of Foreclosures According to records kept by the Federal Home Loan Bank Board, the number of nonfarm real estate foreclosures in 1926 was 68,000. This number increased to an all-time high of 252,000 in 1933. Annual declines thereafter finally brought the number of foreclosures to an all-time low of 10,000 in 1946. There were 18,000 foreclosures in 1952 and the number rose gradually every year until 1960, when they totaled 51,000. The number of foreclosures increased sharply each year thereafter, rising to 117,000 in 1966. A slight reversal has been experienced since then. In 1970, foreclosures dropped to about

101,000. The rising foreclosure rate has been a matter of considerable study.[1] The rate for 1966 was more than six times the 1952 rate and over twice the 1960 rate. Although the trend raises serious question concerning the quality of much mortgage credit, when viewed in perspective the present condition is not yet alarming. Every year during the 1930s saw more foreclosures than are currently being experienced, and the number of outstanding loans then was much smaller. Certain areas of the country, however, have cause for some concern. Unemployment, high loan-to-value ratios, extended payment provisions, and other forms of relaxed credit terms, such as junior lien loans, have played important parts in the rising foreclosure rates.

The Need for New Foreclosure Laws[2] The diversity, delay, and costliness inherent in the application of the present foreclosure laws have stimulated some thought along the lines of corrective federal legislation as the only means of achieving desirable uniformity, speed, and economy. Real estate law, however, has generally been considered properly within the state sovereignty, and efforts are now being directed toward motivating state action. In 1957, in his economic report to the nation, President Eisenhower noted that outmoded foreclosure laws add unnecessarily to the risks and costs of mortgage lending and should be revised. He urged the states to give this matter their early attention.

At the present time, statutory redemption periods range from 2 years in Alabama and 18 months in Kansas to none at all in 24 states. Estimated representative costs of a complete foreclosure proceeding vary widely by states, ranging from $100 in Alabama or Texas to as high as $500 in New York and $1,200 in Illinois. The average time involved in the total foreclosure operation also shows a great variation among the states. The time required from the date of initiation of foreclosure process to the date of acquisition of title free of all rights of redemption will normally be as short as 1 month in such states as Georgia, Hawaii, Texas, and Virginia, or as long as 26 months in Alabama, 19 months in Kansas, 17 months in Illinois and Washington, and 16 months in Iowa, North Dakota, Oregon, and Wisconsin.

As suggested in earlier discussion, the major difficulties in present-day foreclosures may be traced to four principal sources. These are: (1) the statutory period of redemption; (2) the deficiency judgment; (3) lack

---

[1] Leo Grebler, "A Searching Analysis of the Quality of Mortgage Credit," *The Mortgage Banker*, February 1964, pp. 32–36. See also Robert M. Fisher, "Foreclosures and Delinquencies: Dimensions of a Problem," *The Mortgage Banker*, April, 1964, pp. 24–28, 46; and further, see Leon T. Kendall, "The Quality of Mortgage Credit in Real Estate's Adjustment," *The Mortgage Banker*, June 1964, pp. 24–27.

[2] Much of the material in this section is adapted from William C. Prather, "Foreclosure of the Security Interest," *University of Illinois Law Forum*, Fall 1957, pp. 420–61.

of consistent rules for entitlement to rents, profits, and other possessory rights; and (4) the public sale.

Recent studies indicate that an elimination of troublesome features of these provisions in the foreclosure laws may be accomplished without substantial injury to either mortgagors or mortgagees. Home Owners Loan Corporation experience up to 1938 showed redemption in less than 1 percent of the cases of foreclosure despite substantial periods of redemption permitted in most cases. The experience of the same corporation with deficiency judgments through March 31, 1951, indicated whole or partial satisfaction of less than 8 percent. Confusion is arising in connection with the determination of rights to rents, profits, and possession because the laws of many states do not clearly define the rights of the parties. A study of the late 1930s in New York revealed that, over a number of years, more than 99 percent of "public" sales were concluded by sale of the mortgaged property to the mortgagee.

These facts suggest that the situation could be markedly improved by certain definite steps:

1. Limit the statutory redemption period to not more than six months.
2. Eliminate deficiency judgments.
3. Clarify the rules for entitlement to rents, profits, and other possessory rights during the redemption period by legislation where necessary.
4. Eliminate the public sale.

Since the major purpose of a long period of redemption is to permit a borrower to recover from excessive deficiencies, the elimination of the deficiency judgment would largely offset the need to retain the right of redemption.

A statutory presumption giving a mortgagor the rights to possession during the redemption period would enable both parties to make appropriate provision consistent with the advantages and risks of possession by a mortgagor while in default. A provision for appointment of a receiver to collect rents or a requirement of collateral indemnification against waste may be incorporated in the mortgage to offset the statutory effect to the extent deemed necessary by the mortgagee.

The theory of public sale is to ensure competitive bidding for a property under foreclosure. In nearly all cases, the outcome of the foreclosure proceeding is a foregone conclusion: the mortgagee acquires title. Thus, all the additional costs of court proceedings, public advertising, and sale to *protect* the mortgagor become, in fact, an additional burden on him, because nothing is gained in the process.

The proposed modifications of state laws would involve comparable sacrifices by mortgagors and mortgagees. Most noteworthy, as the statistics show, is that all sacrifices would be more apparent than real. Furthermore, the increased value of the property as security, because of the speed and simplicity with which the foreclosure could be effected and the title cleared, would be to the benefit of all parties.

QUESTIONS AND PROBLEMS

1. What is meant by "strict foreclosure" and what alternatives are there to such action?
2. What special procedures are necessary to determine a proper bid for property available through a tax sale?
3. At the present time, in California and certain other areas, there is an active market in second and third lien deeds of trust containing a power of sale. In a time of declining real estate values, what technical position would these liens have?
4. Why is it that some state statutes prohibit the use of a power of sale written into the terms of a mortgage?
5. What advantages may be gained by providing for the appointment of a receiver in event of default by the borrower on a mortgage loan?
6. How valuable to the mortgagee is the right to obtain a deficiency judgment?
7. Should the deficiency judgment be abolished? Why or why not?
8. May a foreclosure sale sometimes be desirable even though the mortgagee would prefer a voluntary deed? Why?
9. What special advantages does a mortgagee have in bidding at the foreclosure sale incident to his own proceedings? Is this arrangement fair?
10. Mortgagor owns a property. A holds a first mortgage against it and B holds a second mortgage. Mortgagor defaults on his mortgage payments. A forecloses without joining B in the action? The property is sold at the foreclosure sale to C. What are B's rights?
11. In question 10, what would your answer be if B's lien was not recorded?
12. How may a receivership be used to advantage in connection with a mortgage in default?

5

Mortgage Adjustments

Need for Mortgage Adjustments As pointed out in previous chapters, mortgage contracts are so drawn as to indicate definite penalties to follow any breach therein. Our most heartrending melodramas would have lost much of their appeal except for their recitals of the dire consequences which follow a failure to keep up mortgage payments on the old homestead. Nevertheless, experience testifies that, in spite of provisions for prompt action in case of a default in mortgage payments, many such commitments are not met in strict accordance with the letter of the contract. Instead, whenever mortgagors get into financial trouble and are unable to meet their obligations, adjustments rather than demands for the proverbial pound of flesh are likely to follow. Some of these adjustments best meet the needs of the mortgagee, to be sure. Others are accepted at times when strict adherence to the letter of the contract would give the holder of the mortgage a financial advantage. Various types of mortgage adjustments are discussed in the pages that follow.

Voluntary Conveyances On the theory that the mortgagor is a free agent, he may sell his equity to the mortgagee at any time after the mortgage becomes effective. Such sale must be conditioned upon the appearance of a new form of consideration—not present before—and complete freedom from fraud or duress. Because there are so many ways of taking advantage of a distressed mortgagor and of freezing out those with junior claims against him, the burden of proof governing the absence of fraud or duress usually rests upon the mortgagee.

For example, suppose that the mortgagor is unable to meet his obligations and faces foreclosure of his equity. In perfect good faith and to save time, trouble, and expense, the mortgagee may make or accept a proposal to take title from the mortgagor upon paying a nominal sum to the latter for his equity. Suppose also that shortly thereafter the former mortgagor's fortunes improve; or suppose that depressed real estate values recover sharply. The former mortgagee may face a suit for recovery on the ground that he used duress to wrest title from the mortgagor. He might have difficulty in proving his honest intentions and in demonstrating that, at the time of the purchase, he paid the fair value of the mortgagor's equity. At that time the property might have possessed little or no value over and above the amount of the mortgage.

Where such voluntary conveyances are used, the common practice in lien states would include a warranty deed from mortgagor to mortgagee. A quitclaim deed would probably suffice in title states. In either event the mortgagor should insist upon a satisfaction piece to make sure that he is no longer bound under his note and mortgage. Otherwise, he may find that he has sacrificed his equity and still is under financial obligation to the mortgagee.

In addition to the legal questions involved in voluntary conveyances, the mortgagee frequently faces very practical financial issues as well. If there are junior liens outstanding, they are not wiped out by a voluntary conveyance. Indeed, their holders may be in a better position than before if the title to the property passes into stronger hands. Unless in some manner these junior liens may be lifted from the property in question—possibly by agreement with their holders to transfer them to other property owned by the mortgagor or even on occasion to cancel them—the mortgagee may find it necessary to foreclose instead of taking a voluntary conveyance. By this means he has a lawful method of becoming free from the liens of the junior claimants.

Purchase of Mortgage by Grantee Sometimes the grantee under a transfer of title prefers to hold his estate free from mortgage encumbrances. If there is only one mortgage outstanding and if its holder agrees to its redemption, no complications are likely to arise. If, however, there are junior liens of record against the property, their interests must be considered. If the grantee has taken title subject to the liens against the property, he may be relieved of the burden of the senior mortgage by paying it off, again with the approval of the mortgagee. If he does so, however, he will be well advised to redeem this mortgage through a nominee in order to protect his investment against junior claimants. Since he has taken on no personal obligations to pay their claims, such a procedure does no violence to their interests. But a grantee who assumes the mortgage when he purchases the property may elect not to follow this practice. If he takes over the mortgage through a nominee who subsequently forecloses his mortgage, the holders of junior liens may be frozen out as the result of the foreclosure sale. When the mortgage is transferred to a nominee, it is kept alive.

Occasionally a mortgagor borrows money, perhaps from a friend whose primary concern is not financial gain, but aid to an intimate friend or associate, for the purpose of redeeming a mortgage. Even here the new lender should purchase the mortgage and keep it alive if there are junior liens outstanding. Otherwise, his friendly gesture may inadvertently result in a major advantage to the holders of junior liens by elevating their positions in case the senior mortgage is canceled. His own claim may then become of junior quality only.

Assumption of Mortgage It has been pointed out that a mortgage is essentially security for a personal debt. The mortgagor is expected to sign a note which accompanies or becomes a part of the mortgage. By agreement, it is possible for the mortgagor to obtain release from his personal obligation after he assumes it; or if the mortgagee consents, he may be relieved of such obligation at the time the mortgage is executed. This would be an unusual type of agreement for the mortgagee to become a party to, but it would be one that would find sanction at law because it is a matter of voluntary agreement, resulting in a contract.

When the mortgagor transfers his rights to another, the question arises, "Does the grantee undertake to relieve the mortgagor of his personal obligation?" If this is the intention of both parties, the assumption of the obligation by the grantee may accomplish the purpose. The deed, after reciting the nature of the mortgage which encumbers the property, will contain a clause to the effect that the grantee assumes and agrees to pay the amount of the obligations owed to the mortgagee, as part consideration of the conveyance of title. Where an assumption is undertaken by the grantee, it should be couched in such language that there should be no doubt about his intent.

An assumption agreement takes the form of a contract of indemnity. It undertakes to shift the responsibility for the payment of the debt from the shoulders of the grantor to those of the grantee. Thereafter the grantor stands in the position of surety for the payment of the debt. However, such an arrangement binds only the parties to it—the grantor and the grantee. Since the mortgagee is not ordinarily a party to such an agreement, he is not bound by it. As a consequence, he may still hold the original mortgagor and every grantee in the chain of title who has assumed the personal obligation of the debt. He may see fit to release the original mortgagor and any subsequent grantee. Occasionally questions are raised about the ability of the mortgagee to reach back of any nonassuming grantees. Some courts seem to take the position that that interrupts the right of the mortgagee to hold all assuming grantees in the chain of title.

In case the mortgagee undertakes to hold all grantees who assume personal responsibility for the debt, he should make sure that they are joined in any suit for foreclosure. If they are so joined, any deficiency judgment may bind grantees who have disposed of their interest in the property years before. If one of these is financially responsible, the mortgagee may collect from him even though he has not owned the property covered by the mortgage for some time. Or the mortgagee may see fit to let his judgments stand on the record without pursuing his remedies under it. In this case, it continues to be a lien upon all real estate owned by all assuming grantees until it is released of record or expires by limitation.

During the intervening years until the statute of limitations runs out, any transfer of property by any assuming grantee will be complicated, because a new grantee will not usually be willing to take title encumbered by the lien of a deficiency judgment arising out of a foreclosure sale affecting another property. Consequently, sooner or later some grantee will probably move to cancel the deficiency judgment by agreeing with the holder to pay it off.

Any such grantee who pays off a deficiency judgment would then have recourse against any predecessor assuming grantee, and of course against the original mortgagor as well, unless he has already been released by the mortgagee. There are occasions when a transfer of title is conditioned upon the securing of a release of the grantor by the mortgagee.

Release of Grantor from Assumed Debt Should the security appear to provide ample protection for the mortgagee, or should the grantee's financial standing be adequate, the mortgagee may see fit to release the grantor from the burden of an assumed mortgage. If he does so, there may be questions raised about his release of antecedent grantors, including the original mortgagor. In any event the mortgagee is not likely to weaken unduly his capacity to collect the debt. In the absence of a release from the mortgagee when a mortgaged property is transferred, there is always one sure way for the grantor to obtain release from an assumed mortgage—that is, to sell the property free and clear of all encumbrances, letting the grantee do his own financing. Even this proposal is based upon two assumptions: (1) that the mortgage contains a prepayment clause, permitting the grantor to pay off at his discretion; and (2) that the grantee has access to funds that will permit him to refinance the mortgage.

Sometimes even where there is no provision for prepayment, the grantor may still prefer to get the grantee to do his own financing, provided that the grantor can prepay the loan without too great a penalty. If the grantee will accept a loan from the same mortgagee, there may be little or no penalty. In such case, the old mortgage may be continued with a release granted to the grantor. In many instances, particularly in a tight money market, it is not convenient for the grantee to refinance the mortgage. In such case it is futile for the grantor to insist upon selling the property free and clear. The grantee may be willing but unable to purchase on those terms.

"Subject To" In contrast to the assumption of the personal obligation to pay the debt, the grantee may refuse to accept this responsibility. In this case he takes title "subject to" the mortgage. So long as he thinks it will be to his advantage—assuming his continuing financial ability—he will keep up payments on the mortgage and observe its other covenants. Under normal conditions, if he purchased the property at a fair price, it will be to his advantage to avoid default on the mortgage as the best means of protecting his own equity.

But should the grantee reach the conclusion that it will no longer be to his advantage to make further payments, or should he become financially unable to do so, he may default in his payments. By so doing, he runs the risk of losing whatever equity he has in the property. He cannot be held personally liable for the debt. The mortgagor and all subsequent assuming grantees are still personally liable and may be held for any deficiency judgment.

It is not ordinarily to the advantage of the grantor to sell property subject to the mortgage. He would much prefer that a responsible grantee assume it instead. But there are occasions when the most advantageous sale can be made subject to the mortgage. Indeed, in some situations the only buyer insists upon such an arrangement. If the mortgagor is about to default and expects to lose his property anyhow, he loses little by finding some prospective purchaser willing to take a chance on the recovery of the value of the property in question. Milkers frequently take title subject to the mortgage.

In case of a gift of property encumbered by a mortgage, the donee takes the property subject to the mortgage. Since he does not acquire the property as the result of a contract, he is not required to make any commitment that would bind him personally to pay the debt. Again this rule is subject to exceptions. If the gift is conditioned upon the willingness of the donee to assume personal responsibility for the debt of the donor that is secured by the mortgage, then, of course, the donee assumes the mortgage rather than takes title subject to it.

Purchase of Mortgage by Grantor Not all defaults result in foreclosure actions. Sometimes the mortgagee will approach a financially responsible grantor—or the original mortgagor—for the purpose of giving him a chance to take action which does not involve a foreclosure suit and resulting deficiency judgment. By demonstrating to him that the present grantee has defaulted and that a foreclosure is imminent, he may induce the grantor to follow an alternative course for the purpose of protecting his own interests. One course open to him is to purchase the mortgage—perhaps through a nominee—thus keeping the mortgage alive. By this means he may preserve his right of indemnity against the grantee. By temporizing, through a reduction of installments or otherwise, he may hold the mortgage until the grantee recovers his financial health or until depressed real estate values are improved.

The purchaser may find it to his advantage to secure a voluntary conveyance from the grantee at the same time he purchases the mortgage. Or he may secure an agreement to repossess the property—leaving the question of ultimate title unsettled until a later date. Of course, if he should purchase the mortgage and secure a voluntary conveyance from the grantee without giving a satisfaction piece in return, he could in effect own the property and still hold the right of indemnity against the grantee should his nominee foreclose the mortgage. Since the grantee faces foreclosure and deficiency judgment anyhow, he would probably be no worse off if he followed the plan outlined above.

It is possible for the grantee to purchase a mortgage at its maturity rather than repay the amount it represents. Instead of asking the mortgagee for a satisfaction piece in return for the amount due, he could request an assignment instead. This might give him some advantage if the property is sold, but it would not provide for him any sort of contract of indemnity such as the mortgagor or a previous grantee could secure by a similar purchase. Generally speaking, if the grantee pays off a mortgage, it is expected that the mortgage will become merged with the title.

Insurance Clauses Every mortgage should (and most of them do) contain provisions for insurance of the property as protection to both mortgagor and mortgagee. The exact nature of the insurance varies with geography, the nature of the property, and the experience of the parties. Fire insurance is standard. Windstorm insurance is commonly used. Extended coverage is gaining in use. Rent insurance and other less well-known types are not as generally needed.

The "mortgage clause" is commonly included as a rider in insurance policies against properties that are mortgaged. Under it, both mortgagor and mortgagee are protected, "as their respective interests may appear." This usually means that the interest of the mortgagee is taken care of first, with the remainder applicable to the interest of the mortgagor. Incidentally, the application of this division may not be as simple as it appears. Depending upon a variety of factors, including the age of the building, the neighborhood in which it is located, and the extent of the damage by fire or otherwise, the major interest of the mortgagee may be to use the proceeds of insurance to liquidate his claims. Meantime, the mortgagor may prefer to use such proceeds to repair or rebuild the damaged structure.

The mortgage should require the mortgagor to keep the property insured (the forms of insurance should be specified, although sometimes they are left to be determined from time to time by the mortgagee) and to give the mortgagee the right to insure if the mortgagor does not, adding the cost of insurance to the claims of the mortgagee. In addition, the latter has the independent right to carry such insurance on the property as he sees fit. He is never permitted to collect more than the amount of his interest. Also, standard policies protect the rights of the mortgagee, regardless of the defenses that may be set up against the mortgagor. Even where the mortgage makes no mention of insurance, the mortgagee has the right to purchase insurance on his own account for an amount not in excess of his mortgage claims. In such case he must bear the cost of such insurance.

The "foreclosure clause" should be reviewed to make sure what it means in relation to the rights of both the mortgagor and the mortgagee in case of foreclosure sale. In some cases, a foreclosure sale cuts off the mortgagor's equity of redemption so that he no longer has any interest in the property to be protected by insurance. Likewise, if the old mortgagee becomes the new owner, he no longer has an interest as mortgagee to be covered by insurance. The change in his status may cancel his part in the insurance policy. And certainly the old policy was not drawn in such manner that it will cover the interests of a completely new owner who acquires title at foreclosure sale. The purchaser at such sale should act promptly to make sure he has whatever insurance he needs to protect his interests in the property.

It is a common practice for the insurance policies to be kept by the mortgagee. By this means he is always in a better position to check on the kinds and amounts of insurance in force; whether or not the premiums have been paid; and whether the carriers are acceptable to the mortgagee according to the terms of the mortgage.

Assignment of Mortgages Since a mortgage is considered to be an asset owned by its holder, it follows that he may dispose of it as he would any other asset. The person who acquires it should make sure that he succeeds to the rights of the original mortgagee. This process is known as an assignment. In the absence of an agreement to the contrary, the right of assignment does not require the consent of the mortgagor. Presumably his rights and obligations are not affected. He merely owes the assignee instead of the assignor.

The assignee will do well to record his assignment at the earliest possible moment. Otherwise, he may find that his newly acquired asset has diminished in value. Conceivably the original mortgagee could practice double assignment. If he first assigns his mortgage to A who fails to record the assignment, and subsequently to B, who promptly records his assignment, as between A and B the latter's rights would prevail. A would have a claim against the assignor, but not against the property.

Estoppel Certificates In order to make sure that an agreement reached in the assignment of a mortgage states exact facts, estoppel certificates are sometimes used to prevent subsequent representations about a different set of facts. For example, if A is about to purchase from B a mortgage on property owned by C, A would be better protected if he obtained a written statement from C, showing the unpaid balance of the mortgage. Otherwise, representations made by B might be intentionally or unintentionally erroneous. Or a verbal statement by C might later be denied and C might produce evidence to show that the amount owed by him is less than A thought it was. The estoppel certificate protects the purchaser of the mortgage.

Estoppel certificates as such are not usually secured from the assignor, since the form of assignment commonly used includes a recital by the assignor giving the amount due on the mortgage. It is frequently desirable to obtain an estoppel certificate from the holder of a junior mortgage when a senior mortgage is being assigned. This prevents future disagreements about the amount of debt based on the claims of the junior mortgagee at the time of assignment of the senior lien.

Extension Agreements Occasionally, at the maturity of a mortgage or in anticipation of it, the mortgagor may seek permission from the mortgagee to extend it for a succeeding period of time. In responding to such a request the mortgagee may need to pursue several lines of inquiry before arriving at a conclusion. Certainly he should know the condition of the security. Has it been reasonably well maintained, or does it show the effects of waste and neglect? He should determine the existence of intervening liens and their effect upon an extension agreement. Should there be no intervening liens, he has nothing to worry about from this source. But if any exist, will the extension of an existing mortgage which has matured amount to a cancellation of the old mortgage and the making of a new one? If so, will this advance the priority of intervening liens? In most cases the answer to these questions is probably in the negative.

What about the surety status of grantees in the chain of title who have assumed the mortgage? Will an extension of time for the payment of the debt secured by the mortgage terminate such sureties? The best way for the mortgagee to protect himself against the possibilities implied in these questions is to secure the consent of such sureties to the extension. As parties to it they can have no grounds for opposing it. But if they are not made parties, and particularly if changes in the terms of the mortgage through the extension agreement tend to increase the obligations for which the sureties are expected to be bound, then care should be exercised that those sureties who refuse to sign the agreement may not be released by the extension agreement. Perhaps the threat of foreclosure and the placing of a deficiency judgment on the record against them may be used to force an agreement to make them parties to the extension.

The exact nature of an extension agreement depends upon the bargaining position of mortgagor and mortgagee. Since the use of extension agreements is limited to term loans, it is probable that the original loan has not been greatly reduced. If the mortgagor can refinance the loan on more favorable terms, he will probably not apply for an extension agreement. This will suggest that, in most cases, the mortgagee occupies a more favorable position than the mortgagor in dictating terms of the extension agreement. As a consequence, he may eliminate some clauses in the original mortgage, such as prepayment privileges, which favored the mortgagor. He may make changes that favor the mortgagee, such as an increase in the interest rate. The changes made will perhaps be tempered by his ability to secure approval of the extension agreement by previous grantees whom he wishes to hold along with the present grantee. Frequently the latter has no choice but to accept whatever terms are offered to him. The previous grantees may protest and make the granting of the extension agreement uncertain because of their unwillingness to accept harsher terms than they had once been held to.

Alternative to Extension Agreement As an alternative to an extension agreement, the mortgagee may agree informally to a temporary extension, without making any change in the record. If the mortgagor is unable to meet all of the obligations of the mortgage payments, these too may be waived, in whole or in part. For example, the fact that the question of such an agreement is raised is probably proof that the mortgagor cannot pay the matured principal of the loan. Therefore, some informal arrangement may be made to permit him to retain possession of the property in return for meeting monthly payments which may or may not include principal installments. In general, if such an informal agreement is reached, the amounts demanded will be adjusted to the payment capacities of the borrower.

The use of such an alternative to a definite extension agreement may serve the temporary needs of both mortgagor and mortgagee. If the latter feels that the security amply protects his lien, he can afford to be lenient in helping the mortgagor to adjust his financial arrangements during a difficult period. If the mortgagor also feels that he has a real equity in the property, he will wish to protect it if at all possible. But if there is little or no equity above the indebtedness against the property, neither mortgagor nor mortgagee may be too happy about a temporizing arrangement. The former may dislike the uncertainty of his continued possession, since he can be subject to a change of plans of the mortgagee at any time. The latter may decide that his best interests will be served by immediate action rather than by temporizing in the form of a month-to-month informal agreement. Consequently, if he cannot work out a formal extension agreement with the approval of grantees in the chain of title, he may insist upon foreclosure of the mortgage.

Release of Mortgage The impact of mortgages may be released by various practices—intentional and otherwise. We have just indicated that intermediate grantees who refuse to sign extension agreements may be released from their liabilities under a mortgage if the mortgagee nevertheless persists in granting an extension of time to the assuming grantee. If the mortgagee voluntarily releases the grantee who has assumed the debt, that act probably releases all grantors as well. Since they stand merely in the position of sureties, the mortgagee must exhaust his claims against the assuming grantee before he can proceed against the sureties. If the mortgagee settles with the grantee for less than the whole debt and thereby releases him from the mortgage, this act releases all grantors as well. Whether the mortgagee collects a part of the debt from the assuming grantee or none at all, if he refuses to bring action on the amount owed he cannot thereafter bring action against any of those who act as sureties on the debt.

Partial releases are of quite a different character. They are quite common. If the mortgage is secured by more than one parcel, the time may come when the owner desires the release of one parcel, either for the purposes of sale or otherwise. The same principle applies when collateral other than real estate is put up to help secure the loan. When the debt is reduced sufficiently to justify the release of this added collateral, a formal release will usually be granted by the mortgagee. The amount of reduction required for this purpose may be written into the mortgage at the time it is executed. Or, if the mortgage covers only one parcel, a sale of a portion of it—provided the remainder is not unduly decreased in value as a result of the sale—will usually be permitted by a release of the lien of the mortgage upon the portion sold. It should be noted, however, that where the debt has also been secured by intermediate grantees who stand in the position of sureties, a release of the lien on any part of the real estate described in the mortgage, or of any collateral security, without the consent of the sureties will immediately discharge them from their whole obligation unless a partial release has been provided for in the mortgage instrument.

Prepayment Privileges Mortgages are expected to prescribe the manner of the payment of the debt which they secure If this is included only in the note or bond—which may not be reproduced in the body of the mortgage—the effect is the same as if such statement were made a part of the mortgage. By mutual agreement the debt may be paid and the mortgage released at any time before the maturity date. In the absence of mortgagee consent, the debtor has no right to insist upon payment before maturity. Even though the full amount of the debt—including full interest to the date of maturity—be tendered to the mortgagee, he is not bound to accept it before the due date of the mortgage.

Sometimes the mortgagor is embarrassed by the absence of a privilege to prepay. For example, suppose that the due date occurs three years in the future. Suppose also that, for some reason, it is necessary for the owner of the property to refinance it immediately. He may not insist upon clearing the record of its existing mortgage, either to make a new mortgage possible or to be able to sell the property free and clear to a buyer who will take it no other way. Unless the mortgagee is willing to accept prepayment, he is in a position to drive a hard bargain as compensation for his consent to prepayment. The result of such bargaining is likely to be a penalty of some sort. It could be all or part of unearned interest to maturity or even more. While the mortgagee cannot insist upon more than principal and interest if he waits until maturity, as a penalty he may exact all that the traffic will bear. If there is no doubt about the adequacy of security, he is not likely to desire prepayment of the debt. Hence, the mortgagee whose consent to prepayment is sought is not running much risk to refuse the request except on his own terms.

In recent years most mortgages, on residential properties in particular, have included prepayment clauses. Some are unqualified in character, giving the debtor the right to prepay any or all of the debt at any time. Some provide that prepayment must take place at the time any regular installment of the debt is due. Some provide limited prepayment privileges—e.g., not to exceed 20 percent of the principal amount of the debt in any one calendar year. Others set a preliminary period of time within which prepayment privileges may not apply. For example, it may be stipulated that no prepayment will be accepted during the first two years after the execution of the mortgage.

In some mortgages, prepayment penalties are fixed in the instrument. The mortgagee may reserve the right to exact a penalty of three months' interest in case the mortgage is redeemed within three years. Since this is an option, the mortgagee may not see fit to take advantage of it. Or the mortgage may provide that, if it is redeemed from the proceeds of another mortgage to a different mortgagee, a penalty for prepayment may apply. Regardless of penalty clauses in mortgages, their use frequently depends upon competitive conditions at the time prepayment is planned.

The exercise of prepayment privileges by a mortgagor may seriously interrupt investment plans of a mortgagee. The latter thinks that he has made a long-term investment. If the term is shortened abruptly, it seems fair to compensate him in some manner for his loss of income while he is seeking another satisfactory outlet for his funds.

Probably most mortgagees would prefer not to grant prepayment privileges to their borrowers. As a rule, however, under the pressure of governmental agencies and the practices of competitors, the tendency in recent years has been in the direction of granting prepayment privileges. It is not at all clear that such privileges always work to the disadvantage of lenders. Corporate bonds commonly recognize the right of a mortgagee to prepayment compensation by providing for a call premium in case the debt is paid off before maturity. In general, this premium is largest when the bonds have been outstanding only a short time. It is reduced periodically thereafter until it disappears entirely as the bonds approach maturity.

Recasting of Mortgages Once a mortgage is executed and placed on record, it does not necessarily follow that its form may not change substantially before it is redeemed. It may be recast for any one of several reasons. Although the mortgage may contain no provision for future advances, they may be made nevertheless by mutual agreement of mortgagor and mortgagee. If there are no intervening liens, nothing further is required than to change the amount of the obligations which the mortgage secures. The result may be recorded only on the books of the mortgagee, without changing the record of the mortgage. If the original note and mortgage call for a lesser amount than the unpaid principal plus the advances, a change in the mortgage may be required to give the mortgagee full protection.

If a patient mortgagee permits the amount of the debt to increase because of delinquency, this too may call for a recasting of the mortgage. Again the subjects of intervening liens and of total debt must be considered. Or should multiple properties be offered as security for the original mortgage, any request for release of any of the original security from the lien of the mortgage must take into account possible changes in the mortgage.

Where a monthly payment direct reduction loan plan is used, with a level monthly payment throughout the life of the mortgage, the time will come when the unpaid balance is but a fraction of the original loan. At that time the mortgagor may request a recasting of the mortgage to provide for a reduction in the interest rate or in the monthly payments, or both. Possessed of a seasoned mortgage and a favorable experience with the mortgagor, the mortgagee is not likely to brush aside such a request. He would probably reduce the monthly payments gladly, since that enables him to keep a good investment for a longer period of time. He may agree to some reduction in the rate of interest more reluctantly. But if the mortgage contains prepayment privileges, he will probably lose it through refinancing by a competitor unless he makes reasonable concessions to the mortgagor. Again, rather than lose the investment he will probably prefer the change in interest rates. A windfall into the lap of a mortgagor may enable him to make a substantial reduction in his real estate loan and justify an immediate request for a recasting of his mortgage as outlined above.

Recasting of mortgages to admit interests not present at the time the mortgages were executed is sometimes necessary. For example, the mortgage may make no provision for an easement of a public utility company which requires access to the rear of the site covered by the mortgage. Since the installation of the services of the utility will add to rather than subtract from the value of the security, the mortgagee will usually be glad to approve the change. Nevertheless it will require a recasting of the mortgage to the extent indicated.

Power of Attorney In many business transactions it is common for one party to authorize another to act for him without any formal written instrument being required for this purpose. But in authorizing most acts which involve decisions concerning real estate rights, such authorization must be in writing. This writing is commonly known as a power of attorney. The principal who gives the power may be anyone, including a corporation, competent to execute real estate instruments. The agent who receives the power can be any natural and competent person or may be a corporation such as a bank or trust company. When used in connection with transactions involving real estate finance, the power given the agent should be set forth specifically in the instrument. A power of attorney should be made a matter of record so that the signature on the mortgage, for example, of someone other than the owner of the property may not cloud the title. Powers of attorney are subject to revocation by the principal and are generally terminated as a matter of law upon his death or insanity. Such a power does not terminate upon the death or insanity of the principal, however, when his agent, or attorney in fact, has a "power coupled with an interest," as where there has been such a transfer of title, or legal or equitable interest, in property to the attorney in fact that he can exercise the power in his own name.

Loan Servicing Loan servicing simply means that the lender has the responsibility for seeing that the loan is paid according to the contract; or that, in case this is not done, something else will follow that will work to the best advantage of both borrower and lender. One important step in loan servicing can be taken at the time the loan is closed. At that time the lender should make sure that the borrower fully understands the nature of the contract he is entering into. Such questions as the importance of making all payments as they fall due, the necessity for keeping the property in good repair at all times, and what it will mean to the borrower when the loan is entirely paid off—all these are proper topics for discussion at the time the contract for the loan is signed.

To facilitate loan servicing once the loan is put on the books, the following minimum requirements must be observed: (1) a file of all pertinent papers, including correspondence, on each outstanding loan; (2) a ledger sheet for each borrower; (3) a tax record that should be kept up to date; (4) an insurance record; and (5) a system of follow-up of delinquent borrowers.

Notices of Payments Due If the payments on mortgage loans are due at intervals of longer than one month, notices are customarily sent out reminding the borrower of the due date of the payment. On monthly payment loans, there is a wide difference of opinion on the subject of sending notices. The arguments against notices include the element of trouble and expense and the probability that the borrower will remember the date anyhow. On the other side of the question it is argued that: (1) The borrower needs a notice. (2) Since he probably owes other monthly bills, the creditor who reminds him of his obligations is most likely to be paid first. (3) The enclosed self-addressed envelope facilitates payment. (4) The return of the bill with the check aids the bookkeeper.

Past-due notices are much more common than notices of payments not yet due. Some send them out immediately after the payment is due and unpaid. Others wait for some time on the theory that the payment is just delayed and not overlooked. Some borrowers adjust their debt-paying habits to the nature of insistence by their creditors.

Late Payments A subject of never-ending debate in mortgage loan circles is the best method of dealing with late payments. It has many ramifications. For example, if A owes a payment on June 1 and does not make it until July 1, he will probably skip his July payment, making it in August. This means that he has deferred all payments one month. If he cannot make his June payment until the first of July, he probably cannot double up payments on that date without getting behind with some other creditor. On the other hand, if he is merely careless, he should be discouraged from falling behind in his payments. The borrower who meets all payments on time or in advance of the due date is the one all lenders like to deal with. Deviations from this desirable practice probably cannot be fitted into compartments. They must be dealt with on a case basis. This creates problems for loan servicing.

Late-charge penalties are used in some instances and are overlooked in others, even when the mortgage permits their assessment. Their purpose is obvious. Their effectiveness is not so obvious. If the borrower is only occasionally late in his payments, he may not be assessed any late charge. If he is careless in his paying habits, late-charge penalties may change his habits if the penalty is heavy enough to be felt. But if the borrower is unable to meet his payments on time, he will be even less able to meet them when late penalties are added. Each lender must decide how to handle late payments, including the policy of treating all borrowers alike or of dealing with each as a separate case.

Moratorium Laws At the depth of the depression of the 1930s, various steps were taken to bring some measure of relief to distressed mortgagors. One type of relief took the form of moratorium laws which extended the time of payment of the debt. Such laws represented what is known as a limited interference with the freedom of contracts. They have been given the descriptive title of "depression jurisprudence." In spite of the fact that the two contracting parties entered into their agreement voluntarily at the time the mortgage was executed, the legislature stepped in to determine that, in the public interest, the weaker party to the bargaining process needed and was entitled to a modification of the contract. One common form of such a moratorium was to suspend or forbid foreclosure sales during the emergency.

As with many other types of legislation, once a decision of this character is reached and made effective, it is fairly easy to extend its operation more or less permanently. For example, some moratorium laws which began in the period of emergency during the decade of the 1930s were made permanent by removing the time restriction on their effectiveness. Out of these moratorium laws has developed the concept that legislation should protect the mortgagor in default against unduly large deficiency judgments. Recent "fair value laws" on this subject reflect this type of thinking. Some of these seem to suggest a revival of the practice of strict foreclosure. The effect is the same if courts deny deficiency judgments on the ground that, at the time of the sale, the property was worth the amount of the debt even though it did not bring that amount at the foreclosure sale.

However, not all moratorium laws have been extended beyond the emergency they were set up to meet. Some granted relief for the period of the emergency and ceased to be effective when the emergency passed. Even here, a pattern has been established which may be utilized in another emergency or as a permanent part of our legislation.

QUESTIONS AND PROBLEMS

1. A transfers property to B, subject to a first mortgage lien held by C and a junior mortgage lien held by D. If B desires to clear the property of mortgage liens, how may he use a nominee to advantage?
2. When a mortgagor assigns his property and his obligations under his note and mortgage on the property to another, how is the mortgagee affected?
3. How may a mortgagor obtain a release from liability on a note and mortgage on real estate when the obligations under such note and mortgage have been assumed by another?
4. What dangers are encountered by mortgagees and unreleased mortgagors when property is sold "subject to" a mortgage?
5. What is an estoppel certificate and why is it necessary?
6. In general, how may the surety status of a grantee in the chain of title, who has assumed the mortgage, be affected by an extension of the existing mortgage?

7. How is a partial release used in a mortgage?
8. How important is the prepayment privilege in a mortgage note?
9. What are the procedural problems involved in servicing a mortgage loan?
10. What decisions must mortgage lenders make in connection with treatment of late payments by borrowers?
11. What was the nature of mortgage moratorium laws adopted by various states during the depression of the 1930s?
12. Do you think changes in our real estate financing techniques since the 1930s may have reduced the need for state moratorium laws? If so, in what ways?

6

Junior Liens

Dependence upon Junior Financing Prospective purchasers of real estate, particularly purchasers of homes, have always been short of capital with which to make substantial down payments. The use of high percentage loans in recent years does not indicate a change in capital accumulations by most people. Instead, it represents a change of pattern in the means used to meet their needs. When lower percentage loans were the order of the day—as represented both in the lending policies of financial institutions and in the laws which regulated their operations—there was still the need for bridging the gap between a 60 percent loan and an inadequate down payment. This gap could be bridged in any one of several ways. One way that was not admitted to be such a bridge was to make the appraisal of the property so high that the loans was in reality for at least 80 percent of the cost of the property instead of the presumed 60 percent.

The other bridge, labeled as such, was a resort to a junior mortgage. As at first commonly used, it was a stopgap rather than a complete answer to a perplexing problem. If the property sold for $10,000, with a $6,000 first mortgage against it, and the purchaser had only $2,000 cash to make a down payment, someone came along with the missing $2,000 in return for a short-term second or junior mortgage. Short-sightedness induced both borrower and junior mortgagee to become parties to such a transaction, without either of them stopping to seek an answer to the question, "What will happen when the short-term junior mortgage matures?" Unlike the short-term senior mortgages used earlier, junior mortgages were never expected to be subject to automatic renewal year after year.

Junior Mortgages In simple real estate financing transactions, such as those involving single residences, the character of the mortgage structure is easily defined. The senior or prior mortgage is usually called a first mortgage. All others are given the class name of junior mortgages. In any particular situation, there may be one or more junior mortgages or none at all. One junior lien, usually called a second mortgage, is sometimes used to bridge the gap between the price of the property and the sum of the first mortgage and the amount of money available to the purchaser to use as a down payment.

Traditionally, second mortgages are short term and carry a higher rate of interest than first mortgages. They frequently cause trouble for mortgagors who are unable to pay them off at their early maturity date. Such mortgagors are then at the mercy of the holder of such paper, who may consent to renew the mortgage for another short term in consideration for the payment of a stiff renewal fee. While the mortgagor is struggling to reduce his first mortgage balance, he is faced with successive heavy renewal charges and high interest rates for junior mortgages.

In other cases, second mortgages may run for somewhat longer periods of time—perhaps as long as five years. Since there is no "business" of second mortgage lending that is organized into financial institutions, the pattern of lending depends in every case upon local conditions and the demands of those individuals who are willing to take the risks that accompany this type of lending. Where second mortgages represent the advance of money needed to bridge the gap between the amount of the purchase price of the property and the sum of the amount of equity funds of the purchaser and the amount available on a first mortgage, the mortgagee who advances the money and takes a second mortgage as security is likely to be an experienced, shrewd person who takes pains to protect his own interests. At the same time he does make possible the purchase of property that would otherwise not be placed at the disposal of a purchaser who cannot finance the purchase otherwise. If, on the other hand, the second mortgage is a purchase-money mortgage needed to enable the seller to dispose of property that he might otherwise be required to hold longer than he wishes, the terms of the second mortgage may be somewhat more to the liking of the purchaser.

The second mortgage reads like a first mortgage, except that it is expected to make reference to and accept the priority of the first mortgage. Unless the mortgagor is careful in writing the second mortgage, he may elevate the priority of the second mortgage to that of a senior lien upon the event of redemption of the first mortgage.

The best way for the mortgagor to protect himself against this contingency is to include, in the second mortgage instrument, a waiver clause committing the holder of the second mortgage to waive its priority, not only over an existing first mortgage, but over any succeeding first mortgage written for an amount not in excess of the amount of the existing first mortgage. This is commonly known as the "lifting clause," since it permits the mortgagor to lift the first mortgage and replace it with another one without disturbing the junior status of the second mortgage. For the protection of the holder of the latter, the lifting clause should contain the limitation that the new first mortgage shall not be for a greater amount than the one it replaces, carried at the time the second mortgage was executed.

Other junior liens, subsequent in priority to second mortgages, are sometimes used. For example, suppose that a contractor purchases a building site, financing it through a first mortgage containing a waiver clause in favor of a construction mortgage. With the execution of the latter, the earlier first mortgage becomes a second mortgage. Suppose that the sum of these two is $10,000. Suppose also that a purchaser of the property at $14,000 has only $2,000 for a down payment. The contractor may see fit to accept the $2,000 in cash, take back a purchase-money third mortgage for $2,000, and sell the property to the purchaser who assumes the first and second mortgages. That means a pretty heavy load of junior mortgage financing for the purchaser to carry.

Junior mortgages are highly speculative. Those who find it advantageous to take them in financing real estate sales are frequently forced to dispose of them promptly in order to free their limited capital for other uses. The sale of junior mortgages at discounts ranging as high as 50 percent is not unusual. The purchaser may be a casual buyer or one who finds trafficking in this kind of paper profitable. For one with capital, courage, and foresight, junior mortgages offer acceptable speculations.

Not all junior mortgages carry the same degree of risk. Some alert speculators are so well acquainted with the territory in which they operate and are such keen students of real estate trends that they are able to minimize their risks by making their commitments on a highly selective basis. Not only must they know the neighborhoods in which the properties on which they are willing to purchase mortgages are located, but they must be good judges of human nature. In one case the mortgagor may have such a low moral hazard that he can be depended upon to make good on a junior mortgage, regardless of the value of the property securing it.

Junior Mortgage Discounts Because of the greater risks accepted by those who hold junior mortgages, it is expected that they shall bear rates of interest commensurate with the nature of the risks assumed. Laws against usury, if applied strictly, would interfere with some of the practices surrounding the use of junior mortgages. These laws are frequently circumvented by discount operations. For example, suppose that a single residence valued at $10,000 carries a first mortgage of $6,500. Suppose also that a prospective purchaser has only $2,000 available as a down payment. In order for the vendor to realize the additional $1,500 required to complete the price of $10,000, it may be necessary for him to take a second mortgage for $1,800 or even $2,000. He will then hope to sell this second mortgage for at least $1,500. The discount enjoyed by the purchaser will enhance the effective interest rate which he realizes on his investment.

This does not mean that two prices will be quoted for the property, one for cash and the other involving a second mortgage. As a matter of fact, if the seller hopes to realize $10,000 from the sale, he will probably ask more. He will then consider offers submitted upon the basis of financing arrangements, among other considerations. While the purchaser of such a property may not realize it, he will probably pay several hundred dollars more for it if a second mortgage is used as a part of the purchase price.

In the sale of highly speculative real estate in active markets, second mortgages may serve little purpose other than to create future trouble for the mortgagor. For example, the first mortgage may be large enough to cover the real costs of land and improvements. The down payment may pay a reasonable profit to the seller and the sales costs. The second mortgage is so speculative that if nothing is ever realized upon it the seller has not really suffered a loss from holding it. Nevertheless, its existence places a burden upon the mortgagor and his assigns. It may be very difficult meantime for the holder of such a second mortgage to obtain an advantage from it.

The discount on junior mortgages will usually continue to apply even after the senior mortgage has been written down to a point where the property might easily be financed with a single mortgage. This the mortgagor may not know. If he does not, he will probably continue to pay heavy discounts to obtain renewals of the junior financing. For example, suppose that a property costing $10,000 is financed with a $6,000 first mortgage, a $2,000 second mortgage, and $2,000 cash. Suppose that the income of the mortgagor is just sufficient to enable him to meet his obligations on both mortgages, pay his taxes, maintain his property in good condition, and pay the normal living expenses of himself and his family. In due time his savings, amounting to $2,000, are represented in the amortization of the first lien to $4,000.

At this point it should be possible to increase the first mortgage back to the original $6,000, using the increase to pay off the junior mortgage. Both the mortgagor and the holder of the senior mortgage would be better protected if this were done, assuming that the mortgagor is dependable and can carry a $6,000 lien on his property comfortably. Any circumstance that would make a renewal of the second mortgage difficult might eventually jeopardize the position of the holder of the first lien.

The latter is not likely to take the initiative in absorbing the second mortgage into an increased first lien. If the mortgagor does not know of the possibility so that he can take the initiative, he may go on year after year renewing the second mortgage. If his payments on the first mortgage are on a standard level basis, he never gets any relief here to permit him to accumulate funds to pay off the junior lien. His equity is increasing but his liquid resources are not.

Different Use of Discount Sometimes discounts on junior mortgages are used in ways different from those mentioned above. Suppose that A sells his property to B, reluctantly taking back a purchase-money junior mortgage for $2,000. Suppose that B is not financially responsible and has difficulty in keeping up his payments. Since he is unable to meet the mortgage principal at its maturity date, it is informally extended. In other words, A does not press for payment for fear that he will have the property back on his hands when he has no use for it any longer.

Along comes C, who is willing to take over the property from B and assume the first mortgage, provided something can be done to reduce the second mortgage. A might be very glad to discount the mortgage 50 percent in order to get $1,000 cash and be relieved of the worry of trying to make occasional collections from B. Or if C is a shrewd bargainer and is known to meet his financial obligations promptly and without fail, A might even be talked into canceling $1,000 of his second mortgage in return for the assumption of the other $1,000 by C. If he does so, it should be the second $1,000 that is canceled rather than the first. By this is meant that A might agree to cancel the entire mortgage after $1,000 has been paid on the principal. If he merely cancels $1,000 of the $2,000 mortgage, title to the property might again get into the hands of someone who is no more capable of meeting his obligations than B was. While C is still bound on his mortgage assumption, he may have lost his financial responsibility, moved out of the jurisdiction of the mortgage, and so forth.

Market for Junior Mortgages Because of the relatively high return on second mortgage paper, speculative-minded investors sometimes favor commitments in this field of real estate finance. Most financial institutions which are regulated in the interest of those who supply their funds are prohibited by law from accepting junior mortgages as primary security for their advances, or from their purchase. Occasionally a second mortgage is taken as supplemental security to bolster weak security behind a senior lien or one that subsequently may become weak. This leaves the purchase of second mortgages almost entirely in the hands of individuals. Trafficking in them is no game for an amateur to play. The chances for loss are great. Even where losses are not suffered, this field of real estate finance grows much worry and uncertainty.

The successful speculator in junior mortgages must know much more than the legal details about the drawing up and assignment of mortgages. This phase is important, and its neglect may be serious. But he must also be a close student of the market in which he operates, possessing a knowledge of such subjects as population changes and trends, general business conditions and cyclical changes in them, and real estate values and how to determine them. He must be able to judge soundness of construction, the effects of depreciation and obsolescence, and a host of other things that may affect the quality of his commitment. As an apprenticeship for the art of junior mortgage financing, successful experience in senior mortgages is sometimes used. It seems axiomatic that one who cannot succeed in dealing with senior mortgages should not tackle the greater hazards of junior mortgage financing.

In recent years an increasing volume of junior mortgages has been generated by builders and realty dealers, particularly in rapidly growing communities. To assist investors in the acquisition of desirable junior liens, corporations have been organized to accomplish selective purchasing for resale. Such corporations buy the mortgages (or trust deeds) at discounts ranging from 10 percent or less to as high as 40 percent. The corporations then sell the obligations to investors at such a discount that when combined with the stated rate of interest on the mortgage note the yield to maturity will be satisfactory. Acceleration of payments by the mortgagor will have the effect of increasing the investor's yield beyond his normal expectation. Against the possibility of default on the mortgage note, in some cases the investor is protected by a warranty agreement providing for repurchase by the selling corporation in event of delinquency on the part of the mortgagor. In the absence of such an agreement, of course, the investor may find himself assuming risks beyond those compensated for in his expected return on his investment.

The U.S. Securities and Exchange Commission and certain state regulatory officials have expressed concern over promotional techniques whereby the investor is "assured" his fixed rate of interest on a "secured" investment. The trust deed business in California, for example, has burgeoned in recent years because of the unusual population growth and the general scarcity of funds for real estate loans. A recent study of a committee of the state legislature found cases in southern California developments where first trust deeds had been written for over $16,000 against houses which sold for less than $14,000. Needless to say, the underlying security for junior liens in such transactions could be nothing but pure blue sky.

Occasionally a first mortgage institution is induced to take over a second mortgage from a good customer such as a contractor. Suppose that contractor A holds a second mortgage for $3,000 on property he has sold to B. Suppose that institution C has agreed to grant a first mortgage on the same property. In case A would rather not bother with collections on his second mortgage, C may be willing to purchase the second from A under some such terms as the following: Instead of paying cash to A, C may give A credit on an account as supplemental security to protect C's investment in the second mortgage on B's property. When the second mortgage is paid off, the account will be released to A.

Such an arrangement may be advantageous to A because, generally speaking, a mortgagor will probably default in his payments less frequently if his mortgage is held by a financial institution than if it is held by an individual. In addition, A is relieved from collection and bookkeeping problems. It can be advantageous to C for two reasons. The interest rate on the second mortgage is high; and C has pleased a good customer by buying the second mortgage.

In the illustration used, there is not likely to be too much question raised about C holding the second mortgage against B's property, because it already holds the first mortgage on the same property. It is usually to the advantage of the holder of the first mortgage to be in a position to check up on payments on a junior lien. Default on the latter may cause trouble for the former.

Senior and Junior Mortgages The existence of a junior mortgage is never a matter of indifference to the senior mortgagee. Neither should be the gambling instincts of the mortgagor nor the buying habits of his spouse. While the lien of the first mortgage takes priority over that of the second mortgage, this becomes most important in times of crisis, when the mortgagor finds that he can no longer meet his obligations. What will normally please the first mortgagee most is an assurance that no such crisis will ever arise during the life of his mortgage. Therefore, anything that creates an undue drain upon the income of the mortgagor may work against the best interests of the first mortgagee. For this reason he cannot be indifferent to the existence of a second mortgage, the obligations of which may create a crisis in the financial affairs of the mortgagor.

Some real estate financial institutions even go so far as to hesitate to grant first mortgages if the mortgagor expects to depend upon a second mortgage to help him finance his property. Others study carefully the amount and nature of the proposed second mortgage to determine whether or not to place a first mortgage on the property. The Federal Housing Administration has definitely frowned upon the use of second mortgages in connection with first mortgages insured by it. As a general rule it has refused insurance where a second mortgage is used. The one exception applies to Section 505 of the GI Bill of Rights, discussed in Chapter 26.

From the standpoint of the holder of the junior mortgage, he has a definite interest in the actions of the senior mortgagee. If the latter refuses to grant any leniency to the mortgagor in a period of reduced capacity to meet his obligations—regardless of the willingness of the junior mortgagee to grant a temporary moratorium—the senior lien may be foreclosed at a time when the junior mortgagee will be hesitant to buy the property to protect his own interests. It is always to the interests of the junior mortgagee to try to cooperate with the senior mortgagee. On occasion the holder of the junior mortgage may find it to his advantage to purchase the senior mortgage to avoid difficulty with its holder. A better alternative might be to work with the mortgagor to refinance the property with a new first mortgagee, on the basis of merging the two mortgages if possible.

Foreclosure of Junior Mortgage The holder of a junior mortgage has the legal right to foreclose his mortgage whenever the mortgagor defaults in his obligations. The possession of this right and the decision to exercise it are two quite different concepts. If the default occurs at a time when the junior mortgagee thinks the property is not worth more than the unpaid principal of the senior lien, foreclosure would produce nothing more valuable than a deficiency judgment. Meantime, if the mortgagor is keeping up his payments on his senior lien—or has made arrangements satisfactory to its holder—and if taxes are current, the holder of the junior lien may find it most advantageous to mark time, hoping for a recovery in real estate values, in the fortunes of the mortgagor, or both. He may even agree with the mortgagor, in writing if necessary, not to press his claims for a specified period of time.

If, however, the junior mortgagee thinks the property is worth more than the unpaid principal of the senior lien, particularly if he doubts the capacity of the mortgagor to improve his debt-paying ability, he may take steps to protect his interests before they become more involved. There are several possibilities open to him. He may buy out the interests of the mortgagor for a nominal sum, perhaps through a dummy purchaser, in order to keep his own mortgage alive better. In such case he hopes to dispose of the property soon to a purchaser who can carry the obligations against it.

He may bargain with the mortgagor directly, agreeing to accept a voluntary conveyance in lieu of a foreclosure suit and a subsequent deficiency judgment. In such case he would probably cancel his junior mortgage, merging his claims into the title to the property. His acceptance of a deed from the mortgagor would probably be conditioned by the absence of any other junior liens of record and by his confidence that the mortgagor would not later claim duress in passing title to the property should real estate values stage an early recovery. In accepting a voluntary conveyance he may take title subject to the first mortgage if he hesitates to assume it. Even where there are subsequent junior liens of record, their holders might not think too highly of their value and might be willing to cancel them for a nominal sum. If this is less than foreclosure costs, the mortgagee may see fit to accept a voluntary conveyance of title.

Should there be any doubt about either of these matters, the junior mortgagee might find it advantageous to bring foreclosure suit, joining all subsequent junior lienors in the suit. If foreclosure is resorted to, the interests of the senior mortgagee must be taken into account. Several alternatives are open to the junior mortgagee. He may sue only the mortgagor and the subsequent lienholders, leaving the senior mortgage undisturbed unless its holder decides to enter foreclosure suit also. He may pay off the senior mortgage, with the consent of its holder if that is necessary. He may bargain with the latter to let his first mortgage stand undisturbed or to take back a new mortgage if the senior mortgagee is a party to the foreclosure suit.

In bargaining with the holder of the first mortgage, there must result a meeting of the minds. Depending upon a variety of factors, the holder of the first mortgage may be willing to accept a lower interest rate, some reduction in principal, or an easing up of payment requirements; or he may make other concessions to the new titleholder. He may insist upon much harsher terms in the new mortgage as his price for granting it. His estimate of the current and prospective value of the property and of the debt-paying capacities of the former holder of the junior lien will color his judgment on these issues.

Indeed, there are occasions when, if the senior mortgage as well as the junior is in default, the holder of the former will approach the holder of the latter to work out a plan by which the latter may take title to the property, even though the junior lienholder thinks he has no equity in it. Suppose for some reason that the holder of the senior lien does not wish to take title to the property. He may offer such terms to a financially responsible holder of a second mortgage as to create an equity where none existed. He may not only be willing to compromise his own claims, but agree to advance additional funds for the purpose of rehabilitating the property to make it more salable or rentable. Such an arrangement may well work to the advantage of both parties to it.

Merging of Mortgages For the better protection of the mortgagor, junior mortgages should be long-term amortized instruments of real estate finance. Sometimes an arrangement is made with the holder of the first mortgage that he will serve as collection agent for the owner of the second mortgage. Suppose that the first mortgage is for $6,000 and the second for $2,000. In this case the mortgagor may make monthly payments to the first mortgagee as if he had a single mortgage for $8,000. Various plans are used in crediting these payments. Under one, all payments of principal installments may be applied against the unpaid balance of the first mortgage, until it has been reduced to $4,000. Meantime, the holder of the second mortgage would be credited with interest only. When the first mortgage is written down to $4,000, its holder may agree to recast his loan, writing it up again to $6,000, thereby releasing funds to redeem the second mortgage.

This practice of merging two mortgages is not too commonly used, but it has possibilities. Until the time comes to merge the two, the first mortgagee not only has the advantage of more rapid amortization of his claims, but he has the added protection of an interest of the junior lienholder that will not be lightly cast aside. While the first mortgage is being amortized, its holder has an opportunity to become acquainted with the debt-paying capacities of the mortgagor. By the time the debt is written down from $6,000 to $4,000, the former should know the latter well enough to determine whether or not to increase the first mortgage indebtedness. The mortgagor certainly has a better deal than if he faced periodical renewals of junior financing. And the second mortgagee who can wait for his money probably stands a better chance of being paid in full in cash.

Redemption Clause While the holder of a second or junior mortgage would normally be much pleased to have his loan paid off, there are occasions when he might prefer to have his mortgage instead of the money. Suppose that the term of the second mortgage is three years. The holder is not obligated to accept payment until the maturity date of his mortgage. Suppose also that the mortgagor has a good opportunity to refinance the property, merging the second mortgage with the senior lien. Without the consent of the holder of the junior lien, the mortgagor might not be able to take advantage of this opportunity.

The best way to be assured of having such an opportunity is to include in the second mortgage a redemption or prepayment clause. A common method of expressing such a clause is to state that "on or before" the maturity date of the mortgage, the amount of the mortgage may be paid and the mortgage canceled, at the option of the mortgagor. In the absence of some kind of a redemption or call clause, the holder of the second mortgage might exact a heavy penalty as the price of accepting payment on the mortgage before it matures. Because of the junior position of the second mortgage and the uncertainties surrounding its collectibility, it is ordinarily not difficult to include a prepayment clause in a second mortgage. What is said here about a second mortgage would apply with equal if not greater force to third and subsequent mortgages.

Hierarchy of Mortgages In contrast to the fairly simple mortgage structure which characterizes the financing of single-family residences, the hierarchy of mortgages sometimes used in the financing of corporations requires the services of a Philadelphia lawyer and two assistants to decipher. Not only are there second and third mortgages outstanding under that name, but frequently several layers of mortgage liens are so designated that the names given them confuse rather than enlighten the casual investor who may be attracted to them. This is particularly true in the financing of railroads and public utilities, where existing corporations may be the result of combinations or of a combination of combinations of corporations which had various types of mortgages outstanding at the time of merger or consolidation. When such combinations take place, the existing mortgage indebtedness is usually assumed and remains outstanding. By the time the new corporations execute some mortgages on their own account, complications can easily develop which require a careful study of wordy legal documents to decipher.

Even names are sometimes deceptive without being intentionally so. An owner of a single residence who uses a first mortgage seldom does anything to raise a question about the legal nature of this type of lien. On the other hand, corporation A might combine with corporation B to form corporation X, which assumes first and second mortgages against real estate owned previously by A and B separately. If now X issues its own first mortgage, with the same real estate as security, this mortgage constitutes a third rather than a first lien as its name implies.

Or suppose that corporation C, with a first mortgage against its real estate, gets into financial difficulty and is forced to raise new money. Suppose also that its only method of doing so is by the issuance of a senior mortgage. But there is already a senior mortgage outstanding. With the reluctant consent of the mortgagees, their claims may be subordinated to those of the new mortgagee whose mortgage is given the title of "prior lien mortgage." By this means the "first" mortgage, by subordination, becomes a junior lien. Meantime the wording of the "first" mortgage may not be changed. On its face it still carries the impression that it constitutes a senior lien. Sometimes the bonds issued under this mortgage are stamped to show the change in status indicated above. This is not always done. In other ways corporations frequently build up complex hierarchies of mortgages.

Baltimore Ground Rents In Maryland, particularly in the city of Baltimore, a system of financing real estate has been used since colonial days under the general name of "ground rents." At the outset, what amounted to perpetual leases were granted on vacant land to be used for building construction. While the actual term of the lease might have been only 99 years, it was renewable in perpetuity. The lessor retained title to the land and granted its use, under conditions stipulated in the lease, to the lessee in return for an annual rental. Since in the early use of ground rents there was no provision for giving the lessee the right to acquire title by purchasing the fee, he could obtain the cancellation of an irredeemable lease only by the process of bargaining the title away from the lessor. Even where redemption rights were given the lessee in the lease contract, they expired by limitation in case they were not exercised within the time fixed in such contract.

In general it appears that the lessor was better acquainted with ground rents than the lessee, and for that reason the lease contract was likely to favor the former rather than the latter. Consequently, the right to purchase the fee was not commonly included. Eventually public policy decreed that irredeemable ground rents were undesirable. Through a succession of laws, beginning in 1884, Maryland determined that all subsequent leases for as long as 15 years should be considered to contain an option for the lessee to purchase the fee at a sum not larger than the capitalization of the ground rent at 6 percent. All ground rent leases executed subsequent to 1884 have been considered to be redeemable.

Pennsylvania Ground Rents In Pennsylvania a somewhat different system of ground rents developed in the early days. While the effect is the same as under the Baltimore irredeemable ground rents, the form is different. In Pennsylvania the title passed to the vendee in return for an agreement to pay a perpetual rent. Under both systems the result is the same as if the grantor had taken a perpetual mortgage on the land equal to its value. In some cases the vendee was permitted, during a specified period of time, to obtain a release from and discharge of the obligation to pay an annual rent, upon payment of a stipulated sum which amounted to the capitalization of the rent. If this privilege was not exercised within the time specified, the rent became perpetual and the arrangement irredeemable. It was still subject to subsequent cancellation through bargaining. As in Maryland, the Pennsylvania legislature in 1885 passed a law prohibiting the execution of irredeemable ground rents in the future.

Financing Construction under Ground Rents In both Maryland and Pennsylvania, financial institutions have been accustomed to finance the construction of buildings where ground rents are used. Mortgages used for this purpose are really leasehold mortgages with the ground rent contract acting as a prior lien. Nevertheless, in those areas where this method of financing has been employed for many years, there is no hesitancy to take leasehold mortgages. Since the ground rent contracts are assignable, in case a mortgage on the structure is foreclosed the mortgagee may succeed to the position of the mortgagor with respect to his rights and obligations under the ground rent plan. The mortgagee then has a property to be disposed of subject to the ground rent.

It is more or less a matter of indifference to the mortgagee whether he finances a property where the mortgagor owns the site and needs to borrow a large part of the cost of the structure or one where the mortgagor does not own the site but needs to borrow a somewhat smaller proportion of the structure cost. If the improved property is worth $12,500, of which the lot is valued at $2,500 and the structure at $10,000, the mortgagor can probably make the purchase with a down payment of $2,500. This would be equivalent to a 100 percent loan on the structure, if the mortgagor owned the lot free and clear of all encumbrances other than the first mortgage on the improved property. Or it would be equivalent to a 75 percent loan on the structure, subject to a prior lien of $2,500 in case of ground rent.

Ground Rent Assignments Not only are properties subject to ground rent bought and sold in the areas where this system of real estate finance is commonly used, but the ground rent contracts are freely traded in. Since they are freely assignable and since they represent underlying liens, they are usually recommended for investment of trust funds and other similar requirements of sound investment programs. With a fixed rate of return over the life of the ground rent contract, prices fluctuate as interest rates change. The statutory right of redemption has placed ceilings over values, since the contract may be canceled by redemption at the option of the grantee or vendee.

Speculation in ground rents sometimes gives a source of profit to contractors not available elsewhere. Since the value of the ground rent is determined by the income realized from it, ground rents on vacant land are not easily disposed of, because the income realized is nil. Income potential may be referred for some years before it is realized. As soon as a suitable structure is erected upon the site, the ground rent contract acquires value. Speculative and operative builders may obtain an additional profit from selling, on a capitalized income basis, ground rents which they purchased at a much lower price.

Current Uses of Residential Ground Rents Except in Maryland and parts of Pennsylvania, ground rents have been little used in this country. Several reasons account for this. In the newer sections of the United States, early land grants passed title more easily than in the two states where ground rents were more common. Other methods of financing construction also developed in the newer areas. While some settlers in these newer sections from Baltimore and Philadelphia tried out ground rents in their new home communities, no real financial pattern developed from these sporadic uses. In the last few years, however, net ground leases have been adapted to an increasing extent to single-family dwellings in new developments, particularly in Hawaii and California.[1] In Hawaii, leasing has been the custom, and Kaiser Industries has offered lots exclusively on a leased basis in its new Hawaii-Kai development.

---

[1] William O. Shenkel, "Residential Net Ground Leases," *Journal of Property Management*, Vol. 29, No. 4 (March-April 1964), pp. 180–93. See also *The Wall Street Journal*, February 25, 1963, pp. 1, 16.

Annual ground rents are a percentage of the appraisal value of the lot for a term of 55 years. The Irvine Company in Orange County, southern California, has 88,000 acres under development and is using long-term ground leases for houses selling from $50,000 to $200,000.

Developers save the most desirable sites for leasing, and thereby overcome initial unfavorable reactions to leasing as opposed to buying the underlying land. Usually the owner of the leased land does not do the subdividing or housing construction. Rather, he grants a "master lease" to a subdivider who makes the improvements, such as streets and sewers. The subdivider may then either build a house on the lot or sell it. In either case, the cost of the improvements will be added on to the price of the house or to the cost of the lease. Many landowners have incorporated a hedge against inflation in the lease terms. They have required that the lease rentals shall be renegotiated halfway through the primary term of the lease. For example, leases at Laguna-Niguel subdivision in California require that ground rents be adjusted after 30 years to compensate for changes in the U.S. government cost-of-living index during the interim period.

Leaseholds are eligible for FHA insurance if the term is for 50 years or not less than 99 years for renewable leases. The Veterans Administration will guarantee leasehold loans if the primary term of the lease is at least 14 years beyond the maturity date of the loans. Leasehold loans are permissible under national banking regulations provided the lease extends at least 10 years beyond the loan maturity date. Federally chartered savings and loan associations may take liens on leaseholds with a primary period of, or renewable for, at least 10 years beyond the terminal date of the loan. Insurance companies may also take leasehold loans according to the laws of the states governing investment policies.

Besides the obvious advantage to the purchaser of avoiding lot costs at time of purchase, it has also been pointed out that restrictive covenants and a continuing repair and maintenance obligation in the lease do much to forestall depreciation and obsolescence.[2] The interest of the developer extends beyond the sale. On the other hand, the inherent disadvantage to this form of tenancy in the purchaser's eyes lies in the emotional appeal and sense of independence, without a terminal date, that is associated with homeownership.

Fee Ownership Certificates One method of financing income property that has some vogue in some parts of the country is the fee ownership certificate. The holders occupy the position of common stockholders, except that they usually have all the risks of, but do not enjoy the

---

[2] All full consideration of residential lease covenants is contained in William M. Shenkel, *An Analysis of Long Term Residential Leases*. A report prepared for the Bureau of Indian Affairs, Department of Interior, March 1963 (Second Printing).

gains that might accrue to, the speculative holders of common stock. Perhaps an illustration taken from actual experience will make clear the true nature of such certificates. Suppose that an apartment house is financed by the use of as large a mortgage as it will stand—say $350,000. Suppose also that the promoter decides that he can sell 2,000 units of fee ownership certificates at $100 each, provided that he can show a return of 8 percent upon them. By the use of a lease to a company organized for the purpose, he receives a contract for a fixed rent of $16,000 per annum. The lessee agrees to pay all carrying charges, including the payments on the mortgage. The lessor then sells fee ownership certificates representing an undivided interest in an indivisible fee. He retains a management contract in addition to the profit he made on the deal. If conditions are favorable, the "common stockholders" will receive their 8 percent return on their investment. If they are too favorable, the lessee will probably exercise his purchase option and buy the fee ownership certificates at the option price of $105. But if future conditions should fail to justify the rent, the lessee would probably give up and leave the fee ownership certificate owners holding the bag, getting what rent they could and dividing net earnings among themselves if any are available. In other words, fee ownership certificates suffer from the weaknesses, but do not enjoy the strength, of common stock. An additional weakness has created difficulties in financing through fee ownership certificates. As certificate holders have moved to inaccessible places, or encountered domestic difficulties, the redemption by the lessee of all of the certificates to recapture the full title of the property becomes a near impossibility. Some certificate holders or persons entitled to dower and curtesy rights cannot be found, or may be located in remote places anywhere in the world. The current tendency is to issue subordinated debentures instead of fee ownership certificates and retain the title in comparable situations.

Later Discussion of Junior Liens In subsequent chapters of this text, further discussion of junior liens will be pursued. This is especially true in the chapters on syndication, long-term leases, and purchase and leaseback. Because of the importance of these subjects, it seems best to discuss them separately, rather than to include in the chapter on junior liens all of the material that is relevant to the subject.

Mechanics' Liens Mechanics' liens are frequently misunderstood by those who are in a position to gain from their use. Many of our statutes represent modifications in practices formerly governed by common law or by equity. Mechanics' liens have no such heritage. They are distinctly creatures of statute, with no background of antecedent policies. The first mechanics' lien law was passed in Maryland in 1791 as a means of attracting needed building labor. In effect, such a law gives certain types of creditors a preferential claim over other creditors of a debtor who owns real estate. These protected in this manner include the creditors who provide materials for structures which become a part of the real estate; the workmen who perform the labor of building the structure; the contractors who take responsibility for seeing that proper use is made of the materials and the labor; and even the subcontractors who have no immediate and direct responsibility to the owner of the property, but serve him indirectly through their relationship with general contractors. As a matter of practice, the owner customarily deals only with the general contractor. He probably could not identify any others protected by mechanics' liens. Yet, in three fourths of the states, any amounts paid by the owner to the general contractor could conceivably be collected a second time under mechanics' liens.

At the outset it must be recognized that a mechanics' lien, if filed in proper order, constitutes a lien against real estate. It is not automatic in operation, but must be foreclosed like any other lien to ensure final satisfaction, so far as the court of equity can ensure it. Also, the mere fact that material has been supplied or that labor has been performed does not fulfill the requirements of a mechanics' lien. There is no lien until notice of it is properly filed and recorded in the appropriate public office.

Because of the confusion arising from some statutes that have not been too carefully drawn, many conflicts result from their interpretation. Generally speaking, priorities of liens are expected to be determined by the order in which they are filed. This is not universally true. In some cases the first overt acts undertaken in the performance of the contract may determine the order of priority. Here is a fruitful source of confusion that should be clarified by more explicit statutes. The time for filing mechanics' liens varies from 30 days to six months after the work has been performed or the material has been delivered.

Mechanics' Liens and Mortgages Conflicts between mechanics' liens and mortgages concerning their priority arise quite frequently. Not all of them can be resolved amicably, and one party or another is often forced to resort to court action to get the issue settled. Nevertheless, there are some principles which have common application to the question at issue. One is that purchase-money mortgages normally enjoy priority over mechanics' liens. This naturally follows from the fact that title and purchase-money mortgage are generally created simultaneously. In other words, the grantee takes the title encumbered by a purchase-money mortgage. Hence his first opportunity to incur an obligation that would give rise to a mechanics' lien would take place after the purchase-money mortgage has been executed. If its holder is diligent in protecting his interests, he will see that his mortgage is placed on record at the same instant of time that the grantee's title finds its way into the records.

Likewise, ordinary mortgages against improved property that are on record before the delivery of materials or the performance of work on the structure would take precedence over mechanics' liens. Even though some recent laws tend to give protection to holders of mechanics' liens by giving them priority over existing mortgages, this principle has not acquired much support as yet. Exceptions will be noted later in this chapter.

Most of the conflicts arise out of the simultaneous appearance of mechanics' liens and construction loans. The latter are presumed to provide much of the funds needed to pay for materials and to compensate labor used in the construction of a building which is to constitute the chief security for the construction loan. Since, by definition, the building does not exist before the material is delivered and the work is performed, confusion over the priority of construction mortgage liens and mechanics' liens may easily arise. In general, the weight of opinion favors priority to the construction mortgage which is made a part of the record prior to the filing of mechanics' liens. Even this preference is subject to disputes on occasion because of the cloudy character of the statutes mentioned above. If the mechanics' lien is interpreted as becoming effective at the time work on the project begins instead of at the time of filing the lien, this might readily cause confusion if work has begun before the construction mortgage is filed, even though such lien is placed upon the record before the mechanics' lien is recorded. Indeed, mechanics' liens have been known to attach under any of the following sets of circumstances: at the time the contract for materials or labor is agreed upon; at the time the first materials are delivered or the first labor is performed; when the construction is started; on the date of filing the lien; or on the date the owner is notified that the lien has been filed.

Because of possible confusion arising from the above situation, some mortgagees insist that no materials be delivered to the site and that no work be performed on the structure until the construction mortgage has been filed. If work has been started, affidavits are sometimes required from all who may be protected by mechanics' liens, showing that all such work has been paid for, before the construction mortgage will be executed. In extreme cases, materials delivered to the site have been taken back to their source, excavations have been filled, and the building site has been restored to its original condition. After all bills incurred up to that time have been paid and receipts have been obtained, the construction mortgage is then placed on record to give it priority, and the work of construction starts over again.

Other complications resulting in conflicts between mechanics' liens and mortgages arise even after questions are submitted to the courts for answers. In some cases a theory is prevalent to the effect that mechanics' liens should take precedence even over prior lien mortgages to the extent of the value added to the property by the improvement which gave rise to the mechanics' lien. Under this theory, if the foreclosure sale produces an amount insufficient to satisfy the claims of the mortgagee and the holders of the mechanics' liens, then the mortgagee is entitled only to the part of the proceeds that the ratio of the value of the property before the improvements represents in comparison with the value after the improvements have been made. For example, suppose that the mortgagee's claim is $6,000, the mechanics' liens amount to $2,000, the proceeds of the sale amount to only $6,000, and the value of the property before the improvements, $8,000; then the mortgagee would be entitled only to $4,800 instead of $6,000.

In still other cases the mechanics' lienholders are entitled to priority up to the full amount that has been added by the improvements. In the above illustration the mechanics' lienholders would get $2,000 and the mortgagee only $4,000, in spite of his supposed prior lien of $6,000. This principle is known as the severability doctrine, which undertakes to separate improvement cost as a special basis for preference.

Discharge of Mechanics' Liens Seldom does a mechanics' lien progress to the point of actual foreclosure. If foreclosure is resorted to, it may be instituted any time after the lien has been recorded and must be started within the time limit established by law. The procedure to sell the land to satisfy the mechanics' lien follows the same path as is followed in a mortgage foreclosure sale. Other forms of discharge and cancellation are more common. Some liens may be withdrawn because they were filed in error. Others may be canceled by court order if the defendant against whose property they were filed can prove that the amounts claimed are not applicable to this property. Many are either paid in full or compromised, and the record is cleared. Pending court action to settle disputes, arrangements are sometimes made to lift the lien from property A and apply it to property B owned by the same party in order to facilitate the disposal of property A. Sometimes the defendant deposits with the court money or its equivalent in order to shift the lien to this asset. Again the purpose is to facilitate the sale or further financing of the property against which the lien was first placed.

Where the mortgagor acknowledges the debt, he may be willing to exchange some other form of assurance of repayment for the lien. For example, he may give the lienholder a note in return for the release of the lien. He should make sure that the lienholder is willing to go through with this kind of arrangement. Acceptance of the note by the lienholder might not necessarily induce him to release his mechanics' lien.

Some mechanics' liens are filed for protective purposes only. For example, if the financial affairs of a property owner are considerably involved, those eligible to file mechanics' liens may elect to do so merely to establish the security for their claims. As soon as the owner of the property straightens out his financial tangles, he may be able to pay off all lienholders, thus discharging their liens. Occasionally nuisance liens are filed. Their disposal may cost the property owner time, or money, or both.

Occasionally mechanics' liens are discharged because their holders fail to pursue their rights within the time allotted to them for this purpose. The time for foreclosing mechanics' liens varies from 60 days to six years, with one year most common.

QUESTIONS AND PROBLEMS

1. What is the difference between a claim secured by a promissory note and a lien?
2. Recently, there has been a marked increase in the use of junior liens in areas of extensive real estate development. Specifically, how do these liens arise?
3. If you were considering purchase of a third lien trust deed, how might your investigation differ from that which you would make if the lien were of first priority?
4. Why do many real estate financial institutions hesitate to grant first mortgages to a mortgagor who expects to depend upon a second mortgage to help him finance his property?
5. What alternatives are available to a junior mortgage lienholder in event of default by the mortgagor in connection with the senior mortgage?
6. Under what circumstances may a junior real estate lien have value even though there is no apparent equity in the property above the claim of the senior mortgage?
7. Under the Maryland "ground rents" system, a lease for as long as 15 years is considered redeemable and the lessee is permitted to purchase the fee for a sum not larger than the capitalization of the annual ground rent at 6 percent. What would be the maximum purchase price of a lot whose annual rental was $360?
8. A ground rent contract is an obligation of the lessee to make future payments. How may this contract take on substantial value to the lessee as a property for assignment to another?
9. What are fee ownership certificates? What are the advantages and disadvantages of this form of financing (a) from the point of view of the company issuing the certificate and (b) from the point of view of the investor?
10. May anyone besides mechanics obtain a mechanics' lien?
11. What are the procedures for the establishment and enforcement of a mechanics' lien in your state?
12. In what ways may a mechanics' lien be discharged?

7

Real Estate Bonds, Investment Trusts, and Cooperatives

Real Estate Bonds In following this discussion of real estate bonds, the reader should not be confused by the subject of notes or "bonds" which evidence the primary form of obligation behind a real estate mortgage. As pointed out earlier in this text, the mortgagor is expected to execute a promissory note which is sometimes called a bond. Then he pledges the real estate as security to insure the payment of his note. When we speak of real estate bonds at this time, we have quite a different meaning in mind. Real estate bonds constitute a series of notes. For example, if the amount to be borrowed is $500,000, instead of issuing one note for that amount the mortgagor, through the use of a deed of trust, will perhaps mortgage the property to a trustee. Against this are issued perhaps 300 bonds each carrying a face value of $500, and 350 bonds each carrying a face value of $1,000. Bonds of less than $500 have been used occasionally but are not very popular because of the high cost of floating them. The costs of engraving, accounting, and so on, are as much for a $100 bond as for a $1,000 bond. By the use of bonds a broad market for participation in real estate financing is tapped.

The use of real estate bonds has had an interesting history. In the early days of financing even larger properties, dependence rested almost entirely upon single mortgages. Then a recognition of a sizable market for participation in this type of financing among small investors resulted in the development of real estate bonds. During the decade of the 1920s in particular, this form of financing was very popular. Indeed, it was so popular that it overreached itself, and many investors lost heavily on purchases of real estate bonds. The common use of leasehold bonds, whose exact character was not generally understood by those who bought them, added to the losses when the dark days of the 1930 depression brought with them wholesale defaults of such bond issues. Some bond houses, failing to forecast accurately the probable breadth and depth of the depression, tried for a time to pay interest on some defaulted bonds from their own resources. Even this was only a temporary stopgap; it postponed for a time but did not prevent bond foreclosures.

The popularity lost by real estate bonds during the 1930s has never been recovered. Several factors account for this. One is undoubtedly the recollections of those who lost heavily on their purchase. Another is the decline of demand for new money for this type of real estate mortgage financing. Relatively few new office and hotel buildings were constructed between the early 1930s and the 1950s. Only recently has construction of office buildings taken a substantial upturn.[1] Although this upturn has been selective as to cities, whereas the boom in the 1920s was general, it has been particularly pronounced in certain cities, such as New York, Chicago, Washington, Dallas, and Houston. In Manhattan, for example, two new buildings were completed in 1947 with a total of 682,000 square feet of floor space. In 1948, the record was three buildings with 226,000 square feet; and in 1949, three buildings with 312,000 square feet. By contrast, over the past 10 years (through 1972) there has been an average annual increase in floor space exceeding 5,000,000 square feet. Numerous hotels and motels are also being built in recent years. Financing for construction of this type is now normally provided by mortgages privately placed with large institutional investors, particularly insurance companies. The participation of the small investor in large ventures of this type which have utilized real estate bonds in the past is now largely limited to subordinated debentures. Often the bonds issued today are convertible into common stock or are with stock warrants attached. These features give the lenders a chance to share in the growth in property values. This is commonly done in shopping center financing.

Description of Bonds The form of the definitive bond is included as a part of the indenture, for purposes of identification. The subjects covered are as follows: (1) amount of bond issue, both currently offered for sale and reserved for future offer, including conditions necessary before future bonds may be offered; (2) maturity date and interest rate; (3) option to redeem outstanding bonds, with dates and call premiums; (4) call dates and premiums for sinking-fund purposes; (5) conditions for making changes in indenture, and vote of bondholders needed to sanction such changes; (6) negotiability and registration of individual bonds; (7) acceleration in case of default; (8) immunity of stockholders

---

[1] John McDonald, "The $2-Billion Building Boom," *Fortune*, February 1960, pp. 119–22.

from personal liability on the bonds; (9) corporate seal and signatures of officers. Then follows the form of coupon attached to the bond, the form of the trustee's authentication, and the form of registration of the bonds.

Security for Real Estate Bonds Since real estate bonds are essentially notes secured by a mortgage on real estate, the trustee is interested in measuring the security which protects the bondholders. Since the latter have little capacity of performing this service for themselves, the trustee is expected to protect bond purchasers by taking an interest in the nature of the security behind their investments. As in other real estate mortgages, two elements of safety are sought:

1. Since the mortgaged property is a going concern, its income potential takes first place. A rule of thumb ratio calls for income twice as great as the amount needed to meet obligations. This rule may be said to be based upon the principle of discounted optimism. On the theory that the optimism may visualize a situation twice as favorable as it really is, if it is discounted 50 percent it is still safe.

On the other hand, if leasehold bonds are issued in such amounts that the expected income is less than the demands against it, the results are bound to cause trouble. For example, suppose that net income from a property available for bond payments at the peak of prosperity, with high rents and a low vacancy ratio, is only $12,000 as against bond interest and retirement allowances of $10,000. A small increase in the vacancy ratio or a slight decline in rent levels can easily result in a net income less than is required to meet bond interest and amortization commitments.

2. In addition to the going concern value of the property, based upon its income potential, those interested in real estate bonds must consider also the liquidation value of the property. While this is determined in part by the income potential, it is based upon other variables as well. It is conceivable that a speculative use of a given property might produce a net income of $15,000, while any other use might earn only $6,000 net. In case the latter contingency becomes effective, the question arises, "What will the property then be worth?" In case this amount is $100,000 or less, it would not be safe to issue $100,000 of bonds against an earning capacity of $15,000 even though this would show a bond interest ratio of more than two times.

It follows, therefore, that, in appraising the soundness of real estate bond issues, both the liquidation value of the property in case of default on the bond issue, and the income potential of the property from the standpoint of its use by a going concern, are important. Of the two, the long-range income potential is more significant. Since the use of property gives its value the net return made possible by this use is the basis for the valuation placed upon the property. Vacant property has only potential use. Care should be exercised in the use of pro forma income statements which assume the presence of unrealized income, gross and net. Much more reliable is the income statement based upon actual experience, which takes into account all probable charges against the gross income before arriving at a net figure.

Parties to Bond Issue As in all other bond issues, usually three parties are concerned: the issuing corporation, the trustee, and the bondholder. The contents of a typical deed of trust or indenture of a first mortgage bond issue are briefly summarized in the paragraphs that follow. First, the borrowing corporation and the trustee are carefully identified. Next in order is the recitation of the authority of the borrowing corporation to borrow money and to issue bonds as evidence of such indebtedness.

The Bond Indenture The bond indenture describes the security behind the bond issue under several captions. These include legal, as well as physical, descriptions of buildings and other tangible property. Intangibles, such as patents, copyrights, trademarks, licenses, and good will, are also incorporated as security.

The definitions section of the indenture includes numerous formal definitions of such terms as "trustee," "bond," "outstanding," "current assets," "current liabilities," "funded indebtedness," and "net income." Under the subject of the particular covenants to which the company subscribes appear the following items: to pay all debts as they come due; to maintain the corporate existence of the obligor and preserve its rights; to conduct the business in an efficient and proper manner; to restrict dividends so long as the bonds are outstanding; to give no prior liens, except that purchase-money mortgages may be issued for an amount not to exceed a fixed percentage of the cost of fixed assets acquired thereby; to restrict subsidiary operations according to a detailed formula set forth in the indenture; not to guarantee obligations of other corporations; not to make loans to officers, directors, or stockholders; to restrict compensation of officers and directors according to terms of the indenture; to render proper accounting; to keep specified amounts of insurance; and to restrict expansion programs to a relationship to net assets as set forth in the indenture.

Sinking-fund provisions of real estate bond issues usually give the issuing company considerable leeway. The required deposit may be a low minimum, such as 2 percent of the original amount of the bond issue annually. Additional deposits will normally be related to annual net corporate income, with a maximum regardless of the net earnings. In lieu of cash, the mortgagor may deposit bonds of this issue, or any combination of cash or bonds. When it is advantageous to do so, the trustee may use sinking-fund cash to retire the bonds.

Default on Bonds When a default occurs, either the trustee or the holders of the contractually required percentage of the outstanding bonds may file notice with the mortgagor that the bonds are due and payable immediately. If the mortgagor makes up all defaults at any time before a judgment shall be entered in favor of the bondholder, the default shall be considered cured and the trustee may rescind the declaration of default. In the meantime, upon a declaration of default, the trustee may enter the property, exclude the mortgagor from possession, and manage the property as if it were owned by the trustee. The trustee may sell the estate, as an entirety or in such parcels as the trustee and the holders of a majority of the bonds may determine. As an alternative, the trustee may foreclose the indenture or use any other remedy available to it to protect the interest of the bondholders.

The indenture provides that, should any part of the security be taken over by the exercise of eminent domain or otherwise, the proceeds shall be paid to the trustee for the benefit of bondholders. However, should the mortgagor wish to use these funds to acquire new land or to construct buildings, it may do so. Meantime, the trustee has the right to contest any award and may charge to the mortgagor any costs incurred in such contest. In case such proceeds are not used for the purchase of land or the construction of buildings to be used in the business, they may be used by the trustee to redeem bonds outstanding. In such case the pattern of bond redemption set forth elsewhere in the indenture shall be followed.

The Trustee The trustee assumes no responsibility for any statements of facts contained in the indenture. It makes no representation concerning the validity or the sufficiency of the indenture or of any bonds or coupons, or as to the security afforded by the indenture. It assumes no responsibility for the application by the mortgagor of the proceeds of the bond issue. If the trustee acts in good faith on any matter affecting the interests of the bondholders, it may not be held responsible for any mistakes due to forgery of documents, and so forth. In case of doubt about the ownership of a bond, the trustee need not act until it has been reasonably satisfied.

The mortgagor pays the compensation and expenses of the trustee. The claims of the trustee take priority over the claims of the bondholders. It is not presumed to have notice of any default under the bond indenture unless and until it has been so notified in writing by the holders of the required percentage of the outstanding bonds. The trustee may buy and sell bonds and be dealt with in the same manner as any other bondholder. The trustee may resign at any time or may be removed at the request of the holders of a majority of outstanding bonds.

Recent Balancing of Supply and Demand The impetus behind recent new construction of office space has resulted from two major forces of demand which have arisen from the general economic expansion: (1) increase in the labor force, and (2) increase in space requirements per worker. The decrease in supply of office space as certain office buildings have been demolished has also tightened the rental market. If the normal building cycle follows true to form, it is reasonable to assume that the present boom in office space construction will continue until the vacancy rate becomes excessive at minimum rentals. In light of anticipated future demand, however, the present rate of building does not seem to forebode any catastrophe such as followed the 1920 boom. Generally, building is now not undertaken until the builder is supported with long-term leases to substantial tenants to take occupancy upon completion and with long-term financing free of balloon clauses. In the financing of this construction, as previously noted, real estate bonds have not been used as commonly as in previous years. New construction, however, is extremely important to all real estate bondholders because of its competitive effect on the whole rental market in capturing desirable tenants, softening rental rates, and hastening the obsolescence of older buildings.

Real Estate Investment Trusts[2] Effective January 1, 1961, special income tax benefits were accorded a new type of investment institution by an amendment to the Internal Revenue Code (Sections 856–858). Under this amendment, a real estate investment trust meeting prescribed requirements during the taxable year may be treated simply as a conduit with respect to the income distributed to beneficiaries of the trust. Thus the unincorporated trust or association, ordinarily taxed as a corporation, is not taxed on distributed taxable income when it qualifies for the special tax benefits. Only the beneficiaries pay the tax on such distributed income. To qualify as a "real estate investment trust" for tax purposes, the following requirements must be met:

1. Ownership must be in an unincorporated trust or association managed by at least one trustee, with transferable certificates of beneficial interest or shares, and ordinarily taxable as a domestic corporation.
2. There must be at least 100 beneficial owners.
3. The trust would not be a personal holding company even though all of its gross income constituted personal holding company income.
4. The trust does not hold any property primarily for sale to customers in the ordinary course of business, that is, dealer property.
5. It must elect to be treated as a real estate investment trust.

At least 90 percent of the income of a real estate investment trust must come from real property rentals, dividends, interest, or gains from

---

[2] Much of the material contained in this section was originally published in an article in the January 1966 issue of The Ohio State University *Bulletin of Business Research*. For fuller discussion, see that article titled "Real Estate Investment Trusts: Their Experience and Prospects," by Leo D. Stone.

the sale of securities or real estate. Seventy-five percent or more of the trust income must be directly attributable to real property, and another 15 percent must be derived from real estate or any other source from which a regulated investment company would derive most of its income, such as interest and dividends. There is also a 30 percent test, which requires that not more than 30 percent of the gross income of the trust come from short-term gains on security sales (held less than six months) and gains on the sale of real estate held for less than four years.

When the new law initially went into effect, it appeared that if the real estate required active management and if the trustees participated in such management, the trust would not be accorded exempt status. The final Treasury regulations have defined the duties and powers of the trustees, shareholders or beneficiaries, and independent contracting managers, however, with some liberality. The property manager may perform and bill the trust for operating costs; he may hire and fire employees; he may collect rents and remit differences with proper accounting for collections and expenses. The trustee is permitted to make some important decisions, such as whether to make major repairs.

When the law was passed, real estate investment trusts where the trustee was required to be "passive" were prohibited in many states. As a result, enabling legislation was required before such trusts could be formed. At the present time, the states generally have laws on the books permitting the establishment of real estate investment trusts that may qualify for special federal income tax benefits.

Types of Trusts The two principal types of real estate investment trusts are equity trusts and mortgage trusts. In the early years of this new trust form, the equity trust form was generally used, but more recently the mortgage trust is assuming importance.

The difference between the assets held by the equity trust and those held by the mortgage trust is fairly obvious. The equity trust acquires proprietary interests, while the mortgage trust purchases mortgage obligations and thus becomes a creditor with mortgage liens given priority to equity holders. Of course, as time progresses more heterogeneous investment policies are being developed, combining the advantages of both types of trusts to suit specific investment objectives. Such combinations are called "hybrid" trusts.

For purposes of description, equity trusts have been categorized into five groups.[3] These groups, their advantages, and their disadvantages are as follows:

1. *Blank Check Trusts.* A blank check trust is one that is organized

---

[3] John C. Williamson, "The Real Estate Investment Trust Act—The Catalyst Which Is Making Real Estate 'Go Public'," *Journal of Property Management*, Vol. 27, No. 2 (Winter 1961), pp. 68–79.

to buy properties judged by the trustees to meet the investment goals of the trust. Participating interests in the trust are sold on the strength of the reputations of the promoters, trustees, and independent contractors with management responsibility. The advantage of this type of trust is its flexibility; but a major disadvantage results from the lapse of time between the date the investors' shares are offered to the public and the time when the funds can be profitably invested. During this period, the investors' shares tend to suffer depressed conditions in the securities market.

2. *Exchange Trusts.* Exchange trusts involve the exchange of property for shares in the trust immediately after its organization. Such a transfer qualifies as a tax-free exchange for income tax purposes, and the trust acquires the shareholder's cost basis with respect to the property for depreciation purposes. The disadvantage of failing to acquire a stepped-up basis for higher depreciation deductions is offset by the tax-free diversification that the investor achieves. The trust also benefits in that it obtains a seasoned property with a known income potential.

3. *Purchasing Trusts.* A purchasing trust is one that has been organized to purchase property described in a prospectus. The advantage of this form is that the potential investor is fully informed about the property to be acquired. Possible disadvantages to the purchasing trust may lie in the lack of diversification and, from an administrative point of view, in the difficulty of gathering sufficient historical data to meet state or federal securities registration requirements.

4. *Mixed Trusts.* Mixed trusts are organized to invest part of the funds raised in a specific property and the balance on a "blank check" basis. Being a hybrid, this trust will have the advantage of providing almost immediate income; but since a part of the funds will be invested over a period of time, the overall return will be relatively low until, at least, the total investment has been made.

5. *Existing Trusts.* Existing trusts are those which were in effect at the time the federal income tax law was revised to permit special treatment and which have since reorganized to qualify under the pertinent Revenue Code Sections. These trusts have the advantage of seasoned management and virtually no new organization costs. They also have an investment history to show prospective investors. Many of their properties will have been written down to the point that depreciation charges are not as great as they would like, but they can cope with this problem by advantageous upgrading.

The equity trusts are distinguishable from the mortgage trusts in many respects regarding investment objectives served. Equity trusts receive rent as a primary source of income, while mortgage trust income is largely in the form of interest income and discounts earned through mortgage amortization. Capital gains in the equity trust come largely through the sale of the real estate. The mortgage trust derives its capital gains from selling mortgages at prices above cost, as a result of a change in money rates or because the mortgages have become more secure instruments. As owner of the physical property, the equity trust may obtain a depreciation deduction as a tax benefit not available to the mortgage trust, but by the same token it must assume the owner's management responsibilities. The mortgage trust income from interest and discounts is fixed in nature, whereas the rental income of the equity trust may be fixed, as in a "net lease," or volatile, where the rents are determined as a percentage of sales. Expenses of operation may also be involved in determining the return to the equity trust. Because they are constantly amortizing, the assets of the mortgage trust are considered more liquid than the real estate owned by the equity trust.[4]

A review of these characteristics suggests at least two distinct markets of real estate investors that the trusts may serve. The equity trust may well be used by the relatively small investor who desires to participate in the ownership and operation of large improved real properties—such as commercial, industrial, or apartment buildings. The mortgage trust, on the other hand, has developed importantly as a vehicle of institutions with increasing surpluses of uninvested savings needing a safe and fixed return or with underutilized mortgage underwriting talent that can be applied to a profitable new venture.

Equity Trusts as an Investment Because of their unique appeals and a growing awareness among investors of their potential, equity trusts are now widely held across the country. At a time requiring discrimination in real estate purchases, it is of vital importance to the individual investor that he have available to him information on the whole range of real estate investment opportunities, and professional guidance in the selection of the investment commitments. He also needs a maximum of liquidity—an element not present in his outright purchase of a sizable real estate parcel.

The real estate investment trust is well adapted to fulfilling these requirements. By affording the individual investor an opportunity to pool his resources with those of persons of like interests, funds are asembled to permit purchase of buildings, shopping centers, land and developments—or whatever seems to offer the most attractive returns. Investment must be approved by a board of trustees who are ordinarily well qualified to make such decisions. The trust certificate holder buys an interest in diversified holdings, and his shares are usually readily salable in the over-the-counter market. The tax exemption places the small shareholder in a position for tax payments similar to what he might

---

[4] Jack R. Courshon, "The Real Estate Trust Holding Mortgage Loans," *The Mortgage Banker*, April 1962, pp. 30–31, 33.

have if he had made the same investment as an individual real estate operator.

The advantages of the trust to the small private investor depend, in the final analysis, on the fundamental soundness of real estate as an investment. The attractiveness of real estate as an investment closely follows its economic value. These values are largely determined by growth in population and its purchasing power in relation to a uniquely immobile and indestructible site with improvements thereon. According to many real estate analysts, the probable physical and economic life of residential buildings is from 80 to 90 years. The indestructible nature of land and the physical durability of buildings makes it possible for the same parcel to experience diverse successive uses over a period of years or centuries. It follows that improvements with the least specialized purposes have the greatest flexibility of use and probable longest economic life.

It is a mistake to assume that land values always rise. Even in a prosperous, expanding economy certain segments of the real estate market, whether classified geographically or functionally, may experience distress. It is for this reason that, if one is to take advantage of the possible physical and economic durability of real estate, investment decisions should be made by competent, foresighted appraisers with a full appreciation of local and general economic conditions. As the management counsel of mutual funds provide this judgment for investors in such funds, so also the trustees of real estate investment trusts provide this service to their investors.

Leverage Much had been written about the advantages of real estate investment as an opportunity for leverage on equity capital. Leverage, also called "trading on the equity," is the use of borrowed capital to increase the profitability of the equity, or shareholder's interest. The use of borrowed capital is profitable as long as the assets financed by borrowed funds earn more than the borrowed money costs. Of course, if the earnings on the borrowed funds do not equal the borrowed money costs, the leverage works in reverse. For this reason, only stable operations such as public utilities and real estate, with high predictability and stability of earnings, can use leverage to a great extent. An example of the effects of leverage are given in Table 7-1.

This example suggests two conclusions:

1. Leverage properly used can be an extremely profitable technique.
2. Leverage improperly used reduces an investment to a speculation and is extremely dangerous.

For these reasons, trading on the equity should be done cautiously and only by knowledgeable technicians. It has been found to be more

TABLE 7-1
Effects of Leverage

	Venture A* All Equity Capital $250,000			Venture B* Equity Capital, $250,000 Borrowed Capital, $125,000		
Item	Average Year	Better Year	Poor Year	Average Year	Better Year	Poor Year
Gross income.......	$50,000	$65,000	$35,000	$75,000	$97,500	$52,500
Operating expenses...........	30,000	33,600	26,400	45,000	50,400	39,600
Net operating income..........	$20,000	$31,400	$ 8,600	$30,000	$47,100	$12,900
Fixed charges (interest on borrowed capital)..........	—0—	—0—	—0—	7,500	7,500	7,500
Return on equity capital.....	$20,000	$31,400	$ 8,600	$22,500	$39,600	$ 5,400
Rate of return on equity Capital (before taxes)............	8.0%	12.6%	3.4%	9.0%	15.8%	2.2%

* This example assumes an operation in both instances providing gross revenue equal to 20% of its capital with operating expenses equal to 60% of gross revenue in average year.

useful in real estate, because of stability of income, than in any other area of business activity. The real estate investment trust makes extensive use of the leverage opportunity.

Real Estate as a Hedge against Rising Price Levels Anyone who bought real estate during or shortly after World War II realizes how rising price levels or production costs of new structures—residential, commercial, or industrial, where production is to a demand—can cause the property values to rise. A study of price levels in America from the Revolutionary War days to the present, where periods of as long as 20 years are considered as a span, has shown a steady rise.

The value of real estate that maintains its economic utility tends to move with the cost of reproduction of a new facility to render a comparable service. Particularly where leverage is used to finance ownership of a larger property subject to possibly higher reproduction cost, a properly selected, functional real estate property can serve as a hedge against higher price levels.

Tax Shelters in Real Estate Investments Much has been written pointing out the tax advantages that may be derived from liberal depreciation allowances deductible from taxable income. The advantage lies in the fact that the functional or economic life of a property often extends far beyond the depreciable life used for income tax purposes. In many instances, the decline in value as a result of depreciation or obsolescence has been substantially or totally offset by rising replacement costs of similar properties when demand for such properties is high in relation to supply. Thus, older properties may sell today at prices above original cost of construction, and yet they may have been substantially depreciated for income tax purposes.

This possibility has been greatly enhanced by the use of accelerated depreciation methods. Such methods permit heavier depreciation charges in the earlier years of the life of the building, and they thus effect a deferral of income tax.

It should be pointed out, however, that to the extent a depreciation charge is taken, the investor has recognized a retrieval of his capital, and not income on his investment. A statement of income and expenses may demonstrate why this is true:

Total revenues received	$100,000
Total cash expenses	60,000
Net cash earnings	$ 40,000
Depreciation charge allowable	
(Write-off to reduce property carrying value)	30,000
Net taxable income	$ 10,000

If this property is managed by a tax-exempt real estate investment trust and the $40,000 of net cash earnings are distributed to trust certificate holders, only one fourth of the earnings (in the ratio of $10,000 to $40,000) will be taxable to the individual recipients. The other three-fourths will constitute a nontaxable return of capital. For tax accounting purposes, the individual investor cannot measure his precise return on his investment by his cash receipts. Distributions paid out of depreciation (as the $30,000 above) instead of net income ($10,000 above) are considered a return of capital until the investor receives the full cost of his shares or sells them. After full recovery of costs he realizes taxable gains.

From a practical investor's standpoint, however, where the trust shares have a ready marketability, a current yield may be effectively determined by comparing the cash dividend received (trust payout) with the current market price. A history of gain or loss in capital may be derived from comparing issue price and market price. Because a large portion of real estate investment trust distributions is usually nontaxable, the after-tax value of such dividends is often substantially greater to the individual taxpaying investor than a like amount of fully taxable dividends of an ordinary corporation.

Recent Expansion in Mortgage Investment Trusts Since the start of 1969, mortgage trusts have blossomed as the new capital source in the real estate markets. Important mortgage bankers and more than a dozen bank holding companies have promoted their own trusts. BankAmerica Corporation has its BankAmerica Realty Investors; The Chase Manhattan Bank promoted Chase Manhattan Mortgage and Realty Trust; Wells Fargo & Co. sponsored Wells Fargo Mortgage Investors; and Bankers Trust originated BT Mortgage Investors. Although some of these trusts engage in equity financing, the predominant purpose of such trusts usually is to take advantage of the mortgage originating, servicing, and financing advantages inherent in an interrelationship between a well-established mortgage banker or commercial bank and its companion trust.

The explosion in mortgage trust development was largely occasioned by the tight money market of 1969 and thereafter. With prime business borrowers absorbing all lendable funds from the banks, traditional mortgage lenders were unable to take care of the real estate market, particularly the demand for construction and development loans. A financing gap developed, and the mortgage trusts were brought along to make a material contribution toward closing that gap.

The principal types of investments are permanent (long-term) mortgages and interim (short-term) mortgages. Permanent mortgages are typically placed to finance a permanent structure for the long-term owner and generally run for a period of 10 to 30 years. The income from these loans is highly predictable over a long period of time and the risks are relatively slight. Recently, straight contractual interest rates have been supplemented by arrangements for bonus interest (known as a "kicker") under certain conditions and by equity participations. Interim mortgages are usually originated for development and construction loans. Development loans are issued for the acquisition of land and the installation of roads, sewers, and utilities. Such loans average about 18 months' duration and are usually limited to from 60 to 65 percent of appraised value after development. Construction loans cover all types of income-producing property with advances being made at appropriate stages throughout the construction period. These loans also run about 18 months on the average and are usually not in excess of 75 percent of the value of the improved property.

The interest rates on interim mortgages may easily run from 3 to 5 percent higher than for permanent mortgages, reflecting the greater risks involved in development and construction loans. This is a highly speculative area demanding expertise in appraisal of market feasibility and real estate values, commercial credit, and interim mortgage administration. There are many reasons why a builder may default on his obligation: reduced demand for real estate because of economic adversity or overbuilding; poor cost management; or excessive delays because of strikes or bad weather. By the same token, these loans can be highly profitable to the skilled development and construction lender. After establishing an equity base from a stock issue, mortgage trusts can generally expect a spread between their money costs on bank credit lines and their interest return on development and construction loans of the order of 3 to 4 percent. If the outstanding equity shares of the trust maintain a constant price/earnings ratio, as the earnings increase on a per share basis as the credit lines are expanded, a subsequent equity issue may be marketed at a correspondingly higher price, thus affording the basis for even more lines of credit, and so on. This effect is called "contradilution," and has led some to call mortgage trusts "money machines." One must hasten to point out, however, that the theory does not always work in practice. The general stock market may bring downward pressures on equities or the trust management may not inspire the necessary confidence to maintain the price/earnings ratio per share and the trusts shares may decline to a market value below book value. In that event, new stock issues would dilute existing shares and expansion from that source would be difficult to justify. It is thus apparent that good management is the key to success for any mortgage investment trust.

Financing of Cooperative Apartments To combat high rents following World War I and at intermittent intervals since, cooperative apartments have been promoted in some American cities, notably Chicago, Los Angeles, New York, and Philadelphia. The pattern of their financing is as follows: First, there is organized a corporation whose assets consist of the land and building which constitute the apartment. Then as large a mortgage as can be obtained will be obtained, with the land and building as security. Each apartment is assigned a price dependent upon the arrangement, the relative location, the number and size of rooms, and so on. The purchaser of this apartment secures the right to use it so long as he meets his obligations to the corporation, together with a block of stock which represents his purchase price. The total amount of stock issued is expected to be sold for an amount sufficient to make up the difference between the net proceeds of the mortgage mentioned above and the total cost of the project. The cost here includes land cost, all construction costs, selling costs, and profit to the promoters.

If the building to be used for the cooperative venture is already in existence, the financing follows the pattern outlined above. If the building is not yet built, the promoter may prefer to play safe by "selling the blueprints" instead of the building. In other words, he has plans drawn for the proposed building and selects a site for its location. Then his salesmen sell apartments from the plans, making sure to get a substantial down payment, 25 percent or more, but giving a contract for purchase which enables the promoter to return the deposit should he decide not to go through with the deal. If by this means he finds that the venture is not likely to attract sufficient buyers, he can abandon or postpone the construction. If, on the other hand, buyers are sufficiently numerous to justify completion of the program, construction will proceed. The remainder of the buyer's commitment, above the down payment, will be due at some future date, perhaps at the time of possession.

The above plan assumes complete ownership by all who occupy apartments in the project. It is sometimes designated as the 100 percent plan. In addition, a modification of this plan, variously designated as semicooperative, group ownership, joint ownership, 40 percent plan, and so on, is sometimes financed by only a portion of the tenants with the remaining units rented to nonowners. Under either the 100 percent plan or any variation of it, the ground floor may be used for stores. These stores may be included in the cooperative scheme or may be rented separately at whatever they will bring in the market.

Cooperative Idea Not New Although cooperative apartments received their greatest publicity in the period immediately following World War I, the idea was not originated at that time. As a matter of fact, the basic principles involved have very wide application even though the name cooperative apartment is not always used. In Philadelphia it has long been customary for two families to own a double house, each having title to and use of its separate unit. Or one man may own both units, ocupy one, and rent the other. In other cities the same practice is followed. Ownership of two- to four-family properties by one or more of the occupants is very common. Apartments as such which followed the cooperative principle were at least known as early as the last quarter of the last century in this country. Even before that, they were known in Europe.

Types of Ownership of Cooperative Apartments The three common types of ownership of cooperative apartments are: trust, corporate, and individual. In the trust type, legal ownership is in the name of a bank or trust company. Purchasers of units are given certificates of beneficial interest or participation certificates. The ownership of such a certificate carries the right to lease a unit in the building. The lease defines the rights and obligations of its owner, including any restrictions upon sale and transfer, subletting rights, and so forth. Management of a trust type of apartment ownership may be vested in the trustee or otherwise, as defined in the agreement.

In the corporate type of ownership, title rests with the corporation of which the purchasers are shareholders. Management is determined by the board of directors. Here also, restrictions may be placed upon the sale of stock and the transfer of leases by those originally entitled to them. The stock is frequently pledged with the directors of the corporation as additional assurance that its owners will meet their obligations to the corporation. This practice parallels the pledging of certificates with the trustee—in the previous type described above—for the same purpose.

In the third type of cooperative ownership, individuals have title to the units assigned for their use. Ownership may take one or two forms: tenancy in common or condominium. Under the tenancy in common type of ownership the purchaser receives by deed an undivided interest in the whole with the right to occupy a particular unit. Under the condominium concept, the purchaser acquires by deed a fee simple title to a specific unit and common ownership of the public areas and the underlying ground. Tenancy in common has many of the disadvantages of the traditional cooperatives. Condominiums have recently received numerous statutory assists and are becoming increasingly popular. Prior to 1963 only six states had condominium laws on their books. Now this form of ownership is legal in nearly all states. It will be discussed in detail in succeeding paragraphs.

Refinancing of Cooperative Apartments Whatever the form of ownership of traditional cooperative apartments, it is probable that all evidence of ownership at the outset will be subject to a blanket mortgage covering all the units in the project. Separate financing of individual units is not favored by mortgagees. As a consquence, leases are almost always subject to the underlying mortgage. It sometimes becomes advantageous for the trustee, the corporation, or other titleholding body to refinance an existing mortgage. Such refinancing can be best facilitated by including in the lease proper provisions for subordinating it to a plan of refinancing which may be offered at a date subsequent to the date of the lease. The purchaser who buys a unit subject to such a lease is interested in the nature of any such refinancing clause in the lease.

Management of Cooperatives Under the 100 percent plan, tenants and only tenants are stockholders of the corporation which owns the cooperative apartment. They elect the board of directors, which in turn provides for the management of the apartment building. Each tenant owner is assessed an amount per share of stock sufficient to meet all expenditures incurred in operating the apartment, including: labor; materials; management fees; repairs to the lobbies, elevators, and so on; water; electricity; insurance premiums; taxes against the property and the corporation; interest upon and amortization of the mortgage; and perhaps something for contingencies.

In some cases the Massachusetts trust plan of organization has been used. The tenant-owners receive trust certificates instead of voting stock. The management is placed in the hands of a self-perpetuating board of trustees chosen from the original tenant-owners. This plan seems to have worked somewhat more successfully than some corporations, since it eliminates the campaigns for elections of directors. Failure of election to the board may leave scars which are not easily healed. Where the Massachusetts trust form is used, the results are essentially the same as those attained by the use of the corporation.

Advantages and Disadvantages of Cooperatives Most of the advantages claimed for cooperative apartments center around housing shortages and rising rents; the desire for stability in the use of housing accommodations; the economies of owner-occupancy; and the satisfaction of doing with one's own as the tenant-owner wishes without seeking the approval of anybody else. Specific advantages are sometimes listed as follows: (1) no rent raises at the whim of a landlord; (2) economy of operation where owner-occupancy rather than tenant interest prevails; (3) redecoration of living quarters as the owner desires and at his own expense, leaving such costs to be as much or as little as the owner prefers; (4) security in occupancy so long as the owner meets his obligations; (5) less vacancy, less expense of operation; (6) prestige of ownership; and (7) the tax advantages accruing from the ability of the owner to deduct his share of real estate taxes and mortgage interest in computing his personal income tax. This saving may be substantial. If he were merely a tenant in an apartment owned by someone else, such deductions would not be avilable to him.

The disadvantages of cooperative apartments can be grouped under two main heads, those concerning their operations and those concerning sins of their promoters. The specific charges against promoters include: (1) too high prices, involving great profits to promoters; (2) financially weak promoters, causing losses to purchasers because the former fail to meet obligations to the latter; (3) costs of cooperative apartments too high when passed on to purchasers. Weaknesses of cooperative apartment operation include: (1) vacancies bear heavily upon former owners who lose their investments and upon remaining owners who must pay additional costs of operation; (2) restrictions exist upon sale of interests, since new owners must be approved by management; (3) in severe depression, even those who customarily meet their obligations promptly may be wiped out, since they cannot carry the entire project.

Condominiums[5] A new word has recently appeared to describe a revised form of cooperative ownership that is having increasing acceptance in the United States. The word is "condominium." The concept dates back to ancient Rome, but its recent revival stems from a desire

---

[5] Charles E. Ramsey, "Condominium: The New Look in Co-ops" (Chicago Title and Trust Company, Chicago, Ill., 1961). See also a bibliography on this topic prepared by Ernest Henry Breuer, State Law Librarian, New York State Library, Albany, New York (1962).

to avoid some of the financing weaknesses and dangers of conventional cooperatives.

"Condominium" means individual ownership in fee simple of a one-family unit in a multifamily structure coupled with ownership of an individual interest in the land and in all other parts of the structure held in common with all other owners of one-family units. This type of ownership modifies the extent of control that may be exercised by the various co-owners over each other and establishes remedies to assure harmonious relations. It is distinguished from conventional cooperative financing in that it provides residence in a multifamily structure on an ownership rather than a rental basis.

One of the earliest applications of condominium in this country was apparently in 1947 when a group of World War II veterans elected to live in an apartment house and sought to qualify for loans insured by the Veterans Administration. This qualification required that each participant become an owner, and not a tenant, of his separate unit. Such ownership, in turn, necessitated application of the principles of ownership of air space and a sharing of the common physical elements—the land, passageways, roof, and so on. The National Housing Act of 1961 gave the condominium its major assist, however, by authorizing FHA mortgage insurance on property so held.

In capsule form, condominium may be distinguished from conventional cooperative in the following major aspects:

1. In condominiums individuals become owners of their units; in ordinary cooperatives individuals may be stockholders of the corporation owning the apartment or trust certificate holders, but they are technically renters.
2. In condominiums individuals vote in proportion to their proportion of ownership; in ordinary cooperatives each individual has one vote regardless of the size of his unit.
3. In condominiums individuals are taxed separately on their units; in ordinary cooperatives individuals pay their share of taxes on the whole property in their monthly carrying charges.
4. In condominiums individuals are liable for mortgage indebtedness and taxes only on the property to which they have title; in ordinary cooperatives each individual is dependent upon the solvency of the entire project.

The increased use of the condominium has necessitated legislation to deal with many questions not necessarily answered by the common law. A review of the recently enacted Ohio law will show the types of questions asked and the answers provided.

The condominium statute provides for a declaration containing:

1. A legal description of the land
2. The name of the condominium property, including the word "condominium"
3. Purposes and restrictions in the use of the property
4. A general description of the building, including principal materials and the number of stories, basements, and units therein
5. Unit designation, together with access areas
6. A description of the common areas and facilities, and the percentage of the total interest appertaining to each unit
7. A statement that each owner shall be a member of a unit owners' association which shall be established for the administration of condominium property
8. Designation of the person to receive service of process for the unit owners association
9. A method for amending the declaration, requiring approval of not less than 75 percent of the voting power

The declaration must be filed with the county recorder and the county auditor.

The unit owners' association is operated by a board of managers duly elected by the membership. This board will normally provide for the prompt repair of common areas, assessment of common expenses, and the distribution of common profits. A lien upon an individual unit is provided for failure of a member to pay his properly allocated share of common expenses. Common profits, like losses, are assigned to the unit owners according to their percentages of interest in the common areas and facilities as set forth in the declaration. These percentages also determine members' voting strength in the unit owners' association.

Major decisions, such as the election not to repair badly damaged property, or to declare the property obsolete and in need of extensive rehabilitation, require an affirmative vote of not less than 75 percent of the voting power of the unit owners' association. Additionally, to qualify for FHA mortgage loan insurance, those limitations required by the FHA must be written into the declaration, the bylaws of the unit owners' association, or a separate co-owners' agreement incorporated by reference into the plan of ownership.

Quite a few people prefer community living but with individual rights such as a condominium provides. With FHA mortgage insurance now available, financial institutions are in an excellent position to provide funds for this type of real estate ownership.

Within the past few years condominium has spread to many uses other than housing accommodation. Doctors, dentists, and other professionals have found this method affords them a means to ownership of their offices in buildings devoted solely to their use. In New Jersey, a shopping center condominium was recently developed, permitting separate ownership of stores.

Perhaps the most exciting trend in condominiums has been their development in resort areas. The condominiums can provide for living or for investment and may include restaurants and commercial businesses, as well as apartment and hotel or motel facilities. Many owners of second homes prefer a property that others will rent. Investment condominiums are typically clustered or high-rise, so that a resident manager can handle them economically. A number of these developments have been syndicated recently and others are currently being marketed. An obvious question the prospective investor should ask in regard to these ventures, of course, is what is the availability of tenants throughout the year.

QUESTIONS AND PROBLEMS

1. Review briefly the financial history of real estate bonds.
2. What protective covenants would you expect to find in the bond indenture?
3. What are the responsibilities of the trustee to the holders of real estate mortgage bonds?
4. What dangers to mortgage bondholders lie in the fact that their lien security is in trusteeship?
5. How may eminent domain proceedings or other forms of involuntary conversion of mortgaged property affect the underlying security, and how should the bond indenture deal with these possibilities?
6. As a real estate bondholder, what protection would you expect to find in the sinking-fund provisions of the bond indenture?
7. Under what conditions does a real estate bond qualify as a sound investment?
8. Recently, a considerable portion of long-term real estate financing has been done by subordinated debentures. What are the advantages of this form (1) to the borrower and (2) to the investor? What are the disadvantages?
9. Why have private placements become increasingly more important as a means of finding investors in new real estate bond issues?
10. What is a real estate investment trust, and what special tax treatment is accorded it?
11. Distinguish between the principal types of real estate investment trusts, and show how each may be useful.
12. What are the common types of ownership in cooperative apartments?
13. What are the advantages and disadvantages of ownership participation in a cooperative apartment?
14. How does the condominium differ from the cooperative apartment, and what are its advantages or disadvantages?

8

Land Contracts

Meaning One form of real estate finance that has been commonly used over the years is the land contract. In some respects it has been treated like an unwanted stepchild, in spite of its usefulness. The term "land contract" is more frequently used in real estate offices than among members of the legal profession. There it is recognized—if at all—under a variety of aliases including "real estate contract," "installment sales contract," "agreement to convey," and "contract for deed." From one point of view, the latter term is well chosen. The land contract is accurately described as a contract for a deed. But the implications of that concept are not always properly observed.

Perhaps one of the reasons why this form of financing has been somewhat neglected is that, in many cases, the members of the legal profession have little part in its use. They may take a major part in its aftermath but frequently are bypassed when the contract is signed.

Informality Surrounding Use The above statement suggests that the drafting of land contracts is too often left to laymen. This is true. The circumstances surrounding the drawing up of land contracts are exceedingly informal. Both vendor and vendee approach the subject with a lack of attention to details that is absent in transactions involving much less responsibility on the part of all concerned. In his eagerness to economize, the vendee may consider the services of an attorney to represent his interests an unnecessary cost.

Under the land contract, the vendor retains the title in his name. So far as the deed record shows, he is still the owner of the property. But the land contract or contract for deed is supposed to tie the hands of the vendor in future transfers of title to make sure that he or his assigns must transfer it finally to the vendee or his heirs or assigns.

The land contract may be used as a substitute for either a vendor's lien or a purchase-money mortgage. Like the former, it is often a fragile type of evidence of the vendee's equity and would normally not be preferred for a long period of time over the purchase-money mortgage, if the latter is available. In states, however, that have long redemption periods during which the vendee has the right to possession and to collection of rents even though in default, sellers of land may refuse to give a deed and take back a mortgage until a very substantial part of the purchase price has been paid.

Uses in Sale of Lots In general, land contracts are used under either of two sets of circumstances. In the sale of vacant lots where the purchaser makes a small down payment—frequently no more than enough to cover the salesman's commission—land contracts find common use. Since the default ratio in such sales has been exceedingly high, it is difficult to visualize any other form of financing that is equally practical. Certainly it would not be expected that the development company which sells the lot on a very small down payment should transfer its title to the purchaser and take back a purchase-money mortgage to account for the remainder of the purchase price. Much of its activities would involve foreclosure suits under such circumstances, because of the frequent defaults by purchasers of vacant lots.

Partly because of these defaults, land contracts used by development companies are so drawn that they place major emphasis upon the protection of the vendor. The printed forms used in such cases contain the information required to fit the lots being sold and require but few items to be filled in at the time of sale. Purchasers who buy the lots put implicit trust in the seller and almost never even think about asking a member of the legal profession to inspect the contract to determine whether or not it protects their interests.

Other Uses The other major type of use of land contracts describes the sale of improved property in which the purchaser usually has but a small amount of money to use as a down payment, if any, and depends upon his income rather than his capital accumulations to liquidate his obligations to the vendor. Again the vendor can scarcely afford to transfer title with only a small down payment or none at all and take back a purchase-money mortgage for all or nearly all of the purchase price. Defaults in this use of land contracts are also common but not as common as with the sale of vacant lots.

The type of improved property—frequently for residential use—which becomes subject to sale under a land contract frequently possesses some major disability that makes its disposal in the ordinary way difficult. The neighborhood may be questionable, the structure may be old, the arrangement of the rooms may leave something to be desired, the market for the property may be sluggish, and so forth. This element of major disability may not necessarily be present, but it frequently is. Any type of property can use the land contract should the vendor and vendee agree. But where disabilities are present, the seller must seek a purchaser whose amount of available capital is so small that he cannot be too choosy in his purchase Likewise, the purchaser must seek a seller who is attracted by only a small down payment or none at all.

Because of the informality surrounding the use of land contracts and, as a result, the frequent failure to give attention to matters that might later create headaches for both vendor and vendee, the remainder of this chapter will deal with the essentials of land contracts required to protect both parties. The subjects discussed represent actual practices where more than ordinary attention is given to essential details of the contents of land contracts.

Vendor and Vendee Assuming that the property which is to be the subject of the land contract is owned by one person, several questions arise about signatures to the contract on his account. Is it sufficient for him to sign for himself, or should his spouse sign also? Since it is a contract for deed, the latter to be delivered when the requirements of the land contract have been fulfilled, it is always safest to have the spouse sign also. Her failure to do so might give her a valid excuse for refusing to release her dower interest when it comes time to transfer title by deed. So far as the intent of the vendor is concerned, his signature alone could indicate that.

Shall the purchaser be indicated in the land contract as the vendee, or shall the contract indicate that he and his spouse are to be considered as joint tenants, with the right of holding the title later in the two names rather than one? Without undertaking at this time to answer this question, let us state that it at least merits greater consideration than it usually receives. If only one name is to be indicated as the vendee, shall the spouse sign the contract along with the vendee? Again caution would recommend both signatures. While the spouse probably has no dower interest in a land contract, one never knows what a court of equity might decide on a subject not too well defined in either law or equity. It is freely admitted that there appears to be less reason for the spouse of the vendee to sign than for the spouse of the vendor to sign. If nothing else is gained, however, the signature of the former is likely to impress her move with the seriousness of the obligation the vendee is undertaking.

Description of Property Inclusion of the legal description of the property avoids complications. Since this kind of description must later appear in the deed at the time title passes, it is better to start with it in the land contract. In the absence of this type of description, the property must be so described that its identification is certain without too much expense or difficulty. It is never sufficient to attempt to describe a property by street number alone. In addition to complications that may arise even at the date of sale, street numbers are sometimes changed. This may create additional unnecessary complications that are easily avoided at the outset.

Existing Mortgage Should there be a mortgage of record against the property at the time the land contract is drawn up, it will of course give its holder a prior lien over the contract. Likewise, a subsequent mortgage of record without notice of the existence of the land contract would normally take precedence over the contract. Either one of two policies may be followed in making payments to the mortgagee under an antecedent mortgage: (1) The vendor may continue to make the payments, perhaps using the land contract installments for this purpose. (2) The vendee may agree to make the payments directly to the mortgagee. Perhaps the vendee will assume the mortgage, thereby accepting personal responsibility for it.

In any event, the mortgage should be accurately described in the land contract with sufficient particularity to make sure that the vendee understands its terms. While, for his own protection, he should have the record of the mortgage carefully studied by someone acquainted with such matters, this is seldom done. The amount of the mortgage, its due date, the method and manner of payments, and so on, should all be set forth in the land contract; or at least by reference to the record they should be made a part of the contract. In order to make sure of his own protection in regard to the amount of the unpaid balance of the debt, the vendee should secure from the mortgagee a statement of such balance, together with a statement of any unpaid installments and any other pertinent information that will help the vendee see the whole picture. Such information should be calculated as of the date of the contract.

In case, the vendor expects to continue to make the payments on the mortgage, the contract should give the vendee the right to pay directly any amounts due or that may become due in the future but may not be paid on time by the vendor. Any payments so made should apply on the debt of the vendee to the vendor. Since the mortgage represents a lien prior to that of the vendee, any default by the vendor that could result in a foreclosure sale could thereby jeopardize the position of the vendee.

The vendee should also be given the similar right to pay taxes, insurance premiums, or other obligations of the vendor if his neglect to pay these as they fall due could interfere with the rights of the vendee. In all such cases the amounts so paid should be credited against the debt of the vendee.

Insurance Clause Upon taking over possession of the property, the vendee acquires an interest in any insurance on it. It will be to the interest of the vendor to require the vendee to pay the cost of this type of protection. While it is common practice to state in the contract that the "insurance now in force shall be continued," this hardly gives the vendee a very intelligent picture of the amount of protection from this quarter. In case the vendor is not insurance-minded, he may be carrying insufficient coverage. Of course the vendee can check with the carrier to learn the kinds and amounts being currently carried. In addition, he may wish to add to the amount or provide other types of insurance protection at his own expense.

At the time the contract is signed, insurance carriers should be notified so that they can add the vendee to their policies, to be indemnified along with the vendor in case of loss, "as their interests may appear." If the carrier is not notified of the change in ownership of the property, it may refuse to pay for the loss if it occurs. Incidentally, these interests not only are separate, but they may be in conflict in case of serious loss covered by insurance. Since the vendor usually dictates the terms of the land contract, he will probably provide that in case of destruction or serious damage to the structure he shall have the option to apply the insurance proceeds to the liquidation of the unpaid balance of the debt or to the replacement or repair of the building. If the former policy is followed, any surplus will go to the vendee. If the latter policy is chosen, arrangements must be made to make up any deficit of repair or replacement expenditures over the amount of insurance recovery.

Rights of Tenants Land contracts should spell out in detail the rights of tenants in possession of any part of the property. In addition, the vendee should check with the tenant to find out if the term of his lease, the amount of rent for which he is obligated—including a statement of prepayments or delinquencies—and all other pertinent facts conform to the representations made by the vendor. The latter might not be dishonest. Even though honest, he can be mistaken. There may even be conflicts of interests between tenant and landlord which should be resolved before the vendee becomes a party to them or has his interests affected by them.

Upon investigation the vendee may decide that he would be well advised not to go through with his part of the land contract, if he finds that the rights of the tenants would interfere too seriously with his own plans. It is always better to discover these rights before rather than after the contract is signed. If any tenant rights are to be bought off, this is better taken care of before rather than after the contract is executed. Even though the tenant's rights have expired, the time and expense of dispossessing him are factors to be taken into account.

If the tenant is not in possession of the property and the vendee has no notice of his rights, he is not bound by them. The tenant in such case would still have recourse against the vendor, but he could not lawfully interfere with the interests of the vendee.

Payments under Land Contract Even the questions arising concerning the payments to be made under the land contract by the vendee to the vendor cannot be simply stated as so many dollars per month, with nothing further said about them. The time and place of making such payments should be carefully defined. The down payment may have been made in the office of a real estate broker, in the directors' room of a local bank, and so forth. It is probable that future payments are not expected to be made at the same place. The rate of interest should be stated specifically, including any change of rate that may be contemplated during the life of the contract.

The contract should outline in detail just what the payments cover. If the monthly payments include interest, this should be stated. If, in addition, they include something for taxes, insurance, and so on, this too should be specifically stated. The contract should leave no doubt about the time and manner of distributing the ingredients of monthly installments. For example, is interest to be credited monthly or semi-annually? Will the tax payments be held by the vendor as a trustee, or will they be credited against the unpaid balance of the principal each month and then added again to the principal each half year as the taxes are paid by the vendor?

What about prepayments? Is the vendee permitted to make prepayments as his resources permit? If so, at what times and in what amounts? No doubt the vendor will ordinarily be glad to encourage prepayments in order to increase his security. Nevertheless, the details concerning them should be included in the land contract in clear form, so that all parties will understand them. Will prepayments provide a cushion against possible future defaults? If so, in just what manner will they operate? These questions can and should be answered in the contract at the time it is executed.

Mortgage Clause Whether or not there is a mortgage against the property at the time the land contract is executed, it is customary to provide that the vendor shall be permitted to mortgage the property for an amount not to exceed his equity. In such case the mortgage is given priority over the land contract. This provision enables the vendor to get at least part of his money out of the property should he care to do so. Presumably the interests of the vendee would not be adversely affected even in case of default on the mortgage by the vendor, since the rate of interest and terms of repayment on the mortgage are not likely to be more burdensome than those on the land contract.

However, if the contract does contain a mortgage clause, it should be couched in such terms that there can be no grounds for future disputes about its meaning. So far as possible, all features of the mortgage should be detailed in the contract. Since the interest rate which will govern such financing a few years hence cannot be accurately forecast at the time the contract is executed, it is sufficient to provide that the rate shall be that amount obtainable in the market at the time the mortgage is sought. Care should be exercised to prevent placing ahead of the vendee's interest any mortgage terms that would be unusually difficult for him to meet should the vendor default on the mortgage.

If care is exercised in drafting the mortgage clause in the land contract, and if later the vendor gets into trouble because he has failed to observe the requirements of the contract, the vendee should not be made to suffer. For example, suppose that the contract contains a prepayment clause giving the vendee the right to make advance payments as he sees fit. Suppose also that subsequently the vendor takes out a mortgage which gives him no prepayment privilege. He might easily find himself in a position where the amount of the outstanding mortgage exceeds his equity in the property, constituting a violation of his contract. If he gives prepayment privileges to the vendee, he should make sure that he receives prepayment privileges in his mortgage.

Another type of mortgage clause is frequently made a part of land contracts. The vendor may agree that when the amount of the indebtedness to him has been reduced a stipulated amount—say 25 percent—he will deed the property to the vendee and take back a purchase-money mortgage for the remainder. This clause may be inserted both as a means of providing a continuing investment for the vendor and as a further assurance to the vendee that he can obtain title to the property upon reaching a stipulated goal. The form of this clause should leave the vendee in a position to accept this option if he sees fit or to arrange some other alternative plan of financing instead. He might even prefer to continue the land contract, even though he has the right to have title transferred to his name.

If this type of mortgage provision is inserted in the land contract, its terms should be in such detail that there can at least be no doubt about the nature of the mortgage to be written at a future date. It is probable that the vendor—as an inducement to the purchase of the property—would agree at the time of executing a contract upon mortgage terms somewhat more liberal than could be obtained in the open market. Such liberality should not be nullified at a later time by giving the vendor an opportunity to hide behind indefinite or vague terms in the mortgage clause.

Provision for Deed As noted above, the vendee looks forward to the time when he will hold title to the property purchased under a land contract. The contract should definitely stipulate the conditions under which deed will be available to the vendee and the kind of deed to be used. Presumably it will be a full warranty deed. If so, the contract should so state. If not, the nature of the deed to be used should be set forth without equivocation.

It is not sufficient for the vendee to take the word of the vendor that a deed will be forthcoming. Before signing the contract, the vendee should make sure, as the result of a proper search of title, of the exact nature of the vendor's interest in the property. In other words, the vendee wants assurance that the vendor has good title. If he has not, he cannot pass it on to the vendee. Then the vendee should be protected against interests which refuse to join the vendor in passing title. For example, it is elementary that the spouse should sign the contract, thereby committing herself to sign away her dower interest when the proper time comes. Her refusal to do so might make it impossible for the vendor to pass good title to the property. Suppose that a life estate in the property exists in the name of someone other than the vendor and his spouse. In such case the owner of this estate also should sign the contract or in some other manner should indicate his willingness to release his life estate at the time the deed is called for.

Since the vendor may see fit to dispose of his interests in the land contract before title to the land passes to the vendee, the latter is properly concerned with several features of the vendor's assignment of his interests. In the first place, he wants to make sure that the assignee understands the exact nature of the contract and that no new interpretation will be placed upon its provisions.

Then he is concerned with another question which may be very vital to his interests: Will his deed, if and when he is entitled to receive it, be signed by the original vendor, or can an assignee be substituted for him? If the latter is permissible, a second question follows: Would it be possible for the vendor to pass title to a grantee, known to be financially irresponsible, by the use of a special warranty deed which gets the grantor out from under any responsibility for the character of the title? If so, even though the vendee under the contract receives a full warranty deed from the assignee, he does not get the full warranty deed which he thought he was to get when be executed the contract.

While the vendor should not be restricted in his disposal of his interest, it should be stated in the contract that both the vendor and his assigns must give a full warranty deed in passing their interests along to someone else. To protect the assigns of the vendee, provision should be made in the contract that the deed may pass either to the vendee or to his assigns. While it is generally assumed that a deed shall be accompanied by an abstract of title brought down to date—or whatever substitute is common in the community—this should be definitely stated in the contract.

Restrictions upon Assignment by Vendee There are occasions when the vendor prefers to place restrictions upon the right of the vendee to assign his interests in a land contract. For example, suppose that the vendor knows about the thrifty habits of the vendee and the housekeeping ability of his spouse. He may be willing to sell them a piece of property because he feels sure that they will take good care of it and will make every effort to live up to their contract obligations. At the same time the vendor might be quite unwilling to sell the property, under the same terms and conditions, to a specific friend of the vendee. What is to prevent the vendee from assigning his interest in the land contract to this friend? Perhaps he signed the contract in the first instance for this purpose; or perhaps such an assignment is an afterthought and is planned without knowledge that the vendor distrusts the new vendee.

The vendor, at the time the contract is executed, can restrict the negotiability of the vendee's interests by the insertion of a clause providing that the vendee may not assign such interests without the consent of the vendor. In the event of a dispute over the application of such a clause to a specific case, the courts would probably look to the reasonableness of the vendor's refusal to approve an assignment as the basis for a decision. It is not probable that the vendor could use his veto power, without justification, to the financial injury of the vendee.

In any event the right of prepayment clause would undoubtedly protect the vendee against prejudicial vetoes by the vendor if the property could be financed in any other manner. Refusal of the vendor to sanction a proposed assignment could be nullified by paying him the amount of the unpaid balance of the debt, thereby canceling his interest in the property.

Failure to Pass Title As stated above, unless the vendee makes sure of using all precautions to protect his interest at the time he executes the contract, he may find that, when the time comes to secure title, the vendor is unable to transfer title to him. For example, his wife may not release her dower interest. Unless she has agreed to this in effect at the time she signed the land contract, she cannot be forced to do so. The vendor may find that he cannot secure the release of a life estate; there may be an indestructible contingent remainderman's interest; and so forth. Consequently, the vendor cannot give the vendee a good merchantable title. Since he cannot perform his part of the contract, a suit for specific performance is fruitless.

Here is another place where the vendee needs competent legal advice to know his interests and the best manner of protecting them. Otherwise he may be "bought off" by the vendor at a price that is too low. Since he cannot sue for specific performance, he can bring action for damages. He should be able to recover whatever he has paid on the principal of the debt and the cost of improvements made with the consent of the vendor, and perhaps also an amount representing any increase in value that the property has enjoyed since his execution of the contract.

Since land contracts frequently contain penalty clauses against default by the vendee, it would not be amiss to include a stipulation to the effect that, in case of default by the vendor, a penalty of a stipulated amount shall be paid by him to the vendee. In the absence of such a provision in the contract, his chances of collecting a penalty through court action are not good.

Default by Vendee Because of the informality surrounding the execution of land contracts, the inexperience of the vendee, and the common absence of legal counsel to advise him, the vendee frequently interprets the contract to be a kind of option. He assumes that, if he decides to default on his contract, all he needs to do is forfeit his rights under it and walk away from it. He may find that conditions established by his signature on the contract are not quite this simple. To be sure most land contracts specifically provide that—at the option of the vendor—a default by the vendee may result in the forfeiture of the rights of the latter. In addition, the vendor reserves the right to retain as liquidated damages any amounts paid by the vendee, including any improvements to the property made by him.

The vendor may not see fit to exercise this option. If he thinks the unpaid portion of the debt exceeds the value of the property, and if he thinks the vendee is financially responsible, he may insist that the contract be lived up to. As an alternative, he may insist upon a cash settlement as the price of releasing the vendee from his contract. Depending upon the vendee's experience and the nature of advice available to him, the amount of cash demanded may not bear too definite a relationship to the amount of loss presumably suffered by the vendor.

If the vendee has had experience with such questions or if he has competent legal advice, he may decide not to forfeit any equity he may have in the property without a struggle. Even though he has technically violated the contract by defaulting in his payments, he may insist upon retention of possession of the property and may actively resist any effort on the part of the vendor to dispossess him. He too may do a little bargaining and agree to vacate and release the vendor only upon consideration that the vendor pay him a substantial sum of money—perhaps the amount by which the vendee has reduced the principal amount of the debt.

While negotiations are in progress, the vendee continues in possession of the property. Depending upon a combination of circumstances, including the pulse of the real estate market, the attitude of the vendee toward committing waste, and the forecast of a favorable or unfavorable decision in a court of equity, the vendor may be willing to pay a persistent vendee in default something to purchase a release from the contract. Perhaps the amount paid may even be considered by the vendor as a price of ridding himself of a nuisance. Even without such nuisance payment, something may be paid even though the vendor expects to suffer a loss, if he thinks that the vendee is financially irresponsible.

Loss of Payments under Land Contracts Under a long-term land contract, regular payments over a considerable period of time may have reduced the original indebtedness substantially. Since it is customary to stipulate in the contract that, in case of a default on the part of the vendee, all payments made may be retained by the vendor in lieu of liquidated damages, on the face of it appearances seem to indicate that a default might nullify all the equity the vendee has built up in the property. Because courts of equity, if appealed to, may construe a land contract as an equitable mortgage, it is not clear what rights the vendee may possess in relation to payments already made.

It does not appear fair that he should be permitted to ask for the repayment of any amounts paid to the vendor. Why not give him an equity of redemption similar to that given the mortgagor? At least he should be permitted to find a means of protecting his equity even after a technical default. Giving him an equity of redemption would probably carry with it an obligation covered by a deficiency judgment, if any applies.

Foreclosure Sale Failing to dispossess a vendee in default, either by a request for observance of the forfeiture clause in the land contract or by an offer of compensation for release from the contract, the vendor may pursue his rights in a court of equity. Since the law on the subject is not well defined, the equity court may render any one of several decisions. It may grant the vendor the relief he prays for, decree that the forfeiture clause in the contract be made effective, and dispossess the vendee from the property. It may even render judgment against the vendee for any installments in default.

As an alternative, it may determine that the vendee still has an equity in the property which he is entitled to recover by continued occupancy of the property for a period of time—fixed in the decree—sufficient to absorb or live up this equity. In other words, without any additional payment, the court may grant the vendee what amounts to free rent for a determined period of time. At the end of that period the vendor is entitled to recover possession of the property unless a new agreement is reached with the vendee in the meantime.

As a second alternative, the court of equity may decree that the land contract is in effect an equitable mortgage. As such it must be foreclosed like other mortgages to determine what disposition shall be made of the proceeds of the sale. Where such an alternative is followed, the procedure from then on follows the path taken by mortgage foreclosure and sale of the security, discussed elsewhere in this text. In general, courts of equity tend to protect the interests of the vendee in default so long as there appear to be reasonable grounds in his favor.

Strict Foreclosure of Land Contracts In some cases the rule of strict foreclosure is applied to land contracts. In other words, even after default a court of equity may fix a time within which the purchaser under a land contract may pay up his indebtedness to the vendor if he can find an alternative method of financing the deal. Failing to finance the property within the time fixed by the court may be followed by a complete loss of equity by the vendee, leaving the vendor with undisputed and unqualified title to the property. Except in times of extremely tight money, the vendee who is entitled to financial assistance will probably be able to find it. If his equity is so thin that no one will be willing to take the risks involved in assisting him, even a foreclosure sale would result in no recovery for him. If, on the other hand, he has a substantial equity in the property and cannot find someone willing to finance him he should be able to find a purchaser for his equity, enabling him to enjoy some recovery of previous outlays. If he fails to make use of either of these possibilities, strict foreclosure may follow.

Recording of Land Contracts State laws provide for the recording of conveyances of land and instruments affecting title. Land contracts generally are considered instruments affecting title and are consequently admissible to record. Recording land contracts is not essential to their validity; it merely gives notice of their existence to third parties.

In some cases the contract contains a stipulation that it shall not be recorded. This is included at the instance of the vendor who receives only a small down payment or none at all. If such a contract is recorded and there is an early default, clearing the record may take time and involve expense to the vendor. Even so, such a contract is occasionally recorded, in violation of its terms. This does not invalidate the contract. It may subject the vendee to a suit for damages if the vendor suffers loss by being unable immediately to effect a sale to another buyer who refuses to take title with the cloud of the recorded contract against it, and who is unwilling to wait upon the purchase until the record can be cleared. Probably such a right of suit for damages would seldom be exercised.

On the other hand, failure to record land contracts against vacant lots because of small down payments affords the vendor a particularly good opportunity to take advantage of the vendee, should he care to do so. The complete absence of possession by the vendee, or of any evidence of it, makes it easy for the dishonest vendor to sell the land and deliver good title to a third party, even though the vendee be not in default.

If, however, the vendee makes a substantial down payment, or as he builds up an equity with subsequent payments, he may feel safer if his contract is recorded. Under either of these sets of circumstances, the recording of the contract should meet with little opposition from the vendor. However, immediate and continued possession of the property by the vendee will normally serve as a satisfactory substitute for a record of the contract. All parties who might wish to acquire a lien prior to the claims of the vendee are put on notice to determine by what right the vendee occupies the property. Physical possession is not necessary to protect the rights of the vendee if sufficient evidence of possession exists to warrant a further inquiry by other parties.

Judgments and Land Contracts Since judgments against a debtor become a lien against any real estate held in his name from the instant of entry of the judgments upon the record, the vendee of a land contract should make sure that there are no unsatisfied judgments on the record at the time the contract is executed. If there are, they probably have preference over the land contract. As to judgments filed after the contract becomes effective, it appears that the vendee is not chargeable with notice of such entry. Consequently, he runs little risk by continuing to make his payments to the vendor. The judgment creditors can best reach the vendor's interest in these payments through court action. Through garnishment or equity proceedings, judgment holders could probably secure a diversion of such payments to a liquidation of their claims.

Complications sometimes result in conflicts between land contracts and mechanics' liens. Because mechanics generally have from 30 days to 6 months in which to file their liens, the vendee should inspect the property before signing a land contract, to determine if there is any evidence that work has recently been done or material delivered that might give rise to a mechanics' lien. If so, receipts from those who did the work or supplied the materials might be a necessary precaution against prior claims. In case the vendee finds that he is responsible for mechanics' liens that were not accounted for in the contract, he may pay them, obtain a discharge of the liens from the record, and take credit for his payments on the debt. If he is not personally responsible for them, he can disregard them, since his claims would precede theirs.

Improvements Directed by Vendee The land contract usually provides that no major improvements or physical changes will be made in the property without the consent of the vendor. The reason for such a provision is obvious. Before the vendee has built up a substantial equity in the property, he might wish to make major changes which would please his peculiar tastes but might not be acceptable to a subsequent purchaser, in case the vendee defaults on his contract. Even the removal of trees and shrubs might result in a decrease in the value of the property. Therefore, any major change should be subject to a veto by the vendor, at least until the vendee has built up a substantial equity.

Should this clause be omitted from the contract or should it be violated by the vendee, the cost of any improvements directed by the vendee could not be assessed against the interest of the vendor without his authorization. As a consequence, a mechanics' lien would attach to the interest of the vendee only. In case the vendee's interest was later forfeited before the mechanics' lien had been attached, no lien would continue. The person filing the mechanics' lien must thereafter look to the vendee for satisfaction. In case the vendee directs and the vendor authorizes the improvement, the whole property could be held as security for any mechanics' liens that might be properly filed, subject of course to prior liens.

Lease and Option Contracts One form of land contract that is even more informal than the forms just discussed is the lease and purchase option contract. The conditions of its use may follow a pattern of this nature. Suppose that A owns an inexpensive property in a neighborhood that is on the decline. Suppose that his efforts to sell it have met with complete failure. Suppose also that he would prefer to sell it rather than rent it. He may be able to combine renting it with an option to purchase. B may find that the property meets his needs. He would like to purchase it but has nothing to use as a down payment. Meantime he requires a place for his family to live in.

Landlord and tenant arrive at an agreement which contains these elements: First the tenant is permitted to use the property for a specified period of time—e.g., one year—at a rental that represents fair rent to both parties. At the end of the period, if he has faithfully met his obligations to the landlord, he may exercise his option to buy the property at a price that should have been agreed upon at the time the arrangement was set up. The exercise of the option may or may not require any additional down payment in cash—probably not. The tenant now becomes a vendee and the landlord a vendor under a land contract. Subsequent developments follow the pattern already outlined in this chapter. The monthly payments, which may not be substantially increased, if at all, are applied as installments on a debt rather than as rent.

As already indicated, this kind of deal is likely to be quite informal at the time it is made. It may not even be in writing. As a matter of fact, neither party may feel that he is bound by it. The saving clause for the landlord is contained in the interpretation he wishes to put upon the manner in which the tenant has met his obligations as a tenant. Even though the tenant pays the rent promptly, the landlord may contend that he had neglected other obligations, such as the proper care of the property. The tenant, by definition, has an option which he may ignore as he sees fit. If, however, both landlord and tenant are satisfied with the original deal, the lease may readily ripen into a land contract.

Conceivably it could bypass the contract stage and become an outright sale, with passage of title at the end of the lease if the tenant can finance the transfer.

Because so many uncertainties and possibilities are involved in such an arrangement, it does not appear that the tenant will find it desirable to incur the expense necessary to secure legal counsel to protect all his rights at the time the deal is made. Even should an unscrupulous landlord deny his option to purchase, the tenant has at least had use of the property at its fair rental value. The chief loss he has suffered is the possibility of making an alternative deal for another property that is no longer available to him at the end of his lease period.

Combined with this type of contract is an arrangement that frequently works to the advantage of both vendor and vendee. The arrangement described below could of course be a part of any land contract, but it is particularly applicable here. By definition the structure is probably not modern. It may even need major repairs, such as a new roof or a new paint job. The vendee has little opportunity to add to his monthly cash payments, but he may have some time which he can devote to repairs and improvements to the property.

So the land contract sets up a schedule of allowances which may cumulate to a sizable "sweat" equity. For example, the vendor may agree to allow $180 for the labor of reroofing the house, $275 for the labor of giving it two coats of paint, and so on. Meantime, the vendee agrees that the materials required for these jobs shall add $400 to the debt against the property. The results please both parties. The property becomes more valuable than it was before the repairs and improvements were made. The added value benefits the vendor because the security for his claims is now proportionately higher than his added investment. The vendee benefits because he has a greater equity in a better property. Even though the vendee is not a skilled building craftsman, he can probably do many things about the place with his own labor. Perhaps he can obtain the assistance of a more experienced friend on a trade-work basis. The vendor is likely to have greater experience than the vendee and will find it to his advantage to advise and assist the latter in making his contributions of time and labor.

Market for Land Contracts In general, the market for land contracts is limited to their sale to individuals acquainted with this type of real estate financing. They know the nature of the risks involved and usually are financially able to bear them. Occasionally a financial institution, such as a savings and loan association, buys them In such case precautions are taken to protect the purchaser against loss. For example, suppose that a property owner disposes of his real estate at a price of $10,000, accepts a down payment of $1,000, and takes back a land contract for $9,000. If he is sufficiently anxious to raise cash, he may make a deal somewhat as follows: He may sell his contract to a financial institution—with or without a discount—and agree to keep $3,000 on deposit with the purchaser as supplemental security. Usually when the contract balance is written down to $6,000 or when the vendee under the contract is able to finance his property by some other means, the deposit will be released and the vendor permitted to obtain unrestricted possession of the net selling price of his property.

QUESTIONS AND PROBLEMS

1. What is a land contract?
2. What other terms are commonly used synonymously with "land contract"?
3. What dangers are attendant upon the use of land contracts by laymen without professional assistance?
4. Under what circumstances are land contracts commonly used?
5. When a vendee on a land contract acquires property subject to a mortgage which was placed on the property by the vendor, what precautions should the vendee take with regard to future borrowing by the vendor where the property may be used as security?
6. What provisions should be made for a deed where property is purchased under a land contract? Might an escrow arrangement be established to the advantage of the vendee?
7. What alternative remedies does a seller under a land contract have in event of default in payment of the purchase price by the buyer?
8. B entered into a land contract to purchase real estate from S. The purchase price was to be paid over a 10-year period by monthly amortization. At the end of five years, B defaulted, failing to make his required payments. The contract provided that in event of default for a period of 30 days the seller could declare a forfeiture under the contract and repossess the property. If the courts should consider the land contract an equitable mortgage, what might be the rights of B and S?
9. What problems arise when a purchaser under a land contract wishes to make major improvements to the premises?
10. Vendee X installed new plumbing fixtures in a building which he is buying under a land contract. No provision was made in the contract regarding improvements, and Vendor Y did not consent. Plumber Z made the improvements. What right, if any, does Z have to enforce a mechanics' lien?
11. Under what circumstances may a lease and purchase option contract be advantageous?

9

Financing Long-Term Leases

Meaning of "Lease" A lease represents a commitment by one party—called the "lessor"—to turn over to another party—called the "lessee"—the use of real estate in return for rent or other consideration. In general, there are two broad classes of leases. The short-term lease leaves the financing and the management in the hands of the lessor. He is expected to supply not only the use of real estate but the necessary services required to make the real estate usable, such as janitor and elevator services. Even though such an arrangement between lessor and lessee might continue indefinitely, this type of lease is considered short term. Since such a lease presents no problems of financing that are peculiar to the fact that real estate uses are subject to rental payments, we shall not be concerned in this chapter with short-term lease financing.

The other type of lease, usually covering a longer period of time than the one just described (though actually it might be for a shorter period) is a type of real estate transaction in which the lessee takes over the management and frequently the financing of the property. The lessor gives up to the lessee the operation and maintenance of the property. The rent paid represents a net return upon the investment, unless it includes in addition an amount needed to pay taxes in case the lessee does not assume them also. If a building already exists on the site leased, it will probably be purchased by the lessee. Or it may be obsolete or inadequate for the purposes of the lessee. In either case the building will be demolished and will be replaced by a building constructed for and financed by the lessee. Where the lessee constructs and finances the building, its ownership and disposition at the termination of the lease should be specified in the lease.

Complex Nature of Long-Term Leases One of the subjects that give rise to conflicts of interests between real estate brokers and attorneys is: Who should take responsibility for drawing up long-term leases? Lawyers contend that they know best how to protect the interests of all parties concerned, because there are so many possibilities for error unless all legal angles are properly explored. Few would dispute the existence of many possible legal complications. On the other hand, real estate brokers contend that most of the questions to be settled in drafting long-term leases involve business practices with which the lawyer may not be fully acquainted. Some years ago the National Associaton of Real Estate Boards canvassed its members who dealt in long-term leases to determine what questions were encountered in lease negotiations. The results of the study showed that there were 350 such questions, which could be grouped into 44 convenient classes. Probably others would now be added if the study were repeated.

The answer to the controversy mentioned above seems quite obvious. Long-term leases are so important to both lessor and lessee that both real estate brokers and lawyers should be asked to make their contributions to the drafting process. Even though divided responsibility may produce further controversy, the interests involved are too important to risk giving the drafting responsibility to one not acquainted with all angles of the subject.

Drafting of Leases Because there are so many ways in which a long-term lease can be drawn with the result that either the lessor or the lessee is placed at a disadvantage, both should be represented by attorneys acquainted with this type of instrument. The interests of the lessor and of the lessee are not identical. One may enjoy a temporary gain at the expense of the other. In the long run, a lease that is not intended to be fair to both parties may not be fair to either. The lease must be so drawn that it represents a complete meeting of the minds of lessor and lessee on all questions about which information is available. In addition, it should anticipate and deal with all questions which are likely to arise during the life of the lease and which affect the relationship between the parties to it.

Provisions of Long-Term Leases In addition to giving the identity of the property and of the parties to the lease, the long-term lease should deal with the following: (1) The subject of improvements has many facets. If the lessee takes over the existing improvements, by purchase or otherwise, maintenance, replacement in case of fire or other cause of damage, erection of new improvements by lessee, ownership of improvements at the expiration or earlier termination of the lease, and so on—all need careful definition in the lease. (2) Then, of course, rents and their payment; insurance—kinds and amounts; purchase options; renewal privileges; rights of the parties in case of forfeiture of lease by lessee; condemnation proceedings—total or partial—and their consequences for both parties; taxes, present and future—all should be carefully spelled out in the lease so that there can be no reasonable grounds for disagreement later.

Rentals on Long-Term Leases Flat rentals—sometimes called fixed—are agreed upon in advance to pay the same amount each year for the life of the lease. A succession of flat rentals for predetermined periods of time receives the name "graded or step-up rentals." For example, the rent may be $4,000 a year for the first 5 years, $5,000 a year for the next 10 years, and $6,000 annually thereafter. Conceivably the succeeding periods could carry step-down instead of step-up rentals. In case there is doubt in the beginning about the amount to be charged for succeeding periods, the rent for the first period only may be fixed in the lease. Then at the end of predetermined periods of time thereafter, the amount to be paid for the succeeding period is determined by agreement, or by arbitration in case the parties cannot agree.

Advantages to Lessor The lessor may prefer to lease his property for a long term rather than sell it. The possible advantages that may accrue to the lessor are: (1) The amount of the principal is fixed for the term of the lease. (2) The lessee assumes most of the responsibilities of managing the property. (3) All new capital expenditures, such as the cost of the erection of a building, are borne by the lessee. (4) The rate of return is presumably fixed for the life of the lease. This is subject to limitations that will be discussed below. (5) By leasing the property instead of selling it, the lessor may save taxes. His income is spread over a long period of time as against a larger capital gains tax in case of sale.

Another type of advantage presumably accruing to the lessor is the improvement in his position from the investment in the building by the lessee. A vacant site, having only potential use, is a more speculative holding than the same site after it has been improved by a suitable structure. This added investment by the lessee not only provides the basis for a return to the lessor, but it assures the latter that the return will not be defaulted by the lessee except under the most dire circumstances. Since a default in the rental payment may result in the forfeiture of the building to the lessor, the lessee will not permit such a default if he can possibly avoid it.

The lessor may prefer to continue his investment in the real estate as against the acquisition of cash for which he has no satisfactory alternative use immediately. The lessor may also feel that, by leasing his property, he is, in effect, receiving a higher price for it than if he sold it.

Advantages to Lessee When a lessee prefers to hire the use of property owned by another instead of buying it, he hopes to gain the following advantages: (1) His capital investment is reduced, thereby making his funds available for other uses. (2) In case his capital is limited, the lease makes unnecessary the large loan that would be required to finance the purchase of the property. (3) The speculative advantages which may result in an increase in the use value of the property may accrue to the advantage of the lessee who pays a flat rental during its life. If the rent is $6,000 a year for the life of the lease and later becomes worth $10,000 a year, the lessee gets the advantage.

On the other hand, the owner may insist upon a sale even though the lessee might prefer a long-term lease. In such a case perhaps both interests can be served by finding a third party willing to buy the property provided the long-term lease is consummated. Or the same results could be attained if the original parties entered into the lease, and subsequently the lessor disposed of his fee underlying the lease. He might be able to realize a higher price after the new building is completed. Particularly is this true if he effects the sale through the use of land trust certificates, described later in this chapter. Of course, if he insists upon a sale rather than a lease, he is on safer ground to follow the first practice suggested above.

Long-Term Lease Covers Land Only In general, long-term leases cover land values only. The lessee is usually expected to build a building on the site or replace one already in existence. All construction arrangements should be anticipated in the lease. The rent on long-term leases is usually net to the lessor, with the lessee obligated to pay taxes, maintenance costs, and so on. As assurance that a building arranged for in the lease will be built, the lessor frequently requires a bond for his protection until the building is erected. All improvements to the land revert to the lessor at the expiration or other termination of the lease, in the absence of arrangements to the contrary.

Financing the Leasehold The right of the tenant to use the property during the term of the lease is called his leasehold. Irrespective of the value of any improvements that he may add to the property, this right may acquire value. In some instances the value has been very large. For example, suppose that a site was leased for 99 years, renewable forever, at $6,000 per year, at a time when this rent measured the current value of the land use. Suppose that, through a shift of business districts or otherwise, the rental that could be obtained from this site increased to $50,000 per year. The owner of the lease would enjoy a profit of $44,000 per year in perpetuity, should this new value continue. The present value of this annuity of $44,000 per year would measure the value of the leasehold as such. In case of a reappraisal rental arrangement, to be applied at intervals throughout the life of the lease, the lessor rather than the lessee would enjoy the fruits of any increment in value that might accrue. Hence the leasehold as such would never acquire any substantial value.

In addition to whatever value the leasehold acquires, the lessee usually owns the building erected upon the site, so long as he meets his obligations to the lessor. He may have purchased the building originally from the lessor or, more commonly, he may have caused it to be erected at his expense. In either event, it requires financing. To obtain the funds for this purpose it has been customary in some instances for the lessee to issue, against his interests in the leasehold and the building, what have generally been called first mortgage leasehold bonds. This term may be misleading to the uninitiated. While it is true that it is the first mortgage bond issue which uses the leasehold and the building as security, underlying it and taking precedence over it is the lease. Should the lessee default in his obligations to the lessor, the leasehold bonds may become valueless. As an alternative to the use of leasehold bonds, sometimes a single mortgagee will finance the operation, taking a mortgage on leasehold and building as security.

Because of the junior position of the holder of the leasehold mortgage, he will insist upon various protections. Since his resources are necessary to finance the building, the erection of which adds needed protection to the interests of the lessor, he looks to the latter for protection in turn. He wants to be sure of ample notice before action to cancel a lease on account of a breach by the lessee. The mortgagee may elect to succeed to the position of the lessee in such case by keeping up rental payments and by meeting other obligations to the lessor. He much prefers to finance a building under a lease where any increments of land value accrue to the benefit of the lessee instead of the lessor. Reappraisal leaseholds are very difficult to finance for this reason.

The mortgagee also prefers that the lease include a purchase option at a price not too greatly in excess of the value of the land at the time the mortgage is executed. An option at a fantastic price is no option at all. One at a reasonable price enables the lessee, or if necessary the mortgagee, to purchase the fee as a measure of protection at a future time. The lessor's desire to retain his investment in the property may be tempered by the necessity for granting a purchase option as the price of enabling the lessee to secure the financial assistance required to construct the building. As noted above, the lessor's interest is better protected by the presence of the building. The lessee will be well advised to make sure that the terms of the lease will enable him to finance the building, before he signs the lease.

In addition to a purchase option, a renewal option is favored by mortgagees. This is particularly true if the lease is about to expire. The shorter the term of the lease, the less likelihood of financing the leasehold. For example, if the lease has only two years to run to maturity, no mortgagee would advance to the lessee more than he was sure of realizing during two years by subtracting from the assured net return from the use of the property all rents, taxes, and other carrying charges for which the lessee is obligated. If there is a renewal clause, it extends the potential life of the lease, unless its terms are unacceptable.

Leases and Mortgages One question which sometimes complicates real estate finance is: When a mortgage is defaulted and the mortgagee takes steps to protect his interests, which takes precedence—the mortgage or a lease on the property which constitutes the security for the mortgage? The answer to this question appears to be quite simple. If the lease was in existence at the time the mortgage was executed, the mortgagee in possession must respect the tenant's rights. If the lease is favorable from the standpoint of the mortgagee or the prospective future owner of the property, the tenant is not likely to be disturbed so long as he meets his obligations. In case he defaults, action will probably be taken against him to bring him into line. But if the lease favors the lessee, the mortgagee is not permitted to cancel it without the approval of the tenant.

So far we have assumed that the mortgagee has notice of the prior rights of the lease as against the mortgage. This notice may take the form of a recorded lease or recognize that the lessee or his successor is in possession at the time the mortgage is executed. Complications may arise if the lease is not recorded and if the lessee is not currently exercising his rights of physical possession.

Leases which become effective subsequent to the execution and recording of a mortgage enjoy no such priority. In case of a default on the part of the mortgagor, the mortgagee in possession may alter the terms of the lease and offer the new terms as the condition upon which the lessee may retain use of the property. If the lessee refuses to accept such new terms, he forfeits whatever rights he may have enjoyed up to the time they are offered him. In addition, he may be required to pay again any rents that he may have paid in advance to the mortgagor. It is frequently to the advantage of the lessee whose lease postdates a mortgage to make a satisfactory settlement concerning a new lease with the mortgagee. Any agreement so reached binds the mortgagee as well as the tenant. And since the mortgagee is likely to become the owner of the property after the foreclosure sale, the future may be better taken care of for the tenant. Failure to arrive at a satisfactory settlement leaves the tenant in a position where he may be dispossessed at the will of the mortgagee.

Joining Lessor in Financing Building Because it is not always easy to secure leasehold financing necessary to pay the cost of constructing an expensive building on a vacant site, particularly in a financial market which is not accustomed to the use of mortgages against leaseholds, it may be necessary on occasion for the lessee to enlist the cooperation of the lessor in financing the construction. If the lessor is willing to let the mortgage cover the value of the land as well as that of the building, he should make sure that the lessee has a sizable part of the building costs covered by his own money.

For example, if the building is to cost $150,000 and the land is worth an equal amount, it is probable that a first mortgage could be obtained for at least 50 percent of the value of land and building, or $150,000. This would mean that the lessee would have use of the property without making any capital investment in it. If, instead, the mortgage was written for only $100,000, the lessor would have $50,000 of the lessee's capital funds as a cushion of value to protect his interests. In case of default, the lessee could be frozen out and the lessor would acquire a $150,000 building for $100,000 If the loan is amortized, as it probably would be, the mortgage would be reduced year by year, but the equity of the lessee would not decrease. Hence, the risk borne by the lessor would decline with the passage of time.

If such an arrangement is made, the lessor will expect to exercise considerable control over the type and manner of construction of the building to make sure that it fits the site and that it meets the needs of the lessee. The desires of the lessor in case the lessee defaults will not be overlooked in such determination.

Financing Subleases A long-term sublease is sometimes financed in a manner similar to that described above for long-term leases. So far as the mortgagee is concerned, his interest is primarily in some questions that would call for answers if he became interested in financing a long-term lease. The difference between financing leases and financing subleases is important and may become the governing factor. In financing the lease, the mortgagee is interested in measuring the difference between the value of the land and building on the one hand and the capitalized rent to the owner on the other. In financing subleases, the latter element would be replaced by the capitalized rent paid to the sublessor instead of to the owner. Presumably the owner of the sandwich lease would have an equity that would reduce the security behind the sublease in comparison with that behind the lease.

Leasehold Bonds Leasehold bonds can sometimes be floated successfully where a leasehold mortgage to a single mortgagee might be impossible. Two reasons account for this difference: (1) Bonds sold to numerous purchasers spread the risk inherent in junior financing operations. (2) Resort to many suppliers of funds makes it possible to finance larger properties than might otherwise be feasible.

This situation tends to favor leasehold bonds issued against properties large enough to absorb the costs of investigation, engraving of bonds, sales expense, and underwriting commissions, in contrast with smaller business properties which cannot afford such costs The common practice in Baltimore of financing structures underlying which are ground rents is an exception to this rule.

Recording of Long-Term Leases Not all states provide for recording of long-term leases. One reason for this omission is the failure to agree upon the nature of a lease. In some states it is looked upon as a real estate interest and is recorded as such. In others it is looked upon as personal property. In the latter states recordation of leases along with deeds and mortgages is not looked upon with favor. Indeed, in some states there is doubt whether a long-term lease is real estate or personal property. To play safe, some leases are recorded as both. Where the lessee occupies the property, there is less concern about recordation, since possession is notice that may not be ignored by parties with a possible financial interest that may come into conflict with that of the lessee.

Mortgage Waiver in Favor of Lease Even where the mortgage exists against the property at the time the lease is executed, it is to the advantage of the lessee to secure a waiver from the mortgagee giving the former the right to retain possession of the land even though the property were to be sold under foreclosure of the mortgage. If such a waiver is obtained, the position of the lessee is protected as long as he meets his obligations under the lease. On the assumption that the lease calls for payments equal to reasonable rent on the property, the mortgagee's position could easily be improved by the lease. If he acquires the active interest of a financially responsible lessee to add to that of the lessor, his chances of obtaining satisfaction on his mortgage should be enhanced. Even if the mortgagor defaults and the mortgagee is forced to buy the property at foreclosure sale, he still has the lessee bound to a lease which the latter will protect, if he can do so, as long as he thinks he has an equity in it. Even should the mortgagee who becomes the owner of the property prefer to dispose of it, his chances of doing so are enhanced if it has a favorable lease against it.

One advantage might be enjoyed by a mortgagee who refuses to waive the priority of his mortgage in favor of a subsequently placed lease. If he thinks that a financially weak mortgagor, with title to vacant property which is, temporarily at least, a liability instead of an asset, may be forced to default on his mortgage, he may prefer to wait until he takes over title by foreclosure before disposing of the use of the property. In such case he may elect not to waive the priority of his mortgage in favor of a long-term lease.

Termination of Long-Term Leases Some long-term leases run only for a specified number of years. No provision is made for any successive use of the property by the lessee. In the absence of any agreement to the contrary, the lessor would acquire whatever improvements the lessee had made during the life of the lease. In anticipation of this situation, the lessee would make no additional improvements and might even neglect repairs to buildings during the last years of the lease.

There would be no incentive to spend money for the benefit of the lessor. Consequently, the improvements that the latter might acquire at the termination of the lease could be quite obsolete and valueless.

Lease renewal or fee purchase options encourage the lessee to maintain and even further to improve the structures. In the absence of such options, some years before the expiration date of the lease the lessee may negotiate for a new lease, to run for a new period of time. If successful in these negotiations, he can then safely proceed with improvement programs. At the opposite swing of the pendulum, the lessor may be given an option to purchase, at the expiration of the lease, any remaining improvements which may have been added by the lessee. The price to be paid for such improvements may be reached by agreement or by arbitration.

Financing the Underlying Fee There is a recognized conflict of interest between financing the leasehold and improvements thereon and financing the fee underlying the leasehold. Any protections which the lessor sacrifices in making the lease may be necessarily yielded as a condition to securing the signature of the lessee; but at the same time, such sacrifices may decrease the value of the interest of the lessor. Should the lessor subsequently find it necessary or desirable to finance his fee in any manner, the terms of the lease will be carefully scrutinized by the party furnishing the finances. For example, a reappraisal lease or even one that provides for a graded rental would normally be more favorable to the interests of the lessor than would one calling for level payments throughout the life of the lease. On the other hand, where the land value is declining rather than increasing, flat rentals might be preferred by the lessor if they reflect at least current land values. This would be exceptional In like manner purchase options are not always favored by those who finance the fee.

The fee underlying the lease can be financed in either of two ways. Under a favorable lease to a responsible tenant, the value of the fee is determined by the terms of the lease and by the level of interest rates in the financial markets. The latter may become very important. Omitting any speculative advantages which the fee owner may enjoy, a fee worth $100,000 when its rent would be capitalized at 8 percent would drop to $80,000 if the capitalization rate became 10 percent. And, of course, one factor which helps to determine the capitalization rate is the credit rating of the lessee.

Like any other real estate interest, the fee underlying a long-term lease can be mortgaged. This mortgage, as a lien upon the senior interest in the real estate, constitutes a prior claim which takes precedence over the lease and consequently over leasehold mortgages or bonds. As an alternative to a mortgage, the fee owner may assign his interests to any purchaser. The assignee would necessarily take title subject to any claims against the fee of which he has notice. Presumably he would have notice of both the long-term lease and of any mortgage against it. Since the fee involves less risk than the leasehold, it follows that financing the fee is much easier than financing the leasehold. In many instances rates of return upon fees underlying leaseholds are comparable to rates of return upon government bonds.

Participation Bonds One pattern of financing leases is to create one leasehold bond issue against the lease and the building but to divide it into two parts. Part A, the senior participation portion, may account for 60 percent of the entire issue. Its rate of interest may be 7 percent, and it may be amortized over a 25-year period. Part B, the junior participation portion, may pay 9 percent interest but enjoy no amortization until the senior portion has been completely paid off. When part A has been retired, part B will then acquire senior status. Meantime, to induce the purchase of the junior portion of the bond issue, it may be sweetened with a bonus of common stock of the company which owns the leasehold.

Effect of Lease on Value The existence of a lease to a financially responsible lessee may make great differences in the value of income property. For example, a war surplus plant in New Jersey was sold to an industrialist for $375,000. The purchaser subsequently changed his mind about the use of the building and decided not to occupy it. Instead he sold it to a couple of speculators for $750,000. The speculators in turn leased the property to a nationally known corporation at $64,000 annual net rental for a period of 15 years. Thereupon the property was then mortgaged to a life insurance company on a basis of capitalized net income for the full purchase price of $750,000. In other words, the owners recovered the price they paid for the property and still enjoyed as income the difference between the annual net rental of $64,000 and the interest on the mortgage of approximately half that amount.[1]

Types of Leases In appraising commercial property for lending purposes, the type of lease used is a matter of prime importance to the lender. Of the many types in use, the most common only will be mentioned here. In the net lease the tenant contracts to pay all operating expenses, taxes, and insurance. A modification of this form places the burden of taxes and insurance upon the lessor. At the other extreme, some percentage leases provide for a fixed minimum rent regardless of the amount of business done, while others have no such minimum.

The appraiser must study the type of lease used in order to determine what stabilized income to expect. In the net lease to a financially responsible tenant, the amount to be expected is most easily calculated.

---

[1] *Mortgage Bankers Association of America Yearbook* (Chicago, 1947), p. 346.

particularly if the rent is fixed for the life of the lease. Even where it is graded, the amount is easily ascertainable if the steps are definitely set forth in the lease as to both time and amount of rent changes. While the net lease may hold down the income accruing to the holder of the equity, it probably best suits the needs of the lender on a mortgage against the property. Next to this type, the lender will probably prefer the percentage lease with a minimum guarantee.

Leasehold Formulas Brokerage of leaseholds is not as simple as some think. On the contrary, the longer the term of the lease and the greater the amount involved, the greater the need for specialized knowledge on the part of leasehold brokers. The lessee acquires an interest that declines in value as the termination of the lease is approached. Meantime the lessor gives up rights that may increase in value without a corresponding increase in payment to him. The broker should not only be capable of evaluating the lease at the time it is made, but he should be able to advise both lessor and lessee about their future commitments. These involve principles concerned with sinking-fund amortization, straight-line amortization, the Inwood coefficient, the Hoskold premise, the Babcock premise, and so on. The technical nature of these formulas precludes their discussion in a treatise of this kind. The broker who deals in long-term leases should be familiar with them.

Such knowledge may lead to profitable business for the broker. For example, under what circumstances would it be to the advantage of the lessor under a long-term lease to sell the fee to the lessee? And under what conditions will the lessee be well advised to merge the fee with the lease? The income tax status of each may help to find answers to these questions. The broker who can calculate the relative advantages of either sales or purchases of fees underlying long-term leases can frequently develop for himself quite desirable business deals.

Present Value of Future Rentals In calculating the value of long-term leaseholds, the element of interest must be taken into account. For example, suppose that a well-secured leasehold agreement provides for an annual payment of $12,000 per year to the owner of the lease. Let us assume that the factors of management and risk hazard are negligible and that the nonliquidity factor is not heavily weighted. Such a lease might well be calculated on a basis of 8 percent interest. If the lease runs for 15 years the owner may think that his lease is worth $180,000 because he expects to receive $12,000 per year for 15 years from it. But discounted at 8 percent interest, the present value of the lease would be only $102,714. Whether the owner would be willing to sell the lease for the lower amount would depend upon numerous factors, including his need for cash. He might easily prefer to retain his investment for the full life of the lease. Again the tax considerations would enter into his calculations.

Speculation in Real Estate Equities Shrewd speculators who have unusual success in purchasing real estate equities on business properties can frequently earn a high return upon their money. If the property in question is outside an established business district, there is probably considerable uncertainty about its future stability. The chances for loss in a period of decreased demand for goods and services are great. In periods like the 1930s, equities in such properties are entirely wiped out if the equity holder is unable or unwilling to keep up payments on his mortgage. If the property is carried in the name of a corporation with no other assets, the real owner can avoid personal liability for the mortgage debt. If this plan is followed, however, the lender will advance a smaller percentage of value in making a loan.

A financially responsible owner who is successful in selecting real estate for purchase, and who is not faced with early difficulties in collecting rents, can earn high returns upon his own investment by trading on his equity. For example, suppose that a store building in a new neighborhood, with an investment of $100,000, is leased to net 9 percent. Suppose that a 60 percent loan at 6 percent has been obtained with the property as security. This will allow $13\frac{1}{2}$ percent return upon the equity. In less than eight years the owner of the equity will have recovered his entire investment if the loan against the property is a straight loan; it will take him a bit longer if it is an amortized loan. Meantime any increase in rent that can be collected as the new neighborhood is stabilized accrues to the benefit of the equity holder. This increase would become greatest under percentage leases as the business of the tenants grows.

Competition for loans in established commercial and industrial districts will permit a slightly lower rate of interest on mortgages. But confidence of equity purchasers in such districts will enable them to purchase equities at much lower rates of return. As a result, the chances for high returns on equities and for loss of principal invested in them are much less in established business districts than in surrounding, less well-defined areas.

Lending institutions are much more likely to be interested in making loans against commercial real estate when the borrower can show that the property has been leased to financially responsible tenants. Such leases are looked upon by lenders as supplemental security for their loans. The equity owner in commercial property is always a speculator. The lending institution tries to avoid sharing his speculative losses, since it is not permitted to share his speculative gains.

LAND TRUST CERTIFICATES

Meaning One method of financing long-term leases that has had considerable vogue in some sections of the country, particularly during the decade of the 1920s, is the use of land trust certificates. This plan of financing did not originate at that time. It is simply an application of the much older idea of the Massachusetts trust. In effect it provides for the ownership of a parcel of land by a number of owners, each of whom owns one or more land trust certificates. Other names used to designate such certificates of ownership are fee ownership certificates, certificates of equitable ownership, participation certificates, and ground rent certificates. The latter should not be confused with Baltimore or Pennsylvania ground rents.

The manner in which such certificates are used follows a pattern somewhat as follows: The owner of a business site leases it to a financially responsible tenant. The latter agrees to build a suitable building on the site. Let us assume that the annual net rental is to be $17,000 a year. If $1,000 is sufficient to pay the fee for managing the project in the interest of the owners of the site, $16,000 remains to pay for the use of the land. Capitalized at 8 percent, the indicated value of the site is $200,000. With the lease to a financially responsible tenant as security, the owner then proceeds to sell the site, vesting legal title in a managing trustee. Equitable title will rest with the owners of the land trust certificates. Let us assume that these certificates have a face value of $1,000 each and pay an annual return of $80.

Land trust certificates have been used also where the owner of the land and the building decides to raise money for some other use by selling its land, leasing it back, and retaining ownership of the building. The same process will be followed as if the seller of the land and the lessee were two different parties.

Legal Nature of Land Trust Certificates If the land trust certificate holders are the unequivocal and unconditional owners of the site, there appears to be no question of the nature of such certificates, in the eyes of the law. As often happens in such cases, courts reach decisions on such questions in answer to a suit brought for another purpose. In the leading case on the subject of the nature of land trust certificates,[2] the question raised was the right of a state to levy a tax on land trust certificates. In seeking an answer to this question, the Supreme Court of the United States found that land trust certificates evidence an interest in land. Therefore they are not taxable as personal property. If the land is located beyond the borders of the state which levies the tax, the tax levied by the state will not apply because one state may not tax land or interests in land situated beyond its borders. If the land is located within the state which levies the tax, such levy must be in a uniform manner according to the value of the property taxes. Since the tax in question did not follow this rule, it was declared to be unconstitutional. Three justices dissented from this opinion. The im-

---

[2] *Senior v. Braden,* 55 Sup. Ct., 800, 295 U.S. 422.

portant part of the decision, from the standpoint of real estate finance, is the finding by the Supreme Court of the United States that land trust certificates evidence ownership in land and are not personal property.

Land Trust as Mortgage One question that has caused considerable confusion in the consideration of the legal nature of land trust certificates involves the inclusion in the lease of the right of the lessee to purchase (or to repurchase) the land. In the leading case covering this phase of the subject[3] the Lazarus Company of Columbus, Ohio, had sold the site on which its department store was situated to a local bank as legal owner. The Lazarus Company leased back the site for a period of 99 years. Meantime the beneficial interest in the land was sold to land trust certificate holders, with the local bank serving as trustee.

In addition to the payments under the contract for the use of the land, the Lazarus Company retained an option to repurchase the fee at stipulated scheduled prices throughout the life of the lease. This option was subsequently exercised. Meantime the company claimed the right, for federal income tax purposes, to deduct a depreciation charge sufficient to amortize the cost of the building in 40 years. Without discussing the prices at which the Lazarus Company could repurchase the land, the Supreme Court of the United States addressed itself to the depreciation charge. In discussing the findings of the Board of Tax Appeals, which had reversed the decision of the Commissioner of Internal Revenue, the court upheld the depreciation charge in the following language:

> We think the Board justifiably concluded from its findings that the transaction between the taxpayer and the trustee bank, in written form a transfer of ownership with a lease-back, was actually a loan secured by the property involved. General recognition has been given the established doctrine that a court of equity will treat a deed, absolute in form, as a mortgage, when it is executed as security for a loan of money.

Highlights of Lease A review of numerous leases using land trust certificates in recent years reveals a more or less common pattern of their contents. In addition to the identification of the lessor and lessee and a description of the property involved, the following highlights are significant: (1) The term for which the lease is to run, subject to earlier cancellation by exercise of a purchase option by the lessee, is stated. (2) The amount of annual rental to be paid and the manner of its distribution are stipulated. (3) A depreciation fund is frequently established, to consist of an annual deposit of a stipulated part of the net earnings of the lessee with the lessor. While the deposits into this fund are dependent upon earnings, minimums are usually established

---

[3] *Helvering* v. *F. & R. Lazarus & Co.*, 60 Sup. Ct. 209, 308 U.S. 252.

for each year of the lease. Both the percentage of earnings and the minimums are frequently stepped up at intervals during the life of the lease. Maximum payments may also be stipulated in the lease, to be observed at the option of the lessee. He is permitted to make any payments in excess of requirements that he may see fit. In lieu of depositing cash, an equivalent amount of land trust certificates, as measured by face value, may be used by the lessee for this purpose. (4) Amounts in the depreciation fund may be invested in U.S. government bonds; or in land trust certificates of the issue involved, upon approval of the price to be paid therefor by the lessor and the lessee. (5) If the certificates are made callable in the land trust indenture, the lessor agrees to call enough from time to time to absorb such of the depreciation fund as shall be requested by the lessee. Call prices are fixed, usually on a declining basis at intervals during the early life of the leases. After 10 years or so the call price remains stationary at only a nominal premium. (6) Purchase options are commonly included in leases where land trust certificates are used. They are exercisable by the lessee on short notice—30 days being common—at step-down prices fixed in the lease. The price provides the amount needed to pay the call price of the land trust certificates. In addition, there may be minor debits and credits to be adjusted in case the lessee exercises his purchase option.

Financing the Building Where land trust certificates are used to finance the site, they become the senior lien against the entire property. The building can be financed with leasehold bonds, debenture bonds, equity funds, or any combination of these types of securities. In any event, the financing of the building will place the contributors of the funds needed for this purpose in the position of junior claimants. This is not always a comfortable position to occupy, particularly in times of depression. For example, the Biltmore Hotel, of Dayton, Ohio, was financed by a combination of land trust certificates against the site, leasehold bonds to construct the building, and equity financing in the form of stock, plus a chattel mortgage to pay for furnishings and equipment. During the depression of the 1930s, stock, chattel mortgage, and leasehold bonds were completely wiped out, leaving the land trust certificate holders as owners of land, building, and equipment. Even this improvement in their status did not prevent the land trust certificates from selling at a heavy discount, so drastic was the reduction in earnings of the hotel property.

Rental Trust Certificates A financing device similar to land trust certificates has been given the name "rental trust certificates." The legal ownership of leases and subleases is vested in a trustee. Against such ownership, certificates of beneficial interest are sold, usually in denominations of $500 or $1,000. They represent fractional parts in an undivided estate in the leases and subleases. The trustee collects all rents due under the leases and subleases. Quarterly payments are made to the holders of the rental trust certificates. Payments up to a certain percent a year are considered to be a return on the investment. Any payments over this amount are considered to represent amortization of the investment. Before making any distribution, the trustee deducts from the rentals received any expenses incurred by him, plus his own fees. Rental trust certificates simply represent a means of distributing the ownership of leases and subleases among a sizable number of people.

QUESTIONS AND PROBLEMS

1. What are the usual distinctions between long-term and short-term leases?

2. What principal advantages may a property owner hope to gain by becoming a lessor on a long-term lease?

3. What are flat rentals? Step-up rentals? Percentage leases?

4. What limitations do percentage leases impose on tenants who might desire to utilize leasehold values as security to finance property improvements?

5. A is a tenant-in-possession under a long-term lease. The lease is not recorded. B is a mortgagee whose instrument is recorded. The mortgage lien was placed on the property while A was in possession. Does B hold subject to the terms of A's unrecorded lease?

6. What is a sandwich lease and how does it derive value? May it become a vehicle for speculation?

7. What principles are utilized to calculate the value of a long-term leasehold?

8. If you were a lending officer of a financial institution, what principal conditions and provisions would you expect to find present before you would accept a long-term lease as security for a loan to the lessor?

9. Why should a long-term lessor require bond to ensure that the lessee will complete his undertaking to construct a building on a land parcel?

10. What are land trust certificates and what purposes do they serve in financing real estate?

11. White and Black are investors. White holds leasehold mortgage bonds whose proceeds were used to finance an office building on the land parcel. Black holds land trust certificates. Who has the senior lien?

12. What are rental trust certificates and why may they be used?

10

Purchase and Leaseback

Meaning In recent years an adaptation of principles well known to those acquainted with real estate finance has received wide acclaim as a new method of financing business property. It contains two steps which are taken simultaneously, although they appear to be separate and distinct. First, an institution, such as a life insurance company, a college or university, a religious body, or a charitable institution with funds to invest, purchases the real estate owned and used by a well-established business corporation—usually a retailer or a manufacturer. Second, the property is leased back to the seller by the purchaser. From these two steps we obtain the name— "purchase and leaseback." Other names used to designate this practice are "sale and leaseback" and "liquidating lease."

The property need not be in existence at the time such an arrangement is made. Some contractors agree to purchase a site to be selected by the lessee, construct a building according to his plans and specifications, turn the complete product over to him for his use, and finance it according to the purchase and leaseback principle, all without any capital outlay by the lessee.

A variation of this plan occurs when an owner assigns a long-term lease to secure a mortgage, executed to a financial institution, with the stipulation that the mortgagor assumes no liability on the mortgage. In such case the mortgagee must look to the lease to satisfy his claims, unless he can induce the lessee to add guarantees of some sort.

Lease Terms The test of investment quality in such an arrangement depends primarily upon the financial stability of the lessee. The customary term of such a lease ranges from 20 to 40 years. Leases on retail property are customarily for longer terms than on industrial real estate. The lease may provide for a renewal or even for a repurchase at or before the expiration date. The rental is net to the lessor. The lessee pays all taxes and assessments, insurance, maintenance and repair costs, utility charges, and so on. The net rent is fixed at such a level that it is expected that, within the original term of the lease, the lessor will have recovered at least the purchase price of the building; and in the meantime he will have enjoyed a final net return at least comparable to currently available returns on government or Aaa corporate bonds. In some such leases the rate of return is not flat for the entire life of the lease but may be graded, with highest rates in the early years, followed by declining rates for successive periods. This practice permits the lessor to write down his investment more rapidly. For example, under the lease of store buildings by Union College to Allied Stores Corporation, rental payments for the first 5 years are 6.7 percent of the selling price; for the last 5 years of the 30-year lease, 3.7 percent; and for a second period of 30 years, 1.5 percent.

In the event of the failure of the lessee to meet any of the charges assumed by him, the lessor is empowered to make the payments required and collect from the lessee. This follows the usual pattern of long-term leases. Defaults—whether due to nonpayment of rent, assignment for the benefit of creditors, or any other action of the lessee that may jeopardize the position of the lessor—usually give the latter the right to terminate the lease. Condemnation clauses are usually well defined. Total destruction of structures is dealt with both in leases and in state laws governing them.

Reasons for Recent Use As pointed out above, the principles involved in purchase and leaseback arrangements are not new. Indeed, at least one instance of the specific practice has been cited as early as 1882.[1] The widespread use of this device has been confined to recent years. The reasons are as follows: (1) Equity capital from outside capital markets has been scarce in the last few years. The alternative was to resort to borrowed capital, which traditionally was limited to 50 to 60 percent of the appraised value of the real estate offered as security for the loan. Where more capital was needed, the opportunity to secure 100 percent of value was eagerly accepted. Even where the borrower could get along with a 50 percent loan, he might prefer to sell his real estate and lease it back for reasons that will be developed later. (2) Financial institutions have at times been hard put to find outlets for their tremendous resources. The amount of these resources in the coffers of life insurance companies pressing for investment will be discussed in Chapter 14. Other reasons for the use of purchase and leaseback arrangements will be discussed later in this chapter.

---

[1] Arthur M. Cannon, "Danger Signals of Accountants in 'Net Lease' Financing," *Journal of Accountancy*, April 1948, p. 312.

Types of Real Estate Used As already indicated, the most common use of the device of purchase and leaseback is in the mercantile field of business. It is not strange that this is so. Traditionally many large distributors, including some very strong institutions and some chains, have not looked with favor upon real estate ownership. Leases of property owned by others have been common. In explaining the reasons for the sale of its properties to the Union College, the president of Allied Stores wrote his stockholders as follows: "This Company has long recognized a preference for renting land and buildings, where leases were obtainable on favorable terms, rather than investing its own funds in real estate." Also, merchandise corporations are thought to be more stable than some other users of real estate. Sears, Roebuck and Company; Federated Department Stores, Inc.; Spiegel, Inc.; Wiebolt Stores, Inc.; Allied Stores Corporation; and numerous other department stores have used the purchase and leaseback device extensively [2] Chain stores in fields covering shoes, variety merchandise, wearing apparel, drugs and cigars, and foods; restaurants; and candy and even smaller individual stores have been similarly financed in substantial numbers.

Next in order of use are industrial corporations. Not all that have become interested in this type of financing have been permitted to use it, because of the highly specialized character of their operations. The real estate used by a department store would at least be available for use by another department store. But that used by some manufacturers might be worth very much less for any other alternative purpose. Among the well-known industrial corporations that have made some use of this device are the Continental Can Company, E. I. du Pont de Nemours & Company, General Electric Company, Westinghouse Electric Corporation, and United States Rubber Company. It is not necessary that a company achieve the strength of an industrial giant, however, to utilize the purchase and leaseback method of financing. Many lesser industrial corporations of sound credit have taken the same route.

Office buildings in the large cities, and even in many smaller ones, have been sold and leased back to their former owners. To some extent, banks have also used financing of this type. Construction companies engaged in building more office space regularly use the commitment to purchase and lease back as a means of financing major construction. They have worked extensively with life insurance companies in this manner.

Sources of Funds Life insurance companies constitute the major source of funds for purchase and leaseback financing. Other sources of funds include college and university endowment funds and charitable

---

[2] As reported by Mark Levy, "Institutional Purchases of Real Estate," *The Appraisal Journals.* July 1949, pp. 308–10.

and religious investment funds. Like life insurance companies, educational institutions have been hard pressed to earn on their investment funds something more than is available from the ownership of bonds. Pension funds have engaged in purchase and leaseback financing to a limited extent. Since liberalization of the income tax laws permitting accelerated depreciation deductions, affluent individuals in high tax brackets have found these investments attractive when they can largely offset rental income against depreciation and interest deductions.

Legislative Changes Prior to 1942, only five of the less well-populated states permitted life insurance companies domiciled within their borders to purchase real estate for investment other than that used for residential purposes. In these five states insurance companies have long been permitted to hold such real estate "as their purposes may require." In 1942, Virginia amended its law to permit its insurance companies to buy commercial property for investment. Other states followed in quick succession, so that now nearly all grant permission to purchase business property for investment.

One legislative program, recently adopted first in Connecticut, and called after the name of that state, does not mention real estate as such, but permits an insurance company to invest up to 5 percent of its assets in loans or investments not permitted under its charter or in sections of the general statutes. Other states have followed the lead of Connecticut. New York took the lead by changing its legislation to permit its insurance companies to invest not to exceed 3 percent (later raised to 5 percent) of their admitted assets in income-producing real estate. Most other states have followed New York's example, with percentages varying from 3 in some states to 20 in Utah and with no limit in Wyoming. The average in terms of assets of all insurance companies affected is between 4 and 5 percent. This makes available at the present time around $9 billion for this purpose, not all of which has been utilized to date.

Although specific statistics on life insurance company acquisitions on a purchase and leaseback basis are not available, the *Life Insurance Fact Book* published by the Institute of Life Insurance in 1971 indicates that realty investments of life insurance companies reached about $6.3 billion at the close of 1970. Since 1946, the total amount of such investments has grown from $735 million, or 1.5 percent of the total assets of life companies, to the 1970 figure representing 3.0 percent of their total assets. Gradually, existing percentage limitations are being increased in some states. In a few states, laws require the specific use of the purchase and leaseback device rather than the general power to purchase income-producing real estate.

Statutory Provisions Regarding Investment Real Estate In some states, legislation permitting the insurance companies to own real estate to be leased to others undertakes to regulate such investments. For example, in New York the cost of such property must be amortized at not less than 2 percent annually. In most other states this requirement is either absent or appears in modified form. In Pennsylvania the value of the improvements, but not the cost of the real estate, must be written off at 2 percent per year. In New York all income over 4 percent must be used to amortize the cost of the real estate. The Connecticut type of statute, mentioned above, is based upon the prudent investment theory. Without any specific statutory regulation, it anticipates that the insurance company will invest its money prudently—which certainly implies that at least the book value of improvements will be reduced as rapidly as they depreciate in value.

New York apparently tried to regulate the investment policies of insurance companies not domiciled in that state but interested in doing business within its borders. Its law provides that the superintendent of insurance may refuse a license to any company whose "investments do not comply in substance with the investment requirements and limitations imposed on like domestic companies." Since most insurance companies wish to do business in New York, the laws of that state set the general investment standards for the entire country.

Legal Character of Lease Contract The purchase and leaseback contract contemplates an actual sale of the property with delivery of both legal and equitable title to the purchaser. Upon attaining the status of ownership, the purchaser then executes a valid lease upon terms agreed upon at the time the two-step agreement was made. Since the sale follows traditional real estate transfers, there is nothing peculiar about it. It is the lease that must be scrutinized most carefully, because each lease is drawn to meet a specific situation. Here there is ample opportunity for mistakes that amateurs would not recognize until it is too late. One very important question is: Is the lease so drawn that it tends to substitute a mortgage for the sale?

For example, as has been pointed out elsewhere in this text, a deed given to secure a debt becomes an equitable mortgage. If the lease contains a purchase option, does this amount to a relationship between the lessor and lessee that a court may construe to be that of mortgagor and mortgagee instead? In fear of this possibility, some lessors refuse to grant repurchase rights. The lessee, on the other hand, would prefer an option to repurchase the property if he thinks it may appreciate in value during the term of the lease. Presumably the court will weigh all the evidence in each case before reaching a decision about the existence of an equitable mortgage when a repurchase option is included in the lease. Doubtful cases may lean in the direction of a mortgage interpretation.

As at least a partial offset to the uncertain attitude of courts concerning the legal character of the lease contract where repurchase options are included, some leases provide such options only in conjunction with cancellation privileges. For example, the lessee might be permitted to request cancellation of the lease at stated intervals during its life, in consideration for his willingness to repurchase the property upon such cancellation. The amount of the purchase price is usually the amortized value of the lessor's purchase price, plus a premium of 1 to 4 percent, depending upon the remaining life of the lease. If the lessor elects not to sell, then the lease is expected to be terminated as of the cancellation date.

In other words, this is not an absolute right to repurchase, since the request may be refused by the lessor. If the specialized character of the building results in pressure upon the lessor to grant the request, the effect is the same as if the lessee had a right to repurchase the property. This situation may be weighed by a court asked to determine whether or not an equitable mortgage exists in a purchase and leaseback arrangement. This possibility has deterred the inclusion of any reference to a repurchase clause in some leases recently executed. On the other hand, the lessee may not dare to request a cancellation of the lease for fear of refusal by the lessor, followed by termination of the lease and dispossession of the lessee. The result is the same as if the lease were noncancelable.

Two Kinds of Purchase Options In some leases there is not only the definite purchase option, or the one tied in with a lease cancellation clause, but both. For example, in a Sears, Roebuck lease[3] running for 40 years with renewal options up to 99 years, the cancellation clause provided for repurchase at amortized cost plus a small premium at any time from the 11th to the 35th year. From the 35th to the 45th year no cancellation provisions were included. After the 45th year, the lessee could purchase the property at its land value only, as determined by arbitration in case the lessor and lessee are unable to agree upon a price.

In addition, should the lessor reject the purchase option tied in with the cancellation clause, the lessee enjoys the following specific purchase options: (1) at any time during the first 10 years, at cost less 1 percent annual depreciation; (2) from the 11th to the 35th year at the prices mentioned above; (3) from the 36th to the 45th year at the price fixed for the 35th year; and (4) at land value any time after the 45th year.

Accounting for Lease Obligations As a matter of accounting procedure, should it appear that a lease is in fact an equitable mortgage, recognition should be given to this fact, at least in the form of a footnote, on the balance sheet of the lessee corporation. Even where the probabil-

---

[3] Cited in *Mortgage Bankers Association of America Yearbook* (Chicago, 1947), pp. 82 ff.

ity of interpretation of the lease as an equitable mortgage is not present, the commitment to pay a definite rental for a long period of time is a fixed charge that may affect the credit standing of the lessee.

Reports to the Securities and Exchange Commission, for example, must include, in a supplementary schedule, definite information about annual rentals on real estate leased by the reporting corporation or its subsidiaries where the lease has more than three years to run. In less specific terms the American Institute of Certified Public Accountants has given its approval to a recognition in financial statements of fixed rentals and other obligations set up under long-term leases. This information is thought to be of significance to anyone relying upon these financial statements for credit or investment decisions.

Advantages Claimed for Lessee The advantages usually claimed for business corporations which sell their real estate and lease it back include the following: (1) This plan will provide more funds for expansion of business and for working capital at lower cost and for a longer period of time than will be available from any other source. (2) The funds so released from the sale of real estate can be invested to better advantage and at a higher rate of return when used to expand business operations. (3) This device simplifies the financial plan of the business corporation, makes possible a smaller debt structure, and avoids the hazards of refunding bonds or other forms of debt. (4) It enables a business corporation, admittedly not skilled in the solution of real estate problems, to pass them along to the purchaser of the property. (5) It is a flexible form of financing the business, resulting in a minimum of investment in fixed assets. (6) Where cancellation clauses are included, they enable the lessee to select a new location for his business, should he see fit to do so. (7) The tax advantages will be discussed later.

In considering the above-named advantages, we must not overlook the fact that, as in the financing of all long-term leases, the financial capacity and stability of the lessee is of prime importance. Purchase and leaseback arrangements are most often available to well-established business enterprises with a long record of successful operation under an outstanding management. Presumably such a management weighs the advantages and disadvantages of alternative financing plans before selling its real estate and leasing it back.

Admittedly not all of the above-claimed advantages are of equal weight. For example, does the purchase and leaseback plan relieve the lessee of concern about real estate problems and permit him to pass them along to the lessor for solution? Under the terms of the lease, the lessor receives a net return. All problems involving taxes, maintenance, repairs, insurance, and so on, remain with the lessee. In other words, the lease does not relieve him of the disadvantages of real estate management and operation. Unless it contains a repurchase option, it may relieve him of any advantage that might accrue from appreciation in the value of the real estate, however. To this extent the lease may be a disadvantage to the lessee instead of an advantage.

This may be a very significant factor to take into account. In the past, at least, 100 percent locations have continued to show appreciation in site values for long periods of time. Whether or not there is any appreciation in value, any remaining value at the expiration of the lease would accrue to the advantage of the lessor, even though his investment had been amortized in the meantime. Should any loss suffered in this manner by the lessee be substantial, it would necessarily need to be taken into account as an additional cost of rentals paid for the use of property owned by the lessor. As an offset, the amount of differential gain between the rentals paid and the return on the funds released by the purchase and leaseback plan would need to be taken into account.

Absence of Restrictive Covenants It is not unusual in bond indentures, and in other types of contracts setting up obligations and covenants of debtors, to place restrictions upon further debt-incurring practices of the obligor. Sometimes these follow a pattern of requiring the consent of bondholders, for example, before other specified debts may be incurred. In other cases, the prohibitions are absolute and make no provisions for seeking consent. It is noteworthy that to date leases arranged under the purchase and leaseback formula have not included such restrictive covenants. Apparently the lessors have been satisfied with the real estate security for their commitments, supplemented by the unrestricted credit standing of their lessees. The future may find the appearance of restrictive covenants in similar leases. Meantime, should the courts decree that a specific lease represents an equitable mortgage, it may in turn violate restrictive covenants in outstanding mortgage bond issues.

The bond issue existing at the time the purchase and leaseback arrangement becomes effective may not interfere with the sale of the real estate, but its indenture may contain a covenant to the effect that the corporation which issues the bonds will not issue any more bonds or will not mortgage its property further without the consent of the holders of a fixed percentage of outstanding bonds. Should a court determine that a specific lease is an equitable mortgage, the above-mentioned covenant may be violated. The corporation would then be subject to whatever penalty the bond indenture provides.

Tax Exemption of Lessor Prior to 1950, certain classes of investors enjoyed a sweeping federal income tax immunity which provided a direct stimulus to purchase and leaseback programs. Had it not been that nonprofit enterprises were totally exempt from corporate income taxes, it is not likely that this plan would have developed to its present proportions. By specific provision of the Internal Revenue Code, educational, charitable, and religious institutions were exempt from the payment of income taxes. In practice, life insurance companies were also given virtual exemption because of the formula permitted by the Treasury Department for the computation of their taxable income. Hence, institutions in these classes that became lessors under the purchase and leaseback program had little concern about the tax consequences of their receipt of one type of income as compared with receipt of another type.

Nonexempt investors cannot be as free in their choices of investment outlets. If a financial institution lends money on an amortized real estate mortgage as security, it need report for income tax purposes only that part of the payments which represent interest on its investment. Amortization of principal is not considered to be taxable income. But if it purchases the real estate and leases it back, it must report as taxable income all rents received, minus only such amounts as are properly deductible for allowed depreciation.

For example, on an amortized loan for $500,000 for 20 years at 6 percent interest, payable annually, the first year's receipt would be $43,600, of which $30,000 would be interest and $13,600 a principal installment. Only $30,000 would be taxable. Assuming interest computed on the reducing balance of the loan, the taxable income would decline year by year. If the nontax-exempt institution purchased a property for $500,000 and leased it back at a net return of 8 percent, the annual income would be $40,000 for each and every year. Assuming that the land is valued at $200,000 and the building at $300,000 for tax purposes, the latter amount only would be depreciable. At a rate of 2½ percent, the allowable depreciation for tax purposes on a straight-line basis would be $7,500, leaving a taxable income of $32,500 for each year. Over a 20-year period the lessor would pay much more in corporate income taxes from its net return of 8 percent on a purchase and leaseback arrangement than from its 6 percent interest on a real estate mortgage.

An amendment to the Internal Revenue Code in 1950 made tax-exempt organizations subject to income tax on their "unrelated business net income." Included in unrelated business income are rentals received from property leased to others for a period exceeding five years, where the lessor with the tax exemption borrowed funds to effect the purchase or acquisition of the property and such indebtedness is still outstanding. The purchase and leaseback situation commonly fits this pattern.

The taxable business lease income of exempt organizations is determined by application of the following formula:

$$\frac{\text{Business lease indebtedness at end of tax year}}{\text{Adjusted basis of premises covered by business lease at end of tax year}} \times \text{Annual business lease rental (less allocable expenses)} = \text{Unrelated business taxable income}$$

The following example is adapted from the *Income Tax Regulations*.[4] Assume that an exempt educational institution purchased a building 12 years ago for $600,000. It used borrowed funds and leased the building for a period of 20 years. At the present time, the end of the 12th year of ownership, the building has an adjusted tax basis of $500,000, and the unpaid balance of the indebtedness to acquire the property is $200,000. The annual rental from the lease is $55,000. Taxes, interest, and depreciation total $20,000 for the year. Unrelated business taxable income from the business lease is computed as follows:

$$\frac{\$200,000}{\$500,000} \times \$35,000 = \$14,000$$

A study of this example shows that the current tax law has moved in the direction of limiting the flexibility of a tax-exempt lessor in dealing with a taxable lessee. Note, however, that the annual business lease income equal to the proportion of the actual capital investment of the tax-exempt investor is still excluded from taxable income. Thus, the leasehold rental income of a tax-exempt investor who does not borrow to finance his acquisition of property is still tax-exempt.

There has also been a reduction in the tax advantages afforded life insurance companies. Whereas their taxes through the mid-1950s were negligible, these companies now find an increasing percentage of their income subject to federal tax. The amended tax formula results in a substantial increase in the proportion of life insurance company investment income subject to tax. The new formula, however, still leaves these companies with a decisive advantage over the ordinary corporate investor, whose income from interest on mortgage loans or from leasehold rentals is fully taxable. The tax impact of a decision by a life insurance company to buy and lease property back to the seller continues to be less under present tax laws than when the same decision is made by an ordinary corporation.

Tax Advantages to Lessee The federal government is far less concerned with the income sources of the lessors described in the preceding section, and the collectible income taxes therefrom, than it is with the outgo payments of those who are fully taxable and who are expected to pay taxes at normal rates. The purchase and leaseback arrangement enables many lessees to report larger expenses for income tax purposes. As a consequence, they report less taxable income. Principal among the lessees who may benefit from this arrangement are property owners who have become committed by previous tax filings to a straight-line method of computing depreciation. For example, suppose that the owner of a property has executed a mortgage of $500,000 at 6 percent for

---

[4] Reg. §1.514 (a)-1.

20 years with annual payments on interest and principal in the amount of $43,600 per year. The total interest deductions for 20 years would amount to $362,000. If a straight-line method of depreciation was adopted, on the basis of 2½ percent of $300,000 invested in the building for depreciation allowance, deduction for this purpose for 20 years would be $150,000. Suppose that instead, the owner of the property sold it for $500,000 and leased it back at 8 percent net. The total deductions for rent during the 20-year period would be $800,000. In the latter case, the deductions for tax purposes would exceed the interest and depreciation deductions in the former case by $288,000. Assuming a corporate income tax rate of 48 percent, this would mean that the government would collect $138,240 less under a purchase and leaseback arrangement than under a 100 percent amortized mortgage plan. Under such conditions the government becomes a major loser by the purchase and leaseback.

Since the adoption of the Revenue Code of 1954, a considerable portion of the tax advantage to the lessee of the purchase and lease-back arrangement has been offset by the adoption of liberalized rules for the use of accelerated depreciation methods. On properties bought since 1953, the declining balance or the sum-of-the-years'-digits method of depreciation, providing proportionately large deductions in the early years of ownership, may be freely elected. Where it is possible to obtain substantial tax deferrals in this manner, without recourse to the leasing device, the ownership of property becomes more appealing than it formerly was. Recent revisions in the Internal Revenue Code, however, have neutralized much of the advantage of accelerated depreciation where property is to be sold. The new rules provide for recapture as ordinary income the excess of speedy depreciation over straight-line depreciation at the time of sale. There are certain exceptions, but even in these cases a minimum period of 10 years to 16 years and 8 months must elapse before all excess depreciation may be treated under capital gain rules.

An additional advantage of the purchase and leaseback arrangement is that over the term of the lease the full value of the property may be deducted in rents paid, while with property ownership the value of the land can never be depreciated. In the foregoing case, for instance, only $300,000 of the total investment of $500,000 could be depreciated, whereas rental deductions might be taken for the full $800,000 of rents paid.

Still another advantage may accrue to the lessee corporation if the sale is made at a profit. Suppose in the case cited above that a gain of $100,000 was realized in the sale of the property. Under the capital gains tax, the 30 percent limitation would result in not more than $30,000 being paid to the government on account of this gain. But the resultant higher basis for rent payments would reduce future income taxes by about $48,000, with a savings of $18,000, disregarding the time factor in the payment of taxes.

Renewal Options Options to renew a lease, at its expiration, for another term, perhaps for the same length of time as the original lease, are sometimes used as a substitute for a repurchase option. Renewals are usually provided for at much lower cost than the rent originally charged. The reduction may be 1 or 2 percent or as much as 5 percent or more of the original cost of the property. Where such renewals are permitted, two questions arise, the answers to which may affect the amount of tax deductions: (1) Shall the cost of improvement paid for by the lessee be spread over the remaining life of the original lease only, or shall it be spread over this period plus the period of lease renewal? (2) Shall rentals paid during each period be deducted as they accrue, or shall they be averaged over the life of the lease plus the life of the extension? For example, if the rental during the first 20 years is $25,000 annually, and the rental is only $10,000 per year for the next 20 years, shall these amounts determine annual deductions for tax purposes or will the average of $17,500 be so used? The answer seems to rest upon the probability of renewal of the lease. This, in turn, frequently hinges upon the favorableness of renewal terms.

Sales to Establish Losses Occasionally, purchase and leaseback plans involve unusual features. If they are set up for the purpose of obtaining an additional tax advantage, they are usually scrutinized very carefully by the Internal Revenue Service. For example, a foundry located in St. Louis, Missiouri, and carried on the tax records at $531,700, was sold to a small college for $150,000 and leased back in the conventional manner to the original owner. The difference, $381,700, was taken as a business loss. The Commissioner disallowed the deduction. The government contended that the transaction represented a gift for the most part and not a sale of the property at its fair value. For a gift to an educational institution, the donor was entitled to deduct not more than the usual allowance from its total net income for this purpose and not the difference noted above. Even after taking legal deductions into account, the result might still be a gain to the vendor instead of a loss.

Advantages to Lessor The advantages of the purchase and leaseback device to the purchaser who becomes the lessor center around the following: (1) The term of the investment is relatively long, and there is no need to bother about early prepayments. (2) The amounts invested are relatively large. (3) Only well-seasoned, well-managed corporations are accepted as lessees. (4) The rate of return after amortization of the principal of the investment is relatively high. (5) The lessor has more control over real estate which it owns than over that on which it merely holds a mortgage. (6) There may be a substantial remainder of value after the lease expires which will serve as a hidden reserve for the lessor. (7) There may be possible income tax advantages in this method of financing real estate.

Whether the long term of the investment is an advantage or may prove ultimately to be a disadvantage depends upon the future level of prices. During the period when many of the leasebacks now in effect were executed, real estate has been priced at high levels. In making their arrangements, the lessors have had the advantage of the services of the best appraisers to help them fix prices they were willing to pay for the properties purchased. They have not blindly purchased real estate merely because the sellers were willing to lease it back for a long period of time. Mortgages likewise have been written for as long a period as the leases discussed in this chapter. Presumably, where mortgages were used the mortgagor has had a cushion of value, over and above the mortgage, which served as protection to the mortgagee.

The amounts invested have been relatively large in comparison with many other individual investments made by insurance companies and other institutional investors which have engaged in leaseback financing. As a consequence, the cost of servicing these large investments may be less than for smaller commitments. Only well-seasoned, well-managed corporations have been accepted as lessees. Indeed, some insurance companies have dealt only with large corporations with assets of at least $100 million. Few of the leases have involved corporations with assets of less than $10 million. With only a limited amount permitted to be used for the purchase of investment real estate, the purchaser has been able to select his purchases with great care.

The relatively high rate of return has been due to several factors. Since the lessee saw a distinct advantage in the leaseback plan and since he found a limited market for his real estate because of the necessity for tax-exempt protection to the lessor, the latter has been able to charge what the traffic will bear. Then, too, the purchase and leaseback plan provides a form of investment that is less liquid than listed bonds, for example. While a purchaser could sell its real estate subject to the lease, it must find a purchaser which enjoys the same tax-exempt status as itself.

Finally, there is greater risk in taking title to the real estate at a price which represents 100 percent of its value than in granting a 60 percent loan with the same real estate as security. In general, the rate of return has been sufficient to permit the amortization of the investment in the building at least, and in some cases in the land and building, within the term of the original lease, and still leave a rate of return upon the reducing balance of the investment somewhat higher than the best return obtainable upon government or Aaa corporate bonds.

The alleged advantage of greater control over the real estate that is owned and leased back to the seller, in comparison with a mortgage on the same real estate, is of doubtful validity. In practice, quite the contrary may prove to be the case. Real estate mortgages commonly contain restrictive clauses giving the mortgagee considerable control over subsequent financial operations of the mortgagor. In general, leases seldom give the lessor such control. Restrictive clauses have not been much used in the leases discussed in this chapter.

In the absence of repurchase and renewal options, the potential remainder value to the purchaser-lessor may be real for several reasons. While the structure value is amortized over the period of the lease, its effective life may be much longer. If the structure will render effective service for 50 years and is completely amortized in 25, its value at the end of the lease would probably not be 50 percent of its original value—changes in price levels being disregarded—but it could be a substantial percentage of the original value. Any residual value in the structure would add to the rate of return received by the lessor. If the site is so located that it continues to increase in value, the remainder could very substantially add to the hidden reserves of the lessor. In this case also, any remainder value increases the rate of return enjoyed by the lessor.

The tax advantage of leasebacks is limited generally to the federal corporate income tax. Insurance company lessors could not avoid state and local real estate taxes even if they wished to do so. While educational and religious bodies might possibly avoid real estate taxes and assessments, they commonly require the lessee to pay them as a precaution against too great opposition from the public. The federal corporate income tax exemption has been freely used up to this time. As previously mentioned, abuse of this exemption has been controlled in considerable measure by recent changes in the tax law. Tax-exempt institutions are now required to pay income taxes on unrelated business income, including substantial amounts of rents received under purchase and leaseback arrangements. Changes in regulations governing corporate income taxes on life insurance companies have reduced, but have not eliminated, their preferred status in the field of real estate financing by the use of the purchase and leaseback device.

Future of Purchase and Leaseback The future of purchase and leaseback arrangements depends upon a number of variable factors. The amount of real estate involved in such financing is already substantial. Institutions that have been organized over the years to foster self-help through mutual insurance, education, religion, charity, and thrift have been encouraged by legislation granting them tax exemption, in comparison with ordinary business enterprises. Except for these tax exemptions, it does not appear that purchase and leaseback arrangements would be so popular. In effect, the purchasing institutions have used a legal device to pass along to sellers the use of their tax-exemption privilege. We have seen that Congress has taken away several of the advantages of the leasing arrangement through changes in classification of income of tax-exempt or tax-sheltered institutions and through extension of use of accelerated depreciation methods. Court decisions may invite either extensions or contractions of the use of this program by the manner in which they interpret leases that are brought before them for adjudication. State legislatures may either liberalize the percentage of life insurance company assets that may be invested in this manner, or they may decide that the purchase and leaseback principle is not in the public interest and may legislate against its extension.

Under the present structure of the income tax law the purchase and leaseback is particularly advantageous for investments by pension funds paying no taxes and by individuals in high tax brackets. They can offset rental income by accelerated depreciation charges and mortgage interest costs of the financed portion. These sources are becoming relatively more important, as life insurance companies have recently signified general preference for mortgage-lending programs on income properties at high loan-to-value ratios where the net rent will support the loan. Recently, the New York Insurance Department issued a regulation making 100 percent loans permissible when supported by leases from tenants of unquestioned financial responsibility. This leaves the purchase and leaseback market even more generally today the province of tax-exempt institutions and highly taxable individuals.

Rent Needed To liquidate completely an investment in a leaseback arrangement and provide an annual return upon the reducing investment balance at a fixed rate of interest requires reference to amortization tables for establishment of payment amounts. Tables are available for monthly, quarterly, or annual amortization. For example, Table 10–1 sets forth representative rates where the lease rental is paid annually.

TABLE 10–1
Percentage of Value Needed to Liquidate Investment and Provide Specific Return

Term of Lease (years)	Rate			
	4%	6%	8%	10%
20	7.36	8.72	10.18	11.75
25	6.40	7.82	9.37	11.02
30	5.78	7.26	8.88	10.61
35	5.36	6.90	8.58	10.37
40	5.05	6.65	8.39	10.23

Proprietary Interest in Business The purchase and leaseback device is a kind of a hybrid, representing some features of a loan and some of equity ownership of real estate. Some colleges and universities have gone one step further and have acquired a definite proprietary interest in numerous types of business enterprises. The pattern usually followed is along these lines. First, alumni and friends have organized a nonprofit corporation. This corporation has used endowment funds of the educational institution, at least in part, to purchase a business enterprise. In this case not only the real estate but the entire business has been acquired. The seller paid to the federal government a capital gains tax if he enjoyed a profit and established a deduction for tax purposes if he suffered a loss. In the meantime the operating head of the seller would ordinarily be retained to manage the business on a salary basis.

Before recent changes in the tax law, the educational institution using its tax-exemption privileges, would pay no federal income tax on the profits it received from the business operation. Whether the owner operated the business directly or through a nonprofit corporation which also enjoyed tax exemption, the profits were tax free. Complaints were levied against this type of transaction, because the tax-exempt owner was not saddled with all the expense burdens of its taxpaying competition. For the same reason the price paid for the business might be somewhat higher than could be obtained from another purchaser not enjoying tax-free advantages. Thus, the tax exemption, allowed for quite a different purpose, provided a loophole whereby business enterprises could derive special advantages by being taken off tax rolls.

Current federal income tax rules sharply limit advantages from this type of arrangement by denying tax exemption to unrelated business income of tax-exempt organizations and their feeders. Unrelated business income is that derived from the conduct of a trade or business not substantially related to the purpose for which the organization was granted an exemption. Thus, the manufacture and sale of macaroni and spaghetti by a university would normally be considered an unrelated business.

Life insurance companies have undertaken some proprietary purchases involving no leaseback arrangements. For example, the life companies pioneered slum clearance programs in which large-scale apartment projects for families with moderate incomes replaced the razed properties. Peter Cooper Village, in the former gashouse district of New York City, and Lake Meadows, a former southside Chicago slum, were financed through direct ownership of life companies.

Nationwide, life insurance company acquisitions of residential real estate have not been impressive in recent years in terms of the potential. About three fifths of the total 1970 life company real estate holdings of $6.3 billion represented investments in commercial properties, including office buildings, department stores, factories, and shopping centers—primarily leaseback arrangements. Another 26 percent consisted of home and branch office facilities. Investments in residential properties were only about 10 percent of the total holdings.[5]

QUESTIONS AND PROBLEMS

1. What are the chief reasons for the purchase and leaseback of real estate?
2. What kinds of real estate can be used most successfully in a purchase and leaseback arrangement?
3. What are the general qualifications required of a vendor-lessee for acceptance as a party to a purchase and leaseback transaction?
4. What are the principal sources of funds for purchase and leaseback financing, and why are these sources most interested in this arrangement?
5. To what degree are life insurance companies eligible to participate in purchase and leaseback financing?
6. Do you think that limitations on participation by life insurance companies in this type of financing may affect their attitudes toward mortgage loans on similar properties?
7. Under what conditions is a purchase and leaseback contract likely to be treated by the courts as an equitable mortgage?
8. How would tax treatment of a purchase and leaseback contract as an equitable mortgage differ from its treatment as a true purchase and leaseback transaction?
9. How should obligations under a purchase and leaseback arrangement be reflected on the balance sheet of the lessee corporation?
10. What advantages are claimed for the lessor under the purchase and leaseback arrangement? What advantages are claimed for the lessee?
11. How do current provisions under the federal income tax law limit tax advantages under the purchase and leaseback arrangement?
12. What do you predict for the future of the purchase and leaseback contract as a financing device?

[5] *Life Insurance Fact Book* (New York: Institute of Life Insurance, 1971), p. 83.

11

Savings and Loan Associations

Basic Ideas The foundation stones of modern savings and loan associations are two in number: thrift and homeownership. Neither is currently placed ahead of the other in importance. In the day-to-day operation of an institution of this character, if the savings and investment funds pile up because of lack of mortgage demand, the progressive manager tries to stimulate loan applications. If the latter exceed the capacity of the institution to supply funds, efforts are made to increase savings. Within reasonable limits, liquidity requirements taken into consideration, an attempt is made to maintain a balance between receipts and disbursements. As a matter of fact, until quite recently the statement that interested savings and loan managers most was neither the balance sheet nor the income statement based upon accruals, but the statement showing cash receipts and disbursements.

In the early days there was a definite difference in emphasis. Homeownership by its members was the goal of the early "building societies" organized by our forefathers of English origin and of the "Bauvereine" organized by their German neighbors. The end was homeownership; the means was a kind of forced savings which were no longer considered essential once the home was paid for. The emphasis upon homeownership was so great that our usual concept of saving for a purpose was definitely reversed. Today we are accustomed to think that those who save accumulate funds against their use for a specific purpose which involves their expenditure at a later date. In other words, saving precedes spending. The basic idea in building associations was to encourage the borrower to borrow, with his home as security, funds which he would then repay from future savings. In this case, spending precedes saving.

The ambition for homeownership was not an indigenous American plan. Neither was the plan for cooperative financing of homes. Both were imported from Europe. Except among the German settlers, early American building societies followed the Anglo-Saxon model. Without benefit of parliamentary sanction, the English had made considerable progress with voluntary associations before the first American counterpart was started in Frankford, Pennsylvania, in 1831. The avowed purpose of this first American cooperative home-financing institution, known as the Oxford Provident Building Association, was to "enable the contributors thereof to build or purchase dwelling houses."

This first association could not even qualify as a mortgage finance institution as we know this term today. It gave no heed to the financial needs of those who owned homes already; its purpose was to help its nonhomeowning members to acquire homes for themselves by purchase or construction. Neither was it concerned with thrift as a desirable objective by itself, since it had nothing to offer to the person who wished to save for some purpose other than homeownership.

Management of Early Associations Some of the earliest building associations were not incorporated but were set up as voluntary trusts, with trustees appointed to manage them, much in the same manner that savings banks have been and are managed. In Pennsylvania, where building associations received their earliest growth, the legislature as early as 1850 began approving charters for the formation of such associations with the management to be placed in boards of directors. The life of these first charters was restricted to 10 years; the number of shares at $200 par to 500; and the authorization was limited to associations planning to operate in three counties only—Philadelphia, Schuylkill, and Berks. By subsequent acts, other counties were added. The first general incorporation law for building associations applicable to the whole commonwealth of Pennsylvania was not passed until April 12, 1859.

This general incorporation act limited the life of associations organized under it to 20 years; permitted associations to have not to exceed 2,500 shares of the par value of $200; limited periodical payments on shares to $2 each; prohibited fines against a deceased member's account after death; required the auctioning off of loans whenever cash accumulations amounted to as much as $500; required security satisfactory to the board of directors for all loans; permitted prepayments on loans; provided that "no premiums, fines or interest on such premiums, that may accrue to the said corporation, according to the provisions of this act, shall be deemed usurious; and the same may be collected as debts of like amount are now by law collected in this Commonwealth"; granted the associations incorporated thereunder the right to purchase at foreclosure sale properties on which they held mortgages and to dispose of same; and validated all mortgages granted by associations before they obtained their charters.

Speculation Encouraged One curious effect of this law was its permission of the organization of speculative ventures which assumed the name of a building association. For example, A could subscribe for five shares of stock with $200 par; agree to pay $2 per share weekly; borrow $1,000 for one month on any security acceptable to the board of directors; agree to pay from 1½ to 5 percent per month interest; renew the loan month by month until he decided to liquidate the purchases for which he made the loan; and take his profit, if any, without even having considered the reasons for which the association which advanced him the money was supposed to be organized. As might be expected, the borrowing members were the ones who received the advantages from this type of operation, if their ventures were successful. The investing members were the ones who suffered the loss if the speculative ventures failed to pay off.

Unfortunately, so long as such speculative associations were permitted to operate, the public failed to distinguish between them and the building associations which were organized to encourage thrift and home-ownership. Once an investor lost money in the former, he became gun-shy of the latter.

Terminating Associations The pattern of early building associations took as its basic assumption that every member would stay with the project until he had acquired a home and paid for it in regular installments. When all had been served in this manner, the association was expected to dissolve, since it had reached its objective. Hence, the name "terminating association." True to the basic idea upon which it was founded, borrowing from the association was thought of as being so desirable that it was expected to command a premium. Savings to finance borrowing had to be forced by the imposition of various kinds of penalties. The bylaws of one early association provided: "Each and every Stockholder—who shall neglect or refuse to pay his monthly dues—as often as the same shall become due and payable, shall forfeit and pay the additional sum of ten cents monthly, on each and every dollar due by him." In other words, if the member had subscribed for only one share, on which he was obligated to $1 monthly dues, his fines for neglect in paying any dues for one year could be $6.60.

Likewise, repayments of loan and interest thereon were carefully safeguarded, and stiff penalties came to be the order of the day for those who fell behind in their obligations. The same association provided:

> Any stockholder who shall fail to give satisfactory security within one month, for money loaned upon his bid, shall be fined one dollar for each and every share loaned upon, and charged with all expenses incurred on account thereof; and if the interest on a loan at any time continue to be in arrears, and

unpaid for the space of six months, the Board may order legal proceedings to be instituted for the recovery of the principal and interest.

Suppose that an association had 30 members, each of whom subscribed for one or more shares having a face value of $200. Suppose each paid monthly dues of $1 per share, and that the total number of shares was 200. If all paid their dues promptly, the monthly contributions should add up to $200. Each time the accumulated capital amounted to as much as $500, it was auctioned off to the bidder willing to pay the highest premium for its immediate use. While the auction method of determining loan premiums was commonly used, some associations had a fixed premium rate, and gave the loans to borrowing members in the order of filing of applications or by lot.

Payment of the premium followed either of two patterns: (1) It was paid in the form of a discount from the amount borrowed. For example, if the amount of the loan was $1,000 and the highest premium offered was 10 percent, the borrower received only $900, but paid interest upon the full $1,000. (2) The premium was sometimes added to the monthly payments for a fixed period of time, perhaps for the entire life of the loan. In other cases it was paid in annual installments for the period required by the rules of the association.

Each member was entitled to borrow up to $200 for each share subscribed for by him. As soon as a loan was made, the association acquired new sources of funds—interest upon this loan and a premium from the successful bidder. Fees and fines for late or missed payments of both dues and loan repayments also added to the receipts or were charged against the accumulated credits to the members' accounts.

Forfeitures Since fees and fines were apparently not sufficient to induce dues and interest payments to be made on time, a third "F" was added in the form of forfeitures. The association quoted above provided in its bylaws that:

> If any stockholder . . . shall continue to neglect or refuse to pay his, her, or their monthly dues and fines, for the space of six months, his, her, or their share or shares of stock may be declared forfeited by the Board of Directors, when the same shall revert to the Association; after deducting all fines the defaulting stockholder shall be entitled to receive any balance of his, her, or their monthly payments, and shall from thenceforth cease to be a member of this Association.

Contemporary Defense of Early Associations A most interesting defense of these early building associations was published in 1869 by one Edmund Wrigley, who had had 18 years' experience as an official of numerous associations. The ambitious title given his little book of slightly more than 100 pages is: *The Working Man's Way to Wealth; A Practical Treatise on Building Associations: What They Are and How to Use*

Them. His arguments in favor of the plan building associations used run as follows:

1st. In that it is perfectly democratic, admitting each individual corporator or member to a full, free and unrestricted voice in the creation and management of Associations formed under it [Pennsylvania enabling act of 1859], and a constant oversight of its operations and affairs.

2d. In that it is entirely mutual and equal in distributing its benefits, giving to all its members their equal portion of all its profits and gains.

3d. In that it is much more liberal in its return of profits and gains than any other known plan of saving and accumulating from small sums of money. Having,—owing to its entirely mutual character,—no preferred class to share its profits, no heavy sinking fund to create and hold in reserve against contingencies hardly within the bounds of possibility, and no necessity for expensive banking houses and clerk hire; and

4th. In that it is the only plan by which the working man can become his own capitalist, and create a source of wealth from which he can supply all reasonable demands, without the aid or interference of the outside capitalist. In short, that it is a system "of the people, by the people, and for the people." One that, with ordinary judgment, enterprise and strict integrity brought to bear in its management, cannot fail of permanent benefit and profitable results to any community or body of people adopting it, and faithfully carrying out its principles.[1]

Share-Accumulation Sinking-Fund Loan Plan The early American associations used a loan plan that few members of the associations ever understood; and not even the elected nonsalaried managers could forecast its full meaning. It operated in this manner: Suppose that A subscribes for five shares of stock and later borrows $1,000 from the association. He gives a mortgage on his home for this amount. In effect this is an unamortized term loan without any definite term stated. Each month he pays the interest, which is credited to the income of the association. In addition, he continues to make his regular payments on his shares.

More often than not, the interest rate was 6 percent. The borrower would pay each month to the association $5 for interest and an additional $5 dues to be credited on his share account. This was the beginning of the practice, to become standard for savings and loan associations, of requiring the borrower to pay 1 percent of his original loan principal per month, regardless of the percentage of loan to property value, and so forth. While most modern lending practices have adjusted monthly payments to a variety of factors, some savings and loan associations have not been able to get away from the 1 percent per month formula.

High percentage loans were common in the early building associa-

---

[1] Edmund Wrigley, *The Working Man's Way to Wealth; A Practical Treatise on Building Associations: What They Are and How to Use Them* (1869), pp. 5–6.

tions. While the borrower was expected to have some capital to put into his home, the amount required was likely to be a token amount only as a gesture of good faith on the part of the borrower. Even this rule was relaxed, when the board of directors felt that the property was being acquired at a bargain, if the borrower enjoyed a reputation for honesty, sobriety, and industry. In any event both the real estate acquired and the member's stock were put up as collateral to protect the loan.

At the end of the year the earnings of the association, minus any expenses, which were small, and any losses, which had to be calculated annually, were credited to the share accounts on a pro rata basis. The credits to the share account thus cumulated from dues and from credited income. Charged against this account were unpaid fees and fines. Whenever these net credits were equal to the amount of the original mortgage, the shares were declared to be matured and were used to offset and cancel the loan. In the beginning, this terminated the member's need for the association. He had reached the goal for which he had set out. Other members would continue paying their dues and borrowing funds needed to finance the purchase or construction of their homes. The "last man" would in effect borrow his own savings and hence have no obligation to pay interest.

Early Withdrawal Practices Meantime, if any member changed his mind about staying with the project until it had run its course, either because he moved away from the neighborhood or for any other reason, another "F" was added to the fees, fines, and forfeitures mentioned above. Withdrawal of funds was penalized by the forfeiture of a large part of credited dividends—commonly 50 percent or more. In some of the early associations, as much as 90 percent of credited dividends was withheld on premature withdrawal. Such penalties bore heavily upon the one who suffered the penalty but benefited those who stayed with the project.

In order not to embarrass the operations of any associations too greatly, any request for the withdrawal of funds by any member had to be submitted to the association 30 days before such withdrawal could become effective. Then each withdrawing member's name was placed on a list to await his turn, which came only after those ahead of him had been satisfied. When each member's withdrawal request was reached, his shares could be redeemed by devoting to this purpose "one half of the funds in the treasury" on each meeting night. Such withdrawal procedures were fixed in the bylaws, presumably by the members of the association. By restricting withdrawals in this manner, a part of the funds coming into the association could be used to make loans, thus keeping the association from dying by the process of having its funds withdrawn as fast as they came into the treasury. Because the withdrawing member was required not only to give 30 days' notice but to take his turn, he never knew when he would be able to get back his investment or any part of it. This plan of withdrawal has been commonly used in some sections of the country until quite recently.

Since the maturity of the shares, which resulted in the cancellation of the mortgage, was governed not only by monthly dues paid by the borrower but by the amount of such variables as premiums on loans, fees, fines, and forfeitures assessed against him and other members and losses for which other members might be primarily responsible, no borrower ever knew when his mortgage would be fully paid. Indeed, he might have credits to his share account almost equal to his mortgage account, only to find that heavy losses would reduce the former substantially without affecting the latter in the slightest degree.

Prepayments of loans faster than the pattern contemplated under the share-accumulation sinking-fund plan were often permitted. In some associations they were even encouraged by providing that if a loan were completely repaid within eight years after it was made, the borrower would receive a refund equal to one eighth of his loan premium for each year less than eight that the loan was outstanding.

Share Loans Even some of the early building associations permitted their members to borrow against their stock as collateral. This plan was encouraged as an alternative to the withdrawal of their funds. Loans could frequently be arranged more quickly than withdrawals and at less cost to the borrower, with forfeitures taken into account. No borrower was ever permitted to borrow up to the full amount of his share credits or even up to the withdrawal value of his account. The borrower could either repay his share loan or continue to pay on his stock until it matured. At maturity he was entitled to receive the par value of his shares less the amount of his loan, any unpaid interest, fees, fines, and so on. Borrowers on share accounts were forced to compete with borrowers on real estate by paying higher premiums than those offered by the latter if the share loan was to be granted. Sometimes premiums offered were very high, 30 percent or more.

Serial Associations In order not to put a premium upon late joiners in a terminating association, anyone joining after the date of organization was forced to make an initial contribution equal to the existing credits per share. Lack of accumulated capital foreclosed this possibility after the credits were of substantial size. This denied participation to many who would have liked to join the association. With the machinery all set up and in operation, an American idea was added that had not been commonly used in England. Why not start a new series with new members? Thus was the serial association born. In effect it amounted to a succession of terminating associations. Whenever it appeared that there was sufficient demand, a new series was started. This meant increasing the number of meetings, perhaps to one a week instead of one each month.

Managerial duties increased, and the secretary and attorney began to receive compensation in the form of fees. Directors, who supplanted the trustees of early voluntary associations when the corporate form of organization was introduced, still served without compensation. The mere introduction of the use of serial associations did not change the methods of operating these associations. The same methods of lending their money on mortgages were continued. Nor should we think of serial associations with their weekly meetings as something belonging to ancient history. Some of them are still in existence and are rendering a service to their members in the face of competition from institutions following more modern methods of operation. The groups still using them possess, to a high degree, a community spirit based upon personal friendship rather than upon impersonal business relationships.

Savings Members Gradually the need for more attention to the desires of savings members began to be felt in the operation of building associations. In some cases the member who started with full expectations of acquiring a home by this means changed his plans or had them changed for him. Perhaps the lady of his choice said "No" instead of "Yes." There were other members who were not ready to buy or build a home even when the credits to their shares accumulated to a point where they reached their face value. Other thrifty people wanted an opportunity to accumulate savings but had no interest in homeownership. Even the member who had secured a debt-free home through the aid of his building association wished to continue as a member of the association, because he had acquired thrifty habits and liked them.

While homeownership was the major objective of these building associations, there was nothing to prevent a member from taking out cash by the maturity of his shares instead of through the process of giving back a mortgage as evidence of a loan. Hence, the practice of maturing shares in cash gradually developed. Even in such an event some members, well satisfied with the returns they had received from their investment, were loath to withdraw the cash due them. They preferred to leave their investment intact or even to add to it as before.

MODERN ASSOCIATIONS

Change of Character of Associations With the emergence of the savings member who did not borrow from the association, the whole character of the association underwent a radical change. From a purely local community association of friends, anxious to help one another acquire homes, it was on the verge of becoming a financial institution equipped to serve two distinct groups of people, many of whom had no direct interest in the others. On the one hand, there were the thrifty people who needed the assistance of a financial institution equipped to care for their savings against the time when they would be needed for any purpose. On the other hand, another group of people needed financial assistance in financing the homes of their choice. Some might save systematically until they accumulated enough to make the down payment on a home. Thereafter they preferred to make payments on a mortgage debt instead of on share accounts to be later offset against the mortgage. Others might continue to build savings accounts after the mortgage was paid off. Still others preferred to borrow the amount needed over and above the funds accumulated by other means to buy a home.

This change in character broadened the scope of operations and brought other changes in thrift and home-financing institution operations. Among these was a gradual change in name to recognize the new position of savings members. The word "savings" began to be used in some combination with "building" and "loan." Gradually the modern standard pattern of the savings and loan association began to take shape. This is the one most commonly used today, except in Louisiana where those operating under a state charter are still called "homestead associations," and in Massachusetts where the corresponding name is "cooperative bank." This latter name has become so well established that even federal savings and loan associations are commonly spoken of in that state as banks.

Except for surviving evidences of the serial type of operations in a few sections of the country, most associations today are thought of as having a permanent life. Because of the local character of their early development, there are differences in their pattern of financing which are somewhat confusing to their customers who move from one section of the country to another. Differences in names have already been mentioned. In Ohio, in 1868, within one year after the first association was established within that state, the legislature gave such institutions the right to accept deposits on which a fixed rate of interest was paid. This was certainly a definite recognition of the new importance of savings members.

With the change in the character of these associations, the older emphasis upon forced savings gradually disappeared. With its disappearance went most of the use of fees, fines, and forfeitures. Investing members were encouraged to bring in their savings in either regular or irregular amounts and at regular or irregular intervals, and to withdraw them as they needed them. Penalties took the form of loss or reduction of income. Borrowers were put on their own responsibility without reference to the performance of other borrowers. Delinquencies were dealt with in terms of those responsible, but losses were not charged against those who met their obligations promptly.

In Ohio, the separation of borrowers from savings members became so complete that there appeared to be some doubt about the ability of savings and loan associations to maintain their tax advantages because of their presumed mutual status. This fetish of mutuality was continued by having each borrower become a member by the purchase of a dollar's worth of shares. In the more recent organization of federal savings and loan associations, even this dollar purchase is eliminated in favor of a statutory declaration that a borrower is automatically a member of the association.

Types of Accounts With the new emphasis upon savings accounts came a classification of shares into groups that undertook to represent the needs of various types of investors. For the investor whose shares had matured but who nevertheless wished to retain his investment, "full-paid shares" (sometimes called "income shares") were provided. These came to have a face value of $100. Dividends were paid in cash. "Prepaid shares" set a pattern that has since been followed by E bonds issued by the government. Purchased at $75, they matured at $100 through the credit of dividends over a series of years. There is no magic in these amounts: $700 could be left to grow into $1,000; or $360 to grow into $500; and so on. The prepaid share is simply the plan arranged for the lump-sum investor who does not need his dividends in the form of cash as they accrue. Many of these then became full-paid shares. "Installment thrift shares" encouraged the small investor dependent upon earnings to set aside a definite amount each month to add to his account in his savings and loan association. This type of share emphasizes the advantages of regular savings habits. To clinch the argument in their favor, some associations either penalized failure to make all payments on time by the assessment of fines for late payments or rewarded the shareholder who met all payments as scheduled by giving him an extra bonus in the form of an increased dividend payment

In contrast to the emphasis upon regularity of payments under installment thrift shares, the Dayton plan (originated in Dayton, Ohio) encouraged thrifty people to make additions to their investments when and as their resources permitted. Each account holder established his own pattern of savings, and his contributions were rewarded in proportion to his individual accomplishments. In keeping with the removal of pressure to save, these shares were given the name "optional savings shares." While some associations still favor the practice of encouraging regular savings, most savings and loan associations have long since adopted the practice of accepting savings at the option of their owners.

Savings and loan associations started out as mutual institutions with no distinction among the claims of those who contributed capital. Later, some were organized with a permanent capital in the form of nonwithdrawable "guarantee stock," so-called because it was supposed to serve as a cushion to absorb possible losses which might otherwise have been assessed against ordinary shares. Where guarantee stock was used, its ownership was concentrated in the management. Other investors received as evidence of their commitments a variety of certificates—fullpaid, prepaid, installment, accumulative, and so forth. These corresponded to the types of shares already discussed. The accumulative certificate was similar to the Dayton plan share.

Deposits, used by some Ohio associations, were sometimes protected by nonwithdrawable stock. In other cases no cushion of investment was provided, since shares as well as deposits were freely withdrawable. In fact, in many instances shares and deposits were so similar in character that great confusion resulted. Some investors never were sure whether they owned shares or deposits.

In recent years there has been a distinct movement in the direction of simplifying the capital structure of savings and loan associations. The pattern followed by mutual associations—the predominant type—calls for only two types of accounts: savings accounts and investment accounts. The former are optional as to amounts and times of deposit, although systematic saving is still encouraged in some quarters. Earnings are credited to these accounts. Investment accounts serve the needs of lump-sum investors who prefer to receive their earnings distributions in cash.

With the passage of the Housing and Urban Development Act of 1968, savings and loan associations were permitted to use the terms "deposit" and "interest" in place of "share accounts" and "dividends." They were also allowed to issue notes, bonds, debentures, and long-term certificates of deposit for the first time.

Dividend Policies Like most other operating policies of savings and loan associations, the current practice in relation to declaration of dividends shows an abrupt break with the past. In the early days all dividends were required to be distributed in the form of credits to share accounts. Gradually, small reserves were permitted, and later undivided profit or surplus accounts began to be added to balance sheets. Currently, approximately 90 percent of the net earnings of savings and loan associations are distributed as dividends. The other 10 percent is added to reserve and undivided profit accounts. Associations differ in the amounts which they allocate to these two accounts, but in general the annual additions to the reserve accounts is considerably greater than the additions to the undivided profits account.

Savings and loan associations are now subject to corporate income taxes. According to the tax formula under which they operate, credits to a reserve for bad debts are deducted before arriving at the amount of taxable income; credits to undivided profit are considered a part of income that may be taxable. As a consequence credits to undivided profit are much smaller than they have been in the past.

Reserves are presumed to provide the association with a means of absorbing losses. Undivided profits can be used for any purpose, including absorption of losses. In addition, many managers hope to pay dividends from undivided profits, if necessary, during years when earnings cannot support adequate dividend policies. During good earnings years, dividends are paid on a basis of competitive rates rather than of available earnings of the association. This permits a retention of some part of good earnings for distribution at a later time.

Dividend rates vary with the general level of money costs. In 1970, for example, during a period of rising interest rates, the average rate paid increased from 5 percent in January to 5.33 percent in December. Geography plays a considerable part in determining dividend rates. In money-plentiful areas—such as parts of New England—some dividend rates are a bit less than average. In money-scarce areas—such as California, Nevada, and Alaska—higher rates are common. In 1966, Congress authorized the establishment of ceilings on dividends paid on savings balances by members of the Federal Home Loan Bank System. This was the first time for statutory control of dividend policy. In 1970, these ceilings were extended to include all savings institutions whether or not they were members of the Federal Home Loan Bank System. This action was largely directed at eastern mutual savings banks that paid rates above the ceilings allowed controlled members. Federal Home Loan Bank Board ceilings on dividend rates at December 31, 1971 are set forth in Table 11-1.

Withdrawals Early building societies discouraged withdrawal of funds before the shares matured. Forfeiture penalties were very heavy. Later, when greater recognition was given to savings members, these penalties were gradually relaxed until they quite generally disappeared. Even then withdrawal at the will of the investor was discouraged in several ways. Until quite recently these associations have looked upon liquid assets as idle assets. Partly as the result of the sad experiences of the 1930s, when investors placed great pressure upon the savings and loan associations by demanding withdrawal of funds even when fear alone dictated such demands, and partly because of the accumulation of unusual liquidity in the form of government bonds purchased during World War II, the attitude of the associations toward liquidity and withdrawals has changed materially.

Even though the laws under which they operate recognize the frozen nature of their assets and consequently permit them to go on notice, if necessary, when withdrawal demands accumulate most of their managers recognize that, in most sections of the country, failure to meet

TABLE 11-1
Interest Rate Ceilings on Savings at Federal Home Loan Bank Member Associations

	Percent
Regular passbook	5.00*
90-day notice	5.25
Certificates:	
90–179-day maturity	5.25
180–364-day maturity	5.50†
1–2-year maturity	5.75‡
2–10-year maturity	6.00§
$100,000 minimum denomination:	
60–89-day maturity	6.50
90–179-day maturity	6.75
184–364-day maturity	7.00
1–10-year maturity	7.50

* Massachusetts associations authorized to pay up to 5.25 percent on any regular savings account and up to 5.50 percent on a certificate account of $1,000 or more with a fixed or minimum term or qualifying period of at least 180 days, to maintain parity with mutual savings banks.
† $1,000 minimum denomination.
‡ $5,000 minimum denomination.
§ $10,000 minimum denomination.
Source: United States Savings and Loan League.

all reasonable withdrawal requests promptly is tantamount to an admission of failure. Increased primary liquidity ratios, combined with insurance of accounts which should forestall most fear withdrawals and with access to secondary liquidity through the Federal Home Loan Bank System, should make withdrawals much easier in the future than in the past. Savings and loan associations cannot afford to carry as much liquidity as commercial banks. Therefore they should not encourage the investment of "hot" money which will probably leave them as soon as its speculatively minded owners find a more satisfactory form of commitment for their funds. Neither should they represent to their investors that they pay on demand. Nevertheless, their performance should be somewhat more liberal than their promises.

The great bulk of funds invested in savings and loan associations comes from middle-class Americans. These people do not save money as such. To them saving has come to mean deferred spending. They save for a purpose or a series of purposes. Some of these purposes are definite in amount and in timing; others are more indefinite in both amounts and timing. When the time arrives that the investor wishes to withdraw his funds from a savings and loan association to pay the costs of something for which he has been saving, he is entitled to withdraw such funds as he needs. The management that caters to this kind of investor and anticipates his needs will attract his patronage.

The amount of liquidity needed to meet withdrawal requirements and to serve the needs of borrowers varies, of course, with economic conditions and, to a smaller degree, with the habits of the customers of each savings and loan association. Since those conditions cannot be foretold accurately, liquidity policies must be adjusted to meet the greatest needs rather than the smallest. From this point of view, it appears that a desirable liquidity policy should include the following elements: (1) at least 10 percent of withdrawable accounts in cash, government bonds, and "near-money" assets; (2) insurance of accounts to minimize fear withdrawals; and (3) membership in the Home Loan Bank System to provide secondary liquidity as needed. Naturally, keeping 10 percent of withdrawable accounts in nonearning cash and low-earning investments will reduce association earning power somewhat. Experience shows that current investors in savings and loan associations are not primarily interested in a speculative rate of return. Their first question is, "Is my investment safe?" The next one is, "Can I get my money back when I need it?"

In spite of the fact that savings and loan associations normally pay a higher rate of return than their competitors, they have had no monopoly in attracting the savings funds of the thrifty people of their communities. This circumstance supports the position taken above. The investing public is not yet able to discriminate in its choice in order to select the investment outlet that provides the best combination of safety, reasonable availability, and a fair return commensurate with safety and availability.

Liquidity Reserve Regulation The present liquidity reserve requirements being enforced by regulatory authorities are somewhat less onerous than those recommended as desirable in the foregoing paragraphs. Prior to 1968, the Federal Home Loan Bank Board was authorized by statute to require associations that were system members to maintain from 4 to 8 percent of their savings and borrowings due within a year in cash and U.S. government obligations. An amendment to the law in 1968 increased the span from 4 to 10 percent and expanded the assets qualifying as reserves to include federal agency obligations, bankers' acceptances, and certificates of deposit.

Within the general requirement, the Board has introduced a new requirement of short-term liquidity. Effective January 1, 1972, associations were required to hold at least 2½ percent of savings and borrowings due in one year or less in the form of cash, U.S. government or federal agency obligations due in 18 months or less, and bankers' acceptances and certificates of deposit due in not more than 6 months.

From December 27, 1950 to March 1, 1961, the overall liquidity requirement was maintained at 6 percent. Since that time, the rate has fluctuated between 5½ percent and 7½ percent where it stood at year-end 1971.

Several states have their own liquidity reserve requirements. Hawaii, Indiana, Maine, Massachusetts, Nevada, New Hampshire, New Jersey, North Carolina, North Dakota, and Washington have statutory requirements. Oklahoma and Wisconsin have acted by regulation. The requirements range from a lump sum of $10,000 in North Dakota to a 10 to 14 percent range in Washington, based on asset size and community population density. Some states impose a 5 percent requirement, and others require higher percentages up to 10. In addition to cash and federal government obligations, the states generally permit the inclusion of direct obligations of the states and their subdivisions, securities guaranteed by the United States, and stock in the Federal Home Loan Banks.

At the 1970 year-end, total cash and U.S. government securities held by all savings and loan associations were $15.5 billion and total savings balances and advances from the Federal Home Loan Banks were $157.1 billion. On the basis of these figures, the liquidity ratio on a nationwide scale at that time stood at about 10 percent.

Savings and Withdrawals In some respects the net inflow of savings is more significant than gross savings. Since 1950, the annual ratio of withdrawals to new investments has ranged from 60 to 70 percent, leaving from 30 to 40 percent of new investments in the associations. This shows not only the steady growth of net investments of savings in savings and loan associations, but also that these institutions are serving the needs of their investors by making their funds available as they are needed. The fairly heavy withdrawals indicated above present a sharp contrast with the records of early savings and loan associations, made at a time when withdrawals were discouraged by long notice periods and by heavy forfeitures of credited dividends. While savings and loan associations are not demand institutions, most of them are making funds available to their owners upon demand.

Reserves One interesting change in savings and loan practices over the years that affects real estate finance is the evolution of reserve policies. As has been set forth in the discussion of the early associations, in the beginning no reserves were built up. Adhering strictly to the concept of mutuality, since gains were credited to the accounts of the members it seemed logical to charge them with the losses. As a result, year by year all profits were credited, leaving nothing to absorb whatever losses might occur. Hence there was nothing else to do but prorate such losses over the number of shares subscribed. A further justification for this practice is that dividend rates were relatively high. Consequently, they were expected to contain a risk element which might require that credited dividends be taken away when losses occurred.

Gradually, but in a niggardly fashion, the legislation which fixed the pattern of operation of these associations was amended to give their managements some leeway in retaining earnings for the purpose of setting up reserves against possible losses. Even then the amounts so retained were strictly limited, to make sure that the mutual principle would still be observed by crediting each year all earnings except the amounts set aside in reserves. Through successive amendments to regulatory legislation, these savings and loan associations came to be recognized as entities instead of aggregates of individual members. For this reason, increasing discretion was given to the management to determine the amount of reserves required. Legislative ceilings over reserves have tended to disappear in recent years.

With the introduction of insurance of accounts of savings and loan associations, the pendulum has swung in the opposite direction. To make sure that it might not be called upon to carry too heavy a load, the Federal Savings and Loan Insurance Corporation (FSLIC) has tended to insist upon reserve floors to serve as a primary shock absorber when losses occur. Each insured association is required to build its own reserves for this purpose. Even uninsured associations have built larger reserves in recent years. The rate of increase in reserves is a function of several variables. The two most important are the rate of growth of the association and the spread between the rates of interest charged on mortgage loans and the dividends paid for the use of money. A rapidly growing association may find it necessary to slow down its growth occasionally, take a breathing spell, and increase its reserve ratio.

Since 1964, the FSLIC has had in effect a new regulation to standardize reserve requirements for its insured members. For purposes of classification, institutions are currently tested by two ratios: (1) the "benchmark," which measures the percentage that the federal insurance reserve account shall be of the total savings account; and (2) the ratio of adjusted net worth to specified, or "risk," assets.

The bench mark test requires that all insured associations shall have a minimum of 5 percent of savings in the reserve account by the time they have achieved their 20th anniversary in business. For institutions less than 20 years old, the requirement is prorated; thus, at the end of the first year, the requirement is 0.25 percent; at the end of the second year, 0.50 percent; and so on. In addition to this bench mark level, an association must reserve for "scheduled items" (20 percent in 1965 and later years). Scheduled items are defined to include all slow loans not insured or guaranteed, 20 percent of slow loans that are insured or guranteed, all real estate owned, investment securities in default, and similar properties.

In applying the second ratio, institutions are classified by present ratio status, amount of specified assets, and age. Since July 1, 1966, any institution having a ratio of adjusted net worth to specified assets of 10 percent or over is not required to add to its reserve. Where ratios are between 8 percent and 10 percent, the required addition is an amount equal to 5 percent of net income after federal income taxes but before dividends. For institutions with ratios less than 8 percent, age and size become important. If the institution has been in business at least 20 years and has specified assets over $10 million, it must credit to the reserve account the greater of 5 percent of net income or 6 percent it credits 5 percent of net income, without alternative. There are three of growth in net assets. If its specified assets are less than $10 million, formulas applicable to institutions that have not reached their 20th anniversary:

Category (by specified assets)	Formula
(1) Less than $25 million	5 percent of net income
(2) $25–50 million	Greater of 5 percent of net income or 5 percent of growth in specified assets
(3) Over $50 million	Greater of 5 percent of net income or 6 percent of growth in specified assets

During 1970, provisions requiring reserve allocations based on percentage of growth in specified assets or 5 percent of net income were suspended indefinitely to provide some flexibility for dealing with unusual stringencies in the mortgage market at that time. This left the reserve requirement at an amount sufficient to meet the bench mark test and 20 percent of the scheduled items. By legislative authority granted in 1970, the FSLIC also has authority to extend the 20-year bench mark standard to 30 years at its option.

Closely related to its reserve policy is the association's attitude toward undivided profits or surpluses. Retained earnings afford two major advantages to the association: (1) They provide free capital upon which no dividends need be paid. For example, suppose that general reserves and undivided profits equal 15 percent of assets. Suppose that the current dividend rate is 4.75 percent, but, in a lean year, the association earns only 4.25 percent net on its total assets. It can still pay 4.75 percent dividends on its accounts without using past earnings. (2) If its earnings are not even that good, it can use retained earnings in the form of surplus or undivided profits to meet insurance reserve requirements and to continue its regular dividend payments even in lean years. This helps to maintain the confidence of investors and to retain their funds for real estate financing purposes.

Hesitancy to Use Reserves Even though reserves are developed for the purpose of absorbing such losses as may occur in the future, the institution which builds them frequently hesitates to use them when losses appear. For example, in a time of depressed real estate values, a financial institution may have on its books a reserve equivalent to 10 percent of its mortgage balances. If it is forced to foreclose some of its mortgages and take title to the real estate which secures them, it may hesitate to put this real estate on its books at its immediately realizable cash value, charging the loss against its reserves. Instead it is more likely to carry the real estate at the same amount as its foreclosed mortgage. Indeed, it may add foreclosure costs and delinquent interest to the real estate account, unless it is prohibited from doing so by the laws under which it operates.

If it hesitates to take a loss on foreclosed mortgages, if one exists, the financial institution may hesitate also to sell its real estate at a realistic figure. It may prefer to sell it at prices inflated enough to justify its inflated book value, even though the purchaser has little or no down payment. The inflated real estate thus again becomes an inflated mortgage, and the book reserves remain untouched. If an upsurge in real estate values squeezes the water out of inflated values, the questionable reserve may become more real. Otherwise, taking of the loss is postponed but not eliminated. Meantime, holding real estate against a hope of recovery in real estate values may not always be a paying business. It might be better to take whatever can be obtained for some of it and charge the loss against the reserve that was built up for just such a purpose.

Measuring Losses Many real estate financial institutions, like many other business enterprises, probably have difficulty in defining, with any degree of accuracy, the amount of loss suffered in any mortgage transaction that results in a foreclosure sale. Even the net proceeds of the sale, after sales expenses are taken into account, subtracted from the unpaid principal amount of the debt plus interest added to the time of the sale, will not produce an accurate measure of loss. Other items of expense, such as the cost of time spent by the salaried attorneys, appraisers, and even supervisory officers, are essentially a part of the loss. Bookkeeping costs between the time of default and of disposal of the foreclosed property might well be added. These and other items normally charged to overhead expense could easily be prorated over mortgage losses instead.

On the other side of the operating statement, there is a tendency to overestimate the amount of loss properly chargeable to foreclosed real estate. For example, while it is customary to build reserves against possible losses, they are likely to be the result of an afterthought. More often than not, additions to the reserve account are the residual amounts left over after direct expenses and dividends are provided for. A more realistic approach would be to consider additions to reserves before dividends are declared.

Some students of this question are inclined to go so far as to recommend that a serious attempt be made to measure the risk element in each mortgage and build a reserve accordingly to offset it. The practicability of this prescription is open to question. A middle course follows the path of occasional review of the mortgage portfolio for the purpose of classifying its contents into risk classes. Then each class or group of mortgages—in the aggregate—may be assigned a reserve ratio that seems best to suit the situation. For example, group A might consist of low percentage mortgages, on properties in the best locations, and which have a low moral hazard. The elements of risk in such mortgages might be considered so negligible that they can be disregarded. In other words, no specific reserve is set up against them. In group B the risk factor might justify a deduction of 10 percent of the income annually to build a reserve against possible losses; group C, 20 percent; group D, 30 percent; and so on. Logically, the interest rates charged on mortgages in each of these groups should be adjusted to the risk factor.

Another method of trying to accomplish the same results by following a rule-of-thumb procedure is to add to the rate of return upon riskless investments the cost of servicing loans, and to subtract the sum from the interest rates charged on the mortgages carried in the portfolio to find the risk ratio. For example, suppose that the effective rate of interest on government bonds is 5.10 percent and that the average cost of servicing loans, including general overhead expenses, is 1 percent. If the average interest rate on mortgages is 7 percent, the equation 7 minus (5.10 plus 1) would leave 0.90 percent. This would be presumed to measure the risk factor. Logic would dictate that this 0.90 percent be set aside in a loss reserve to protect the association against possible future losses.

In case the mortgagee follows a practice of using variable interest rates, the higher the rate charged, the greater the amount to be set aside in the reserve. This practice too is consistent with good business policy, since one excuse for the higher rates of interest on the mortgages is the greater risk assumed.

If either of the above plans, or an acceptable substitute, were followed, losses would be accounted for currently instead of at the time of crisis only. If the mortgagee should be fortunate enough to avoid the use of the loss reserves set up, so much the better. But any actual loss which had been accounted for in the manner indicated should cause no embarrassment at the time it occurs, provided it did not result in a greater drain upon the reserve account than had been anticipated. Logically, a loss so measured and anticipated in building a reserve to provide for it would really not be a loss at all. It would simply mean that a hoped-for excess profit had not been realized.

Second Mortgage Associations For the most part, savings and loan associations have insisted upon holding first liens against the properties on which they have granted loans. One notable exception was the type of association developed in Philadelphia years ago. There the first lien was normally held by a trust company. The savings and loan association then held a junior lien. Most of the institutions which used this plan were small neighborhood associations. It has been estimated that at one time Philadelphia had more than 3,000 neighborhood institutions, all small in size and many taking second mortgages as evidence of their claim against their borrowing members. With this large number of associations there could be no "business" of savings and loan operation. They were all one-night-a-month associations, with a secretary who served 20 or more associations at one time, each meeting on a different night so that he could be present at all meetings when dues and interest were paid. Although Pennsylvania was one of the three leading savings and loan states before the 1930 depression, it has been reliably estimated that not as many as 50 people made their living there from operating savings and loan associations.

Savings and Loan Holding Companies Over the last few years, several holding companies have been formed placing under common control groups of stock-type savings and loan associations. This activity has been greatest in California and Texas, although other states have participated to a lesser degree. The original popularity of savings and loan holding companies as vehicles for public ownership lay in the spectacular growth rate of savings and loan associations. In particular, the West Coast has been consistently a money-scarce area for lenders on real estate security. Holding companies could offer the advantages inherent in more specialized management. They could achieve broader insurance coverage for holders of large accounts by placing up to $20,000 in each of several subsidiaries, thus attracting institutional investments on a large scale from the lower dividend-paying areas in the East.

First Charter Financial, Great Western Financial Corporation, Financial Federation, and Imperial Corporation of America are representative holding companies that are listed on the New York Stock Exchange. First Charter Financial had savers' accounts in 1971 totaling $2,343 million in 54 branches in the San Francisco Bay and Greater Los Angeles areas. Great Western Financial had $2,745 million in savings in seven associations broadly serving all of California. Financial Federation reported $973 million in savings in 11 associations throughout southern California. Imperial Corporation of America was more diversified with $1,279 million in savings distributed among 14 associations, of which 5 were located in California, 6 in Texas, 2 in Kansas, and 1 in Colorado.

After early spectacular rises, savings and loan holding company stocks experienced substantial declines. A change in the federal income tax law to a new formula that rendered earnings of savings and loan associations taxable; a rise in mortgage foreclosures; a narrowing of the spread between dividend and mortgage loan rates; a sense of increased hazard in new ventures in land development and construction; and the prospect of further regulation by the Federal Home Loan Bank Board and the states involved dampened the ardor of public investors for these shares. As the mortgage risks have declined recently in California, the equity values of the holding companies have increased. An unfortunate side effect of the volatility of these share prices has been the confusion in the minds of some savers with accounts in the subsidiary institutions. It is not always clear to them that their accounts are not jeopardized by the market gyrations of the holding company shares. In fact, this tinge of uncertainty toward the savings and loan business has somewhat affected the sense of security that savers had before the publicly-held holding companies entered the field.

QUESTIONS AND PROBLEMS

1. What were the origins of the savings and loan association?
2. What were fees, fines, and forfeitures? How and why were they invoked?
3. What were terminating associations and how did they differ from serial associations?
4. Describe the share-accumulation sinking-fund loan plan.
5. Under the practices of early associations, what penalties were assessed against a member who withdrew from the organization before completion of the project for which the association was organized?
6. What were Dayton plan associations, and how did they expand the scope of savings and loan activities?
7. What factors govern dividend policies of savings and loan associations?
8. What liquidity problems are created by the right of investors to withdraw funds from savings and loan associations?
9. What policies should be followed to maintain liquidity of a savings and loan association?
10. What methods can you suggest for determining what amount should be appropriated as a reserve for losses on mortgage loans? Are your methods in accord with those adopted by the FSLIC?
11. How have savings and loan holding companies affected the savings and loan business?

12

Savings and Loan Associations (continued)

Lending Policies As specialists in the field of real estate finance, savings and loan associations are the primary sources of financial assistance for a great many mortgagors. For that reason their lending policies become a matter of great importance to anyone interested in financing real estate. Although each association is managed by its officers and its board of directors, we must first take a look outside of the management if we would understand its lending policies. These are determined in part by general economic conditions, in part by governmental actions, and in part by competitors.

General economic conditions play a major part in setting the lending pattern of any association at a particular time. If the general level of interest rates is low, savings and loan associations must take this into account or go out of business. If new money is coming in slowly, loan applications will be more carefully screened than if idle funds are piling up. If collections of outstanding loans become more difficult because of reduced incomes of borrowers, refinancing of loans for new borrowers will not be as easy. If real estate activity begins to slow down in the face of the maintenance of a high level of cash receipts, the association may be forced to liberalize its lending policy to keep its funds employed.

Governmental actions affect the lending policies of savings and loan associations both positively and negatively. On the negative side, regulatory bodies set boundaries beyond which associations may not go. It is not uncommon to prohibit loans on property located more than 100 miles from the home office of the association. Experience has taught that adequate servicing of loans requires a concentration of security within a readily accessible area. Likewise, similar restrictions prohibit:

the taking of a junior lien as the primary security for a loan; loans on unimproved property; the making of loans without the signed reports of appraisers; loans to officers and directors except on their own homes; loans in excess of statutory or regulatory percentages of loan to appraised value; and so forth.

On the positive side, the actions of governmental agencies frequently determine the lending policies of savings and loan associations, whether the latter like such actions or not. In recent years the lending patterns approved by such agencies as the FHA and the Veterans Administration in setting up regulations for GI home loans have set in motion irresistible forces which savings and loan associations dare not ignore. Even though the assistance offered by these agencies is not used, lending policies are nevertheless colored by their programs. Low-interest rates, high-percentage loans, prepayment privileges, common use of the monthly payment direct reduction loan plan, and so on, have all been forced upon lenders of all types by governmental agencies. Indeed, the actions of some governmental agencies have forced other similar agencies to change their own restrictions in order to permit the institutions they regulate to stay in business. State laws respond to changes in federal policies. One federal agency is even sometimes required to adjust its plans to the changes effected by another federal agency.

Competitors, with or without the assistance of governmental agencies, frequently serve notice upon savings and loan managements that they must change their lending policies, "or else." An aggressive management that adopts a liberal lending policy and convinces the potential borrowers in its market that it has a more advantageous lending plan can soon develop imitators among its competitors. Indeed, the competitors who fail to conform to changes which appear to be permanent in character will probably cease to be competitors.

With this background of lending policies to which the management of each association must conform, we now turn to those elements of a lending program which are subject to the discretion of individual association management.

Types of Property As home-financing institutions, savings and loan associations not only give first attention to single-family dwellings, but they are probably best equipped to make sound loans in this area. Next in order come two- to four-family dwellings; small properties combining business and residential uses; residential real estate consisting of more than four-family units; large business property; special-purpose real estate; and so forth. As a general rule, these institutions have encountered least difficulty with loans against owner-occupied homes as security. Over the years the personal relationship between the borrower and the lender has worked to the advantage of both. By knowing the capacities of the borrower, the lending institution has been able to make adjustments in times of stress without taking too great risk and without losing a customer. Even in times of reduced income, the homeowner must have a place to live. As a choice between retaining possession and a chance to continue to own his home, on the one hand, and moving into a rental property, on the other, he will cling to the former if possible. Meantime the lender prefers not to take the security away from the borrower except as a last resort. When most homeowner borrowers default on their obligations, the market is likely to be glutted with distress real estate. The lender prefers not to own much of it at such a time.

In order to meet the real estate needs of a community, lending institutions must assist in financing other types of property as well as homes. Frequently a savings and loan association is about the only source of financial assistance for this purpose. In times of excess cash, some operators look outside the home-financing fields for loans. As a general rule, the farther savings and loan associations get away from owner-occupied single-family dwellings, the more risk they run. This is true not only from the nature of the property but from the limitations upon their own capacity. Business properties and, particularly, special-purpose real estate possess hazards with which savings and loan operators may not be too familiar.

What is said here is recognized in the laws which regulate this type of financial institution. For example, the rules and regulations governing the operation of federal savings and loan associations provide that not more than 20 percent of an association's assets may be invested in mortgages on real estate other than closely defined residential properties. Generally speaking, managers recognize their limitations in making loans outside of the field of family residences and do not approach this 20 percent limitation upon other real estate security. It is for the protection of investors in institutions whose managers may not admit their limitations that such a restriction is necessary. Some managers will not consider applications for loans on special-purpose properties. Others are attracted by the higher rates of interest obtainable therefrom and the lower percentage loans usually granted

Moral Hazard One factor which helps to determine the answer to a particular loan application is the moral hazard of the loan. Even though the real estate is offered as security, the lender does not look forward to the time when he will take over the security to satisfy the loan. Neither does he relish the possibility of bickering and continued pressure upon the borrower in order to collect payments as they fall due. Two questions should be settled to the satisfaction of the lender before he grants the loan: (1) Will the borrower be likely to be able to meet his obligations? (2) Will he be willing to do so without causing trouble? Together, the answers to these two questions provide a measure of the moral hazard. Even though the property appears to provide ample security for the loan, if the borrower has difficulty in carrying it because loan payments represent too heavy a burden, the loan is not a good one for the lender to have on his books.

In seeking answers to questions about the capacity and the character of the borrower, lending institutions make free use of credit reports from local credit bureaus. Membership in such an agency is a must for real estate financing institutions. Even individuals who deal in real estate mortgages will do well to make use of the files of credit bureaus. Here the debt-paying capacity and habits of prospective borrowers are spread upon the records. In addition, references are sometimes useful, provided they come from people who know the applicant for the loan more than socially. Finally, the lender can ascertain from a conversation with the applicant and his wife much information that will be useful to him in measuring the moral hazard.

The FHA considers the moral hazard so important in reviewing applications for mortgage insurance that it has developed a definite rating sheet for borrowers to determine the following: On the subject of the attitude of the borrower, it tries to measure his social and economic characteristics and his motivation in relation to the transaction under consideration. In other words, does he think in terms of homeownership or of cheap rent for the period of time his mortgage commitment will provide? On the subject of ability to pay, the FHA looks into the applicant's employability and earnings stability; the relation of his total obligations to the demands of the loan applied for; and the relation of his income to these obligations.

Of the five "Cs" of credit that are subject to examination by financial institutions—capital, character, capacity, collateral, and conditions—character and capacity measure the moral hazard. In specific instances, in the face of adverse economic conditions and in the presence of continued declines in the value of the collateral, the character of the borrower has been such that he has continued to meet his obligations so long as his earning capacity permitted. On the other hand, in spite of capacity and collateral value, a discontented borrower can make plenty of trouble for a mortgagee.

Perhaps the moral hazard is greatest in cases where the property falls into the hands of milkers who, with little or no investment in it, proceed to take all they can out of it before the mortgagee is permitted to take over. By taking from the property all they can in rent without paying interest or principal installments, taxes, or repairs, they complicate the problems of the mortgagee who finally secures possession after exhausting both patience and legal barriers set up by the milker in control of the property. Such a person usually evades any personal responsibility for his own acts in regard to the property.

In contrast, the experience of the Home Owners' Loan Corporation demonstrates the low moral hazard in making loans to most people. In spite of high percentage loans made by the HOLC to more than a million homeowners during the greatest depression the country has ever experienced, more than 80 percent of the mortgagors made good on their mortgage obligations. The determination to keep homes threatened by foreclosure of mortgages that they could no longer carry enabled these homeowners to carry through to a successful conclusion the payment of mortgages more nearly adjusted to their capacity to pay. In the experience of the HOLC, private mortgage lenders can no doubt find plenty of food for thought.

Neighborhoods To an increasing extent savings and loan associations are giving serious attention to the neighborhood in which a property is located before approving an application for a loan. In many instances their general knowledge of their potential markets is such that they can visualize the neighborhood influences for good or ill as soon as the address of the subject property is given them. In other cases they do not depend solely upon general impressions but make a careful and systematic study for the purpose of discovering adverse neighborhood influences. Sometimes the results of this study are dramatized in the form of a security map of their market. Using an ordinary map of the city in which they operate, they may outline the most desirable lending areas in one color—perhaps green. Blue may designate areas that are still good but have passed their peak of values. Yellow may designate declining areas that are on the downgrade. Here we find older neighborhoods with obsolete properties, many of which may show evidences of neglect. Red spots on the map are danger signs. Absentee ownership and blights of one kind or another have left their unmistakable marks in the heavy risks assumed by those who finance properties in such areas.

Once such a map has been prepared, it must be used with discretion. If all lenders bid for loans in the green and blue areas, overlending may result. On the other hand, there are still good opportunities for sound loans in the yellow and even occasionally in the red areas. By lower percentage loans, shorter mortgage maturities, and higher interest rates, mortgage risks may be reduced or compensated for. It is better to consider each loan application from a red or yellow area strictly on its own merits rather than to attempt to set a quota of loans to be granted in these areas.

Many savings and loan operators give attention to the assistance offered them by the FHA, which developed a most useful rating sheet for neighborhoods. It includes the following items: (1) relative economic stability; (2) protection from adverse influences; (3) freedom from special hazards; (4) adequacy of civic, social, and commercial centers; (5) adequacy of transportation; (6) sufficiency of utilities and conveniences; (7) level of taxes and special assessments; and (8) appeal. On the basis of a mathematical rating given to each of these factors, the FHA determines whether or not to insure mortgages in a given neighborhood. In some neighborhoods no insurance will be approved, regardless of other factors affecting mortgage risks.

Loan Percentages In analyzing the percentage of loan to value of the subject property, savings and loan associations have had their lending policies largely determined by outside influences in recent years. Before 1933 loan percentages were fixed more or less theologically. Some lenders set an upper limit of 50 percent; others, of 60 percent, and still others, of 66⅔ percent. The latter was considered tops. To make sure that, in periods of excess funds, institutional lenders did not exceed these ceilings, regulations and legislation usually reinforced the resolutions of those regulated by fixing statutory limits on loan percentages. In applying these ceilings, however, it should be kept in mind that the amount of loan approved was measured in terms of the relationship between the loan and the appraised value of the property as fixed by the lender. As a result, it was easy to permit a particular loan to exceed the ceiling by liberalizing the appraisal. As a matter of fact, it was easy to make a liberal appraisal without recognizing it as such at a time when appraisal procedures were not too scientific. This circumstance, coupled with less attention to the moral hazard than is being currently given, probably required fairly low loan percentages to insure reasonably safe loans.

In recent years the improvement in appraisal techniques and the pressure by governmental agencies for more liberal loans has forced many savings and loan associations to revise their ideas about loan percentages. In some cases conventional loans are still held down, even though the same institution makes FHA and GI loans on a higher level. In other cases even conventional loans are pitched at the higher level if necessary to get the business. Of course, some borrowers need and prefer only low percentage loans.

Other factors influence the percentage of loan to appraised value. Amortized loans usually are available at a higher percentage of loan to appraisal than are straight or term loans. The period of the business cycle has considerable influence; this factor, incidentally, may have a result quite contrary to expectations. Liberal loans are granted in periods of prosperity, when both borrowers and lenders are optimistic. Lower percentage loans are the rule in depressed real estate markets. Logically the reverse should obtain. Smaller losses would probably result if the common practice were reversed.

Maturity of Loans In the early days of savings and loan associations in this country, a magical formula was adopted requiring a payment of 1 percent of the original principal of the mortgage per month, such payment to include principal installment and interest. This was more or less irrespective of the rate of interest charged, although in the beginning 6 percent was the standard rate. This rate was commonly used because it was the legal rate in most states. If the rate were 6 percent, this meant a maturity date between 11 and 12 years after the mortgage was executed, if all went well and if no prepayments were accepted. Responding to outside pressure, for the most part, maturities have been extended in recent years so that 25 or 30 year, and even longer, maturities have been used by savings and loan associations.

Recent Developments in Lending The rapid growth of the savings and loan business has focused attention on the increasing need for broadened investment powers. Tax increases affecting savings and loan associations, greater competitiveness of commercial banks, and imbalances between money-surplus and money-scarcity areas creating demands for extraterritorial lending programs—all of these conditions have created pressures causing adoption of a loan participation program, increased powers to finance land acquisition and development for residential use, higher loan-to-value ratios, and more extensive lending on structures housing more than four families.

Since March 1, 1957, federally insured savings and loan associations have been empowered to acquire mortgage loan participations from U.S. instrumentalities and from other federally insured lenders. From a volume of $158 million in 1958, participations have increased substantially. In 1970, associations were particularly aggressive in purchasing loans outside their own business as a means of keeping savings most profitably invested. They purchased $3,745 million of loans and participations. Of this total, $1,108 million came from other associations and $2,637 were acquired chiefly from commercial banks, insurance companies, and mortgage brokers

Since November 16, 1959, federally chartered associations have had the power to finance the acquisition and development of land primarily for residential use. Under current regulations, institutions may grant a developer one-package financing which provides for the purchase of land, its development into building sites, and the construction of homes on those sites. To date, these loans have been used more extensively on the West Coast than in any other section of the country.

The Housing Act of 1964 effected a statutory extension of basic savings and loan lending areas to 100 miles (rather than 50 miles as previously provided) from the home office. The act raised from $35,000 to $40,000 (increased in 1970 to $45,000), the maximum loan that can be made by a federally chartered savings and loan association on a single-family home. The same law removed limitations on aggregate amounts that federally chartered associations may invest in loans outside the basic lending area or in participations. Each of these types of investments, however, continue to be subject to the limitation of 20 percent of the assets of the association. In addition, federally chartered associations were permitted to make loans secured by leaseholds if the term of the leasehold does not expire, or is renewable so as not to expire, for at least 15 years beyond the terminal date of the loan. In 1970, this period was reduced to 10 years. Authority to make urban renewal and property and home improvement loans was also expanded.

The Housing and Urban Development Act of 1968 extended the lending and investment authority of savings and loan associations substantially in certain directions. They were authorized to finance mobile and vacation homes and to make loans up to $5,000 for the repair, equipment, alteration, or improvement of any real property. They were authorized, further, to enter into repurchase agreements and the sale of participations in pools of government-backed mortgages. The act also permits them to invest in certificates of deposit of banks insured by the FDIC. On an international basis, they were authorized to invest in foreign housing aid loans guaranteed by the Agency for International Development.

In 1971, upon Federal Home Loan Bank Board authority, the lending area of federal savings and loan associations was expanded to within 100 miles of any branch provided the location of the property is within the same state as the home office. The Board also liberalized members' authority to invest in public housing loans in declining areas.

Mortgage Turnover In spite of any contract arrangement for the maturity of loans granted by savings and loan associations, it has been customary over the years for many such loans to be repaid in not more than half the time that it would take to mature the loan according to the terms of the mortgage which secures it. Indeed, in a large number of cases the payoff may come at the end of only two or three years. Such payoffs may be due to prepayments; or they may result from the sale of the property with a new mortgage issued, a part of the proceeds of which is used to pay off an existing loan.

In attempting to measure the rate of mortgage turnover, two ratios are in common use. The ratio of new loans to the amount of principal reduction in loans on the books contains an uncertain amount of distortion, because "new loans" include those written against property already used as security for loans that are being paid off. For example, should the mortgagor sell his property and the purchaser refinance his loan with the same association in a manner that requires a new mortgage, the entire amount of the new mortgage is considered a new loan. It does not represent an addition of a like amount to the mortgage portfolio. Only the difference between the unpaid balance of the old loan and the amount of the new loan is really a new loan. In fact, in considering all associations as a group, a new loan made by one association to pay off a loan at another adds only the difference between the two loans to the total loans of all associations. In like manner, if the same borrower takes out a new mortgage for a larger amount than the unpaid balance of the old mortgage, the difference only is really a new loan.

The ratio of principal reduction to the amount of loans held at the end of the year is a more significant test of mortgage turnover. The reduction in principal balance reflects three things: (1) regular installments paid to amortize the loan principal; (2) prepayments over and above these regular installments; and (3) payoffs of loan balances from whatever source is available. When a mortgage is canceled for any reason and a new one is made by the same or a different savings and loan association to the same or a different borrower, using the same property as security for the new loan, not all of the reduction in principal balance is real. If the new loan is larger than the old—as would usually be the case—there has been no real reduction. Instead, there has been an increase, as noted above. As a consequence, when all associations are considered as a whole, neither new loans nor reductions in principal balances are as large as anticipated. But since the excess reductions stated merely offset the excess new loans, the ratios of reduction in principal balance to the amount of loans held at the end of the year are reasonably reliable.

Since the amortization principle first had common acceptance among early savings and loan associations, few of them have used demand or one-year loans which were actually expected to be renewed automatically so long as interest and taxes were kept current. Savings and loan associations have, from time to time, made some use of term or straight loans. The most common maturities of such loans have been two, three, or even occasionally five years. Term loans have not generally been looked upon with favor by this type of lender. Where granted, they have been used at the insistence of the borrower.

As has already been indicated, savings and loan associations were the first types of real estate financing institutions to use the principal of amortization in getting the loans paid off. Amortization is no cure-all for the ills that may afflict a borrower. To be effective, the period of amortization must be adjusted to the debt-paying capacities of the borrower. A short maturity loan, with principal repayment provisions that are too great for the borrower's income, can precipitate a default just as quickly as can a loan whose entire principal falls due at an early date. In either case the mortgage is really a deferred certificate of ownership. The lender really purchased the property when he made the loan but did not acquire title to it until some time later—when he foreclosed his mortgage.

Prepayments Mortgages may be written to invite, discourage, or prohibit prepayments before maturity. A federal savings and loan association mortgage usually contains a clause to the effect that the borrower shall pay not less than a certain number of dollars per month. Many state-chartered savings and loan associations follow the same practice. The "not less than" invites larger payments whenever the borrower is in a position to make them. Many homeowner borrowers look forward to the day when they can own their homes free and clear of all encumbrances. Consequently, most of their savings may be applied to reduce the principal of the mortgage against the home.

The lending institution which grants prepayment privileges without restrictions of any kind runs the risk of losing money on some loans. For example, suppose that in a highly competitive market the lender absorbs the loan costs. Its out-of-pocket costs for appraisal, attorney's fee, and so on, may be considerable. If the loan is on the books for a few months only and is then completely paid off because of a windfall to the borrower, a refinancing operation, or a sale of the property to someone who prefers not to assume this particular mortgage, the original lender may not recover all its costs before it loses the mortgage. To protect itself against such a contingency, a savings and loan association may include in its mortgage a clause to the effect that, if the mortgage is paid off within a specified period of time—usually one to three years—the mortgagee reserves the right to exact a prepayment penalty of 90 days' interest.

Such a penalty is not always demanded, even though it is a part of the loan contract. Even though the attention of the borrower was directed to this clause when he signed the mortgage, he will probably resent the application of the penalty. The lending institution may decide that it does not care to purchase ill will with a three months' interest charge. Whenever a borrower pays off a loan, the lender likes to have the goodwill of the borrower. It may attract loans to friends of the borrower. Some lenders waive the prepayment penalty clause if the borrower uses his own funds for repaying the loan but apply the penalty if the loan is refinanced by a competitor. Presumably the borrower gains an advantage in refinancing his loan and can afford to share it with the original lender, who may otherwise lose money.

Some lending institutions discourage, but do not prohibit, prepayment privileges. They permit some prepayments—grudgingly. Some permit prepayments of not more than 20 percent of the principal within any period of 12 months. Such an arrangement grants the borrower the right to reduce his loan considerably faster than is contemplated in the mortgage contract. It is an effective deterrent to refinancing with a competitor. Since only 20 percent is permitted in the loan contract, any prepayment beyond this amount must be with the consent of the mortgagee. This consent may cost the mortgagor dearly if the result of total prepayment is the loss of a loan by the original lender. Savings and loan associations do not generally use the restricted prepayment privilege.

In some mortgage contracts there is no provision for prepayment. Unless the loan is repaid according to the terms, any change must be purchased from the mortgagee. The latter may and occasionally does permit prepayment—restricted or not—without any penalty. When no prepayment clause is included in the mortgage, the mortgagee is likely to resist prepayment by assessing prohibitive penalties if the privilege is requested. Savings and loan mortgages made in recent years usually include full prepayment privileges although the historically high interest rates have inspired some tendencies in the opposite direction.

Interest Rates For many years the percentage of loan to appraised value was commonly used to measure and to offset the risk element of what were then considered to be unusually risky loans. As already indicated in an earlier part of this chapter, fairly low ceilings of loan percentages were established both by managements and by regulatory bodies. Higher risk loans might be financed below these ceilings. Interest rates were fixed with less regard to risks assumed. They were likely to be standardized for all loans granted within any economic period. Even today, some associations charge the same rate of interest on all conventional loans. Their managements seem to feel that they cannot justify variations in rates or that they should just as well charge rates that are commonly accepted in their markets. Because such rates are likely to be higher than those charged on FHA and GI loans, some associations refuse to make insured or guaranteed loans.

Other associations use the interest rate as a means of compensating for risks assumed in making real estate loans. On this basis, loans that entail greater risks and costs are required to pay higher interest rates. Small loans, even though lacking the element of great risk, may still be charged the higher rate because of the higher costs per dollar of bookkeeping, servicing, and so on. Associations which use various interest rates on mortgage loans frequently start with a base rate on a loan equal to perhaps 40 percent of the appraised value, using as security property in good neighborhoods built less than 12 years before and with low moral hazard. Additions to this base rate to compensate for added risks are sometimes established more or less on a rule-of-thumb basis. In other cases, an elaborate schedule is used which takes into account such items as: tenant- or owner-occupancy; specific age of property; design and construction of main buildings; maturity of loan; location of security; loan percentage; life insurance protection with mortgagee as beneficiary as his interest may appear; amount and apparent stability of income of borrower; other obligations of borrower; special hazards; and so forth.

Those who have used discriminatory interest rates on mortgage loans have found little difficulty in explaining to their borrowers the reasons for this practice. These interest rates are like the prices of shoes. Shoes can be purchased at from $5 to $25 or more a pair, depending upon the quality. Discriminatory interest rates measure qualitative differences in service rendered to borrowers. To the occasional borrower who might question whether discrimination is being practiced against him, the association should be able to state the conditions under which his loan too will merit the lower rate of interest. In some cases interest rates are reduced, with or without the request of the borrower, when risks are reduced through amortization of the loan balance.

One factor that influences the level of interest charges on real estate loans is the amount and aggressiveness of competition. If competition is weak or absent, higher rates may be charged. If the race for available mortgage loans is close, rates may be cut by the successful bidder. When mortgagors recognize this possibility, they may shop around for low rates as they sometimes do for liberal loans.

Appraisal Policies In the days of early building societies, appraisals of property offered as security for mortgage loans were neither as accurate nor as necessary as they are today. The pressure from friends and neighbors to maintain payments was greater than any pressure possible under current practices of borrowing from strangers. Such attention as was given to appraised values took the form of visits to the property by officers and directors of the association. Gradually this service was recognized in the form of token fees paid to those who were selected to view the property offered as security for a loan. In order to avoid any appearance of favoritism in passing out appraisal fees, members of appraisal committees were changed from time to time. In a simple economy, with inexpensive properties not greatly different from each other, probably little harm was done when it was assumed that any officer or director of a building society was competent to set an estimated value upon property offered as security for a loan.

In some modern associations, all appraisals are still being made by committees of board members whose major source of income may be as butchers or bakers or candlestick makers or in any other trade or business not even remotely associated with real estate and construction. In others, only full-time officers and key employees of the association are used for this purpose. In still others, an outside experienced appraiser may be used on a fee basis. His conclusions are then checked by an independent appraisal made by an employee or officer, also experienced in this work. With the increasing complexity of problems concerned with real estate value and with recent pressures for higher percentage loans, more and more attention must be paid to the qualifications of those who establish the risks assumed by mortgagees.

As a partial offset to what has just been said, we find reasons to question whether the mortgagee needs to give as much attention to the value of security offered for a real estate loan as was the case before the 1930 decade. When the FHA, for example, insures a real estate loan, it does so after an appraisal of the property by an appraiser selected or approved by it. In other words, since the risk is in large part shifted from the lender to the FHA, the latter rather than the former determines whether or not the loan shall be made. It is possible, of course, for the lender to grant an uninsured loan on its own appraisal if the FHA appraiser is unable to arrive at a conclusion that will meet the needs of the borrower. This is not likely to happen, since the FHA loan applied for is probably more liberal than the association would be willing to grant in conventional form, unless the FHA turns down the neighborhood, the moral hazard of the borrower, and so forth, rather than the ratio of loan to appraisal. In such case, the lender might, on occasion, disagree with the FHA and make an uninsured loan.

The same reasoning applies to GI loans guaranteed by the Veterans Administration. Here, too, appraisal responsibility is largely shifted from the lender to the VA. Since the entire responsibility is not so shifted, it is well for the lender to make his own appraisal, under both the GI and FHA plans.

Appraisal Records Until recent decades, savings and loan associations have not been too meticulous in recording the results of appraisals with the loan file. Indeed, in many instances the records were not filed because there were no real appraisals to be recorded. Office appraisals were frequently used. They are still used in a minor number of instances. By this is meant that at the time the loan application is filed the borrower answers all questions about his property to the satisfaction of the association officer or employee who takes the application. In addition, the officer may be sufficiently familiar with the property to make a careful inspection unnecessary, according to his ideas on the subject. The conclusion drawn by the association representative may be that the loan is sound. It is executed without any statement being made in the record about the value of the property.

Another practice, even more common until 1930, has been aptly called a "horseback" or "windshield" appraisal. The appraisal committee of the association, or some member of it, drove past the property, gave it a casual outside glance only, and reported to the lending officer that it was satisfactory security for the loan requested or for some lower figure. The writer has had personal knowledge of as many as 15 such appraisals being made in one hour. Again nothing may have been put into the record to indicate the estimated value of the property.

With more enlightened management and more alert supervisors, there came a time when it seemed desirable to have the record show a value of the property offered as security for a real estate mortgage. In case of a crisis it appeared desirable to have a statement, signed by the appraiser or an appraisal committee, indicating someone's estimate of value. While this could not be used as a basis for recovery of a loss suffered by the association, in the absence of proof of fraud or gross negligence it did tend to inject an element of conservatism into appraisal practices. These first appraisal reports should perhaps be called, instead, "certificates of appraisal." Many of them supplied no evidence of the basis of appraisal, but only the conclusion to the effect that the undersigned thinks such-and-such property is worth so many dollars.

Currently, both progressive managements and careful supervisors require more or less elaborate, signed appraisal reports to accompany loan papers and to remain a permanent part of the file of the borrower until the loan is liquidated. Such reports cannot be made honestly without an inspection of the property, inside as well as outside. Some associations keep these appraisal reports long after they are required to do so. They may be useful at some future time if a new loan is applied for with the same property as security. If old appraisal reports are not used with discretion, they may hinder rather than help future lending operations. Appraisals should always reflect current and, as far as possible, future values. Past values are less useful in real estate appraisals for financing purposes.

For example, suppose that association A appraised a new property in 1960 at $20,000 and made a loan of $15,000 upon it. Suppose in 1972 an applicant requested a loan of $22,000 on the same property. Although the latter might be a more conservative loan, owing to the changed price level, the association might well be more willing to make the later loan if it had not made the earlier one and if its records did not show that the 1972 loan requested was larger than the value of the property 12 years earlier. These old records tend to color new appraisals.

Decisions on Loan Applications Except in very small associations, where the appraiser may also be the loan officer, the one who fixes a value upon a property is not expected to decide whether or not to grant the loan applied for. Property value is only one of the elements to take into account in reaching such a decision. It should be weighed carefully, along with all the other pertinent factors discussed earlier in this chapter. It is even open to serious question whether the appraiser should know the amount of the loan applied for. If he does, this knowledge may tend to color his conclusions. This suggests also that, if the property is being sold, the appraiser should not even know the selling price. His objective should not be an answer to the question, "What will this property sell for in the current (possibly inflated or possibly depressed) market?" Instead, the lending institution wants his answer to the question, "What is this property worth as security for a long-term real estate loan?" The latter question involves forecast, but so does the decision to make the loan.

Numerous factors with which the appraiser may lack acquaintance help the loan officer to reach a conclusion concerning the loan application. The responsibility for appraisals rests with the appraiser; the responsibility for loan decisions rests with the loan officer, the loan committee, or the board of directors, depending upon the practice followed in a particular association. For that reason the payment of an appraisal fee should not be contingent upon the granting of the loan. Such a practice tends to make a loan officer out of the appraiser.

Appraising of Conditions In arriving at its decision on a loan application, the committee or the individual that faces this responsibility must be not only a coordinator but also a forecaster. Even assuming an accurate picture of the moral hazard as measured by the character and the capacity of the borrower, and an equally accurate report about the value of the collateral offered as security for the loan and of the other capital owned by the borrower, there still remains the need for an appraisal of the most difficult of the five "Cs." The longer the term of the loan, the more difficult the appraisal of future conditions becomes. This is true for two reasons: (1) Foresight becomes progressively more dim as the maturity of the loan recedes into the future. (2) The longer the term of the loan, the less rapidly the principal balance is amortized.

In spite of the difficulties in forecasting future economic conditions for the country as a whole and for the community in which the property is situated, the success of a particular mortgage loan may depend upon the answer to questions concerning such a forecast. The value of the property at the time the loan is made is important. So is the earning capacity and the character of the borrower. But if the lender ignores future considerations and follows a policy of drifting with the tide, he may find too late that he has been using hindsight instead of foresight in reaching decisions on loan applications. It is not sufficient to shrug off the future by saying that nobody can tell what will happen 15 or even 10 years hence. Granted the truth of the statement, mortgage lenders nevertheless have responsibilities for using to the best of their ability, rather than ignoring, evidences of future economic conditions.

Purposes of Mortgage Loans Of all mortgage loans granted by savings and loan associations, home purchase invariably is given as the purpose which accounts for the largest dollar volume of loans. This is followed in order by home construction, which generally amounts to about three fourths of the dollar volume needed for home purchase. Refinancing generally amounts to approximately one fifth to one fourth as much as the amount needed for home purchase. Reconditioning loans total one half of the amount needed for refinancing. In some years the ratio is considerably less than one half. A catchall classification of "other purposes" may approximate or even exceed the amount needed for refinancing. "Other purposes" frequently include the use of funds quite unrelated to real estate.

Recent Growth During the past 50 years, savings and loan associations have experienced periods of growth, decline, and growth again. From 10,009 active associations in 1922, with total assets of $2,802 million, the number of associations reached a peak in 1927, with 12,804. The peak in assets for this period was reached in 1929, with $7,791 million. From 1930 to 1936 assets experienced an annual decline to a low of $5,165 million in the latter year. The amounts given here are for total assets less pledged shares. The number of associations declined in every year from 1927 to 1949. At the latter date the total number of operating associations was only 5,983, or less than half the number in the years from 1925 to 1929, inclusive. By the end of 1970 the number of associations stood at 5,738. After a low in assets was reached in 1939, an increase was experienced in every year thereafter to 1970. Total assets were then $176 billion.

Meantime, the amount of first mortgage loans held by all associations was $2.4 billion in 1922; this increased to $6.5 billion in 1929, declined to $3.2 billion in 1936, and thereafter increased year by year to $150 billion in 1970.

The book value of real estate owned increased from a negligible amount in 1922 to $238 million in 1930 and to $1,163 million in 1935. Thereafter it declined to $1,026 million in 1937, to $117 million in 1943, and to only $12 million in 1948. By 1970 it had increased to $900 million, not excessive in view of the tremendous growth in assets.

Government bonds in the portfolios of savings and loans associations, both direct obligations of the United States and those guaranteed by the government, became significant for the first time in 1936, when the total amount owned was $99 million. Most of these holdings were HOLC bonds. The total declined to $71 million in 1940 and thereafter increased quite rapidly to a peak of $2.4 billion in 1945. Since that year there has been a decline to a low of $1.5 billion in 1948, followed by a steady increase to about $12.0 billion in 1970.

The first year for which reliable information is available on the subject of reserves and undivided profits is 1936. In that year the total was $490 million. This changed but little until 1942 when $500 million was reached for the first time. Since then, increases were recorded each year, until the amount reached over $12 billion in 1970. The ratio of reserves and undivided profits to mortgage loans in all savings and loan associations since 1940 has been approximately 10 percent. In 1970, it stood at about 6.8 percent. Although this percentage reflects a significant decline in the last few years, the reserves still stand in marked contrast to practices formerly followed. In early days, neither reserves nor undivided profits were permitted to accumulate. Both losses and gains were supposed to be distributed year by year as they accumulated. Even the first legislation on the subject fixed ceilings over reserves instead of floors under them. As participants in mutual institutions, their members were expected to share in their fortunes, good and bad, in proportion to their commitments. While this attitude of mutuality is still being maintained, the great concern with building reserves and undivided profits emphasizes the long-range obligations of a going concern instead of the short-range requirements of an institution that might be liquidated at any time.

Comparison with Competitors Table 12–1 shows the distribution of home mortgage loans outstanding at the end of 1970 by selected types of lenders. The security for the mortgages upon which this table is based includes only one- to four-family homes.

The table shows the importance of savings and loan associations in home mortgage financing.

TABLE 12–1
Percentage Distribution of Home Mortgages, Year-End 1970

	Percent
Savings and loan associations	44.8
Life insurance companies	9.5
Commercial banks	15.1
Individuals and others	9.6
Mutual savings banks	13.4
Federal National Mortgage Association	7.6
Total	100.0

Source: *Statistical Abstract of the United States* (Washington, D.C.: U.S. Government Printing Office, 1971), p. 440.

QUESTIONS AND PROBLEMS

1. What are the chief factors affecting lending policies of savings and loan associations?

2. Why do savings and loan associations prefer to make loans on single-family dwellings over other forms of residential or commercial real estate?

3. Why do these institutions make loans on nonresidential properties, and under what restrictions do they operate?

4. What has been the trend of the percentage of loan to appraised value in recent years, and what conditions have influenced this trend?

5. What justification can you give for granting savings and loan associations broader lending powers? What recent changes in this direction have been made?

6. What distortion is inherent in the ratio of total new loans to the amount of principal reduction as a measure of the rate of mortgage turnover?

7. Can you suggest a more accurate measure than that indicated in question 6?

8. If no provision is made for a prepayment privilege under a mortgage loan, under what conditions may the mortgagor make prepayments?

9. How have many savings and loan associations hoped to gain an advantage by permitting loan prepayment without penalty?

10. What criticism can you give of an institutional practice of standardizing interest rates for all conventional loans made within a certain economic period?

11. How can discriminatory interest rates be justified as a part of an integrated lending policy?

12. Why has more attention been paid to appraisal policies in recent years? How has this affected the development and maintenance of appraisal records?

13. In your opinion, what importance should be assigned to a forecast of future economic conditions in making a decision on a long-term mortgage loan application?

14. What factors have contributed to the recent growth of savings and loan associations? What new competitive factors are affecting their growth rate?

13

Financing of Real Estate by Banks

Current Real Estate Lending by Banks In this chapter are discussed real estate lending practices of three kinds of banks: mutual savings banks; state-chartered commercial banks; and national banks. No attention is paid to the relatively insignificant role currently played by private banks in the field of real estate finance. Since the policies of all commercial banks have much in common, they will be discussed as one class, except for the differences noted below. Real estate mortgages are expected to involve long-term commitment of funds, regardless of the specific terms for which mortgages are written. Therefore it is to be expected that both experience and regulations should dictate that only capital, surplus, and time deposits be used by commercial banks for making real estate loans. Since mutual savings banks are not looked upon in the same light as commercial banks, most deposits in the former are considered to be time deposits.

As of December 31, 1970, the total savings and time deposits of all banks in this country were $321 billion. Of this total, commercial banks held $249 billion and mutual savings banks $72 billion. The relatively small number of saving banks, scattered throughout the country, that are owned by stockholders are classed as commercial banks for our purposes, since their operations more nearly parallel those of state-chartered commercial banks than of mutual savings banks.

The real estate mortgage holdings of all banks as of December 31, 1970, are set forth in Table 13–1. It is interesting to note the concentration of real estate mortgages on residential property as security, with "other" types of real estate in second position and farm real estate in third position.

MUTUAL SAVINGS BANKS

Origin of Mutual Savings Banks[1] The origin of mutual savings banks in this country has much in common with the origin of savings and loan associations. Both had their impetus outside of the group to be served. Both had a semireligious background. Like their predecessors in England and on the continent of Europe, the clergy, philanthropically minded people, and others interested wished to encourage thrifty habits and frugality among the growing numbers of working peoople. The sponsors of these "frugality banks" recognized the need for institutions

TABLE 13-1
Mortgage Holdings of All Banks as of December 31, 1970 (000,000 omitted)

	Nonfarm Residential	Farm	Other	Total
Commercial banks	$45,716	$4,342	$23,281	$ 73,339
Mutual savings banks	49,936	119	7,893	57,948
Total	$95,652	$4,461	$31,174	$131,287

Source: *Statistical Abstract of the United States* (Washington, D.C.: U.S. Government Printing Office, 1971), p. 440.

which could care for the savings of those dependent upon wages for a living against the time when incomes might be reduced for one reason or another. Even the names of some of the early savings banks attempt to describe their purposes. The first to start business in this country was the Philadelphia Savings Fund Society, which opened for business in the fall of 1816. It is fitting that the first institution of this kind should have been started in the city made famous by the thrift teachings of Poor Richard. This was soon followed by the Provident Institute for Savings, started in Boston in the spring of 1817. The idea of such banks soon spread to other cities. All contemporary accounts of their operation lay emphasis upon the services rendered to humble people of small means who would probably squander their earnings except for the exhortations of savings banks to save something against the time of need.

Concentration of Mutual Savings Banks Today mutual savings banks are found in only 18 states. Most of them are concentrated in three states—Massachusetts, New York, and Connecticut. In these three states,

---

[1] Much of the material in this chapter on the subject of mutual savings banks is adapted from John Lintner, *Mutual Savings Banks in the Savings and Mortgage Markets* (Boston: Division of Research, Graduate School, Harvard University, 1948). See also the monograph prepared for the Commission of Money and Credit titled *Mutual Savings Banking* (Englewood Cliffs, N.J.: Prentice-Hall, Inc., 1962).

savings banks have attracted much more savings funds than have all other types of banks and savings and loan associations combined. Outside New England, New York, New Jersey, Delaware, Pennsylvania, and Maryland there are only a few mutual savings banks—9 in the Middle West and 12 in the far West, including Alaska. The three states first mentioned above account for three fourths in number and more than that in proportion of assets of all mutual savings banks in the country. Massachusetts has 172 savings banks; New York, 121; Connecticut, 69; other New England states, collectively, 75; New Jersey, 20; Pennsylvania, 8; Delaware, 2; and Maryland, 5. Outside of this area the only other states having such institutions are: Ohio, 1; Indiana, 4; Wisconsin, 3; Minnesota, 1; Washington, 9; Oregon, 1; and Alaska, 2.

Management of Mutual Savings Banks Savings banks have no stockholders. By a curious use of language, their owners are called "depositors." The return they receive upon their investments is called "interest" in spite of the fact that no one makes a commitment to pay them a fixed return. There is no backstop of stock to protect deposits against the shocks of losses. As a mutual institution only, the deposits, plus whatever reserves have been retained in the business to absorb losses, may be looked to for the purpose of meeting the effects of unusual losses.

Since the depositors are not considered to be stockholders, they have no voice in the management of their own funds. This task is entrusted to a self-perpetuating board of trustees. The original board was selected by the organizers of the bank. Vacancies resulting from resignations, deaths, or other causes are filled by the remaining board members. This system has worked quite satisfactorily over the years. In actual practice it differs only in form from the manner of selecting the boards of directors of many American corporations whose stockholders enjoy voting rights that are seldom or never exercised. In such corporations, boards of directors are virtually self-perpetuating bodies.

Growth of Savings Banks There can be no question about the need for savings banks, the quality of the services rendered, or the nature of the responses by the people who took advantage of these services. The number of such banks increased steadily for a time, both in total assets and in number of depositors. The number of banks grew steadily until it reached a maximum nearly 100 years ago. Since then the number of banks has shown a considerable decline which is especially marked in recent years.

In 1820 there were 10 mutual savings banks in the United States with total assets of $1 million dollars. The number increased to a peak of 674 in 1875, when total assets amounted to $850 million. Since that date the number has declined to a low of 494 in 1970. By the end of 1970, total assets amounted to about $79 billion.

Undoubtedly the growth of savings and loan associations and savings departments of commercial banks played their part in other sections of the country, leaving the bulk of savings business in the above-described "savings bank" area to the mutual savings banks. The recent rapid growth of federal savings and loan associations in New York and New England suggests that there may be other reasons for the failure of savings banks to expand into new areas in recent years.

Savings Banks and Their Investors Since the owners of deposits in mutual savings banks expect to withdraw their savings on demand, the banks must operate in such a manner as to meet these requirements. The laws under which they operate permit them to "go on notice" for 30 to 90 days before paying withdrawal demands. Except in times of emergency, they make no use of this protection. To make common use of it would discourage patronage. While some banks have suffered more than others, in general withdrawal demands have not frequently been unduly burdensome to most savings banks. Since withdrawals are closely associated with confidence of the investors, the strong reputation of savings banks has helped to keep down "fear" withdrawals.

For the protection of safety of deposits, the states in which savings banks operate have enacted laws restricting the investments of such institutions to "legals" which are supposed to be of high quality. Within statutory limits which set forth the categories of investment opportunities available to savings banks, the management has wide latitude of choice in selecting what seems to it to best serve its requirements for safety, liquidity, and return.

Restrictions upon Real Estate Lending All mutual savings banks receive their charters from states. The laws regulating their operation represent quite a wide range of patterns in their mortgage-lending programs. The ratio of maximum loan to value varies from 50 to 90 percent (except for FHA and GI loans). In New York, for example, in the case of one- or two-family owner-occupied dwellings, constructed within 10 years of the loan, a savings bank may invest up to the lesser of 90 percent of the appraised value of the property or $25,000. The bank may invest up to 75 percent of appraised value on other property used for residential purposes or for business, manufacturing, or agriculture. In Massachusetts, savings banks may invest up to 80 percent of appraised value in certain circumstances, but no loan of such a class may exceed $25,000. Connecticut also authorizes 80 percent loans in amounts not to exceed $20,000.

Savings banks are also subject to restrictions on the percentage of assets or deposits that may be placed in mortgages. In New York, the maximum amount of conventional mortgage loans that may be held by a savings bank is 65 percent of the assets of the bank. There is no ceiling, however, on the proportion of assets that may be invested in

FHA or VA loans. In Massachusetts, generally, 70 percent of deposits may be invested in mortgages, plus an additional 15 percent of deposits in federally underwritten mortgages. Similarly, in Connecticut 85 percent of assets may be invested in mortgage loans, but all loans in excess of 70 percent of assets must be FHA or VA.

State laws regulate maximum terms for loans, as well as other characteristics. New York provides the terms on its "90 percent" loans shall not exceed three fourths of the useful life of the property or 30 years, whichever is less. Massachusetts and Connecticut have a 25-year maximum term for their "80 percent" loans.

Because trustees of mutual savings banks are traditionally conservative, self-imposed restrictions may be even more rigid than those imposed by law. In general they prefer loans on single-family dwellings. Only the largest institutions, whose investment funds present constant pressure for investment, get into the fields of investment in apartment-house, commercial, and industrial mortgages.

Lending territories are usually determined by their short distance from the home office, so that the problems of servicing will not be so difficult as they are when property securing mortgage loans is located at great distances. In recent years the pressure of investment funds has recommended removal of distance restrictions when mortgage loans are insured by the FHA or are guaranteed by the VA. In New York state, where more than half of all assets of mutual savings banks are located, recent changes in legislation governing lending territory have been expanded to permit such banks to make even conventional loans in the neighboring states of Connecticut, Massachusetts, New Jersey, Pennsylvania, Rhode Island, and Vermont. Similarly, Massachusetts and Connecticut may make loans in their own and adjoining states. In the case of the latter states, however, the loans must be located in a city or town situated within a specified distance of the bank. By way of contrast, there are no state territorial limitations for savings banks located in some other states such as Delaware, Maryland, Pennsylvania, Rhode Island, Vermont, and Washington. In all cases, geographic limitations do not apply to FHA and VA loans.

The National Association of Mutual Savings Banks has presented an illuminating tabulation to show the extent of extraterritorial lending by savings banks in nonsavings bank states. Significant figures are presented in Table 13–2.

Mortgage Experience of Savings Banks Before the depression of the 1930s, savings banks had long been the major source of mortgage money in the areas in which they operated. From the time that savings banks became significant caretakers of savings funds until the 1930 depression, real estate mortgages had been looked upon with favor as satisfactory investment outlets for funds deposited with them. During the last quarter

TABLE 13-2
Mortgage Holdings of Mutual Savings Banks on Properties Located in Nonsavings Bank States, by Type of Loan, Selected Years, 1951–1970 (in millions of dollars)

Year	Type of Mortgage			Total Nonsavings Bank States	Total Mortgage Loans	Nonsavings Bank States as Percent of Total
	FHA	VA	Conventional			
1951.........	n.a.	n.a.	n.a.	499	8,428	5.9
1955.........	1,258	1,689	26	2,974	17,396	17.1
1960.........	2,622	3,634	68	6,323	26,213	24.1
1966.........	7,233	6,015	363	13,611	46,555	29.2
1970.........	8,110	6,807	1,234	16,150	57,275	28.2

Source: *National Fact Book of Mutual Savings Banking* (New York: National Association of Mutual Savings Banks, 1971), Table 77, p. 56.

of the last century and the first three decades of this one, mortgages always absorbed at least a third and frequently as much as a half of the total resources of savings banks.

For example, in Massachusetts more than half the assets of all savings banks were invested in mortgages by 1924. This proportion continued without important change for the succeeding 10 years, never in this period dropping below 50 percent of total assets. As the effects of the 1930 depression began to take their toll, an abrupt shift from real estate mortgages to U.S. government bonds became evident. A similar shift, but not so abrupt, was shown in the decrease in corporate securities, with a corresponding increase in government bonds. The percentage of assets invested in mortgages experienced an uninterrupted decline from 1932 to 1946. In the earlier year, 54 percent of savings banks' assets in Massachusetts were invested in mortgages; in the latter year the percentage was only 24. Meantime, by 1946 over 63 percent of total assets were invested in government bonds, while in 1932 only 8 percent were so invested.

The amount of real estate mortgages foreclosed during this period is not an important element in accounting for the decline in the mortgage portfolio. Most of the acquisitions of real estate temporarily reduced the amount of mortgages on the books, to be sure. But since much of it was disposed of by means of purchase-money mortgages, it found its way back on the books as mortgages again. The net decline in the mortgage portfolio as a result of these foreclosures was probably not more than one third as great as the net decline resulting from all causes. This statement does not completely offset subsequent possible additional losses where purchase-money mortgages in turn must be foreclosed because they contained an unrecoverable element of inflation at the time they were issued. The major decline must be accounted for as the result of a shift of management policy from real estate mortgage investment to government bonds. This was reflected not only in the use of new money coming into the banks but in that of money which represented repayments of mortgage principal as well.

What happened in Massachusetts was matched, in some degree at least, in the operation of savings banks throughout the country. After 1932 the mortgages held by all savings banks in the United States decreased year by year. While there was some recovery in the decade of the 1940s, by the middle of that decade the total amount of mortgages in their portfolios was still less than in the previous decade. Meantime, corresponding figures for savings and loan associations on a national basis showed an increase of approximately two thirds. The percentage increase in residential mortgages held by insurance companies from the middle 1930s to the middle 1940s was even greater.

Changes in Policy The factors that accounted for this change in policy concerning real estate mortgages as investments are not too clearly defined in the record Patriotic desire to help finance the needs of the government during World War II undoubtedly played some part. The decline in the demand for real estate financial assistance was also a factor. Demand for mortgage money is a flexible concept. Competitors of savings banks apparently found a demand for their funds that were available for mortgage loans, since the total amount of mortgage holdings by savings and loan associations in Massachusetts—federal- and state-chartered combined—increased approximately 33 percent from 1936 to 1946. Meantime, mortgage holdings of savings banks declined 24 percent. Dollarwise, this difference is not so striking. The mortgage holdings of savings and loan associations increased approximately $112 million; those of savings banks declined $252 million. These amounts taken together confirm a decrease in overall demand for mortgage financial assistance. The supply of real estate buyers had undoubtedly declined for a part of this period, while the supply of government bonds for most of it was ample to meet all requirements. During this period, interest rates on mortgage loans declined somewhat, but government bond interest rates declined relatively more.

The above evidence leads to the conclusion that, for reasons best known to their managements, the savings banks of Massachusetts definitely decided to restrict their holdings of real estate mortgages. This of course was their right. The only purpose of emphasizing it here is to show that borrowers had that much of their opportunities contracted. They were required to look elsewhere for real estate financial assistance.

Reasons for Decline The search for the reasons for the decline in the volume of real estate mortgages held by savings banks suggests two outstanding conclusions. In the first place, their managements resisted strongly the acceptance of "newfangled" lending plans. Long accustomed to the use of one-year or demand mortgages, the savings banks with some reluctance made a concession to the popularity of competitors' loan plans when they secured legislative permission to write loans for three years instead of one. At the end of three years such mortgages were frequently kept alive as demand instruments. The monthly payment direct reduction loan plan did not immediately appeal to savings bank managers even after further changes in legislation permitted them to use it. Likewise, the high percentage loans made by federal savings and loan associations and other competitors did not cast a shadow which was heeded by savings banks. Even their legislative authority to make FHA loans—which were high-percentage, monthly payment, direct reduction loans for the most part—was not freely used. Refusing to read the handwriting on the wall, the savings banks watched their mortgage business flow toward their competitors. They still clung to short-term loans limited to not more than 60 percent of their appraisals.

In the second place, it does not appear that this loss of mortgage business was accompanied by any great measure of regret. Perhaps it would be more accurate to state that savings banks were willing to lose mortgage business rather than compete for it, under the terms desired by borrowers and aggressively offered by competitors. During the depression they had suffered losses from this type of investment even though they had limited their loans to low percentages of appraised value and even though they had the legal right to demand repayment of the debt at their convenience. The loss suffered on mortgage loans was relatively greater than on all other types of investments. In the face of this experience, they hesitated to grant high percentage loans whose repayment could not so easily be demanded because the new and more popular loan contract did not fix a maturity date for the entire amount advanced.

Also, it can be said further that many savings bank managements had reached the conclusion that mortgage lending, whether high percentage or low, whether amortized or not, and whether insured or not, had ceased to be a proper kind of business for a savings bank to engage in. Aside from purchase-money mortgages, used to assist in the disposal of foreclosed real estate, they did not look with favor upon granting new loans to average borrowers. This conclusion was reached in spite of the fact that, over the years, the excess of earnings from real estate mortgages, in comparison with the returns from investments carrying less risk, more than compensated for the losses suffered on mortgages during depression years.

The experience of the Massachusetts savings banks does not seem to have been shared in the same degree by those in New York. At least in the period following the close of World War II, the latter again became aggressive bidders for real estate mortgages, particularly those insured by the FHA or guaranteed by the VA. During the years 1947 and 1948, GI loans increased rapidly, with less increase in this area in 1949. FHA loans showed a sharp increase in 1948 and an even greater increase in 1949. During the period of 12 months ending September 30, 1949, total mortgage investments of New York savings banks were greater than for any previous 12-month period.

Indeed, savings banks generally have experienced another change of attitude toward mortgage investments since about 1947. This change was due in part to a desire to decrease their holdings of U.S. government bonds. When they liquidated sizeable quantities of bond holdings, they again turned to corporate bonds and to real estate mortgages as outlets for their funds.

Meanwhile, their continued growth posed investment problems, which were solved in part by a return to favoritism of mortgages. Less than one fourth of their assets were in mortgages at the end of World War II. By 1954, about one half of their assets were in mortgages. In 1960, the ratio of mortgage loans to total assets ranged from about one half in Pennsylvania, Maryland, and Maine, to nearly three fourths in New York and Vermont. During the period from 1950 to 1960, of total net uses of funds received by mutual savings banks amounting to $17.8 billion the amount channeled into residential mortgages totaled $16.9 billion, or 95 percent. This percentage was even greater than that for savings and loans, which placed only 85 percent of their net total fund uses to residential mortgage loans.

Several factors have combined to make mortgages especially attractive to savings banks. Regular amortization, improved marketability, better yields than were otherwise available, and federal underwriting have provided liquidity and earning power in the same investment, together with security of principal. Their investment program was given nationwide significance by legislative changes in most savings bank states permitting out-of-state lending both conventionally and through the purchase of FHA and VA mortgages derived in other sections of the country.

Recent proposed federal chartering of mutual savings banks would reinforce the increasingly important role of these banks in the national mortgage market. For example, this chartering would permit federal mutual savings banks to hold up to 80 percent of their assets in conventional mortgages—which is more liberal than the present provisions in nearly all savings banks states. Furthermore, there would be no limit in federally underwritten mortgages, whereas most states now have such limits. By 1960, savings banks were the largest VA mortgage holders, having grown from the smallest holders of the main institutional lenders. Similarly they were second only to the life insurance companies in FHA loans. They are now in first position in both VA and FHA loans by wide margins; and by federal chartering, the positions would be further reinforced.

Volume of Mortgage Holdings By September 30, 1970, the mutual savings banks of the United States held a total of $57,275 million in real estate mortgages. The distribution of these mortgages was as follows:

	Amount (in $ million)	Percent
In-state....................	$34,876	60.9
Out-of-state................	22,398	39.1
Total................	$57,275*	100.0

* Does not add due to rounding.

The percentage distribution of the types of loans of these banks at the end of 1970 was:

	Percent
Conventional.................	51.5
FHA........................	27.8
VA.........................	20.7
Total................	100.0

Breakdown by type of property was:

	Percent
Residential..................	86.2
1-to-4 family...........	64.7
Multifamily............	21.5
Nonresidential...............	13.6
Farm.......................	0.2
Total................	100.0*

* Does not add due to rounding.

Analysis of Risk Experience Sample studies of savings bank operations in Massachusetts led Lintner to conclude that loans made on single-family residences were safer than those on two- to four-family properties; and that the latter represented better security for mortgage loans than larger income properties such as apartment houses, store and office buildings, store and apartment buildings, commercial garages, and so forth. He also found that there is considerable correlation between the time of granting the loan and the amount of loss that should be anticipated. For example, in years of feverish real estate activity, with unusually great demand for financial assistance by borrowers, optimism of management is likely to invite risks which may ripen into subsequent losses. It is probable, however, that rates of interest have been higher in such periods, thus providing some cushion to absorb later losses. In periods of less activity in mortgage lending, on the other hand, greater caution minimizes losses.

Among the other relationships found by this sample study are those listed below. While they are not startling in character, they do afford statistical support for general impressions held by those best acquainted with mortgage loan operations. It is highly probable that similar studies of mortgage lending practices of other types of financial institutions would lead to similar conclusions. Lintner's conclusions follow:

1. There is a direct relationship between the loan-to-value ratio and the probability of loss. In other words, the higher this ratio, the greater the chance for loss. This conclusion ignores the support of insurance of mortgages by the FHA and the guarantee by the VA so far as the lending institution is concerned. However, it raises some interesting questions about the possibility of losses that may be borne later by the insuring and guaranteeing agencies.

2. The risk of loss on loans using newer properties as security is somewhat less than on loans against older properties as security. Numerous factors combine to produce this conclusion.

3. Geography helps to determine the loss ratio. The closer the security is to the office of the lender, the lower the loss ratio. This of course is a reflection of the ease of servicing such loans. Those against properties located some distance from the city in which the office of the lender is located cannot be watched over as carefully as effective loan servicing demands.

4. Mortgages against owner-occupied properties carry less risk than against those occupied by tenants. The two major factors that lead to this conclusion are the uncertainty of income derived from rented properties and the lack of incentive on the part of both tenant and landlord to maintain rental property in top physical condition. At times of default in mortgage payments, waste and neglect are more likely to take their toll on rental properties than on those that are owner occupied.

5. Amortized loans are less likely to result in loss than are straight loans. In the amortized loans the principal is constantly reduced, usually at least as rapidly as the value of the property declines. Under the straight loan plan, on the other hand, the principal amount of the indebtedness remains the same as it was when it was first placed against the property, regardless of what happens to real estate values. As pointed out elsewhere in this text, the common use by savings banks of demand and one-year loans resulted in the same amount of indebtedness against

the property for indefinite periods of time. If the interest and taxes were being paid promptly, the savings bank was content with its investment and saw no reason to call its loan. In case of default in interest or tax payments, the lender was hesitant to insist upon payment of the principal of the loan and thereby run the added risk of acquiring more real estate in a market that was probably already glutted. As a consequence, the indebtedness of the borrower might increase at a time when the value of the security might be declining.

6. Neighborhoods influence the risk factor. Unless this probability is recognized at the time the loan is granted and is compensated for in the form of lower loan-to-value ratios and more rapid loan amortization, it may contribute materially to losses. Particularly when term loans are the vogue, as described in the preceding paragraph, the decadence of a less desirable neighborhood may be reflected in more than usual declines in the value of real estate located therein.

7. Lintner found a direct relationship between the size of the city in which single properties are used as security for mortgage loans and the amount of risk assumed by the mortgagee. Higher appraisals, the influence of greater spread of unemployment, reduced incomes in the large cities in times of economic depression, and other factors account for this conclusion.

8. There is an inverse relationship between the risk factor and the age of the mortgage at the time delinquencies occur. This applies with greater force to amortized loans than to straight loans, since, with the former, the older the mortgage the smaller the loan balance, as applied to each loan.

Institutional Securities Corporation An interesting facilitative organization of the New York mutual savings banks is the Institutional Securities Corporation. Started in 1933, the corporation experienced rapid growth after World War II. It is wholly owned by New York state mutual savings banks, which may also invest money with it at interest through purchase of debentures or trust or agency-participation certificates. At December 31, 1971, funds placed with the corporation included $5 million in capital stock, $52.3 million in debentures, and $140 million in trust or agency-participation certificates. The corporation provides facilities for nationwide direct servicing of mortgages, appraisal and inspection of real estate, examination of mortgage servicing agents or contractors, mortgage tabulating service, purchase and management of FHA and VA mortgages under trust or agency agreements, and servicing and administration of mortgages under participation agreements. In 1957, Institutional Securities Corporation organized Instlcorp, Inc., which it totally owns. The subsidiary was set up to provide a facility through which pension funds may purchase collateral trust notes secured by mortgages. Instlcorp performs the home office duties for its pension fund clients in much the same manner as the parent corporation acts for its savings bank clients. Since 1966, savings banks have also been permitted to participate in the purchase of collateral trust notes of Instlcorp. Recently, this subsidiary has been particularly active in financing the creation of new low and moderate income housing and rehabilitation under the National Housing Act. At the end of 1971, Instlcorp was servicing mortgages totaling $144 million on properties located in 28 states, the District of Columbia, and Puerto Rico. Of the total serviced, about $69 million represented security for collateral trust notes held by 107 savings banks and the remaining $75 million were FHA and VA mortgages held by various pension funds.

Proposed Federal Chartering of Savings Banks In 1963, the National Association of Mutual Savings Banks proposed congressional legislation to authorize the establishment of federal mutual savings associations. Charters for the new associations would be available to all existing mutual thrift institutions, although none would be required to convert. For mutual savings banks, such legislation would set up different methods in selection of the controlling group and would foster new attitudes particularly toward lending and borrowing policies. Some nomenclature would be changed, as "association" substituted for "bank." The new associations would be under supervision of the Federal Home Loan Bank Board and would have available insurance of accounts provided by the Federal Savings and Loan Insurance Corporation, which might be renamed to describe its new scope. The proposed legislation would permit lending on homes and combination home-and-business property anywhere in the United States. Territorial restrictions would be enforced on a basis comparable to that presently applied to federally chartered savings and loan associations. The proposal would grant authority to buy and sell loan participations; authority to make loans on leaseholds; and authority to make personal loans. Conventional loan balances, however, could not exceed 80 percent of total assets.

Adoption of this proposal received a rebuff when it was deleted from the Housing and Urban Development Act of 1968. At some future date, however, it may be reconsidered.

COMMERCIAL BANKS

Nature of Commercial Banks As the name implies, commercial banks—whether national or state chartered—are the reservoirs of credit for the commerce of the country. Unlike savings and loan associations and savings banks, they are not mutual in character. Their financial plan is based upon stockownership, frequently quite closely held; the investors look upon their commitment as a source of profit through the dividends they receive. The people who supply most of the funds of commercial banks, the depositors, have no voice in management and do not share in the dividends distributed to the shareholders.

Bank depositors are divided into two groups. Demand depositors consist of individuals, corporations, and other groups of people, who place their working capital in their local banks for safekeeping, to be drawn out as needed by the owner. Such funds are not looked upon as investment money. They are simply placed where they are more secure than if they were left in the home or the office. Because they are withdrawable on demand, the bank's use of them is necessarily greatly restricted. In contrast, those who place time deposits in commercial banks look upon such an operation as an investment on which they expect an interest return. Because such funds are expected to remain in the bank longer than are demand deposits, they can be invested in long-term commitments, including real estate mortgages. While commercial banks reserve the right to require 30 days' notice before time deposits can be withdrawn, this right is seldom exercised.

Savings Growth in Commercial Banks Up to the turn of the century, savings accounts in commercial banks were incidental to the major operations of these banks in other financial fields. The law which created national banks made no mention of savings accounts. In 1903, a significant ruling of the Comptroller of the Currency gave the green light to the opening of savings accounts by national banks. The effect of this ruling was that, since the legislation establishing these banks failed either to authorize or to prohibit savings accounts, each bank was free to make its own choice on this question. Nearly half of the national banks chose to open savings departments within the next decade. Then the Federal Reserve Act of 1913 specifically sanctioned such departments by encouraging their operation.

The development of savings departments in state-chartered commercial banks more or less paralleled that of savings departments in national banks. In general, state banks gave favorable consideration to savings accounts somewhat ahead of national banks. Even then it was not until 1917 that the savings deposits of all commercial banks in the country equaled the deposits of all mutual savings banks. Thereafter the commercial banks forged ahead rapidly until the depression years of the 1930s. In 1932, the commercial banks fell behind for the first time in a decade and a half. Taking the lead again in 1935, the commercial banks never lost it. In recent years, their savings and time deposits have been more than double those of savings banks.

There are, however, many who question the propriety of commercial banks taking advantage of the total increased mortgage lending potential created by their present time deposits, because of the increased need for liquidity in connection with their commercial banking function. They point out that a great part of the increase in savings and time deposits is represented by certificates of deposit (CDs), which the banks first began issuing in 1961. Two types of certificates are issued. One type is the large-unit (probably $100,000 or more), negotiable certificate issued to the larger business firms; the other is the small-unit, non-negotiable certificate issued to smaller businesses and individuals. A corporation, which was previously carrying funds in a commercial account at no interest, can now place the same money at interest with the bank and receive a certificate therefor which is as negotiable as a stock or bond. If it needs the funds again, all it has to do is sell the certificate in the market. About $2 billion of time deposits were generated by commercial banks by CDs in 1961. From that time until July 31, 1967, the total grew to $44 billion. Of this amount, over $18 billion represented negotiable CDs. This latter amount, alone, represented approximately 10 percent of the estimated total savings and time deposits of $186 billion. Savings and loan associations as well as other corporations have extensive holdings of CDs for funds deposited in commercial banks.

In light of this reliance on the liquidity of these instruments, the attendant hazards should be noted. Since these certificates are for a term at a higher money cost, the funds they represent must be put to work at a relatively high interest rate to yield a profit. On the other hand, since CDs have early maturities, all banks could be stripped of CD money quickly if short-term rates rose above the highest rate for CDs. Banks making mortgage loans with reliance upon the permanency of CD money would then be pressed. This, of course, points up the need for a reliable secondary market for conventional, as well as federally underwritten mortgages. The problem of secondary markets is discussed in Chapter 27.

Trusteed Funds In addition to the resources in savings accounts that may be used for mortgage lending, commercial banks may have trusteed funds in their trust departments which must be invested. In general, such funds have been left with the bank by individuals who may have very definite ideas about their investment. As a consequence, one trust may be so set up as to prevent the investment of its funds in real estate mortgages. Another may set limits upon the amounts that may be so invested. It might even specify the types of real estate security acceptable for real estate loans. Still another may leave wider discretion to the trustee. Since trusts are enjoying substantial growth, it is likely that an increasing amount of money for real estate lending will be available from this source.

History of Real Estate Lending by Commercial Banks As originally passed in 1863, the national bank law permitted national banks to make loans on both real and personal property as security. A year later the law was amended in such manner that the term "real property" was taken out. Thereafter and until the second decade of this century, national banks were not permitted to make loans on real estate directly. However, they were permitted to accept real estate mortgages as secondary collateral to prevent losses on loans previously made in good faith on legal types of collateral. When trust companies and state-chartered commercial banks began to look with favor upon loans against real estate as security, national banks, sometimes with the tacit acceptance of their supervisors, began to experiment with real estate loans, disguised as secondary collateral in the manner described.

Meantime, state-chartered commercial banks were given more flexible powers in the making of real estate loans. From their earliest beginnings they were permitted to make such loans in the areas in which they operated. In only a minority of the states were there major restrictions upon such operations by the time that national banks were first authorized to make real estate loans; i.e., after the change in the original law of 1863. According to the reports of the Comptroller of the Currency, by the end of the first decade of this century state-chartered banks and trust companies had nearly one sixth of their assets invested in real estate mortgages, while national banks had only a negligible amount so recorded.

Throughout the history of commercial banking in this country, it has been quite evident that national banks have been more effectively supervised than have state-chartered banks and trust companies. At the outset the charters of the latter undertook to establish some standards of operation. Subsequently, for a long time there was no adequate method of examining bank operations to make sure that even the meager charter provisions were being observed. Indeed, there was no attempt at examination of state-chartered banks until quite late in the 19th century. As a consequence, state-chartered commercial banks effectively made their own laws on the subject of real estate lending operations.

Until state banks and trust companies used their authority to grant real estate loans in a manner to place competing national banks at a distinct disadvantage, the latter kept out of the field of real estate mortgage lending. But when the competitive advantage possessed by state banks began to embarrass the operating plans of national banks, supervision of the latter was relaxed in a manner to give more leeway in making mortgage loans, even though the laws under which they operated failed to sanction such practices.

It is fortunate that commercial banks—both state and national—did find it advantageous to grant real estate loans. In many sections of the country there have been neither savings banks nor savings and loan associations to assist in the financing of real estate purchases. Even today there are areas where mortgage money is restricted to that made available by commercial banks. While this is less true than formerly, it still describes some real estate markets.

Federal Reserve Act As originally enacted in 1913, the Federal Reserve Act opened the door to real estate loans by national banks by providing that they could make loans on improved and unencumbered farms for periods up to five years and for amounts not in excess of 50 percent of their value. No national bank could invest for this purpose more than one fourth of its capital and surplus or one third of its time deposits.

In 1916, this law was amended to permit national banks to make loans on improved and unencumbered real estate other than farms. The same limitations were imposed as stated above for farm loans, with the further restriction that, on real estate other than farms, the maturity of the loans was limited to one year instead of five. It is significant to note that one-year loans on urban real estate was the common pattern at that time for many of the competitors of national banks in some areas. Consequently the one-year limitation placed national banks in a competitive framework in such markets. Not all of the state banks limited real estate loans to one year as a matter of practice. Because of this, a demand arose almost immediately for further liberalization of the lending powers of national banks in the real estate field. This demand presently received the active support of the Comptroller of the Currency. No changes were made, however, until the passage of the McFadden Act of 1927. This law permitted five-year, 50 percent loans on urban real estate.

In 1935 the Federal Reserve Act was further amended to permit national banks to lend up to 60 percent of the appraised value of the property for a period of 10 years, if 40 percent of the loan was amortized during the ten years. In 1955 lending provisions were liberalized by increasing the permissible percentage of the loan to the appraised value of the property from 60 to 66⅔ percent for 40 percent amortized residential mortgage loans not exceeding a 10-year maturity. National banks were also permitted to make an amortized residential real estate loan in an amount not to exceed 66⅔ percent of the appraised value of the property if the amortization schedule under the loan was sufficient to extinguish the entire loan within 20 years. In 1959 the lending provisions were even further liberalized. These banks were permitted to lend up to 75 percent of the appraised value of the property where the term of the loan was not over 20 years, if the payments were sufficient to amortize the entire loan within the period ending on the date of its maturity. The five-year, 50 percent limitation was retained for unamortized loans. In 1964, the Federal Reserve Act was amended to permit national banks to make home loans up to 80 percent of appraised property value, amortized over a period not to exceed 25 years. A further liberalization in 1970 permits national banks to make home loans up to 90 percent of appaisal value with an amortization not to exceed 30 years.

Other provisions in the law governing real estate loans by national banks include the following:

1. National banks may make real estate loans which in the aggregate do not exceed 70 percent of time and savings deposits or 100 percent of capital stock and surplus, whichever is greater.

2. Real estate loans which are fully guaranteed or insured by governmental authority are exempted from the maturity and loan-to-value limitations on national bank real estate loans.

3. Construction loans with maturities up to 60 months made by national banks on industrial or commercial properties will not be classified as real estate loans provided the bank has a firm takeout agreement whereby a responsible permanent investor will acquire the mortgage upon completion of construction.

4. Construction loans on residential and farm buildings are also exempt from real estate loan limitations where their maturity does not exceed 24 months; they are considered as ordinary commercial loans.

5. National banks are permitted to make loans on leaseholds that have at least 10 years to run beyond the terminal date of the loan.

6. Loans made to manufacturing or industrial businesses are exempt from real estate loan limitations even though the bank takes a mortgage on real estate as security where the bank relies primarily on the general credit standing and earning power of the business as the source of repayment.

Volume of Mortgage Loans Held by Banks For all commercial banks of the country, real estate mortgage loans constitute about one eighth of total assets and about one third of the amount of time deposits. Loans on residential properties, including apartments, account for approximately two thirds of the dollar volume of all mortgages, with all other types of real estate security making up the other one third. In number of mortgages held, residential loans represent an even higher percentage than is true for dollar volume. Approximately nine tenths of the total number of loans on real estate as security are residential loans.

The distribution of mortgage holdings among different sizes of commercial banks varies somewhat, although the differences are not too significant. In general, the largest banks have a smaller percentage of assets invested in real estate mortgages. The greatest concentration is recorded for banks in the smaller asset categories, though not in the very smallest groups.

Grouped as a single type of financial institution, commercial banks hold about one sixth of the dollar volume of all real estate mortgages in the United States. Of the loans against real estate as security, those on smaller properties—one- to four-family—represent a smaller proportion of the total than do those secured by multifamily apartments and commercial property.

Fluctuations in Mortgage Holdings Unlike savings and loan associations whose major outlet for funds is real estate mortgages, commercial banks vary greatly in the dollar volume of mortgages held. Two conditions account for these fluctuations. In the first place, many commercial banks—particularly the larger ones—would prefer to invest their funds elsewhere. Consequently, whenever the demand for money for commercial loans is great, they show less interest in real estate mortgage commitments. In the absence of a commercial loan demand of sufficient magnitude to absorb their available funds, some of them become more interested in loans against real estate as security.

In the second place, commercial banks have in the past approached the business of making loans on real estate with considerable caution. In general, they have followed smaller loan-to-value ratios than have savings and loan associations. Also, in periods of smaller demand for real estate mortgage credit, commercial banks are generally content to let their competitors make most of the available loans. In the middle 1930s commercial banks were not active bidders for mortgage loans. Their proportion of total mortgage debt dropped considerably from its level at the beginning of the depression. By contrast, in the post-World War II period the proportion of total real estate mortgage debt held by commercial banks rose to a point approximately double the ratio of the middle 1930s. It must be remembered that insurance of loans by the FHA and the guarantee of loans by the VA entered into the picture in the postwar period. Commercial banks made more generous use of both insurance and guarantee of mortgages than did some of their competitors. The use of insurance and guarantee is reflected also in loans made by the larger banks. In general, the larger the commercial bank which holds mortgages, the more generous the use of insurance and guarantee of mortgage loans.

For farm mortgages the fluctuations were even greater. The percentage of decline in total farm mortgage holdings from 1929 to the middle 1930s was greater than for mortgages against urban real estate. Likewise, the percentage of increase in the post-World War II period was greater for farm mortgages than for urban mortgages.

Geographical Distribution of Mortgage Holdings by Banks Holdings of real estate mortgages by commercial banks throughout the country exhibit wide variations among the different states. Those at the top of the list—measured in terms of percentages of mortgages held to total assets—are California, Michigan, New Jersey, and Virginia. At the other end of the line, large states with much smaller percentages of assets invested in real estate mortgages include New York, Massachusetts, and Illinois. Wide fluctuations are to be accounted for by several factors including: strength of competition from other lenders, particularly savings and loan associations, savings banks, and insurance companies; attitude of bank managment toward real estate mortgages; and differences in legislation on the subject.

Particularly significant is the relationship of real estate mortgages to the amount of time deposits. Here the geographical variation is not nearly so great as the percentage of loans on real estate to total assets. In general, the states whose commercial banks enjoy the greatest amount of time deposits also have the highest percentage of them invested in real estate mortgages.

Differences among States It is not pertinent to attempt in this text a detailed analysis of different state laws governing the operation of banks chartered and supervised under them. There are major differences in policy governing real estate lending operations of state-chartered commercial banks. Several factors account for these differences. Among them is the political strength of competitive financial institutions. For example, where aggressive managements of savings and loan associations are jealous of the encroachments of commercial banks on what they consider to be their field of operations, this aggressiveness is likely to be reflected in the character of commercial bank supervision.

Since the supervision of commercial banks and of competitive financial institutions is frequently either under the same control or under closely related controls, it becomes a nice question of balance to determine which type of institution to favor in supervisory activities. The problem is likely to become even more acute in future years as commercial banks and their competitors assume more common characteristics. For example, there is no question but that savings institutions are beginning to see the need for maintaining greater liquidity in order that they may attract and hold more funds of thrift people who may wish to ask for and expect the withdrawal of their funds on short notice. Meantime, commercial banks—both state chartered and national—are becoming more and more like savings institutions; they are inclined to compete more vigorously for savings and to give more consideration to the investment of savings deposits in real estate mortgages. It is not surprising that the operations of savings institutions accuse commercial banks of trying to become savings and loan associations; nor that commercial bankers are disturbed about the trend of savings institutions toward the assumption of some functions heretofore looked upon as the sole prerogatives of commercial banks. It is highly probable that the requirements of the customers of these institutions will determine the future character of their operations.

Types of Real Estate Loans As pointed out above, commercial banks have made more use of the insurance and guarantee of real estate mortgages than have savings and loan associations. The largest banks which engage in the business of real estate lending have relatively more of their loans—both in number and in dollar volume—either guaranteed or insured. The smaller banks use insured or guaranteed loans to a lesser extent. The FHA and the VA set the pattern for interest rates, maturity dates, and loan-to-value ratios. Conventional loans on residential real estate generally carry a somewhat higher rate of interest, are written for a shorter period of time, and cover a smaller ratio of loan to value. Those made in recent years are generally amortized or partly amortized.

Loans on property other than one- to four-family residences are usually not insured or guaranteed; they frequently are wholly or partly amortized; they usually run for a shorter period than do loans on one- to four-family residences; and interest rates are somewhat higher, though there is considerable variation in this regard.

Changing Character of Bank Loans on Real Estate Since 1930, several significant changes have been made in the character of real estate mortgages held by commercial banks. Some of these changes have paralleled those made by their competitors during the same period, while others cannot be so classified.

Loan-to-value ratios have increased sharply, particularly during the periods when FHA and VA loans have been in vogue. Maturities of real estate loans have lengthened materially, particularly for loans on residential property as security. In all of these changes, commercial banks have responded to the same types of pressure that have affected their competitors—savings and loan associations, savings banks, and insurance companies.

Another significant change in the mortgage-lending practices of commercial banks—shared by insurance companies and, in a smaller degree, by savings banks, but not by savings and loan associations—has been the general introduction of loan amortization. In the earlier years commercial banks used straight or term loans quite commonly. Some real estate loans held by commercial banks were partially amortized as long ago as the middle 1920s. This practice has been continued. In addition, many fully amortized loans have been granted by commercial banks in recent years. Again the influence of FHA and VA loans is reflected in this change. Savings and loan associations did not share in this change in recent years, since they have been using fully amortized loans for many years. The change to fully amortized loans—particularly in the financing of residential properties—came for life insurance companies and for savings banks concurrently with the change for commercial banks—and for the same reasons.

Methods of Acquiring Mortgages Commercial banks follow either of two practices in acquiring mortgages on real estate. Some have mortgage loan departments that are so well organized that they are active competitors within their markets for real estate loans. Indeed, their advertising for mortgages may be pitched on a very aggressive plane. If their time deposits are large and dependable over a period of years, they are likely to be more active bidders for real estate mortgages. As pointed out in Chapter 7, they may even have become sponsors of mortgage investment trusts. They not only originate the loans which they carry in their portfolios, but they service them as well. In some communities that lack specialized real estate financial institutions, commercial banks may be the most reliable agencies for making loans on real estate.

Other commercial banks, which place less emphasis upon real estate mortgages as sources of income, may not even have a mortgage department worthy of the name. Such mortgages as they may acquire from time to time are purchased from mortgage bankers or dealers. As pointed out in Chapter 15, commercial banks that purchase their real estate mortgages are likely to be "in-and-outers" so far as their mortgage acquisitions are concerned. Some of them may even let their mortgages be serviced by their loan correspondents, particularly if the security is located in a city other than the one in which the bank is located. Finally, some commercial banks prefer not to engage in mortgage lending under any circumstances.

Recent Trends During the years since World War II the proportion of nonfarm mortgage loans held by commercial banks has increased a bit more rapidly than those held by all competitors combined. Of the total of nonfarm mortgages held by commercial banks at the end of 1970, approximately two thirds used residential property as security. Of the total volume of residential loans about one seventh were insured by FHA or were guaranteed by VA. Commercial banks showed a three-to-one preference for FHA loans over those guaranteed by VA. Farm loans constituted 6 percent of all mortgage loans outstanding in bank portfolios at the end of 1970.

QUESTIONS AND PROBLEMS

1. How do mutual savings banks and commercial banks differ in their general purposes?
2. How have the differences in the purposes of mutual savings banks and commercial banks affected their lending policies with respect to mortgage loans on real estate?
3. Where are most of the mutual savings banks located? Why are they not found in other parts of the country?
4. What were the reasons for the decline in the volume of real estate

mortgages held by mutual savings banks during the 1930s and the war years of the 1940s?

5. Why did mutual savings banks adopt a more favorable attitude toward lending on real estate mortgages after the close of World War II?

6. How has recent legislation liberalized the lending practices of mutual savings banks?

7. What conclusions may be drawn from Lintner's studies of savings bank operations in Massachusetts? What value do such studies have as a guide to loan policy?

8. Why have commercial banks been so slow in entering the real estate lending field?

9. How important statistically are commercial banks as a source of mortgage money to finance real estate purchases?

10. How has the character of real estate loans made by commercial banks changed since the 1930s? Answer the same question for mutual savings banks.

11. How do commercial banks and mutual savings banks acquire their mortgages?

12. Do you expect the commercial banks to be relatively more important or less important as a source of real estate financing in the future? What considerations have influenced your opinion?

14

Financing of Real Estate by Life Insurance Companies

Life Insurance Companies as Lenders on Real Estate Security Like some other types of financial institutions, life insurance companies have followed a pattern in lending on real estate as security that has adjusted itself to changing economic conditions. At one time farm loans were popular outlets for investable resources of insurance companies. Later, enthusiasm for this type of investment cooled materially. From time to time mortgages on urban real estate have been favored. Since life insurance companies, unlike savings and loan associations, for example, were not organized primarily for the purpose of financing homes, it is to be expected that they will seek the outlets for their investment funds which will best meet the requirements of the investor at the time the investment is made.

One of the reasons why real estate mortgages are in current favor with life insurance companies is the pressure for investment of enormous resources at a time when interest rates on other types of investment are relatively lower.

Life Insurance Assets According to the *Life Insurance Fact Book*, total assets of life insurance companies in 1890 were $771 million. They doubled in each decade until, in 1960, they totaled about $120 billion. As of December 1970, they were estimated at $207 billion, indicating continued rapid growth. In recent years insurance companies have experienced quite a change in their investments in real estate mortgages. In 1930 slightly more than 40 percent of all assets were so invested. This percentage declined to a low point of just under 15 percent in 1946. Since that year there has been a consistent increase in the proportion of assets invested in mortgages. At the end of 1970, the percentage

14 / Financing of Real Estate by Life Insurance Companies   241

was approximately 35.9. Meantime, because of the very rapid growth of total assets, the dollar volume of mortgages held at the end of 1970 was over twice as great as the 1958 volume.

The magnitude of the investment problems of life insurance companies is indicated from the fact that in 1950 new investments amounted to $12.3 billion; in 1959, to $19.8 billion; and in 1970, to $62.3 billion. New investments represent not only new assets but refundings and pay-offs of old investments. For example, purchases of short-term securities, usually involving reinvestment of the funds several times during the year, amounted to $38 billion in 1970. Of the remainder, approximately $10 billion were derived from matured or redeemed bonds, mortgage amortizations or prepayments, and sales of holdings.

Earnings on Investment The net average return on life insurance investments in 1923 was 5.18 percent. In the following year this average rate of return started on a long, steady period of decline which reached a low of 2.88 percent in 1947. Since 1948 there have been annual increases to about 5.30 percent in 1970. The continued decline in the earnings rate for insurance companies through the mid-1940s helped to account for a return of interest in real estate mortgages, because they have consistently paid higher rates than government bonds or even Aaa corporate bonds. The yield differential has generally remained even as bond yields have risen.

History of Mortgage Lending by Insurance Companies In the early days of life insurance company operation, such institutions were primarily dependent upon real estate mortgages for investment outlets. As late as 1860, approximately 60 percent of their assets were represented by mortgages. Another 20 percent of total assets were represented by premium notes owed by policyholders who had not yet paid their insurance premiums in full. These are hardly to be classed as investments of the same quality as real estate mortgages. Consequently, more than three fourths of conscious and purposeful investments of life insurance companies in 1860 took the form of real estate mortgages.

A couple of decades later, corporate bonds and the obligations of political subdivisions began to be included in the investment portfolios of life insurance companies. By 1890 mortgages had shrunk relatively to about 40 percent of assets. By 1900 their percentage had been further reduced to 30 percent, where they stayed until the decade of the 1920s. By 1930, real estate mortgages were again 40 percent of total assets. As a result of the depression of the 1930s, real estate mortgages dropped to less than 20 percent of the total assets of life insurance companies and remained there until 1949. But because of the exceedingly rapid growth of such assets in recent years, as set forth above, the amount of real estate financing by insurance companies is a continuing factor of tremendous importance.

Restrictions upon Real Estate Loans by Insurance Companies Most of the states have passed laws governing the operations of insurance companies. These fall into two classes: laws governing the operations of companies domiciled within the state; and those controlling activities of companies domiciled elsewhere, but doing business within the state that passed the law. Since the major purpose of both types of laws is the protection of the policyholders, the features of the legislation dealing with investments are more or less incidental to this major purpose. For this reason, a brief discussion of legislation of the latter type must be presented.

While most laws dealing with insurance companies domiciled within the state permit investments in real estate mortgages, such permission is usually hedged about with various types of restrictions. Only the most common restrictions will be discused here. Those interested in the less common types are referred to the laws of the various states for such information. In general, the permission to make loans on real estate is limited, for example, to "improved land," including farms. While such improved land is supposed to be unencumbered, such encumbrances as taxes, assessments, easements, and building restrictions are excepted.

One common type of restriction that impinges heavily upon real estate finance, and that will probably be subject to review from time to time, is the upper limit of individual loans and the limit of assets which may be devoted to this type of investment. For example, in New York an insurance company may not invest more than $30,000 or 2 percent of its total assets (whichever is greater) in a mortgage on a single property. If the company's assets are less than $1 million, it is effectively restricted to loans on residential or small business properties, including farms. If its assets exceed $100 million, this 2 percent limitation loses much of its meaning. In New York, also, not more than 50 percent of the total assets of a life insurance company may be invested in all real estate mortgages held by it at one time. Again the size of the company has an important bearing upon its competitive position in the field of real estate finance.

Where legislation governing the operation of life insurance companies makes specific mention of such subjects as leaseholds and land contracts, they too are subject to the restrictions defined in the law. For example, no loan may be made by an insurance company domiciled in the state of New York on a leasehold whose unexpired term is less than 21 years. In Minnesota the corresponding term is 40 years; in Ohio 99 years, renewable forever; and in Texas for a period at least 10 years beyond the term of the loan.

Where restrictions of the kind mentioned above are included in the law which governs the operation of insurance companies domiciled in another state but doing business in the state which passes the law, the purpose is to protect the domestic companies against unfair competition as well as to protect the policyholders.

Restrictions setting the upper limits of loans in relation to the value of the security therefor are considered to be quite conservative in today's markets. Such loan-to-value ratios usually range between 66⅔ and 75 percent for conventional mortgages. FHA and VA loans are usually exempted from these as well as from most of the other restrictions discussed herein. In general, while a few laws make gestures in the direction of a recognition of the importance of appraisals in the administration of such loan-to-value restrictions, they cannot be said to give the full protection intended. In the absence of appraisal standards which are not yet available, such limitations are more theological than practical. In making this statement there is no intent to imply that loan-to-value restrictions operate any differently for insurance company lenders than for any other kinds of real estate financial institutions.

In respect to one type of restriction, not mentioned above, insurance companies usually enjoy greater freedom than their competitors. They are not usually required to amortize their real estate loans nor to limit them to any maximum maturity. Recent changes in policy on such questions have been dictated more by competition than by law. For example, insurance companies are making freer use of amortized loans on residential properties than was their practice a quarter of a century ago. Recently, several states have passed laws permitting higher loan-to-value ratios, usually 75 percent, if the loan is fully amortized within a prescribed term of years.

Geographical Limitations Here is an area in which laws governing insurance companies operate quite differently from those governing the operations of other types of lending institutions. For example, in Chapter 12 it was pointed out that savings and loan associations are usually discouraged from making loans outside of a narrowly restricted lending area defined in the regulatory laws as being within, say, 100 miles of the home office of the association. Until recently savings banks have been subjected to geographical limitations somewhat more liberal than those for savings and loan associations, but nevertheless restrictive.

Geographical limitations for insurance companies are much more liberal. For the most part the lending area for them is considered to be the United States. In some state laws even Canada is added. One potent reason for this difference is that insurance companies are commonly national in their markets for writing insurance policies. It has been thought fair to allow them to invest their funds in areas from which they have been obtained in the usual course of conducting their insurance business. Indeed, some states have been so insistent that this be done that their legislation is slanted in this direction. For example, Texas laws require that a foreign insurance company, as a consideration for the right to do business in that state, must invest at least three fourths of the reserves required to protect Texas policyholders in Texas real estate finance and in Texas securities.

Geographical Distribution of Mortgage Holdings At the end of 1969, the states which supplied the largest holdings of farm mortgages in the portfolios of life insurance companies were, in the order named: Texas, California, Iowa, and Illinois. The largest holdings of FHA nonfarm mortgages were in the following states, in the order named: California, Texas, Washington, Ohio, and Florida. Corresponding figures for VA nonfarm loans place the following states at the top of the list: California, Texas, Virginia, Ohio, and Illinois. Other nonfarm mortgages showed greatest totals in the following states: California, Texas, New York, Illinois, and Florida. The "other nonfarm" classification includes mortgages on commercial and industrial properties. Total real estate mortgages held by insurance companies at the end of 1969 were greatest in the following states: California ($9.8 billion), Texas ($6.9 billion), New York ($3.8 billion), Illinois ($3.3 billion), Ohio ($2.9 billion), and finally, in Florida ($2.9 billion).

Self-Imposed Restrictions While it can be said that savings and loan associations, for example, are all interested in making loans on real estate as security, the same generalization cannot be applied to all life insurance companies. Great differences appear in the mortgage-lending operations of the latter. These differences are accounted for by variations in size, investment experience, and mental attitudes of those who manage the companies. As may be expected, smaller companies are less well equipped to handle mortgage lending than are their larger competitors. Some companies limit their mortgage holdings to residential properties as security, while others lend on commercial, financial, and even industrial property as well.

In spite of the pressure of funds for investment and for reinvestment, life insurance companies occasionally experience something akin to the "in-and-out" policies of commercial banks in their mortgage investment programs. This is particularly true of advance commitments. At times they will gladly indicate to their correspondents their willingness to purchase agreed-upon quantities of mortgages for future delivery. On other occasions they become more cautious and prefer to consider purchases only as mortgages are offered to them. In unusual situations—where money rates appear quite uncertain—they may even withdraw from the market temporarily.

Mortgage Experience According to a study published by the National Bureau of Economic Research,[1] mortgage experience of a sizable sample

---

[1] R. J. Saulnier, *Urban Mortgage Lending by Life Insurance Companies* (New York: National Bureau of Economic Research, 1950). A considerable part of the statistical material of this chapter has been adapted from this study and from the *Life Insurance Fact Book*.

of life insurance companies exhibits the following characteristics. Geographically speaking, a high concentration of loans was made from 1940 to 1946 in the northeastern section of the United States, New England excepted. Large metropolitan areas attracted loans on family dwellings and accounted for 90 percent in number and nearly half of the dollar volume of life insurance mortgage loans. These were followed in order by loans on apartment houses and loans on other types of income properties, including stores.

On the whole, the distribution of real estate loans in recent years has shown a distinct trend toward apartment complexes and commercial and industrial properties. Mortgage holdings of one- to four-family residential properties represented over half of all mortgage holdings from 1950 through 1964, reaching a high of 61 percent in 1956. Since 1964, this proportion has steadily declined. At the 1970 year-end, it was about 35 percent. At that time, over 55 percent of total mortgage holdings were on apartment developments and commercial properties, with the balance on farms. It should also be noted that in the autumn of 1967, the life insurance industry committed over $1 billion to alleviate blighted urban conditions. An additional $1 billion was pledged in 1969, with the result that by the 1970 year-end nearly $1.6 billion had been pledged or committed to mortgages under this program.

The predominance of FHA loans in the period from 1940 to 1946 was particularly marked, being 57 percent in number and 31 percent in dollar volume of all home loans closed or purchased. The VA loans had not yet had a chance to come into favor during this period. Two thirds in number and 43 percent in dollar volume were written for 20 years or more. Increases in the maturity of loans and in the loan-to-value ratios of real estate loans made by life insurance companies during the past quarter century have been especially marked.

The types of mortgages held by life insurance companies at the end of 1947, 1959, and 1970 are shown in Table 14–1. The relative shift from

TABLE 14–1
Types of Mortgages Held by Life Insurance Companies (000,000 omitted)

	1947		1959		1970	
	Total	Percent	Total	Percent	Total	Percent
Nonfarm loans						
FHA.............	$1,398	16.3	$ 8,523	21.7	$12,001	16.2
VA...............	844	9.8	7,086	18.1	5,394	7.2
Conventional.......	5,538	63.6	20,744	53.0	51,331	69.0
Farm loans...........	975	10.3	2,844	7.2	5,649	7.6
Total..........	$8,755	100.0	$39,197	100.0	$74,375	100.0

conventional to FHA and VA loans between 1947 and 1959 is quite noticeable from the table. The dollar volume of conventional nonfarm loans increased nearly 10 times from 1947 through 1970. The outstanding FHA and VA loans increased markedly in significance and then went into a decline relatively, although maintaining fairly constant dollar amounts during the 1960s. The increasing relative importance of conventional nonfarm loans in a large measure is attributable to recent demands by business for external financing which have diverted funds that might otherwise have flowed into home mortgages under FHA and VA programs.

Preference for Larger Loans Although life insurance companies make loans on single-family residences, many of them prefer the larger loans in this category. Seldom will they compete actively for smaller residential loans except when they are buying them in bulk. To an even more marked degree, they prefer loans on multifamily dwellings and on commercial properties such as hotels and office and loft buildings. Even in the field of industrial real estate, they are an important financial influence.

Another development in the mortgage market affecting life companies is the rapidly growing importance of local lenders, especially savings and loan associations and commercial banks. Insurance companies are experiencing increasing difficulty in competing for conventional residential loans. For this reason, also, these companies are seeking loans on income property occupied by tenants with superior credit ratings. The advantages of purchase-and-leaseback arrangements have been sharply curtailed during the past few years by changes in the federal income tax law. Out of the leaseback experience, however, life companies have learned that they can accomplish an approximate equivalent by 100 percent loans. Since the definite approval of such loans in New York state, insurance companies have been looking with increasing favor on 100 percent loans on income property when the tenants are of unquestioned financial responsibility and the net rent will support the loan. Relative freedom from maximum loan limitations and territorial restrictions gives the life companies an advantage over their competitors in regard to this type of property.

Proportion of Assets in Mortgages In 1890, 40 percent of insurance company assets was invested in real estate mortgages. For the next 40 years this ratio varied from year to year until in 1930 it was again 40 percent. From 1930 the ratio declined steadily until in 1945 it was just under 15 percent. Increases since 1945 brought the ratio of mortgages to total assets up to 35 percent in 1971. During this latter period most of the shift in investments was from government bonds to mortgages. The present ratio is somewhat lower than during the immediately past years because of the extremely attractive yields in the bond markets during 1969, 1970, and 1971. At the end of 1970 life insurance companies held about one sixth of all real estate mortgages in the country.

Mortgage Loan Department Because of the geographical extent of mortgage loan operations, the problem of organization of the mortgage loan department of a life insurance company is quite unlike that faced by its competitors in this field of operations. Investment in mortgages can be national in scope for any particular company. Their origination and servicing must be conducted at the local level to be most successful. Because of differences in practices among insurance companies, several plans of operating mortgage loan departments are in common use. The more extensive the mortgage-lending operations, the larger the number of loans outstanding and the more far-flung their geographical distribution; the more varied the kinds of property which secures them, the more complicated the mortgage loan department becomes.

The institution which has outstanding a large number of insured or guaranteed loans on residential property, widely scattered geographically without any great amount of concentration in any contiguous area, may well find one type of mortgage loan department most satisfactory. One which has a similar amount of money invested in a small number of large commercial and multiple-family residence loans, concentrated in a few metropolitan areas, might find a different form of organization best adapted to its needs.

There are two major types of organization to be considered. In addition, variations and combinations of these two types are in use. These two major types are branch offices and outside correspondents. They have been known to succeed each other, following a pattern of alternation that is dictated by experience which ends in disappointment. If one system is tried continuously to the satisfaction of the management, it is not likely to be disturbed. But if its results are unsatisfactory, regardless of the reasons, it is not uncommon that a major operation is performed in order that a change of pattern may be substituted.

Where the branch office type of organization is used, it is manned by salaried employees of the insurance company. Here the control is direct. Both lending and servicing facilities can be set up by the home office, and supervisory personnel can see to it that company policies are carried out to the letter. Under this plan of organization, the lending institution can literally build a loan portfolio according to its own pattern, instead of picking and choosing among the types of loans offered for its purchase.

Branch offices may be located in the same physical quarters as the respective local offices of the insurance division of the insurance corporation, or they may occupy separate space. In either event, the employees of the mortgage loan department are under the supervision of the home-office staff engaged in mortgage loan operations. In addition they may be subject to some measure of direction by the roving field representatives who visit them from time to time. Arm's-length supervision of small staffs needed to man branch offices may be one of the reasons why this plan of organization is less commonly used than the correspondent system next described.

Loan Correspondents As an alternative to branch offices for the purpose of making and servicing loans, some insurance companies prefer to appoint outside companies or individuals to handle this part of their mortgage business. From the standpoint of loan origination only, the service performed by such a correspondent is that of a finder, for whose service a finder's fee is paid. Here both the mortgage banker and the mortgage broker are used. Both of these are described elsewhere in this text. Some insurance companies use either in ways that best suit their purposes. In some instances, the finder's job is completed when he points out an opportunity for making a real estate loan. Or he may take the next step and assemble information about it, leaving decisions to be made by salaried representatives of the insurance company.

Perhaps, instead, the finder assembles the information, prepares the necessary papers, and in fact does all but the closing of the loan, leaving only the latter function to be performed by the more direct representatives of the lender, if they find it desirable to complete the transaction. Finally, in the case of mortgage bankers (or mortgage companies, as they are sometimes called) the finder may use its own funds to close the loan, which is then offered for sale to the insurance company. Some of the sellers of such mortgages are properly classed as correspondents of the insurance company purchaser, because of their contractual and continuing relationships. Others are not properly called correspondents, since the relationship between buyer and seller is casual and discontinuous.

Where the finder is compensated for the service of finding mortgage opportunities only, other arrangements must be made for servicing the loans which he originates. Where the correspondent is a mortgage banker, he may also service loans made by him for the insurance company or sold by him, receiving therefor a separate service fee. A variety of plans are used to provide compensation for loan correspondents. Among them are monthly payments, a percentage of collections made, and a percentage of original loans. As pointed out elsewhere in this text, a high finder's fee may be accompanied by a low servicing fee and vice versa.

Even those insurance companies that have had extensive experience with both branch offices and loan correspondents seem to encounter difficulty in deciding which plan is better. One reason for this apparent indecision is the problem of changing conditions. At one period of the business cycle, one plan appears to meet requirements best; at another period, another plan may be preferred. Some companies combine the two, using branches to establish patterns and loan correspondents to operate within patterns so established. Some companies alternate plans. Some use both at the same time. Historically speaking, correspondents appeared first. They still predominate.

Undoubtedly, branch operation provides a better opportunity for close control than does the loan-correspondent plan. For that reason, times of stress are likely to emphasize the contributions of branches in contrast with those of the more independent correspondents. On the other hand, aggressive correspondents who produce results satisfactory to their principals are likely to find continued demand for their services.

Alternative Investments The institutional purchasers of mortgages usually have alternative outlets for their funds. Their investment committees are constantly weighing the advantages of purchasing high-grade corporate bonds, municipal bonds, and similar investments against those accruing from the purchase of real estate mortgages. Since bond issues carry less overhead and involve less trouble in servicing even when the servicing of mortgages is farmed out, they are likely to be favored. Unless the net interest spread is definitely in favor of real estate mortgages, the latter are likely to suffer from time to time as far as their purchase by large institutional holders is concerned.

Originating and Service Fees In a study made by the National Bureau of Economic Research, originating fees paid by life insurance companies to correspondents varied from 0.25 percent to more than 2 percent. In at least half the cases studied, the range was from 0.75 to 1.5 percent. The greater number fell in the class paying from 1 to 1.25 percent, with the classes 0.75 to 1 percent and 1.25 to 1.5 percent following closely thereafter.

Orginating or finders' fees are of particular significance where mortgage loans are repaid within a relatively short period of time. If a finder's fee is paid in placing a loan on the books, this reduces the effective interest rate on the loan correspondingly. For example, if the finder's fee is 1.5 percent and the loan is repaid within five years, the 1.5 percent commission must be amortized within the five-year period, unless a corresponding penalty is charged against the borrower for the privilege of prepaying his loan. That is one reason why insurance companies frequently make no provision for mortgage loan prepayments or for such prepayments only when penalties are assessed. One common provision is to permit not more than 20 percent of the loan principal to be repaid within any consecutive period of 12 months. In the recent period of extremely high interest rates, it is not uncommon to have total "lock-in" of the loan for a minimum period, often five to seven years. Currently, finders' fees are commonly paid by the borrower.

Servicing fees in the sample study by the National Bureau ranged from 0.2 to 0.7 percent. More than half the cases studied fell within the range from 0.3 to 0.59 percent. The distribution of the number of companies paying 0.3 to 0.39 percent was approximately the same as those paying 0.4 to 0.49 percent. Those paying 0.5 to 0.59 percent were considerably fewer in number.

Home-Office Operations In addition to the supervision exercised by home-office mortgage loan departments of life insurance companies, some such departments are largely depended upon to originate and service loans. This is particularly true of some small companies, of those which have only an unusually small proportion of their assets invested in mortgage loans, and of those which concentrate their mortgage loans in one or a few areas with close geographical contact with the home office. Some home offices make no use of either branch offices or loan correspondents either for loan originations or for loan servicing. Some rely in part upon loan finders of one kind or another and do all the servicing from the home office. Some find their mortgage loan operations so widely distributed that they farm out both loan origination and servicing.

In general, the functions of the home-office mortgage loan department may be classified under the following heads: (1) the determination of mortgage loan policies, including the kinds of property on which loans will be made or purchased, the geographical areas in which they are to be favored, and the loan plans to be used; (2) the consideration of loan applications and of mortgage-purchase opportunities and the recommendations to be made thereon to the investment committee; (3) the establishment and operation of a plan of supervising home-office staff, field representatives, branch-office personnel, etc.; (4) the study of performance records of loans on the books; and (5) periodic checks to determine the status of mortgage loan investments. From time to time property management arrangements may be required to handle the management, operation, and disposal of properties acquired through foreclosures of delinquent mortgages.

Except in those intermittent periods when unusually large amounts of foreclosed real estate are acquired, the management of property presents no particularly difficult problem. Under so-called normal circumstances, which produce only occasional property acquisitions, the probability is that a local representative or agent will be assigned the task of property disposal. If a mistake was made in making the loan, the insurance company will absorb its loss, if any, as one of the calculated risks of the mortgage loan business. If foreclosure results from causes that could not have been foreseen when the loan was acquired, the same procedure is followed. Only when there is no reasonable market for foreclosed properties will the problem of property management become acute. Then heroic steps may be needed to minimize losses. The home office will then assume greater responsibility for more direct control of owned real estate.

Ownership versus Lending Financial institutions that have learned from experience that mortgages sometimes turn out to be deferred certificates of real estate ownership have pondered this question: Which is safer, to start with ownership or to end with it? In other words, as an alternative to making a very high prcentage loan against a property owned by the borrower, some lenders are experimenting with direct ownership of income property. When a financial institution takes a mortgage on an existing property, it can only take or leave this kind of investment. If it builds the building instead, it can exercise such choices as location, arrangement, and standards of construction. If it makes a loan, it has no direct control over the property as long as the obligations of the mortgagor are met. When it invests its funds directly in the real estate, management rests with the owner. There is no mortgagor. Equities in owned real estate are out in the open. Equities in mortgaged real estate may be just as definitely established in the mortgagee, even though they may be concealed for a time until legal title passes when a default results finally in foreclosure or in an adequate substitute in the form of a voluntary conveyance.

Other factors are also present in the determination to own the real estate from the beginning in contrast with lending against it as security. These include legal complications surrounding foreclosure proceedings. Tax problems play their part also. With the prospect of high taxes for the indefinite future, financial institutions still arrive at investment policies in the boardroom, but only after the tax angles have been fully explored. In some instances the probabilities lean in the direction of recommending outright ownership of some investment property instead of depending upon interest from mortgages only.

Life insurance companies are among those experimenting with real estate ownership for investment purposes. Such properties are either owned directly by the insurance companies or by wholly owned subsidiaries. The total directly owned real estate in 1947 was $860 million. Of this, $582 million was utilized for company operational requirements. At the end of 1970, the total had grown to $6.3 billion. The life companies' own home and branch offices required about $1.5 billion of that amount. The other $4.8 billion represented direct ownership of commercial and residential properties. Although this is a favorable trend toward making possible more business facilities and housing, it should be pointed out that $6.3 billion is only slightly more than 3 percent of the total life insurance company assets at that time. Many of these properties are held under leaseback arrangements, discussed elsewhere in this text.

Commercial Real Estate as an Investment Because of its increasing importance to the life insurance company investment program, commercial real estate should be analyzed in regard to the primary objectives of safety of principal, liquidity, and yield. Its attractiveness depends upon its ability to meet these objectives.

The safety of principal in a direct investment in real estate must be determined by whether the investor can recapture his capital (1) by sale of the property for an amount equal to his unamortized investment or (2) by a full return of his capital in the amortization process, together with a rent equivalent for interest. The measure of marketability of the property, of course, depends upon such factors as its diversity of uses, site, and architectural appeal. Increasing rates of general price inflation and a rising level of real estate prices have also had important impacts in increasing salability of such properties. Critics of commitments to effect a hedge against inflation urge that such uses of funds are of a speculative, rather than investment, nature and consequently improper.

Where reliance for recapture of capital is on the full amortization process, the financial integrity of the lessee is paramount. This financial condition is required to meet the objections of those who claim that 100 percent financed rental properties are less secure than mortgages granted for lower percentages of the property value. It is suggested by those favoring direct investment that if the financial strength of the lessee is unquestionable in the early years of the lease, by the time financial conditions of the company will have had time to change, the unamortized cost will be adequately secured by excess property values. Even in event of financial reverses, they point out, most corporations reorganize and continue operations, with the result that reorganization trustees affirm real estate leases and preserve the owners' claims to continued rental income.

In regard to the liquidity factor in direct real estate investment, it must be accepted that large individual parcels are not readily salable. This is particularly true in periods of economic adversity. Life companies must therefore evaluate this characteristic in light of their overall portfolio requirements. They must accept the limitations of the degree of liquidity provided provided by the normal amortization of principal implicit in rent income under a long-term lease.

The most attractive feature of this form of investment has been its yield. Directly owned commercial real estate has been consistently acquired to yield effective interest rates $\frac{1}{2}$ percent or more above those on mortgages on comparable property. In addition, recently, bonus interest based on rental overages and equity participations have been written into the loan agreements. In addition, a most important inducement has been the opportunity for capital appreciation either in the residual value after the property has been fully amortized or as result of rising price levels.

There have also been administrative advantages claimed for direct investment. Proponents believe that the supply of commercial real estate at attractive yields is great. It is true that investments in the commercial sector over the last decade or longer have been in tremendous volume. It is not so certain, however, that placement of funds in this area is any less competitive than in other types of investment.

An additional advantage claimed for real estate investment has been the unlikelihood of refinancing or early prepayment so often characteristic of mortgage loans. Although the point seems to be well taken, the advantage seems to be purely one of degree. Both direct ownership and mortgage lending also carry the obligation of periodic reinvestment of funds released by amortization.

Still another advantage claimed for direct investment in real estate is that it permits management, by specially tailored terms of purchase and leaseback, to control net income to some degree. For some purposes, many of them tax-related, this possibility is desirable.

On the other side of the coin, in addition to the questions raised in the foregoing discussion, the problems of staffing skilled persons to administer such real estate investment programs are great, often prohibitive for small insurance companies. Many fear the possibility of having to manage the property in event of reversals. There is also still a strong prejudice among older, senior executives against direct ownership of real estate.

Private Placements One method of financing that is essentially a part of real estate finance was developed during the 1930s and has since grown to enormous proportions. This is variously known as private placement, direct sale, private sale, and so forth. In effect, the business enterprise that needs money obtains it directly from the financial institution that is expected to be the ultimate investor in the securities purchased. There is no middleman such as an investment banker, a security underwriter, or a security salesman.

While not all of the securities that have been purchased by financial institutions in the form of private placements can be classified as real estate bonds, enough of them fit into this category to warrant a brief discussion of private placements in a text on real estate finance. As a matter of fact, the successful experience of financial institutions with large real estate mortgages laid the foundations for their participation in the broader field of private placements.

Origin of Private Placements Private placements of securities as we know them currently originated in the early 1930s. The depression of the 1930s focused attention upon the need for security in an uncertain world. In a very real sense, life insurance companies were the beneficiaries of the misfortunes of investors and speculators who lost money from the decline in the prices of stocks and bonds. Disillusioned and discouraged security purchasers in great numbers turned to life insurance as a more certain means of protecting their dependents. This also had the effect of placing upon the insurance companies the burden of investing funds supplied by their policyholders.

For more than two decades we have witnessed a marked trend in the direction of institutionalizing the savings of the American people. Many who lack confidence in their capacity to manage their own affairs have shifted the burden to financial institutions such as life insurance companies. As a result, life insurance companies have become the largest single class of institutions entrusted with the care of the savings of thrifty people. Following the many bank failures in the early 1930s, life insurance companies for a time were about the only source of funds available to industrial enterprises in need of financial assistance. Demand matched supply when those in need of loans went to those who had money to lend.

Influence of Security Regulation Another factor that has influenced the wide use of private placements was the enactment of the Securities Act of 1933, which gave an agency of the federal government police power over the sale of securities offered in the open market. The element of cost in preparing applications for approval by the Securities and Exchange Commission, while an item of some importance, is probably not the major factor considered by those who sought to bypass such need for seeking approval of the issuance of securities to be offered for sale. The time element was undoubtedly much more significant in the early stages of the use of private placements of securities.

For example, if corporation X should decide at a regular meeting of its board of directors that it should raise money by the sale of a mortgage bond issue at a time when the market for such bonds was reasonably favorable, it would have to prepare its registration statement and supporting documents for submission to the SEC in support of its application for the approval of the sale of its securities in the open market. Thereafter the SEC must be given sufficient time to examine the evidence before reaching a decision. Consequently, from the date of a determination to borrow money to the sale of the bonds in the open market, a few months' time could easily be consumed. Meantime, the market for this class of security might easily turn against it in a fast-moving world. Instead of disposing of the bonds in a favorable market, as had been hoped, the issuing corporation might find itself in a position where it could not dispose of its bonds under reasonably favorable conditions.

By contrast with the above method of an open-market offer of its bonds to all and sundry investors, the corporation could negotiate with a single financial institution such as a life insurance company—or a few such institutions—for the sale of the entire bond issue. Since in such case there would be no public offering of the securities, the SEC would have no jurisdiction over the sale of the bonds. The time, trouble, and expense of preparing registration statements and supporting documents could be saved. Within a few hours instead of a few weeks or months, the borrowing corporation could negotiate a deal with the institutional purchaser or purchasers of its bonds and know just what to expect. Details of preparing the bond issue could follow.

Presumably, also, in the absence of middlemen, the borrowing corporation could realize a bit more from the sale of its bond issue. The amount so saved, if any, depends upon several considerations, including the relative bargaining ability of the seller and the buyer of the bonds.

Continued Use of Private Placements Even after the conditions that gave rise to private placements in the early 1930s had been succeeded by easier money markets, the use of private placements continued. In some years the tempo of their use has been faster than in the early 1930s. In each of several recent years, more than 30 percent of the proceeds of all new security issues came from private placements. Meantime the investable resources of life insurance companies have mounted year by year. The pressure of putting to work these increased resources have caused an extension of the use of private placements for corporate securities.

QUESTIONS AND PROBLEMS

1. Review briefly the general history of life insurance companies as lenders on real estate security.
2. Are life insurance companies more likely than savings and loan associations to invoke penalties for prepayment of mortgage loans? Why or why not?
3. How do geographical limitations on mortgage lending by insurance companies differ from those governing the operations of other types of lending institutions?
4. By what methods do insurance companies place their investable funds in real estate mortgages? What are the advantages and disadvantages of each method?
5. What reasons can you suggest for the trend toward a decreased proportion of government-underwritten mortgages in insurance company loan portfolios in recent years?
6. Evaluate life insurance companies as investors in mortgages on commercial and industrial real estate.
7. What is the usual range of originating fees paid by life insurance companies to loan correspondents? What is the range of servicing fees?

8. In what types of real estate have life insurance companies invested most extensively as equity owners? Why?

9. How important is private placement to life insurance companies as a means of acquiring corporate securities?

10. What are the most important factors considered in a decision by an insurance company whether to invest in real estate mortgages or corporate bonds?

15

Mortgage Banking

Meaning Mortgage bankers are sometimes known as mortgage companies or mortgage dealers. Those included under this appellation as defined in the membership section of the 1946 Constitution of the Mortgage Bankers Association of America are as follows:

Any person, firm or corporation . . . engaged in the business of lending money on the security of improved real estate in the United States, and who publicly offers such securities, or certificates, bonds or debentures based thereon, for sale as a dealer therein, or who is an investor in real estate securities, or is the recognized agent of an insurance company or other direct purchaser of first mortgage real estate securities for investment only.

The principal activity of the modern mortgage banker is originating and servicing income property and residential mortgage loans for institutional investors. Some mortgage bankers are essentially one-man concerns, with all of the small capital owned by the manager. In other cases, the corporate form of organization is used, with more than one class of security sometimes sold to obtain capital. In some cases, operations are extensive enough to warrant the maintenance of offices in several cities by one corporation. Since mortgage bankers are essentially merchandisers of mortgages, they expect to turn their capital rapidly. Their relatively small equity capital is sometimes supplemented by the use of bank credit. Even when bonds or debentures are sold, the resulting capital of mortgage bankers is not large in comparison with the annual volume of business done.

Departmentalization In the smaller offices, manned by the owner and a couple of clerks, the owner-manager is a jack-of-all-trades. He takes care of all parts of the business. In the large mortgage banks, departmentalization may be carried out in some detail, with each major department operated more or less as a unit. Among the most common of such departments are: (1) the promotional department, which develops new business, processes applications for loans, obtains purchase commitments, and so on; (2) the title department, which drafts papers, records them, takes care of title problems, and delivers the mortgages; (3) the servicing department, which makes collections, and so forth; (4) the accounting department, which keeps all records; and (5) the insurance department, which handles all insurance problems. Sometimes separate departments handle taxes, FHA transactions, and so forth.

Need for Soliciting Business Some mortgage bankers look with disfavor upon dependence on customers calling at their places of business to apply for real estate loans. One comment is fairly typical of this group. In a discussion of the need for soliciting business the following statement was used: "The walk-in customer, with the exception of former borrowers or depositors, is generally someone shopping a poor loan around, or trying to find which lender will make the highest appraisal, or seeking a rate at less than the prevailing one. This group is not helpful to the building of a selective mortgage loan portfolio"[1]

Since the lender has no means of knowing in advance the people who are likely to become applicants for real estate loans, many mortgage bankers find their best source of business to be real estate brokers. Since most transfers of real estate title which give rise to the need for loans occur as the result of sales efforts of brokers, the latter are in the best position to know what loans will be needed. Field agents contact brokers regularly and undertake to render service of a kind that will win their goodwill.

Next in order of solicitation are builders. Some field agents make a practice of calling upon builders on their construction jobs, since it is frequently difficult to find them at their offices. When construction loans are granted, the fieldmen who contact the builders to solicit their business sometimes serve as inspectors as well. Where permitted to do so, field agents attend meetings of both real estate brokers and builders, thereby keeping abreast with their thinking on matters affecting the financial problems which they face.

Functions of Solicitors In some mortgage banks the business solicitor is merely a salesman. It is his function to secure applications for loans. These are processed in the office. Other members of the staff appraise the property. Approval or rejection of loan applications is the responsibility of higher-ups in the office, after review of the applicant's credit report and the appraiser's report on the property and the neighborhood. In other banks, the experienced solicitor is given considerable authority

---

[1] Reported in *Year Book* (Mortgage Bankers Association of America, 1947), p. 187.

to make commitments for loans. Some are made before the property is sold. If a broker wishes to know what he may rely upon in the nature of financing, he contacts the solicitor and obtains a commitment, subject to the credit rating of the mortgagor. In borderline cases where the solicitor is in doubt, the application for a loan is referred to the office for decision. But when the solicitor makes a commitment, the processing of the loan application in the office is a matter of routine.

Where the solicitor is permitted to commit the mortgage bank on a loan application, the functions of selling and underwriting are merged. Such a practice merely carries one step further the practice upon which the entire business is founded. A mortgage bank that acts as a loan correspondent for an insurance company is really the salesman, with the insurance company the underwriter. While the latter may not always act favorably upon the decisions of the former, its frequent failure to do so would result in a cancellation of their business relationships. Those banks which place considerable authority in the hands of their solicitors merely follow the same practice.

Some bankers have found that it is desirable to hire solicitors on such a basis as to urge them to specialize in one type of business. For example, a good solicitor of residential mortgage business might not be successful if he spent a part of his time soliciting loans on business property; and vice versa.

Compensation of Solicitors Mortgage bankers find the key to their business success to be the character of their solicitors. Consequently, the method of compensating them to assure the best results becomes paramount. No one formula is universally followed. In some cases they are put on straight salary. Some solicitors, particularly those who are employed part time, are paid on a commission basis instead. Some bankers employ at the same time both full-time salaried solicitors and part-time commission solicitors. A common method includes some sort of volume bonus even for salaried people. The variety of methods using a bonus or incentive payment follow several patterns. One relates the amount of the bonus to the current volume of business produced by the solicitor. Such bonuses are usually paid monthly. In other cases the bonus is computed on an annual basis. In still other cases, a more elaborate system is used, relating the incentive payment to commissions charged, to profit from the writing of insurance policies, or to a similar basis.

Not all loans made by mortgage bankers produce a profit. But to keep the goodwill of real estate brokers, small unprofitable loans must sometimes be handled. Solicitors are paid for securing this class of business even though the loan results in a net loss to the banker.

Payments to Outsiders One problem faced by all institutions engaged in making loans on real estate as security is the question of making payments to those not actively engaged in the business. Such payments usually assume two forms: First, a finder's fee is sometimes paid to the real estate broker or the builder who is responsible for bringing the loan application to the attention of the mortgage banker. This is a sort of bribe to induce the broker or builder to give preference to the banker who pays it. But if all lenders in a given market pay the same finder's fee, it ceases to be effective as a business-producing device. Also, where it is used it becomes habitual whether the broker really "finds" the loan application or not. For example, if A buys a property through broker B and insists upon securing his mortgage loan from banker X, B still expects his finder's fee even though he had no choice of lender. In some markets, finder's fees are the rule. In others they are not used at all. In still others, some lenders use them while others do not. Prompt service may produce loan applications in spite of the absence of a finder's fee.

The other type of outside payment is indirect. The absorption of all or a part of loan fees is a form of payment to outsiders for the loan. This, too, is subject to wide variations, dependent upon the practices of competitors and upon the amount of money pressing for investment in real estate mortgages. Like the payment of finder's fees, the absorption of loan costs tends to lose its effectiveness if all lenders in a given market follow the practice. Sometimes the loan applicant demands that he be paid the finder's fee, if he knows that it is customary in his market to pay one.

Sideline Business Some mortgage bankers are not greatly disturbed if they fail to make a profit from mortgage loan acquisitions. By making the loan they acquire various types of sideline business. Among these are the writing of fire insurance premiums, sales commissions, property management fees, real estate brokerage, sale of leases, appraisal fees, and loan-servicing fees. The latter are normally most important. Depending upon the combination of circumstances, loan-acquisition profits and servicing profits may be alternatives. For example, one banker may be willing to accept a servicing contract at no profit if the commission from disposing of the mortgage is great enough. Another may be willing to forgo such profit if the servicing fee is large enough to show a profit.

One of the arguments used by mortgage bankers with insurance companies interested in establishing branch offices for the purpose of soliciting and servicing real estate loans is that the mortgage banker can render the service at less cost because of its sideline business operations. The branch office of the insurance company would be concerned with loans only. With approximately the same overhead costs, the mortgage banker can conduct several types of business, as listed earlier. In addition, mortgage bankers sometimes render services to real estate brokers and builders, in order to build or keep their goodwill, which insurance companies are not permitted to render.

The recent emergence of real estate investment trusts has provided an attractive new market for mortgage bankers. The well-qualified and diversified mortgage banker is a natural manager to handle the originating, servicing, and advisory functions for a mortgage investment trust. Some mortgage bankers have even seen fit to sponsor mortgage trusts themselves to enjoy the benefits of fuller use of their facilities and talents as publicly derived trust funds are made available to them for placement. Even further benefits to the mortgage banker have been derived from better ability to cope with shortages of construction loan money and urgent needs of qualified builders and developers in times of credit stringency.

Ringing Doorbells From time to time solicitors for mortgage bankers have been able to find business by ringing doorbells and asking if the occupant-owner would like to save money on his mortgage loan. If the loan was a high percentage loan when it was executed a few years previously, and if it is now a seasoned loan, it may merit a lower interest rate, or smaller payments, or both. The solicitor, by promising a new loan with either or both of these features, may develop considerable refinancing business. In general, if the level of mortgage interest rates is low, there is less chance for business by a door-to-door canvass than if higher levels prevailed. The borrower can hardly afford to refinance his loan for an advantage of $\frac{1}{2}$ percent. A full 1 percent is much more attractive.

As an alternative to ringing doorbells, some solicitors have found new business by studying mortgage recordings at the courthouse. If a sizeable mortgage on a property in a good district has been on the books for several years, it has probably seasoned to such an extent that it may be refinanced to the advantage of the borrower. A telephone call or a visit may result in new business for the mortgage banker. Current practices of omitting interest rates from mortgage records has tended to put a damper upon this method of raiding mortgage portfolios.

Procedure in Making Loans As already indicated, flash appraisals and informal commitments are sometimes made in advance of the receipt of loan applications. The more formal procedure is to get the loan application, have the property appraised, secure photographs of it, and get a credit report on the borrower. The latter may be obtained by telephone for the purpose of arriving at a conclusion, with a written report to follow before the loan is closed. If the commitment for the purchase of the mortgage is required before the loan is closed, further time is consumed. In general, the mortgage banker will know what types of loans to submit to each of his principal purchasers to make sure of their acceptance. Where the mortgage banker uses his own funds to close the loan, he can save time at the expense of making a loan that he may not dispose of readily.

Some parts of loan processing may be started in anticipation of the acceptance of the loan by the insurance company. For example, the check on the title is often time consuming. If it can be started before a commitment is received, closing time can be expedited.

Where the mortgage banker sells loans to several insurance companies or commercial banks, he usually wishes to make sure that all receive fair treatment, in order to retain their business. He may distribute the loans made in an equitable fashion. To do so he may prefer to use his own capital in making the loans instead of receiving an advance commitment for purchase. On the other hand, he must cater to the wishes of those to whom he sells mortgages. This means that he must offer only such loans as he knows will meet the approval of the purchaser.

Where a long-standing relationship between mortgage banker and insurance company investor has taught each to know what to expect of the other, authority may be granted by the latter to commit it up to certain amounts in making loans. In other words, the mortgage banker is permitted to close the loan promptly, knowing that the insurance company will not refuse to buy the mortgage. By speeding up the decision to make the loan, both borrower and lender are given more prompt service. Frequently, promptness in making decisions is what gets the mortgage.

Methods of Financing Mortgages In general, mortgage banks finance real estate loans according to one of the following patterns:

1. The loan is made only after the banker has received the prior approval of the insurance company for which it is a loan correspondent. The insurance company which agrees to take the loan may even advance to the mortgage banker the amount of money needed by the mortgagor. Otherwise the mortgage banker uses its own funds, knowing that within a short time it will recoup the amounts so invested from the institution which has contracted to take the loan. In such a transaction, the banker is, in effect, the agent for the insurance company.

2. The mortgage banker may act as a real merchandiser, investing its own funds in the mortgage and then offering it for sale to some investor seeking this type of outlet for its funds. In this case it may keep its own funds invested at all times, selling only such mortgages as it needs to free its funds for the purchase of a new supply. Since its capital is small in comparison with its volume of business, this is not its major objective. Whenever it makes a loan without the prior approval of some purchaser, it runs the risk of acquiring stale merchandise that no purchaser will take off its hands at an advantageous price.

Then it may unwillingly find its capital tied up in nonmerchantable mortgages.

Growing Significance of Mortgage Companies[2] There are over 2,000 institutions listed as mortgage companies in the membership of the Mortgage Bankers Association of America. A number of these, however, undoubtedly perform mortgage banking as an incidental rather than as a principal function. It appears that there are many fewer mortgage companies than commercial banks and savings and loan associations in the country. In fact the number of mortgage companies is nearer that of life insurance companies, their best customers.

Growth in the number of mortgage companies has been spectacular since the end of World War II. Of the 854 companies approved to deal in FHA-insured mortgages in 1954, 445, or more than half, had been in business less than 10 years. During the five years beginning in 1950, 194 of these companies entered the field.

Even more significant than a doubling of the number of mortgage companies since the last war is their growth in assets. From an estimated $160 million of assets in 1945, the total rose to $1.8 billion by the end of 1955, an increase of over 10 times.

By the end of 1955, nearly $20 billion of mortgages were being serviced by mortgage companies. This volume represented over one fifth of the total one- to four-family dwelling mortgage debt outstanding. By comparison, mortgage companies serviced about one eighth of this total mortgage debt in 1951.

The continuation of rapid growth through the 1960s and into the 1970s is indicated by later statistics. At the beginning of 1971, mortgage bankers were servicing an estimated dollar volume of $82.4 billion of mortgage loans. Compared with an estimated total of about $450 billion of U.S. mortgage debt at that time, the debt being serviced by mortgage bankers constituted about 18.2 percent of the total mortgage finance segment of the economy.

The substantial postwar growth of mortgage bankers, as well as their present structure and operational methods, can be attributed largely to the federal mortgage assistance program. The Federal Housing Administration insurance and the Veterans Administration guarantee programs have offered what was needed to create a national mortgage market. These agencies provided minimum property requirements, subdivision standards, and credit review which gave insured or guaranteed mortgages a quality upon which distant lending institutions could rely

---

[2] Statistical data and related information concerning activities during the 1950s presented in this section and elsewhere in this chapter are adapted from Saul B. Klaman, *The Postwar Rise of Mortgage Companies* (New York: National Bureau of Economic Research, Inc., 1959). Current data are derived from *Research Committee Trends Report No. 9* (Mortgage Bankers Association of America, 1971).

with little individual review or investigation. The federal underwriting itself permitted institutional investors to make loans of higher risk than would otherwise be prudent or legally possible from the standpoint either of loan-to-value ratio or of distance from lender to liened property.

The FHA or VA mortgage has emerged as a standard article, subject to ready trade in the national marketplace. It has an additional unique feature. It is eligible, under certain limitations, for purchase by another federal agency, the Federal National Mortgage Association (FNMA). The availability of this resource as a buyer in the market at times of temporary credit stringency has provided a stability in the supply of mortgage funds that did not previously exist.

The mortgage banker, operating in a localized area, has been the natural beneficiary of the increased need by nonresident investors for a local agency to originate and service mortgages. Accordingly, the marked increase in federally underwritten mortgages has given impetus to mortgage banking. Nearly half of an estimated total of $38.9 billion federally underwritten FHA and VA loans outstanding at the end of 1955 was being serviced by mortgage companies. In 1951, mortgage companies were servicing only about one fourth of a comparable total outstanding debt of $20.7 billion. This same trend is reflected in the proportion of mortgage holdings of life insurance companies, mutual savings banks, and the Federal National Mortgage Association which are serviced by mortgage bankers. In 1955, nearly two thirds of their total home mortgages and about four fifths of their FHA and VA mortgages were so serviced, compared with one third and two fifths, respectively, in 1951. At the beginning of 1971, on one- to four-family loans, 58.1 percent of FHA loans and 55.8 percent of VA loans were being serviced by mortgage bankers, while only 3.4 percent of the conventional loans were so handled.

From the foregoing statistics, the parallel nature of the growth of federal underwriting of mortgages and the institution of mortgage banking is clear. After 1956, the VA-guaranteed mortgage diminished somewhat in importance although it is experiencing a resurgence with extension of veterans' benefits to those with more recent military service. The FHA, however, has continued to insure a substantial volume of new mortgages generated. The stake of mortgage bankers in the continued functioning of an active FHA program is unquestioned. They recognize that they and FHA are drifting down the same stream together. Their great fear is that the FHA program of broadening and strengthening the home loan market may be undermined by incompatible and unrelated problems. The 1968 extension of the FHA insurance program, however, should further increase the need for mortgage banking services.

Mortgage bankers are also deeply concerned with the support they may be able to rely upon from the Federal National Mortgage Association in a tight market. To them, this agency stands in much the same relationship as the Federal Reserve System to commercial banks or the Federal Home Loan Bank System to savings and loan associations. Yet its objectives have not been set forth with sufficient definiteness in this regard to induce reasonable reliance at all times.

Purchasers of Mortgages The great majority of real estate mortgages acquired by mortgage bankers find their way into the portfolios of life insurance companies. The second most important customer in recent years has been the mutual savings banks. Through new legislation, savings banks in some states are permitted to own mortgages on properties located at a distance from their home offices and they have been utilizing mortgage bankers to an increasing degree. Other investors through mortgage companies include chiefly commercial banks, savings and loan associations, and the Federal National Mortgage Association.

A survey of about 90 representative mortgage companies for the years 1953–55 gave good indications of the relative importance to mortgage bankers of their various customers. In 1953, for example, mortgage companies at the median sold 85 percent of their total mortgage loan volume to life insurance companies. In the same year, the median percentage of sales to mutual savings banks was 3.6. By 1955, the median percentage of mortgage loan volume sold to life insurance companies had dropped to 80.8, while the comparable percentage of sales to mutual savings banks had increased to 14.6. It is apparent from these statistics that savings banks gained substantially in relative importance as mortgage banking clientele during the period. In fact, one sixth of the mortgage companies reported that over half of their sales volume went to savings banks in 1955, compared with one ninth in 1953. Other investors, including commercial banks, savings and loan associations, and the Federal National Mortgage Association, acquired a greater dollar volume of loans through the surveyed companies in 1955 than in 1953, but the percentage of the total sales volume was small and decreased during the period. It also appears that the large mortgage companies are far less dependent upon life insurance companies than the medium-sized and small ones. This condition leaves open the question whether the large companies attained their magnitude because they developed diversified sales outlets, or attracted new types of investors because of their size.

An estimated 40.6 percent of the total dollar amount serviced by mortgage bankers in 1970 was held by life insurance companies, 18.8 percent by mutual savings banks, 15.6 percent by the Federal National Mortgage Association, and 25.0 percent by other investors, including commercial banks, savings and loan associations, pension and welfare funds, and individuals. These figures indicate a continuation of the relative increase in importance of mutual savings banks, the Federal National Mortgage Association and other investors, as compared with life insurance companies, as mortgage banking clientele during the late 1950s and the 1960s.

The demand of commercial banks for the services of a mortgage banker largely emanates from the rural areas where cash is more plentiful than local investment outlets. City banks that are interested in real estate mortgages as investments frequently originate their own mortgages. Country banks depend upon mortgage bankers instead. Frequently, if their cash resources are large, they may pay higher premiums for loans than will insurance companies. Some smaller mortgage bankers cater to this trade because of the high premiums paid for loans. Larger companies usually find it more advantageous to deal instead with the few insurance companies for which each is a correspondent. Then, too, the demand for loans by country banks is likely to be intermittent, depending upon the state of their cash and upon their outlook concerning future business conditions. They are in-and-out buyers.

One further difference between commercial banks and insurance companies as purchasers of real estate mortgages is that the former are subject to fewer rules than the latter. Because the insurance companies are mass purchasers, they find it necessary to standardize the rules under which they operate. For example, a specific company may set a minimum of 720 square feet of floor space for a single residence that it will finance. In such case it is useless to offer it a loan on a smaller house, regardless of its quality. Or the insurance company may not be interested in VA loans. Commercial banks normally do not have enough mortgage experience at any one time to make them unwilling to consider the purchase of any loan which the mortgage banker may offer to them.

However, because of the restrictions under which commercial banks are forced to operate in the purchase of mortgages, the mortgage banker may make sure that he can dispose of a "bank" loan before he makes it. Some use a submission sheet in offering mortgages to commercial banks. It contains a description of the property; the terms of the loan and the price asked for it; the necessary information about the borrower—such as his occupation, annual income, and credit rating; the amount of the appraisal, FHA or otherwise; and any other pertinent information about the application. Sometimes submission sheets are sent out on the same day to several commercial bankers. The first one to accept by telephone, telegraph, or letter gets the loan, and it is closed on that basis.

Savings and loan associations do not ordinarily purchase mortgages from mortgage bankers. They do not like to pay any premiums for the purchase of mortgages. Occasionally an individual may liquidate his mortgage holdings by selling them to a savings and loan association through a mortgage banker. Or on occasion such a buyer may purchase an individual loan which he would have liked to make originally but which for some reason he did not have the opportunity to make. One exception to this rule about savings and loan associations' purchases of mortgages from mortgage bankers occurs when the association, like the country bank, operates in a community where savings funds greatly exceed investment opportunities. In such cases a mortgage banker, or a mortgage broker in a neighboring city which can use excess funds, serves as the investment agent for the savings and loan association.

The Federal National Mortgage Association is an agency created by Congress to provide a secondary market for federally underwritten mortgages. In view of the importance of mortgage bankers in the origination of these mortgages, it is to be expected that the FNMA should become their customer. Activity of the FNMA in the insured mortgage market has provided an important new business channel for mortgage bankers. The history and current status of the FNMA is discussed in Chapters 27 and 28.

Mortgage loans are sometimes sold to individuals, estates, or trustees. Here there is even less rigidity in purchaser requirements than in the case of commercial banks. Loans purchased by such buyers may be safe but off-color loans. Perhaps they should be called off-standard. For example, insurance companies will not ordinarily consider a loan against a motel or a motor freight terminal. It may carry a high rate of return and represent a low percentage loan. Because of the difficulty in placing such loans, the borrower usually pays all costs, including the fees to the mortgage banker.

On the other hand, some mortgage bankers prefer not to deal with individual investors except when off standard property is involved. Volume of sales to one individual is not likely to be large. Each may have his own ideas about appraisals, location, and so on, so that the time spent in trying to sell an individual a mortgage may be out of proportion to the amount of business generated. In general, the individual purchaser of mortgages expects a higher yield on his investment than does an insurance company, for example. One reason for this demand is the high-income taxes paid by the individual. To net a yield comparable to that enjoyed by an insurance company, the individual must obtain a higher interest rate.

Occasionally a mortgage banker has found that he can get a better price for a large inventory of mortgages than for a single mortgage or a small number. Hence by the use of his own capital, supplemented by bank loans, he accumulates whatever inventory he can carry before offering it to institutional buyers. In doing so he is taking the risk that interest rates will change before he is able to liquidate his holdings. For example, if the larger purchaser will pay a 2 percent premium on $500,000 or $1,000,000 of 9 percent loans, the mortgage banker will work toward that amount as his goal. Meantime, if investment committees of large buyers decide suddenly that they no longer want to buy 9 percent mortgages, the mortgage banker may find sticky merchandise on his shelves. Since his bank loans are for short periods of time, he must adjust his price to the new bid price of the buyers and, if necessary, take his loss.

Pension Funds Although as yet they have been an elusive market, pension funds offer appealing possibilities as customers of mortgage bankers. As an industry, mortgage bankers are becoming increasingly cognizant of the magnitude of the pension fund market, and they are more aware of their own excellent position to compete for fund investments.

In essence, pension funds are simply accumulations of money over the working life of an individual to provide income to him during his retirement. Before World War II, these funds were largely established by corporations or by governmental units on a voluntary basis and on a relatively small scale. In the postwar labor climate, desirable pension plans became an important method of attracting scarce workers into employment with a particular firm. Favorable tax treatment was accorded acceptable pension plans. Pensions became an important issue at the labor-management bargaining table. Under this impetus, the amount of investable funds held to underwrite retirement and related benefits grew spectacularly.

In 1950 private pension and retirement funds held assets of $11.7 billion. By the end of 1970 these funds had increased over 12 times, totaling $141.2 billion. At the same time, the assets in government-sponsored funds increased from $25.7 billion in 1950 to $117.3 billion in 1970. Thus, from about $37.4 billion in 1950, the total pension funds had grown by 1970 to a formidable $258.5 billion. Furthermore, the annual rate of growth of private funds alone had increased from about $1.5 billion per year in 1950 to about $9.5 billion annually in 1970. The total assets of the private funds alone are projected at over $250 billion by 1980—nearly one and a quarter times the present size of the total life insurance industry.

The shifting of the flow of these funds from bank accounts and corporate bonds and stocks into mortgages has been a slow process. The present percentage of pension trust funds invested in mortgages is insignificant compared with the potential. The reason for the small proportion of funds invested in mortgages seems to be that investment committees and counselors, and even bank trust departments, are unfamiliar with the safety and ease with which these investments can be handled through mortgage bankers. Many trustees have been concerned that there is no market quotation on mortgages. As the secondary market for mortgages improves and their security becomes better defined, this objection can be overcome. The trustees have also had an abiding fear of additional, unanticipated costs of handling mortgage investments. In this respect the mortgage banker is admirably equipped to relieve their burden. Over a period of time, as the mortgage banker reaches the decision-making groups and dispels their fear of the unknown, he will find a lucrative market. He can demonstrate, for example, that in its important aspects a federally underwritten mortgage can be handled as safely and simply as bonds and stocks through the proper employment of mortgage banking services.

Considerable thought is also being directed toward the development of a security based on a package of mortgages which would be serviced on a "carefree" basis by others than fund administrators. This security would be made available in a denomination conveniently large, and, although probably bearing a rate slightly lower than the composite interest rate for mortgages serving as the underlying protection, it would still yield an attractive return and at the same time exonerate the fund management from responsibility and possible embarrassment in connection with delinquencies.

At the beginning of 1971, of a book value of $95.8 billion in non-insured private pension funds, only $4.2 billion was invested in mortgages. Although this is a relatively insignificant amount, a few factors could change this. These funds have on the average from 40 to 50 percent of their holdings, at market value, invested in corporate common stocks. Such investments, obviously, are extremely sensitive to the general complexion of the stock market. A weakened securities market could stimulate demand for real estate mortgages with their liberal and certain yield. Furthermore, even in a stable stock market, as the benefit payments required under pension fund obligations swell and certain funds reach the point where the cash income does not cover the disbursements, the low yield of common stocks coupled with the uncertainty of capital gains may become less attractive than real estate mortgages.

On an increasing basis, pension funds are venturing into the mortgage market. The International Ladies' Garment Workers' Union and the International Brotherhood of Electrical Workers have approximately $150 million each in mortgage investments. Recently the AFL-CIO moved to form a mortgage investment trust to help about 130 smaller unions place about $200 million in government-guaranteed mortgages. The trust will enable a union with only $100,000 to participate in a larger pool and thus gain the benefits of freedom from administrative burdens. There are now about 200,000 private pension funds in existence. Many are small, but nearly all are growing. As they move into the real estate mortgage market, they create a heavy demand for the mortgage-banking function.

The recently launched program of mortgage-backed securities guaranteed by the Government National Mortgage Association (GNMA) was partly inspired to lure more pension fund money into real estate financing. The details of this program are discussed in Chapter 28 in connection with GNMA activities. Important advantages to the pension fund investor are: GNMA securities are competitive in yield with high-grade corporate securities; they carry the guarantee of GNMA and the full faith and credit of the U.S. government. The securities are designed to avoid the paper work and documentation involved in handling mortgages; there is simply one piece of paper—the security—calling for regular payments of interest with repayments of principal either monthly or at maturity. The guarantee relieves the investor of mortgage delinquency problems. There is a steady cash flow generated by the interest payment and amortization process. Secondary markets are developing for this type of security. Finally, pooled mortgages from a particular state or area may be selected as backup securities, if the investor prefers. Thus, in February 1970, the New Jersey state retirement fund specified that only New Jersey mortgages be used to back a GNMA-guaranteed security that they purchased.

Others besides mortgage bankers interested in real estate mortgages, such as savings and loan associations and commercial banks, are also seeking means of tapping the increasing amount of investable assets in pension funds. They hope to gain access to these sources in the future through servicing and other participation type agreements. For example, a New York City savings and loan association has a program permitting institutional lenders to purchase as little as a 1 percent interest in a mortgage package. The savings and loan association services the loans and reports monthly to each participant on its share of the principal and the interest payments on the mortgages in which it participates.

A similar program on a national scale was originated by George W. Warnecke & Company, of New York City, through its subsidiary, Central Home Funds, Incorporated. This company offers pension funds and other institutional investors mortgage trust notes, individually secured by carefully selected mortgages against owner-occupied homes in many states. The Marine Midland Trust Company of New York City serves as trustee, and servicing is through locally approved FHA lenders for the life of the mortgage. Collections go to the trustee and it pays the noteholders.

These mortgages provide an attractive yield. Only fully government-insured or guaranteed liens are selected. The noteholder never gets directly involved in selection or servicing; it does not have to qualify to do business in a number of states to get geographical distribution in its mortgage portfolio; and it never appears as an interested party in a mortgage foreclosure proceeding.

There is no fixed redemption period on the mortgage trust notes. Their principal amount is amortized, however, as monthly payments are made by the individual homeowner. To offset this inflow of funds, fixed monthly purchases of notes can be arranged to keep the pension fund fully invested at all times.

Other companies are similarly engaged in originating real estate mortgage participations for pension funds. In fact, their investment activities include conventional first and second mortgages, federally underwritten mortgages, construction funds, purchase and leaseback transactions, and industrial and commercial financing. Loan participations may be set up by use of the mortgage trust indenture. The scope of real estate investments provided by these companies is designed to appeal to a broad spectrum of institutional investor objectives.

Types of Loans Mortgage bankers typically provide their major services in arranging permanent financing for new rather than existing properties. They frequently assist builders by establishing short-term credit for new construction. This credit may be arranged for the builder directly from a commercial bank, or the mortgage banker may advance the construction costs and borrow from the commercial bank in its own name. In either event, the funds for construction are ultimately provided by the commercial bank. Mortgage bankers usually gain an additional fee when they finance the builder themselves, but the typical 1 or 2 percent additional compensation involved often does not justify the higher risks and larger staff required in observation and supervision of the construction process.

From a survey of representative mortgage bankers a high degree of concentration of real estate loans on one- to four-family properties is clearly shown. By statutory limitations and practice, most FHA and VA loans are on one- to four-family dwellings; and, with few exceptions, the conventional mortgage loans derived by mortgage bankers are on similar properties.

The small proportion of conventional loans on income properties handled through mortgage bankers can be explained in the decision of most institutional investors to originate such loans directly. Lending on larger building units requires specialized knowledge of appraisal techniques and legal problems, and the loans are usually large enough and in sufficient volume to justify the institutional lender in maintaining its own staff for direct negotiations with such borrowers. This practice is particularly common among insurance companies and savings banks in the highly industrialized areas of the country, especially in the East.

Exclusive Outlets The goal of every mortgage banker is to establish relationships with investment institutions which are so satisfactory to both the buyer and the seller of mortgages that the seller will always know where he can dispose of his inventory and the buyer will know where he can secure supplies of new mortgages. Some of these relationships crystallize into exclusive contracts. The mortgage banker agrees to sell only to one or to a very few investors; and each of these in turn agrees to buy in that market only from the mortgage banker whose name is signed to the exclusive contract. The signatures to the contract are not as important in the long run as the manner in which both parties deal with each other. If each is satisfied with the service it receives from the other, no formal contract is needed. If either is dissatisfied, a formal contract will probably be terminated at the earliest opportunity.

Most investment institutions do not object to the mortgage banker having more than one purchaser of its mortgages. In fact, they prefer such an arrangement, since it removes pressure from the investor to absorb all offerings of the seller at all times. In taking on its list of investors, however, the mortgage banker should exercise care in avoiding too much competition among them. For example, one investor may prefer FHA or VA loans; another, conventional loans; a third, apartment or commercial loans; a fourth, FHA 221 loans; and so on.

Indemnity Policies In spite of the general practice of securing prior approval of the purchaser of the mortgage before it is granted, the mortgage banker still has a responsibility for making sure that the loans he processes do not result in a loss to the purchaser. For example, if such a loan is paid off within the first year, it is frequently replaced with another of similar amount, premium free, or the mortgage banker may return whatever premium was collected in disposing of the mortgage. In still other cases, only the loss that is due to a negative yield will be made up. In some cases these obligations of the mortgage banker are a part of the contract between the insurance company and its correspondents. In other cases, unwritten understandings are sufficient to fix responsibility. In general, the mortgage banker is more likely to be dependent upon the continued business of the purchasing insurance company than the reverse.

The prepayment privilege in mortgages is particularly troublesome in mortgage banking because of the premiums and other fees paid by the investor in acquiring the mortgage. Because of the common practice of competitors who originate loans to include this privilege, its exclusion might result in a loss of business. From the standpoint of the investor, if he permits prepayment freely, he may lose money if the privilege is exercised early in the life of the loan. One common answer to the problem is to permit limited prepayment privilege—to become operative only after two years, for example. Another is to permit prepayment on any interest date but with a penalty of a few months' interest or of a flat percentage of the amount of the mortgage. In still other cases, the amount of prepayment without penalty is limited to 20 percent per year.

Fees Paid by Borrower The borrower normally expects to pay two classes of fees: (1) All expenses of making the loan are expected to be paid by him. Such fees for FHA and VA loans are standard. There is no such standardization for conventional loans. Sometimes they cover out-of-pocket costs. At other times they cover what the traffic will bear. Costs cover appraisal fees, title insurance, if any, title check fees, and office expense. As pointed out elsewhere, competitive practices help to determine the amount of costs charged to the borrower. Sometimes appraisal fees are charged only if the loan is made; sometimes whether or not the loan is approved; and sometimes they are absorbed by the lender. (2) Off-standard loans—those made against properties that holders of mortgage paper do not like as security—frequently cost the borrower a fee in addition to those mentioned above. Instead of a sellers' market for such mortgages, it is generally a buyers' market. Because the mortgage banker may have unusual difficulty in disposing of them, he expects the mortgagor to pay his fees.

Small Commercial Loans Large corporations have less difficulty in financing real estate than do smaller concerns. Likewise, small commercial properties fail to attract funds that are usually available in the financing of larger properties. Smaller properties, owned by less well-known firms, are more difficult to appraise; the credit rating of the borrower is not likely to be as high; and the costs of servicing may be greater than for larger buildings owned by stronger corporations. Instead of making the loans needed by the smaller firms, on a basis of shorter amortization periods and higher rates if necessary, there is a tendency for financial institutions to bypass this lending area. This makes a kind of no-man's-land of small commercial loans, sought after by no lenders and shunned by most of them.

Financing of Special-Purpose Real Estate A special-purpose property is one whose highest and best use is limited to one type of business. Examples are bowling alleys, filling stations, hotels, and theaters. Most industrial real estate belongs in this category also. While each of these may be used for one or more other purposes, the conversion cost will be high and the loss of efficiency great. In considering the financing possibilities of such properties, three factors must be carefully weighed: (1) the value of the property as appraised by competent appraisers; (2) the financial standing of the mortgagor; and (3) the credit rating of the lessee in case the mortgagor is not the user of the property. If all three factors are favorable, either local or out-of-town financing will probably by readily available. If all three are negative, no one wants to risk much on such property. It is the analysis that results in plus and minus ratings that must be most carefully made.

For example, it is conceivable that the lender's impression of the property is so favorable that he considers its resale value or lease opportunities high in case he should find it necessary to foreclose his mortgage. Such a situation is rare and tends to deny the definition of special-purpose property recited above. But where it exists it may result in easy financing regardless of the standing of the mortgagor or the lessee. In most cases it is expected that the security of the mortgage against special-purpose property will depend upon the successful operation of a business which uses the real estate. For that reason the lender will give much attention to the business of the firm whose net income is expected to pay, directly or indirectly, the carrying charges on the loan.

Without getting into a technical discussion of the methods of analyzing the probability of success of a business enterprise, the following factors usually attract the attention of the lender: (1) nature of the industry—basic or a fad; (2) position of the enterprise in the industry; (3) rent or other cost of building occupancy in relation to rent-paying capacity of occupant; (4) occupant's adequacy of capital and his access to more capital if needed; and (5) experience and know-how of occupant.

In case a lease is involved, the lender should study it carefully to discover its unfavorable features, if any exist. Among the questions which require answers are: (1) Is the lessee a strong company in its own right, or is it a "paper" subsidiary without adequate resources to protect the lender? (2) Is the lease subject to easy cancellation without penalty which might jeopardize the position of the lender? (3) Are there any special hazards that might result in a severe reduction in the net income of the lessee?

Mortgages on special-purpose real estate, in recognition of the risks involved, frequently contain special covenants for the protection of the lender. Among these are the following: (1) Use of excess net earnings to amortize the loan more rapidly; (2) maintenance of adequate working capital at all times; (3) restrictions upon dividends and bonuses until the mortgage is written down to an agreed amount; and (4) giving the lender a voice in management personnel.

Takeout Letter In some of the larger mortgage banks a major source of new business is the financing of mass housing projects. If a builder wishes to construct a group of 200 houses, each requiring a mortgage of $15,000, the total amount of the mortgage commitment will be $3,000,000. If he approaches a mortgage banker for assurance that this amount will be forthcoming, the latter, in turn, must make sure of his market for the mortgages. By negotiation with an insurance company, he receives what is known as a "takeout letter." This is a commitment that the insurance company will take over the mortgages as the properties are finished. The terms of such letters are necessarily detailed and specific.

Meantime, with this letter as evidence of its ability to dispose of the mortgages, the mortgage banker does the construction financing, using its credit at the bank for funds for this purpose. Bank loans are necessarily short term and are paid off as mortgages are transferred to the insurance company. In some cases the insurance company never gets some of the mortgages agreed upon, because the purchaser of the property occasionally buys it for cash or insists upon doing his own financing. In either case, the mortgage banker obtains the funds to liquidate its bank loans. More than one bank may be used, because of the lending restrictions upon commercial banks.

Servicing Department   The mortgage banker owes two obligations to the investor whose funds he handles: (1) to invest his money safely; and (2) to get it back according to the loan contract. Lending money is fairly simple. Getting it back may be more difficult. Servicing involves more than serving as a clearinghouse for checks transmitted by the borrower. Adequate servicing involves at least four major operations:

1. Current payments made by the borrower must be processed and the net proceeds, after retaining tax, mortgage, and hazard insurance quotas and service fees, must be transmitted to the investor that holds the mortgage. In rare cases the investor insists that all escrow deposits for taxes, mortgage insurance, and hazard insurance be transmitted to it to be held in trust for the borrower.

2. The security must be inspected periodically to make sure that it is not being subjected to waste or unusual depreciation.

3. When the property changes hands and the new owner assumes the mortgage debt, a whole series of records in the office of the mortgage banker must be changed. The collection department must get the proper name and address of the new owner and set up new records to check against delinquency by him. Insurance papers must reflect the change of ownership. The tax department must change its records in order to make sure about new tax bills. The accounting department must set up new records in line with the new obligor on the loan. If the mortgage is insured by the FHA or guaranteed by the VA, the proper governmental agency must be notified. Even where the present mortgage is completely paid off rather than assumed by the new owner, the mortgage banker must protect the interests of the holder of the mortgage by making sure that the proper amount is paid in the proper manner.

4. Finally, in serious cases of delinquency, steps must be taken to protect the holder of the mortgage, by foreclosure if necessary.

Among these four steps in servicing, too many lending agencies think primarily of the first. They may neglect the second. The third is thrust upon them perhaps more than once during the life of the mortgage. At such a time, outside forces call the tune and the mortgage banker must dance to it. The fourth step is the one that nobody likes to contemplate and that no one has ever quite made adequate provisions to meet. Plans of borrowers sometimes go awry, perhaps through no fault of theirs. Delinquencies follow. They are costly to the investor and to the mortgage banker. They are frequently disastrous to the borrower, who may lose his equity if he cannot maintain his payments on his loan.

It is not uncommon for the delinquent borrower to be delinquent in payments on his other financial obligations at the same time. Cumulative pressure from all creditors may make it impossible for him to meet any one creditor's claims fully. It is not easy for a mortgage banker to reach a conclusion about forebearance that is always wise, even though the holder of the mortgage counsels patience so long as there appears ample protection of his interests. We are primarily concerned here with servicing costs. This much appears certain. No fee has probably ever been adopted that is based upon a pattern of chronic delinquency with its letters, its telephone calls, its personal contacts, all pointed toward the collection of nonexistent funds. Temporary delinquencies may be cured. They may be prevented from becoming chronic. But the servicing of even temporary delinquencies probably results in an outlay that is in excess of current receipts for servicing purposes. When times are prosperous, a skeleton crew is sufficient to man the collection department. When unemployment and decreased incomes become the order of the day for our general economy, the number of employees in the collection department of a mortgage bank may be stepped up appreciably.

Cancellation of Contracts In most cases, a formal contract is drawn up covering the servicing of loans by the correspondent for the investor. Such contracts contemplate a continuing relationship based upon continuous purchase of mortgages to be serviced by the agent. It is common for the investor to reserve the right to cancel such a contract either with or without cause. Sometimes the mortgage banker receives a bonus of some kind when a loan-service contract is canceled. Obvious causes for cancellation include: the bankruptcy or other evidence of incapacity of the mortgage banker; negligent or inefficient servicing of loans; fraud or misrepresentation; and sale of business or change of management which is interpreted by the investor to be against his best interest. Less obvious causes include a feeling on the part of the investor, which it might have difficulty in substantiating by direct evidence, that the correspondent is not doing and perhaps cannot do the kind of job expected of it. Or even if the agent is doing all that he has promised, the investor might decide to make a change, perhaps for the purpose of giving its business to someone else.

Delinquency Study Various practices are followed to prevent temporary delinquencies from becoming chronic. If the borrower has forgotten to make his payment on time, one notice will probably be a sufficient reminder to him. If he is just careless in his financial affairs, he may need some education on the subject of family budgets and how to balance them. But if he has insufficient income to meet his obligations, repeated notices may be of little effect. Someone has said that a visit over the telephone is worth several notices and that a call at the home is more valuable than both telephone conversations and written communications. Sooner or later the mortgage banker must learn the cause of the delinquency—and the sooner the better. He needs to know a great deal about the borrower and his family. Perhaps he did not learn enough when the loan was made. In any event, when the crisis comes and loan payments are not made on time, a thorough study should be made.

This study should reveal all pertinent information about the sources of income of the borrower; a complete story of the family, including the ages of its members, the names of any members of the household outside of the immediate family, and any peculiar conditions of sickness or otherwise that create a constant or a temporary drain on the family income; the buying habits of the borrower; his commitments involving installment payments and other debts; the specific reasons for the current delinquency, if any can be detected; and the proposals of the borrower for bringing his account current again.

With this information before it, an experienced collection department should be able to arrive at some decision concerning the delinquent borrower. If a temporary emergency only is the seat of the trouble, a period of adjustment is probably in order. If the case appears hopeless, an entirely different course of action is suggested. Foreclosure is not always the best plan to follow. Perhaps the mortgage banker can assist in arranging a sale of the property with some recovery to the borrower or an exchange for one that the borrower can more readily carry. While it is easy for the mortgage banker to take the position that the borrower is the one that is in default, it is at least worth inquiring whether the banker might not share a part of the blame if an inexperienced borrower was induced to make a commitment that he should never have undertaken. Both from the standpoint of good ethics and from that of good business, the greater experience and financial wisdom of the banker can well be applied to the solution of the problems of the honest but inexperienced borrower who finds difficulty in meeting his obligations when his debt-paying capacity declines or his obligations increase more than he had anticipated when he took on the loan. Little case can or should be made for the occasional dishonest borrower who can pay but won't if he can evade his responsibility when he finds that he no longer has an equity in his property.

It is understood that the decision about the action to be taken in the case of a delinquent borrower must be made by the holder of the mortgage. Generally it will be guided by the recommendations of the correspondent banker who is on the job and knows the facts of the case. Probably few mortgage holders would have set policies, either tough or lenient, which they would insist upon applying in all cases, regardless of the conditions surrounding the delinquencies. In reaching decisions concerning delinquent accounts, the past experience of the borrower, as well as his apparent current equity in the property, should be taken into account. That is one good reason why the record of the account should reveal its entire past history, including what happened in previous cases of temporary delinquency.

How Profitable Is Mortgage Banking? For most mortgage bankers, little definitive information has been collected that would afford specific answers to the two basic questions upon which their business has been founded: (1) What is the cost of putting a mortgage loan on the books? (2) What does it cost to service a real estate loan? In the operations of mortgage bankers in a city of several thousand people, variations have been noted of as much as 100 percent in charges to borrowers, apparently for the same type of service; of premiums to purchasers of mortgages ranging from 0 to 3 percent at the same period of time and for approximately the same type of loan; and of service fees ranging from $\frac{1}{6}$ to $\frac{3}{4}$ of 1 percent. As was pointed out earlier in this chapter, there is an apparent choice made by some mortgage bankers between high premiums and low service fees and low premiums and high service fees. And as was also pointed out earlier, many mortgage bankers are content to make their profits from sideline activities.

The *Research Committee Trends Reports* of the Mortgage Bankers Association of America publish annually representative operating ratios for mortgage bankers servicing portfolios of various sizes. These ratios provide valuable standards for cost accounting studies by individual mortgage bankers. Particularly as competition becomes keener and profit margins are narrowed, the price of staying in business may easily become more knowledge about their own basic costs of doing business.

Studies of loan-servicing costs soon develop some conclusions that should be obvious to all. For example, regardless of the size of the loan, certain minimum costs are inescapable. If it develops that this minimum is as much as $1.25 per month, or $15 per year, then any loan of less than $3,000 balance is a losing proposition on a loan service basis of $\frac{1}{2}$ percent. This not only suggests an avoidance of small loans but a step-up percentage of loan-service fees whenever the unpaid balance is brought down to the break-even point. If the loan is completely amortized, it reaches a point sooner or later when the fee needed to provide a profit would be exorbitant. When the balance is only a small fraction of the original amount of the loan, the loan-servicing costs should be at a minimum.

Absence of Supervision One feature of mortgage banking business that has attracted some individuals to engage in it in recent years is the absence of government supervision. In spite of the growing importance of this method of financing real estate, it has so far escaped regulation of its activities. Probably this is due in part to the investment of equity funds in their operations rather than the appeal to the general investor. During the decade of the 1920s, the mortgage bankers of New York became involved in the sale of "guaranteed" mortgage certificates to the extent that a mortgage commission was appointed in 1935 to help clear up the defaults in this type of financing. Within a short time this commission took over the affairs of 21 companies which had sold $700 million of certificates to 200,000 investors, using 15,000 mortgages as collateral for these certificates. This was an emergency operation and has not been followed by any general plan of public supervision of mortgage bankers.

Future Problems of the Mortgage Banker[3] The exceedingly rapid rise of mortgage banking in the postwar years has by its very nature engendered certain competitive conditions which will become increasingly important from this time forward. The industry has flourished in the development of a national market for federally underwritten mortgages at favorable yields to investors in new housing construction. In fact, the conditions have been so favorable for growth in the field of mortgage origination and servicing that it is only reasonable to assume that more intense competition may be anticipated both from outside the industry and from within. The outside competition may be expected chiefly from commercial banks and savings and loan associations. Competition from within the industry may involve a shakedown of the type experienced by the commercial banks and savings and loan associations in the late 1920s and early 1930s if too many are drawn into the field as result of the enchantment of the lucrative years just past.

Commercial banks are becoming increasingly interested in programs of originating and servicing mortgages for investors other than themselves. In fact, commercial banks are in a particularly favorable position to move into mortgage banking because they have immediately available any funds necessary to provide interim financing or to maintain a mortgage inventory for sale. The American Bankers Association has been actively pointing out the advantages of a broad mortgage program to its membership, and the commercial banks are becoming more conscious of the advantages to be gained by offering mortgage origination and service facilities for bank-administered pension and welfare funds. These funds have been important investors through mortgage bankers in recent years.

---

[3] Saul B. Klaman, "Challenges Facing the Mortgage Banker," *The Mortgage Banker*, November 1959, pp. 18–19; see also Miles L. Colean, *Mortgage Companies: Their Place in the Financial Structure* (Englewood Cliffs, N.J.: Prentice-Hall, Inc., 1962).

To maximize their current opportunities, some banks have acquired mortgage banking expertise by buying out mortgage banking firms. Some firms so acquired have simply been absorbed into the bank assets and operations; others, secured by the one-bank holding company route, have maintained their separate integrity as mortgage bankers.

Savings and loan associations are also taking new cognizance of potentials in the national secondary markets. Whereas they previously limited their competition to local markets, they now find it possible to participate in loans made anywhere in the country. Through participation techniques, small savings and loan associations are enabled to handle much larger construction programs than would otherwise be possible. It is a short step from active participation in loan origination in the national market to adoption of a policy of sales of loans to other investors. Although insured savings and loans are now limited in the sale of such loans to 20 percent of their portfolio, such a limitation allows a substantial participation, and the limitation can always be changed.

Only experience will determine the extent to which too many entries into the mortgage banking industry will cause it embarrassment. Particularly if the economy can escape a serious reversal, it is possible that the weaker members of the industry will be absorbed by the stronger institutions and that a counterpart of the disasters among commercial banks and savings and loan associations will not occur.

Mortgage bankers can do much to strengthen their present position in the economy by their decisions from this point forward. They particularly need to reduce their dependence on FHA and VA mortgage activity. So long as they are primarily identified with a government program, they are subject to the whims of Congress and federal administrators. Within the industry, many are suggesting an expansion of areas of service into related activities and improvement of the present services. Mortgage investments account for only about 2 percent of over $135 billion available in personal trust and estate funds; less than 3 percent of $55 billion of assets of fire, casualty, and marine insurance companies; and about 20 percent of over $18 billion of funds held by credit unions. The potential in regard to pension funds has already been discussed. Furthermore, some mortgage bankers are beginning to cultivate the individual investor.

Much can be accomplished to shorten and render more certain the time lag between mortgage commitment and loan closing. From the institutional point of view, another important need is to improve coordination of the flow of investable funds with mortgage availability. Mortgage warehousing is doing much to alleviate this problem, but mortgage bankers have difficulties in maintaining inventories which commercial banks will not have if they enter the field. Such an eventuality would place a premium on increased capital and give the larger mortgage company a decided advantage.

Many companies are also considering expansion into real estate operations and insurance as logical auxiliary fields which might take on primary importance if income from servicing mortgages should begin to fall short. This diversification would relieve the company from such a high degree of dependence on the federal housing programs and give it greater stability.

QUESTIONS AND PROBLEMS

1. What is a mortgage banker?
2. Why are mortgage bankers important to both borrowers and lenders?
3. How does a mortgage banker originate new business?
4. What is a finder's fee? Do you approve of payment of finders' fees? Why or why not?
5. How does a mortgage banker finance the mortgages which it originates?
6. How do you account for the spectacular growth of mortgage companies since the end of World War II?
7. Who are the principal purchasers of mortgages generated through mortgage companies?
8. What types of loans are most attractive to mortgage bankers? Why?
9. How is the mortgage banker compensated for his services?
10. What is a takeout letter and how is it used to aid in construction financing?
11. What are the obligations of a mortgage banker to the investor in the real estate mortgages which the mortgage banker originates and services?
12. If you were a mortgage banker today, what areas would you be exploring for possible expansion of your services?

16

Miscellaneous Sources of Real Estate Finance

Range of Sources of Real Estate Finance Operators of savings and loan associations are fond of harking back to January 3, 1831, as the birth date of the first association organized in this country for the financing of the homes of the workingman and his family. One hundred thirty-four years is a long time, even in the life of a business. We should not infer, however, that the growth of institutions created for the financing of real estate has kept pace with the growth of population. Instead, there have been many stops and starts, with many types of lenders coming into the picture and going out again without leaving much evidence of their permanence as sources of funds for mortgage lending. With many of them real estate finance has been a kind of sideline, to be pushed only when the demand for other wares declined somewhat.

Markets for this type of financing have not been as well organized as those for the financing of our great industrial, railroad, and public utility corporations. In recent years' all this has changed. With the support of various governmental plans for shifting a part of the risk from the shoulders of lending institutions, real estate finance has acquired new backers. Not only savings and loan associations but commercial banks, insurance companies, savings banks, mortgage banks, religious and charitable foundations and funds, trustees of estates, and a miscellaneous collection of individuals currently find virtue in providing funds for mortgage loans. Some of the individuals act on their own account, and some act as agents for others.

Mortgage Loan Brokers Closely related to the mortgage banker, yet distinct from him, is the mortgage loan broker. The relationship is so close that there is frequent confusion among those who fail to see any major difference. In other cases the mortgage loan broker is considered, often without justification, to be the black sheep of the mortgage-financing family. On another branch of the family tree, the mortgage loan broker is closely related to the better understood real estate broker whose activity is centered around the sale of real estate. Indeed, the same individual acts frequently in the dual capacity of real estate broker and mortgage loan broker.

Unlike the mortgage banker, the mortgage loan broker never invests his own capital in a mortgage. He is strictly an agent and not a merchandiser. To be sure, he may act from time to time as an agent without a principal, since he frequently is put in the position of peddling a loan application until he finds an investor interested in it. When this is accomplished, the broker then becomes the agent of the investor for the purpose of closing the deal for a loan.

Mortgage loan brokers may operate "under their hats"; from a small office devoted to this business only; or in conjunction with insurance brokerage and other related businesses. They may even use their real estate brokerage offices as their places of business. They may be individuals, partnerships, or corporations. They seldom advertise their business in any formal way, but depend upon personal contacts to secure their loan applications. Their chief function is to originate real estate loans for insurance companies, commercial banks, and others, usually in the order of importance indicated here.

Method of Operation When a mortgage loan broker secures a lead about someone in need of assistance in the financing of a real estate purchase, he contacts the prospective applicant. After learning about the needs and capacities of the applicant, he tries to determine if any of his possible principals would be interested in the loan. If so, and if he feels sure which one will give favorable consideration to an application, he will probably ask the applicant to fill out a form bearing the name of such a principal. If he is not so sure about the principal, the broker will probably use a form of his own. The information so obtained is in the nature of a prospectus about the proposed loan.

This is then submitted to one or more principals. If any are interested, they will indicate the terms upon which they will consider the loan and request a formal application according to these terms. The appraisal is made by a representative of the insurance company or other prospective lender. As an alternative to the submission of the prospectus, the broker may contact the field representative of the lender, if one is readily available. If he is favorably impressed with the property after a casual inspection, the detailed application is requested.

With the submission of an application for a loan and its acceptance by an insurance company or other lender, the work of the mortgage loan broker is about finished. The appraisal is made by a representative of the lender. The loan closing usually takes place in the office of an attorney acting for the lender. The lender advances to the attorney the funds required for the loan. The fee paid to the broker is truly a finder's fee. For finding the loan he receives compensation that is comparable to that paid to mortgage bankers for the same service.

Loan Servicing Where the mortgage loan broker finds the lender, it is obvious that he assumes no added responsibility for the loan. Since the broker has no organization set up for the purpose of servicing loans, the lender must look elsewhere. The mortgagor is instructed to remit by mail or to make his payments to a local bank or other collection agency designated by the lender. In some cases, the mortgage loan broker joins forces with a mortgage banker. The former usually receives the finder's fee, and the latter takes care of all else concerning the loan. Occasionally the finder's fee is divided between the broker and the mortgage banker. In other cases, the mortgage loan broker works in conjunction with a bank, a savings and loan association, or an individual who invests a part of his funds in real estate mortgages.

Sources of Business The sources of leads for business for mortgage loan brokers are numerous. Records of building permits are carefully scanned. News items that lead to loan applicants are studied regularly. Classified columns in newspapers are sometimes used to attract loan applicants. Such advertisements may attract those whose applications have been turned down elsewhere. Personal contacts with builders, attorneys, and others produce some loan applications. If applications for new loans are not numerous, the mortgage loan broker may try his hand at refinancing existing loans. By scanning the courthouse records, he can frequently detect probable high interest rates by his knowledge of the practices of lenders of record. Even the old standby of doorbell ringing is not overlooked in the search for loans to refinance.

In case the mortgage loan broker doubles as a real estate broker, he may also "double" his personal source of income. In selling a property which requires new financing, the real estate broker may offer his assistance in securing the kind of loan needed. Then he can pursue his usual practices in offering the loan to any of his several principals, to secure the funds needed to finance the property. If he is successful in placing the loan with one of them, he earns two commissions—one from the seller of the property for finding a buyer; the other from the holder of the mortgage for finding an investment outlet for his funds.

One reason why the mortgage loan broker is sometimes called the "black sheep" of the mortgage loan family is the assumption that he deals only in off-standard loans. Some people ask, "Why is it necessary for a loan broker to peddle a loan when there are so many organized financial institutions ready, able, and willing to make real estate loans?" The assumption behind this question is not always warranted: namely, that the borrower is acquainted with real estate financial institutions. This is not always true. In many instances the need for a real estate loan is the first occasion for the borrower to become interested in this subject.

As pointed out above the mortgage broker is simply a finder of mortgage money. As such he operates no differently from any other person engaged in the same kind of activity. It is customary for all sorts of people to assist a real estate purchaser to finance his purchase. Frequently it is the only way by which a deal may be closed. Architects, contractors, lawyers, and others make recommendations about financial institutions. The mortgage broker simply makes a business of finding the right source and expects compensation for the service rendered in finding a loan.

Not all of the lending opportunities discovered by a mortgage broker result in loan closings. Occasionally he is unable to find a principal willing to make the loan. This is characteristic of the whole mortgage-financing business. Some loans cannot be placed with any institution. Others are turned down by one, only to be made by a competitor. Even loans that are peddled unsuccessfully by mortgage loan brokers may be later made by a lending institution to whom the borrower makes a direct application.

Incidentally, the term "black sheep" is not confined to mortgage loan brokers. Whenever one lending institution makes a loan that a competitor has turned down, there is a raising of eyebrows about the lending policies of the institution that makes the loan. This does not necessarily mean that the institution will make a risky loan that has been refused by some other lending institution. It is not unusual for A to make a loan that B refuses to consider favorably. On the same day, perhaps B will make a loan that has been declined by A. In such a situation, which one is the black sheep?

It should be kept in mind that the mortgage loan broker is never in a position to make a decision about a loan application. He merely offers a loan, which the principal whom he hopes to represent may or may not accept. Because there is no absolute standard by which the acceptability of loan applications can be measured, the broker frequently does not know whether the loan sought is an acceptable one until he has offered it to one or more lending institutions.

Mortgage Specialists Throughout the country there are a small number of mortgage specialists who are equipped to arrange the financing of large transactions involving apartment houses, office buildings, and industrial and commercial property. Since the total number of such transactions is relatively small, such specialists operate in a few of the largest cities only. Owners, purchasers, and even brokers call upon the services of these specialists on occasion because of their acquaintance with both the methods of financing large holdings and the sources of funds needed to consummate such operations. While such specialists sometimes engage in sales or lease brokerage, they confine their attention to the larger properties and make no pretense of conducting a general real estate business. In conducting their operations they make use of both private placements and public financing.

Real Estate Brokers Even though the real estate broker does not think of himself as a mortgage broker, he may act like one and be compensated accordingly. In some markets it is customary for all lending institutions to pay a finder's fee to real estate brokers who bring loans to them. This practice usually starts when one lending institution undertakes to obtain an advantage over its competitors by offering a finder's fee. In self-defense the competitors then match the fee first paid. This tends to nullify the advantage secured by the institution that pioneered the practice. Nevertheless, once a practice of paying finder's fees is started, it is not easy to abandon it. Consequently, the real estate broker expects to collect his fee even in cases where the borrower insists upon patronizing the institution that is accustomed to pay it. In such a case it can hardly be said that the broker earned the fee, since he did not originate a loan for the lending institution. In markets where the payment of finder's fees to real estate brokers is customary, the broker does not think of himself as a mortgage broker.

Where finder's fees are not generally used, the real estate broker nevertheless is required to assist buyers and sellers to finance property offered for sale. The success of any particular deal frequently depends upon the ability of the experienced broker to assist the inexperienced buyer to finance the property. In such a case the real estate broker is still a finder, but without receiving compensation in the form of a finder's fee. His services benefit the lending institution as well as the purchaser. He is frequently in a position to take the business to any one of several competitive lending institutions. If the purchaser, inexperienced in real estate finance, has confidence in the broker, he is likely to be guided by his advice in making a loan application.

The institution to which a real estate broker takes a loan application assists the plans of the broker. By making the loan, it enables the broker to earn a selling commission. Sometimes the broker overlooks this reciprocal service and considers the lending institution which receives much of the business recommended by him to be under obligation to him. Where finder's fees are not paid for this service, the broker expects compensation in some other form. The form of compensation most frequently expected is a willingness on the part of the lending institution to return the favor by occasionally making an off-standard loan that it would otherwise not care to grant.

Such a situation poses a problem for the lending institution. It fears the risk element of the loan application, for one reason or another. It also fears to offend a real estate broker who originates acceptable loan applications. Without departing too far from its lending principles, the lending institution will try to find a means of helping out a friendly broker. If possible, some modification of the first request that will add protection to the loan will be approved. Perhaps the borrower can put up supplemental security of some kind. Or maybe he can get along with a somewhat smaller loan. Or perhaps the seller can be induced to take back a small purchase-money second mortgage. To keep the goodwill of the broker, the lender will spend more time on such an application than would normally be spent, in the hope that an otherwise unacceptable loan application can be made acceptable.

Individuals The statistics of mortgage lenders that are quoted from time to time by various agencies always include a miscellaneous category which carries the caption "Individuals and others." As a residual classification, no one seems to know too much about the composition of this group. Savings originate from two sources: (1) Corporate savings represent the undistributed earnings of corporations that are retained in the business for expansion and other purposes. (2) Individual savings represent the amounts accumulated by the great mass of income receivers who spend less than they earn. Their savings aggregate into the sums used for expansion of both new and old business units.

Some people save in order that they may spend more at a later time. Others save because their incomes exceed the amounts needed to meet their consumption requirements. Still others save from habit. Whatever the reasons for saving, funds accumulated by this means are available for investment. Some investors prefer to place their investable surplus with financial institutions for reinvestment. A smaller number prefer to handle their investment programs directly. From this latter group come those who place a part of their funds in real estate mortgages.

Some individuals make mortgage lending a business. While it will seldom be a major activity, it is followed with sufficient frequency to designate it at least as a major outlet for funds. Others grant a loan or purchase a mortgage as an experiment. They may become casual investors in this type of paper. The difference between the approaches of these two types of individuals may be marked. The first probably makes a careful study of real estate prices, population trends, neighborhood changes, and so on, so that he may be classified as a professional investor in real estate mortgages. This does not insure him against loss, since he may be like some so-called professional speculators in the stock market. They study and chart and scheme and still arrive at the wrong answers. Casual investors in real estate mortgages may take a flier because they want to see how they come out; because a friend or neighbor asks for a loan secured by real estate; and so forth.

The casual investor frequently makes no pretense of knowing all the answers about real estate lending operations. If he purchases corporate stocks, he probably does so on the hot tip he receives from his next-door neighbor—who may be a clerk in a grocery store—or from his barber or his garage mechanic. With the same nonchalance he may put his money into a real estate mortgage. If the venture turns out successfully, so much the better. If it ends in trouble and perhaps in a suit to foreclose the mortgage, his losses are probably no greater than they would have been had he taken a flier in the stock market.

The relative importance of casual and professional individuals who lend money on real estate as security is unknown. As stated above, even the importance of all individuals as one group is subject to conjecture.

Prevalence of Individual Lenders In the aggregate, individual lenders constitute a large but probably declining source of funds to be advanced upon real estate as security. There are no completely reliable statistics which show the proportion of all mortgage lending undertaken by individual mortgagees. The best estimates available seem to indicate that it is somewhere in the neighborhood of 15 to 20 percent.

In the early days, before there were financial institutions equipped to serve the mortgage needs of borrowers, individuals of means constituted a major source of real estate finance. This class is still active in some of the smaller communities not yet adequately served by financial institutions. Such lenders may enjoy several advantages over their institutional competitors. They can act more promptly if occasion requires. They are subject to no restrictions fixing the maturity of the loan or the percentage of loan to value. They can deal in either first or second mortgages as the occasion may require. In days gone by, some preferred junior mortgages because of the higher return they could earn. With the general lengthening of the term of mortgages, the tendency toward higher percentage loans, and the progressive decline in interest rates throughout the country, the opportunities for individuals in both the senior and junior mortgage fields have narrowed considerably. The multiplicity and growth of financial institutions bidding for this business, together with the emergence of governmental agencies which favor financial institutions as against individual lenders, have all combined to make individual lending as a business somewhat less important than formerly.

Many individual mortgagees attain their status through necessity rather than choice. If A has a property that is for sale but is not readily financed in the usual manner, he may be induced to take back a purchase-money mortgage as a major part of its purchase price. If this deal works out to his satisfaction, he may subsequently seek similar opportunities to invest funds in other mortgages against property in which he has no financial interest. Or he may worry through the problems of collecting the mortgage on the property that he sold and be glad to forget this means of earning a return upon his invested capital.

Nonbusiness Loans A great many individual lenders do not look upon their ventures into the field of real estate finance as business operations at all. Some buy properties for the use of their children or other members of their families. For reasons best known to themselves, they may take back liberal mortgages on such properties. One very potent reason may be to keep their gifts within the limits of tax exemptions under our inheritance laws. Suppose that the property which A gives to his daughter costs $30,000. A gift of the property free and clear of all encumbrances might subject most of that amount to inheritance tax. By taking back a sizable mortgage, he may spread the gift over a sufficient number of years to avoid the inheritance tax, if year by year he cancels a portion of the mortgage, again in the form of a gift. By successive annual cancellations of a part of the mortgage, the entire property passes from father to daughter without being affected by the inheritance tax.

The forms of mortgages based upon family relationship should not be taken too seriously. Interest rates, repayment terms, and so on may be drafted in a manner to take care of the interests of the mortgagee should the mortgagor see fit to dispose of his equity in the property. In such case the grantee would be obligated to observe the terms of the mortgage as written. Meantime, the mortgagee may forgo and even forgive interest payments, using his discretion about collecting all, only a part, or none of them.

In addition to nonbusiness loans on real estate based upon family ties, a considerable number of mortgages where there are no such ties would properly fit into this classification. Businessmen frequently assist their younger associates to acquire homes and sometimes even business properties by advancing the money needed for the purpose. Again the rate of interest collected may not represent a competitive rate but may be limited to what the lender might hope to earn on a similar investment in government bonds. Terms of repayment are also frequently adjusted to the capacities of the borrower instead of to what would normally be required for this type of loan.

From time to time businessmen have engaged in housing ventures for the purpose of providing living quarters for their employees. Sometimes the venture has been undertaken by a corporation and sometimes by an individual. In any event, the objective has been the provision of housing accommodations and not the profit that can be made from such a venture. Terms of sale has been fitted to the major objective and are not necessarily competitive with other real estate lending plans available in the same community.

Estate Loans Classed along with real estate loans by individuals, we frequently find those made by executors of estates. Such individuals may get into the business of real estate finance accidentally or on purpose. In disposing of real estate, they may sometimes take back purchase-money mortgages. In other cases, they may seek out this type of investment for funds entrusted to their care. Traditionally, the courts under whose jurisdiction they operate have looked with favor upon real estate mortgages as desirable outlets for estate funds. Within the limits of his trustee obligations, the executor may favor loans to the families which are the beneficiaries of the estate. Some executors, on the contrary, keep clear of any entanglements that might develop from this quarter.

Like other individual lenders, executors of estates are somewhat more free than financial institutions in determining lending policies, including maturity of loans, interest rates, and repayment requirements. However, they are more likely than individuals using their own funds to adhere to money-lending practices common to the market in which they operate. Again like other individual lenders, they are inclined to confine their mortgage holdings to small properties, particularly residences. In some instances this rule is not observed when a good opportunity for financing apartment houses or busines property is presented.

The pattern of lending normally adopted by estate trustees is likely to be the one with which each individual trustee is best acquainted. If he is a county seat lawyer, he may prefer farm loans. If he is a city banker, on the other hand, loans on urban real estate, particularly residences, may be selected. While the court which sanctions his appointment supervises his operations in a general way, the specific investments made of funds in the estate are more likely than not to be left to the discretion of the trustee. If losses occur because of mistakes in judgment only, the trustee is not held liable for them.

Credit Unions Cooperative credit unions are being established in considerable numbers in this country, following the pattern earlier established in Europe. At the end of 1970, credit unions in the United States had assets approaching $18 billion. In general, their purpose is to develop a pool of credit for their members, to be drawn upon in time of need. As a rule it is expected that the contributions to this pool by the members will be small but regular. The withdrawals from the funds of the union may be needed to meet emergencies which call for more money than the borrower could command from any other source. In spite of the fact that such emergencies are unpredictable and that, as a consequence, liquidity of the resources of these credit unions should be emphasized, in recent years some of them have engaged in long-term real estate financing.

A major reason for this change in investment policy has been the high level of employment in the postwar years. Members of these credit unions have had available funds to invest in credit union certificates but have had less than usual occasion to call upon the unions for loans. Instead of keeping these excess funds idle or investing them in low-rate short-term opportunities, mortgage loans have been looked upon with favor, particularly in financing homes for members. In some cases the managements have undertaken long-term commitments of this character with their eyes open. They recognize the difficulties they might face if too much of their resources were frozen in this manner so that they could not meet demands from their members for loans to meet future emergencies. They hope that, if and when that time comes, they can dispose of their real estate mortgages, without loss, if it becomes necessary to use this method of realizing the cash required by their members.

Private Real Estate Syndicates Private real estate syndicates are usually made up of a few local friends and business associates who think they see a speculative opportunity in real estate operations. They operate informally, sometimes to their disadvantage, and the public seldom knows of their existence. They pool their resources to establish a fund, either for the purpose of purchasing an equity in a property already encumbered by a mortgage or upon which a mortgage is placed as a part of the deal, or for the purpose of paying for a property so that they may own it free from encumbrances. Different circumstances may dictate one or the other of these methods of financing the property.

Each separate transaction is set up as a joint venture, even though the same individuals may participate in successive deals of this kind. Title to the property purchased may be taken in the name of one member of the syndicate who serves as its manager or in the name of some corporate trustee. In either event, the terms of the syndicate agreement should be set forth with greater particularity than is usually followed. Misunderstandings and miscalculations may be better avoided by more explicit written agreements. Even though an elaborate agreement be drawn up, it is usually known only to participants in the syndicate. No representation is made to outsiders that would lead them to consider this type of syndicate as a general partnership.

As in any other business venture, numerous questions may arise in the future that should be anticipated at the time the deal is made. Among them are the following: (1) responsibility, compensation, and authority of manager and trustee, if one is used; (2) method of voting upon issues to be settled by members—one vote per man or votes distributed according to amount of financial contribution to the resources of the syndicate; (3) improvement policies—modernization of old building or even replacement as the best means of realizing greatest profits from the venture; (4) assessments of members and methods of collecting them; (5) methods of dealing with members who refuse or are unable to meet assessments; (6) methods of disposal of syndicate interests of members wishing or forced to dipose of them; and (7) names of syndicate members, the amounts of their individual contributions and the manner of sharing profits or losses.

This type of syndicate is normally used to finance a real estate speculative venture. It can, however, be used for investment purposes as well. The kinds of properties dealt in include: vacant land thought to be about ready for subdividing; apartment or office buildings, or even factories; or any kind of property the present owners of which may be in need of immediate financial rescue. In other words, real estate syndicates may be associated with financial distress.

The qualifications of members of real estate syndicates of this type should include the following: (1) They should have available resources that could be devoted to such a venture for whatever period of time is necessary without embarrassment. (2) They should have the courage required to embark upon a type of business operation that may involve considerable risk. (3) They should have the patience needed to stay with the program which they undertake until they test their best opportunities for profit from it. In some cases this may take several years, with annual expenses and taxes to pay but no income to offset them. (4) They should be well-enough acquainted with each other to be able to act in harmony, come what may. Ventures of this kind require a high degree of mutual confidence, both among the members and in the syndicate manager.

Various practices are followed with respect to the determination of issues to be settled involving the interests of syndicate members. Under one method of operation, the chief contribution made by the members is financial. They pay their money over to the manager and let him make all decisions concerning its use. This has the advantage of avoiding conflicts of opinions, but places a considerable burden of choice upon one man. Under other methods, all major decisions are made by syndicate members. This is the more democratic approach, but may result in differences that are not easily resolved. If a trustee holds title to the property in trust for the members, it is not expected that he will be required or permitted to make major decisions affecting their interests. The agreement should make this clear, to avoid future complications.

Syndicates for the Small Investor Within the last few years, a number of large syndicators have brought syndication down to the level of the small investor. Certificates of participation have been sold in units as low as $500, $1,000, or $5,000—amounts which were previously considered too small. The result has been that, instead of a few participants of substantial means and risk-taking ability, the syndicate membership may be composed of thousands of small investors who have been intrigued by promises of a tax-sheltered high return per year. It has been estimated that in 1962 about $3.5 billion of assorted types of real estate were syndicated among over 100,000 individual investors. The annual average invested during the 1950s was about $2 billion. Such dollar volume places the syndicates in a class with mutual funds as an investment medium. This fact, coupled with the speculative nature of the operations, has caused the Securities and Exchange Commission considerable concern.

A typical example of the operation finds the syndicator and his chosen associates advancing $100,000 for the general partnership interest. Limited partnership interests are then offered to the public in $1,000 or $5,000 units for a total of $4.4 million. With the $4.5 million of equity funds the syndicate can buy a real estate complex costing up to $10 million, mortgaging the property for the difference. The promised high return to limited partners must to a great extent be conditional on the income potential of the property. Furthermore, at least a portion of the return is considered for tax purposes to be a recovery of capital for depreciation of the property. Many investors assume a permanently rising price level which will offset actual dollar depreciation in real estate. If this condition does not hold, however, the investor finds that his depreciation deduction is a true cost as well as a tax item, and that his return is lower by that amount.

In an operation of this kind the syndicate general partners share few of the risks. They may have originally bought the property through another business entity and sold it to the syndicate at a profit. Through another company which they own they may receive substantial remuneration for management services. Above all, as the general partners, all earnings and capital gains not contracted away to the limited partners accrue to their benefit. They stand to gain all residual benefits. For a $10 million real estate holding, for example, $1 million net income should not be excessive for a one-year operation. Distributions on the capitalization might be as follows:

```
Net rent income (before interest).....................  $1,000,000
Less:
   Mortgage ($5,500,000 @ 7%)............  $385,000
   Limited partners ($4,400,000 @ 12%).....   528,000
                                                          913,000
         Residual to general partners (syndicators)........ $   87,000
```

On the $100,000 invested by the syndicators the return for the year would be 87 percent. Upon later sale of the property at a capital gain, the syndicators' participation usually would take a major portion of the gains above a refund to limited partners of their original investment.

From the example it is apparent why those charged with protecting investors are afraid that many may be lured into this type of venture without appreciating that the 12 percent return is not certain and that the risk is relatively high.

Recently, the flood of new capital has been swelling the demand for sound properties. It has become increasingly difficult for new owners to pass on their higher costs in the form of rent increases. Syndicators are experiencing unusual difficulties in finding properties that will bring in enough income to justify the high payments to investors after deducting normal operating costs.

Since January 1, 1961, New York state, the largest market for real estate securities, has required filing of prospectuses of public issues with the Real Estate Syndication Section of its law department. During the first year of operation, the section rejected or succeeded in having withdrawn one out of every four proposed offerings. Even so, the section cleared $1.3 billion of real estate securities for public offering during 1961. After some curtailment in activities during the mid-1960s, there has been a veritable stampede into real estate investment through syndicates during the late 1960s and early 1970s. Investors have been aggressively seeking a hedge against high rates of inflation, tax shelters, and highly predictable returns. The most respected Wall Street underwriters are now bringing out S.E.C.-registered limited partnerships to invest in properties. California is particularly active in intrastate syndications. Promoters of some syndications do not specify what properties they will buy. These have been called "blind pool syndications" and should be recognized as pure venture capital funds. The National Association of Real Estate Boards has issued a public statement cautioning the public against the "speculative nature" of real estate syndicates.

Limited Partnership Syndicates for Publicly Assisted Housing The limited partnership business form has recently emerged as a favored vehicle for the ownership of residential rental real estate for low and moderate income groups where constructed under the aegis of the National Housing Act or similarly directed state statutes. The limited partnership form is attractive because it offers to all limited partners the major advantage of a corporation—liability for firm business obligations limited to a specific capital contribution—and does not incur the disadvantage of the corporate form of not being able to pass business operating losses through to the firm owners. The limited partnership is not treated as a separate taxable entity like the corporation. The partnership losses, therefore, are distributable directly to the partners in accordance with their loss-sharing ratio, whereas in a corporation such losses can only be offset against corporate income of other periods.

In establishing the limited partnership, great care must be taken that the contractual terms identify it in effect as a partnership and not as an "association" as understood by the Internal Revenue Service. An association is taxed like a corporation. The six criteria for treatment like a corporation are the presence of:

1. Business associates
2. An objective to carry on the business and divide the gains therefrom
3. Continuity of life
4. Centralization of management
5. Limited liability
6. Free transferability of interest

A corporation must have more corporate than noncorporate characteristics to be classified as a corporation for tax purposes. Criteria 1 and 2 above are common to both corporations and partnerships. It is, therefore, commonly understood that a business firm will receive treatment as a partnership if two of the criteria 3 through 6 are absent.

Most limited partnerships have a centralization of management similar to corporations, so differentiation normally will take place in 3, 5, and 6. Under the Uniform Partnership Act, after which most state statutes are patterned, the general partner has the power to dissolve the partnership at any time, thus denying it continuity of life. Otherwise, a terminal date may be provided for in the partnership articles. The criterion of limited liability is negated by the very fact that one partner is a general partner with unlimited liability. Finally, free transferability of interests can be limited by requiring permission of the general or other limited partners to effectuate a change of ownership. Such a restriction has been deemed by the Treasury regulations such an impingement as to constitute a legal curtailment of transferability of interests. By proper combination of these provisions, tax treatment as a partnership can be achieved.

The sole general partner of a limited partnership is often a corporation. The advantage of this arrangement lies in the limited personal liability the builder-sponsor of a project can achieve by holding his interest in the limited partnership in his corporation. An incorporated general partner can also provide better continuity of management. To avoid "dummy" characteristics in the sole corporate general partner, the Internal Revenue Service follows internal guidelines (called "safe harbor rules") imposing certain ownership and minimum capital requirements. In regard to ownership, limited partners may not own, individually or in the aggregate, more than 20 percent of the corporate stock. The tax rules of attribution of ownership relating to members of the partners' families also apply. The net worth requirement of the corporate general partner depends upon the total contributed capital of the partnership: If the contributed capital is less than $2.5 million, the corporate general partner must have a net worth at least equal to 15 percent of the total partnership capital, but not to exceed $250,000. Where the contributed partnership capital is $2.5 million or more, the corporate general partner must maintain at all times a net worth of at least 10 percent of the partnership capital.

It is a uniform rule that property can be depreciated only to the extent of its tax basis, usually cost. In a general partnership, where all partners have unlimited liability, the tax basis, or cost, includes both equity contributions and debts for which all partners are responsible. Thus, the full cost, whether financed by equity or debt, can be claimed as a depreciation deduction over time for income tax purposes. A consistent application of this rule to limited partners would seem to limit their depreciation deduction to their equity interest, since they assume no liability beyond that amount. In this instance, however, there is an exception where none of the partners has any liability in connection with the property acquisition.[1] This is true in regard to a mortgage on real estate acquired by a partnership on a "subject to" basis without assumption by the partnership or any of the partners of any liability on the mortgage. Under such conditions, the full cost of the property, whether acquired by funds provided by equity or debt, may be taken as a depreciation deduction by the partners, whether general or limited. Thus, where a depreciable property was financed by $9 of debt for each $1 of equity, the partner has leveraged his depreciation deduction to 10 to 1. Over time, the taxpayer partner may claim $10 of depreciation deductions against taxable income for each $1 of equity invested. In a 50 percent tax bracket, his cumulative tax savings could amount to $5, or five times his equity investment.

Although the Tax Reform Act of 1969 extended the recapture provisions of the income tax law whereby excess depreciation taken by accelerated methods is treated as ordinary income rather than capital gain upon sale of the property, more liberal treatment was accorded government-assisted projects and rehabilitation expenditures for low-income rental housing. Furthermore, a new 60-month straight-line write-off was provided for rehabilitation expenditures for low-income rental housing where the dwelling units are held for occupancy by persons of low or moderate income consistent with the policies of the Housing and Urban Development Act of 1968. Publicly assisted housing has thus become particularly attractive for syndication to the taxpayer in the high bracket who is seeking deductible losses to pose against income he is receiving from other sources.

In summary, the appeals of the limited partnership syndicate for publicly assisted housing lie in combining maximum depreciation deductions, relatively favorable capital gain treatment under the recapture rules,

---

[1] Treas. Regs. §1.752-1(e); see also Sheldon Schwartz, "How to Find Tax Shelter as a Limited Partner," *Real Estate Review*, Vol. 1, No. 2 (Summer 1971), pp. 54–59.

and government-assisted financing with delegated management responsibility and limited liability. Such a marriage of investment advantages has made it possible for many builder-sponsors to complete qualified construction projects without any equity investment of their own.

Miscellaneous Sources of Real Estate Finance Without undertaking to exhaust the list of sources of real estate finance, the following should be mentioned. Since they are not so important as those described earlier and since they present no peculiar problems, no detailed discussion of their operations will be undertaken. These sources are: (1) corporate employers who assist their employees to finance homes; (2) trade unions, a part of whose funds are sometimes used to finance homes for their members; (3) land developers who encourage home construction by the use of devices such as land contracts and waivers to subordinate their claims to construction loans; (4) lodges and associations that may have in their treasuries funds not needed for some years; (5) trustees, both individual and corporate; (6) foundations; (7) educational, religious, and charitable institutions; and (8) governmental agencies of various kinds, some of which are discussed separately in this text.

A new source of investment funds that is likely to play a major role in real estate financing in the future is pension funds. By 1970, the estimated resources of such funds had already reached over $258 billion, having grown from less than $38 billion in 1950. Whether these funds are administered by insurance companies, banks, trust companies, investment committees of employing corporations, or governmental agencies, they are expected to be invested in a manner to provide safety, availability as needed, and a return consistent with safety and availability. More and more, mortgage bankers and others who originate real estate mortgages for sale are looking to the resources of pension funds as prospective funds for real estate financing.

Sale of Miscellaneous Types of Securities Over the years, nearly every type of security that has ever been used in the financing of any type of business in this country has been tried in the financing of real estate projects. Common and preferred stock, participation-mortgage certificates, debenture bonds, collateral trust bonds, installment certificates, second mortgage notes, land contract-collateral trust notes, and so on, have all been tried. Some of these belong to ancient history. Nevertheless, the patterns set by them may again be used if circumstances warrant. For that reason, a brief description of some of them is pertinent to this study.

Use of Debentures In American experience, debenture bonds are unsecured promises to pay a definite amount of money at a definite time. Because there is no specific security mentioned in the bond indenture, they are sometimes said to be based upon credit. That is true. But a part of the credit of the issuing corporation is the amount of its equity in its property. If a debenture bond issue follows a mortgage, the debenture bonds are necessarily less well protected than is the mortgage. But if there is no mortgage outstanding and if the bond indenture contains protective clauses prohibiting the use of a mortgage, the debenture bonds may be adequately protected.

In some corporations owning real estate, the funds needed are obtained from the sale of debentures, without any underlying mortgage. Following the debentures will come one or more classes of stock. Debentures are used also in the reorganization of real estate corporations which have defaulted in their obligations on their mortgage bonds. When a new financial plan becomes effective, income debentures sometimes take the place of the mortgage bonds.

Use of Stock Various types of real estate have been financed, in part at least, through the sale of stock. One more or less common plan is to obtain as large a mortgage as possible against a particular real estate project and to finance the remainder of the cost with one or more classes of stock. In many instances there has been no remainder. Enough has been obtained from the mortgage or the mortgage bonds to pay the entire cost incurred by the promoters. Nevertheless even here there would normally be stock to evidence residual ownership of the enterprise and control of its operations. If all goes well with a venture of this type, the mortgage will eventually be amortized from the earnings of the mortgagor. The stockholders will then own the real estate free and clear of all encumbrances, regardless of their small investment in it.

Even where misfortune befalls a real estate venture financed by a mortgage, so that the mortgagor is forced to default in his obligations, any reorganization that follows will not necessarily freeze out the stockholders. On a reduced scale of holdings and, perhaps, after meeting some kind of an assessment, they may be included in the new financial plan. Unorganized and inarticulate bondholders do not ordinarily care to assume the functions of management. They are normally willing to carry along the stockholders for this purpose.

When a defaulted mortgage is held by a financial institution, the chances of the participation of the stockholders in any plan of reorganization are not so favorable. The mortgagee may prefer to take over the property and either manage it for its income return or dispose of it to the best advantage possible. As a matter of experience, much income property taken over by mortgagees as a result of the depression of the 1930s proved to be a very satisfactory investment in the years that followed. Patience, accompanied by a sound management program, frequently paid good dividends. In other cases, particularly if the original loan represented a high percentage of value and if the default followed quickly after the granting of the loan, the mortgagee was not so fortunate in recovering its investment.

Whenever stock is used to help finance a real estate project and it becomes necessary for the mortgagee to foreclose its mortgage, the chance of any recovery except from the security is not great. A deficiency judgment could be obtained, but usually the corporation has no assets except the property which secures the mortgage. Unless there is some kind of a guarantee of the mortgage, recovery is limited to the liquidating value of the security.

Use of Preferred Stock Preferred stock is used in financing real estate projects in two ways. In some cases, a mortgage is executed for as large a percentage of the value of the property as it is possible to obtain. Then preferred stock is offered in an amount sufficient to cover the remainder of the cost of the property. Common stock is reserved for the promoters. Normally it represents no investment of cash. The promoters hold it as a kind of certificate of hope. If all goes well, it may eventually acquire some value. If necessary to sweeten the offer of preferred stock, its purchasers may be given a bonus of common. In any event the promoters would make sure of retaining the control.

Since in a case of this kind the common stock represents no investment other than the time of the promoters, their hope of making their holdings worth something springs from a program somewhat as follows: If net earnings are sufficient to meet carrying charges on the mortgage, to pay dividends on the preferred stock, and to leave any surplus, the latter is used to amortize the mortgage. After it is paid off, the preferred stock will then be redeemed. Finally the holders of the common stock will own the real estate.

The other use of preferred stock follows a default in a mortgage. When a reorganization of a real estate corporation becomes necessary, the holders of mortgage bonds are sometimes asked to take preferred stock in place of their bonds. Whether they retain their old bonds and waive the fixed obligation of the mortgagor to pay interest unless it is earned, or whether they exchange their bonds for mortgage income bonds, debenture income bonds, or preferred stock, is frequently a matter of indifference. The rearranged contract may produce the same result under any one of these patterns.

French Plan One elaborate plan for combining mortgages with stocks in financing real estate was the "French plan." Its somewhat involved parts were as follows: First, there was organized the Fred F. French Security Company, later merged into the Fred F. French Investing Company, Inc. One subsidiary was the Fred F. French Management Company, and another was the Fred F. French Operating Company. The method of operation started with the selection of a suitable site for an apartment house. Next, a new corporation was organized to own the site and the building to be constructed on it. As large a mortgage as could be obtained was executed against the site and the proposed building. Preferred stock was then offered to make up the difference between the cost of the land and building and the amount of the mortgage.

With each share of preferred stock the purchaser received, as a bonus, one share of common stock. Whenever a share of bonus stock was issued to a purchaser of preferred stock, another share was given to the Fred F. French Investing Company, Inc. By purchasing one additional share of the common the Investing Company maintained control of each real estate project. It was the expectation that the common stock would acquire value after the mortgage and the preferred stock were redeemed.

Meantime the various French companies sold the securities, constructed the buildings, and operated them, charging in each case the going rates for such services. A considerable number of apartment houses in New York City were constructed under this plan of financing, including the Tudor City group. The latter were financed in various separate projects. The depression of the 1930s hit very hard not only the separate real estate corporations but the French companies as well.

Mandel Plan A variation of the French plan, operated on similar principles, was given the name "Mandel plan." About the same sort of program of selling securities, constructing apartment houses, and managing them was set up. The major difference appeared in the use of the bonus common stock. Instead of giving the holders of preferred stock in the A corporation common stock of that corporation, the Mandel plan organized a holding company to own the common stocks of each of the separate real estate corporations. This holding company was called the Henry Mandel Associates, Inc. Then the purchaser of the preferred stock of the A corporation was given a bonus of common stock in the holding company. This plan tended to diversify the risk of the common stock. If some of the real estate corporations earned more than others, all holders of common stock would be treated alike. Control of the holding company was centered in the parent investment company, as in the French plan.

Early Real Estate Trusts During the decade of the 1920s, investment trusts of various kinds were developed on a broad front in this country. At a time when a flood of new investment funds was being contributed to by millions of people who never before had purchased stocks or bonds, we witnessed a series of changes in security prices that bewildered even the experts. Into this picture the managers of investment trusts brought two qualities that made a strong appeal to experienced and inexperienced investors alike. In effect, they announced: "We are experts. We know what to buy. Furthermore, we will provide every investor, large or small, with the safety that accompanies diversification." And so, presumably, the two qualities needed most by investors in an uncertain security market were available for the asking—expert management and diversification of risk.

It is not surprising that in the large list of investment trusts organized at this time were some which invested their funds in real estate. Since investors were no more capable of selecting income real estate than they were the stocks and bonds issued by railroads, public utilities, and industrials, such real estate trusts met a favorable response for a time. For example, the Diversified Real Estate Investment Trust No. 1 was organized in 1928 to deal in business properties on the main streets of Los Angeles, California. It sold certificates of beneficial interest with a face value of $50, totaling $1,000,000. In this particular trust, profits were to be used first to amortize the outstanding certificates. After all certificates had been paid in full, their holders were then entitled to receive two thirds of future profits, and the managers of the trust, one third. Certificates had a 10-year maturity. At the maturity date in 1938, the trust was to be liquidated. The proceeds of the liquidation were to be applied first to the redemption of any certificates or credits thereon that were still outstanding. The residue was to be distributed, two thirds to the certificate holders and one third to the management.

A so-called real estate trust of this character, engaged in buying and selling real estate, sounds much more like a speculative pool than like an investment trust. In this respect it paralleled the management trusts which speculated with other people's money in stocks during the latter part of the 1920 decade.

Second Mortgage Companies In areas of extensive junior financing, numerous companies have been organized to deal principally in second mortgages. The major activity of many such companies is to purchase for resale whole second mortgage notes secured by subordinate liens on improved real estate. The companies so engaged buy the mortgage notes chiefly from builders and real estate dealers at discounts ranging from 10 to 37½ percent. The notes are then sold to the public. They normally have a nominal interest rate, but they are offered to the public at a discount sufficient to yield the purchaser a much higher rate on the unamortized balance.

Company services include careful selection of mortgage notes to be offered, possibly a continuous reinvestment program for note purchasers who seek maximum earnings on their funds, and often a repurchase agreement with each mortgage sold whereby the corporation agrees to buy back any mortgage note in a purchaser's hands upon proper notice in event the mortgagor defaults in his payments. At least one company has permitted purchasers of mortgage notes to invest accumulated funds in cumulative preferred stock of the mortgage company as part of its reinvestment program. These shares might later be exchanged at par toward the purchase of additional mortgage notes yielding 10 percent.

In a flourishing real estate market these companies have prospered. As the market has weakened in certain areas, however, such companies have run into serious difficulty. Particularly where they have made repurchase agreements, their equities are seriously impaired by more numerous defaults. Where the defaults become sufficiently significant, the public second mortgage noteholders cannot be made whole under the warranty agreement, and they may become losers as a consequence of the subordinated position of their mortgage security.

Equity Participations of Institutional Lenders[2] In recent years, institutional lenders have become increasingly interested in equity participations in projects in which they have a lending interest. There are several forces at work in the economy that have induced this trend. Savings deposit institutions have had to respond to increased interest payment demands of depositors and higher costs of administration. Statutory restraints have been liberalized. Certainly equally important has been the willingness of hopeful borrowers to grant some degree of equity participation to tilt the scales in their favor in a tight market for mortgage money. Philosophically, mortgage loan officers feel entitled to equity participation when they provide up to 100 percent of the financing and in many cases assume equity-type risks.

Usually associated with equity participations is a less secure legal and financial position. This may take the form of a second mortgage, a wraparound loan, a mortgage or purchase and leaseback of a subordinated fee, or a subordinated convertible debenture. Often, lenders will accept higher loan-to-value ratios, lower interest rates, and slower repayment terms as well. Occasionally, they may provide the "front money" to prime the pump for the flow of construction money at an early stage of development. To be of interest to institutional lenders, the projects usually involve investments in excess of $1 million. Thus, the borrowers are highly experienced and reliable developers, and they are working with prime real estate.

Perhaps the most usual form of participation, which may be incorporated in the conventional financing forms such as mortgages and leases, is a stipulated percentage of gross or net income above some agreed base figure. The more commonly accepted measure is gross income because of its ease of determination. This kind of provision is common in financing motels and nursing homes.

A less used form of equity participation, more commonly associated with stable income streams, has the investor or lender taking an actual conveyance of title to all or part of the property at the expiration of the tenant's lease or at the end of the mortgage payback period. This

---

[2] See also Cornelius C. Rose, Jr., "Equity Participations," *The Mortgage Banker*, June 1968, pp. 44–47.

arrangement, of course, has the disadvantage of many years of deferral in the opportunity to participate.

A common method of development financing involves the splitting of the real estate into a fee and a leasehold estate. The investor buys the land at its fair value and leases it back to the developer. The investor then makes a mortgage loan on the leasehold estate. The lease normally provides for a base rate plus overages based on sales volume of occupant tenants of the developed property. In this case, the investor has a fixed return, plus possible overages, and he retains the residual property values through fee ownership. The developer, on the other hand, has the advantage of a high loan-to-value ratio, a 100 percent depreciable asset, and lower payout requirements, since he does not need to amortize the investment in land.

Since this method is unusually complicated, an example may be helpful. Assume a development with a building costing $3,220,000 on land valued at $580,000. The investor, often an insurance company or its subsidiary in this case, buys the land for $580,000 and leases it to the developer at 9 percent constant, or $52,200 per year. The investor then makes a 75 percent loan on leasehold improvements, which totals $2,415,000, to bear 9 percent interest and be amortized over 30 years (9.66 percent constant). The investor then contracts to receive a participation (say 30 percent) of "net defined income," which is determined by deducting from effective gross income all debt service payments, ground rents, and cash expenses, to arrive at cash flow. On a defined net income of $100,000, the investor's participation would be $30,000. His total return and yield would be computed as follows:

Ground rent..........................	$ 52,200
Contract interest rate................	217,350
Participation in defined net income...	30,000
Total.............................	$ 299,550
Total investment ($580,000 + $2,415,000).........	$2,995,000

Yield to investor is thus about 10 percent plus reversion of land.

The developer's return, of course, is determined by relating his residual cash flows to his equity investment, initially $70,000 of cash flow as a return on ($3,220,000 − $2,415,000) $805,000, but subject to adjustment as effective gross income changes.

A related type of financing is the "sale and buy-back," or installment sales contract. Under this arrangement, the investor buys the property from the developer and simultaneously sells it back to him under a long-term installment agreement whereby he retains legal title. The developer-buyer obtains an equitable interest in the title and may claim depreciation. His payments are set approximately equal to the current mortgage constant for the purchase price, plus a contingent payment related to property performance. The buyer normally has prepayment privileges in the form of contract termination options which when exercised will also result in a profit windfall to the investor.

The recent period of historically high-interest rates has brought the wraparound mortgage into considerable acceptance. Often, when an owner requires additional financing he arranges for the placement of a new first mortgage in a larger amount than is presently owing on an existing property. A part of the proceeds of the new loan is used to satisfy the old mortgage. Sometimes it is not possible or even good judgment to pay off this prior mortgage. Prepayment penalties may be high or interest rates may be attractively low on the existing mortgage. In this case, a wraparound mortgage may be arranged whereby the owner obtains the benefits of additional financing without the prior mortgage being extinguished. The second lender takes over servicing the prior mortgage out of payments he receives from the owner as debt service. For example, assume that Jones owes $400,000 on an apartment building secured by a first mortgage requiring debt service of $40,000 annually with interest first deducted at 6 percent. In order to expand the building at a cost of $300,000, the owner arranges with an insurance company for a wraparound mortgage of $700,000 bearing interest at 8 percent and requiring debt service of $64,750 (9.25 percent constant) annually. At the closing, the owner executes mortgage documents supporting his $700,000 obligation and receives $300,000 cash. The insurance company relieves him of his $400,000 savings and loan obligation and will proceed to pay it off at the rate of $40,000 per year out of the $64,750 it receives. By servicing the prior debt at a lower interest rate, the insurance company leverages its own return to well above the 8 percent nominal return on its mortgage note.

Recently, there has been a decided emergence of "front money" transactions. Quite commonly, experienced developers team up with partners who have no development experience but who can provide cash outlays necessary to carry a development through its initial stages. The split on net income and relative positions in regard to control of the venture are negotiated. Terms of a joint venture of this kind might follow the general outlines of this example: Brown, a developer, enters into a joint venture agreement with Green, the "money partner," to acquire and develop land and build a condominium on it. With the land to cost $500,000 and the improvements to cost an additional $4,000,000, the project might be projected to gross $5,500,000 on sale of the units. Green lends $500,000 to the venture to buy the land. A construction loan is arranged for $3,700,000. To make up the deficiency between building costs and the construction loan and to provide working capital, each partner contributes $300,000. As sales of the condominium units are made, the proceeds are distributed according to the agreement as follows:

1. The construction loan is repaid.
2. Green receives back the $500,000 advanced for land purchase.
3. Interest is paid on Green's loan at the rate of 10 percent per annum.
4. Any proceeds left over are distributed equally to Brown and Green to return their capital contributions and pay out the profits.

In large projects, the institutional investor's position is usually secured throughout the construction period by fee ownership or a first mortgage lien on the property. Arrangements may provide that as buildings are constructed and sold the investor will release the property and participate in the profit or, if buildings are leased, that he will share in certain leasing overage benefits with the developer.

Many institutions are developing a specialty of standby commitments for 100 percent of the cost of a building project. By this arrangement, the developer is assured an unconditional takeout when the project is completed. This gives him the financial strength to arrange for a construction loan and time to arrange cheaper, more conventional permanent financing. In event the standby commitment is used, in normal course the institution becomes a partner with the developer under terms providing for substantial participation in profits in addition to loan repayment requirements, including interest.

Morgage Insurance Companies[3] Prior to the provision of mortgage insurance by the federal government during the 1930s, the field was exclusively occupied by private companies. These companies sold insurance coverage principally on mortgage loans on large commercial and high-rise apartment buildings with little or no emphasis on insurance on loans for single-family dwellings. Further, their operations were for the most part on a regional basis with inadequate regulation, and the insured loans were not regularly amortized. Under the impact of the Great Depression, these firms either failed or ceased operations as a matter of good judgment.

From the depression period until 1957, the mortgage insurance and guarantee field was left to the federal government with its Federal Housing Administration and Veterans Administration programs. In 1957, however, the Mortgage Guaranty Insurance Corporation was organized and licensed by the Wisconsin Insurance Commissioner. It is now authorized to do business in 48 states and the District of Columbia. From the time of its organization to December 31, 1971, its insurance in force has increased sharply, amounting to $5.1 billion at the 1971 year-end.

---

[3] The material in this section is based on the *Statement of the Federal Home Loan Bank Board on Inquiry into Mortgage Insurance Companies* (Washington, D.C.: Federal Home Loan Bank Board, June 26, 1964).

The business is generated about equally from new housing and from sale of existing homes. The bulk of the company's business has been with savings and loan associations. Recently, however, a growing number of banks, credit unions, and insurance companies have been using this protection. In 1972, there were eight private insurance companies from which the Federal National Mortgage Association would accept insurance in its conventional loan programs. The Mortgage Guaranty Insurance Corporation is the most important, however, by a wide margin. It accounts for over 70 percent of the loans insured by private companies.

These companies offer insurance to approved mortgage lenders against financial loss on first mortgage loans where mortgagors fail to make required payments. This insurance is ordinarily not utilized unless the loan exceeds 80 percent of appraised value. Mortgage Guaranty Insurance Corporation coverage, for instance, insures the top 20 percent of the mortgage loan regardless of balance, to a maximum limit of 95 percent of appraisal value. Such protection makes it possible for lenders to increase the volume of conventional loans by lending at loan-to-value ratios that would be excluded under their normal lending policies.

An institution becomes an approved lender by applying to an insurer and having a master policy issued in its favor. Factors considered by the insurance company as part of its approval process include: size, supervisory history with regulatory agencies, appraisal experience and qualifications, operating policy, and membership in the Federal Savings and Loan Insurance Corporation or (for commercial banks) the Federal Deposit Insurance Corporation. Most applicants have been savings and loan associations, although commercial banks and others have recently become interested in the service.

By the terms of the master policy, a "default" is declared when payments have not been made for four months. The insured institution must give notice to the insurer within 10 days after the insured loan has become in default. The insurer may then direct the insured institution to initiate appropriate legal proceedings. In any event, the proceedings must be instituted within nine months of the time the loan first went into arrears. Within 60 days after completion of the legal proceedings, the insured institution files notice of loss and conveys its title to the insurer. The amount of loss payable to the insured institution includes the principal balance due under the mortgage, back interest, real estate taxes, hazard insurance premiums, all expenses incurred in preservation of the property, and all legal expenses, including court costs and reasonable attorney's fees. In the determination of the loss payable, the insurer may exercise an option not to acquire the property, but to leave it with the insured institution, and thereby limit liability to 20 percent of the allowable claim. The effect of this option is to shift the risk of 80 percent of the allowable claim to the institutional lender, which for satisfaction of its claim must look to the value of the property it has as security.

These insurance companies approve only loans that meet their underwriting standards. When approved, one of two types of loan policies will normally be issued. The policy most frequently used provides for a year term with annual renewals, called the "annual plan." The premium for the first year is 1 percent of the amount of the loan; and for succeeding years it is ¼ of 1 percent of the declining balance of the loan. Under the second plan, a single premium is paid in the amount of 2½ percent of the initial amount of the loan to cover a 10-year term. The premium under all plans is paid by the borrower. The policies are subject to cancellation by the insured institution, and it may then receive a partial refund of premium. The insurance companies also require that the borrower pay an appraisal fee of $20 to accompany each application for insurance where the loan exceeds 80 percent of appraised value. This fee provides a fund to finance additional appraisals by agents of the insurer to verify the quality of the lender's appraisals.

Private insurance companies now cover over 3 percent of the total home mortgage debt outstanding. It is also interesting to note that they are now extending this type of insurance to multifamily, commercial, and industrial properties. Commercial Loan Insurance Corporation, a subsidiary of MGIC Investment Corporation, for example, extends loans to every type of commercial and industrial real estate, including shopping centers, factories, nursing homes, retail stores, and warehouses. As in insurance of home mortgages, the protection extends to the top 20 percent of the outstanding loan balance. A five-year noncancellable policy may be purchased for a single premium of 2.9 percent of the loan, or for an annual premium of 1.2 percent of the loan for the first year and ½ of 1 percent of the outstanding principal balance at the beginning of each year thereafter. The renewal premium is ½ of 1 percent of the outstanding principal balance at the beginning of each renewal term.

Lease guarantee insurance has been assuming importance in recent years. It has been typical in the financing of shopping centers and other commercial or industrial developments that the bulk of the mortgage payments be covered by prime tenants. These tenants, occupying a major part of the space, therefore command lower rental rates because of the developer's reliance upon their credit. Since many mortgage lenders will accept minor lessees whose leases are insured in lieu of a prime tenant, there is often an advantage in increasing the occupancy percentage for insured minor tenants and cutting back the space allotted to major tenants. The insurance premium is usually only a fraction of the differential gain from the higher rents obtained through the shift in space allocation.

The character of the risk inherent in private mortgage insurance is well-stated in a prospectus filed in 1961 with the United States Securities and Exchange Commission by Mortgage Guaranty Insurance Corporation:

In common with insurers of other types of risk, the mortgage loan insurer proceeds on the assumption that past experience, adjusted for applicable changes in conditions, will prevail on average in the future.

Application of this basic assumption to the field of mortgage loan insurance is believed to involve substantially greater dependence on broad estimates, and consequently less likelihood of accuracy, than most other forms of insurance. Losses on first mortgage loans do not necessarily follow a generally steady and reasonably predictable pattern from year to year. Under favorable economic conditions, losses are likely to be small. The great risk in the residential mortgage loan insurance field would appear to be a period of adverse general economic conditions of substantial duration. However, a localized depression affecting an area in which a significant amount of loans has been insured might also affect its operations materially. . . . Whether and when a period of adverse economic conditions will occur and the extent of the losses which may be suffered by first mortgage residential lenders and insurers are all unpredictable.[4]

How the inherent risk is being dealt with in Wisconsin is described in a 1963 prospectus of the Mortgage Guaranty Insurance Corporation:

Regulations of the Wisconsin Insurance Department require MGIC to maintain two separate reserves for losses, a case basis reserve and a contingency reserve. . . . The contingency reserve is designed to protect against the effect of adverse economic cycles. MGIC is required to credit to this reserve (by charges of surplus and not to income) an amount equal to 50% of all premiums earned. Subject to the approval of the Wisconsin Commissioner of Insurance, this reserve is available for payment of losses to the extent losses in a given year exceed 30% of the premiums earned in that year. Funds credited to the contingency reserve, to the extent not used in payment of losses, must remain in the reserve for fifteen years.[5]

A recent study was made under the direction of Dr. Chester Rapkin, former chairman of the Urban Studies Group of the Institute of Environmental Studies and professor of finance at the Wharton School of Finance and Commerce at the University of Pennsylvania, to determine the soundness of the MGIC insurance protection. By computer analysis, MGIC was subjected in "model" form to 30 different combinations of foreclosure experience and economic decline. The study concluded that the company ". . . appears to have the size and balance to withstand

---

[4] "Prospectus," Mortgage Guaranty Insurance Corporation, October 17, 1961, p. 5.

[5] "Prospectus," Mortgage Guaranty Insurance Corporation, May 14, 1963, pp. 17–18.

immediate catastrophic losses, and only with assumptions of acute and unprecedented mortgage foreclosures exceeding even the worst period of the 1930's does the simulation analysis place the model company in jeopardy."

Similar requirements are imposed upon the other insurers, but the question will always remain whether the reserves are sufficient to meet the requirements of a future occasion. Should the reserves run short, there is not the availability of Congress to appropriate for inadequacies in protection that are considered a likelihood in the case of the federal underwriting programs.

QUESTIONS AND PROBLEMS

1. How do the functions of the mortgage loan broker differ from those of the mortgage banker?

2. How important may your real estate broker be as an aid in financing a purchase? How may he assist?

3. How important is the individual lender as a source of funds for real estate loans? What is the trend in volume of loans from this source? Why?

4. How important are credit unions as a possible source of funds for financing real estate?

5. How does a real estate syndicate operate? What are its principal appeals to investors? What are its dangers?

6. In acquiring and financing real estate through the corporate form, what are the usual functions of the following types of securities: (*a*) debenture bonds, (*b*) preferred stock, and (*c*) common stock?

7. What is the French plan?

8. What is the Mandel plan, and how does it differ from the French plan?

9. What is a second mortgage company? What would you anticipate might be the most important problems of such a company?

10. Give examples of current techniques being used to provide equity participation for institutional investors.

11. What are mortgage insurance companies, and what services do they offer to the mortgage lenders?

17

Loan Applications

Meaning of Loan Application A vague idea on the part of an individual who would like to own a specific parcel of real estate is not the material of which loan applications are made. Many people who inquire about real estate loans are "lookers." They have not yet reached a decision to act in the purchase, construction, or financing of a property. They are seekers after information concerning the proper method of financing a property they would like to own. All such inquiries should be encouraged. If more people would consult financial institutions before they make commitments to purchase real estate, they could avoid many mistakes. If the inquiry indicates that the person seeking advice is a looker instead of an applicant for a loan, he should be treated in a courteous manner, but of course no loan application will be presented for his signature.

The loan application is made out only for one who has reached a decision about a purchase or who already owns a property, and who presumably will be able to carry out his plans, provided he secures the financial assistance which he seeks. The purchase of the property, where a new acquisition is involved, has been the result of negotiation. Likewise, the securing of a loan to finance it is probably subject to similar negotiations in many instances. The loan application should be looked upon as a preliminary offer on the part of the applicant. The lender may counter with a somewhat different proposal.

Legal Nature of Loan Application The acceptance of a loan application places the lender under no legal obligation, even though it be made out on a form provided by the lender. The applicant will usually be asked to sign the application. This makes the instrument one side of a contract—the offer. Unless and until the lender indicates his willingness to accept this offer—in other words, to approve the application—no contract exists. Even after such approval has been indicated, it would be very unusual for either party to attempt to hold the other to a contractual relationship. Conceivably, this could be done after each party has affixed his signature to the loan application.

Reasons for Loan Application The loan application is not an end in itself. It is the means to a determination of a proper answer to the all-important question: Shall the loan committee approve the application for a loan? Properly planned and executed, it opens several doors to compartments containing significant information of use to the loan committee. There is considerable merit to the older plan of requiring the applicant for a mortgage loan to appear in person before a loan committee for interrogation. Since this cannot be done conveniently in modern times, the loan application can be used as a substitute for the personal appearance of the applicant. So far as possible, the loan officer who takes the application should fulfill his obligation to be the eyes and the ears for the loan committee. From this point of view, he can make effective use of the loan application.

Among the specific reasons for taking the loan application are the following: The preliminary information about the property is obtained by this means. In addition to information about its location, much more information of use to the loan committee can be obtained at the time the application is made. While it is never safe to rely upon the prospective borrower's estimate of the value of his property, it is well to learn what he thinks about it. Since he is trying to obtain a loan with his real estate as security, he will gladly tell all he knows about the property. In doing so he may drop a few remarks that are not obvious from an inspection of the property but that may have a bearing upon its value. A skillful questioner can learn much about the property that will prove useful to the loan committee as a supplement to the report of the appraiser.

Primarily, the loan application must be relied upon for information about the borrower. Credit reports are essential and should be freely used. They too can be supplemented by the impression made by the applicant at the time he furnishes the information required for the loan application. Without appearing to be too inquisitorial, the officer or employee who takes the loan application should obtain much necessary information directly from the applicant. If we are to take seriously the moral hazard and the debt-paying capacities of the applicant in approving or rejecting loan applications, we must learn about them. The best time to acquire this information is when the loan application is being made.

While the loan application is being made, the first step toward adequate loan servicing is being taken. It is a trite but true saying that a loan well made is half collected. While the representative of the lending agency is getting "a line on" the applicant, he can give the applicant the story of his institution's lending policies. Instead of assuming that every applicant for a loan knows all about the obligations he seeks to assume, it would be a better approach to assume that he knows little or nothing about mortgage loan practices.

The loan application should be a continuing source of information about the applicant that may prove useful at any time during the life of the loan. A review of the information obtained at the time the application is filed will frequently supply the key to a solution of the problems which borrowers sometimes face when their dollars are not numerous enough to pay all creditors on time.

Loan Applications for Income Property Applications for loans which use income property as security follow a different pattern from that used for owner-occupied residential real estate. In the latter case, the application form should be capable of recording most of the information desired of the applicant. In the former case, the application may be less significant than the supplementary information which accompanies the application. For example, a comparative income statement, giving details of receipts and expenditures directly applicable to the specific property involved, is a must. While other income of the applicant—particularly if an individual is applying for the loan—is worth knowing about, it is the income-producing capacity of the property that is most determining. Vacancy statistics over a period of time sufficiently long to be representative of probable future operations are significant. Where commercial real estate is offered as security for a loan, the lender will want to know all about the tenants, the character of leases and the expected income therefrom, the details of operating expenses, the quality of the management of the property, and the status of the neighborhood in which the property is located.

In addition to comparative income statements, comparative balance sheets will also be required of the applicant. The nature of the applicant—whether an individual, a partnership, or a corporation—is pertinent. The other assets of the applicant will be required to determine what supplementary security that is offered will be investigated, even though the income-producing capacities of the real estate offered for security for a loan will be more significant. The other obligations of the prospective borrower—their amount, maturity, and seniority—must be known to the lender. Emphasis is placed upon comparative balance sheets as well as comparative income statements. The lender is interested both in the current financial condition of the applicant and in the progress made during recent years.

Informal Applications If your reaction to what is said above is that it sounds a bit ambitious in view of the probability that many applications will probably never be granted, perhaps we should be a little more selective in accepting formal applications for loans. Few would deny the desirability of getting all pertinent information for those who are to become borrowers. The best time to get it is when the applicant is seeking the loan. As one requesting something which another has the power to grant or to withhold, the applicant is probably willing to give all the information that seems to have any reasonable bearing upon his request.

To avoid cluttering up the files with information likely to prove useless and to avoid taking too much time of the staff members who take loan applications, a preliminary or informal application is frequently quite useful. The one who takes applications for loans should be fully conversant with the lending policies of his employer. In addition, he should have sufficient discretion to make some decisions on his own, frequently on the spot. In general, applicants for loans can be grouped into three classes: (1) those whose requests are likely to be granted; (2) those whose requests will most certainly be denied; and (3) doubtful cases.

After determining that an applicant is likely to qualify in group 1, a formal application should be taken. Without presuming to act for the loan committee, the one who interviews the applicant should be in a position to tell those in group 2 that, for reasons which should be stated if possible, it is not probable that the application will be approved. If the applicant nevertheless insists upon filing a formal application, it probably should be accepted, even at the expense of a waste of time. If the one who takes the application is sure of his ground, he can ask a minimum number of questions and thus save time. Doubtful cases should be referred to the loan committee for decision.

An interview lasting only a few minutes should be sufficient to determine the need for a formal application. During the course of this informal discussion, the applicant should be encouraged to do much of the talking. By this means he will tell much that is useful to the interviewer. It may develop early in the conversation that it will be useless to file a formal application because it is not consistent with the policy of the lender to grant this particular loan. For example, the prospective borrower may insist upon terms which the lender is not willing to meet: for example, a 25-year loan, a 6 percent interest rate, a 100 percent VA loan, a monthly payment inadequate to carry the loan, and so forth.

It is well to find out what the borrower has in mind as early as possible. If he is quite insistent upon terms which the lender is unwilling or unable to grant, there is little need for taking the further time of either applicant or interviewer. If, on the other hand as is usually true, the prospective borrower is merely trying to get the best terms obtainable, he is usually willing to listen to the other side of the case and may be won over to the loan plan offered by the lender.

While first impressions are not always conclusive, the interviewer should be able to size up the attitude of the applicant by the manner in which he answers questions. If he is evasive in his answers or contradicts himself on significant points, or if he appears to be a difficult person to deal with, it may develop early in the conversation that the granting of the application would be likely to create trouble for the lender. While an interviewer who turns down an application solely on these grounds should be sure of his position, he can save trouble for the lender if he finds out about the character of the prospective borrower before rather than after the loan is granted.

Frequently the preliminary interview develops into a first lesson in real estate finance instead of a loan application. If it appears that the applicant has ambition but little or nothing to back it up, the interviewer may well take a few minutes to give friendly advice and assistance that will postpone an application for a loan. By so doing he can make a friend, create goodwill for his employer, and lay the foundation for future business.

Whenever it becomes necessary for the interviewer to deny an application for a loan, whatever the reason may be, the applicant should know the reason for the refusal, particularly if it appears that the lender would like to do business with him if he could. If the interviewer knows that his employer cannot make a loan at this time, it does not follow that he cannot make a friend. A friendly refusal may lead to a subsequent renewal of the application on terms more favorable to the lender.

Who Should Take Applications? Regardless of what manner of loan solicitation is employed by a mortgage-lending institution, it appears obvious that a direct representative of the lender should interview the applicant and take the application. Even where loan finders are used and where fees are paid for their services, they should bring the applicant to the office of the lending institution instead of bringing only a loan application. Filtering loan applications through an outsider may produce factual information. It cannot take the place of a personal interview. As stated above, the interview may develop much useful information that may not answer any specific question on the application form. Also we cannot overlook the element of bias in permitting a finder to take loan applications. Since his fee is dependent upon the granting of the loan, it is obvious that he will make the application as favorable as possible.

Whether the interviewer should be an officer or an employee of the lending institution is a question on which there will probably be no general agreement. His title is not as important as his capacity to do the job assigned to him. In many respects the interview with the applicant for a loan is the most important contact which the lender will ever have with the borrower. Mistakes made at this point are almost sure to be reflected in later experiences. For that reason the interviewer should be a mature person, able to size people up quickly, and thoroughly acquainted with the lending policies of his employer. He must not only be instructed what to do but should be trained to perform the specific job assigned to him.

Use of Application Form Presumably the lender will use a specific application form which includes the items about which information is sought. The form should be filled in by the interviewer by using the responses which are made to his questions by the applicant. These questions should be sympathetic but searching. In many cases the information sought may be obtained by direct questions. In some instances it will be gleaned from the general conversation of the applicant. By directing the conversation, the interviewer can usually lead the applicant into a position of supplying the needed information. While the applicant is telling his story, he is under close observation by the interviewer for the purpose of establishing an overall impression of sincerity, purpose, objectives, and capacity.

Much information of a useful character can be obtained in the form of questions by the applicant. He should be encouraged to ask all the questions he desires. This will help the interviewer to find out what is in the mind of the applicant. By giving frank, concise answers, the interviewer will encourage the applicant to do the same. By the time the application blank is filled out, the interviewer should have a pretty definite idea of its acceptance or rejection. If he has any doubts about its acceptance, he should be wary about making any promises to the applicant. If the application is denied because of any specific evidence contained in the form signed by the applicant, such as lack of income to carry the loan, even an implied promise of probable approval will mislead the applicant and create ill will toward the lender.

Contents of Application Form There is no magical application form that will meet all needs. The experienced and successful interviewer could write his own questions as he goes along and could record the applicant's answers in a form that would give an adequate basis for its use. The inexperienced interviewer can fill in all answers provided for on the best organized application form and end up with a product that fails to provide the information needed for making decisions. Presumably, the form used will be that one which experience has demonstrated to be most useful to the lender. The information recorded upon it should be obtained by an expert interviewer and should be as specific as possible. Loan committees can reach decisions quickly on open-and-shut applications. The great bulk of loan applications are not of this kind. They require careful study. The answers in many cases may be of borderline character. Here especially is the place where the well-presented loan application is useful in reaching decisions.

Unusual Uses of Loan Applications Elsewhere in this text, open mortgages or mortgages for future advances have been discussed. If a lender has granted a loan for $16,000 which is subsequently amortized to $8,000, and the borrower wishes it raised back to $16,000, shall the lender grant the request without hesitancy, provided there are no intervening liens? Or shall a new loan application be filled out, giving reasons for the advance, together with any changes in status of the borrower since his original loan was granted? Presumably all lenders satisfy themselves as to the soundness of future advances. Some prefer to follow procedures in taking loan applications therefor almost as if they were making entirely new loans.

In some cases where title to property is being transferred, the lending institution whose mortgage is being assumed asks the new owner to fill out a loan application as if he were applying for a loan. In case the mortgage does not contain a clause requiring the consent of the lender to the sale of the property, the lender could only request the new owner to make out the loan application. He could not require it. If the original mortgagor wishes release from the mortgage, the lender may make a new application from the vendee a condition to the consideration of such a request. Under ordinary circumstances there should be little difficulty in securing the consent of the new owner of the property to filling out a loan application. While the original mortgagor acts as a surety for the repayment of the loan, the lender will deal primarily with the new owner. Consequently he wants to know as much about him as if the loan were being made directly to him.

Credit Rating of Applicant No lender is safe in making real estate loans without knowing all that he can learn about the credit standing of the applicant. Sources of credit information are essentially three in number: organized credit agencies, such as the local retail credit bureau or the commercial agency; friends of the applicant for the loan; and the applicant. All three are useful. The first two are frequently used as alternatives. If the credit bureau has adequate and current information, friends and acquaintances of the applicant will not be contacted. Many lenders find that friends are not too fruitful as sources of credit information. They will usually give honest opinions, but they may not know too much about the financial affairs of the applicant. They know him socially but may know nothing of his debt-paying habits or capacities.

In many respects the most reliable source of credit information is the applicant for the loan. By skillful questioning the interviewer can learn more from him than from all other sources combined. The statements made by him can then be checked with information from other sources.

Curiously enough, reports by credit agencies do not always tell the story which the lender wishes to hear. The applicant who has never sought credit may not even be recorded on the books of the local credit bureau. But if he has always paid cash for his purchases, he will probably keep up the payments on his mortgage. The applicant with a credit rating will probably be a good borrower if he has a reputation for paying bills promptly. Slow but good payers may get into trouble, perhaps without causing loss to the mortgage lender. Chronic borrowers from small loan companies and applicants whose records show unpaid judgments and long-standing accounts for necessities or even conveniences are not normally sound risks for mortgage loans.

At best, credit information from sources other than the applicant are likely to show capacities only. What the lender who makes a long-term commitment to a borrower on a real estate mortgage needs to know in addition are the intangible elements of credit which cannot well be ascertained from the basis of a dollars and cents formula. These intangibles include such elements as incentive and mental attitude. Credit agencies gather little information on these subjects. The interviewer must somehow manage to learn them from the applicant and must pass them on to the loan committee.

Even when the interviewer and the loan committee obtain all available information about the credit standing and the debt-paying habits of the borrower, too much dependence should not be placed upon it. Experience shows that within a few years the mortgagor will probably sell the property, and the obligations on the mortgage will fall upon the shoulders of a new owner. Even though the original mortgagor is legally bound on his note, his economic capacity to meet his obligations may change, he may move out of the jurisdiction in which the property is located, and so on. Hence the credit rating of the borrower is important but should not be depended upon exclusively in reaching a decision on a loan application. In the final analysis, the security for the loan may be the best assurance of its collectibility.

Applicant Information The interviewer cannot learn too much about the applicant. Some things he must learn if he is to protect his employer properly. The occupation age is of great significance. By this is meant that the age of the applicant has a meaning only as it relates to his future earning capacity. A wage earner employed at a job which requires physical skill and strength might be old at 45. A professional man of 55 may not be as old from the standpoint of occupation age. The period of employment in the present job aids in determining the applicant's stability. If he has taken a new job recently, the past experience will be more useful on this point.

It is well to find out about the applicant's employability in other jobs in case for any reason he should lose his present one. The stability of his present employer is important also. The current earnings of the applicant and of members of his household who contribute to the family budget are musts. No only the amount of earnings of these other people, but particularly the part contributed to the family exchequer, help to determine the desirability of granting loans requested.

In measuring incomes not too much attention should be paid to unusual sources such as overtime. Also, it is the take-home pay that is significant. Deductions for social security, income tax, hospitalization, and so on, do not help the borrower meet his obligations on his loan. Incomes of children may be temporary for one of two reasons: (1) The employment of children may not be as secure as that of adults. (2) Even if an adult son or daughter living at home currently contributes to the family income, this arrangement may be only temporary. Long before the mortgage has been repaid, such a son or daughter may have established a new home, and the parents will lose the financial contributions. What the lender wants to know is: What is the long-range debt-paying capacity of the applicant for the loan? Another way of stating this question is: How long will the applicant probably earn enough to meet the carrying charges on the loan for which he is making application?

Unusual family financial burdens are matters of great importance to the lender. The number and ages of the children will help to determine usual expenses and can be weighted accordingly. It is the unusual last straw that may be too heavy for the camel. Contingencies can only be guessed at. Certainties should be made known to the lender. A skillful interviewer can secure information that may not be suggested by the application form and yet would be determining in the approval or disapproval of a loan application.

Installment Commitments Assuming that the applicant for a real estate loan is a normal person, he will probably be interested in the purchase of other articles of value, such as a television set or an automobile. It is probable also that these may be purchased on some kind of an installment plan. The mere fact that the borrower has commitments of this kind is no bar to the granting of a real estate loan. At least, the lender should be acquainted with all the facts before he acts favorably upon a loan application. In many instances the interviewer may establish such a friendly relationship with the applicant that future installment commitments may be talked over with him before they are made. From the standpoint of both borrower and lender, the important problem to avoid is the creation of an installment debt greater than the borrower can hope to carry.

The occasion for taking an application for a loan may give the interviewer an excellent opportunity to give the applicant some good pointers on the subject of family budgets. Where such a task is undertaken, it must be done in such a skillful manner that the applicant will not feel that he is being "preached at." From his point of view, he came into the institution to borrow money and not to listen to a sermon on what to do with his income.

Condition of Property To an increasing extent, lenders are taking a direct interest in the physical condition of the property on which loans are to be made. Some go so far as to refuse a loan on a property that has been owned for some time if its condition is distinctly bad. They take neglect of the property as evidence of lack of interest on the part of the borrower or financial inability to maintain it properly. Others will make a loan, provided that steps are taken to cure the defects by making proper repairs. Some are willing to rely upon the verbal promise of the borrower to make the repairs promptly. Others insist that the agreement be made in writing. And some withhold enough from the proceeds of the loan to pay the cost of needed repairs.

If the appraiser's report shows the need for specified repairs to put the property in reasonably good condition, and the estimate of the cost is $1,200, the lending institution sometimes tells the prospective borrower that it cannot grant the $16,000 loan requested if the property is to remain "as is," but that it will gladly grant a loan of $17,200, if $1,200 is to be used to make the specified repairs. As a part of the interview at the time the loan application is filed, the attitude of the applicant toward needed repairs can be ascertained. If he is aware of the need of repairs at that time, so much the better. If he is not, he can still be asked to state his position on the question, should the inspection of the property disclose a need of repairs for the protection of the security for the loan. His reaction will also help the interviewer to determine whether or not he has pride of ownership to a degree that makes him want to keep his property in good condition.

Supplemental Security With real estate as the primary security for a loan, it is not unusual for a mortgagee to require supplementary security as well. This may take the form of other real estate or real estate interests, bonds or other securities, other valuables, or even cash or its equivalent. For example, an account holder in a thrift and home-financing institution might wish to finance a home by mortgaging it to the same institution. Instead of withdrawing funds from his account to use as a down payment, he may prefer to keep the account intact, borrow the larger amount needed, and use the account as supplementary security for the real estate loan. Whenever supplementary security is demanded, the mortgagee requires it because of the unusual risk element in the loan. As repayments on the principal reduce the amount of the risk, the supplementary security is usually released to the mortgagor. This release may be arranged for at the time the mortgage is executed or may follow a subsequent request by the mortgagor.

Occasionally releases are effected as the result of a recovery of or increase in real estate values. In a period of rising prices, the risk may be diminished as readily by an increase in the value of the security as by a decrease in the amount of the indebtedness. Where supplemental security is demanded, the right of substitution of one acceptable kind for another is usually granted the mortgagor. For example, should a second piece of real property be used as supplemental security, it may be released from the mortgage coverage, if occasion requires, by substituting an acceptable amount of government bonds in its stead.

If the supplemental security takes the form of cosignatures on the mortgage, they will be scrutinized very carefully. If there are to be cosigners of the note and mortgage, then there should probably be co-applicants for the loan. Many cosigners think of their obligation as a recommendation of the applicant. They never expect to be called upon to make good on their underwriting obligation and would probably resist payment if it were demanded of them. Even courts might sustain their position and relieve them of financial obligations to the lender, unless it appears that they have a stake in the venture. The cosignature of someone having a financial interest in the property would certainly be taken more seriously than that of a chance friend. Cosigners on short-term notes are probably more protection to lenders than if they appear on long-term mortgages. By the time the crisis arrives for the mortgage, the cosigner may be so much involved with his own troubles that he can be of little service to the mortgagor or the lender.

Some loans are made upon real estate owned by a corporation of strong financial standing. Others are made to dummy corporations whose only asset is the real estate offered as security for the loan. In the latter case the loan officer is not likely to make too strong a recommendation for a real estate loan. In some cases the real owner of the dummy corporation signs the note and mortgage personally. Then it becomes necessary for the lender to know the financial responsibility of the owner. His other sources of income and their amounts, his assets and liabilities, his reputation and the history of his past financial operations are all matters for investigation by the lender. The signature of the real owner may mean much or little. Even his financial standing may not be sufficient to recommend a loan if his reputation is against the granting of long-term credit to him.

Life Insurance Insurance on the life of the mortgagor is sometimes encouraged by the mortgagee, with the latter as beneficiary. Such insurance serves two purposes: (1) It serves as added security for the loan, thus increasing protection to the mortgagee. (2) It protects the family of the mortgagor in case anything should cause the death of the family breadwinner. At his death, the insurance payments would normally be used to pay off the balance due on the mortgage. In some cases the insurance policy is so written that it amounts to a renewable term policy with the insurance coverage reduced year by year, commensurate with the normal reduction in the unpaid balance of the loan.

The monthly payment made by the borrower is normally made in one lump sum. From this payment is deducted the insurance premium; the remainder is applied to the amortized loan as if no insurance policy were in effect. It follows, of course, that the monthly payments must be larger than if there were no insurance of this type. Sometimes this combination of mortgage and life insurance is represented to be a foreclosure-proof type of loan. Caution should be used in making any such representations. To be sure, the death of the mortgagor while the insurance was in effect would not result in the loss of his home by his family. But should his income be sharply reduced during his lifetime, it might be more difficult for him to keep his mortgage alive because of the heavier monthly payments to meet the requirements of both insurance and mortgage payments. The usual amortized loan plan, supplemented by an independent life insurance policy, would serve the same purpose without adding anything to the cost to the mortgagor.

Risk Rating of Loan Applications The FHA and some lending institutions have translated the information on loan application forms into quantitative terms for the purpose of arriving at a risk rating of the application. Where mass operations in the field of real estate loans are necessarily dealt with, some such practice is probably desirable. It is not apparent that the net results will be any different than if each case is considered on its merits, assuming that the person who passes judgment is competent. Also it should be observed that even when the "statistics" of the loan application indicate either a positive or a negative position, special circumstances might tilt the scales in the opposite direction. In time of crisis the lender finds that he is not dealing with average loans but with a series of specific situations.

From a somewhat different point of view, the one who interviews a loan applicant must try to classify the possible loan that may develop from the application into one of three groups. If he feels that, for any reason at all, the loan if granted is likely to be troublesome to collect, his reasons should be carefully developed for the guidance of the loan committee. In another category he would place the loan that he feels sure will be at least a loss-free, or safe, loan. In other words, even though the borrower might have difficulty in meeting his obligations, the lender would be expected to lose nothing even if foreclosure of the mortgage should follow. Sometimes this type of loan is called a money-good loan. What the interviewer is always seeking are trouble-free, or sound, loans: those that never cause difficulty of any kind because the applicant gives every indication that he can and will meet all of his obligations without question and on time.

The Contingency Factor In considering applications for real estate loans, much attention is properly given to all ascertainable factors of income and expenses of the applicant. Probably less attention is paid to the unseen and frequently unpredictable factor of contingency. This is most difficult to deal with because it cannot be related to any known item of income or expense. For example, before a loan application is approved, the family budget may balance, with some to spare, after providing for carrying charges on the real estate loan, to be credited to a contingency fund. Since this latter is to be built up out of income, it must accumulate slowly. Meantime, if the unexpected happens and hard luck befalls the borrower, his debt-paying capacity may be reduced drastically, temporarily or permanently.

If the income of the borrower is reduced drastically or if his expenses are sharply increased, his capacity to meet his obligations on his mortgage may be seriously interfered with. If the difficulties are only temporary, they may be dealt with as such. If they are of more permanent character, more permanent remedies may be called for. Within the limits of reasonable business operations, the contingency factor cannot be adequately dealt with. The risks of the business must be called into play to help out when these unexpected happenings occur.

Amount of Equity One question that is always raised at the time a lending institution takes an application for a loan is the amount of equity the prospective borrower has or expects to have in the property at the effective date of the loan. The owner's equity interests the lender for two reasons:

1. It is a measure of the cushion of safety which protects the lender at the time the loan is granted. The equity which the lending institution is most concerned about for this purpose may not be the amount which the borrower thinks is the measure of his equity. The lending institution will place more credence in the appraiser's report on this subject. The borrower will likely measure his concept of equity as the difference between the price he paid or expects to pay for the property and the amount of the loan which he hopes to obtain. The appraiser may arrive at quite a different amount, which may be either more or less than the applicant's amount. It is usually less in an inflated market but could be more in a depressed market.

2. The amount of equity which the borrower thinks he has in the property will have great influence upon his desire to keep the property. If he thinks his equity is sizable—whether the appraiser agrees with him or not—he will do his best to keep up his payments on his loan in order to protect his equity. If, on the other hand, he thinks that his equity is small or nonexistent, he has less incentive to continue to meet his obligations if some more favorable opportunity to obtain living quarters is offered to him. The latter may be an alternative purchase or even a rental property.

This attitude of the borrower toward his presumed equity has protected many loans even after a decline in real estate prices has, temporarily at least, wiped out all equity which the borrower once had.

If he is unacquainted with the facts of the case, he may still make his payments on the loan long after he could have purchased a property of equal value at a price less than the balance of principal of his mortgage loan.

At the other extreme, the absence of any real equity has deterred many lenders from granting loan applications. If the loan application is for $18,000 on a property costing $20,000, but on which the lender's appraiser fixes a price of only $17,800, the loan will not ordinarily be granted. Likewise, many lending institutions have refused to make 100 percent GI loans even though they might be 50 or 60 percent guaranteed by the Veterans Administration. These lenders felt that, in the absence of an equity, the borrower would not enjoy a sense of homeownership. They feared that the purchase of a home encumbered by a 100 percent loan would be looked upon as a convenient rental arrangement, to be abandoned when a more favorable housing opportunity was presented. As pointed out in another chapter, this fear about GI loans has not been vindicated to date. Nevertheless it has been an honest fear and has prevented some veterans from obtaining financial assistance in the purchase of homes, at least at the institutions which represented their first choice.

Bases of Mortgage Decisions In reaching a decision about a particular loan application, several factors must be weighed carefully. Unless complete dependence is to be placed upon mortgage insurance or guarantee, this observation applies to all types of loans on all kinds of properties. Among the factors to be taken into account are: the appraisal of the property; the analysis of the moral hazard; and the estimate of the debt-paying capacity of the mortgagor. If too much dependence is placed upon the appraisal factor, to the exclusion of the other two, trouble may result for the lender. Even though the income factor may be satisfactory, the attitude of the borrower may determine whether the obligations of the mortgagor will be met promptly or whether the cost of loan servicing will be unduly enhanced because of the stubbornness of the borrower. It is obvious, on the other hand, that even though the borrower's intentions may be of the best, a serious drop in income might quickly jeopardize his ability to keep up his mortgage payments.

More and more lenders are coming to recognize the need for having expert appraisers set a value upon the property offered as security for the loan. To a lesser degree, we are beginning to give more attention than was formerly the case to expertness in analyzing the other two factors mentioned earlier. It is probable that the loan application merits more attention than it normally receives. It can be used merely to record formal information about the borrower and his property. Or it can be used for more significant purposes as well.

Second Guessing As stated earlier in this chapter, the loan application may prove useful long after it has been approved. As long as the borrower meets his obligations to the lender, there is little reason to review the loan application. But if these obligations are not met in full and on time, it is a pretty good plan to review the file of the borrower and to restudy the loan application. The latter may serve two purposes: (1) It may suggest a solution to the difficulties faced by the borrower. (2) It may give the lending institution a chance to see if a mistake was made in granting the original loan application.

Such second guessing will not cure the troubles of the borrower whose loan is currently in trouble. But on the theory that we can learn as much from our mistakes as from our successes, second guessing on applications that have been approved may help to avoid a repetition of the same mistakes in the consideration of future applications. In general, it is probable that if a loan was good when it was made, it will continue to be of a character to protect the interests of the lender. In addition, it should protect the interests of the borrower, in the absence of unexpected events that seriously affect his domestic relations or his debt-paying capacities.

Negotiation After the loan application has been taken and studied, together with the reports of appraisal of the real estate offered as security for the loan applied for, and after the credit report of the applicant has been reviewed, there comes a time for decision. This decision may be favorable, unfavorable, or favorable with reservations. In many instances negotiation is required to arrive at a conclusion acceptable to both borrower and lender. Negotiation may cover a wide variety of subjects: amount of loan, interest rate, maturity, payments, supplemental security, need for immediate repairs to property, inclusion of taxes and perhaps insurance with payments on the loan, deposit with the lender of equity money in case a construction loan is applied for, and even rental assignments in case of possible foreclosure. When the inexperienced applicant for a home loan is involved, he is likely to ask for what he thinks he needs in financing the home of his choice. Experienced borrowers may plan to dicker a bit, asking for more than they expect to receive or in other ways including trading material in their applications.

Once a decision is reached which is acceptable to both borrower and lender, what amounts to a conditional commitment is in order. This means that when all conditions are met, including of course acceptance of satisfactory character of title, the lending institution will be ready to close the loan according to the terms agreed upon in negotiation, or according to the terms of the application in case no further negotiation is required. This conditional commitment is necessary in order that the applicant may proceed with the purchase, construction, or other arrangements dependent upon the granting of the loan. The closing is essentially legal in character and requires no discussion in this text.

Loan Expense Nearly all loan expenses are customarily borne by the borrower. These include, among others, the initial service fee, if any; the appraisal fee; the legal closing costs; the title examination and insurance fee; the brokerage fee, if any; the credit report fee; and the amounts needed to pay mortgage registration tax, where it applies. This statement is subject to important limitations in highly competitive markets. Mortgagees may be so anxious to lend money that they will absorb the expenses of making the loan, or at least a large part of them. In doing so they run the risk of taking a loss on the deal should the mortgagor exercise his right of prepayment and refinance the loan or pay it off at an early date. Nevertheless, while loan expenses are expected to be borne by the borrower, this is not always true.

Depending upon the factors mentioned above, only the initial fee for the privilege of making the loan may benefit the lender. All other charges are supposed to represent out-of-pocket costs incurred in putting the loan on the books. This statement is further subject to limitations where fixed amounts are charged in making loans, governed by the size of the loan rather than the actual costs incurred. Either gains or losses of small amounts per loan may result from fixed fees. Some costs tend to penalize small loans, percentagewise. For example, while it probably costs more to examine title to a property worth $100,000 than it does for one worth $10,000, the cost is not proportionately greater.

Real Estate Broker If the real estate broker who negotiates a sale could always find a prospect willing and able to purchase the equity of the vendor, the broker would need to know relatively little about real estate finance. On the contrary, most sales must be financed in some manner other than the assumption of existing indebtedness and the payment in cash of the remainder of the purchase price. Because of this, a major function of the sales broker is the discovery of a financial plan that will fit the buyer's capacities and the seller's needs. Price negotiation is a major function of brokerage. But also there are times when a deal falls through, not because of differences in price, but because there appears to be no way of financing the deal. In many cases there is no practicable way of financing a deal if the buyer is trying to purchase property which he cannot hope to carry. In other cases where price is not a stumbling block, an alert broker is able to find an acceptable method of financing the sale where none is obvious. In still other cases, differences in price may be bridged by financial manipulation.

For example, suppose that the seller is willing to take back a purchase-money mortgage for $9,000 and cash for $3,000 in exchange for a property priced at $12,000. The prospective purchaser thinks $11,500 is the top price he will pay. Perhaps the broker can get an agreement on a price of $12,000, including a down payment of $3,000 and a purchase-money mortgage for $9,000, provided the interest rate is 7 percent instead of the 8 percent the seller had hoped to get. If the broker can convince the purchaser that the latter will save money in the long run by this means, he may be able to push the deal over. Conversely, the seller might prefer to sell at $11,500 and take back a purchase-money mortgage at 8 percent interest.

No real estate broker can afford to fail to familiarize himself with all financial arrangements which he might be able to use. In residential property brokerage, every salesman should be an expert in FHA and VA loans. He should know current levels of interest rates on conventional loans. He must be acquainted with the policies of lending institutions within his market and even with the prejudices of those who determine these policies. If, for example, he knows that institution A prefers not to make loans in area X, he had better advise his purchaser to apply for a loan from institution B, which has no such limitation. If a liberal loan is needed, he should go to the best place to get it, even if the interest rate is a bit out of line. Most institutions will be glad to make conservative loans in the most desirable neighborhoods; but then the rate of interest becomes a major consideration. Financial institutions customarily cultivate real estate brokers as possible sources of future business. Brokers in turn should do a bit of cultivating on their own account, because there are times when they need to be on the receiving end of favors to be handed out.

The broker can usually assume that the purchaser and the seller are inexperienced in the field of real estate finance. The cooperation of both may be required to put through a deal. He must not only be their financial adviser but, on occasion, the one to make decisions, subject to their approval. For example, it may be imperative in a specific situation to revise the original terms of a preliminary sales contract. This might call for a down payment of $2,000, a price of $10,000, and an understanding that the remainder will be provided by a first mortgage of $8,000. If such a mortgage is not obtainable because of location, condition of the property, or other disability, the broker may find it necessary to tell the seller that his acceptance of a second mortgage for $1,500 is a necessary condition to the consummation of the sale.

Meantime the broker should anticipate and plan to avoid possible complications by making the original preliminary contract contingent upon the ability of the purchaser to obtain adequate and reasonable financial assistance. He should not accept a substantial and irrevocable binder against a cash sale of the property at $10,000 unless he feels reasonably certain that he can help the buyer finance the property.

If he has made the contacts and learned the lessons suggested above, he should be able, in most instances, to predict fairly accurately the maximum amount that can be borrowed against the property as security. Since this amount is predicated in part upon the moral hazard of the loan, he must know in advance whether or not the applicant can qualify for the liberal loan needed in case the appraisal of the property by the lender stands up to the $10,000 price.

Pressure Loans Thus far in this chapter we have been considering loan applications on the basis of their use in forming the foundation of a judgment concerning the application. Occasionally financial institutions feel inclined to respond to pressure of one kind or another and make loans against their better judgment. Governmental agencies which supervise their operations sometimes anticipate such pressure and relieve it in advance by limiting the kinds and amounts of loans that may be granted to directors, officers, and employees of the institution. This is probably necessary. It is unfortunate that there is not an equally effective method of dealing with pressures from other quarters.

One source of pressure loans is the application that is from a good customer of the institution but that fails to measure up to its standards. For fear of losing a good customer, the logic of the loan application is sometimes cast aside and the loan is granted. For example, a contractor-builder may rely upon the institution for much of his financing. This business, we will assume, is profitable and much sought after by competitors. Along with the good loans that measure up to the standards of the lender, the contractor may occasionally present an application for an off-standard loan or for a standard loan on a substandard property. Such an application places the lender in a dilemma which he would prefer to avoid. He can hardly assume that the applicant has made a mistake which will be readily corrected once his attention is attracted to it. The applicant knows his policies too well for that to happen. Such applications are not easily denied, even though the facts are against them. Most lenders would rather not face the decisions involved in them.

Another type of pressure loan comes from quite a different quarter. Mortgage lenders, like others, frequently must choose the lesser of two evils. For example, some have been very conscientious in their opposition to high-percentage, long-maturity, low-interest loans. They have not thought that such loans are sound risks or that they serve the best interests of the borrower. Nevertheless, they have not enjoyed a free choice in turning down all such applications, because they have disliked the possible alternatives even more. One alternative that has been proposed in the form of numerous bills introduced in recent Congresses is direct lending by the government to low-income groups, to GI borrowers, and, more recently, to low and moderate income groups.

In recent years America has become housing conscious as never before. All sorts of pressure has been exerted upon Congress to provide better housing accommodations for all American families, at government expense if necessary. Most such propoals start with a gesture in the direction of private enterprise, to the extent that it will be asked to provide the accommodations needed. They usually end with a statement to the effect that, if private enterprise cannot do the job, then the government must. The fear of direct government lending has pressured many private lending institutions to make some loans whose applications would otherwise have been denied.

Effects of New Patterns of Financing upon Lenders Under older patterns of financing real estate, the lender appraised the property and the prospective borrower. Then he determined the amount, if any, that he was willing to lend against the property as security. Since he shared the risks with the borrowers, he predicated his answer to a request for a loan upon the risk involved and gauged the amount of the loan, the interest rate charged, and the maturity of loan sought.

Under more recent patterns, the risk to the lender has sometimes been shifted to a governmental agency. With this shifting of the risk, the lender has surrendered much of his control over his operations. The agency which insures or guarantees the loan makes the appraisal and fixes the interest rate and, at least within limits, the maturity of the loan. It even determines whether or not the loan will be granted, for if it refuses to insure or guarantee it, the lender is not likely to carry on his own shoulders the particular type of loan sought.

On the contrary, the type of loan granted an applicant may still measure the estimate of the risk on the part of the mortgagee. If he is satisfied with the neighborhood in which the property is located, the credit rating of the applicant, the property offered as security for the loan, and the ratio of loan to value, he may be willing to grant a conventional loan on terms as favorable as those which apply to an insured or guaranteed loan. If, on the other hand, he is uncertain about any of the above factors, or if for any other reason he hesitates to take the full risk of the loan, he may be willing to make it only if it is insured or guaranteed.

QUESTIONS AND PROBLEMS

1. What is the legal status of a loan application?
2. What various purposes can you suggest that a properly completed loan application may serve?
3. In what major respects should applications for loans on income property differ from those on owner-occupied residential real estate?
4. What purposes can be served by an informal interview between an

applicant for credit and a representative of the lender before a formal application for loan is filed?

5. How may the credit rating of an applicant for a loan be determined?

6. To what extent are other installment commitments of a loan applicant significant to an inverviewer for a prospective lender?

7. What forms of supplemental security available may be significant in the evaluation of a loan application?

8. How is insurance on the life of the mortgagor used to increase his borrowing potential?

9. What is meant by the "contingency" factor in a real estate loan?

10. In what ways is the amount of the owner's equity in a property given as security for a real estate loan significant to the lender? Might this equity be important even though the loan was insured by the federal government?

11. How have the FHA and VA programs for underwriting loans modified the standards applied by a lender in evaluating a loan application? Would these modifications affect conventional loans as well as those which are to be insured or guaranteed?

18

Appraisal for Financing Purposes

Relation of Appraisal to Finance Little can be said within the limits set for a discussion of real estate finance about the important subject of appraisal. That is a branch of real estate study that needs a volume for itself. At this point it is necessary to relate appraisal to finance. If an applicant for a loan is purchasing a property, the price paid may be used by the mortgagee as evidence of value, but he would not consider himself bound by it. Likewise, if the applicant were a seller instead of a buyer, the mortgagee might be interested in the asking price but again would not base his decision upon it. To an increasing extent, we are learning more about the determinants of real estate value. To the mortgagee it is the long-range value of a property that gives him protection for his loan.

Few would claim, at least among those best acquainted with the subject, that appraisal of real estate is an exact science. It is an art whose practitioners are becoming more adept in its use. Its importance in serving the needs of real estate finance cannot be overemphasized.

In appraising property for financial purposes the appraiser must keep in mind the reason for his assignment. A man of means whose ideas fail to conform to those of most people might be willing to pay for a piece of property several times what it will appraise for as security for a loan. To the eccentric purchaser, it might be considered a bargain. Yet no financial institution would dare lend on it more than a fraction of its purchase price. Appraisal processes frequently make use of what is sometimes called the community concept of value: that is, what other people think the property is worth. The mortgagee must always keep this concept in mind because what is a mortgage today may become real estate at some future time if a default, followed by a foreclosure sale, occurs. This does not mean that financial institutions should use a foreclosure formula in appraising property. But neither can they ignore the possibility of subsequent property acquisitions to replace their present mortgages.

It must also be kept in mind that the mortgagee wishes to know the value of the whole property as security for a loan. This means that the appraiser must look at the property from the viewpoint of function and fitness of its component parts to perform the function intended. A corner lot in a neighborhood zoned for business might be worth $10,000 as a site for a filling station, if it were unimproved. But suppose it already has on it a house worth $8,000 for residential purposes. The lot for residential purposes is worth only $4,000. If the house is moved or demolished to make room for a filling station, the cost of moving or demolishing it will about equal its salvage value. What is the value of this property as security for a loan? It certainly is not worth $18,000 = $10,000 + $8,000. It is either a filling station site or a residential property. It cannot be both at the same time.

A financial institution is not likely to value it at either $10,000 as a filling station site or at $12,000 for residential purposes. Loans against vacant land are always risky unless there is ample assurance, backed by a bond, that it will be utilized in the near future. As a part of a residential property the building will probably depreciate quite rapidly in the future. By the time its value has been reduced substantially, its owner may have missed his market for disposing of the site for business uses.

Rent Potential In granting loans on real estate as security, the mortgagee always looks to the potential rent which the property is capable of earning. If the property offered as security is a single residence occupied by its owner, it is producing no rent immediately. Nevertheless, it has a rent potential which measures the rent that it could command if offered to some user other than the owner. As a general rule, expensive dwellings will attract lower percentage loans than more modest housing accommodations. In terms of rent potential, the latter are less risky than the former. Likewise, properties that are in any manner constructed or located to satisfy the whims of eccentric people possess a lower rent potential than those which satisfy the needs of greater numbers of people.

Old properties in declining neighborhoods are greater risks for mortgage lending than are newer properties better located. The rent potential, which can easily be translated into sales demand, is lower with the former than with the latter. Unimproved real estate, having no rent potential of consequence, is usually not at all inviting as security for real estate mortgages. In most cases financial institutions will not lend against vacant lots. Indeed, some of them are prohibited by the laws and rules which regulate their operations from accepting vacant lots as primary security for a mortgage.

Value Many attempts have been made to define value. Two definitions which have been found workable are: (1) Value is the present worth of the future benefits to be derived from the use of a parcel of real estate by a typical owner. (2) Value is the amount which approximates the top price which a purchaser will pay for it if he is well informed; under no immediate compulsion; paying cash needed above the typical available first mortgage loan; and is buying for long-term use or investment.

While volumes have been written on the subject of value, the two definitions above contain the elements of value that usually interest the real estate lender. The emphasis is upon: (1) present worth; (2) of future benefits; (3) to most users; (4) who are well informed; (5) but not compelled to buy; (6) ability to finance; and (7) the long-run character of the transaction. Acceptance of the principles of these definitions as a basis for academic discussions of the subject, and consistency in their use when applied to actual appraisal problems, are not the same thing. Indeed, in reviewing numerous appraisal dockets, it might sometimes be said that the appraiser who is best acquainted with theoretical definitions of value frequently has least success in applying them, while the one who has spent less time in pinpointing concise definitions may arrive at more reliable results in field trials. All of which means again that appraisal of real estate is a very practical activity.

Value and Price Long arguments have consumed much time and energy in dealing with differences between value and price. Without undertaking to repeat them here, let us point out that, for appraisals for financing purposes at least, there is a well-recognized difference. Especially in the period following the end of World War II, lending institutions have carefully avoided current prices in their search for values upon which they could base safe lending operations. In general it may be said that value for lending purposes carries with it a long-range connotation. Price may be short-lived. While most lenders are willing to consider value on a going-concern basis, a few think of it in terms of catastrophe hazard instead. By this is meant that most lenders are willing to assume that their purposes have been served if the long-range value is recorded in terms of the probability that the borrower will meet his obligations without serious default. A few assume, on the contrary, that the borrower will probably default in his payments at some time or other. They want value to be defined in such a manner that their interests will always be protected, come what may.

Since World War II real estate prices have advanced rapidly. Most lending institutions admit that values have risen also, though not so fast nor so far as prices. Hence they have been unwilling to follow prices with lending ratios. They have been searching for the less tangible evidence of long-range value as the basis for their loans. In doing so they have generally tied their value determinations to past price levels. That is, they have assumed in 1970 and later that 1960 prices were a fair index of value at their earlier date. By adding a percentage—40 or 50—to known prices of 1960, they reached an appraisal in 1970 and later that was substantially less than prevailing prices at the later date.

Foresight versus Hindsight This policy of attempting to relate current value to past prices has some interesting, if illogical, consequences. Almost all definitions of value used in the appraisal of real estate speak of "present value of future benefits," or words to that effect. They never attempt to measure past benefits as such. Such definitions suggest the use of foresight instead of hindsight in fixing values for lending purposes. Yet postwar practices quite commonly indicate that hindsight rather than foresight has guided appraisal policies. Indeed, this has often been a failing of financial institutions. Even in periods of depression and their aftermath, ultraconservatism dominates appraisal practices, when all the lessons of the past speak in favor of probable sharp recoveries from depression-low real estate prices. As the peak of real estate prices is approached in the succeeding prosperity period, the lenders whose appraisal policies are directed by hindsight finally turn their conservatism into optimism if they overlend at the peak of prices. When they should be looking ahead to a time of lower prices, they are casting their eyes backward to prices that are probably distinctly higher than values.

In other words, if values are presumed to be more stable than prices, the fluctuations of the latter might take them above the value line at one period of the business cycle and below the value line at another. The appraiser who bases his appraisals on reasonably accurate estimates of future changes confirms this thesis. The one who always bases his appraisals upon past prices and keeps below them thereby denies the greater stability of values in comparison with prices. In addition, he runs greater risks in prosperous periods and misses greater opportunities in recovery stages of the cycle.

Arbitrary Discounts Some real estate lenders ask their appraisers to base their conclusions upon current selling prices. In other words, the lender thereby expresses doubts about the capacity of the appraiser to measure properly "the present worth of future benefits" of the subject property. What is asked of the appraiser is a determination of the comparative soundness of the current price of the property being appraised. If he demonstrates to the loan committee the accuracy of his conclusions on this subject, the committee then proceed to set their own value upon "the present worth of future benefits" by applying an arbitrary rate of discount to the findings of the appraiser. For example, if the committee think the current market is approximately 25 percent too optimistic about long-term values, they will discount the current market appraisal accordingly.

If they apply the same percentage of discount to all properties, they would place a loan value of $8,000 on a property selling for $10,000; a $4,000 loan value on a $5,000 property; and a $16,000 value upon a $20,000 property. If they think higher priced properties are likely to carry a larger element of inflation in periods of optimism, their discounts may result somewhat as follows: $8,000 for a $10,000 property; $4,200 for a $5,000 property; and $15,000 for one selling for $20,000. Even where the appraiser is instructed to report a long-term value rather than a current price, the loan committee may still see fit to apply a lower loan value based upon their greater conservatism. The reductions are not always uniform, nor even consistent. A greater deduction may be given a property in one neighborhood than a similar property in another, in spite of the fact that the appraiser's report probably reflects differences in neighborhood desirability.

The Appraisal Process The end result of any appraisal is to find the value of the property at a definite time, assuming that the property is useful for a specific purpose named in the appraisal. The process followed to arrive at this result may be quite involved. It starts with the collection of data affecting the value of the property in question. Here progress is made from the general to the particular. If the appraiser is undertaking an all-inclusive job, he will start with international relations, because they help to determine the attitude of people toward buying and selling real estate in every city and hamlet in the country. Next, attention would be given to national economic, fiscal, political, and social conditions. Usually these two sets of data are omitted; not that they are unimportant, but that they are a bit too involved for most appraisers to follow and to interpret.

Most data collected start with the city in which the property is located. These data should be kept current so that their collection need not be repeated for each appraisal. The same is more or less true with neighborhood information. Information about the site is collected specifically for the appraisal in question. Size, shape, topography, and fitness for the intended purpose are all carefully recorded. Then the improvements are carefully measured and described.

Three Approaches Wherever possible, the appraiser undertakes to measure the three approaches—or guides—to value. The cost approach is based upon the assumption that the property can be reproduced and that its reproduction cost sets an upper limit beyond which the value will not go. Methods of estimating cost will not be discussed here. The costs are most often measured—for the improvements—in terms of square-foot or cubic-foot units. Since the structure is not always new, its present condition is reflected in value estimates by deducting from reproduction cost new proper allowances for depreciation. This item covers physical deterioration due to wear and tear; functional obsolescence which reflects failure of the building to compare favorably with others which serve a similar purpose; and economic obsolescence due to external adverse influences, such as the infiltration of incompatible groups or uses. Land is not ordinarily depreciated in appraisal reports. It may decline in value, however.

The market approach is comparative. It takes into account all sales, asking prices, offers, and opinions of the value of the subject property and of others with which it can properly be compared. Without being conscious of it, perhaps, the buyer of real estate uses the market approach when he visits numerous properties in search of one to purchase. By comparing one with another he may select the one that not only best meets his needs but that best suits his pocketbook as well. In using the market approach, several cautions must be observed. Only comparable properties should be compared. Time is an important factor. Sales made six months or a year ago may not be a sufficient index of today's values. Terms and conditions of the sale are significant. Only those that were entered into voluntarily and on terms most commonly used are good indexes of value of other properties.

Land is best valued by the market-approach method. Except where it represents monopolistic characteristics, one site can substitute for another to a large extent. Then, too, there is seldom a scarcity of land. Urban land can be created in practically unlimited quantities.

Presumably all data collected under both the cost and market approaches are useful in arriving at value. The mere collection serves no purpose other than to clutter up appraisal forms, unless it is analyzed carefully and its bearing upon the value of the subject property is pointed out.

The income approach undertakes to find the net income applicable to the property being appraised. Gross income ratios serve little purpose. In the first place, they are based upon averages. The property being appraised may not be an average property. On the contrary, it may be far from average, owing to such factors as the size, location, arrangement, age, and condition. Net income may prove to be very useful. In calculating it, however, care should be exercised to make sure that it is the income that can be expected over a long period of time. Over any short period of time, even a year, net income may be completely unrepresentative. A new property might have little or no repair costs during its first year. Or in any given year, because of prolonged vacancies and unusually heavy repair costs, the income could even be negative. This would not necessarily indicate negative value for the property.

Once expected income is calculated, its capitalization will produce the element of value attributable to the income approach. This is then compared with the amounts arrived at by the cost and market approaches to find a final amount which the appraiser is willing to certify as his best estimate of the value of the property.

Market Approach Deceptive Whatever kind of real estate is being appraised, caution must govern the use of the market approach in the appraisal process. In the first place, comparable data may be hard to find when most needed. There may have been few sales of properties sufficiently like the subject property to provide significant comparisons. In the second place, even where there are many sales of comparable property, the results show sales prices rather than the long-term values for which the lender is always seeking. In times of economic depression there may be enough sales to establish price standards. But depression sales are expected to be at sacrifices which fail to measure long-term value. Price recoveries in subsequent periods always leave open the question: What is the value of a specific property that is sold at forced sale?

At the other end of the economic cycle, inflated prices may not deter numerous sales. On the contrary, when the inadequate supply fails to satisfy a stepped-up demand, sales may soon develop into resales of the same properties at increased prices. Hence the price data may again be adequate to establish price standards for comparative purposes. But it is price, not value, that is emphasized in periods of inflation. The appraiser seeking long-term value for financing purposes can easily be deceived if too much emphasis is placed upon current prices at almost any period of the business cycle.

Capitalization Rates The accurate determination of net income from a parcel of real estate is the basis for using the income approach to value. The selection of a capitalization rate must be the next step. This is not always easy. It is arrived at by a process of comparison. The elements of the capitalization rate are usually considered to be four in number. First, the most nearly riskless rate of return is selected as the basis for comparison. This is presumed to be the rate on long-term government bonds. Eliminating the element of speculation and thinking solely in terms of dollar-income return, most people would probably prefer government bonds to any other type of investment. Admittedly they do not protect against changes in price level. They are not expected to provide hedges against inflation.

To the rate of return upon government bonds are added three other elements, as follows: (1) a charge for nonliquidity of real estate as an investment; (2) a charge for management costs; and (3) a charge for the additional risk of real estate investments. Real estate enjoys various degrees of liquidity. A modest standard single house, located in a good neighborhood, can be disposed of quite readily in normal markets. An industrial property might hang over the market for several years without attracting a buyer at a reasonable price. Depending upon the type of property involved, the factor of nonliquidity might add from ½ percent to several percent to the capitalization ratio.

The management factor again varies in importance, depending upon the character of the real estate. The function of management is to select, secure, and retain the kind of user of the property for which it is best suited. For a well-constructed, well-located property rented on a long lease to a single tenant of great financial responsibility, the management factor would not weigh heavily. It would not likely be less than ½ percent under the most favorable circumstances. If the property is not new and is located in a neighborhood whose changing characteristics leave its future in a doubtful classification, and if it is occupied by a variety of tenants whose business success is not too well assured—then the amount to be added to the capitalization ratio can easily be several percent.

The risk factor is always the most difficult one to measure. Good locations, occupied by modern buildings with tenants who are well satisfied and able to pay fair rentals continuously, carry relatively small risk, perhaps ½ to 1 percent. At the other end of the scale, a new business enterprise, not too well financed, manufacturing a product whose market has not yet been established, may carry great risk. Or a commercial lease on a percentage basis, with no minimum rental stated and no recapture clause, might put the owner of the real estate into business partnership with an inexperienced or inefficient tenant whose rent-paying capacity is decidedly uncertain. The risk factor can and frequently does add to the capitalization ratio more than nonliquidity and management combined.

From what is said here, the difficulties involved in arriving at the proper capitalization rate become apparent. Nevertheless, the appraiser must arrive at a tenable ratio which he is forced to use in estimating value from the income approach. As he proceeds from more familiar ground in dealing with residential properties to those devoted to commercial uses, and finally to industrial and specific-use properties, his difficulties cumulate. Since his ability diminishes in this progression, it is not surprising that the interest of lending institutions in making loans also diminishes as the properties more difficult to appraise are presented for loan security.

Summation Values Fortunately we are hearing less about appraisals built up as the sum of separate valuations of land and improvements. In times past it was assumed that one appraiser could use the cost approach to measure the value of the improvements and that another appraiser could use the market approach to estimate the value of the land for its highest and best use—irrespective of its current use. By adding the two amounts a summation value was arrived at. The trouble with such a procedure was that it violated the major premise of all appraisals—to find the present value of future uses of the land and its improvements. A parcel of land cannot be used at the same time for conflicting purposes.

It is always possible to appraise the land without giving attention to the value of the improvements, because existing improvements can usually be demolished, if desirable, to make room for a better use of the land. But the improvements cannot ordinarily be appraised independently of the site on which they are erected. Improvements cannot ordinarily be removed without tremendous loss of value. Only salvage value, if any, remains when a building is demolished or is moved to another site. When the site value increases and the building value declines, there frequently comes a time when demolition of the building is economical. Until that time arrives, any appraisal of the building must be in terms of its use in connection with the site on which it is located.

Qualifications of Appraisers In discussing the qualifications of appraisers, it is necessary to assume that they reach independent conclusions. Many so-called appraisals are merely the confirmation of opinions of others. They should not be classed as appraisals at all. The independent appraiser should possess the following qualifications:

1. His basic education in economics, construction standards, and so forth, should be supplemented by specific appraisal study, preferably that required to merit the use of the designations MAI, i.e., Member of the American Institute of Real Estate Appraisers, or SREA or SRA, certifications of the Society of Real Estate Appraisers, meaning respectively "Senior Real Estate Appraiser" and "Senior Residential Appraiser."

2. He should have the ability to collect pertinent facts about the jobs assigned to him, to analyze their significance, and to draw conclusions therefrom. One of the compelling reasons for specific training of appraisers is their need to know what kinds of facts to collect and what to do with them after they are collected. By themselves, facts may be useful or useless. Many so-called hardheaded businessmen abhor theory. Yet the only reason for their success is that they are good theorists. A theory, if sound, is a generalization from facts. If it is unsound, it is not good theory. Appraisers need to be theorists: they need to learn how to collect facts and to draw proper generalizations from them.

3. Judgment is a quality hard to define, but the absence of it may completely disqualify an appraiser. It means the capacity to separate the essential from the nonessential; to weigh, to compare, and to place the emphasis where it belongs. Frequently we hear that judgment is the only absolute requirement for success as an appraiser. But judg-

ment alone may be sterile unless its user knows what information to apply it to and unless he is trained in the specific field of study. A man might possess excellent judgment as a pharmacist and be utterly useless as a real estate appraiser.

4. Since there is no royal road to a proper conclusion in any appraisal process, the path to be followed requires persistent efforts and meticulous care to make sure that all facts are collected and placed in their proper relationship. As has been said above, a 90 percent average in making appraisals ranks the appraiser very high. But 90 percent success cannot be attained by collecting only 90 percent of ascertainable facts. The missing 10 percent may be those most significant in the particular situation.

5. The appraiser must possess a high degree of intellectual honesty. Not only must he be honest in the sense that he would not knowingly cheat his employer. He must make sure that he will not cheat himself out of a decision by failing to observe all of the rules with which he is acquainted. If, for any reason—either outside pressure, subtle hints, or dictation by another—he fails to reach the conclusion which his training, his set of facts, and his judgment tell him is right, he lacks a prime qualification as an appraiser.

6. His background of experience should give him familiarity with the job to be done and confidence in his ability to do it. Being a successful real estate salesman or a successful builder will not necessarily make one a competent appraiser. But both real estate selling experience and building experience can be very useful to the individual who hopes to turn the knowledge he gains from these activities into appraisal channels. It is a truism that we learn by doing. Many people do without learning why. Others learn why by observing others. Both represent forms of practical application of skills. The English system of formal study first, to be followed by an internship, has much to commend it in the training of appraisers.

7. Knowledge of the neighborhood in which the property to be appraised is located is a great timesaver. It is probable that a competent appraiser can arrive at a proper valuation of a property located in a city which he has never before visited. But the time it would require to reach a sound decision would be much greater than that consumed by an equally competent appraiser "on the ground." That is why financial institutions sometimes select their appraisers according to their familiarity with the neighborhood in which each property is situated.

Real Estate Appraisal Organizations The two leading real property appraisal organizations are the American Institute of Real Estate Appraisers and the Society of Real Estate Appraisers. These two societies have performed outstanding service in the development of appraisal standards and in disseminating education in the appraisal field.

The American Institute of Real Estate Appraisers was founded in 1932. The Institute is affiliated with the National Association of Real Estate Boards (NAREB), and, in addition to demonstrating proficiency in real property valuation, an MAI (Member of the Appraisal Institute) must also hold membership in the NAREB. Furthermore, to be eligible for the MAI designation, the appraiser must be at least 30 years of age; have at least five years of effective appraisal experience; submit three or more acceptable appraisal reports covering work actually performed in a professional capacity; pass two comprehensive appraisal examinations; and have a good reputation for integrity and ability. He is at all times subject to the bylaws, regulations, and rules of professional conduct of the Institute.

The Society of Real Estate Appraisers, previously known as the "Society of Residential Appraisers," was organized in 1935. It originally developed within the framework of the savings and loan business, and consequently was limited in scope to the appraisal of residential properties. The SRA (Senior Residential Appraisers) designation was and is awarded to appraisers qualified to appraise residential properties. Like the MAI, the SRA designation may be held indefinitely without reexamination so long as the appraiser pays his membership dues and follows the code of ethics. Since January 1, 1963, an additional designation has been awarded known as the "SREA," or "Senior Real Estate Appraiser." Holders of this designation must meet standards similar to those for the MAI and, in addition, must continue to maintain highest proficiency in their particular field of specialization. Furthermore, unlike the MAI and the SRA, holders of the SREA must have their work reviewed every five years. If they are to be permitted to continue to use the SREA designation, they must qualify on academic, ethical, and professional grounds.

Broker as Appraiser Many real estate brokers do not pretend to be expert appraisers. Without formal study of the material needed to equip an appraiser to do an expert job, they know their own limitations in the field of establishing values. But their customers do not know them. The prospective seller or purchaser of property depends upon the representations of the broker. When the latter recommends a purchase or a sale at a price, or even when he offers it at a fixed price, he gives the impression that he has appraised the property and has reached a conclusion that the asking or offered price is its value. Too frequently the only appraisal the broker has given the property merits the designation of "horseback," "windshield," or "armchair" appraisal.

Some real estate brokers try to warn their customers that appraisal is not included in their services. When the owner lists his property for sale and requests the advice of the broker about the price to ask, he may be told, "You ask what you think you must get and I'll try to sell the property at that price." In response to a question from a prospective buyer, he may say: "This property is the best buy on my list"; or, "In comparison with the other properties we have looked at today, the price of this one most nearly meets your requirements." The broker might even go so far as to say: "You have looked at various properties and know their comparative values as well as I do. You must make the decision about the value of the one you buy." In spite of such precautionary statements, the broker is looked upon as the man who knows the value of the property offered by him. It is difficult for him to erase this impression from the minds of his customers.

Lending institutions are placed in a peculiar position when dealing with real estate brokers. On the one hand, the broker is a fertile source of mortgage business. In some cases he is the chief source which the lender depends upon. Hence the lender likes to keep the broker happy by making loans needed to finance his sales. Many lending institutions play up to the brokers in their market. Indeed, in some cases they will go so far as to grant loans brought to them by brokers that they would hesitate to grant otherwise. The lender is willing to take a chance on an occasional off-color loan in order to keep the goodwill of a broker who is relied upon for future business.

Nevertheless, the lender is seldom willing to rely upon the representations of value made by the broker. Independent appraisals are required to be made by one or more individuals who have no sales commission at stake in the subject transaction. The broker normally understands this and the reasons for it. So long as the sale is financed, he is satisfied. But if his proposals are turned down too frequently, he will probably cater to another lender.

If the lending institution has confidence in the appraisal ability of the broker, it may use his services as an independent appraiser. In other words, when a loan application comes from a source other than the broker, the lending institution may call upon him to make an appraisal, for which the usual fee will be paid. By this means the goodwill of the broker is maintained so that he will think kindly of the lender when he has an opportunity to recommend a source of mortgage money.

Incidentally, the broker who can appraise property with reasonable accuracy gains two advantages over his competitor who lacks this capacity. In the first place, the broker-appraiser should be in a better position to judge the kind of a bargain being offered by the seller. If he thinks that the asking price is low, he can better find a buyer for the property than if his conclusions lead in the opposite direction. In the second place, if he knows the value of the property, in contrast to the price at which it is being offered, he can advise both buyers and sellers with greater confidence. If the value is substantially less than the price asked, he can save his own time by telling the owner frankly what his opinion is. By this means he can help to effect a quicker sale. He may even advise the owner to raise his price if he thinks it is too low. In dealing with the prospective purchaser, he can talk with greater confidence if he knows the value of the property. He may even advise the prospect to offer an amount substantially less than the asking price in order to deal honestly with both buyer and seller.

Loan Terms The appraiser can be of great assistance to the lending institution by making recommendations concerning loan terms. In granting loans on income property, the lender may find that the various factors to be considered may add up to a positive answer in one case and a negative one in another. For example, a high-percentage loan, at a low rate of interest, for a long period of time, might be turned down; while a lower percentage loan, at a higher rate of interest, amortized at a rate satisfactory to the lender, might be approved. Amortization of loans on income property as security follows no such standard pattern as is normally set up for residential loans. Rapid amortization, particularly during the early life of the loan, might develop a more favorable atmosphere for loan approval than if such quick repayment of the principal was not contemplated.

As has been stated elsewhere in this text, it is not ordinarily expected that the appraiser shall act for the loan committee. The appraisal of the property is only one of the factors considered by those who pass upon loan applications. But, for income property, the situation is somewhat different. The moral hazard, for example, is less significant here. More dependence is necessarily placed upon the report of the appraiser. If he is competent to appraise income property, he probably knows as much about its future possibilities as do the members of the loan committee. For that reason, his recommendations about loan terms are usually quite acceptable to the committee.

Purpose of Appraisal Two schools of thought approach the subject of appraisal from two different starting points. One contends that, at a given time, there can be but one value of a specific parcel of real estate. The other inclines to consider the concept of value from the point of view of the purpose to be served. From this point of view, there could be as many values as there are purposes. Both agree that the purpose does color the value label placed upon the real estate. For example, in condemnation proceedings, the award is likely to favor the person whose property is being taken. Probably the amount awarded will be higher than the price of the property in the open market. For tax purposes, the taxpayer more often than not is assessed on a valuation less than the market price. If a sale is being made on long terms, the price is likely to be higher than if it calls for all cash above the first mortgage. And so a long list of purposes might easily produce a similar list of valuations.

When a lending institution requests an appraiser to appraise a specific property, it is known that the purpose is to form the basis for a long-term mortgage loan. Frequently the appraiser is not told the price that is being paid for the property if a purchase is being financed. But since financing of the property is involved, the appraiser is expected to be more conservative than if he were setting a selling price. Indeed, the same appraiser might fix two or more values on the same property at the same time: one for sale on long terms, one for security for a long-term loan, and so forth. Those who insist that there can be but one value of a given property at an instant of time are usually willing to concede that a percentage of this less than 100 would probably please the lender best, and that a percentage higher than 100 might be needed in some other cases for other purposes.

Unless an FHA-insured loan is being used, the purchaser of a property may never know what value is placed upon it for lending purposes. If he found out that such a valuation is lower than the price he pays, explanations might be in order. On the other hand, if the appraisal made at the behest of the lender should be higher than the price paid—as sometimes happens—then the buyer would probably feel that he is getting a bargain If explanations of differences are called for, the lender should be able to satisfy the buyer that the points of view of the buyer and the lender are not the same.

When a lender takes an application for a real estate loan and gives the impression that the loan will probably be granted if the appraisal stands up, failure to grant the loan may raise doubts in the mind of the purchaser about the price he is expected to pay for the property. If the informed and experienced lender doubts the price as a measure of the value of the property, why should not the purchaser rely upon the opinion of the lender instead of that of the seller or the real estate broker? In many preliminary purchase contracts the purchaser protects himself by inserting a clause to the effect that the purchase is dependent upon his ability to secure financial assistance of a specified amount at a specified rate of interest.

It should be emphasized that, whatever the purpose of the appraisal, the procedure is the same. Complete data will be collected, analyzed, and coordinated. The three approaches to value will be used so far as they are applicable. The difference lies in the definition of value. The lender's concept is always a conservative one, tinged with a caution about future possibilities.

Appraising Single Homes In appraising single-family residences, the market approach is probably most useful if sufficient data concerning recent sales are available. The cost approach is a limiting factor which ordinarily sets the upper limit beyond which the value will not go. As a choice between paying a higher price and reproducing the property, the average informed buyer would prefer the latter. The income approach is seldom applicable in the appraisal of single-family residences, except in areas where they are constructed in large numbers for rent instead of for sale. The owner-occupier of a single residence expects to pay for the amenities of homeownership, which mean nothing to the tenant as such. Hence the use of the income approach would produce a net income measured in monetary terms that could not justify prices usually paid except by the use of unusually low capitalization rates. Such rates are unrealistic, since the ownership of even residential real estate is not so safe as that of high-grade bonds.

Appraising Apartment Dwellings All income property is assumed to have normal use and competent management. If either of these is absent, income and expenses must be adjusted accordingly. The benefits of ownership of such properties flow from the income that the property is expected to produce. In considering the gross income estimate, the appraiser is guided by actual rent received but is not necessarily bound by it. What he is after is average rent received year after year. In looking to the future, the effect of aging of the building must be taken into account. In general, rents on a given apartment building are expected to decline about 2 percent per year. A living unit that commands a monthly rental of $135 when new would probably rent for $110, 10 years later. Eventually rents will drop only to an irreducible minimum beyond which they will not go until the apartment dwelling is ready to be replaced with a new building of some kind.

Vacancy allowances must be accounted for in all apartments. Care should be used to avoid misrepresenting the facts. In unusual cases vacancies could be very low, perhaps 1 percent. In slum areas, with tenants suffering from irregular incomes, vacancies and uncollected rents could easily run more than 10 percent. In appraising apartments, the appraiser tries to approach the vacancy allowance for the specific building as closely as possible rather than to use any general average. He may need to use the average which his experience has taught him to be applicable to this class of structure. In any specific case a vacancy allowance that is smaller than the average for that class of property probably indicates that rents are lower than they need be. A higher than average allowance suggests that rents are too high.

The expense schedule includes taxes, anticipated as well as current, and probably will run 10 to 15 percent of gross income for most apartments. Insurance costs are expected to cover premiums for fire and extended coverage, public liability, and boiler insurance as minimums. Other forms of insurance may include protection against water damage and loss of rents. Operating expenses are "computed" rather than accrued during any one year. They should cover what most managements would expect to incur in a normally competitive market. Allowance for management fees should be taken into account even if the owner manages the property. Depreciation should cover whatever equipment is included. If the latter is of sufficient importance, it may carry separate rates. The building will normally be depreciated at about $2\frac{1}{2}$ percent per year.

When a capitalization rate is selected, the principle of substitution must always be taken into account. Presumably, any investor has alternative investment opportunities. These are not limited to the field of real estate but cover all other fields as well. Hence, in the selection of a capitalization rate, efforts are made to find an alternative investment that is comparable to the subject property in desirability as an investment and whose rate of return is known to the appraiser.

Cost and market approaches, so far as the latter may be available for comparable apartments, are sometimes useful for checking purposes. As a rule, however, the income approach is the most reliable basis for determining value for financing purposes.

Appraisal of Retail Stores The financial institution asked to consider an application for a loan against real estate devoted to retail stores is primarily concerned with the continuous flow of income from rentals of the store units. At the outset the appraiser must appraise the neighborhood as well as the store operator. In doing so he is faced with three questions: (1) If the store has reasonably competent management, is the community large enough and does it have sufficient need for the products or services to support the business which is to occupy the store building? This is sometimes expressed in terms of the drawing power of the area. In turn, it is dependent upon the shopping radius which is conditioned by such factors as location and transportation facilities. If the building is suitable for alternative business uses, this should be taken into account by the appraiser. (2) Can the occupants of these stores pay the rent agreed upon? This question and the one following imply a long period of time rather than the current period during which the loan is applied for. (3) In bad times as well as good, can they pay enough rent to meet the carrying charges on the loan?

If the appraiser finds that the rent contracted for is in excess of the long-term earning capacity of the property, it is the stabilized rent that should concern him most. The excess, if large in amount and if contracted to be paid over a considerable period of time, will probably disappear in some manner. If, on the other hand, the excess is due to the fact that the building is leased for a long period of time to a financially responsible chain store corporation which makes the lease with its eyes open, then the excess becomes a factor in the evaluation process.

Special-Purpose Property The rent potential of special-purpose property limits its financing opportunities. A commercial garage may provide a satisfactory income to its owner so long as it is used for the purpose for which it was constructed. But if this use is abandoned, what alternative use is available? The rent potential of the best alternative use might be much less than that of the original use. A theater or other amusement use of real estate might be even less capable of maintaining income from alternative uses. Church loans are particularly difficult to obtain. They suffer from two major disabilities: (1) The rent potential of a church is small, even negligible. (2) Foreclosure of a church loan is seldom undertaken because of the low-rent potential and because of the psychological effect of such action by the mortgagee. The public seldom understands that the mortgagee institution which takes a mortgage upon a church as security is using, not its own money, but trusteed funds that it is obligated to protect—by foreclosure if necessary. Where church loans are granted, other than business considerations frequently help the mortgagee to decide to take the mortgage. Then all possible forbearance is exercised in collecting the interest and the principal payments.

Appraisers generally classify property such as filling stations, fast food dispensaries, hotels, motels, and theaters as special-purpose property. While they are so constructed and arranged that they have only limited alternative uses, presumably there are competitive opportunities for renting such properties. Again the income approach is the one used primarily for appraisal purposes, with cost and market approaches used for checking purposes. Because of the high degree of specialization of use represented in such types of real estate, the appraiser will frequently need the assistance of experienced managers in the specific field of real estate use. For example, in appraising a theater, the appraiser must learn from operators of other theaters just what items of expense and of income are to be included. In addition, the appraiser must find out all he can about the factors which determine both income and expense.

In appraising special-purpose property it is well to use the cost approach to set an upper limit of value. Likewise, the market approach will be used so far as information about comparable properties is available. But sales and even leases of special-purpose property are not as common as in the case of properties enjoying greater numbers of alternative uses.

Specific-Use Property In a sense all income property is special-purpose property. A one-story store building is primarily useful for merchandising purposes only. But because there are multiple alternative merchandisers who can use it, it is not generally classed as special-purpose property. Some appraisers go one step further and designate as specific-use properties those that are so located, constructed, and arranged that they have little or no competitive uses. In this class are put a considerable proportion of industrial properties. For example, a steel mill is ordinarily built for the use of one corporation only. Normally it can afford to pay much more for the use of this property than can any other user.

In considering the income approach in appraising specific-use properties, it is not the rental income as we ordinarily think of this term that is taken into account. Rather it is the business income from a specific corporation that is important. The appraiser responsible for setting a value for lending purposes on such property will do well to consult investment bankers acquainted with methods of appraising incomes from such businesses. The cost approach again sets an upper limit of value. The market approach may not be used to estimate the value to a competitor corporation as often as to some purchaser with an entirely different and probably less effective use for the property.

A smaller number of appraisers are competent to appraise industrial property than is true for other classes of real estate. The turnover of such properties is ordinarily infrequent, so that market prices afford little assistance. Because of lack of experience in lending on such properties, financial institutions do not look with favor upon loan applications from owners of industrial property.

The appraiser assigned the task of fixing a value upon industrial real estate is concerned primarily with location and structural fitness for the intended use. Location is relative. The property must be at such a place that it has favorable relationships with markets, transportation facilities, materials and supplies, and the kind of labor the business enterprise needs. Land normally is expected to be relatively cheap. An excess of land for expansion purposes is desirable. Taxes are of such importance as to cause business enterprises to abandon their investment in one locality and reestablish the plant in a different one where taxes are more favorable. Available utility services and their cost are elements to be carefully considered by the appraiser. In some cases such questions as the availability of an adequate water supply determine the location of industrial plants.

In any analysis of an industrial enterprise, the factor of management assumes unusual importance because of the absence of alternative demands for the real estate. Unless the product is likely to meet with continued demand in the market and unless the management shows evidence of being able to produce and market its products in a manner that will mean continued profitable operation of the enterprise, it is probably useless to undertake an appraisal of much industrial real estate for lending purposes. It is hard enough to find mortgage money to finance such properties when all factors are favorable.

Appraisal of Vacant Land In the appraisal of vacant land, there is no element of reproduction cost to be considered except, of course, to estimate what it would cost to purchase land at wholesale and to process it for sale at retail. The chief basis of appraisal is the market approach, since each parcel has value when compared with other parcels available for the same or similar purposes. Vacant land normally has no immediate income. From the point of view of the income approach, it is possible to estimate potential income, assuming that the vacant site were improved with a structure that fits it. This is frequently done in establishing a sale price for the vacant land. This is speculative, unless there are definite plans for the construction of such improvements immediately. In the absence of this assurance, lending institutions are not usually interested in making loans on land that is expected to remain vacant. To make doubly sure that temptations of presumed low-percentage loans and high-interest rates may not attract loans on vacant land, most supervised lenders are prohibited from making any loans on unimproved land. Occasionally such loans are taken to supplement security on other loans.

QUESTIONS AND PROBLEMS

1. What is an appraisal and what kinds of data are collected in the appraisal process?
2. What are the differences between value and price for appraisal purposes?
3. What are the three major approaches which the appraiser may take to arrive at real estate value?
4. What are the proper limitations on the use of the market approach to real estate appraisal?
5. In determining value by reference to real estate net income, what are the factors considered in determination of the capitalization rate?
6. A real estate site is appraised at $10,000 for use for a six-family apartment house. Located on the lot now is a house appraised at $7,500. By a summation of values, this property might be appraised at about $17,500. Would you approve of this procedure? Why or why not?
7. What are the qualifications of a good appraiser? Can you rely on your broker for appraisal services?
8. How should appraisals affect loan terms?
9. What particular problems are encountered in appraising each of the following: (a) single homes; (b) apartment buildings; (c) retail stores; and (d) special-purpose and specific-use properties?
10. What are the most acceptable approaches to appraisal of vacant land?
11. How important are the following factors in an appraisal?
    a) A history of past prices.
    b) An estimate of future economic conditions in the community.
    c) Money market rates.
    d) The professional background and other business interests of the appraiser.
    e) Intentions to have the loan federally insured or guaranteed.

19

Title Analysis for Financing Purposes

Evolution of Assurance of Good Title In the evolution of assurance of good title upon which real estate finance must be based, several significant steps can be traced. In some instances even today, title passes with no assurance of the validity of title other than the trust placed by the purchaser in the seller. To save expense, deeds are occasionally accepted without reference to the records. A series of old deeds, showing an unbroken chain of title for a long period of time, may accompany the new deed and may be accepted by the grantee as sufficient evidence of title, particularly if the grantor is a well-known citizen whose word is usually trusted. This course is not recommended. The few dollars saved may be poor compensation for much larger losses that may be suffered, perhaps through no intent of the grantor.

In earlier periods of our history and even in rural communities today, the above course of action may be supplemented by a more or less careful search of the records by a local lawyer who may have some acquaintance with the recording processes in his community. As a matter of fact, even though he is a general practitioner rather than a specialist in real estate law, he may be able to render satisfactory service because of his acquaintance with the peculiarities of the recording system and with the parties involved in the real estate transaction. The results of his researches may be stated orally to his client; may be included in a letter to him; or may be couched in the phrases peculiar to the more formal title "opinion." Where the grantee acts upon the recommendations of his lawyer, he substitutes his trust in him for his former trust in the vendor. For the small fee charged by the lawyer, he cannot be expected to be held responsible for errors in judgment, if any. Gross negligence on his part or willful intent to take advantage of his client are proper grounds for damage suits.

If the attorney discussed above should "abstract" from the record the salient points upon which he bases his opinion and should pass these along to his client as evidence to support his conclusions, he might well call his report an abstract and title opinion. As this abstracting process became more formal, it not only summarized some parts of the record but copied verbatim some other parts. Thus was born the abstract system which forms the basis of title opinions in many sections of the country. Abstracts are never official documents enjoying the importance attributed to legislation and court decisions. Instead, they represent some presumably competent individual's concept of what parts of the records are significant in searching title to real estate.

Abstracts go back to the earliest records available, presumably at least those which recorded the earliest grant from the government to an individual owner. One noteworthy abstract started out somewhat as follows: "Assuming the title in the name of John F. Jones under date of August 17, 1870, to be valid," and so forth. The courthouse had burned and with it all land records preceding this date. From the date of earliest land records, abstracts attempt to include all actions of importance that may affect the quality of title to the land in question. In addition to identifying maps, abstracts deal with deeds, mortgages, releases, taxes, leases, judgments and other liens, wills, pending suits, and a variety of other items that may cover 40 or more categories.

The development of the abstract system tended to separate record search and title examination. Abstract companies and young attorneys are assigned the duty of continuing an abstract once it has been developed. Normally the abstract is passed along with the deed to the grantee. When he in turn becomes a grantor, he is responsible for having the abstract brought down to date by the use of tail sheets which deal with anything that affects the title to the property since the abstract was last continued. When this service has been performed, the abstract is then turned over to the attorney for the new grantee, who bases his opinion of title upon his examination of the abstract. Again he advises his client—orally, by letter, or by a more formal opinion—of his conclusions. His opinion may recite specific items which lead him to question the validity of title or which he thinks his client should know about, even though he concludes that the title is merchantable. As before, the attorney who passes upon title is not expected to guarantee its quality.

The next stage in the evolution of assurance of title makes use of the certificate of title, a little-used plan in most sections of the country today. This is a form of title opinion by which the author may again combine the search of the records with a statement of his conclusions based thereon. The searcher may use the abstract or he may bypass it. In any event he issues to his client a statement in the form of certificate of title, the legal status of which is not always clearly defined. Is a certificate any different from an opinion? Does the author assume any different responsibility when he says, "I certify"? Partly because of the uncertainty surrounding this issue, the certificate is not commonly used.

Title Insurance The insurance of title to interests in real property encompasses a unique combination of characteristics: (1) liability is assumed only after evaluation of the risk; but (2) the protection is against events that, with certain exceptions, have taken place before the policy was written; and (3) the coverage continues without recurring premiums as long as ownership is retained by the insured or his heirs. When the certificate takes the form of a guarantee of title, something new has been added. Companies organized and operating solely for this purpose, or in combination with other financial functions make a business of indemnifying their policyholders against losses that may develop as a result of defective titles. Some are simply title guarantee companies; others combine title guarantee with banking or trust functions; still others combine title guarantee with mortgage operations. Geography plays a part in these combinations. Title and trust companies are probably most common.

Title insurance is based upon several considerations. The records may be incomplete or defective. While they are expected to speak for themselves, the courts may cause them to speak a language not understood by even the experienced searcher. Title insurance affords a means of warning or protecting against risks of acquiring a defective land title either by pointing out the defect and excepting it or by insuring against the potential loss. The title insurance business originated in the United States in the last century, and as of 1957 title insurance was being written by 147 companies. Eleven companies were operating in 5 or more states; 31 were in more than one state; and 77 had branch outlets in their state of incorporation.[1] Most title insurance is written on the West Coast, although it is now being used extensively in many population centers and is available in every state.

Torrens System Under the Torrens system, the state supervises and arranges for an assurance of title. In effect, the state undertakes two obligations: (1) upon application, to determine the character of title of a specific property, at the expense of the applicant; (2) by a system similar to title insurance, to guarantee the character of title insofar as the resources in the insurance reserve are sufficient for that purpose. In Hawaii no reserve has been established, but the general credit of the state is pledged to protect against loss. Twenty states have had legisla-

---

[1] Quintin Johnstone, "Title Insurance," *The Yale Law Journal*, February 1957, pp. 492–524.

tion permitting use of the Torrens system, but 8 states have since repealed it, leaving only 12 with registration statutes still on their books. Only Hawaii, Illinois, Massachusetts, and Minnesota make substantial use of it. The other states in which use is permitted are Colorado, Georgia, New York, North Carolina, Ohio, Oregon, Virginia, and Washington.

Most of the arguments against its use are really against its introduction. Under universal use its simplicity and economy should recommend its continuance. Under this system, unlike the more commonly used abstract system, no attention is given to happenings antedating the latest transfer of title. Once this system is put into effect on a broad scale, the assurance of title should be determinable in a few hours at most instead of in the days or weeks now required. A study made by Horace Russell and David A. Bridewell, general counsel and assistant to the general counsel, respectively, of the Federal Home Loan Bank Board and its agencies, covered the very extensive experience of the HOLC on the subject of systems of land title examination.[2] Their conclusions indicate very definitely that transfers of titles under the Torrens system take less time and involve less expense than under any of the other systems in use in this country. These authorities make valuable suggestions for changes in the systems now used for the purpose of effecting further economies in time and money through the use of the Torrens system. Meantime, however, the interests opposed to its introduction and use evidently weigh more heavily than those in favor of it.

Objectives of Torrens System The major purpose of the Torrens system is to create and to maintain a merchantable title to land. Before such a title is created, any adverse claims must first be determined and dealt with. In defense of his plan Torrens stated that his purpose was to "simplify, quicken, and cheapen the transfer of real estate and to render titles safe and indefeasible." Specific advantages claimed for the Torrens system include: (1) It substitutes the greater certainty of an official adjudication of title for the uncertainty of unofficial examinations and opinions. (2) It cheapens the cost of title transfer by avoiding the necessity for repeated examination of title whenever a title is transferred. (3) It speeds up the process of title transfer. (4) It avoids the increasing accumulation of title evidence over the years which makes future determination of titles increasingly more difficult and expensive.

Torrens Fund in Chicago The Torrens law has been in operation in Cook County (Chicago), Illinois, since 1897. The costs of transferring titles from the old recording system to the Torrens system amount to $50, to cover filing of application, examination of title, publication, and issuance of the first certificate of title. To these costs must be added

---

[2] Reported in *Journal of Land and Public Utility Economics*, Vol. XIV, pp. 133–46.

a payment of $1/10$ of 1 percent of the value of the land to be paid into the indemnity fund and to defray abstract charges. At the beginning of 1968, the amount held in the fund exceeded $2 million. At the present time the indemnity fund is growing at the rate of approximately $100,000 per year. From 1897 to 1968, the total charges against the fund on account of errors have averaged about $3,000 per year. Thus, it is apparent that the amount paid into the fund annually is more than sufficient to pay all claims by a wide margin. The process of registration normally consumes about three months. The cost of transfer of registration, after the original issuance of the certificate of title, is $5 irrespective of the value of the property.

Origin of Abstract Companies Most law offices, except those which specialize in other phases of the law, render service to those interested in real estate transactions. Occasionally a lawyer becomes so much interested in the field of real estate that he specializes in it. He may even decide to substitute the business of real estate abstracting for the general practice of law. This is one way in which real estate abstract companies are established. Some abstract companies, in turn, find it advantageous to become agents for title insurance companies. They may even operate as a dual type of business—doing abstract work for those wishing it and adding title insurance for those who prefer it. In time the agent may become a principal, organizing his own title insurance company instead of depending upon an underwriter to assume the risks of the business.

Meantime, lawyers are supposed to be jealous of both abstract companies and title insurance companies, where the business of serving real estate clients is involved. If the abstract companies or the title insurance companies take business that otherwise is sought by lawyers, the cause for the jealousy is apparent. On the other hand, it does not necessarily follow that the lawyer is bypassed in closing real estate transactions. Instead, he may still be included as the adviser to parties to a real estate transaction, with the specialized part of the work, which he may be glad to be rid of, being taken care of outside of his office.

In some instances, title insurance companies not only make use of local attorneys in searching the records and in other ways, but they encourage the latter to close their own deals and bring their opinions of title to the title insurance companies for insurance. Where the insurance company has an approved list of attorneys, such procedure minimizes the work of the company. In the other cases, the preliminary work is all done by the title insurance company, on order of an attorney who then proceeds to close the transaction, thereby avoiding details of title search which he may not care to deal with.

Lawyers Title Insurance Corporation The Lawyers Title Insurance Corporation was organized in 1925 and was originally financed by lawyers to provide a means of protecting the business of the legal profession in the examination of land titles. Its function is to engage exclusively in the business of title insurance. It employs approved attorneys who search the title, and then adds the element of insurance which individual lawyers are not equipped to supply. In some cities it makes use of abstract companies as well as attorneys. The company now operates over a wider area than any other, having offices in 46 states, including Hawaii, and in the District of Columbia, Puerto Rico, and several provinces in Canada.

Nature of Abstract Recorded instruments constitute the basic evidence of title to real estate. The records are official and are treated as such. An abstract, on the other hand, is not an official document. It may be a full and complete copy of every pertinent record, or it may be a short form or synopsis type, often called a "bobtailed" abstract. Its purpose is to furnish all the material information contained in the original documents and records from which it is compiled, so that they may be studied as completely as if the originals were under inspection. The abstract should show the inception and foundation of the title, together with its devolution to the date of examination. The abstract should document the incidents of the land, its divisions and subdivisions, all adverse claims and titles, liens or charges, and every other matter of record that may affect the title. Although an abstracter is not required to go beyond the record, he may do so if he becomes aware of an item that may have a bearing on the quality of the title.

Abstracts usually include reference to the source of the original title from the government. City and town plats are usually included if such are in existence. All legal actions pending that may affect the title should be noted. Easements and restrictions are carefully noted, since they run with the land. Likewise, zoning and other regulatory ordinances governing the use and occupancy of the real estate and the improvements permitted to be placed upon the land are important parts of abstracts. The status of taxes is always important.

An abstracter—whether a firm specializing in such activities or a lawyer who takes on abstract work incidentally—is responsible only for an accurate portrayal of original documents and records affecting title. Any mistakes in recording or in indexing legal documents will be carried into the abstract without identifying them as mistakes. The abstract makes no pretense of disclosing hidden title hazards. Among the latter may be one or more of the following: (1) forged deeds in the chain of title; (2) deeds by minors or other incompetents; (3) deeds by grantors who represent themselves as single persons when in fact they are married; (4) claims of unknown or forgotten heirs; (5) mistakes in recording legal documents; (6) falsification of records; (7) errors in indexing of records; (8) birth or adoption of a child after a will is made; (9) deeds delivered after death of grantor; (10) impersonation of true owners of land by others not having title to it; and so forth.

When abstracts were first used, they were made by public officers who had charge of the records. In a dozen or so states it is still the law that, when called upon to do so and when compensated according to a schedule of fees, the public official will check the records for specific findings requested of him. Public records are open to the public. Their use by outsiders is not subject to a charge by the public official who is not called upon to make a search of any part of the records.

Legal Definition of Abstract The Supreme Court of Illinois has defined an abstract as follows:[3]

> In a legal sense, a summary or epitome of the parts relied on as evidence of title and it must contain a note of all conveyances, transfers or other facts relied on as evidence of the claimant's title, together with all such facts appearing on record as may impair the title. It should contain a full summary of all grants, conveyances, wills and all records and judicial proceedings whereby the title is in any way affected and all encumbrances and liens of record and show whether they have been released or not.

Lack of Uniformity In many areas there is a lack of uniformity in the practices of abstracters. In general, there are no standard requirements which govern the operations of those who profess to be expert in making or in continuing abstracts. Trade associations have done much to raise standards; but, unfortunately, those who need the benefits of trade association contacts most are those who expose themselves to the practices of others least frequently. Some abstracters have little investment in plant and depend entirely upon the use of public records when their services are sought. Even here they may not be too careful or too wise in the use of information available to them. Such abstracters are sometimes known in the trade as "curbstoners." Others have a great deal invested in what are known in the trade as "title plants." These consist of tract indices, miscellaneous indices, suit and judgment dockets, plats, maps, takeoffs, and photostatic, photographic, and microfilm equipment. The results of abstracts vary widely, owing to differences in the experience, care, and ingenuity of those who do the work.

Some degree of uniformity has been introduced by some state associations of title companies. One of the most ambitious efforts in this direction took the form of a booklet issued by the Wisconsin Association, entitled *Suggestions of What an Abstract of Title Should Contain*. According to its author, the secretary of the Wisconsin Association, this booklet was the outgrowth of recommendations made by the HOLC and the Federal Land Bank. These, together with certain large insurance companies, preferred uniform abstracts to suit their own needs. The

---

[3] 244 Ill., 363, 91 N.E. 475, 135 Am. St. Rep. 342.

impetus given by these agencies led the abstracters of Wisconsin to see the advantages of greater uniformity in abstracts for all users. Some other states have followed the example of Wisconsin in encouraging greater uniformity through the trade associations in their area.

In some states abstracters are licensed and bonded. The license requirements may include an examination, to make sure that the applicant has an adequate set of records and is equipped to make a daily takeoff of new material from the records. Where licensing procedure is first used, it customarily includes the usual "grandfather clause," which blankets in those already engaged in the abstract business. In many states there are no license laws for abstracters. Many abstracters hesitate to sponsor license laws for fear they might include too much regulation of their business by public agencies.

Short-Term Abstracts In some cases a practice of using what has come to be known as "short-term" abstracts has sprung up. Suppose, for example, that a plot of ground is being subdivided and that the abstract of title up to the time of subdivision has been so carefully drawn that no attorney or other local interested party will question the title. The abstracts of the lots into which the plot is subdivided begin with the date of the subdivision. Therefore they are called short-term abstracts. They may even serve all local needs quite acceptably. Outside agencies, such as out-of-state insurance companies which may later be called upon to finance a property located in the subdivision, may refuse to base their decisions upon such short-term abstracts. The cost of revising the abstract or of adding to it at a later date may be considerable.

Abstracter's Certificate At the end of the abstract there should be the certificate of the abstracter, showing the nature of his work, the records searched, and the contents of the abstract. If the abstract does not purport to cover some records, that fact should be stated unequivocally. For example, if the certificate states that the records of the county treasurer, the county clerk, the county recorder, and the clerk of the local courts only have been searched, then any loss occasioned by the failure to include any records from the federal court could not be assessed against the abstracter. However, the certificate of the abstracter cannot protect him if it is couched in vague or obscure language. If he certifies that his searches have revealed no encumbrances, this will be interpreted to mean that there are no encumbrances against the property whose title is at stake.

A typical abstract certificate reads as follows:

We hereby certify that the foregoing Abstract of Title, consisting of 116 sections, was collated by us from the records of Franklin County Ohio; and we believe the same contains every instrument of record in said County, in any way affecting the premises described at title page, as shown by the respective indexes to said records.

Legal Opinion of Title A lawyer studies abstracts for the purpose of arriving at an expert opinion of the character of the title. In his study of a specific abstract, the lawyer is generally limited to the evidence presented in the abstract. If it has been carefully compiled and recently brought down to date, any further study of the primary records would disclose no new evidence about the title so far as the records are concerned. The lawyer who renders an opinion about a real estate title is not asked to insure the title. The fee he is paid for examining it will not warrant his assumption of this risk. Based upon his study of the abstract and/or the record, the opinion he gives is his best judgment concerning the character of the title.

The lawyer cannot be expected to take responsibility for any defect in title not disclosed by the records. Any responsibility borne by the lawyer is based upon proof of his negligence or of his lack of professional skill. Either would be difficult to prove. There is always room for honest differences of opinion among competent lawyers on such questions as interpretations of wills and probable outcome of litigation affecting land titles.

Any defects disclosed by the records are likely to be flagged by most lawyers. As a class, lawyers are inclined to be conservative, technical, conscious of criticism resulting from their own errors, and observers of form and precedent. Consequently, in studying the record, they are apt to be attracted by evidence that raises questions about the character of the title. Even in exceptional cases involving negligence or lack of professional skill, the consequences may not show up until it is too late to do anything about it. The lawyer may be dead or unable to make good on any judgment rendered against him.

Scope of Real Estate Law for Title Examination Purposes One skilled in corporation law or the law of domestic relations is not necessarily qualified to pass upon questions involving title to real estate. Real estate law is technical in many respects. But the lawyer who examines an abstract for the purpose of determining the quality of a real estate title may and frequently does encounter questions involving corporation law, bankruptcy, divorce court proceedings, and many other phases of law. On all questions of this nature the abstracter must first decide what is important and significant to be included in the abstract. Then the examining attorney must pass upon the sufficiency and the validity of the actions taken in various types of legal proceedings, many of which affect the field of technical real estate law only indirectly. That is one reason why five lawyers examining the same abstract may find five different sets of objections to the title of the real estate in question. Each in turn may object to something which his predecessor examiners have approved or at least have not raised objections against.

Defects in Records   A survey of 4,190 titles in California[4] showed that 30 percent contained defects of some kind. In the order of frequency of appearance, errors noted covered the following categories: defects in execution; defective descriptions; tax liens and judgments; encumbrances not covered by escrow instructions; and miscellaneous errors, including potential mechanics' liens and defective proceedings of various types. While there was no means of determining which of the above might have resulted in claims which could be asserted and collected, the potential liability in the cases studied exceeded $10 million.

Meaning of Title Insurance   Title insurance does all that both a carefully drawn abstract and a well-considered opinion by a competent lawyer are expected to do. In addition, it adds the principle of insurance to the above services and undertakes to spread the risk of unseen hazards among all who benefit from it. It must start with careful analysis of the records. The plant of the commercial title company may be even more complete than the public records. Then there must be skilled technicians to examine all evidence of the title to determine its character. If the conclusions warrant, the title company will back up its opinion about the title to a given piece of property by assuming the risk that is not disclosed in the records or in its own files.

What title insurance is supposed to add to the abstract system and the opinion of skilled lawyers may be classified as follows: (1) definite contract liability to the premium payer; (2) ample resources to back up this liability; (3) reserves sufficient to meet losses; (4) supervision by an agency of the state in which the title insurance company operates; (5) protection to the policyholder against financial losses that may show up at any future time because of title defects of any kind, disclosed or hidden.

Types of Title Insurance Policies   There are two types of title insurance policies in common use. The owner's policy guarantees that the title is good. In some cases it even insures the title to be marketable. In other words, it can be used to force an unwilling purchaser to accept the title, because it is guaranteed. While the owner's policy does not ordinarily cover the interests of the purchaser, the insurance of title in the name of the owner reduces the probabilities of loss by litigation. The owner's policy is purchased with a single premium which purports to protect the owner and his heirs forever. There is no statute of limitations which outlaws the life of the policy.

The mortgagee policy insures the status of the lien and the mortgage. Since the interest of the mortgagee in the land is terminated when

---

[4] Reported in *Title News* (official publication of the American Title Association), April 1950, p. 13.

his money has been repaid, the mortgagee policy expires when the mortgage is paid off or canceled. If, as a result of foreclosure, the mortgagee becomes the owner of the real estate, the mortgagee policy becomes an owner's policy as of the date of change of title. Because the mortgagee policy is expected to run for a shorter period of time than an owner's policy, it is usually somewhat cheaper.

The risk rate for owners' policies is commonly $3.50 per $1,000 up to $50,000 and becomes progressively lower as the insured amount increases. For amounts over $15,000,000, the rate is $1.25 per $1,000. Mortgage premiums run $2.50 per $1,000 up to $50,000 and become as low as $1 per $1,000 on amounts in excess of $15,000,000. The minimum premium on an owner's policy is $10 and on a mortgage policy, $7.50. These rates prevail in about half the states. In other states and areas special rates apply. These rates are often under the surveillance of the state insurance commission. They tend to be somewhat higher in areas where the loss experience has been bad. Premiums charged are for insurance only and do not cover examination cost, record search, abstract, or closing expenses. In some localities reissues of title insurance policies on the same property, but to different policyholders, are reduced to 50 or 75 percent of the original premium.

It is customary to write two policies on the same property. For example, if A purchases a property for $10,000, he will probably want a title insurance policy for that amount. If he mortgages his property for $5,000 to B, a separate policy for $5,000 will be written to protect B's interest. If the insurance company should pay a loss claim to the mortgagee for his $5,000 interest, the owner's policy would normally be reduced by this amount.

Where an owner's policy and a mortgage policy covering the same property are issued simultaneously, there is some saving in premium. The rates applicable to the owner's policy are the regular owner's rates, but the premium for the mortgage policy is generally a nominal amount, often $7.50, for an insurance coverage not in excess of the owner's policy.

A third type of policy, less common than the other two, should be mentioned. The leasehold policy is written in favor of the lessee to protect his interest in the property during the term of his lease.

Full Coverage Demanded Title insurance companies usually demand that the policy covering the title to a parcel of real estate be written for the full value of the property, in case the owner's policy is used; or for the full amount of the mortgage, in a mortgagee's policy. The reason for insistence upon full coverage is quite obvious. For example, suppose that an owner of a $50,000 property requested a title insurance policy for only $10,000. It is quite probable that any losses that might be suffered would fall within the $10,000. Consequently, the insurance company would, in effect, be giving 100 percent protection but would be collecting a risk premium on only 20 percent of the value of the property.

Binder or Commitment A prospective purchaser of a parcel of real estate may wish to make sure of his status as owner if and when he consummates the purchase. Until he becomes the owner he cannot have the title insured in his name. Likewise, a mortgagee who is approached to make a loan with the real estate as security prefers to know his status before he agrees to make the loan. In either case a binder (called a commitment in some areas) is used to recite the title insurance company's findings concerning the character of the title to the date of the binder. The binder also recites the acts which must be performed and the requirements which must be met before the title insurance policy can be written. When all necessary instruments have been drawn and recorded, the policy will become effective, assuming that no new complications have arisen to create doubts about the character of the title. Usually the time during which the binder takes the place of the policy is short. In unusual cases, such as a delay caused by inability to close a deal because one grantor cannot be easily and quickly located, the time may be longer.

If there are defects in the title which the insurance company insists must be cured before a title policy will be written, they will usually be noted in the binder. In other words, the binder states that the specified defects must be cured and that, when they are so taken care of, the policy will be executed.

Losses under Title Insurance In effect, title insurance consists of two parts: (1) a determination of ascertainable facts about the character of the title before insurance is granted and a willingness to stand behind such determination; and (2) a wager against the happening of an unascertainable event—beyond the control of the insurer and the insured—which will have an adverse effect upon the title. The primary purpose of the insurance company is so to conduct its investigations that no serious question can be left unanswered under the first heading outlined above. This does not mean that absolute perfection of title is insisted upon as a prerequisite to its insurance. Minor irregularities which are not likely to cause serious difficulty are frequently overlooked. If the latter were to be corrected by the insured before title was accepted for insurance, much business would be lost, because the insured would conclude that, if a title must first be perfected in all details, it probably would not need to be insured.

The initial impulse is to consider losses and loss adjustment expenses of title insurance companies quite low when related to premium income. Their reasonableness will become more apparent, however, when the full character of the business is taken into account. For example, a survey by the American Land Title Association Research Committee taken among its membership showed losses and loss adjustment expenses for 1968 and 1969 to be respectively 4.5 and 4.2 percent of premium income. However, total pretax operating results for both years were only 13 percent of gross operating income. By comparison, for the year 1969, 425 industrial companies reported in Standard and Poor's *Analysts Handbook* showed pretax operating profits averaging 15.4 percent, with finance companies reporting 44.8 percent. Furthermore, according to Best's *Aggregates and Averages* for 1969, surety companies had pretax operating profits of 15.5 percent.[5]

The title insurance business deals with risk elimination as well as with risk assumption. The noninsurance services rendered by title insurance companies greatly outweigh the insurance function. If the preliminary work is properly done, the actual insurance underwriting involves a relatively slight chance of liability. The preliminary work, however, is time-consuming and costly. Many writers in the field have likened title insurance to a service with a warranty. The rate charged, therefore, must not be related solely to the risk assumed, but also to the cost of services rendered.

Experience has taught the management of title insurance companies that certain conditions are conducive to a higher loss ratio. For example, examinations made by other than full-time company specialists are usually less reliable. Losses are most frequent during the early years of the policy, since the passage of time seasons the title. Periods of economic distress and accompanying declines in real estate prices prompt more attempts by buyers to escape the bonds of executory contracts by challenging the title; under the same conditions of economic stress, recoveries on mortgage policies are substantially less. The most common cause of loss is negligence on the part of employees or agents making the title examination. Most losses result from failure to discover unpaid taxes, restrictive covenants, easements, and judgments. There have been practically no losses because of an unmarketable title.

Most title insurers take an optimistic attitude toward their loss expectancy. In fact, some companies maintain no reserves at all. As will be noted later, several states have not seen fit to impose reserve requirements. The impact of this policy is somewhat lightened, however, by the practice of reinsurance, which is common in the business where risks the substantial. Some companies, for example, reinsure all risks in excess of $25,000.

In general, direct costs which are charged to losses include the following: (1) Those caused by oversight or negligence on the part of the employees of the insurance company, or by mistakes in the company's records. Among the subjects of such losses are taxes and special assess-

---

[5] John E. Jensen, "Findings of Second Annual ALTA Research Committee," *Title News*, December 1970, p. 6.

ments overlooked or underestimated, followed in order by prior mortgages, judgments, mechanics' liens, and easements. (2) Losses resulting from borderline cases where there may not be a valid claim should it be carried into the courts. Nevertheless, the title insurance company may find it desirable to pay some such claims as a means of building and maintaining goodwill.

Indirect costs arise from the defense, at the expense of the title insurance company, of attacks upon insured titles. Some of these may be brought with honest intent, while others are simply nuisance suits. If it appears that a company will settle one of the latter rather than pursue it in the courts, this company may find that it becomes the victim of numerous suits of this kind.

In a sense, most of the expense of a title insurance company is incurred as an offset against losses. The establishment, improvement, and maintenance of a plant all serve the purpose of minimizing losses. By having access to a complete and dependable record, presumably the insurer can determine better the nature of the risk assumed in any specific case. Without its investment in its plant, more of its decisions would become gambles rather than fact-finding operations. In other words, title insurance is not looked upon as a form of casualty insurance. When a company issues a title policy it does so in the firm belief that, while the character of the title does not make it letter-perfect, it cannot be subject to successful attack. Only the unknowable—the part not covered by the records or the plant of the insurer—is looked upon as a chance-taking procedure. To the extent that examiners and others are made loss conscious, losses should be minimized.

Extra Fees In general, title insurance companies will not insure a title unless they think it is good. Therefore they do not make a practice of charging extra fees to cover unusual hazards. If unusual hazards are present, they must be cleared up before the title will be insured. There are occasional exceptions to this rule. Tax titles are not liked by many insurance companies. When they are presented for insurance, sometimes an extra fee is charged. Likewise, temporary hazards are sometimes compensated for by extra fees. For example, during the depression of the 1930s, many voluntary deeds were given to save foreclosure costs and resulting deficiency judgments. Since there is always a question as to whether a court of equity may frown upon such deeds at a subsequent time, an extra and unmeasurable hazard is created which is sometimes the occasion for an extra fee. Other extra hazards may result from any one of several causes. For example, an unreleased though presumably paid mortgage may cause future trouble.

Expansion of Coverage In areas where title insurance is commonly used, there appears to be developing a tendency to look to the title insurance policy to protect the purchaser of or the lender against real estate from any hazards that might in any manner affect the character of the title. As a result, title insurance in such cases tends to become indemnity insurance as well. The specific hazards which may be covered by such expanded coverage include the following: (1) loss resulting from mechanics' liens; (2) loss resulting from violations—present or prospective—of covenants or conditions which limit the use to which the real estate may be put (included among these covenants and conditions are: [a] those which govern the type and cost of improvements; [b] those which prohibit the manufacture or sale of intoxicating liquors; and [c] setback limitations); (3) loss resulting from improvement encroachments; (4) loss resulting from the presence and use of easements, which use might result in damage to buildings, trees, shrubbery, and so on; and (5) loss resulting from rights of tenants holding property under unrecorded leases, including rent prepayments.

Lenders rather than owners are responsible for the tendency toward expansion of coverage of title insurance policies. This is an outgrowth of the increased marketability of real estate mortgages. If a lender in one section of the country purchases a mortgage on real estate located in a different section, it is natural to expect the lender to seek all possible protection against future potential losses; hence the urge to expand the liabilities placed upon the title company.

Meeting Added Hazards In cases where the expanded coverage of title insurance policies—by the use of riders covering the added risks discussed in the preceding section—creates added burdens for the title insurance companies, means are sometimes used to minimize the risks. For example, to protect against losses resulting from mechanics' liens, the title insurance company may take over some of the functions of the lender. It may insist upon paying out the funds provided by the lender. In this manner it can follow prudent practices in making sure that all bills are paid to the proper people, thus avoiding the possibility of losses resulting from mechanics' liens. In such case the title insurance company would assume the responsibility of checking all subcontract bids against the plans and specifications to make sure that the money supplied by the lender, plus the equity funds provided by the owner, will be sufficient to pay all costs of construction. Such service takes the title insurance company far afield from the business of strict title insurance but helps to get business that might otherwise go to competitors.

To protect title insurance companies against possible losses due to reversions, various plans are followed. One plan that has gained some popularity is to require the mortgagor to deed his property to a trustee who in turn leases it to the mortgagor. The lease contains a cancellation clause which may become effective immediately upon the violation of any of the lease terms, such as a prohibition against the manufacture or sale of intoxicating liquor. By invoking such a cancellation clause, the trustee could effectively prevent loss to the title insurance company. The lease would bind not only the original mortgagor but all grantees who hold under him.

Abstract versus Title Insurance In attempting to compare the time it takes to determine the quality of a real estate title by the abstract system with that it takes under the title insurance system, a wide variety of practices is encountered. If no abstract exists, a record of title down to date must be compiled in either event. The more complete records normally kept by title insurance companies should favor them, so far as the time element is concerned. Furthermore, the title insurance company probably has more personnel capable of putting together the material needed. In case an abstract already exists, the process of continuation should again favor the title insurance company, so far as time taken to arrive at a decision concerning the quality of title is concerned. If the records of the plant are reasonably complete, a decision should be reached quickly.

While the abstractor also may have a set of records to work from, his continuation of an abstract is only the first step in the process of determining title. Once the abstract is continued, it is turned over to an examiner who may not be able to give it immediate attention. Time is lost which would probably not be taken up by the insurance company. Then the practices of the examiner must be taken into account. If he insists upon reexamining all the abstract—from the first transfer of title from the government down to date—he will probably consume more time than the insurance company will use in reaching a decision about the title. The latter will probably use as a starting point the date of the latest previous insurance policy.

On the other hand, if the examiner of the abstract also takes for granted that the latest previous examination was complete and accurate, he may pay attention only to the tail sheets, thus economizing time in his examination. By this means it is possible for an abstract to be continued and to be examined within about the same time limit as that used by the title insurance company.

Influence of Large Investors The trend toward nationalizing the market for real estate mortgages has had its effect upon the increasing demand for real estate title insurance. Any absentee owner of a mortgage prefers to play safe by asking that titles to real estate on which he holds titles be insured. Large institutional investors recognize that the greatest risk assumed in the acquisition of federally underwritten real estate mortgages may be in the mortgagor's title. Government insurance is conditioned upon the ultimate ability of the approved mortgagee to offer, in exchange for the government debentures for which the law provides, a foreclosed title satisfactory to the FHA. This condition, in effect, requires of investors in FHA mortgages that they have positive assurance of a good and marketable title, for any less may result in the nullification of the government insurance upon which the investors depend for protection in event of the mortgagor's delinquency. In general, only with title insurance does the investor have positive protection against financial loss because of unmarketability of titles and indemnification for losses in event the FHA declines to accept titles for causes which can be amply covered in an insurance policy. Investing in mortgages without title insurance protection involves an assumption that the mortgagee, or his assignee, will be able to obtain government debentures in exchange for foreclosed properties; but, too late, the investor may discover that his assumption is false. For these reasons, most corporate investors regard federally underwritten loans as safer when the title is insured. The secondary market for these loans, therefore, is also a primary title insurance market. Life insurance companies, savings banks, savings and loan associations, and commercial banks almost always require title insurance in these circumstances. A similar practice is followed by the Federal National Mortgage Association. Although neither the FHA nor the VA insists upon title insurance as a prerequisite to federal underwriting of mortgages, even small institutional lenders, including local banks and savings and loan associations, may require title insurance if they contemplate resale of a mortgage in the national market. While abstracts may satisfy local needs, title insurance will probably produce a more ready sale should the holder of the mortgage wish to dispose of it later.

Government Regulation of Title Insurance Companies Experiences of the 1930s took a heavy toll of title insurance companies along with many others. Relative freedom from regulation by governmental authorities was a contributing factor. In recent years, however, in the wake of the *South-Eastern Underwriters* case,[6] which held that insurance transactions across state lines were subject to federal regulation, the states have greatly extended their interest in all insurance companies. This was motivated by the expressed congressional policy that regulation of insurance companies at the state level is in the public interest, but if the states do not meet their responsibilities in this regard the Congress will fill the void.[7] The state legislation has had several major effects beyond forestalling federal entry into the field. Many of the provisions are directed at assuring the financial ability of the insurance companies to meet loss claims. Several states require title insurers to fund reserves with a state agency as a condition of doing business. Restrictions on investments and minimum reserve and capital requirements are imposed in some cases. Some states require reinsurance under certain conditions.

---

[6] *United States v South-Eastern Underwriters Association*, 322 U.S. 533 (1944).

[7] Public Law No. 15 (79th Cong., 1st sess., approved March 9, 1945.)

In some instances, the state statute may have the effect of preserving monopolistic advantages. These advantages have been preserved by requiring extremely high deposits with the state to do business in a certain area (as a minimum of $50,000 to operate in Cook County, Illinois), or by limiting the type of business which may be done (possibly excluding business in any other form of insurance), or by setting high minimum standards for the title plant. As to rate regulations, most statutes simply require that rates be reasonable and nondiscriminatory. Rate schedules and policy forms must generally be filed with the state insurance commission and are subject to commission disapproval.[8]

Title insurance companies generally must file annual reports with their state regulatory agency and are subject to audit. Texas and New York, in particular, carry out extensive audit programs for title insurers. Other states generally have not been concerned to any major degree about the compliance of title insurance companies.

The present situation suggests that there may be substantial dangers in uncritical reliance on the ability of all title insurance companies to meet their full liabilities. One danger lies in the fact that state policies governing the deposit of funds with the state or providing for the establishment of company reserves are generally without any actuarial basis As previously stated in connection with the discussion of loss experience, many companies carry no reserve for the payment of loss claims. The "Model Title Insurance Code" developed in the mid-1960s by the American Land Title Association prescribed for reserves in considerable detail. Since that time, several states have established codes for the regulation of title insurance where none previously existed and other states have revised existing statutory provisions. Deposit requirements now vary from none whatever to up to 40 percent of aggregate capital. The statutes generally also require unearned premium reserves, ranging from as high as 10 percent to as low as 3 percent of the premium charge for the policy. By common practice, the unearned premium reserve is maintained for 20 years, with a 5 percent recovery to income each year. Experience has shown, however, that as much as 80 percent of losses on title insurance usually occur during the first five years the policy is in existence. This suggests that the bulk of the premiums are earned during the first five years, and some states, like California, have set their reserve adjustment policies to take this into account.[9] With considerable irregularity in the regulation of company reserve requirements and the lackadaisical attitude toward audit and other forms of supervision which is evident in many states, the possibility that some companies may find themselves in difficulty at a later date must be the

---

[8] Johnstone, "Title Insurance," pp. 510–11.

[9] William H. Deatly, "Solvency Aspects of Title Insurance Regulation," *Title News*, June 1969, pp. 25–30.

concern of any purchaser of title insurance. Since the insurance cannot be better than the insurer, consideration of the financial status of the title insurance company is indicated as a proper procedure for any purchaser of this kind of protection.

Exceptions Since the title insurance policy is a contract between the insurer and the insured, it may contain such terms and conditions as are agreed upon between the contracting parties. Consequently, any exceptions become matters of great importance. They should be plainly stated in such manner as to make them clear to all concerned. Among the exceptions most commonly found in title insurance policies are: (1) the rights of tenants or others in possession of the property, which are not matters of record and which are not ordinarily found in the plant of the insurance company; (2) any questions which may arise on account of easements, party walls, encroachments, and those that might be disclosed by a survey of the property whose title is insured; (3) laws, government acts, or regulations, including zoning ordinances, restrictions governing use and occupancy of the property, and so on; (4) current taxes and assessments; (5) unrecorded liens; and (6) special conditions which may apply to a particular title and be written into the policy insuring it.

While there is a tendency to standardize title insurance policies, exceptions are frequently subject to bargaining and adjustment. If the insurance company thinks it runs little risk in so doing it may agree to eliminate some restriction or exception to which the prospective policyholder makes strenuous objection. In other cases, a survey of the property as a condition of insurance will usually result in the elimination of the survey exception.

Surveys One important feature of real estate financing that is frequently overlooked is the need for an accurate survey of the property to be financed. Before a mortgage loan is disbursed, it may be desirable to make sure that it is protected by the right property as security. Surveys serve other purposes also. For example, should a request for a partial release of security be presented at any time, a survey will show whether the remaining security is what it is supposed to be. Easements can scarcely be granted safely without a survey. Finally, if the mortgage should for any reason become involved in court proceedings, a survey is almost essential before decisions can be relied upon.

Errors sometimes discovered by surveys include the following: (1) The building which affords the chief security for the mortgage loan may not even be located on the land described in the title. It may be on an adjoining lot instead. (2) Buildings, particularly garages, encroach upon adjacent lots and even upon alleys and streets. (3) Buildings on adjacent lots encroach upon the land described in the title to the property being financed. (4) There may be a material surplus or deficiency of land or its measurements as described in the title. (5) While the building may be located on the proper lot, it may be so situated as to violate setback lines prescribed in the title. (6) Easements may be improperly located or improperly used. (7) Conveyances may not properly describe the property intended to be used as security for the mortgage loan.

Once a proper survey is conducted by a competent engineer or surveyor and a map is submitted by him as evidence of his findings, the next step is to determine what, if anything, is to be done about his findings. If no irregularities are found and if the survey conforms in all respects to the title to the land, so much the better. If inconsequential irregularities are found, they may be disregarded by the lending institution. In some cases it may be best to insist upon corrections before mortgage funds are disbursed. Finally, in some instances, admittedly small in number, the findings of the survey may cause the lending institution to refuse to make the loan.

Surveys of commercial and industrial real estate which is offered as security for mortgage loans are generally more imperative than surveys of residential property. This is true for two reasons. In the first place, much greater amounts of money are usually involved, so that the risk of a mistake is correspondingly greater. In the second place, much more of the land area—even up to 100 percent—is covered by the building. As a result, encroachments upon adjoining property are much more common. Where encroachment consists only of use for flower beds, hedges, and so forth, corrections are easily made. Even secondary buildings such as garages can be moved if necessary. But the encroachment of a major building is much more serious. It cannot be moved if it covers 100 percent plus of the land area it is expected to occupy. Its owner may be forced to purchase the "plus" area, perhaps at a holdup price.

Use of Escrow By "escrow" is meant the use of an impartial third person to represent all parties to a contract in such manner that the contract will be observed without deviation. Escrow can be used with many types of business relations. In the field of real estate it is primarily concerned with closing of title transfers, or placing of mortgages, or both. If the first of these two only is present, the term commonly used to describe the use of the third party is "deed and money escrow." If the second only is present, the term used is "moneylender's escrow."

In the latter case, the mortgagor deposits with the escrow agent the mortgage, properly executed in the name of the mortgagee. The mortgagee deposits with the same agent the money to be lent to the mortgagor. When this agent has satisfied himself that the mortgage represents a valid first lien and that the mortgagee's check is good, he disburses the money according to his instructions and directs that the mortgage, after it is recorded, shall be turned over to the mortgagee. In like manner the use of escrow could serve holders of junior liens as well as those of senior liens. It is particularly desirable to use escrow when the new mortgage produces the means of paying off an existing mortgage, mechanics' liens, a judgment, an accumulation of taxes and assessments, or any other kind of encumbrance against the property.

In the above cases escrow involves only two parties—the mortgagor and the mortgagee. It could involve any number. For example, when A sells property to B, B may see fit to finance his purchase by a loan from C, which he uses to pay off a mortgage due D. In such a case one escrow agent can well represent all four parties, receiving from each the money or legal papers which he should contribute and delivering to each whatever he is entitled to receive in closing the sale and financing the property.

In what is commonly spoken of as a "profit" escrow, it is possible for a real estate operator to make a profit for himself without the investment of his own funds. Suppose, for example, that A contracts to purchase property from B and in turn makes a deal to sell the same property to C at a higher price. By the use of a double escrow, B obtains the price due him, C obtains title to and possession of the property, and A takes his profit without the investment of his own funds. Indeed he can take his profit without having his name appear upon a deed either as grantee or as grantor.

In some cases several properties may be included in a profit escrow, each of which is finally deeded to a different ultimate purchaser. Existing mortgages may be paid off and new ones placed against the properties. Regardless of the complications involved in such deals, escrow arrangments can be made to cover them without confusion and to work to the satisfaction of all parties concerned. These are commonly known as concurrent escrows.

The escrow agent, or escrow holder as he is sometimes called, is supposed to be not only an impartial third party but one experienced in handling arrangements of the kind that require his services. In fulfilling his obligations to both parties to a real estate transaction, he should know what to look for and where to find it in the records. Sometimes it is contended that when an escrow agent is used there is less likelihood that one party or the other can upset a deal by refusing to see it to a conclusion. In practice, however, the use of escrow is surrounded by about the same amount of mutual confidence as any other arrangement for closing real estate deals. Escrow is not a substitute for honesty or a complete meeting of minds. These are presumed to be present in the use of escrow agents. The use of elaborate escrow contracts, sometimes in printed form, which are signed by both parties, does not invalidate what is said above. Nevertheless, escrow is supposed to establish some relationships that are more difficult to break than if escrow arrangements are not used. For example, an escrow in mortgage financing gives the assurance to a borrower that he can get the agreed-upon loan if the title to his property is good.

Probate Escrows When an owner of real estate dies, his property passes to the devisees named in his will—or to his heirs, in case the owner dies without leaving a will. In any event, the probate of the estate takes time and involves expenses such as the payment of the debts of the decedent and of estate and inheritance taxes. In case the will is contested, or in case other complications delay the settlement of the estate, a good market for the disposal of the real estate may be missed. Through the use of escrow, the property may be sold immediately, with the proceeds held by the escrow agent until the estate is closed and all obligations have been met. The remainder is then distributed to those entitled to receive it. The purchaser of the property is protected against taxes, expenses, or the consequences of a will contest. Meantime, if it appears that the final settlement of the estate may be deferred for a year or more, it may be desirable for the court to authorize the escrow agent to invest the funds held by him in a manner to provide safety and liquidity and at the same time to produce some return.

QUESTIONS AND PROBLEMS

1. What is an abstract of title?
2. How does an attorney's opinion or certificate that a title is good, based on review of an abstract, differ in effect from title insurance?
3. What is the Torrens system, and why is it not more widely used?
4. An abstract will not disclose several hidden title hazards. List as many of these hazards as you can.
5. What is the legal responsibility of an attorney for an opinion which he has rendered stating that he considered the title good and unencumbered when it later appears that the title was defective when the opinion was given?
6. In what ways does title insurance render benefits which are not available to a person relying solely on the abstract system and an attorney's opinion?
7. What types of title insurance policies are in common use?
8. What is the loss experience of title insurance companies? How does it differ from that of most insurance companies?
9. How has nationalizing the market for real estate mortgages affected the title insurance business?
10. What exceptions are commonly found in title insurance policies?
11. Do you see any dangers in the manner in which title insurance companies are presently regulated by state authorities? Do you have any suggestions for improvement?
12. How may an escrow agent be utilized as a means of protecting the title in a real estate transaction? Give examples.

20

Mortgage Loan Servicing

What It Is Not A great many people—including some who are engaged in the mortgage business—have little conception of the meaning of mortgage loan servicing. In answer to an inquiry on the subject, they frequently respond in such a manner as to indicate that they think the acceptance of a payment on a loan at the teller's window or the cashing of a check sent in by mail covers the subject. When all goes well with the borrower and he meets all obligations on time, his loan might well be classified as self-servicing. Even here the troubles of the mortgagee may not be completely lacking, as will be shown later in this chapter.

Nor does it follow that all small mortgages are trouble-free. As pointed out elsewhere in this text, mortgagees are not interested in making loans that merely qualify as safe loans. They want to make sure that they are sound loans as well. Even though the value of the security behind a small loan is sufficient to protect the mortgagee in case of foreclosure, this does not mean that the servicing of the loan will not be expensive before foreclosure is resorted to. In most instances, mortgagees will use every available means to assist the mortgagor to keep his property, even at considerable unrecoverable expense if necessary.

It is the larger loans that cause the most trouble. Even with a larger allowance for mortgage loan servicing costs, the amounts available for this purpose may not be sufficient to protect the mortgagee against loss when trouble develops. The theological approach to the subject of loan servicing may have served fairly well in the past. The more successful mortgage lender of the future will probably base his operations in this area upon something more tangible than blind faith that the mortgagor will meet his obligations.

Purposes of Mortgage Loan Servicing A fair synonym for "loan servicing" is "loan collection." By this is meant the recovery of the amounts advanced to the borrower, according to the terms of the instrument which evidences the loan, or as nearly in conformity thereto as the circumstances will permit. Mortgage loan servicing should not mean merely collecting the amounts due the lender at the expense of the borrower. Proper loan-servicing plans protect the interests of the borrower while trying to collect the amounts due to the lender. When a lending institution becomes a party to a contract which commits an inexperienced borrower to repay a loan, it can hardly be assumed that any difficulties encountered by the borrower in meeting his obligations are solely the affair of the borrower.

All real estate mortgage lenders have a dual obligation to meet. In most instances, those who make decisions for the lending institution are acting as trustees for funds owned by people of modest means. Consequently, as trustees, the managers of such institutions are bound to take every reasonable precaution to make sure that funds advanced on mortgage security will be repaid. At the same time, such institutions have a correlative obligation to protect the interests of those whom they encourage to borrow money. They are not Shylocks and do not act as if they were. In order to maintain the proper margin of safety to protect the interests of those whose funds are advanced to borrowers and, at the same time, to give equal protection to those who use these funds in financing their real estate purchases, loan servicing must cover a broader scope of operations than is customarily considered by many lending institutions.

Or, stated in another way, the purpose of loan servicing is to keep a good loan in good standing. Assuming that it was a proper loan to make when it was executed, it is the function of the loan-servicing department to make sure that it does not change its character for the worse. It is possible for good loan servicing to make weak loans stronger. Experience has demonstrated many times that careless servicing of mortgage loans will result in making weak loans out of strong ones.

A mortgage loan servicing policy must have a desirable attainable objective and must pursue methods that most nearly conform to the fulfillment of the purposes established. Neither leniency at one time nor toughness at another is likely to indicate consistency or to produce the kind of results expected in the long run. Whatever is done at any time concerning any mortgage loan should be in keeping with a policy which antedated the action and which the borrower should have understood fully at the time he made the loan.

Delinquency Prevention Prevention of delinquency in mortgages is much less expensive than attempting to put out the fire after it has acquired a good start. It is not always possible to prevent mortgage delinquency. Much more can be done in this direction than is being done at present. The place to start the prevention of delinquency is in the making of the loan. Many real estate purchases are based upon emotional rather than logical considerations. If the lending institution becomes a party to a loan which the inexperienced borrower cannot carry comfortably, trouble is invited. The loan-servicing machinery should be put in order at the time such a loan is made, because it will probably be called into action soon thereafter. It is no kindness for the lender to grant a loan which he feels sure will become a case for loan servicing on an emergency basis. The applicant should be discouraged from making such a loan, even though the lender feels that it is a safe loan so far as the lender is concerned.

Once a loan is made, the lender should not wait until a default occurs in meeting, or failing to meet, a payment on it. Many lenders develop the confidence of their borrowers to the point that if one finds that, for any reason, he is likely to encounter difficulty in meeting his financial obligations, he will consult his mortgage lender for advice. Even before a default occurs, something may be done to prevent it. Some borrowers have even consulted friendly mortgage lenders on subjects that are non-financial in character but which may nevertheless develop into trouble that will be reflected in subsequent mortgage delinquency.

Pride of ownership has probably induced most real estate mortgage borrowers to make commitments for loans. Once this pride diminishes or disappears, trouble is probably brewing. A casual inspection of the property on which a nondelinquent loan is outstanding may anticipate and probably prevent a delinquency in many instances. If a drive past the security for a mortgage loan produces evidence of waste or neglect, a more careful inspection is suggested. Since most mortgage operations provide for inspections at the will of the mortgagee, the excuse given for the inspection may be that it is merely a routine visit. If such an inspection shows that the property is not being properly maintained, a visit with the borrower may result in corrective measures that will keep the loan out of the delinquent mortgage servicing department. At least the visit should develop the attitude of the borrower and place the lender on guard about the next step to be taken by him. If the borrower is beginning to encounter financial trouble, something may be done, through the advice of the more experienced lender, that will help to cure the situation before it is too late.

Reappraisal of Property As a part of the inspection routine, or at least as an accompaniment to it if the more careful inspection is indicated, it is a pretty good policy to reappraise the property in the light of its changed condition and in the light of current economic conditions. Such a reappraisal will give the lending institution a better and more up-to-date impression of its position in comparing the current loan balance with the current value of the security behind the loan. To be sure, such a reappraisal will cost money which probably cannot be assessed against the borrower, as the cost of the original appraisal probably was. But it may save much more in the long run. In any event, it is a proper part of the loan-servicing process.

If such a reappraisal indicates a marked decline in the value of the property, there may be no great cause for concern if other real estate of a similar character has declined in about the same ratio. It is the unusual decline in value, caused by waste and neglect, that may give rise to most trouble for the lender. Meantime, the borrower may not be aware of the extent of the value decline. There will probably be little occasion to discuss this subject with him. The results of inspections are frequently brought to his attention, together with suggestions for making indicated corrections. The inspector may even find it desirable to recommend additional advances by the lender, both for the protection of the loan and for the assistance they may render to the borrower.

Some lending institutions direct occasional inspections and reappraisals of properties serving all of their loans whether or not there is any suspicion of approaching trouble. If it is the policy of the lender to make such inspections, to be followed by reappraisals if needed, no question is likely to be raised by any borrower at the time his property is visited. If necessary, someone at the property may be told that a routine inspection is part of the service which the lender supplies the borrower occasionally. As pointed out elsewhere in this text, such an inspection may be the forerunner of a new advance by the borrower to pay the costs of repairs, maintenance, or a modernization program. If the loan is in good standing at the time the inspection is made, the inspector may help sell a modernization loan.

Reappraisal of Mortgagor At the time a loan is granted, the moral hazard is investigated. It is being given increasing weight in reaching decisions about mortgage loan applications. But this feature of loan security, like the value of the property, may be subject to change. If it should deteriorate for any reason, the lender may face the consequences in future delinquencies. Not only should the lender know about the habits of the borrower at the time the loan is granted, but he should be alert to detect any adverse change later. Whenever a borrower pursues spending habits that result in living beyond his means, some creditor will suffer. More likely than not, all creditors, including the mortgage lender, will suffer. When a person is financially involved, it is not easy for even secured creditors to enjoy full protection as long as other claims go unsatisfied.

If the mortgage lender discovers changes for the worse in the spending habits of a borrower, or if this subject was not sufficiently studied when the loan was granted and subsequent information uncovers disturbing facts, a conference with the borrower is advisable. Perhaps corrections can be made in spending habits before it is too late. In any event, a friendly but revealing approach to the borrower, tactfully handled, can scarcely do harm. It might do much good. Even though the borrower might resent such an approach at the time it is made, he deserves the note of caution it should carry. If he does not change his habits as a result of such an interview, he will at least know that the lender is aware of the situation and that his account will be subject to continuous scrutiny in the future. This may have a sobering effect upon him.

Rapid Turnover of Loans May Be Misleading Some lending institutions are lulled into a false sense of security by the rapid turnover of the loans in their portfolio. Because borrowers are taking advantage of prepayment privileges and liquidating their loans before they would normally mature, it does not always follow that the portfolio is becoming more secure. On the contrary, if loans are being paid off from the proceeds of larger loans—either by the same or new borrowers—the opposite tendency may be developing. It is common in a period of prosperity for small, seasoned loans to be replaced by larger, unseasoned loans, frequently granted to less responsible borrowers. Higher prices of real estate, accompanied by higher percentage loans to those with smaller capital accumulations, account for this change.

Indeed, it is particularly in periods of prosperity, when optimism rules the decisions of both borrowers and lenders, that the seeds of later loan-servicing trouble are sown most widely. Unless extraordinary care is exercised at such times, problem loans may be made without recognition at the time. Curiously enough, loans made in periods of depression cause less trouble than those made in prosperous times. The reasons for this fact are obvious. Prices are lower and will probably advance from low levels of depression years, thus increasing the margin of safety for the lender. Likewise, incomes will probably increase, making it easier for the borrower to meet his obligations. Only those with capital will ask or receive loan assistance. The slow turnover of loans in times of depression is not necessarily a cause for concern to the lending institution.

Loan Insurance and Guarantee Loans insured by the FHA or guaranteed by the VA are not necessarily free from servicing problems. On the contrary, it is probable that many such loans were made by their lenders with less than normal attention to the problems of future loan servicing. If guaranteed or insured loans are made because of the guarantee or insurance, and particularly if they would not have been granted otherwise, trouble may develop. While neither the FHA nor the VA would intentionally sanction a loan which it considered too heavy for the borrower to carry, there is a tendency on the part of some lending institutions to assume that they have shifted their loan-servicing problems to a governmental agency when they make insured and guaranteed loans. This is not the case.

The major purpose of these governmental agencies is to be of service to the borrower. If the borrower could have obtained liberal loans without insurance or guarantee of his mortgage, there would probably never have been either an FHA or a VA lending program. Because sufficiently liberal loans were not available, these agencies were developed. Since their interest is primarily centered in assistance to the borrower, neither the VA or the FHA will permit the borrower to lose his property by foreclosure of the mortgage until every reasonable effort at the solution of his financial difficulties has been made. This means loan servicing by the mortgagee.

Furthermore, much of the cost of loan servicing, even where loans are insured or guaranteed, is not recoverable from the borrower or from a governmental agency. While the principal of the loan and the delinquent interest are intended to be recoverable, the costs of working out programs of forbearance and adjustment are not.

In general, the safety but not the soundness of such loans is insured or guaranteed. This is accepted as a part of the program. For example, when a mortgagee makes a guaranteed loan to a veteran, it must satisfy itself that the borrower's income, present and prospective, is sufficient to meet the carrying charges of the loan. In other words, the burden of the soundness of the loan is not shifted to the VA. In time of crisis, the VA does not undertake to make loan payments continuously, thus keeping the loan account alive on the books of the lender. While this may be done on a temporary basis, sooner or later the degree of safety of the loan will be demonstrated when foreclosure proceedings are directed, to be followed by indemnification of the lender on account of lost principal and delinquent interest.

Mortgage Files A real estate mortgage is not the type of investment, if indeed there are any such in modern times, which may be tucked away some place in the files until the mortgagee is surprised someday to find that it has a loan-servicing case on hand. Even though the mortgage is properly filed in a safe place, the mortgagor's file must be kept handy where it can be reached readily by members of the loan service department. In it there should be a complete and accurate loan application; an equally complete and accurate appraisal report; a credit report together with all other information collected about the loan applicant and the members of his household; inspection reports made from time to time by a representative of the lender; any reappraisal reports that have been made; an up-to-date record of the status of taxes against the property; a similar record of the kinds and amounts of insurance against the property, together with the expiration date of each policy;

and any miscellaneous information about the borrower which may be possessed by the lender. In the latter category even local newspaper clippings may prove useful to the loan-servicing department if they are available at the right time.

Like many other business records, the mortgage file may appear to occupy valuable space which could properly be used to better advantage for other purposes. But once the loan-servicing department is called upon to handle a problem case, it needs all the information available as the basis of its decisions. Not infrequently a careful review of the mortgage file, including a rereading of the loan application and the appraisal report, will supply the key to the solution of the problem. Whether such a review suggests that the loan should never have been made is more or less beside the point. The loan has been made and is now delinquent. The mortgage file is studied as an aid to the discovery of the means necessary either to repair the delinquency or to find some other remedy.

Even before a loan becomes delinquent, the mortgage file should be a useful tool in the hands of the loan-servicing department. As indicated above, the prevention of delinquency pays better dividends than its cure. If the loan-servicing job is to be accepted as a continuous assignment, rather than as an emergency operation to be undertaken only when a crisis occurs, frequent use of the mortgage file will probably be called for. A review of what happened in previous instances when the mortgagor needed a little leeway in meeting his payments will help to establish the pattern of a proper answer to a subsequent request for a brief moratorium or some other type of adjustment. Not all mortgagors are expected to pay every installment on the dot. If they did, the operation of the loan-servicing department would be dull indeed. Nor is a late or missed payment a matter to be ignored. Instead, it rings a bell that should be heeded at once. The kind of response it should receive is frequently found in the mortgage file.

Larger institutional lenders may take advantage of the tremendous progress that has been made in recent years in filing and account status verification by electronic methods. Computers accept information indexed in a console keyboard or punched in paper tape, as well as the information recorded on magnetic ledger cards, and they process information under the control of programs fed into their magnetic core memory units. Output information can be printed on paper or punched in paper tape. For purposes of servicing mortgage loans, information on each customer is recorded on magnetic strips, paper tape or cards, so as to be usable by the computer. Account number, payment due date, interest rate, monthly payment, unpaid balance, date paid to, area code, appraisal, and other pertinent information make early detection of loan delinquency or other irregularity more readily possible.

Furthermore, use of computers radically cuts back the space requirements for mortgage files.

Collections As stated above, a fair definition of the purpose of mortgage loan servicing is to get back the money advanced to the borrower plus the amounts due in the form of interest or otherwise. At the time the loan was made, the borrower promised to make payments in amounts and at times specified in the agreement. For good loan-servicing purposes both the timing and the amounts should best suit the convenience of the borrower. If the amounts exceed his debt-paying capacity, the loan should not be made. If he can meet his monthly payment as of the 15th day of the month more conveniently than on the first day, there appears no compelling reason why he should not pay on the 15th.

Failure of the borrower to pay on the day fixed in the contract constitutes a breach of contract. What follows such a breach is not always clear. Some lenders prefer to get in touch with the borrower as soon as the payment is even one day delinquent. Others allow a few days of grace, thinking perhaps the payment date has been overlooked. As a means of minimizing this possibility, some lenders consistently send out notices of payment dates, to reach the borrower a few days in advance of his obligation date. Others prefer not to send due notices, at least for loans payable monthly. Whatever policy is adopted by a particular lender, it should be followed consistently. The head of the loan-servicing department should be kept informed of all infractions of payment dates. At the time he is notified of a delinquency he should be given a complete briefing of the amount, the nature of the delinquency, a list of all currently delinquent payments, and an experience statement concerning the past practices of the borrower.

The latter is particularly important. If, during the three and a half years the loan has been on the books, there has never before been even a late payment, the action taken should certainly follow a different path than for a borrower who is chronically delinquent. In the former case, informality and the assumption that a reminder is all that is needed to correct the delinquency are indicated. For the chronic delinquent, more heroic measures will need to be taken sooner or later.

First Default In case an informal reminder fails to produce immediate results when the first default occurs, it is essential that the borrower be contacted personally by the loan service department without delay. The attitude of the lender at this time may set a pattern of future dealings with the borrower that may be hard to change. If possible, the borrower should be induced to come in for an interview. Failing in this, a telephone call may be used. The attitude of the loan-servicing agent should be friendly but firm. The purpose of the interview should be to obtain an answer to the question "Why?" An answer—not an alibi—is called for. From the attitude as well as the conversation of the borrower, the loan service agent must discover, if possible, the real reason for the delinquency.

As soon as the reason for the default becomes apparent, the method of taking care of it should be worked out. If the reason is satisfactory to the loan service agent, there still exists a default, and a plan for taking care of it should be agreed upon. It is essential that such a plan be clearly understood by the borrower and that it be within his reasonable capacity to meet, in the light of his other obligations. If he falls behind in his payment on his mortgage loan, he is probably involved financially elsewhere as well. These other obligations should be discovered by the lending institution so that they may be taken into account in any plan of taking care of a delinquency in mortgage payments. Perhaps the borrower needs some friendly advice, coupled with an education about family budgets.

In dealing with such a borrower, a "get-tough" policy on the occasion of the first default is unwise. It is sure to accomplish one undesired result. It will undoubtedly arouse and probably merit the antagonism of the borrower. It may not produce any money. Nor will a plan of catching up on the delinquency which the borrower cannot hope to meet be advisable. Once the lender has all the facts, he may decide to forget the current payment as well as a few future payments. That will simply postpone the maturity of the loan. Such a plan may best meet the needs of the borrower and best protect the interests of the lender. No solution can be found until the problem is fully understood. Then it should fit the problem.

If, instead of finding that the borrower has a satisfactory reason for missing his payment, the loan service agent discovers that the borrower is facing domestic difficulties, is squandering his income, has lost interest in his property, or by his attitude shows that he does not intend to keep up his payments, then a different approach must be taken. On the face of it, this looks like a situation that promises real trouble. At least the lender must plan quick action. He faces two alternatives:

1. He may disregard the interests of the borrower and take whatever steps are necessary to protect his investment in the mortgage. This is the easy path to follow. It is sanctioned by law and hallowed by custom. If the borrower has been willfully negligent in disregarding his obligations to the lender, there will be none to stay the hand of the sheriff in sustaining the lender's right to demand that the letter of the mortgage contract be lived up to.

2. The alternative plan is more difficult to execute. At the time the loan was granted the lender perhaps did the borrower a favor. But that was not the motivating force that dictated the decision to make the loan. The lender made it because he saw an advantage to himself in lending the money. He probably played a major part in "selling"

the borrower upon the desirability of taking the loan. In doing so he failed to gauge properly one or more major weaknesses possessed by the borrower. On the first default, therefore, the lender may see fit to share the blame with the borrower and use his broader perspective, longer experience in financial affairs, and generally riper judgment to help the borrower solve his problems. This is the harder course to follow. Even if it produces a successful conclusion, the lender runs the risk that the results will be only temporary and that the borrower will soon be in difficulty again.

The lender has no legal obligation to go beyond the letter of the contract in dealing with the borrower. If our system of free enterprise is superior to the economic system of other countries, however, it is only because all, rather than a few, share its benefits. Those of us who believe in it wholeheartedly feel that we can make sure that more people share the benefits by helping those in financial difficulties with friendly advice and counsel. In keeping with this philosophy, the lender probably has a strong moral obligation at least to try to help any delinquent borrower to solve his financial problems on the occasion of the first default. It is not only good morals but it is good business for him to do so.

Whatever the cause of the first default and whatever the attitude of the borrower concerning his unpaid obligation, the first default on a mortgage is an event that should not be passed over lightly by the mortgagee. He should take prompt action to learn the cause of the default. The information which he receives will guide his future action. That is why complete and accurate information about the first default is of such great significance.

Taxes One of the causes of loan delinquency is the semiannual tax bill which the borrower has probably not made specific provision to meet. Those lending institutions which collect a pro rata proportion of annual taxes (and assessments, if any) with each regular payment on the loan have two advantages: (1) They help the borrower to budget his tax obligations on a monthly instead of on a semiannual basis. Most borrowers can do a better job with a monthly instead of a semiannual budget. (2) The lender has direct control over the payment of the taxes. From his own records he knows at all times the exact status of the loan, taxwise.

Where taxes are not so collected from the borrower as a part of monthly payments, the lender will wish to know the status of tax payments by the borrower. Some require borrowers to bring in their tax receipts. These are usually reliable and can usually be used to make up the tax file of the lender. Where such receipts are not submitted by the borrower and where for any reason they are open to question, a search of the records will be required to supplement the information needed to complete the files.

When taxes are found to be delinquent, the lender will be expected to take action in two directions—to get back taxes paid, and, if possible, perhaps to change the system of paying them. Mortgages usually give the lender the right to pay taxes and to charge the amounts so paid to the account of the borrower. To avoid penalties, the taxes should be so paid before they become delinquent. That is why a tax-delinquent borrower may be asked to have the lender pay them the next time to avoid delinquency. Since real estate taxes constitute a prior lien taking precedence over a mortgage, no mortgagee will tolerate continuously delinquent taxes.

If delinquent taxes are paid by the lender and if arrangements are made by which the lender will advance the funds to pay future taxes also, some plan of collecting the amounts from the borrower will follow. Either monthly payments may be increased for this purpose, or the borrower will be expected to make a lump-sum payment to cover taxes, in addition to regular payments on the loan. The former plan is ordinarily much more practical. If the borrower failed to accumulate enough to meet his tax obligations before he became tax delinquent, it is not likely that he will be able to do so afterward.

Curiously enough, the borrower may become tax delinquent without becoming delinquent on his loan payments. When this happens, it is a tribute to the loan-servicing department. Public authorities have no corresponding tax-servicing program. Occupying the position of prior lien claimants, they may let private agencies help real estate owners solve their financial problems. When the time comes to use pressure on the tax-delinquent real estate owner, the taxing authority usually has but one formula to apply—a tax sale. While the borrower never quite understands the procedure of tax collection until it is too late, he may be brought to understand the loan-servicing procedure of the lender so that he is careful not to become delinquent on his loan payments.

Insurance Insurance is a subject that many Americans put in the same category with religion. They believe in both, but do not work very hard at either. As a nation we have faith in insurance and recognize the need for its protection. We do not know much about it, and as a consequence we suffer from too much or too little. An aggressive insurance salesman can easily make many of us insurance poor. In his absence or if he approaches us when we are short of ready cash, we may fail to buy the minimum amount necessary for our protection.

At the time a loan is placed upon a property, the lending institution may follow either of two policies on the subject of insurance: (1) It may insist upon the provision of insurance to protect its interests, leaving the borrower to make whatever additional provisions he sees fit. (2) It may follow the more realistic plan of advising the borrower on the subject. Seldom will a lender fail to require the borrower to provide protection for the lender. Too frequently he stops at this point.

More often than not, the lender will not be far wrong if he assumes that the borrower knows practically nothing about real estate insurance. He knows neither the kinds of insurance he should purchase, the amount to buy, nor the best place to buy it. While he has heard of fire insurance, he may know little about extended coverage and the added protection it will give him. Mortgagors do not know whether they should carry life insurance payable to or assigned to mortgagees. If such insurance is suggested to them, they do not know how much or what kinds of policies to carry.

At the time the loan is closed, the lender can render a real service to most of his borrowers if he will go out of his way a bit to discuss such questions with them. In doing so a good rule to follow is the too frequently forgotten golden rule. If, out of his experience with many real estate owners, the loan officer will advise the borrower in terms of what he himself would do as a borrower, loan servicing will be facilitated and the needs of the property owner will be better cared for.

What is said above is recognized as a gratuitous service by the lender. It may not be requested by the borrower. Indeed, it may not be wanted, since he may have his own ideas about insurance. Unfortunately, when he does have them they are not likely to be based upon broad experience. So far as the mortgagee is concerned, he usually writes his own ticket on the subject of insurance. He insists upon what he thinks is needed for his protection when the loan is closed. And then for fear changing conditions may call for new types of insurance, the mortgage is so written that these new types can be required as and when they appear to be needed.

Insurance Records and Their Use The mortgagee is expected to keep an accurate record of insurance written for his protection. Since he usually keeps the insurance policies in his files, he is in a position at all times to know the status of all insurance policies against any real estate which serves as security for one of his loans. Since he satisfied himself about all of them when the loan was closed, he simply keeps them up to date unless new forms or amounts are added. In many lending institutions an insurance clerk is maintained whose function it is to keep all insurance files current.

The mortgagee always reserves the right to pay insurance premiums and to add their cost to the borrower's account. Then to make assurance doubly sure, the lending institution usually carries a blanket policy that will protect it against errors and omissions and borrower's neglect. The payee in such a blanket policy is the mortgagee.

When mortgaged property is transferred, the mortgagee checks insurance policy records to make sure what endorsements are required. Notice to insurance companies is usually the duty of the mortgagee as soon as it knows about such changes in ownership of the property. Here again, neither seller nor buyer is likely to remember that insurance policies as well as title are expected to change hands.

Insurance Settlements As a part of mortgage loan servicing, the mortgagee will probably be expected to assume a major role in settling any claims against an insurance carrier on account of a damage claim. In case proof of loss is not filed promptly with the insurance company by the insured, the mortgagee may perform this service. Since the insurance settlement affects both the mortgagor and the mortgagee—"as their interests may appear"—the latter uses the insurance company's check as partial security for the loan until a determination is made about the disposition of its proceeds.

If the loss is small in relation to the value of the property, probably the proceeds will be used to make repairs as promptly as possible. If the remaining security is ample to give protection to the mortgagee, there will be no hesitancy in turning over the insurance company's check to the insured, properly endorsed by the mortgagee to indicate the release of his claims to it. If the loss is greater, the reverse may be the case. The insured may endorse the check in favor of the mortgagee, who then holds the proceeds in trust until the repairs to the property have been made.

If the loss is great enough to represent essentially the total loss of the insured structure, a decision must be made about its replacement. In some cases the interests of the mortgagee and the mortgagor are in conflict at this point. The former may prefer to have his claims against the property completely satisfied by using the proceeds of the insurance settlement to pay off the principal balance of the loan. The latter will be likely to wish to rebuild the destroyed structure.

If the structure is rebuilt, new investment will probably be required. It would be unusual if the proceeds of the insurance settlement would be sufficient to pay the cost of a new structure. This is particularly true if the building is to be more modern in design than the old one. Should the insured have available the additional money, there will usually be little difficulty in reaching a satisfactory settlement with the mortgagee. Probably the latter will be glad to have the proceeds of the insurance settlement applied to the cost of a new building. By this means it will acquire a loan on a new building. If for any reason this should not be true, the mortgagor should have little difficulty in obtaining the necessary financial assistance from some other source.

The real trouble arises when the mortgagor depends solely upon the proceeds of the insurance settlement to finance the new building; or upon this source plus an additional advance from the mortgagee. In case the latter does not see fit to make such an added investment, the net result may be that the proceeds of the insurance settlement will be used to liquidate the balance of the loan against the property, with any excess going to the mortgagor to be used by him as he sees fit.

In any event, if the amount of the insurance settlement reduces the insurance coverage on the property unduly, both mortgagor and mortgagee will be interested in having the policy rewritten to give the protection needed. Again the loan-servicing department will be expected to take the initiative in effecting this change, since the mortgagor will probably understand little or nothing about what changes in coverage have been made.

Change of Ownership Commonly, owners of real estate are permitted to dispose of their interests without the consent of the mortgagee. Indeed, the latter may know nothing of the transfer of title until the new owner sends in a payment on the loan. In many instances it would be to the advantage of the seller to consult the mortgagee before the sale is consummated. The latter might be willing to cancel the old mortgage and make a new one in the name of the buyer, thus taking the seller out from under any liability on the debt of the buyer. This is particulaly true if the purchaser needs to borrow more money for improvements to the property or if he wishes to take advantage of a prepayment clause in the mortgage to make a substantial advance payment. Even where the buyer needs a larger mortgage than the present unpaid balance of the existing loan, the mortgagee may be willing to make the added advance on a new mortgage instead of having the seller take back a purchase-money second mortgage for a part of the price of the property.

In case the mortgage contains a clause to the effect that the seller may dispose of the property only with the consent of the mortgagee, the latter will have an opportunity to get acquainted with the buyer before the transfer of title takes place. Whether or not this is the case, the mortgagee will certainly be interested in interviewing the purchaser at an early date. While the original mortgagor is still held on the note and mortgage, the new owner will be looked to for keeping up payments on the loan. For that reason, the loan-servicing department will hope to learn as much about him as it knows about the original mortgagor. An interview should develop about the same kinds and amounts of information as were furnished by the original mortgagor at the time he made application for the loan.

Normally, little difficulty will be encountered in obtaining the desired information. The interview serves two purposes. It is expected first to give the mortgagee the information he needs about the new borrower to make sure of his capacity to carry the loan. In case it develops that the purchaser probably cannot meet his obligations comfortably, the mortgagee may be able to sense this early enough to help work out plans to avoid future trouble. For instance, perhaps a trade may be arranged to give the weak borrower a property that he can carry and to place the loan on the property in which the mortgagee is interested into stronger hands.

In the second place, the new borrower can learn from the interview what is expected of him. Not only his obligations on the loan, but insurance, taxes, maintenance, and so on, should all be explained to him in such a manner that he understands them fully. Probably up to this time he has not read his mortgage carefully. If he has, he may not understand fully all its implications.

Probably the new owner assumed the mortgage when he purchased the property. Some mortgages are so written as to make this requirement. In case such a mortgage has not been used, and in case the purchaser has taken title to the property subject to the mortgage, the mortgagee will probably try to persuade him to assume the mortgage. In this case he can only persuade, but may not insist. While the original mortgagor is still held as guarantor on the loan, he may subsequently get into financial straits, so that this guarantee is worthless; he may even move out of the state. It is always to the advantage of the mortgagee to have the current owner of the property feel a personal obligation to keep up the payments on the loan.

Stages in Mortgage Loan Servicing There are essentially four stages in mortgage loan servicing. The first should appear at the time the loan application is approved. Then is the time to discuss all features of the loan with the borrower. This is the beginning of loan servicing. Next is the servicing of loans in good standing. If the loan is properly made, the normal expectation is that it will be collected in due course. Whether or not this goal is reached depends in large part upon the efficiency of the loan service department. The third stage begins when regular servicing breaks down and the loan becomes delinquent. The servicing of a delinquent loan follows a different pattern from regular servicing of a loan in good standing. Finally, if delinquent servicing fails to correct a situation that represents trouble for both mortgagor and mortgagee, complete failure of the loan venture is admitted, and foreclosure takes place.

Final Resort to Loan Security Up to the time of foreclosure of a mortgage, loan servicing has placed emphasis upon the debt-paying capacities of the borrower. Uncertain as these may become in time of crisis, the change of status from a mortgagee to the owner of the security behind the loan may bring even greater headaches. Experience of the past recommends that acquisition of the security be a last resort move, made only after every other method of protecting the position of the mortgagee has been explored and exhausted. Those who hastily plunge into foreclosure proceedings frequently have occasion to regret such hasty action. Even where foreclosure expenses are avoided through the use of voluntary conveyances, acquisition of the security protecting the loan creates new hazards for the lender.

In the first place, the property taken over by the mortgagee is probably in need of major repairs. In attempting to protect his equity, the borrower has probably neglected the property seriously. Taxes may be in arrears. When the mortgagee takes over the property, he must either dispose of it or try to rent it until a more favorable market is available. In either case he must rehabilitate it to make it more attractive to prospective purchasers or tenants. The acquisition of the property has probably occurred in a market already glutted with other distress property. Vacancies may complicate the problems of ownership, since loss of income from property held for either sale or rent cannot always be recovered from future operations. Even vandalism of vacant properties frequently adds to the losses of the new owner. The districts where foreclosures are most common, and the age of the property involved, invite both malicious acts from those who hope to profit from thievery of fixtures and mischievous acts from adolescents who find pleasure in breaking windows and doing other damage to vacant properties.

Causes of Delinquency The causes of delinquency are many. There are two causes that are not always recognized or at least are not always admitted. One source of delinquency is mistakes in making loans. Unless mortgagees know as much about borrowers as they should, and unless they refuse to make unsound loans even though they may be safe loans—then they need not be too much surprised if delinquency follows. In too many cases the borrower cannot hope to carry the obligations of a mortgage on a property purchased by him, even though his capital accumulations are sufficient to make a down payment large enough to provide an ample cushion of safety for the mortgagee. The major cause of delinquency in such a loan is the mistake made by the lending institution in granting the loan in the first place.

Along with this unrecognized, or at least not often admitted, cause of delinquency is another cause closely akin to it. Failure of regular servicing operations sometimes results in delinquency. Whenever the mortgagee is content to look to the margin of safety in the liquidating value of the security to protect his loan, he is inviting delinquency. Not many borrowers expect to default on their loan obligations when they sign a mortgage. But not all of them enjoy incomes sufficient to meet the costs of all that they would like to buy for themselves and the members of their families. If they are permitted or encouraged by their mortgagees to make commitments that they cannot meet, mortgage delinquency is likely to follow. Naturally, a mortgagee cannot dictate to his borrowers about their purchases. But he can so impress them with the importance of keeping up their payments on their mortgage loans that he will help them to realize that proper financing of the home is more important than the purchase of things the acquisition of which can be postponed until the borrower can afford them.

Decrease in Income One prolific cause of delinquency in mortgage loans is a decrease in income of the borrower to the point where he cannot meet all his obligations. An increase in expenses produces the same result. It is no answer to say that, if the mortgagee is able to secure his payments, he can forget about obligations owed to others. Sooner or later any continuous excess of outgo over income will land on the doorstep of the mortgage lender. As soon as it becomes evident that the borrower is overextended in his financial obligations, loan servicing has acquired a special assignment.

The first requirement is to get all the facts. Ordinarily this should not be too difficult. Borrowers generally recognize the superior financial skill of lenders and are willing to seek advice when they get into difficulties. If the loss of or decline in income is due to personal weaknesses of the borrower, one type of adjustment will be suggested. If our economy is suffering from one of its periodic headaches and business generally is declining, another plan may be indicated. If the increase in expenditures is the result of careless habits, the answer will probably be different than if it is due to inexperience and the absence of a budgetary procedure. Each case must be handled on its merits in terms of probable results of adjustments.

In making adjustments, the loan-servicing department must keep in mind the objectives of its operations. If it appears that a plan for solving the financial problems of the borrower can be successfully worked out, it will probably be undertaken. This may involve contact with other creditors to secure their cooperation. Since the mortgage loan will normally take precedence over their claims, other creditors will probably help in the solution of the borrower's problems if they think eventual success is possible.

Cost of Illness Payment for the new baby, an emergency operation, the prolonged illness of the breadwinner of the family, or any other kind of illness that places an unusual strain upon the pocketbook of the borrower is a frequent cause of delinquency. When reserve funds are sufficient to meet such contingencies, the mortgagee is likely to hear about it. The first consideration for an otherwise faithful borrower is to restore the family to normal health. Otherwise, lack of income because of illness or worry about unpaid doctor and hospital bills may have a prolonged effect upon the debt-paying capacities of the borrower. If the value of the property and the prospective income of the borrower justify such a move, the mortgage loan may be increased by an amount sufficient to pay the cost of the illness and to bring the borrower up to date on current indebtedness. Much depends upon the past experience of the lender with the borrower.

Depression Blues Regardless of the income of a particular borrower, depressions are always nightmares for lending institutions. Borrowers find properties on the market as good as theirs priced at not more than the amount of the unpaid principal of their mortgages. Fortunately for most lending institutions, borrowers generally do not know the worst about declines in real estate prices at such times. But whenever a borrower feels that his equity in his property has been seriously reduced or has disappeared entirely, he contracts a bad case of depression blues. He finds that the down payment he made on his property, plus the savings that he has accumulated in the form of reductions in the principal amount of his loan, have all vanished. His faith not only in real estate mortgages but also in the desirability of homeownership is put to a severe test at such times. Even worse, he begins to listen to soapbox orators who tell him in lurid terms the ways in which he has been made the dupe of an economic system of exploitation of the many for the benefit of the few. If he visualizes the holder of the mortgage on his property as one of the few, he may decide that his cue is to cease making payments on his mortgage.

Here is where a reputation for fair dealing on the part of the loan-servicing department can pay large dividends. In the first place, if the borrower has faith in the institution which holds his mortgage, he will probably discount heavily what others say about finance and financiers. At least he will listen to what loan service officers tell him about the causes of the depression and the probable chances for recovery of his lost equity in his property. If he is willing to keep up his payments but cannot because of reduced income, other adjustments will probably be made, dependent upon his past experiences.

Domestic Troubles They are occasions when mortgage lenders wonder if they are financiers or marriage consultants. Domestic troubles cause mortgage delinquencies. In such cases the first job of the loan service department is to get the facts. Certainly a "get-tough" policy, ending in a threat of foreclosure, is not the immediate answer to a default growing out of domestic troubles. If an investigation conducted by the loan-servicing department discloses that the major trouble is the absence of good financial management of the family's affairs, surely a financial institution should be able to make suggestions for the solution of that kind of a problem. Time spent on such a situation may result in a happier family as well as in the collection of the debt due to the mortgagee.

But if the domestic troubles stem from the moral turpitude of one spouse, the loan-servicing agent must decide quickly whether he wishes to offer his services as a domestic relations counselor or whether he thinks the case is one for lawyers to handle. If divorce proceedings follow, the loan payments are likely to suffer. Then the loan-servicing department must decide what means it can employ to insure loan collections pending a determination of the final disposition of the property. If the margin of safety in the value of the property is ample, a waiting period may be the immediate answer. If it is not, foreclosure may be called for, even while divorce proceedings are under way.

Financial Irresponsibility If in spite of patience and exhortation on the part of the loan-servicing department, a financially responsible borrower insists upon being irresponsible in meeting his obligations to the lending institution, this will usually become evident while it is still possible to do something about it. Such a borrower will cause trouble in times of easy money and marked prosperity just as readily as in times of opposite tendencies. Upon threat of foreclosure, he will probably pay up past delinquencies and become current on his loan payments—for a brief period of time. Soon he will fall back into his wayward ways and become a case for delinquency servicing again.

If such a borrower cannot be converted to regular paying habits, it is a good plan to get rid of him while the mortgage market is easy. He probably has a good equity in his property so that he can refinance his loan with some other lender. If his mortgagee lets him know that patience is no longer considered to be a virtue, that he must refinance, and that once a foreclosure suit is started it will be pursued to a conclusion, he will probably pay off his loan. He may even use his own funds for the purpose. If not, he will borrow the necessary funds elsewhere. Incidentally, he may have learned his lesson and may become a regular payer of his obligations to his new mortgagee. Probably not. At least it is well for the mortgagee that cannot succeed in making him pay regularly to get his mortgage retired before his irresponsibility is backed up by inability to meet his obligations.

Clashes in Personalities In the servicing of delinquent loans, clashes in personalities appear to be all too easy to develop. On the one hand, the borrower, probably unable to meet his contractual obligations, is inclined to assume a defensive position. He is trying to defend himself, his family, and his home. He must speak for himself. His emotions frequently get the better of his logic. The loan-servicing agent, on the other hand, does not speak for himself, since he has no personal investment at stake. He must speak for the lender. In fact he is the lender, in the eyes of the borrower. Therefore what he says and his manner of saying it must reflect the interests of his employer. Again it must be emphasized that, even in the presence of an emotional delinquent borrower who is quick to misunderstand and to misinterpret anything that is said to him, the attitude of the servicing agent should be in keeping with the basic philosophy of the institution which he represents.

The loan-servicing agent occupies a difficult position. He dare not respond in kind if an abusive borrower speaks his mind—or rather gives vent to his emotions. To do so might relieve the harassed agent, but it would seldom serve the best interests of his employer. The latter is not interested in a display of repartee. He wants his representative to find a way—the best possible way—of getting the money that is due him. This means first finding the facts, then ascertaining attitudes and intents and making adjustments accordingly.

If the borrower can but will not meet his obligations, the sooner he learns that the lender will take whatever steps are necessary to protect its interests the better. Long arguments or loud talking are not necessary to get this point across. A calm, measured, but direct statement by the servicing agent will be most effective in such cases. If, on the other hand, the borrower is anxious and willing to pay but is temporarily or permanently unable to do so, he deserves and has a right to expect advice and assistance. His problem resolves itself into a matter of strategy. What is the best method of helping him attain his objective? Again the attitude of the loan-servicing agent should reflect the basic objective of his employer.

Nature of Adjustments Until all facts concerning a delinquent borrower are in the hands of the loan-servicing officer, he cannot know what decision to render concerning any specific borrower in default. If the borrower still has an equity in his property and if he can carry on with a reasonable reduction in his monthly payment, it is probable that the amortization period can be extended without undue risk to the lender. If it appears that the debt-paying capacity of the borrower is only temporarily on dead center, the lender can probably forego a few payments, again extending the maturity date correspondingly.

If, on the other hand, it is evident that the borrower is unlikely to be able to carry his present loan comfortably, and if he has a fair equity in his property, perhaps the lender can assist him to trade his equity for that in a more modest property that will meet his needs within reason and that is encumbered with a mortgage that he can carry. A proposal for such a solution is likely to meet with disappointment on the part of the borrower and even with active resistance. But as the borrower better understands the alternatives, he may change his attitude toward such an adjustment.

Servicing Income Properties Most lending institutions that make loans on "income" properties use a strict "income" approach in servicing mortgage loans. The income status of such properties may change quickly and drastically. Lacking the amenities of owner-occupied residential properties, values adjust themselves more readily to changes in income derived from such properties. For this reason more care should be exercised in making loans on income properties. Normally, a greater margin of safety will be demanded by the lender. A shorter period of maturity is usually applied. Regular servicing is watched more carefully to avoid delinquencies. And more prompt action is taken if payments are missed.

If delinquencies occur on income-property loans, facts may be ascertained and sometimes adjustments made. In such cases, however, it is the mortgagor who is expected to make the adjustments. If a part of the income that should be applied to mortgage payments is being diverted to other uses, this can be corrected. If the mortgagor is able to reduce the principal balance of the loan, the future payments may be brought within the income-producing capacity of the property. If the liquidation value of the mortgaged property is in question, the mortgagor may be able to add other property to help secure the loan. In general, the loan-servicing pattern to be followed will conform to an income approach.

Loan-Servicing Costs Few mortgage lenders have much conception of the cost of loan servicing. No adequate cost studies have been made to measure such costs. Nevertheless, those who contract to service loans for others must make a charge which, supposedly, takes care of all expenses and leaves something for the contributions of the servicing agent. Rule of thumb charges, based upon hope rather than knowledge, are customarily made. The circumstance which saves many servicing contracts from ultimate loss to the servicing agent is that it is usually not called upon to render all the services for which it contracts.

An illustration will show what is meant by this statement. Suppose that the original loan is for $10,000 and the loan service fee is ½ percent. The fee would amount to nearly $50 for the first year, assuming the loan to be a monthly payment direct reduction loan. But by the time the loan balance is reduced to $1,000, the annual fee would amount to only $5. While the $50 should leave some profit to the servicing agent, it takes little imagination to see that the $5 would probably be insufficient to cover even the minimum costs of servicing the average loan for a whole year. Fortunately for most servicing agents and for those institutions which do their own loan servicing, most loans never remain on the books until they have balances too small to leave servicing payments in the self-supporting class. In other words, the common practice of payoffs before maturity—because of refinancing or otherwise—reduces the servicing obligations below contractual commitments. Otherwise, as principal balances are reduced, it would appear logical to increase interest rates sufficiently to offset the increase in loan-servicing costs. As a matter of fact, this is done frequently in farm-mortgage practices, where complete payoffs before maturity are less common than in urban mortgage financing.

QUESTIONS AND PROBLEMS

1. "Loan servicing" is fairly synonymous with "loan collection." What are the indicia of a good loan collection policy?
2. What may a lender accomplish through periodic reappraisals of the mortgaged property and the credit standing of the mortgagor?
3. Does a rapid turnover of loans on the books of the lending institution always indicate that the loans are becoming seasoned and more secure? If not, what may it reflect?
4. Has the expansion of the federal loan insurance and guarantee program simplified or complicated mortgage-servicing problems? In what respects?
5. What would you expect to find in a complete and up-to-date lender's file on a loan that is being serviced?
6. What are the four stages of mortgage loan servicing?
7. List all the reasons you can why a loan may become delinquent. From an analysis of the list, what would you say should be the background and abilities of an able loan-servicing officer?
8. What action should a lender take when the first default occurs? How may his disposition of the delinquency vary depending upon whether the default is unwarranted?
9. Why does nonpayment of taxes constitute a breach of the mortgage covenants? How may lenders often avoid this default through their collection policy?
10. What is the proper responsibility of the lending institution in seeing that the mortgaged property is insured?
11. What problems are raised between a mortgagor and a mortgagee when insured property has been completely destroyed, the insurance proceeds have been received, and the mortgagor desires to rebuild?
12. What particular problems may be encountered in servicing income properties which are not likely to be so important in servicing owner-occupied residential properties?

21

Financing Subdivisions and Development Projects

Origin of Subdivision Activities In the early days cities gradually encroached upon neighboring farm land and, by a process of attrition, bits of fringe land were gradually absorbed for city use. The business of anticipating future urban use of rural land did not develop commonly until the last quarter of the 19th century. Even then it had a slow, spasmodic growth until the second decade of the 20th century. By that time it had become well-enough established to be ready to take full advantage of the opportunities offered to it in the roaring 1920s.

Kinds of Subdivision Activity While there are many variations of subdivision activity, those that enjoyed earliest success stemmed from two major types. The parasitical subdivider acquired control over a small tract of land—20 acres or so—on the edge of a city, spent a minimum amount in marking it out into building lots designated by white stakes at the corners, and put on a selling campaign. If the campaign was successful, he probably disposed of all or nearly all of his lots in a single season. Indeed, in many cases the sale required only a few days, starting with a brass-band type of advertising splurge. In many instances a brass band was literally used, and a carnival spirit prevailed among the large crowd that gathered on the opening day to satisfy their curiosity and perhaps to buy a lot. It was not uncommon for a kind of contagious enthusiasm to attack such a crowd. The sight of some people signing purchase contracts induced others, who came only to see the show, to come away with receipts for their down payments also.

The success of subdivisions of this kind depended upon mass selling over a short period of time. In addition to the campaigns which attracted large crowds, follow-up visits by salesmen to the homes of those whose names were not secured on the dotted line at the first visit to the site always emphasized the rapidity of sales to others. Every lot on the plat that was marked "Sold" called attention to the decreasing number of lots still available. The scarcity-value concept, once planted in the mind of the prospective purchaser, helped to put over many a sale. Unless the sale was essentially completed in a single season, this parasitical kind of subdivision was hard to sell at a later date.

Once most of the lots were disposed of or at least contracted for, the promoter of parasitical subdivisions lost interest quickly and moved his operations to greener pastures. With no organization of lot owners and no promoter interest in favor of the installation of streets and other facilities for making the lots usable, they might remain for years in a state of idle land. In time even the white stakes might disappear through the unintentional action of the elements or through the intentional acts of small boys. In one such subdivision, the original sale of the lots preceded their subsequent purchase and absorption into an adjoining development project by more than 40 years. At the end of that time it was even difficult to find some of the owners. While this is admittedly an extreme example, it shows what can happen to parasitical subdivisions.

A Century-Old Subdivision Project One of the earliest attempts at organized subdivision activity was sanctioned by legislation passed in Pennsylvania on March 7, 1853. It took the form of an amendment to the law passed three years earlier for the chartering of building associations in the counties of Philadelphia, Schuylkill, and Berks. By the law of 1853, the privilege of forming mutual corporations was extended to land associations. Taking advantage of the growing popularity of building associations, the land associations appealed to the same market, but on a different plan of operation.

Speculators purchased acreage adjacent to or near an existing city or village on thin equity. Their charters limited such purchases to not more than 50 acres and required land associations to dispose of all lots within 10 years. After the land was acquired, it was platted.

Finely prepared maps and plans of the ground, nicely laid out, with the principal streets of the city or village continued to it, and intersecting it at right angles; the visible ends or improved terminations of these aforesaid principal streets being perhaps two or three miles off, with many a green field and hay-cock meadow and pasture intervening, yet undefiled with the pick and spade of the cellar-digger.[1]

---

[1] Edmund Wrigley, *The Working Man's Way to Wealth; A Practical Treatise on Building Associations: What They Are and How to Use Them*, pp. 18–19.

The 50 acres were cut into lots 20 × 100 feet, providing perhaps 20 lots per acre, after making due allowance for land dedicated to streets. The speculators who owned the land—paying perhaps $10,000 in cash and giving back a purchase-money mortgage for $40,000—then formed a land association with 1,000 shares of a par value of $200 each. This association then purchased the land above described, paying $10,000 down, assuming the mortgage for $40,000, and giving back a second mortgage for $150,000, for a total price of $200,000. The 1,000 lots in the subdivision averaged $200 in price. Purchasers bought stock in the association, similar to their purchases of stock in building associations, on the installment plan. If the sale were successful and if the lots were paid for by the members of the land association, the speculators did quite well for themselves.

And what have the stockholders to show for their money? A lot of ground, two or three miles out in the rural districts, with the taxes to pay on them for many years before they are available to build upon, with the street improvements all to be done and paid for, without the possibility of selling even at cost—firstly, because of the great number of similar lots all suddenly forced into the market at one time; and secondly, for the reason that the stockholder has anticipated a value that it will take several years to realize. . . . Cattle will still graze upon many acres of ground in the rural districts around the city of Philadelphia, that were sized through Land Associations ten or fifteen years ago.[2]

Could this have been written by a contemporary about subdivision activity in 1855, or did it merely forecast what was to happen in 1925, 70 years later?

Development Projects A second type of subdivision activity merits the name "development project." Instead of being a single-season operation, it started on the theory that it would take years to complete. A larger tract of land, containing a few hundred or, in some cases, a few thousand acres, was acquired for the purpose of creating a satellite city near if not immediately adjacent to an already populous community. Topography frequently dictated in part the choice of location for such a project. Since the ultimate success of such a venture depended upon the use of building sites by homeowners and others, the development company was constantly under pressure to do everything possible to encourage the use of sites after their sale. While the development company did not overlook the advantages of mass selling through sales campaigns, it did not base its success solely upon such campaigns.

Unlike the single-season subdividers, who had no interest in the actual use of the land, developers must be credited with some of the outstanding residential communities in the country. To mention only a few,

---

[2] Ibid., pp. 21–22.

the Country Club district of Kansas City, Missouri, Mariemont near Cincinnati, the Roland Park district of Baltimore, Kew Gardens in New York, and Shaker Heights in Cleveland—all are outstanding examples of advanced ideas in city building. Those responsible for such developments have been pioneers in city planning as well as in other programs for maintaining high levels of real estate uses in American cities. The work of these pioneers is now being carried forward by organized efforts in urban renewal all over the country.

Changing Pattern of Subdivision Activity Both types of subdivision activity discussed above blossomed to the fullest extent during the hectic 1920s. The single-season subdivision withered and died at the end of that decade. We have heard practically nothing from it since. At least, no flood of new subdivisions of this type have been advertised recently. Some of those that flourished earlier have since been absorbed into adjacent development projects, and some have been recovered by the potato patches for which they are best suited.

Development projects have had a checkered career during the period since the crash of 1929. Some have proceeded on their successful way, but at a slower pace. Others have passed from weaker ownership to stronger and are still in existence. Some have changed their complexion considerably. And some have not yet recovered from the depression of the 1930s, as the population has moved in another direction. They, too, are being overrun with weeds and show signs of neglect, except for the islands which represent the homes of the hardy pioneers who built houses here and there throughout the development before the crash.

Although the public has generally lost interest in buying vacant lots as such, this breed of promoter has many lives. During the late 1950s and early 1960s, there was a revival of sales to absentee purchasers on a mail-order basis—$10 down and $10 monthly until fully paid. An estimated $300 million to $500 million was paid or committed through land sales contracts for the purchase of such parcels in 1962. The bulk of the offerings on this basis has been western range and desert lands in Arizona, California, Nevada, New Mexico, and Utah. Lands in Florida, Texas, and some foreign countries have been promoted in similar fashion. The typical brochure implies good climate and soil, nearby water and other utilities, available home financing, recreational opportunities, and likely appreciation in site value. The true condition is usually one not far removed from raw land in an unattractive area. Water, if available, may be brought in at the cost of several thousand dollars for the well. No provision has been made for sewage disposal, road maintenance (if indeed there are roads), or fire protection. In many cases, the land is subject to gas and oil reservations with rights of surface entry, and even to grazing rights. Usually institutional lenders will not make loans for home construction on these lots, very often because the promoters can not give the purchaser a clear title as well as for other obvious reasons.[3]

The states involved and the U.S. Attorney General have moved to protect against further spread of this type of selling with some well-timed legislation and indictments for mail fraud. Title XIV of the Housing and Urban Development Act of 1968 is the Interstate Land Sales Full Disclosure Act (ILSA). This law is designed to enable the buyer to be as familiar as the seller with property being offered for interstate sale. Offerings of property protected by this law must be filed with the Office of Interstate Land Sales Registration of the U.S. Department of Housing and Urban Development. The thrust of activities of this office (OILSR) is to achieve a complete disclosure of all material facts relating to the property. The required property report covers such items as: distances over paved and unpaved roads to nearby communities; existence of liens on the property; purchaser's obligation to pay taxes, special assessments, or acquisition costs; availability of such amenities as recreational facilities, garbage collection, sewage disposal, utilities, paved streets leading to public access routes, schools, and medical and shopping facilities; and soil and foundation conditions as a base for building improvements. If the buyer of the property does not receive a copy of the property report before or at the time of signing his purchase agreement, he may void the contract at his option. Both civil and criminal penalties are provided for developer-sellers for false statements of material facts or failures to state all material facts. Although this law has greatly strengthened the hand of authorities in interstate sales, it should be recognized that several types of transactions are exempted from coverage by this statute. These include: promotions in which the number of lots to be sold is less than 50; sale or lease of subdivisions in which all lots are at least five acres or more in size; sale or lease of improved land (with a building thereon) or where the seller agrees to make such improvement within two years; sale of real estate investment trust securities; sale or lease to a person whose purpose is to construct improvements thereon or to resell; sale or lease of real estate that is free and clear of all liens and encumbrances provided the purchaser and his spouse personally inspect the property concerned and if the seller executes an affidavit to that effect; sale or lease of real estate by any government agency or by court order; and sale or lease of cemetery lots. Since much is obviously left to state authorities in this area of regulation, OILSR cooperates closely with the state agencies by way of exchange of information and general assistance.[4]

---

[3] Stanley Mosk, "Subdivision Promotions in the West—The Problem and Proposals for Solution," *State Government,* Vol. XXXVI, No. 3 (Summer 1963), pp. 142–47.

[4] William H. McMullin, "Truth in Selling: The Interstate Land Sales Full Disclosure Act of 1968," *Real Estate Review,* Vol. 1, No. 1 (Spring 1971), pp. 94–98; see also *HUD-15-F(2),* published by the Office of Land Sales Registration, August 1970.

An entirely new factor has come into the picture to help materially in changing the pattern of subdivision activity. The earlier idea of lot selling is based upon the assumption that most people prefer to select a homesite, have a home constructed upon it to their order, and then select the items of home equipment needed for comfortable living. This program is not only based upon an assumption of the existence of distinct individual tastes but upon the further assumption that most people can and will pay the price of satisfying these tastes. It is most expensive in operation, because it necessarily involves retail prices at all stages of home production.

Development-Construction Projects By contrast, the high prices of residential real estate in the post-World War II period have given great impetus to a movement that had been in the making for some years before the war. Heroic efforts are being made to substitute wholesale methods of producing, financing, and marketing homes for the retail method mentioned above. In the field of house construction, we are still seeking workable prefabrication formulas. In the field of site production and distribution, we are also experimenting with wholesale programs. Bypassing high-priced and scattered building sites in development projects such as those discussed above, builders are acquiring raw land at wholesale prices; developing it according to a unified pattern; building houses in great numbers and by the use of whatever economies they can lay hands upon; equipping them with home appliances such as refrigerators, washing machines, stoves, and even television sets and air-conditioning units; and then using as many wholesale methods of finance and of sale of the entire package as have been developed to date.

With encouragement from both governmental agencies and the public, this new pattern of substituting the sale of a fully equipped home for the sale of an unimproved lot is making great headway. For the most part it is catering to the middle-class market and even to a more modest type of home development. The tailor-made house will always be demanded by those who prefer a greater degree of individuality than that offered in a mass-housing project. Some, of course, will prefer a specific location for one reason or another. While it appears that the inclusion of building construction as a part of subdivision activity complicates the problems of the promoters of such a venture, in some respects it may simplify them instead. The development company has always had the problem of encouraging construction—but at arm's length. The development-construction company certainly has more control over the entire project and can better avoid some of the mistakes made by its predecessor.

It would be a mistake to assume that the new pattern of subdivision activity is necessarily more stable than its contemporary ancestor, or that its promoters have necessarily avoided all of the errors committed by their predecessors. At this point we are not passing judgment upon either of these questions. We are merely pointing out this addition to the pattern of subdivision activity. Nor shall we undertake to deal in detail with all the problems of any of the three types of subdivisions mentioned above. Instead, we shall confine our attention to the financial problems associated with the business of acquiring land at wholesale and disposing of it at retail. The financial arrangements may be eminently satisfactory, and yet the project may be a dismal failure—for reasons that form no part of the subject matter of this text.

Financing Parasitical Subdivisions In discussing each of the three types of subdivision activities mentioned above, we are interested in two types of financial problems: (1) those concerned with the wholesale acquisition of the land; and (2) those involving the transfer of title at retail to the lot purchasers. In considering, first, the acquisition of land to be subdivided, several alternative plans are available. The subdivider may buy the land outright and take title to it either in his own name or in that of a corporation organized for the purpose of relieving him from personal liability for whatever follows. Frequently he acquires the land at an advantageous price some time—perhaps a few years—in advance of its sale for subdivision purposes. If he acquires ownership, he may have the title transferred to a trustee for the purpose of making sure that deeds to individual lots may be forthcoming promptly whenever final payments warrant the passing of title to the purchaser.

Sometimes the subdivider forms a partnership, either with the owner of the land or with someone who is willing to match his capital against the sales ability of the subdivider. In such event the owner or purchaser keeps title in his own name or in that of his designee, in case he prefers not to be known as a party to the project. The subdivider may have no ownership interest in the land but may be interested only in the profits to be derived from the sale of the land at retail. In the case of a partnership of this character, the distribution of the initial costs of surveys, legal fees, and preliminary advertising are agreed upon between the partners.

Occasionally the subdivider may prefer to keep his plans secret from the owner to avoid an increase in the price of land that is being used for truck gardening or is merely idle awaiting future developments. If he is buying the land for cash, either directly or through a dummy, no complications arise. But if he has only a part of the purchase price to use as a down payment, he may need to negotiate with the seller to take back a purchase-money mortgage for a sizable proportion of the purchase price. This may not be difficult to arrange, but the terms of the mortgage may not fit into the plans of the subdivider. He cannot hope to pay off the mortgage at one time, but will need releases of portions of the security as deeds to individual lots are required.

Since this contingency will not occur for several months at the earliest, the subdivider sometimes uses a purchase-money mortgage without disclosing his plans to the seller. Subsequently, he arranges to redeem the mortgage through some other form of financing, or makes a new deal with his present mortgagee by which the latter will release the mortgage against any one lot upon receipt of a stipulated sum of money. In case the seller knows of the plans of the subdivider at the time the land is sold to him, the mortgage can be so drawn as to provide for partial releases as stipulated sums are paid.

Ordinary mortgages on land available for subdivision purposes, either from a financial institution or from individuals, are not easily placed by subdividers. Most financial institutions are rigidly restricted in regard to the making of development loans. Individuals would usually be willing to grant only low percentage loans, even if they could be interested in this type of speculation. The individual who would take a chance on even small loans on unimproved land could probably be induced to provide equity capital on terms not too much more restrictive.

Lease and Release One plan of financing both parasitical subdivisions and development projects is known as the lease and release pattern. Suppose that A owns acreage which is ripe for subdividing purposes. B leases the acreage for a period of years, determined in part by the total area, agreeing to pay 8 percent annual rent upon an agreed valuation of $1,200 per acre for land that would probably not find a ready market for more than $750 per acre. The title remains in the name of the seller. As a part of the deal, he agrees to permit the land to be subdivided and a plat to be recorded, dedicating the necessary part of the land to streets and other public uses. The seller also agrees to deed any specific lot (assuming five lots to the acre) to any person designated by the subdivider, upon receipt of a cash payment of $500. Although the fractional part of the acreage released would not quite require $500 per lot, even after streets are provided for, the release price is usually somewhat higher than this fraction would indicate. If all lots are finally deeded, either to purchasers or to the subdivider, the total payment for the land will be only $1,200 per acre. To avoid complications arising from death, and so forth, such deeds are sometimes drawn by corporate trustees which hold legal title to the land for such purpose.

For the protection of the lessor under such a plan, payments made by lot purchasers should also be made to the same trustee, to be disbursed only according to a prearranged program of meeting sales costs and other expenses as they accrue, with sufficient profits to protect the interests of the seller-lessor being kept in a trust fund until each lot is released. Limitations of space will not permit a detailed discussion of what happens in case of default in annual rental payments if lots are not sold readily, or what happens to the unsold lots at the termination of the lease by expiration or otherwise. All such questions should be anticipated and dealt with in detail in the lease agreement. Suffice it to say that, under the lease and release plan, the owner of the land is virtually a partner of the subdivider.

Options Occasionally a subdivider has been willing to undertake the promotion of a parasitical subdivision with no more definite a relationship to the land than is provided by an option to purchase it. In such case he has little or no financial risk in the venture, since his original costs for surveys, and so forth, are small. Any sales that he makes are handled in much the same way as under the lease and release program. Even where options are used, the rights and obligations of both parties should be clearly set forth in the agreement. One of the clauses in the option agreement will probably be drawn to provide a substitute type of arrangement to succeed the option in case the early sale of lots is sufficiently impressive to suggest its ultimate success. Where options are used, even the original lot sales may be only tentative, subject to cancellation and refund of the down payment or binder, in case it appears that buyers are not likely to make satisfactory response to the lot offerings. This is a precarious type of financing that is not recommended from the point of view of the owner of the land, the subdivider, or the lot purchaser.

Pricing of Lots in a Parasitical Subdivision In the pricing of lots in a parasitical subdivision, the pattern used is frequently somewhat as follows. Assuming that the land is contracted for at $1,200 per acre and that it subdivides into five lots per acre, the cost per lot may run $300 by the time streets are accounted for. The lots will probably carry price labels averaging from $1,000 to $1,500. Some may be higher and some lower in price. On only small down payments and a long term to amortize the balance, the quoted price may be rigidly adhered to. Liberal discounts are given for additional down payments, with real concessions for cash purchases. One inducement to cash payments and large down payments is the saving of interest accumulations on the land contracts used to finance lots sold on terms. The latter are sometimes subject to bargaining, particularly if the purchaser has enough cash to purchase more than one lot. Lot sales which are not for all cash are usually executed by the use of land contracts. The default rate of these contracts is very high. Since the larger the down payment the less likely the chance of defaults, the subdivider is usually willing to pay a high price for insurance against defaults.

Remnant sales of lots unsold at the end of the first season are sometimes tried by parasitical subdividers. After the flush of a sales campaign has subsided, the promoter may be so anxious to get the remaining lots on contract that he will offer large discounts comparable to those given for cash sales. This is a dangerous practice. For example, suppose that A contracts to purchase Lot 24 at $1,200 and pays 10 percent down. At $10 per month he makes three additional payments, leaving a balance, disregarding interest, of $1,050. Suppose that the purchaser of Lot 25, as nearly identical with the adjoining Lot 24 as possible, contracts to pay only $1,000. If the purchaser of Lot 24 learns of the reduction in price, he may default on his purchase.

Operating Costs By definition, parasitical subdivisions involve no improvement costs. Occasionally a street may be plowed to simulate a paved roadway. Surveys locate lot posts. Advertising and sales commission may be high, since the chief source of business is frequently high-pressure selling. The advertising must be sufficiently generous in amount and in frequency to prepare the prospective buyers for response to a campaign opening day. Then the salesmen must be compensated at a rate to attract those who can get results. Suppose, for example, that the sales commission amounts to 10 to 15 percent of the retail sales price; advertising to $30 per lot; discount for a cash sale, to 20 percent; and legal and engineering costs, to $12\frac{1}{2}$ percent. On a $1,200 lot which costs $300, the selling commission would be $180 (using the higher percentage of 15); advertising, $30; discount, $240; and other costs, $150. The profit to the subdivider would still be 100 percent on cash sales made during the opening season. The overhead costs may be very low. A promoter may use his home for his office and the home telephones of his salesmen for business purposes. Preliminary contracts may be signed on the site or at the home or the office of the purchaser. Final land contracts might even be signed in the office of the attorney for the subdivider. If collections on land contracts are made by a trustee or other financial institution, the promoter may need no office to which the public is invited. As a consequence, the promoter may have no need for an office or a staff of employees.

Sale of Contracts For purchasers who are unable to take advantage of cash discounts, the usual formula calls for a down payment sufficient to cover the direct sales cost. Since the salesman gets his commission from this down payment, he will try to collect as much as possible as a down payment. The binder on a preliminary contract will be considerably less—whatever the purchaser happens to have available. The higher sales commissions are usually paid for cash sales. Down payments of less than the amount of the sales commission mean that the salesman will be required to wait for a part of his commission until future monthly payments are made. This means that he may never get his commission in full. Whatever form of wholesale financing the subdivider has used, he is anxious to cash in on his operations as quickly as possible. The fear of defaults, together with his desire to realize his profits for investment in a new venture induces him to dispose of his contracts at a heavy discount if he can find a buyer. If he is successful in getting most of his lots sold on contract in a single season, and if he sells them for only a 10 percent down payment, he can afford to sell the contracts at a discount of 40 percent (in the illustration used in the preceding section) and still realize more than a 50 percent profit after paying all expenses. Since "Sell out and get out" is the motto of many parasitical subdividers, the sooner they get out the better they like it.

Form of Organization of Development Projects In contrast with parasitical subdivisions which are frequently controlled by individual proprietorships or partnerships, development projects are almost always incorporated. There are several reasons for this. In spite of the fact that they involve less risk than parasitical subdivisions, they are always speculative ventures. Consequently, those who contribute the equity capital insist upon limiting their risks. The amount of money needed is usually much greater than the promoters possess. They must interest others in making capital contributions. While the control may be centered in the hands of the promoters, it is well to have favorably known civic and business leaders on the board of directors, for several reasons: (1) This is an excellent way to get them to be among the first to move into the new development. (2) Their names add prestige to the company. (3) Their counsel is frequently needed as a balance against the enthusiasm of the promoters.

Another form of organization, less common than the corporation but still used by development companies, is the syndicate. In effect, a single individual, who is usually the promoter, enlists the interest of a small group of speculators who see the profit possibilities in a development project. By pooling their resources devoted to this purpose, they get together sufficient funds to finance the project. So far as the public knows, only the promoter may be considered to be the owner of the property. It is recorded in his name and he, in turn, transfers title as lots are sold and completely paid for. Meantime a syndicate agreement, establishing the relationships between the manager and those who contribute the money, is drawn up and signed by all parties. This kind of financing may continue until the project is entirely closed out, or it may be succeeded by a new arrangement when profits are sufficient to repay the original capital contributors.

Where the development company controls land not within the corporate limits of the adjacent city, it is usual to incorporate a separate political unit to manage the public affairs of the area. At the outset the company controls its politics, fixes tax rates, determines bond issues, and so on. Almost always, when this occurs, as the community develops there appears an opposition party wishing to place the control in the hands of the residents. When the control changes hands, the new group may have real or imagined grievances against the company which cause the pendulum to swing away from its wishes. If and when this occurs, there may be a temporary retardation in future progress of the community. Sooner or later, if the company is at all diplomatic, it can usually work out a program that will meet the approval of those in civic control of the political unit.

Financing Development Projects The financial problems of development projects differ from those of parasitical subdivisions both quantitatively and qualitatively. There is a large amount of money involved, and it must cover a much larger number of items. By definition, a development project covers a much larger area—so large that it cannot hope to be disposed of in a single season. Its promoters must devote years to its sale. While there is present something of the contagious enthusiasm mentioned above in the discussion of the sale of lots in a parasitical subdivision, it manifests itself in different ways when applied to a development project. The latter must be disposed of by a steady campaign of convincing prospective buyers that the promises made about it are in process of fulfillment. The contagion in the latter case is not something that is of sudden appearance; it develops slowly over the years as those affected by it watch the progress of continued growth.

One of the problems of a development project that differentiates it from a parasitical subdivision is the element of location and size. Any small acreage anywhere in close proximity to a city can meet the needs of the parasitical subdivision—and the closer the better. Only a large area, several times the acreage of a parasitical subdivision, can be considered for a development project. Topography plays a part also. In subdivisions, the flatter the land the better, because there are less waste and more lot possibilities. In development projects, broken topography, for at least a part of the area, is desirable. Parks, recreational facilities, including perhaps a golf course, and so forth, require something more than flat land if any is available. To acquire the larger acreage needed, the developer may be required to start operations some distance from the city center, perhaps even some distance from its present periphery.

Transportation Distance immediately raises the question of public transportation. Private automobiles may be used by the members of the family; but for servants, guests, and so on, it is always safer to provide some means of public conveyance. In the earlier days this meant street-car lines, the extension of which to the development project frequently required a considerable subsidy by the development company. Even where modern bus service requires a lower capital expenditure, some subsidy may be required to meet operating deficits for service to a sparsely populated area. Eventually, as population increases, such facilities will undoubtedly become self-supporting. Meantime, a temporary subsidy is a frequent part of the financing problems of a development company. In some cases it has been necessary to provide independent bus service as a feeder line to public transportation lines in the adjacent city. In order to work out the transportation problems, it is not uncommon to enlist the interest of the key officials of public transportation companies in the real estate development to be served. The fact that the name of the president of the local transportation company appears on the board of directors of the development company is no accident.

Preliminary Costs Even before land is acquired for development purposes, a sizable amount of money may be spent to test the capacity of the areas selected to meet the requirements. Options, legal surveys, soil tests, surveys to determine answers to drainage questions, platting possibilities, and so forth—all cost money. If more than one area is under consideration, options may be taken on both until some questions can be answered about them. To do the job right, experts may be consulted and some studies may be conducted before decisions are reached. Expenses incurred for all preliminary purposes must be met currently as they are incurred, even though they are later capitalized when the project is started.

Improvement Costs Unlike the parasitical subdivision, the development project does not offer bare land for sale. It must deal in building sites. The difference is material. Land in the form of bare lots carries with it the vague hope that someday, somehow, it will be made available for use. Lots in a development project must be made available for use at the time they are sold. This means the installation of streets, sewers (or provision for septic tanks in some cases), water lines, and so on. In addition, utilities such as gas, electricity, and telephone service must be provided. Occasionally, lots in a section of the project may be sold in anticipation of the installation of the facilities needed for use of the lots. But a definite program, accompanied by a timetable for their installation, is probably on the schedule before the sale takes place. Not infrequently the sale goes on while the streets are being paved and other improvements are being installed. This show of activity is a good inducement to purchasers who have been considering the acquisition of a lot but have been a bit uncertain about its availability for use until they see work proceeding.

Since the development project will require years for completion and sale, it is usual to improve it in sections rather than all at once. When one section is essentially disposed of, another will be opened for sale and improvement. The stage of the business cycle and, more particularly, the progress of sale and building within the area, fix the timetable for opening new sections. Frequently the plans for future use of areas not immediately improved change, so that a different layout of streets, lot sizes, and so on, may take place before new sections are opened. For that reason, only parts of the land under control for future use may even be platted at the outset. The remainder constitutes the reserve for future use.

Various plans are followed to finance the installation of improvements. The two major plans are: (1) Improvements are installed at the expense of the development company, with the lot price fixed high enough to include their cost. In such case the improvements may be neither as generous nor as permanent as future needs will demonstrate to be desirable. (2) In case the area is separately incorporated, bonds may be issued to cover the cost of street improvements and the installation of water and sewer lines. These bonds are serial in character and are expected to be redeemed by assessments against the building sites served. This means that lots are sold subject to such assessments. It means also that more pressure is put upon the company to dispose of lots as soon as they are improved, to avoid carrying the heavy load of assessments against unsold lots. Bonds are sometimes issued for these improvements even where the development project is a part of an already incorporated political subdivision.

The last straw that sometimes breaks the camel's back is the loan of unpaid assessments for street and other improvements. In case the development company is overoptimistic about lot sale possibilities and causes too much land to be improved before it can be sold, trouble may result. If the improvements are paid for directly, the cash will probably be in sight before the improvements are installed. But if the improvements are to be paid for from the proceeds of the sale of bonds, cash outlays are postponed to a future date. Then, if the lots are not sold or if the purchasers fail to meet their share of the assessments, the entire burden falls upon the company. Failure to meet these assessments will eventually cause trouble. A safe policy to follow is to keep in reserve enough cash to meet such contingencies. Such a conservative practice is seldom followed.

Utilities such as gas lines and electric and telephone wires are frequently installed by the respective utility companies, with the cost being paid by the development company. Such cost may be recoverable at a future date under conditions set forth in the contracts between the companies involved. One plan that has had some vogue is to permit the development company to recover its cost, without interest, when half the lots in a given area have been built upon. Occasionally, if the probabilities of early use of the lots seem to justify the expenditure by the utility company, all or a part of the installation cost may be borne by it. While its stake is not as great as that of the development company, it may be willing to do a modest amount of pioneering.

Financing of Buildings Development companies are frequently required to provide financial assistance for the purpose of constructing buildings. At least three kinds of buildings are sometimes included in such assistance: residential, business, and public. As indicated above, the continued success of a development project is conditional upon a show of building activity in the form of new residential units. When some people show their confidence in the area by building new homes, others are encouraged to think of and plan for new homes also. Whether new construction is created for the immediate use of owners who expect to occupy the finished product, or whether new homes are being built for sale by speculative contractors, the result is approximately the same. The more frequently the sounds of the hammer and the saw are heard, the greater is the interest created among prospective lot purchasers.

Consequently, the development company is always glad to encourage new house construction. It will gladly advise lot owners about methods of financing construction and do everything possible to help arrange financial assistance for private home builders. For contractors building houses for sale, it will go even further. Sometimes it will sell them lots with little or no down payment, taking back a purchase-money mortgage for the remainder of the purchase price. Although this is normally a first mortgage, it will contain a waiver clause agreeing to the subordination of the lien of this mortgage in favor of a construction loan. With a liberal construction loan, the builder can frequently buy the lot and construct the house with practically no investment of his own funds.

Since every sale of a speculatively built house is likely to encourage the builder to purchase at least one more lot, the development company offers special inducements to its salesmen to concentrate attention upon efforts to sell such houses. Since the company probably combines lot selling with real estate brokerage, it can give special inducements for the sale of new houses. For example, if the brokerage commission for the sale of a house is 6 percent, the salesman may get 4 percent and the employer 2 percent. If, however the salesman sells a new house for a builder, he may be permitted to receive the entire 6 percent.

Even with the inducements offered above, the builder may hesitate to pioneer in the construction of houses in a newly opened development project or in a new section of one that has been in operation for some time. Here the company must make new approaches to the builder to get construction going. One method is to donate an occasional lot to a desirable builder. This gift will serve as a cushion against a possible loss in selling a house in a newly opened section. A more direct assurance can take the form of a guarantee by the development company against loss by a builder. In either case, the company will probably select the site and exercise considerable control over the type and cost of building to be constructed upon it.

Lot salesmen frequently refer purchasers of building sites to a particular contractor when they are seeking someone to do their building. By this means the contractor is placed under obligation to the salesman. One excellent means of discharging this obligation is to buy another lot from him. Such purchases will ordinarily not be made except in anticipation of their early use. But the builder has alternative choices in selecting building sites and may use one rather than another, partly in response to previous favors and partly because he thinks aggressive salesmen will help him to dispose of finished houses.

Business Building Financing Every new residential section must be served by shopping centers of some kind. The development company is just as much interested in encouraging the right kind of shopping centers as it is in encouraging residential construction. This encouragement may take various forms. Special inducements may be offered to tenants particularly desirable for the shopping center. Market surveys, financial advice, and miscellaneous subsidies may be used to assemble an attractive array of businesses for the shopping center concourse.

In the financing of a shopping center there are three principal categories of investment funds.[5] The first category encompasses the basic land and construction costs and charges which are proportionately applicable to the basic construction costs. The justification to the investor for advancing these costs lies in prospective net income from rentals. Certain minimum rentals must be established to meet creditors' financing charges if adequate financing is to be assured. In addition to the basic construction costs are secondary construction costs which are more appropriately amortized by separate income derived by standby charges or surcharges on operating costs. Examples of facilities identifiable as secondary costs include central utilities; central television antennas; rental sign space; costs of construction in preparation for future expansion, which should be amortized against future tenant rents; and special expenditures for certain tenants, which should be covered in lease terms. The third type of costs in shopping center development arises in connection with the improvement of surrounding areas. If the shopping center is developed as an adjunct to an already existing residential area, these costs, of course, are nil. If the surrounding areas are yet to be built up, the development company must expect to recover these costs through land sales or construction of appropriate residential properties for sale or rent. In some instances, the development company plans the shopping center to service its adjacent residential sections. In others, the primary objective may be to derive the principal profits from the shopping center and to create the residential development for subservient purposes.

In some cases the development company is so anxious to make sure

---

[5] Victor Gruen, "Close Look at Costs of Shopping Centers," *The Mortgage Banker* (May 1960), pp. 24–29.

that the kind of shopping center is entirely in keeping with the kind of neighborhood being created that it will maintain a monopoly over the construction of buildings to be devoted to business uses. Owning the site, it may frequently be able to secure mortgage finance funds sufficient to construct the buildings. This is more likely to happen if it can show the lender an impressive list of prospective tenants anxious to rent space in the new buildings. Once a building or a shopping center is constructed and rented, the company may see fit to dispose of it in order to release its capital for other purposes Or, if it possesses sufficient financial resources, it may prefer to maintain its investment in order to enjoy a continuous return. In a pioneering center, the rate of return at the outset may be too low to invite outside investment in the property. It may be necessary for the company to hold the property until it can increase rents to a level which will show a satisfactory return upon the investment, so as to induce investors to become interested in its purchase.

Public Building Financing As soon as even a few families occupy houses in a new development project, there is a need for public buildings for community use. The minimum to start with is a place for a school and a place for public meetings of one kind or another. Others can be added as population needs dictate. The answer to needs for public buildings at the outset is likely to take the form of temporary or makeshift buildings. A building constructed as a field office for the development company may serve as a meeting place for the village commission. The home of the president of the development company may provide space in its basement for the first school. As the population increases, the site dedicated to school use may be improved with a temporary structure containing a few rooms.

As soon as the area attracts enough homes to establish a credit rating for the community in financial circles, a new schoolhouse, a city hall, and so forth, may be erected from the proceeds of a bond issue. Until this time comes, all community buildings, including those used for recreational facilities, usually contain some element of financial subsidy by the development company. Even after the community has attained considerable size, the company will be expected to make contributions, in some form, for churches and other public buildings needed for contented living by its inhabitants.

Wholesale Financing of Development Projects As noted above, the financing problems of development projects are much more complicated than those of parasitical subdivisions. Quantitatively, the former cover many times more acres than the latter. Qualitatively, the former cover many activities not included at all in the latter. The patterns of wholesale financing of the larger area, extending over a longer period of time, must be very different from those covering a small acreage, to be sold out in a single season if possible. By comparison, the financing of parasitical subdivisions is exceedingly simple, involving as it does only the control over land. The financing of development projects covers the financing of land, in one category, and the several other financial requirements discussed earlier, in another.

The financing of the land alone may follow any one of the plans discussed in describing the financing of subdivisions. It may be by outright purchase for cash, by the lease and release device, or by the use of a purchase-money mortgage with provision for partial release of the mortgage at the time the title to each lot is transferred. Because of the amount of land and the length of time involved, the option plan is hardly suited to development projects.

The funds needed to pay for the land or to make the down payment on it may be obtained from the resources of the promoter; from a partner or partners, of whom the landowner may be one; from a syndicate; or from a corporation's sale of stock. The latter may be common or preferred stock or both. If preferred stock is used, it is sold to more conservative investors, while the promoter and those more speculatively inclined hold the common. Preferred stock is frequently callable, so that when it is retired the owners of the common stock will be entitled to any residual profits, in return for the greater risks assumed by them. Whatever the pattern of stocks used, the promoter-manager will always want to make sure that he retains control over the policies of the enterprise.

Bonds are not suitable types of securities to be issued by real estate development corporations. The speculative nature of the project and the uncertainty of income speak strongly against the assumption of fixed charges. Likewise, the issuance of mortgages for cash suffers from the same disability. Neither the mortgagee nor the mortgagor can feel comfortable under such a financing program. The same comment applies, to a lesser degree, to purchase-money mortgages. The use of a purchase-money mortgage puts the seller and the buyer into a kind of partnership even though the law does not recognize it as such.

Banks are hesitant to make even short-term loans to development companies because of the nonliquid character of their assets. Hence the financing of development companies is largely dependent upon equity capital. This takes the form of original capital, supplemented by the plowing back of future earnings.

The funds needed to finance land acquisition constitute the easiest part of the financial problems of development projects. In many cases the total amount needed for this purpose is only a fraction of the total capital eventually invested in such an enterprise. Considering all of the other financial demands against the project, the land cost might easily be only one fourth or even one fifth of the total investment. This is another good reason for preparing the land and putting it on the market in sections instead of trying to offer it all at once. The profits from each section are needed to finance the preparation of the next section.

Plowing Back of Earnings It is common practice for American business corporations to grow from the retention of a large part of their earnings. Therefore the adoption of this policy by real estate development companies is not unusual, except for its intensity of use and the narrow margin of safety frequently employed. By this is meant that the original capital is sufficient only to start the enterprise, with complete dependence upon future sales to keep it going. Should the first season of operations meet expectations, the progress ahead would seem to provide a clear road to final success. But if, for any reason, sales are slow in developing, a single season may find the enterprise so mired in overhead expenses that it must collapse before it has a real chance to get started. Then some stronger financial control may take over at great loss to those who planned the enterprise.

Marked success at the outset may even lure the promoters into the path of final failure. If early sales bring in great amounts of cash, plans may be laid for too rapid expansion. Promoters of real estate development projects are notorious for their optimism about the future. When actual sales confirm optimistic hopes, the ground work is being laid for an expansion of future plans. Overextension of commitments, so that demands for cash may exceed future receipts, may jeopardize the financial stability of the operations at any time. Conservative reinvestment of earnings may result in continued consolidation of position and stabilization of resources to protect against whatever shocks the future may provide. Reckless use of resources on a shoestring basis may weaken the foundation of the structure so that even a slight shock will result in its collapse.

Use of Commitments of Institutional Investors Even though buyers of newly constructed homes may be available, there is still the problem of disposing of the final mortgages. This is an important consideration where the mortgages are FHA-insured or VA-guaranteed and current interest rates have risen above maximums set for federally underwritten mortgages. The originator of the mortgages must have an appropriate plan of disposition if he is to avoid tying up his own capital, and possibly impairing it. If he is especially fortunate he may have a firm takeout commitment from an institutional investor on all mortgages generated by the project. In many cases the institution making the construction loans also does all of the final financing. Or it may decide to keep only the conventional loans and leave the loan originator to his own resources to dispose of the FHA and VA mortgages. In this event, a takeout letter will be sought from a private investor or from the Federal

National Mortgage Association (FNMA). The takeout letter will give the necessary prior assurance of a satisfactory permanent market for these mortgages and thus enable the construction to proceed. In the absence of a takeout letter, the institution making the construction loan may decide at the time it extends its credit to the contractor that it will take over any unsold mortgages at a forfeiture price. For example, it may guarantee 92 percent on the mortgage, if the contractor cannot dispose of the loan to better advantage. In that case, funds are advanced on the construction loan up to 92 percent of the total amount of the mortgage. Eight points are withheld to keep the total of the loan consistent with the forfeiture price. If the mortgages can be sold in the meantime to FNMA or a private investor at a price in excess of 92 percent, the contractor is credited with the difference. If not, the institution making the construction loan must decide whether to retain the mortgage at 92 percent or sell it and absorb the loss. In practice, the mortgages are usually retained.

Under present conditions of high loan-to-value ratios, contractors endeavor to mortgage out all of their costs, leaving only profits at risk. They are generally successful in accomplishing this objective in the housing field. Conservative lenders, however, may leave contractors short of this goal, particularly by declining to finance unsold properties. A financially responsible and competent contractor may sometimes be granted an exception to the requirement of prior sale, in anticipation of winter construction, to provide an agreed number of slabs to be placed on a speculative basis. As houses are sold at these locations and as the deposits are received, loans may then be granted to bring the houses to completion. Other deviations from normal credit terms may be made in accordance with the capacity of the contractor to justify credit from his banker or other credit source.

Influence of FHA The dependence placed in recent years upon FHA financing of new residential construction has given the administrator of this mortgage insurance program a large measure of control over the areas in which loans will be insured. Specifically, in the field discussed in this chapter, the FHA not only determines whether or not it will insure loans in any given area but controls the method of wholesale financing and the types of improvements required. For example, it will not insure mortgages on properties located in a development project unless the land is free and clear of all encumbrances and unless the improvements in the nature of streets, sewers, and so on, meet the standards established by the FHA. In the interpretation of its regulations on this subject, however, the FHA has tried to be helpful. Suppose that the entire project covers 400 acres. Suppose also that only 10 percent of this acreage is being offered to the public in the form of improved building sites. This 10 percent will be accepted by the FHA, provided it meets the standards set up. The remaining acreage held in reserve for future development and sale is disregarded as if it were not under the control of the development company.

Among the subjects in which the FHA is interested[6] are the following: suitability of improvements; total area; protections; civic, social, and commercial centers; transportation facilities; utilities available; taxes and assessments; special hazards, if any; street maintenance programs; extent of improvements; width of streets and pavements; grading; drainage systems; relation of streets, parks, and other publicly dedicated land to total acreage. Some of the regulations of the FHA represent requirements, and others are merely recommendations.

Pricing of Lots The pricing of lots in a development project follows the pattern described above for parasitical subdivisions in part and differs from it in important respects. In the first place, prices are quoted on a long-term basis and are likely to be somewhat higher than those quoted for lots in parasitical subdivisions. If improvements have been installed by the company, their cost will be added. Since the complete sale of the lots is postponed for several years, the granting of discounts even for cash purchases may not be a wise move. Rumors of flexible prices make future sales at quoted prices more difficult. Occasionally cash discounts are granted, but only on a *sub rosa* basis. Sometimes indirect discounts are allowed, as when a cheap lot is accepted at an inflated price as a down payment on a higher priced lot at a standard price.

During depressions, when development company sales have approached the vanishing point and when the need for cash is pressing, discounts are given in the form of credit for future assessments. For example, if the quoted price of the lot is $1,200 and future assessments total $400, the lot may be sold for the difference, or $800. Installment sales are not common during depressions; the $800 cash sale may be a boon to the company whose treasury is depleted.

Operating Costs Unlike the promoter of a parasitical subdivision, the development company has numerous additional costs which must be reflected in the price of its building sites. In the first place, it must have an office, preferably located in the downtown section, where it can be reached conveniently by lot purchasers wishing to make payments on their contracts. This means overhead expenses for rent, bookkeepers, and so forth, which must be maintained throughout the life of the development. Carrying charges are increased to account for the amounts needed to pay a return upon the larger capital investment. Advertising costs must be calculated upon a long-range basis rather than upon a single-season operation The effects of advertising are frequently cumulative. This is particularly true of the sale of lots in a development project.

---

[6] See FHA Bulletin No. 3 on *Land Planning*.

The prospective purchaser with insufficient interest or resources today may become a buyer at some future time when his resources permit, if his interest is cultivated by a persistent advertising campaign.

Taxes and assessments paid by the development company probably must be considered as expenses, because they cannot always be capitalized and added to the price of the building site. For example, if a lot is priced at $1,200 and does not sell for three years, its price is still likely to be $1,200, in spite of the fact that the company has meanwhile paid out $275 for taxes and assessments. In addition to the capital costs of installation of improvements and utilities, the area being offered for sale must be kept fresh looking by newly painted signs indicating street names; by the mowing of parkways and even vacant lots; and by the acceptance of other community obligations that may be assumed later by a municipality, but that at the outset must be borne by the development company.

Financing of Sales Formerly the sale of lots in development projects followed either of two patterns: (1) Cash sales are made to those able to pay cash and particularly to those planning to build a house soon. Cash sales are accomplished by the immediate transfer of title to the purchaser. This is a much simpler operation than the sale of improved property, because seldom is any question raised about the nature of title held by the vendor. (2) A land contract is used in case the lot is purchased on installments. The down payment is expected to cover at least the direct sales expenses. More is obtained if possible. Where land contracts are used, the monthly payment may vary, but is expected to cover a pro rata proportion of annual taxes and assessments as well as interest and something toward amortization of the principal. If street improvements are installed after the lot is purchased, the purchaser is obligated under his contract to pay the additional amounts needed to cover the assessments required to pay the interest and amortize the improvement bonds. The added cost of such improvements is a frequent cause of default on the land contract, since many installment purchasers lack the resources to pay this extra cost.

In recent years cash sales have been much more common than formerly, though they are not used exclusively even today. If the purchaser desires to use an FHA loan to finance the construction of his house, he must first clear the building site of all encumbrances.

Financing of Resales Generally speaking, purchase of vacant lots at retail prices is not a very profitable venture for the purchaser. The original retail price is likely to forecast the future use of the building site if not indeed the highest price it may bring in the open market. Financing of resales is not easy. For example, suppose that A contracts to pay $1,200 for a lot, paying $120 down. Suppose that his added payments to cover principal installment, interest, taxes, and assessments during the succeeding two years amount to $300. His cash investment to date is $420. He still owes probably $1,020 on his contract. To break even it would be necessary for him to find a buyer willing a assume his contract for $1,020 and pay him $420 in cash. It is probable that the development company will be glad to sell a comparable lot for $1,200, with a down payment of $120. Even if quoted prices have been increased 10 percent, the new price of company lots will be only $1,320 and the new down payment only $132.

If the lot purchaser has paid for his lot in full and is willing to take his loss by selling at the price quoted by the company for its remaining lots, the lot owner still faces a financing problem. The company can sell on such terms as it sees fit. The owner of the individual lot must find a buyer willing to pay cash. In addition, the logical salesman of his lot is a company salesman. But the latter can earn three or more times as much in selling a company lot as in selling a lot owned by an individual, since he must divide the commission on the latter with his employer.

Consequently, neither the opportunity for sale at an advantageous price nor the financing of a sale in competition with the development company recommend the purchase of vacant lots at retail prices for speculative purposes.

Creating New Cities The most recent type of subdivision activity developed in this country may truly be designated as city building. Land sales are not a major part of such programs. Even building sites have been overlooked in the effort to create a home ready to move into. Two separate programs are being pushed simultaneously, different from each other yet closely related in their objectives. In spite of surface indications that they are quite distinct in their approach to the solution of America's housing problems, a careful analysis shows that their similarities are more significant than their differences.

One gives the impression of subdivision activity in reverse. It undertakes belatedly to correct some of the consequences of earlier mistakes made by subdividers who failed to anticipate the density of population now evident in some of our larger cities. Because of the rapid growth of our largest cities, the great freedom given to those who developed our cities as we now know them and the absence of clairvoyance on the part of both public and private planners, most of our great cities suffer from the wastes of slum areas where uneconomical uses of land require heroic measures for recovering real estate values. In such areas all of the conditions necessary for comfortable living already exist, except modern structures. Utilities are already available; stores, schools, churches and other offsite community needs are at hand. What is needed is a reassembly of small, individually owned parcels of land into one larger holding sufficient in size to justify a redevelopment program.

Such a reassembly is represented in a huge face-lifting operation which affects a section of middle Manhattan, New York City, covering the area from Fourteenth Street to Twenty-third street and from First Avenue east to the river. With encouragement from the city authorities, the Metropolitan Life Insurance Company bought up the individual parcels of land, secured the abandonment of all streets from Fourteenth to Twentieth and from Twentieth to Twenty-third, and replatted the resulting area for two large housing projects. Stuyvesant Town occupies the area from Fourteenth to Twentieth Streets, and Peter Cooper Village covers the area from Twentieth to Twenty-third Streets.

These projects are owned entirely by the Metropolitan Life Insurance Company and are held by it as an outlet for some of its investment funds. Stuyvesant Town was erected on land that—by agreement with the City of New York—was not to be saddled with an increase in real estate taxes for a period of 20 years. Meantime the city actually collected taxes that previously were only assessed but not always collected. Peter Cooper Village was not subject to any such arrangement, though veterans of World War II were given preference in the allocation of housing space. While this kind of project does not represent homes for sale, it does embody a new plan of creating a "new city" to house American families.

Even earlier the Metropolitan had created a similar "new city" in the Bronx, where it acquired 129 acres formerly occupied by a religious organization. Within this area it created a city of 51 separate buildings housing 12,273 apartments and 200 stores. They are capable of providing housing accommodations for 42,000 people. Only an enterprise headed by management of vision, courage, and tremendous financial resources could undertake such a project. The area to be covered must be of sufficient size to justify an investment that can be relatively independent of surrounding real estate uses. The pattern set by the Metropolitan in New York City, and already followed by it in several other cities, has blazed the trail for redevelopment of other slum areas by other institutions with large resources.

Of course, a great impetus has been given to slum clearance and rehabilitation by the urban renewal program of the federal government working in conjunction with local government entities and private developers. This program has taken on national significance in recent years and is discussed in detail in Chapter 29.

Selecting New Sites The other method of creating new cities differs from that just described in several major particulars. Its promoters select a new site not already built up, and create a new city from farm land. While close proximity to the city whose population provides its customers is desirable, it is sometimes necessary to go out some distance in order to secure control over the amount and kind of acreage desired. When such a site is located, it is acquired for the purpose of development and construction as a consistent whole rather than as a series of uncontrolled, piecemeal uses by individual owners. The company which has the vision, the courage, and the access to the resources needed for the purpose is not interested in selling land, building sites, or even merely completed homes. It sells the opportunity to live in the new, coordinated community through the medium of a purchase of a house and lot.

The planning at least must encompass the entire acreage acquired. From the start its promoters must "see" the completed project in order that they may provide all of the improvements, utilities, and community services needed for complete living as a part of the community. The actual construction may cover only a part of the total area at the outset. As each section is completed and disposed of, other sections will be successively added. Only completed houses are sold. In some cases the sale includes all the equipment needed for comfortable living, described elsewhere in this volume as packaged real estate.

In the financing of these projects, Section 608 and, more recently, Sections 220, 221, 235, and 236 of the FHA have been very helpful in inducing private financial institutions to invest large sums in building construction. Since the amount of loans approved for insurance by the FHA for such purpose is dependent upon appraisals made for this agency, it is probable that the construction loans may provide at least all of the money needed for erection of the buildings. Nevertheless, the purchase of the land; the installation of streets, sewers, and so forth; the provision of schools, recreational facilities, and so on; the arrangement for public transportation; and other elements of cost not directly concerned with the specific building site and the buildings to be erected thereon: All of these add up to considerable sums of money which only a well-organized group can command.

Not all of such projects are concerned primarily with the sale of completed houses. Some provide rental housing accommodations for those who wish, at least temporarily, to rent rather than to buy. Some combine both rental space and houses for sale. Like the housing projects owned by the Metropolitan Life Insurance Company, these other efforts to create "new cities" are limited to our largest city areas where the demand for new housing accommodations is very great, or to the housing needs of new industrial areas. To house the population needed to supply labor to the huge $400 million steel plant constructed by the United States Steel Corporation, Fairless Hills and Levittown, Pennsylvania, were created as "new cities." In such areas great new projects can be created quickly without too great fear of failure or stagnation because of a glutted market. While such projects can and do take time for development, they cannot be expected to consume as much time as the development and sale of development projects described earlier in this chapter.

Large Corporations as Developers During the early 1960s, a number of large publicly held corporations have become interested in the real estate development-construction business—corporations whose historical central activity has not been housing. Since 1960, such important firms as Aluminum Company of America, Reynolds Metals, Koppers Co., Inc., Christiana Oil, Humble Oil, McCulloch Oil, Sunset International Petroleum, and Union Carbide have taken equity positions in broadscope development programs.[7]

These corporations have at least three basic reasons for becoming deeply involved in homebuilding. In the first place, profit squeezes have led many materials producers to seek diversification in operations. The housing market, with its relative assurance of constantly increasing demand factors, has been more appealing than that for new specialty items of uncertain acceptance. Second, many such corporations have strong financial positions, including excess cash or lines of credit permitting borrowing at money costs less than those charged most builders. They can thus obtain a special advantage from increased leverage on borrowed capital. A third reason, often most important, lies in the public relations aspects of a captive outlet for corporate products. The long time lag between product innovation and wide usage in construction can be reduced when manufacturers provide field testing under their own control. Firms engaged in urban renewal add luster to their corporate image for public service promoted through local news media.

Large corporations usually find the "new city" development-construction type of operation the only one of sufficient magnitude to be attractive. The housing market is analyzed in terms of labor supply at competitive prices, stability of employment, diversification and types of industries, and the ratio of homeowners to total population. Future development sites are chosen with due regard for city growth trends, existing availability of housing, family incomes, unfulfilled needs of potential customers, and the city master plan. Communities may be established for homes in various price ranges, so that families may upgrade their housing under the same development sponsor as their needs and income grow. Trade-in plans may be carried out not only for moves from one community to another within a metropolitan area but also for shifts from one city to another where the same developer can offer a somewhat standardized product. The product in these cases is more than a house—it is promoted as a way of life. The community must therefore offer an acceptable standard of convenient shopping, school, religious, and recreational

---

[7] Gurney Breckenfeld, "The Emerging Giants," *House & Home*, Vol. XXIII, No. 1 (January 1963), pp. 67–71, 113–15.

facilities, as well as the more commonplace public utilities and rights-of-way.

Undoubtedly these "new city" development-construction projects are in direct competition with development projects. The popularity of the former will hurt sales of building sites in the latter. Yet there will continue to be a need for the latter, at least in metropolitan areas smaller than our largest ones, to meet the needs of those who still prefer to plan their own house construction.

QUESTIONS AND PROBLEMS

1. What are the characteristics of a parasitical subdivision? Do you know of one?

2. What services should be performed by a developer before his subdivision activity merits the term "development project"?

3. Point out forms of subdivision and development activity which are not characteristic of practices before World War II.

4. How is a purchase-money mortgage used in financing a parasitical subdivision?

5. How is a lease and release used to finance a parasitical subdivision or a development project?

6. Gray buys a lot for $3,000, paying $100 down and $35 per month, with interest at 8 percent annually on the unpaid balance. Taxes are $40 annually and special assessments for street improvements amount to $80 per year for 10 years. How long will it take to pay for the lot and how much will Gray have paid for it when he finally receives an unencumbered title?

7. What kinds of deed restrictions and other forms of protection to lot owners should be incorporated in a soundly conceived development project?

8. What conditions should govern the selection of new sites for development projects?

9. What forms of organization do development projects usually take?

10. What are the various ways in which developers may finance the installation of improvements?

11. How has the increasing importance of FHA financing affected development standards?

12. How have the developers' problems changed with the movement of the big city population into suburbia?

13. What problems do you visualize for large publicly held corporations as builders of housing?

22

Financing Farms and Rural Development

Meaning of Farms The American farm combines, in its real estate relationships, both residential and business uses. It affords a place for the owner-operator and his family to live while it provides them with their means of livelihood. In times past, the farmer has been looked upon as a grower of crops and farm animals. To an increasing extent he has become a businessman. Like any other type of business, farming requires capital. Requirements for this purpose cover real estate capital, machinery, working capital, and contributions to cooperative ventures.

Real estate capital, with which we are primarily concerned in this study, covers the cost of land and its more or less permanent improvements. The latter include the home, various types of farm buildings, fences, drainage, and, in some cases, irrigation and terracing. These costs add up to the greatest proportion of the capital investment of the farmer.

Determinants of Amount of Investment The amount invested by an individual farmer in his real estate is governed by several unrelated factors. The type of farming, of course, helps to set the pattern of investment. The size of the farm in turn helps to determine the use made of it. The period of the business cycle is a major factor in the pricing of farms. The price paid measures the kind and amount of financing needed. One interesting feature of farm financing that has assumed greater importance in recent years is the competition of city folk in the purchase of farms. There has always been a feeling on the part of many city dwellers that ownership of a farm is quite desirable. More recently, several new factors have accentuated this feeling. In groping for security in an uncertain world, people seem to feel that farming offers a better than usual sense of protection to farm owners. Many people feel that nothing can happen to interfere materially with farm ownership. Some city people have purchased farms as a hedge against inflation. Others have purchased run-down farms as a means of equalizing income tax burdens. Whatever the incentive which impels city people to purchase farms, the effects of their competition complicate the financial problems of farmers who hope to make a business of farming.

Sources of Farm Capital Traditionally, the typical cycle which eventually leads to farm ownership, by those who make farming a business as owner-operators, begins with the small savings of a boy on the farm. These are added to as the young man works as a hired hand until the equity capital necessary for a venture on his own takes form. Seldom can a young man hope to own a farm unless he inherits it. Ownership comes in the middle life of the farmer who buys a farm. Until the person ambitious to become a farm owner acquires some capital through savings, he will probably maintain his status as a laborer working for someone else.

With some capital accumulated through savings, the farmer may become his own manager through one of the following processes: (1) He may enter into partnership with someone else. (2) He may become a tenant instead of a laborer for hire. (3) He may use some kind of credit arrangement to add to his equity capital the amount needed for acquiring a farm.

Partnership Partnerships are commonly used in farm operation. One partner, frequently the inactive one, owns the farm and takes into partnership a younger man with experience and usually some capital. Sometimes even the capital is absent. The owner of the farm matches his capital against the skill of the younger man. Father and son and father and son-in-law partnerships are very common. Two brothers may become partners. Or partnerships are arranged in which no blood or marital relationship exists between the participants.

Farm partnerships have the advantage of encouraging long-range planning which may end in a transfer of title to the land at the death of the older member of the firm. They are frequently entered into without written or formal agreement. The imposition of personal income taxes probably did more to require an accounting of income between partners than had ever been done before. As a general rule, farmers have not been accustomed to distinguishing sharply between income and capital investment. This has been true of partnerships as well as of other types of business organization on the farm.

Because of the prevalence of the father-son origin of farm partnerships, the problem of lines of authority takes on interesting patterns. The older man tends to make the decisions at the outset, but, if all goes well, more and more he defers to the wishes of the younger partner, until finally the original position is reversed. Eventually the son may, to all intents and purposes, become the owner, with the father being supported by the son as his share in the fruits of the partnership.

Leasing In the absence of a father-son partnership, and particularly if the farm owned by the father is not large enough to support two families, the younger man may lease a farm instead. While he is expected to have some capital, he can enter the farming business by using the real estate capital of someone else. In return for the use of this capital he pays a share of the crops, or a cash rental, or a combination of the two. Some farmers prefer a lease to farm ownership, especially in times when the price of land is very high. By renting land owned by someone else, they can continue to add to their savings, pending a decline in prices.

Some farmers own the place which provides them with a home and lease additional land for productive purposes. Sometimes the partnership arrangement discussed above is made possible by leasing adjoining or nearby land. By this means not only is additional land acquired, but a home needed for the younger member of the partnership is made available also. Some city people who own farms but are unacquainted with their operation are very glad to shift the burdens of management to a tenant skilled in farm operation.

The lease arrangement avoids some of the difficulties occasionally encountered in partnerships. Under a proper form of lease, the landlord is concerned only with end results. Meantime, management is centered in the tenant. At the same time, tenancy lacks the stability of a partnership arrangement. Leases are likely to run one year at a time or on a year-to-year basis. Some of the work on a farm and some of the investment by the tenant must necessarily look beyond this short period for results.

A modification of farm leasing takes the form of a manager-operator agreement. The owner of the farm hires a manager who operates the farm, with all capital being supplied by the owner. By a kind of profit sharing plan, the hired manager is permitted to share in the results of his labors over and above a stipulated salary for his services.

Like partnerships, leases are frequently informal and oral rather than written. As in other business matters, a more formal written lease is recommended. Like other leases, farm leases should include all practicable provisions to make sure of complete meeting of minds between the tenant and the landlord. In general, a lease that leans too far in the direction of protecting either party to the disadvantage of the other is not likely to endure for long or to produce satisfactory results.

A comprehensive text on the subject of farm financing makes the following recommendations on the subject of farm leases: The lease arrangement should be in writing; it should be definite; it should fit the type of farming to be engaged in; it should state the rental rates;

it should provide for change or modification upon mutual agreement; it should provide a method of settlement of misunderstandings; it should be legally signed by both parties to the agreement.[1]

Use of Credit As a business loan, the financing of farm real estate is expected to be repaid from the income from farm operations. While the lender will look to the appraisal of the security for the loan as a basis for his decisions, neither he nor the borrower expects to have the loan repaid from the proceeds of the sale of the property. Here, as elsewhere in real estate finance, a distinction must be made between a safe loan and a sound one. A lender may feel safe in making a loan if the liquidating value of the security will be at least equal to the amount of the loan. But a borrower who would expect to use this means of meeting his obligations would not be making a sound business commitment.

Because most farms are family operated, the personal equation in farm loans is particularly significant. The lender gives great weight to the moral hazard. An ambitious, experienced farmer can obtain real estate financing of greater advantage to him than he could if his reputation for integrity and skill were less favorable. The lender knows that he is taking the risk of managerial ability and acts accordingly. In analyzing the moral hazard, the family is included in the lender's calculations. As a family-operated business, farming reflects the type of family as well as the type of head of the household. The attitude of the wife toward farming and farm life may be nearly as important as that of the borrower. Farm productivity, in terms of dollar income, is frequently definitely related to the interest taken by the wife in farm operations.

Increasing Demand for Credit In looking into the future, it seems probable that farmers will depend more upon credit facilities in financing their operations than has been true in the past. The reasons for this change are: (1) The average size of farms is increasing. Increased mechanization makes possible the handling of more acres with the same man power. (2) This increased mechanization calls for larger capital investment. (3) Soil exhaustion requires greater attention to and investment in rehabilitation and conservation programs. (4) Many farmers are reaching an age when they are no longer able to continue to handle their acreage. With higher prices of farms, the transfer of these holdings to younger men will call for more credit than was needed when the present farmers acquired their holdings.

Factors Considered by Lender In addition to the moral hazard, the lender on farm real estate takes into account various factors that may not be present in considering urban real estate as security for loans.

---

[1] I. W. Duggan and R. U. Battles, *Financing the Farm Business* (New York: John Wiley & Co., Inc., 1950), p. 67. Much of the material in this chapter is adapted from this book.

Loans are made not on acres alone but upon the productivity of those acres. Erosion and wastage as well as fertility must be studied, since the loan will be repaid over a long period of time. The lender must look to the productivity of the farm over a series of years as the source of repayment of his loan. Hence he tries to measure it as best he can.

The size of the farm is important. Since it must first afford a living to its owners, the lender wants to make sure that there will be enough left to pay taxes and operating expenses—including reasonable allowances to maintain the productivity of the land—and still leave a balance of income from which the mortgage can be amortized. Even a well-operated small farm might be a poor lending risk because of the absence of a debt-paying balance of income.

As a businessman seeking a business loan, the farmer must be able to demonstrate his efficiency as a manager. Operating costs should be consistent with a productive unit of the kind that a borrower should offer as security for a loan. Evidence of lack of balance in the investment of capital or in the use of labor will not produce a high credit rating for lending purposes. For example, some farms are inefficiently operated because their owners or operators economize too much in the use of laborsaving machinery; others lean in the opposite direction and are burdened with more mechanization than the particular farm can support.

To an increasing extent farmers are required, for one reason or another, to keep accounting records of their operations. When the owner of a farm makes an application for a real estate loan, he must be in a position to tell what he owns and what he owes. His net worth will go a long way toward determining his borrowing capacity. Not only will the lender be interested in the use of a microscope, but he will want to use his telescope also. He will want to know in detail the current condition of the business and also the progress of the operations as compared with those in preceding periods. An increase in assets or a decrease in debts indicates an increase in net worth. The opposite tendency in either would speak against an extension of too much credit to the applicant for a real estate loan. Changes in price levels are taken into account in measuring changes in net worth.

In some respects an income statement is even more useful in measuring debt-paying capacities than is a balance sheet. The latter is somewhat of a liquidation measure; the former tests the farm operation as a going concern. As might be expected, adequate and accurate income statements for farm operations are more rare than balance sheets. They are becoming more common. County extension agents are rendering worthwhile service in encouraging accounting records. The farmer who keeps them is a better credit risk than one who does not.

Types of Farm Mortgages As stated above, farm mortgages should be paid out of income. The type of mortgage most likely to meet the needs of most farmers runs for a long period of time—10, 20, 30 or, in some cases, as long as 40 years; is payable in annual or semiannual installments; and carries a low rate of interest, since the average return on farm capital is low. Some years may show higher than average returns, but others will show lower rates of return, depending upon prices of farm products, crop yields, and other factors.

Term loans fail to meet the needs of most farmers. If a lump-sum mortgage falls due at an inopportune time, when renewals are not favored and refinancing is unavailable, trouble for the borrower may result. Foreclosure marks the end of the trail for many such mortgages.

Purposes of Farm Mortgages Farms may be mortgaged to obtain funds to meet any of the needs of the owner. A new automobile, a large hospital bill, or an educational program may be financed by a mortgage. In general, it is expected that, like any other business loan, a farm mortgage will be used to finance a business need. Such needs grow out of the following pattern:

1. The mortgage may assist in financing the purchase price of a farm. Presumably the borrower will first have capital to use as a down payment and will hope to borrow the remainder of the purchase price. Sometimes the loan takes the form of a purchase-money mortgage to be held by the seller of the property.

2. The mortgage may finance the cost of permanent improvements. Barns, silos, drainage facilities, and so on, are all part of the productive capacity of the farm. As such, their financing must be placed in the same class as the purchase of the land. The financing of home improvements which are in keeping with the kind of farm on which they are located is also to be classed as for business improvements.

3. The funding of short-term obligations by the use of a mortgage is commonly followed. If the debts have been incurred for long-run productive purposes, and if they cannot be paid from current income, the use of mortgage credit to refinance such debts is justified. On the other hand, the funding of an overextended current debt incurred for consumption purposes might handicap the future operations of the farmer. However, the existence of such debts might produce similar results, so that the mortgage might be the lesser of two evils.

4. Mortgages are frequently used to refund an existing mortgage. The latter might have matured, or it might contain less favorable terms than are available in the current market. Such terms may include a lower amortization schedule, a reduced interest rate, or a longer maturity of the debt. Every borrower on mortgage security is likely at some time or other to face the possibility of refinancing his loan. In each specific case the advantages to be gained must be weighed against the costs of paying off the old loan and the placing of the new one. Prepayment privileges may not be provided for in the mortgage. In this case, penalties may be applied if prepayment is sought.

The maturity of a term mortgage or one that is not fully amortized usually calls for some kind of a refunding operation. While the holder of such a mortgage may permit it to remain overdue so long as interest and taxes are paid, this is a precarious position for the debtor to be in. The holder of the mortgage may change his mind and demand payment of an overdue debt. For this reason, refunding operations are desirable if the money market is favorable at the time the mortgage falls due. In case the mortgagee is an individual, his death may precipitate a crisis in event that the mortgage is past due. In the settlement of the estate, prompt action may be taken to collect the debt, by foreclosure action if necessary. The frequency of use of individual mortgagees in farm financing makes this issue more significant here than in the financing of other kinds of real estate.

Amortization Plans The disadvantage of straight loans for farm financing in comparison with amortization of the debt from income has already been mentioned. Several forms of amortization of farm mortgages are in common use. The so-called standard or constant payment plan provides for a level payment each semiannual or annual period. As the principal installments result in a decline in the balance of the indebtedness, successive interest charges are progressively smaller. With level payments the amount of each principal installment increases, thereby speeding the date of complete amortization of the debt.

The Springfield plan provides for equal amounts to be applied to principal reduction, plus interest for the current period. Since the interest declines steadily, there is a corresponding decrease in each total payment of principal installment plus current interest. Under this plan the principal is seemingly paid off faster during the early years of the loan than under the standard plan. As the years pass, however, the amortization of the principal balance of the loan is not accelerated as under the standard plan.

A modification of the standard plan of amortization takes the form of a change in interest rate after a fixed number of years. Curiously enough, the change in this case results in an increase in the rate of interest instead of the expected decrease. As the principal balance of a mortgage is substantially reduced with a series of payments, it should become a safer mortgage for the lender and therefore should merit a lower interest rate. In one case—used by the Metropolitan Life Insurance Company—the rate increases by ½ percent after the 15th year. This helps to compensate the lender for higher service charges as the amount of the loan is reduced. Meantime, level payments are made each semiannual period throughout the life of the loan.

In some farm financing plans only a portion of the principal is amortized during the life of the loan. This invites refinancing with a smaller mortgage when the original loan matures. While this gives the borrower the advantage of smaller payments, it exposes him to the risks that surround any mortgage plan which calls for a lump-sum payment at a time which may prove to be quite embarrassing in a tight money market. Renewal or refinancing with another lender at such a time will necessarily be on the lender's terms. Lenders sometimes prefer the partial amortization plan, because it enables them to keep their funds better employed. Also, at frequent intervals the lender may review his commitments and decide whether to renew the loans—perhaps at higher interest rates—or to demand payment of the debt.

Some flexibility in amortization schedules is brought about under compulsion. For example, in times of stress lenders do not ordinarily wish to take over the security behind farm mortgage loans. If the financial condition of the borrower is such that he cannot meet full payments, the lender may be forced to accept less. Both the willingness and the ability of the lender enter into such postponements. In many cases the postponement of principal installments merely adds to the maturity of the loan. The borrower who depends upon successive postponements of making principal installments may find himself in a precarious position, because such an arrangement represents a change in the loan contract which the lender may not always grant.

Prepayment Privileges Borrowers with farm real estate as security prefer to have the privilege of prepayment of their loans as and when their incomes permit. In years of high income the debt can be reduced more rapidly than contractual payments permit. In case the borrower wishes to sell the farm, prepayment privileges are always advantageous if the prospective purchaser prefers to pay all cash or to do his own financing.

The lender, on the other hand, frequently prefers not to grant prepayment privileges, since this necessitates reinvestment of his funds. Restricted prepayment privileges are sometimes granted. They may take the form of limiting the amount that will be accepted in any one year—such as 20 percent of the principal amount of the loan—or of assessing a penalty of 1 to 3 percent. In still other cases, no prepayment is permitted for a specified period of years, after which the privilege may apply. Penalties may or may not be applied when the time for prepayment privileges arrives.

Prepayment may be permitted by mutual agreement in spite of the absence of a permissive clause in the mortgage contract. If the income of the borrower is unusually large, and if the lender can readily invest his funds elsewhere to his advantage, he may be willing to accept prepayment. But if the purpose of the prepayment is to arrange for refinancing elsewhere, the lender may be unwilling, in the absence of a contract to the contrary, to accept prepayment without a penalty.

Sinking Fund for Future Payments Because of the irregularity of farm income, some farm mortgages provide that the borrower may build up in high-income years what amounts to a sinking fund to take care of installments in lean years. If such funds are credited with the same rate of interest as is charged on the mortgage, the effect is about the same as if prepayments had been allowed. The difference lies in the fact that prepayments might not be considered by the lender as an offset to no payments when farm income is low. Both the Federal Land Bank System and some private lenders on farm security encourage the practice of developing a fund to take care of some future payments.

Timing of Payments Unlike mortgage payments on residential properties in urban areas, where the monthly payment direct reduction loan plan has become the common pattern, farmers make their payments less frequently. Payments are most commonly made on an annual, semiannual, or quarterly basis. Which of these plans is followed is determined by the nature of the farming operations. In areas where cash crops are harvested once a year, annual payments best meet the requirements of the borrower. Where tradition dictates a semiannual contract, borrowers frequently become six months in arrears unless their cash income permits payments more often than once a year. In the infrequent cases where income is collected more frequently, the payments may even be met quarterly without inconvenience to the borrower. For example, dairy farmers might readily meet quarterly payments on their mortgages.

Rehabilitation Financing Where farmers undertake a program of soil rehabilitation or a conservation program, the amounts so invested cover a series of years. Some mortgages are so written as to provide for advances as needed for this purpose. The repayment of these advances is arranged in such a manner as to permit the anticipated increase in yield to pay the cost of the program. In order to play safe, only a portion of the anticipated increased yield—perhaps 75 percent—is required to repay the loan. In some cases only a small part of the advances is required to be repaid annually until the entire program is completed. Then the repayments are increased to amortize the advances over a period comparable to those of ordinary farm mortgage loans.

In financing any such operations, the lender must make sure that the borrower proceeds under the guidance of experts, so that the funds advanced will be spent in such a manner that their recovery within a reasonable time may be expected. The usual period for repayment of such loans runs from 5 to 15 years. This is an area of financing in which neither the lender nor the borrower is presumed to be expert. Both need the advice and guidance of specialists capable of fitting a conservation program to the needs of a specific farm.

Appraisals for Farm Loans The average appraiser who appraises property for the purpose of making loans on urban real estate would be of little use to lenders on farm property. Since farm loans are made on the business of farming, the appraiser must be able to set loan values on more than land and permanent improvements. He must be able to measure the selling price of the land and also its earning capacity. The latter is conditioned by the character of the management of the farm, so that this must be reviewed also.

Unlike loans against urban real estate, farm mortgages do not really constitute the first private claim against the property offered as security. Since the farmer-borrower and his family make their living from the operation of the farm, their living expenses constitute the first deduction from farm income. To be sure, their standard of living will probably be lowered in times of reduced income, but they nevertheless depend upon farm income to pay their family expenses. Then, unless the lender is willing to foreclose his mortgage at the first sign of default, he must allow the borrower enough to continue to pay operating expenses, including ordinary repairs and maintenance costs. All of these considerations must be taken into account in appraising farms for lending purposes.

The American Bankers Association defines a good farm mortgage as follows: "The test of a good farm mortgage loan is whether the farm offered for security will provide sufficient income to provide a living for an average family, pay operating expenses including taxes and insurance, and leave enough margin to pay interest and principal on the loan."[2]

Because the lender must always take into account the possibility of foreclosure as a last resort, he must consider the problem of future salability of the farm. Here even apparently extraneous factors must be studied. Among them are such subjects as the condition of roads, the proximity of schools, and the availability of markets.

Search for "Normal" Value Since farm mortgages are commonly written for from 10 to 30 years or more, the appraiser is constantly searching for the long-range "normal" value which can be depended upon for lending purposes. In periods of high prices for farm products and for farms, the "jitters" factor in appraisal processes assumes large proportions. How much should current prices be discounted in the search for a stable value which would protect a long-term loan? Since all appraisals are attempts to measure events to take place in the future, inflation is a particularly formidable stumbling block to accurate forecasting. The tendency to use past values as a bench mark in measuring future values is easily understood. It is not always realistic, however. It is conceivable that what appear to be today's high prices may prove in the future to be yesterday's low prices instead.

In searching for normal value, the appraiser must forecast the future trend of prices of commodities whose values are for the most part fixed

---

[2] The American Bankers Association, *Farm Real Estate Financing* (New York, 1949), p. 3.

in world markets. If he is too pessimistic, he discourages the borrower who is unable to obtain the amount of the loan that he needs. The farm appraiser's task is not an easy one.

Sources of Funds for Farm Mortgages The sources of funds for loans on farm mortgages as security are, in order of volume: individuals and others; Federal Land Banks; insurance companies; and commercial banks. The miscellaneous group of individuals and others account for approximately 40 percent of farm mortgage loans. Individual lenders are present when the seller of a farm takes back a purchase-money mortgage as part payment for his property; when a father or other relative sets up a young man in the farming business; or when the funds needed by the borrower are obtained for a person of means who is willing to invest funds in farm mortgages.

In spite of the prevalence of farm mortgages held by individuals, this class of loans is ordinarily made with less attention to safeguarding the interests of both mortgagor and mortgagee than is true of institutional lenders. In many cases no expert appraiser is asked to give an opinion of value. The borrower and the lender agree upon the value of the property for lending purposes. Particularly if a purchase-money mortgage is involved, the needs of the borrower rather than the value of the property may determine the amount of the loan. This may later cause trouble for both borrower and lender.

As a general rule, the term of mortgages made by individuals is shorter than is that of mortgages held by financial institutions. Interest rates are relatively high where no family relationships are involved, with wide variations in specific cases. Short terms and high interest rates result in higher than average installment payments. Unless the payments are carefully geared to the income-producing capacity of the farm, trouble may result.

Included in the miscellaneous category of farm mortgage lenders are the usual sources of real estate finance with urban land as security. They cover savings and loan associations, mortgage loan companies which represent life insurance companies and other institutional investors, and so forth. In some localities, school funds are invested in farm mortgages. Endowment funds of educational and charitable institutions provide sources of farm mortgage finance. As with individuals who invest in farm mortgages, there is no common pattern of mortgage lending by miscellaneous sources. Expert appraisals may be lacking, and attention to details of sound mortgage lending may be overlooked.

In general, individual and miscellaneous lenders do not hold enough mortgages to give them a wide distribution of risks. With limited resources they may not be able to pursue policies more flexible than those set forth in the mortgage instrument. Under the best of circumstances they may not be able to help the borrower meet unusually difficult financial problems. Since the lender usually dictates the terms of an unstandardized loan pattern, he is likely to make sure that his interests rather than those of the borrower are taken care of.

Life Insurance Companies Life insurance companies have experienced a long and varied history as holders of farm mortgages. They tend to concentrate their farm loans in the best-developed areas and upon relatively large individual loans. In some cases they make loans directly through their branch offices, and in other cases they purchase farm mortgages from mortgage bankers and others. Even commercial banks sometimes have purchase agreements with life insurance companies by which the bank may hold a mortgage for a short period of time—as much as two years—and then dispose of it to an insurance company.

Some insurance companies offer long-term farm financing at low rates of interest. Some of these loans may run as long as 40 years. Several amortization plans are used, most of which provide for some kind of prepayment privileges, provided that these advance payments arise from farm income. While farm mortgages held by life insurance companies currently amount to $5.6 billion, less than 3 percent of their assets are invested in this class of paper. This is a much lower percentage than was formerly so invested.

Commercial Banks In their real estate lending operations, commercial banks are subject to various kinds of limitations. The laws and regulations under which they operate set standards which must be observed. For example, the total amount of real estate mortgages held by a national bank may not be in excess of the larger of (1) its paid-in capital and unimpaired surplus; (2) 70 percent of its time and savings deposits. In addition to legal restrictions, policies established by boards of directors of commercial banks limit their real estate lending operations. Some will make no farm loans under any circumstances; others favor this type of lending. Still others prefer a balanced program in which farm loans play some part.

In rural areas, commercial banks constitute the largest segment of institutional lenders who hold farm mortgages. Here again, governmental restrictions determine the kinds of loans made. National banks may make unamortized five-year loans up to 50 percent of appraised value. They may also make amortized loans. On such loans they may lend up to $66 \frac{2}{3}$ percent of the appraisal value on a 10-year maturity if 40 percent of the principal amount is to be amortized over the life of the loan. As an alternative, they may lend up to 90 percent of the appraised value for a term not longer than 30 years if the loan is secured by an amortized mortgage, deed of trust, or other instrument under the terms of which the installment payments are sufficient to amortize the entire principal of the loan within the period ending on the date of its maturity. Most commercial bank loans on farm mortgages tend to be of the relatively shorter maturities.

Federal Land Banks From 1917 through 1947, the 12 Federal Land Banks made, through 1,233 national farm loan associations, long-term mortgage loans to 1,100,000 farmers and ranchers. The total amount of these loans was $4.1 billion. About half of this amount was advanced during the years 1933 to 1935, mostly to refinance outstanding farm mortgages where foreclosure was threatened. As of the end of 1970, the amount of farm mortgages held by Federal Land Banks was slightly more than $7.1 billion.

Such loans are limited to 65 percent of the normal value of the security when used for agricultural purposes. Only those who derive the principal part of their income from farming operations are eligible for Land Bank loans. Such persons may obtain loans to purchase land for agricultural purposes; to make improvements in the form of buildings or otherwise; to refinance debts at least two years old; and to provide funds for long-term agricultural purposes.

Land Bank loans may be made for periods of from 5 to 40 years. Appraisals are made by experienced Land Bank appraisers. All such loans must be collateralized by first mortgages. In addition, each borrower must purchase stock in the Land Bank which makes the loan equal to 5 percent of the amount of the loan. This, too, is held as collateral to protect the loan. Finally, the national farm loan association which recommends the loan must endorse the note given by the borrower.

Under the law, interest rates on Land Bank loans may not exceed 6 percent. Farmers obtaining loans from this source are required to pay interest at rates based on the cost of money in the investment market and the cost of operations. From 1935 to the early 1950s, most loans made carried a 4 percent rate. From 1933 to 1944, Congress subsidized a part of the interest on these loans. Because of higher money costs in the 1960s and 1970s, rates have risen to the point that current loans have generally been made at 6 percent.

Servicing of Land Bank Loans Land Bank loans are serviced through the national farm loan associations. When the borrower gets into financial difficulty, forbearance is exercised whenever the borrower is deemed to have a reasonable opportunity to catch up on his obligations. Deferments, extensions, and suspended-payment plans have been developed for this purpose. Loans are sometimes recast and a new plan of amortization is set up. When foreclosure has been necessary, deficiency judgments have not been enforced for amounts greater than the difference between the fair value of the property and the amount of investment shown on the books of the lender. As soon as full recovery is realized, any additional claims are voluntarily released, provided there is no evidence of bad faith on the part of the borrower.

Farmers Home Administration In 1946, Congress set up the Farmers Home Administration to lend appropriated funds to farmers unable to obtain financial assistance from any other source. Included in its purposes are direct loans for the purchase, improvement, or enlargement of family-type farms. Under the National Housing Act of 1949, the Farmers Home Administration is authorized to make loans and grants to farmers for the purpose of constructing or repairing farm homes and other farm buildings. To be eligible for such a loan the farmer must be unable to obtain a loan elsewhere. He is supposed to be able to repay the loan from income.

Direct farm ownership loans are made to help farmers buy family-type farms, and to enlarge and develop such farms. Loans are made for periods up to 40 years at 5 percent interest. Each loan is repayable on a plan best suited to the needs of the borrower. Prepayments are invited. Farm operations of borrowers are supervised to insure the best results from their efforts. By this means repayment of the loan is best assured. Loans can be made up to the full fair and reasonable value of the farm. Loans are made to farm tenants, laborers, or owners of small and underimproved farms. Veterans and married borrowers with dependent families are given preference. The borrower is required to measure up to standards of character, industry, and successful farming experience.

In addition to the farm ownership loans just described are rural housing loans. These loans are available to farm owners and owners of nonfarm tracts in rural areas and small rural communities with populations under 10,000. The owners need not be farmers. The funds must be used for construction and repair of homes and essential farm buildings. Terms vary in accordance with the borrower's ability to repay, but the maximum maturity is 33 years and the interest rate is flexible. Housing loans may also be made to residents of rural areas who are 62 years of age or over to buy previously occupied housing as well as to build or improve their own homes. These senior citizens can use a housing loan to finance the cost of a building site as well as the dwelling.

Farmers Home Administration Loans and Grants Farm ownership loans on June 30, 1971 came to $265 million. Of these loans, about $5 million were made directly and $260 million were under the insurance operation. At that time, the amount of farm ownership loans outstanding, direct and insured, was close to 3 percent of all farm real estate debt.

An important function of the Farmers Home Administration has been the improvement of rural housing where other financial resources were not available. Because of the generous credit arrangements it is permitted to make, the Farmers Home Administration often ends up giving its borrowers better terms than they could have obtained from a private lender if they had been able to meet ordinary credit standards. This program, therefore, is a form of subsidy to those who can qualify for its benefits. The demand for these loans has increased markedly since 1961 when the authority of the agency was expanded to permit direct loans for housing purposes to persons other than farmers on nonfarm sites in rural areas. In fact, the limits of the lending program would now seem to be set by the size of the appropriation to the Farmers Home Administration for this purpose that the Congress is willing to approve.[3]

In 1964, the law was liberalized to allow grants to finance low-rent housing for domestic workers. These grants are available to broadly based nonprofit associations or to public bodies that will undertake provision of eligible housing as a public service. In 1966, authorizations for such grants were extended to financing cooperatively owned housing and rental housing for rural families other than senior citizens.

Insured Mortgages Private lenders are permitted to make farm ownership loans through the Farmers Home Administration. These loans may not exceed 90 percent of the value of the farm and are fully insured by the federal government. Payments may be amortized over periods up to 40 years at 5 percent interest, of which 4.5 percent goes to the lender and 0.5 percent is retained by the Farmers Home Administration. The 0.5 percent retained is placed in an insurance reserve fund. After five years, lenders have the option of selling the paper to the federal government.

Insured housing loans may be made to individual farmers, groups of farmers, and public or private nonprofit organizations to finance housing facilities for domestic farm labor. Insured loans may also be made in rural areas to individuals, corporations, and partnerships to provide rental housing for elderly rural people.

The Housing and Urban Development Act of 1968 authorized direct and insured loans in rural areas (expanded in 1970 to include populations up to 10,000) to low and moderate income persons and families and to provide rental or cooperative housing for such persons and families where assistance is not available under Sections 235 and 236 of the National Housing Act. The interest rate is set by the Secretary of Agriculture after considering the cost of money through the sale of notes and the payment ability of the applicants. It may not be lower than 1 percent. An interest supplement sufficient to render the loans marketable will be paid from, and reimbursed by annual appropriations to, the rural housing insurance fund. Even nonrural residents may avail themselves of this provision if they are employed in rural areas. An additional provision of the 1968 Act authorized financial and technical assistance to provide housing and related facilities in rural areas to

---

[3] Miles L. Colean and Richard J. Saulnier, *The Real Estate Lending Activities of the Farmers Home Administration* (A Report to the Mortgage Bankers Association, 1963), pp. 7–19.

rural trainees and their families under extremely favorable repayment and interest requirements. On June 30, 1970, Farmers Home Administration rural housing loans totaled about $2.6 billion, of which nearly $600 million were direct and just over $2 billion were insured. Approximately 65,000 homes were financed through this agency in 1970.

Rural Development In the interest of general rural development, the Farmers Home Administration is authorized to make or insure loans for many purposes other than those related to farm operations or providing rural housing. It assists rural community groups and farmers to finance recreation and rural development enterprises where credit cannot be obtained at reasonable rates and terms from other sources. Such facilities include ponds, lakes, and parks, sports areas, camping facilities, fishing and hunting preserves, access roads, and domestic water, irrigation, drainage, and waste disposal systems. A borrower's total indebtedness for these loans cannot exceed $4 million. The maximum term is 40 years with the interest rate at 5 percent. The average loan is about $130,000.

Emergency Loans In times of emergency as declared by the President or a natural disaster as determined by the Secretary of Agriculture, the Farmers Home Administration also makes emergency loans. Eligibility is determined by a Farmers Home Administration county committee, consisting of three local citizens with farm knowledge and experience in the distressed area. Loans made for operating expenses are repayable the next year. Equipment and livestock loans may be repaid within five years. Real estate loans may extend up to 20 years. The maximum interest rate is 6 percent.

Volume of Farm Mortgage Debt According to the Agricultural Research Service of the U.S. Department of Agriculture, the farm mortgage debt at the end of 1970 was approximately $29 billion. This compares with $6.6 billion in 1939 and $4.8 billion at the end of 1945. The relative holdings of various mortgagees as of the beginning of 1940 and 1971 are shown in Table 22–1.

At the beginning of 1971, the total assets of U.S. agriculture were estimated at $317 billion; total debt, $60 billion; and farmers' equities, $257 billion. Thus, equities were about 82 percent of total assets. The $29 billion of real estate debt approximated 14 percent of real estate assets of $212 billion; and nonreal estate debts of about $31 billion were about 30 percent of nonreal estate assets of $105 billion. Although these figures suggest that farmers are in a generally sound financial position, the conclusion is limited by the usual fallacy exhibited by averages. While many farmers are either free of mortgage debt or have their obligations written down from the application of large profits in the early postwar years, the younger farmers who purchased their land at the peak of high prices still face mortgage burdens greater than the averages

TABLE 22–1
Percentage Distribution of Farm Mortgage Loans by Principal Lenders, as of January 1, 1940 and 1971

Type of Lender	1940 Percentage	1971 Percentage
Commercial banks	8	14
Federal Land Banks	31	23
Federal Farm Mortgage Corporation	11	†
Life insurance companies	15	20
Farmers Home Administration	*	3
Individuals and others	35	40
Total	100	100

* Less than 0.5 percent.
† Outstanding loans of the Federal Farm Mortgage Corporation (created by Congress in 1934), made in the name of the Land Bank Commissioner, were all sold to the 12 Federal Land Banks on June 30, 1955.

quoted above would indicate. For example, the average mortgage written during recent years amounted to about $20,000 compared with the 1947–49 average of $4,230. Also, non-real estate debt undoubtedly bears heavily upon those who owe on the largest mortgages. At the end of 1970, non-real estate debt of American farmers was about equal to the real estate mortgage debt. While the amount of non-real estate debt owed by owners of mortgaged property is of considerable concern to those who hold such mortgages, non-real estate debt of farmers is even more important to holders of farm mortgages. As has been pointed out elsewhere in this chapter, farm mortgages cover both real estate and business uses. Hence any burden of defaulted non-real estate debt owed by farmers might result in taking away from the debtor his capacity to earn enough to meet the obligations on his farm mortgage.

QUESTIONS AND PROBLEMS

1. What are the common sources of farm capital?
2. Why are partnership and leasing arrangements relatively common in financing farm operations?
3. What are the chief purposes of farm mortgages and how should mortgage terms be arranged to fulfill these purposes?
4. Discuss the applicability of the following provisions in a farm mortgage: (*a*) amortization; (*b*) prepayment privileges; and (*c*) sinking fund for future benefits.
5. What criteria should be used in appraisals for farm loans?
6. Why are individuals the principal source of mortgage loan funds utilized in financing farms?
7. Discuss the commercial bank as a source of funds for financing farm real estate?

8. What has been the experience of life insurance companies as investors in farm mortgages?

9. Under what conditions may a farmer borrow funds through the Federal Land Bank System?

10. How does the Farmers Home Administration offer financial assistance to farmers in buying farms? To nonfarming owners?

11. What is meant by "rehabilitation financing"?

12. It has been stated that the balance sheet of American agriculture suggests that farmers in general are in a sound financial condition. Would you qualify this statement?

23

Federal Home Loan Bank System

Hoover Conference on Homeownership With the real estate business in the doldrums and getting worse day by day; with increasingly large numbers of homeowners facing the threat of foreclosure by mortgagees who were hard pressed to find the means of liquidating the claims of those whose funds they held for investment; and with the whole structure of home mortgage financing about to collapse: President Hoover called a conference on home finance and homeownership to meet in Washington, D.C., December 1930.

The keynote of the conference, as expressed by President Hoover, is found in the following sentence: "It should be possible in our country for anybody of sound character and industrious habits to provide himself with adequate housing and preferably to buy his own home." It will be noted that the emphasis was placed upon individual responsibility and homeownership. Homes rather than housing dominated the thinking of those who planned this conference.

While the conference was called at the insistence of representatives of the real estate business and those interested in real estate finance, it included other groups as well. Distressed homeowners as such were not represented. There appeared to be no way to select competent representatives of this group. The conference was arranged by a planning committee under the joint chairmanship of the Secretary of Commerce and the Secretary of the Interior. As early as August 1930, this committee started planning the scope and objectives of the conference.

Approximately 600 people were invited to this conference. Among the diverse interests represented were real estate, real estate finance, city planning, building construction, education, social work, and government. The members of the conference were divided into an elaborate list of 31 committees covering practically all subjects concerned with homeownership. Each committee presented a report which was printed as a separate bulletin of up to 150 pages.

This conference gave its attention to numerous questions, many of which can be classified under the headings of causes of and remedies for the situation faced by the conferees. Under the head of causes, the following stood out:

1. The instability of real estate values in this country—due to a combination of factors which we need not stop to discuss here—resulted in low-percentage loans in relation to values. Even normally low percentages were further reduced in periods of economic distress, so that refinancing became very much restricted when most needed.

2. Low-percentage first mortgages required supplementary financing for many real estate owners. This took the form of short-term second and third mortgages. Refunding of these short-term obligations was costly under the best of circumstances, because of the prevalence of heavy discounts. Under circumstances which represented less than the best, mortgagees, fearing the future, pressed for liquidation of their claims, precipitating numerous foreclosure actions.

3. The prevalence of short-term primary financing in some sections of the country resulted in increases in demands for repayment when the mortgagor had least opportunity for refinancing with other lenders on mortgage security. Because these short-term mortgages made no provision for amortization, the mortgagees lacked this source of liquidity with which mortgagors could have been assisted. Unsatisfied demands for repayment of matured mortgages invited increased foreclosures.

4. Short-term funds invested in long-term mortgages became frozen at a time when the demand for the withdrawal of these funds was greatest. In general, whether a real estate mortgage is written for a long or a short term, it is to be considered a frozen asset unless the debt secured by it is actually amortized. If you list the cities where commercial banks were in greatest difficulties during the early 1930s and then make another list of localities where banks were heavy lenders on real estate mortgages, you will find a striking coincidence.

5. Inefficient and unsystematic appraisal practices resulted in the virtual purchases of many real estate parcels at the time mortgages were placed against them. Many lenders had only vague ideas on the subject of appraisal techniques. They let some of their borrowers make their appraisals for them by shopping around for loans until they found the highest bidder for their business. If what is said in this paragraph seems to be in conflict with what is said under "1," keep this in mind. Some loans were actually 40 or 50 percent loans. Others, labeled 40 or 50 percent loans, were actually 110 percent loans because of excessive

appraisals. Frequently the amount of the loan was agreed upon, and the appraisal was adjusted to make the loan fit the announced lending policy of the mortgagee.

6. The dependence of real estate lenders upon purely local sources of loanable funds created an uneven flow of mortgage money in different parts of the country at the same time. Under normal economic conditions, one city might have a plethora of funds and a dearth of loan demand; another city might have a great backlog of loan demand and insufficient funds with which to meet it. In the absence of any kind of mechanism to shift funds from one section of the country to another for this purpose, real estate lenders were shut off from access to national capital markets.

7. There was a lack of standards for quality of construction. Lenders did not ordinarily undertake to tell contractors and owners what type of structures to build. Indeed, some of them had no yardstick by which to measure construction quality. They merely responded favorably or unfavorably to applications for loans. Since the nature of the response to such applications was conditioned, in part at least, by their anxiety to put to work the surpluses of cash that they might have on hand, in times of surplus jerry-builders undoubtedly received more encouragement and support than in times of shortages. Jerry-built structures always complicate real estate markets and make refinancing even more difficult in times of economic stress and tight money.

8. Too many real estate parcels were held by weak holders who lacked the capacity to meet their obligations when their economic circumstances were disturbed ever so little. Like some of their more fortunate friends and acquaintances, they, too, made an emotional response to the sentimental appeal for homeownership. But lacking the financial resources with which to back up their emotions, they fell easy prey to foreclosure action as soon as the economic road became rough. These foreclosures flooded a market already glutted with unwanted properties, caused wider fluctuations in all real estate values, and raised doubts in the minds of even strong holders about the desirability of investment in real estate.

Earlier Attempts at Legislation As early as 1918, a group of savings and loan association leaders lobbied for a "mortgage rediscount bank" and succeeded in having a bill introduced in 1919 to accomplish this purpose. Although hearings on this bill were conducted by the House Banking and Currency Committee, it was never reported to the House by the Committee. A similar fate met another bill introduced in 1928. The apparent lack of urgency for the passage of such a law, at a time when most home-financing institutions were getting along pretty well without the assistance of the federal government, resulted in its failure to arouse much interest in the subject on the part of members of

Congress. It required a major depression to dramatize the need for what later developed into the Federal Home Loan Bank System.

Recommendation for Legislation As one tangible result of the Hoover conference, the President announced at a press conference in November 1931, that he planned to recommend to the Congress legislation for the purpose of setting up in the home-financing field a system of banks comparable to the Federal Reserve System, which serves the needs of the commercial financial institutions of the country. In December 1931, and again in January 1932, he made formal recommendations to Congress along these lines. The proposed legislation was intended to serve both as a recovery measure and as a preventive program for the future. Before the subject became law on July 22, 1932, it had to run the gauntlet of conflicting interests.

Prolonged hearings developed three divergent points of view about the proposed legislation. The real estate groups, which had been primarily responsible for the original Hoover conference, contended for a mortgage discount system which would enable mortgage holders to acquire liquidity when needed by selling mortgages to some kind of national mortgage banks. The commercial banks were not convinced of the need for any new legislation and opposed the passage of any new bills, looking toward a new credit system in the home-financing field. The savings and loan leaders worked for a credit reserve system instead of a mortgage discount program. With some support from insurance companies and others, the credit reserve principle finally prevailed. Thus was born the Home Loan Bank System, which has for its major objective provision of liquidity for its member institutions.

Practical Politics at Work The final passage of the Home Loan Bank Act affords a good illustration of the operation of practical politics in a democracy. Because of the bitter struggle over this bit of legislation, every vote was important. A few needed votes were enticed in support of the bill in exchange for adding a provision that sounded fine but was completely unworkable from the start. A second was added to provide that distressed homeowners, as well as member institutions, should be given access to the facilities of the Home Loan Bank of their district. But since such access must be on the same terms as those provided for member institutions, it was evident that no distressed homeowner could possibly qualify for a loan. The reason for this will become clear as we discuss qualifications for membership. This section was repealed in less than one year.

Five-Man Board The administration of the Home Loan Bank Act was entrusted to a bipartisan five-man board appointed by the President with the consent of the Senate. The overlapping terms of the board members were for six years. Their powers of control over the Home Loan Banks were inclusive and, in general, comparable to the powers of control exercised by the Federal Reserve Board over the Federal Reserve banks. As will be shown later, additional powers were added by the Congress from time to time. The first board members appointed by President Hoover in the summer of 1932 were never confirmed by the Senate, so that their terms expired with the accession of the new President and the new Senate on March 4, 1933.

The five-man board was abolished during World War II under the war powers of the President. It was superseded by a single commissioner in the person of the former chairman. In 1946, a board of three members succeeded the commissionership by Executive Order of the President. Since this action had the tacit approval of the Senate, it thereby acquired the effect of law.

Location of Home Loan Banks The law provided that the Home Loan Bank Board should establish not less than 8 nor more than 12 regional banks. The latter number was chosen. At first no bank was established in the same city with a Federal Reserve Bank. Rumor reports that the first chairman of the board, whose home city was Newark, New Jersey, wanted his home town, rather than New York City, to be honored with a Home Loan Bank. To be consistent, other banks were located in Cambridge, Massachusetts, instead of Boston; Evanston, Illinois, instead of Chicago; and so on. Later this situation was changed so that the 12 banks were located in Boston, New York, Pittsburgh, Indianapolis, Chicago, Cincinnati, Winston-Salem, Little Rock, Topeka, Des Moines, Portland (Oregon), and Los Angeles. The latter two were later combined to form a bank in San Francisco with branches in Portland and Los Angeles, and the Winston-Salem bank was moved to Greensboro. A 12th district was reestablished in 1963 and began formal operations in 1964, with the bank now located at Seattle.

Capital of Home Loan Banks The law provided that each member of a Home Loan Bank must purchase stock equivalent to 1 percent of the unpaid principal of the home loans held in its portfolio, or $2,500, whichever was greater. Each bank was required to have a total capital of not less than $5 million. Any amounts needed by a bank over and above the amounts contributed by the members could be invested by the U.S. Treasury at the call of the Home Loan Bank Board. The maximum investment of the Treasury in all Home Loan Banks was limited to $125 million. At the outset most of the capital was owned by the Treasury. In order to make sure of getting the entire amount due from the Treasury, the Home Loan Bank Board built the capital of the regional banks rapidly from this source until it was practically exhausted, regardless of the amounts invested by the members.

Later it appeared advantageous for the members to own the stock of these banks. The 1 percent of home loans stated above as the basis for stock purchase by the members was interpreted to be a minimum, and members were encouraged to purchase additional amounts. Also, some members purchased additional amounts of stock to increase their borrowing capacity at these banks, since this was limited to 12 times the amount of stock owned by them. A part of the contributions made by members was used to redeem the stock owned by the Treasury.

In June 1950, the second session of the 81st Congress amended the Home Loan Bank Act by requiring that, within one year after the enactment of the amendment, each member of a Home Loan Bank should acquire and maintain stockholding of not less than 2 percent of its home mortgage loans. At the end of the year each bank was to retire at par an amount of stock held by the Treasury of the United States equal to the amount of its stock held by its members in excess of 1 percent of their home mortgage loans. Annually thereafter it was to retire Treasury-owned stock equal to one half of the net increase in member-owned stock since the last previous retirement. Such retirement of Treasury-owned stock was subject to the limitation that it should not operate to reduce the aggregate capital stock, reserves, surplus, and undivided profits of the Home Loan Banks below $200 million. All stock of all Home Loan Banks has been owned by their members since July 2, 1951. Effective January 1, 1962, the stockholding requirement by member institutions was reduced from 2 percent to 1 percent of home mortgage loans. However, members have not been permitted to sell back any of their excess stock. Furthermore, any member which has borrowed in excess of 12 percent of its total loans must hold stock equal to one twelfth of the principal balance due its regional bank. As of the end of 1970, member-owned stock amounted to $1,607 million. Compared with Federal Home Loan Bank obligations outstanding, the equity holdings provided a cushion of about 16 percent.

Other Sources of Funds In addition to the capital of the Home Loan Banks, other sources of funds consist of:

1. Consolidated bonds and notes which are sold in the open market by the Home Loan Bank Board as they are needed, with the proceeds distributed among the various regional banks on the basis of their probable loan demands. These bonds and notes carry such maturity as best seems to meet the needs of the system. Interest rates reflect the cost of money for that type of paper at the time the bonds and notes are issued. By the sale of these bonds and notes, the member institutions have access to the capital markets of the country. This represents an abrupt change from the prevailing dependence upon local funds that obtained before this bank system was started. At the end of 1970, outstanding bonds and notes amounted to $10,183 million.

To facilitate the distribution of these bonds and notes the Home Loan Bank Board maintains a New York office headed by a fiscal agent. His function is to keep in touch with dealers who serve as wholesale purchasers of these bonds and notes throughout the country. There are about 500 such dealers. These dealers in turn retail the bonds and notes to their institutional customers. In addition to their open-market distribution, these bonds and notes can be sold on short notice—10 days if necessary—through a private offering to selected dealers. These are usually for shorter terms than those offered in the open market.

2. Deposits of members who have excess funds sometimes add to the funds available to other members. Demand deposits pay no return to their owners. Interest rates on time deposits vary with the length of time and with the needs of the banks. Recently a new pattern using a definite maturity certificate of deposit has been introduced into the system. Under the theory of system operations, it is expected that excess deposits in one bank can be borrowed by another bank in the system. Until 1945, member deposits were not very significant in amount. At the end of 1970, they totaled $2,331 million.

Need for a Backstop As stated in the preceding section, the sale of Home Loan Bank obligations gives the members of these banks access to the capital markets of the country. This is predicated upon the assumption that the market will absorb whatever obligations are offered to it. Even during the recent times of stress, such bonds and notes as were offered found a receptive market at conservative rates in terms of the money and capital markets at the time of issue. The recent markets constituted a real test of strength. Advances to members of the Home Loan Bank System rose from $5.3 billion in 1968 to $9.3 billion in 1969, an increase of $4 billion. This outward flow of funds through the system constituted a historic high in support to the membership. There is, of course, always the question whether the open market will absorb the required amount of obligations at reasonable cost to the issuers. Experience thus far gives grounds for optimism.

Congress has granted to commercial banks ample protection by authorizing various governmental agencies concerned with commercial bank operation to take whatever steps may be necessary to provide liquidity as needed. Those best acquainted with the problems involved and sympathetic to the types of institutions which are members of the Home Loan Bank System for years urged Congress to provide a comparable backstop for the debentures issued by this system.

In June 1950, Congress finally provided that the Secretary of the Treasury at his discretion might purchase from time to time up to $1 billion of obligations of the Home Loan Bank System. Each purchase should "be upon such terms and conditions as to yield a return at a rate determined by the Secretary of the Treasury, taking into consideration the current average rate on outstanding marketable obligations of the United States as of the last day of the month preceding the making of such purchase." The Secretary was also authorized to sell such obligations of this nature as he might purchase, at such prices as he might determine. This authority was expanded by the Rate Control Act of 1969 which authorized the Secretary to purchase up to $4 billion of these obligations. The 1969 statute further stated that the Secretary should act whenever necessary to avoid substantial impairment of the Home Loan Bank System because of monetary stringency or rapidly rising interest rates.

The term "backstop" is intended to describe the discretion now resting with the Secretary of the Treasury in the purchase of obligations of the Home Loan Bank System. It is not expected that he will exercise this discretion so long as an open market is available for such obligations. Only in times of emergency, when the market is no longer open, will the Treasury be called upon to purchase such obligations. Such a backstop is needed not alone in the interests of the members of the Home Loan Bank System but in the interests of our whole economy as well.

Liquidity Requirements As a part of the strategy in securing the enactment of legislation providing for the backstop just described, the same law included a provision that has not been quite so palatable to operators of savings and loan associations. It is recognized that the backstop of Treasury purchases of Home Loan Bank obligations would be needed to provide liquidity for bank members in a time of crisis. In order to force such members to provide some of their own liquidity, the Congress has given the Home Loan Bank Board the responsibility for requiring members of the system to maintain—in cash and "near money" assets—not less than 4 nor more than 10 percent of each member's obligations on withdrawable accounts.

In making the above requirement operative, the Home Loan Bank Board is authorized to pass regulations prescribing different amounts, within the above limits, for different classes of member institutions. Such classification of members may be according to "type of institution, size, location, rate of withdrawals, or such other basis or bases of differentiation as the Board may deem to be reasonably necessary or appropriate." These requirements are discussed in Chapter 11.

Meantime, whenever a member fails to measure up to the liquidity demanded for its class of institution, it may not make or purchase any loan. Failure to comply with this liquidity requirement shall constitute grounds for removal of the member from the Home Loan Bank System.

Bank Management Each Home Loan Bank is separately incorporated, with its own stock outstanding. It is managed by a board of directors ranging from 12 to 15 in number. Four are appointed by the Home Loan Bank Board as public interest directors. As a general rule, these members are not directly connected with the home-financing business. The other directors are elected by the members of the bank. In determining eligibility for membership, the Home Loan Bank Board has given attention to geographical distribution. For example, where a regional bank serves several states, each state is given representation on the board of directors, even though a preponderance of members and of their assets are concentrated in only one of the states. The chairman and vice-chairman are appointed by the Home Loan Bank Board. The former is usually a public interest director, and the latter is usually an elected member.

The appointment of bank officers and the determination of their salaries are first passed upon by the board of directors. This action is then subject to review by the Home Loan Bank Board, whose decision is final. This system has generally worked quite satisfactorily, though there have been occasions when it worked very badly. The problem of bank autonomy versus government supervision seems to be impossible of solution to the satisfaction of all concerned. Under an atmosphere of mutual trust, fair-minded men can usually arrive at reasonable and acceptable compromises, whereas suspicion of motives on either side soon degenerates to a point where principles are forgotten and personal differences become paramount. Complete autonomy of these banks without supervision from Washington was never intended by Congress in setting up this bank system. Neither was effectual operation of these banks from Washington instead of supervision.

Each bank is expected to earn its own expenses, add to its reserves, and pay a return on its stock subject to the amount of services it renders its members. Included in its expenses is each bank's pro rata share of the part of the Home Loan Bank Board's operating expenses that are properly chargeable against the regional banks. Assessments for this purpose are usually made semiannually in advance, but may be made as needed.

Within broad limits set by the Home Loan Bank Board, the directors of each bank operate it according to their own best judgment. For example, the Board may decree that the rate of interest on long-term advances to members shall not be less than x percent nor more than y percent. The exact rate within these limits is then fixed by the board of each bank. The Home Loan Bank Board establishes the broad pattern of lending operations. The bank management passes upon each application for an advance to a member to make sure that it conforms to this pattern.

Even issues that are decided by the Home Loan Bank Board but that involve a regional bank or its members are frequently funneled through the regional bank for investigation and recommendation. For example, applications for insurance of accounts, for bank membership, and for conversion of a state-chartered savings and loan association to one with a federal charter are first processed by the regional bank. After all pertinent facts are gathered and studied, the bank is expected to make a report—including all papers in the case—and a recommendation upon the question raised. The Home Loan Bank Board is not bound to follow the recommendation of the regional bank.

Advances to Members The major purpose in establishing the Home Loan Bank System was to give its members access to capital markets broader than the localities in which they operated. Any member may secure advances from his Home Loan Bank for any legitimate purpose. If a member needs funds to meet the requirements of withdrawal demands from its members, it may call upon its Home Loan Bank for an advance. If its opportunities to make mortgage loans exceed its available cash, it may obtain similar advances. Even if a member merely wishes to make a better showing of liquidity for window-dressing purposes, it may look to the same source for the cash it needs.

Advances to any member are limited to 50 percent of its savings balances. When borrowings exceed the 50 percent limit, a 1 percent penalty interest rate is charged. Within this legal limit, the FHLB Board has a more restrictive policy limiting borrowing to not over 25 percent of the member's total withdrawable savings balances. This restriction is lifted for the purpose of meeting withdrawal demand of savers. None of the banks in the system encourages any of its members to exhaust their maximum capacity to obtain advances. To do so might place the member in an embarrassing position should it be unable to obtain advances in case of an emergency.

At the 1970 year-end, 71 percent of the advances to members had maturities under 12 months, and over 98 percent were secured. Outstanding advances to members had risen from $4 billion at the beginning of 1968 to $10.2 billion, a huge increase of 150 percent.

Maturity of Advances In order to meet the various requirements of their members and others for liquidity purposes, the Home Loan Banks have various patterns of advances. (1) Those to members for 30 days or less need not be collateralized or amortized. (2) Advances up to one year need not be amortized. If made to members whose creditor obligations do not exceed 5 percent of their net assets, they need not be collateralized. (3) All advances of more than 1 year but not in excess of 10 years must be both collateralized and amortized. Collateral may be as follows: FHA mortgages, up to 90 percent of the unpaid principal balance; other amortized home loans, up to 65 percent of the unpaid balance; unamortized home loans, up to 50 percent of the unpaid balance; and U.S. government obligations, up to their face value. For advances to nonmembers, any legal investment may be accepted as collateral for advances for one year or less, at the discretion of the board of directors or the executive committee of the Home Loan Bank. All advances of more than one year's maturity must be planned to be repaid in equal monthly or quarterly installments over the life of the advance. Prepayments are permitted, and if any are made they may be applied to the liquidation of subsequent installments. Interest rates vary with the length of the loan period and with the state of the capital market.

Line of Credit Each member may be given a line of credit with its Home Loan Bank to encourage such a member to make use of the lending facilities of the bank. The line so established is ordinarily "the maximum that can be extended with safety, not, however, in excess of the member's borrowing capacity." The maximum borrowing capacity for any member under any circumstances is 50 percent of its total savings balances. Lines of credit established by the board of directors or the executive committee serve as guides to the officers of the bank in making advances to members. All such advances are reported regularly to the directors or the executive committee. Lines of credit are reviewed annually, or oftener if necessary. In setting them up, the extent of their use without collateral is also determined.

Lines of credit may be extended, at the discretion of the board of directors or the executive committee, to nonmembers which are "chartered institutions having succession and subject to the inspection and supervision of some governmental agency." Rates of interest on advances to nonmembers must be at least ½ percent higher than rates on similar advances to members.

Eligibility for Membership Like the Federal Reserve System after which it was patterned, the Home Loan Bank System has both compulsory and voluntary members. All federal savings and loan associations are required to be members. State-chartered savings and loan associations, life insurance companies, and savings banks are eligible for membership on a voluntary basis if their applications are approved by the Home Loan Bank Board. Such approval is not difficult to obtain, provided the financial condition and the character of the management of the applicant pass muster. As a matter of fact, however, few savings banks and insurance companies have applied for membership. At the end of 1970, the members of the system numbered 4,601 savings and loan associations, 47 mutual savings banks, and 1 life insurance company.

Because of the predominance of savings and loan associations in the membership of the Home Loan Banks, other types of eligible thrift and home-financing institutions have been hesitant to join. Life insurance companies may have little need for the services offered by the regional banks. The few that have joined to date have not used these services and, excepting one, later withdrew from membership. Savings banks, on the other hand, may face a situation in the future in which they may regret their lack of access to a credit reserve pool of funds. They can scarcely afford to meet the requirements of membership in the Federal Reserve System. Since their operations more nearly parallel those of savings and loan associations, it seems unfortunate that they should not have access to the Home Loan Bank System through membership in it. That the savings banks themselves are becoming increasingly aware of this condition is indicated from the fact that their membership in the Home Loan Bank System has more than doubled since 1961.

The members of the Home Loan Bank System hold approximately one third of the total mortgage debt on nonfarm one- to four-family homes in the United States.

Advisory Council The law which established the Home Loan Bank System provided for a Federal Savings and Loan Advisory Council of 18 members. One is elected by the board of directors of each Home Loan Bank, and the remainder are appointed by the Home Loan Bank Board. They receive their expenses, but no compensation. The Council meets semiannually, and oftener if requested by the Board. Their functions are limited to conferences with the Board, requests for information from it, and recommendations to it on matters which come within its jurisdiction. Like other councils of its type, this one can be and frequently is a powerful influence in the development of the bank system. Its usefulness at any particular time depends upon the caliber of its members, their attitude toward their duties, and the willingness of the Home Loan Bank Board to cooperate with the Council.

This willingness is particularly important, since the Council has no powers or authority. It may request, but it may not demand. It may suggest, but it may not direct or dictate. The Home Loan Bank Board needs and usually is glad to receive and heed the advice which those best acquainted with thrift and home-financing problems can give it. If the members of the Council approach their duties in a spirit of helpfulness, the Board will usually respond in a like spirit. But if some members of the Council are allowed to use the occasion of a meeting to engage in carping criticism on minor issues or even to attempt to take over the authority and the responsibility of the Board, the results are likely to be negative. On its part the Board or any member thereof can easily convey to the members of the Council a sense of futility if refusal to listen or unwillingness to cooperate is evident. On the whole, the Council has well justified its existence to date.

Conference of Bank Presidents Soon after the Home Loan Bank System was established, the Board recognized the need to confer on a continuing basis with the bank presidents on problems, policies, and procedures. It therefore set up an additional advisory group called the Conference of Bank Presidents. The conference has a formal schedule of quarterly meetings, but special meetings are frequently called. This group seeks in meeting with the Board to achieve a full exchange of views and information. Areas of particular concern are indicated by the formal committees designated by the Conference: legislation and regulations, liquidity, and supervision and examination.

Examination of Members and Others The method of supervising members of the Home Loan Bank System came up for discussion soon after the system was established. With the subsequent legislation providing for the chartering of federal savings and loan associations and the still later law establishing the Federal Savings and Loan Insurance Corporation—all under the general supervision of the Home Loan Bank Board—this problem became somewhat more complicated. It was finally determined that examination and supervision should be separated. Consequently, the Home Loan Bank Board set up an examining division with a head office in Washington and a branch office in each of the Home Loan Banks.

Although the examiners in each district are quartered in the same building as the bank of that district, they are under the direction of a regional examiner who reports to and receives his instructions from the chief examiner in Washington. Although the examining division works in close cooperation with the bank management, it is not under the control of the bank. The examining division has been aptly described as a photographic division. Its chief function is to take an accurate picture of federal savings and loan associations and such state-chartered associations as have insurance of accounts. The cost of annual examinations is assessed against the association examined. The examination of bank members which are not insured is more in the nature of an analysis of reports submitted annually, covering their operations for the preceding year. Special examinations are given to applicants for insurance and for federal charters to determine their eligibility therefor.

To an increasing extent, state supervisory authorities are working with the examining division of the Home Loan Bank Board in checking over the operations of state-chartered associations which are in part under the Board's jurisdiction. In the beginning of the various programs under control of the Board, state supervisors sought the sole right to examine state-chartered associations, with a copy of their report to be submitted to the Home Loan Bank Board. Because of the wide variety of examination practices among state supervisors, not all of which were of uniformly high quality, this was not possible. As more uniformity in both procedure and quality of results has been accomplished, a higher degree of dependence upon state examinations has been made possible. Much progress in this direction has been made in recent years.

In recent years, also, the associations examined have become better acquainted with the requirements of the examiners, who, in turn, have ironed out, through experience, some of the kinks in their earlier efforts. As a consequence, examinations are relatively less expensive, while they are also relatively more effective, than formerly. All those who are concerned with examination procedure, which, at best, may seem to interfere with the orderly operation of a well-managed association, come to do what is necessary to facilitate periodical examinations as soon as they understand their objectives thoroughly. Examiners are not gumshoe artists looking for crooked operators. Their objective is to help management operate its association in a manner that will best serve the interests of thrifty people and borrowers on real estate as security. The aid they give is necessarily indirect, because their work is finished when they "photograph" the operations and current condition of the association. The results of examinations are then turned over to the supervising agency.

Supervision The president of each Home Loan Bank is chief supervisor for the Home Loan Bank Board in his district. This puts him in a somewhat anomalous position. As president of the bank, he is supposed to serve the members of his bank providing them with advances when they are needed In this position he is expected to be a promoter of savings and loan business. As chief supervisor, he is in part a critic rather than a promoter. However, since criticisms are presumed to correct faults so that the member criticized can render better service, perhaps even criticism can be considered to be one element of a promotion program.

Also, many observers believe that supervision is at least 90 percent persuasion, salesmanship, and promotion of better ways of operating savings and loan associations; only 10 percent or less criticism of a "crackdown" character. In any event, a diplomatic bank president can perform the dual functions of promoting thrift and homeownership in his district and of taking whatever action is necessary to keep those examined operating within the limits of their authority and responsibility.

Supervision starts in where examination leaves off. The examiner's report is submitted to the bank president, who submits it to the members of his staff for review. In other words, they examine the "photograph" carefully to see if there is any violation of the rules and regulations. When such are found, they are included in a supervisory letter addressed to the association, with instructions to make any changes indicated and to report back the action taken. Usually this is the only action needed to induce corrective measures. If necessary, punitive action can be directed against the offending management and, if need be, against the association which it manages. On rare occasions the violation of regulations is so serious that the Home Loan Bank Board is asked to review it and pass judgment upon the action to be taken.

All supervisory orders should be subject to appeal—up to the Home Loan Bank Board if necessary. If examiners or supervisors make mistakes, the consequences should not be borne by the association examined without full opportunity for a hearing before penalties are enforced. Indeed, it appears that supervision could be expedited considerably if discoveries by examiners were divided into three categories and were dealt with according to the following pattern:

1. Procedural matters that involve no need for interpretation, and hence are not discretionary, could be corrected at the time of examination by agreement between the examiner and the manager of the association. These include questions, such as methods of accounting and failure to observe rules regarding record keeping, about which there can be only one reasonable interpretation. If the association indicates a willingness to make the suggested changes that are called to its attention by the examiner, this fact should be reported to the supervisor; but no further action need be taken if the change is actually made. Subsequent examinations can determine this.

2. Should the manager refuse to accept any such suggestions for a procedural change, the question should be referred to the supervising officer for decision and action. Likewise, all other questions except those involving changes in management or in the capital structure of the association should be referred to the same authority. Any orders of the supervisor in the district to which the associaton objects should promptly be subject to review in the form of a conference between the association manager or his designee and the supervisor. In most cases differences can be settled best across a desk instead of at the length of a telephone line or by mail service.

3. All matters of sufficiently serious import—such as a change in management, major changes in the capital structure, or appeals from the orders of the district supervisor—should be sent to Washington for review and decision. Either before or after the decision has been reached, the association should have ample opportunity for a hearing. On most serious matters, involving changes in top management, even Home Loan Bank Board members should be expected to act as hearing officers.

All decisions reached at any level should be enforced promptly in the absence of an appeal or a request for a hearing. Even cases appealed should be settled promptly rather than leave uncertainty concerning what final disposition is to be made of an order that is neither enforced nor rescinded. Since the purpose of all supervision is to insure sound institutions, properly managed in the interest of thrift people and borrowers on real estate security, supervising agencies, as well as the associations supervised, have a responsibility to do everything possible to reach this objective, and to avoid doing those things which might confuse and becloud the major objectives.

In all communications passing between the association and the supervisory authorities, a clear line of distinction should always be drawn between orders and suggestions. Orders originate from violations of law and legal regulations. The supervisory authorities have no discretion about them if they perform their duties faithfully. Advice and suggestions should be so labeled and may be offered freely.

Regulation versus Management In the operation of the Home Loan Bank System, we find a situation that is typical of many governmental agencies. A small minority of managers resist the orders of regulatory bodies, even when these bodies are strictly within the law. They resent even the appearance of pressure to keep them in line with operating policies that have been given the stamp of approval by legislative bodies by the process of declaring some alternative policies to be opposed to public policy. In spite of the fact that theirs is a kind of business that has been declared to be affected with a public interest, and therefore subject to regulation, they still prefer to follow in the footsteps of Commodore Vanderbilt, who, in most picturesque language, first resisted regulation of the railroads.

On the other hand, we find some representatives of regulatory bodies who do not hesitate to step over the bounds of legal requirements in order to give orders which they think should be given in the public interest. On occasion their experience may have taught them something that the legislators have not yet learned. Nevertheless, until the legislative body grants the authority, the regulator should hesitate to assume the responsibility for giving illegal orders. Suggestions may be handed out freely, but orders should be used sparingly, and then only when the facts warrant and the path of regulation is clear.

There is a major difference between regulation and operation of a business enterprise. Regulation is essentially negation. Legislation establishes boundaries beyond which operation may not go legally. The major order-giving function of regulators is to police these boundaries and to keep operations within them. Even the legislative functions of an administrative agency such as the Home Loan Bank Board should be clearly in line with the authority granted it by Congress and should be stated in such definite form that they have the force and effect of statutory law. In its legislative capacity the Home Loan Bank Board sets the boundaries of operation that Congress intended it to set. In its administrative capacity, it polices its own boundaries to see that operation conforms to legal standards.

Operation of a business enterprise is essentially affirmative in character. Management, acting within the boundaries set by regulation, must be held accountable for an unending series of positive decisions upon which the success or failure of the venture depends. If we insist upon placing upon business operators the responsibility for the consequences of these decisions, we must give them enough authority to provide freedom of action within the boundaries set by regulation. It is not easy to keep impatient operators of savings and loan associations within the bounds set by regulation. Nor is it easy to keep ambitious regulators outside the field of operation. Yet service to the public, as well as its protection, demands that the distinction between operation and regulation be strictly observed by all parties. It is not sufficient that regulators shall be interested only in protection of thrifty people and homeowners while operators shall be concerned only with serving them. Both regulators and operators must insist upon both protection and service. This can be accomplished only when operators and regulators act in such a manner as to win and merit mutual trust and respect.

Objectives of a Credit Reserve System Development of a formula for making real estate mortgages on small properties liquid has been an elusive thing. Real estate trust issues secured by large properties are often traded freely in the securities markets. But the uninsured mortgage on a small property in one section of the country has little appeal for an investor in another locality. Even the investor in the same city as the property would wish to visit and inspect the property and have it appraised. In other words, he would go to more trouble and expense than if he were purchasing the more liquid stock or bond. The widening market for FHA and VA mortgages, particularly through government-backed mortgage pools in which participations are sold, reflects a favorable trend; it has far to go. Trafficking in these types of mortgages is not based upon confidence in the loan so much as in the insurance or guarantee of its repayment. Recent extensions of the secondary market functions of the Federal National Mortgage Association into the conventional loan field and the creation of the Federal Home Loan Mortgage Corporation as a secondary market facility empowered to buy and sell both federally underwritten and conventional mortgage loans have been good beginnings, but only that, toward achieving liquidity for real estate liens.

By its design, the Home Loan Bank System, except through the Federal Home Loan Mortgage Corporation as discussed in the next chapter, does not and cannot inject liquidity into individual mortgages. What it does is to provide liquidity for the institution which holds the mortgage. As a credit reserve system, it is not necessary for it to undertake the difficult task of making mortgages marketable. It merely accepts them as security for advances to members of the Home Loan Bank System.

In providing this service it gives its members an alternative source of funds. Before the Home Loan Bank System was organized, savings and loan associations were accustomed to obtain cash on occasion from the commercial banks of their locality. Usually such loans were collateralized with mortgages held by the borrower. In this manner local banks aided the plans of mortgage lenders materially. One difficulty with such a plan was the limitation of availability of funds at a time when such funds were most urgently needed.

Of necessity, commercial bank loans were made for short periods of time only. They were extended with care in such manner as to protect the lending institution. When the borrower most needed new advances, the lender was least likely to look with favor upon granting them. In addition, such advances as had already been made were likely to be called at most embarrassing times for the borrower.

The Home Loan Bank System was not intended to take business away from local commercial banks. Instead, it was developed for the purpose of providing more dependable liquidity for its members, for a longer period of time, if necessary, than that for which commercial banks could commit their funds. Some members of the Home Loan Bank System still depend upon their local commercial banks for at least a part of their short-term needs for cash. The reasons for this practice are several. In some cases the close relationship between the savings and loan association manager and his banker is so cordial that friendship dictates the use of local bank credit. On other occasions, the local bank may be so anxious to get loans that it will lend money at lower rates of interest than those currently charged by the Home Loan Bank of the district. Even when local banks are used as sources of cash, the member-borrower enjoys the feeling of security which membership in the Home Loan Bank System affords it.

QUESTIONS AND PROBLEMS

1. What weaknesses existed in the home mortgage financing structure in the early 1930s.
2. At the time of establishment of the Federal Home Loan Bank System, what were the principal points of view as to what a Home Loan Bank should accomplish?
3. How were the Home Loan Banks originally financed and how is their stock held at the present time?
4. In addition to equity capital, what other sources of funds do the Home Loan Banks have?
5. What action does the Home Loan Bank Board take to assure the liquidity of individual members within the system?
6. Describe the organizational structure and the principal management objectives of the individual Home Loan Bank.
7. What are the major conditions under which Home Loan Banks will advance funds to their members?
8. Are the Home Loan Banks in a position to assist their membership in other ways than by advancing funds? How?
9. What kinds of financial institutions are eligible to join the Federal Home Loan Bank System? Which institutions did join? What reasons can you give why other institutions did not become members?
10. How is the Federal Home Loan Bank System supervised? What are the problems in fusion of regulation and management?

24

Affiliates of Federal Home Loan Bank System

FEDERAL SAVINGS AND LOAN ASSOCIATIONS

Background of Federal Savings and Loan Associations When the Home Loan Bank bill was under consideration in 1932, there was some discussion of including in it a provision for establishing a more uniform type of thrift and home-financing institution to take the form of federal savings and loan associations. Since thrift and home-financing institutions in the past had been developed to serve local needs only, it is not surprising that they followed a variety of patterns. In Ohio, some took deposits payable (presumably) on demand and carrying a definite rate of interest. In California, term certificates of investment also carried definite rates of interest. In Louisiana, they were called "homestead associations." In Massachusetts, their counterparts were known as "cooperative banks." In the Middle West, they combined in a wide variety of names using such words as "building," "savings," and "loan" in different arrangements.

An able committee of the United States Savings and Loan League made a careful study of this wide variety of practices, names, and so forth, and drafted a model code for savings and loan associations, selecting for that purpose what appeared to be the most desirable practices from the various plans in use. There was considerable support for including in the Home Loan Bank Act provision for the incorporation and supervision of this code. Because of the quality and the quantity of opposition to the major functions of this law, it was decided not to press for the inclusion of this model code.

So well did the committee's report impress the leaders of the savings and loan business that, after the enactment of most of its provisions into the regulations governing federal savings and loan associations, it became the basis for a proposed uniform savings and loan act to be offered for adoption by the several states. While this model code was never enacted in its entirety in any state, it has furnished ideas to those who have been instrumental in securing amendments in state laws. As a result of these amendments, state-chartered associations have moved closer to the plan of operation followed by federal associations, discussed in this chapter. Whatever practices best meet the needs of thrift people and homeowners served by savings and loan associations can be incorporated into operating plans of all associations, whether under state or federal charter. Over the years, these plans are likely to converge toward a common pattern rather than to diverge into two separate and distinct types of thrift and home-financing institutions.

Provision for Federal Savings and Loans When the bill which became the Home Owners Loan Act was passed in 1933, a little clause on the subject of federal savings and loan associations was inserted before the bill—which met with little opposition to its major provisions—was passed. Surprisingly enough, this clause was apparently included without its earlier opponents giving much attention to it. In brief, it set up a plan for chartering and supervising federal savings and loan associations under the Home Loan Bank Board. An initial appropriation of $150,000 was provided for the purpose of enabling the Board "to encourage local thrift and home financing and to promote, organize and develop the associations herein provided for Federal associations or similar associations organized under local laws." By subsequent amendments the total amount finally made available for this purpose was $850,000. Although the law as above quoted covered state-chartered associations as well as federals, most of the time and money was spent on the latter.

In addition to newly chartered federal associations, the Board was authorized to set up rules and regulations for converting state-chartered associations into federal associations. This provision created a great deal of controversy, especially among state supervisors. In some states enabling acts were passed to permit state-chartered associations to take advantage of this conversion privilege. In other states, the so-called "enabling acts" might be better described as "entangling laws," since the conditions surrounding conversion made the change of charters very difficult. And in some states frank opposition took the form of either no legislation—without which conversion was impossible—or negative legislation.

In one state the constitutionality of the whole idea was attacked. While the U.S. Supreme Court upheld the federal law, it helped to clarify the conditions under which it could be applied.

In 1933, about half the counties in the United States had no savings and loan associations. In its promotional activities emphasis was placed by the Home Loan Bank Board upon those counties that could support an association but had none. Where associations already existed, the Board favored converting of state-chartered associations to federal associations instead of granting new charters. Even here, however, the Board judged for itself whether or not the associations in existence were serving their communities adequately. In the middle 1930s, some existing associations were frozen so tightly they could serve neither investors nor borrowers adequately. With the restoration of public confidence upon the granting of a federal charter, which was necessarily accompanied by insurance of accounts, and with the various kinds of tonics which the Board was able to administer to federal associations, a new federal charter usually gave the converted association a new lease on life. But every conversion also resulted in a decrease in the prestige of state associations generally and of the position of the state supervisor in particular.

Nature of Federal Associations The regulations of the Home Loan Bank Board, together with the law under which they apply, determine in detail the nature of federal savings and loan associations. This type of association is intended to be primarily a local thrift and home-financing institution, mutually owned by its investors. Borrowers are given the right to attend shareholders' meetings and to cast one vote each. No deposits may be accepted upon which a definite rate of return is promised. Every federal association is required to be a member of the Home Loan Bank System and is expected to make use of its facilities if and when it can use them to advantage. Borrowing from other sources is much more definitely restricted. In addition, the federal association must have its accounts insured by the Federal Savings and Loan Insurance Corporation.

Loan plans are simplified. In general, federal associations are confined to restricting their loans to residential real estate as security, with enough leeway to take care of community needs for other types of real estate. Not more than $45,000 may be loaned on the security of any one single-family home; limits on multiple-dwelling units are subject to regulation of the Home Loan Bank Board. Also, not over 20 percent of assets may be loaned on other improved real estate without regard to limitations on loan amount and without regard to the 100-mile limit; and, furthermore, additional sums not exceeding 20 percent of the assets of the association may be used without regard to area restrictions to make or purchase participating interests in loans that are otherwise eligible holdings for federal associations. All loans must be secured by first liens. In addition, federal associations may invest in bonds and notes of the United States and state and municipal governments, obligations of the Federal National Mortgage Association, stock or debentures of the Home Loan Banks, and National Housing Partnerships.

Lending Operations The specific lending programs of federal savings and loan associations are as follows: (1) Installment loans may be made on homes or on combinations of home and business property up to 75 percent of the appraised value. (A home is defined as a residential property which provides not more than four-family units.) These loans must be repaid in monthly installments within a period of 30 years. With the consent of the members of the association, the ratio of loan to appraised value may be increased to 90 percent. Such loans may also be made up to 95 percent of value, provided the excess over 90 percent is covered with private insurance or the association creates a loss reserve. If the loan is insured or guaranteed by an agency of the United States, it may follow the pattern of insured or guaranteed loans. (2) Term or straight loans may be made for periods not to exceed five years, provided that they do not exceed 50 percent of the appraised value of the property. With the approval of the members, term loans may be made up to three years for an amount not in excess of 60 percent of the appraisal. (3) Loans may be made on other improved real estate for an amount not in excess of 50 percent of the appraised value, to be repaid in monthly installments over a period of not more than 20 years. With the approval of the members, the percentage may be increased for apartment loans to 80 percent of appraised value, provided the loan is amortized in 30 years; it may also be increased to the maximum allowable for insured or guaranteed loans. Associations may make construction loans on the security of apartments or commercial property for periods up to three years. The maximum loan-to-value ratio for loans on commercial property is 75 percent, to be amortized over a period not to exceed 25 years.

Federal associations may invest in leaseholds with a primary or renewal period extending at least 10 years beyond the loan maturity date. They may invest up to 5 percent of total assets directly in real estate located in urban renewal areas and in loans secured by first liens on such property. Direct investments, however, may not exceed 2 percent of total assets. These associations may also make 90 percent loans on first mortgages amortized over 30 years to provide single- and multiple-housing accommodations, including rest and nursing homes, suitable for and limited principally to occupancy by persons over 55 years of age. If their general reserves, surplus, and undivided profits are over 5 percent of withdrawable accounts, federal associations may also lend for land acquisition, site improvement, and developmental housing construction. They may make loans of this type up to 5 percent of their withdrawable accounts. The specific terms and limitations under which the loans are made are subject to regulation by the Home Loan Bank Board. In 1964, the Board regulations provided that development loans could be made up to 70 percent of the appraised value of undeveloped land and improved building sites and up to 80 percent of the appraised value of the total property as houses were completed on the sites. The developer was required to begin improvements within nine months of land acquisition and the development loan had to be retired completely by the end of six years. Federal associations may purchase any loans that they are eligible to make. However, loans purchased from affiliated institutions or from an officer or employee must be approved by the Home Loan Bank Board.

In early 1972, the Home Loan Bank Board made a move designed to stimulate lending in poor neighborhoods. It modified its regulations to permit federal associations to make partially amortized loans on residential and commercial buildings. These loans can have maturities of as few as 10 years with monthly installments based on terms as long as 30 years. Since payments under these conditions are smaller than for a straight 10-year mortgage, there is a "balloon" payment required at maturity. Meanwhile, the lender can study the loan and the borrower's performance. If refinancing is justified, the lender may elect to make a new loan at maturity under appropriate terms.

In its 1972 action, the Board also authorized federal associations to make mortgages with diminishing monthly payments. These loans are intended to assist persons nearing retirement. Under this plan, a borrower can make large payments in the 10 years or so before he retires, with smaller payments after his retirement, when his income is lower, until the mortgage is extinguished.

Lending Area The regular lending area is limited to a radius of 100 miles from the home office, or 100 miles from a branch office to the extent that such area is within the same state as the home office. A state-chartered association converted to a federal association may continue to make loans in the area that it served prior to the conversion. At the time of conversion the association must file a map showing the counties in which it is making loans and which it desires to retain as a proper lending area. With respect to loans within the 20 percent limitation, the 100-mile limit does not apply.

Growth of Federal Associations The greatest growth in the number of federal savings and loan associations had been experienced by the end of 1936. By that time 1,200 had been organized. By 1943, the number had increased to 1,466. As of the end of 1970, it stood at 2,067. Total assets of all federals in 1936 amounted to 15 percent of the assets of all savings and loan associations. By 1970, the federals represented about 36 percent of the number and over 54 percent of the assets of all associations. The total assets of all federal associations in 1970 were over $96 billion.

In general, in comparison with other savings and loan associations, federal associations charge a bit lower interest rates on mortgage loans:

advertise more liberally; pay slightly lower dividends; and put a larger percentage of earnings into reserves. The latter is essential because, owing to their rapid growth, their reserves are less generous than those of their competitors.

FEDERAL SAVINGS AND LOAN INSURANCE CORPORATION

Objectives of Insurance of Accounts There are several objectives claimed by the sponsors of insurance of accounts in savings and loan associations. First of all, those who supply such institutions with their funds are, for the most part, middle-class people who can ill afford to lose their hard-earned savings. Insurance of accounts helps to protect these people. In the second place, insurance of accounts helps to instill confidence in people whose investment funds are needed for home-financing purposes but who might be hesitant to place them in an uninsured institution. Third, it is hoped that the assurance of safety through this type of protection will materially reduce fear withdrawals at times when the institution should retain all but the funds needed for necessitous withdrawals, if it is to be permitted to serve its normal functions as a depository of thrift and a source of home-financing assistance. Fourth, insurance of accounts will help to instill confidence in the managers of institutions whose accounts are insured, so that they will have the courage needed to operate their associations in as nearly normal a fashion as possible even when economic conditions are unfavorable. Finally, it is recognized that our financial structure is made up of interrelated parts. If the public ever loses confidence in any one of our financial institutions, others will suffer as well. Hence, insurance of accounts in savings and loan associations helps public confidence in insurance of bank accounts, and vice versa.

Background of FSLIC While no one knows whether or not the Federal Deposit Insurance Corporation is actuarily sound—since it has never been put to the test—there is no question about its acceptance by the public. Immediately after provision by Congress for the insurance of bank accounts, the old boot, the clock, and the tin can buried in the backyard began to disgorge their currency contents. Public confidence in our commercial banking system was miraculously restored. The about-face was immediate and complete. Since that time many of our commercial banks have been blessed—or cursed—with so much money that many of them from time to time have resembled hoarding institutions.

With this example before them, parties interested in savings and loan associations succeeded in having a rider attached to the National Housing Act of 1934 to provide for insurance of accounts in savings and loan associations. Titles I, II, and III of this act are discussed elsewhere in this volume. Title IV, completely unrelated to the other three titles, provides for the insurance of accounts in savings and loan associations.

Pattern of FSLIC The Federal Savings and Loan Insurance Corporation is managed by a board of trustees who constitute the membership of the Federal Home Loan Bank Board. Its operations are under the immediate control of a general manager selected by the board. Its capital stock of $100 million was originally purchased by the HOLC. It has been since transferred to the Treasury Department.

All federal savings and loan associations are required to have their accounts insured. State-chartered associations may elect to have their accounts insured if they can meet the requirements of the trustees of the FSLIC. These requirements consist chiefly of solvency and sound operating policies. Members of insured associations are protected by this insurance up to $20,000 each. The amount was originally $5,000 but was increased to $10,000 in 1950 and again in 1966 to $15,000. Coverage was increased to $20,000 in 1969. This form of insurance provides only for the safety of investments, not for their liquidity.

Failure to obtain from an insured association any amounts requested for withdrawal would not necessarily involve the Federal Savings and Loan Insurance Corporation. The Corporation steps in only when the insured institution defaults. A default occurs only when a "conservator, receiver, or other legal custodian is appointed for an insured institution for the purpose of liquidation."

In event of default of an insured savings and loan association, the remedy accorded the insured account holder will be determined by the insurance corporation. It may pay him off in cash, or it may make available to him a transferred account in another insured institution in the same community.

Since the insurance coverage is limited to $20,000, the question arises, "What happens to the uninsured portion of an account for more than this amount?" By definition, it has no preferential claim against the assets of the association, since it is uninsured. For example, if A owns an account for $25,000 in the X insured association, upon default he may be covered by either of the above plans with respect to $20,000 of his account. The other $5,000 would continue as a claim against the institution in default, subject to any prior claims. What finally happens to this claim will depend upon how much is realized from the liquidation of the assets of the institution. It should be noted that over 95 percent of all investments of insured associations fall within the insurance coverage. Also, the holders of the large uninsured accounts are protected by the supervision given their associations by the FSLIC.

One feature of the operation of the FSLIC seems particularly noteworthy. As long as a financial institution keeps its doors open, the public knows little of its condition and seldom inquires about its operations.

But if a receiver or a conservator is appointed, this news spreads rapidly and sets numerous fires of suspicion and alarm. This in turn may diminish confidence in other financial institutions which are in no wise directly concerned with the troubles of the defaulting institution.

In recognition of these facts, Congress provided that, when an institution insured by the FSLIC becomes financially involved, the Corporation may make it a loan or even a contribution that is not to be repaid. This may be done without the knowledge of the general public. Even where new management is indicated, the change can be agreed upon behind closed doors. The present operating head may become conveniently ill and require a prolonged vacation. Or, if a blood transfusion for the board of directors is called for, an addition or two or even more replacements can be arranged without fanfare. Indeed, a good publicity agent can capitalize such changes to the advantage of the association. But since there has been no default, the financial troubles of the institution need not be dramatized in the public eye.

Where it appears to the Corporation that an insured institution should be liquidated, it may or may not precede such action with an application for receivership. Instead, it may elect to buy all of the assets, paying therefor enough to liquidate all creditors' claims and all claims of account owners, both those that are within the $20,000 limit of insurance and those that run over that amount. Thereafter it will dispose of the assets in such manner as to realize the greatest amount possible. This process may prove less expensive in the long run than a receivership.

Cost of Insurance To meet the cost of insurance of accounts, the FSLIC charges each member $1/12$ of 1 percent premium annually on the total accounts of an insurable type plus all creditor obligations, as determined by its latest annual report. Until June 1950, the insurance premium was $1/8$ instead of $1/12$ of 1 percent.

Starting on January 1, 1962, the FSLIC began a supplementary program to increase the reserves of the Corporation. Insured institutions have been required to make an annual prepayment equal to 2 percent of their net annual increase in savings, less any costs of Federal Home Loan Bank stock purchases. Payments under this program are credited as secondary reserves.

When the primary reserves built from the basic premium charge aggregate 2 percent of all insured accounts, all institutions that have paid premiums for at least 20 years are relieved from further payment of premiums until the reserves drop below the requirement. Similarly, when the total secondary reserves combined with the primary reserves reach 2 percent of all insured accounts, further prepayments are suspended. At this time, each insured institution may utilize a prorated portion of its secondary reserve to apply against its regular premium. This procedure may be followed until the combined total for primary and secondary reserves drops below 1.75 percent of the insured accounts. For the first time in history, at the 1969 year-end, the total primary and secondary reserves had risen to 2.138 percent of the aggregate insured liability, and the Federal Home Loan Bank Board announced suspension of prepayments by insured institutions and declared that the regular premium would be satisfied by a charge against the secondary reserves. At the end of 1970, the ratio of primary and secondary reserves to insured liability continued above the requirement—at 2.048 percent. Should there be an unusual drain upon the reserves, the FSLIC is empowered to levy a special premium assessment against its members, but these assessments may not exceed $\frac{1}{8}$ of 1 percent of the total accounts of insurable type plus all creditor obligations of the member institution. In order to equalize reserves on account of new institutions coming into the system, an admission fee, determined by the Corporation to be equitable, is charged each new member.

Examinations At the time an application for insurance of accounts is submitted to the FSLIC, it may determine that no further examination is necessary; or it may decree that the applicant be examined, at its expense, to determine eligibility for insurance. Such examination may include appraisals, particularly if the applicant owns much real estate. Reasons for refusal to insure the accounts of the applicant include impairment of capital and unsafe financial policies of the management. Sometimes defects in either or both are corrected as a prerequisite to insurance.

All insured institutions are subject to at least annual examinations to make sure that safe and sound management policies are maintained. The cost of such examination is assessed against the insured institution. In lieu of its own examination, the FSLIC may accept the examination made by a public regulatory authority. Examinations of federal savings and loan associations present no special problem, since both supervision of federals and the Insurance Corporation are under the Home Loan Bank Board. State-chartered institutions are sometimes examined jointly by the FSLIC and the state supervisory authority. In other cases only the latter makes the examination.

Supervision The regulations of the FSLIC establish standards of operation which must be observed by insured institutions. Only a brief mention will be made here of some of the subjects covered. Sales commissions for the sale of shares or accounts are regulated, both as to amount and as to method of payment. Membership and withdrawal fees must be identified as such. No insured institution may issue any securities payable on demand or represent itself as paying its investors on demand. Lending area and limitations upon borrowing must be in accord with the laws and regulations under which the insured institution operates. Members are discouraged from operating like mortgage bankers. Sale of loans is limited.

Extent of Operations of FSLIC In 1936 the number of insured associations was 1,575; in 1970, it was 4,365. In 1936 insured associations represented 16 percent of the number of all savings and loan associations; had 25 percent of the assets and 29 percent of the mortgage loans. In 1970 they represented 76 percent of the number; had 97 percent of the assets; and had 97 percent of the loans. As of the end of 1970, the total assets of insured members exceeded $170 billion. As of the same date, the assets of the FSLIC amounted to $3 billion. It had reserves in excess of $2.9 billion.

Loss Experience Over the first 34 years of its operations, the FSLIC has had a phenomenally satisfactory loss experience. As of December 31, 1970, net insurance losses incurred were $133.6 million, an amount just over 6 percent of total premiums collected. In all, it had handled 91 cases.

The Corporation may assist a troubled institution by means of a loan, a contribution, or acquisition of assets. Combinations of these means may be used. In extreme cases, the association may be placed in receivership. This extreme remedy has been used in only 12 of the 91 cases. Thirteen cases were handled by the sole remedy of acquisition of assets, representing losses of $35.7 million. Fifteen cases were handled by acquisition of assets with a contribution, resulting in losses of $51 million. Fifty-one institutions were assisted by contributions and loans, either or both, with resultant losses to the Corporation of $42.7 million. No saver has ever suffered a loss of insured savings at an FSLIC-insured institution.

Further Legislation Affecting FSLIC In June 1950, Congress passed legislation containing several provisions affecting the future of the FSLIC. in addition to the reduction in insurance premium from $\frac{1}{8}$ to $\frac{1}{12}$ of 1 percent, Congress strengthened the Corporation by directing the Secretary of the Treasury to lend it "on such terms as may be fixed by the Corporation and the Secretary, such funds as in the judgment of the Home Loan Bank Board are from time to time required for insurance purposes, not exceeding in the aggregate $750 million outstanding at any one time." As with the authorization for the purchase of the obligations of the Home Loan Bank System, it is expected that the Secretary of the Treasury will lend money to the FSLIC only in emergencies, when it cannot readily dispose of its debentures in the open market.

Furthermore, in 1965, the hand of the FSLIC was additionally strengthened when it was granted the power to require deposits from its members equal to 1 percent of their total savings. At the end of 1970, these savings amounted to nearly $142 billion, thus affording the FSLIC an additional liquidity potential of over $1.4 billion.

FEDERAL HOME LOAN MORTGAGE CORPORATION

In July 1970, President Nixon signed into law the Emergency Home Finance Act of 1970. Title III of this act provided for the establishment of a Federal Home Loan Mortgage Corporation (FHLMC) to serve as a secondary market facility for real estate mortages under the sponsorship of the Federal Home Loan Bank System.

The 12 district Federal Home Loan Banks subscribed to $100 million initial capital for FHLMC. Its directorship is composed of three members of the Federal Home Loan Bank Board.

The new Corporation has authority to buy and sell FHA and VA loans, mortgage participations, and conventional loans. Prior to beginning operations in late 1970, the Federal Home Loan Banks effected purchases of $322 million of federally underwritten mortgages which were placed in a pool to serve as backing for bonds guaranteed by the Government National Mortgage Association, as described in Chapter 28. In October 1970, FHLMC issued its first GNMA-guaranteed bonds, in two issues totaling $315 million. By January 1971, FHLMC announced an auction of $50 million federally underwritten loans, thus becoming established as a secondary market facility similar to the Federal National Mortgage Association, discussed in Chapter 28. Purchases of these mortgages by FHLMC differ from those by FNMA, however, in that FHLMC makes its commitments at a fixed price and allows the yield to float, thus absorbing the risk of changing interest rates, while FNMA pays a stable rate and allows the price to float, thereby placing the burden of rate changes on the builder or mortgage seller.

During 1971, the first year of operation, FHLMC offered two programs: an FHA/VA whole loan purchase program and a conventional participation program. Over $1 billion of loans were purchased in the first year. Under the conventional participation program, FHLMC will buy up to 85 percent of a conventional loan package that may contain: (1) all single-family loans; (2) all multifamily loans; or (3) a combination of single- and multifamily loans, so long as multifamily loans do not exceed 50 percent of the package. FHLMC will inspect and underwrite all loans offered under this program, but it will reject those loans deemed to be improperly documented, overappraised, or, for some other reason, unduly risky. All loans offered must have been closed within one year of the date of offer to sell to FHLMC.

The most important program, currently becoming operative, is the conventional whole loan program. This program took over a year to develop. Purchases of conventionally originated mortgages were withheld pending development of uniform note, mortgage, loan application, and appraisal forms that would permit universality of use among the various states. The whole loan program is initially being restricted to over-the-counter purchases of single-family and multifamily loans, and a 24-month forward commitment for multifamily loans only. The terms of the FHLMC commitment are unique. They provide for a fixed dollar amount and a maximum fixed constant. The constant is based on the current interest rate and a 22-year term. In this way, the builder knows the exact amount of his loan and that his monthly payments cannot be increased. When the loan is presented to FHLMC, if the interest rates are higher the amortization period may be extended up to 30 years with an accordingly higher interest rate. If, on the other hand, interest rates have dropped, the borrower can, if he wishes, extend the amortization period to 30 years and have his payments reduced. His interest rate, however, will remain the same as when originally quoted. A fee of 1½ points is charged for the commitment.

Although the conventional market still is awaiting support, FHLMC has immediately brought about a strong increase in the number of federally underwritten mortgages made and purchased by the savings and loan associations, thus complementing the Federal Home Loan Bank Board's objective in this direction.

Mortgage bankers have been disappointed in the interpretation of the Federal Home Loan Bank Board that FHLMC can deal only with insured institutions. The Board gives as its reason that it cannot exercise the necessary control over the noninsured institutions. Mortgage bankers, for their part, urge that they should be permitted to participate in the FHLMC programs because they are adequately audited by FHA and by their investors through comments and reviews of the servicers' audited financial statements. They point out that, as a consequence of this position, the savings and loan associations without a staff able to perform the servicing are, in effect, deprived of the benefit of FHLMC; and, further, such a policy limits the mortgages sold to FHLMC to the narrow geographic area that can be serviced by the selling institution. Accordingly, many excluded institutions are recommending that the authority of the FHLMC be expanded to permit it to deal with all established FHA-approved mortgagees.

HOME OWNERS LOAN CORPORATION

Background of HOLC The establishment of the Federal Home Loan Bank System occurred too late to prevent the flood of actual and threatened foreclosures that accompanied the depression of the 1930s. By June 1933, they were being recorded at a daily rate of approximately 800. This compares with less than one fourth of that number in previous periods of more normal economic conditions. It soon became evident that drastic measures were needed to at least slow down the increasing stream if it could not be stopped altogether. A new pattern of assistance to distressed homeowners took the form of the Home Owners Loan Corporation, which became effective June 13, 1933. In recommending the necessary legislation to Congress the President said:

> Implicit in the legislation which I am suggesting to you is a declaration of a national policy . . . that the broad interests of the nation require that special safeguards should be thrown around home ownership as a guarantee of social and economic stability, and that to protect home owners from inequitable, enforced liquidation in a time of general distress is a proper concern of the Government.

The resulting legislation—after an unusually short period for hearings on such a revolutionary measure—was passed with almost unanimous approval of the members of both parties.

Resources of HOLC As originally passed, the Home Owners Loan Act set up a corporation known as the Home Owners Loan Corporation, whose directors were the five members of the Federal Home Loan Bank Board. It was capitalized at $200 million, subscribed by the Secretary of the Treasury on behalf of the Reconstruction Finance Corporation, which put up the money. The HOLC was authorized to issue its own bonds up to an amount of $2 billion. Later this amount was increased, by amendments passed by Congress, to a final total of $4,750 million. These bonds could be issued for periods not to exceed 18 years and at interest rates not greater than 4 percent. The interest only was guaranteed by the government. Later the government guaranteed the repayment of the principal as well. Through successive refunding operations, the interest was reduced substantially, saving enough in carrying charges to absorb huge losses suffered by the Corporation.

HOLC Loans The major function of the HOLC was to make real estate loans to distressed homeowners. The most widely used plan followed by the Corporation was to exchange its bonds for the outstanding mortgage which was about to be foreclosed. At the outset, many of the mortgagee institutions were not too enthusiastic about this exchange. With only the interest on the bonds guaranteed by the government and with the uncertainties which surround a new program, bonds sold as low as $82\frac{1}{4}$. With the addition of the guarantee of principal repayment by the government in April 1934, the board of directors of the HOLC were finally able to get their bonds up to par in the open market. From then on the price never dropped below par. And from then on, mortgagees changed their attitude toward these bonds completely. Presently it seemed that all of them wished to exchange all of their frozen assets—some of which were only technically delinquent in their obligations—for a liquid asset worth more than its face value in the open market. In many instances mortgagees encouraged their borrowers to apply for HOLC loans.

No loan on any one property could exceed $16,000 nor more than 80 percent of the appraised value as established by the Corporation. Loans were limited to properties having an appraised value not in excess of $20,000. The loan had to be secured by a first lien on predominantly residential property, containing not more than four-family units and occupied in whole or in part by the applicant for the loan or held by him as his homestead. The original interest rate on these loans was 5 percent. This was later reduced to 4½ percent. The term of the loan was originally 15 years. Later extensions were granted up to 25 years.

Use of Cash by HOLC In connection with the loans described above, the HOLC was authorized to advance whatever cash was needed to liquidate delinquent taxes and assessments, and to pay the cost of necessary repairs, maintenance costs, insurance, and expenses of the transaction. All of these advances were added to the loan and had to be kept within the limitations imposed by the law. The Corporation pursued a policy of encouraging fairly liberal repairs to put the property in good condition at the time the loan was made. As might be expected, properties eligible for HOLC loans frequently required considerable repairs and had large tax delinquencies as well. Total advances by the Corporation for taxes, repairs, and so on, exceeded $400 million.

Where the holder of a mortgage which was eligible for refinancing by the HOLC was unwilling to accept the bonds of the Corporation in return for his mortgage, and if the distressed homeowner was unable to secure financial assistance elsewhere, the HOLC was authorized to use cash to pay off the existing mortgage, making a loan to the borrower for that purpose. In such case the interest rate could not exceed 6 percent nor the amount of the loan 40 percent of the HOLC appraisal. In general, such loans were not encouraged. Wherever possible, pressure was brought upon the mortgagee to induce him to accept bonds in place of his mortgage. Where the property was not encumbered by a mortgage, the Corporation was authorized to lend up to 50 percent of its appraised value at a rate of interest not in excess of 5 percent for the purpose of liquidating delinquent taxes and assessments and of paying the cost of necessary repairs and maintenance.

HOLC Appraisals Loans made by the HOLC were limited to $16,000 and to 80 percent of the value of the property as it was appraised by the Corporation. Organized at a time when the market was already glutted with unwanted properties, the Corporation could have further demoralized the residential market had its appraisers given first attention to market value. In a low and declining market, the inevitable result must have been to push selling prices further downward. Instead, the Corporation adopted a three-way appraisal formula based upon the assumption that, in times of happier economic circumstances, values would enjoy definite recoveries from those reflected in depressed prices.

This three-way formula took into account: (1) the replacement cost of the property, less depreciation; (2) the presumed market value under normal conditions; and (3) the capitalized rent that the property should command in periods when tenants could afford to pay reasonable prices for the use of property. By the use of such a formula the Corporation helped to build a floor under residential property values, instead of letting the bottom drop out from under them.

In its appraisal program the HOLC suffered from one very serious handicap. With foreclosure facing at least a couple of million homeowners, quick action was demanded. Yet a sufficient number of trained and experienced appraisers was unavailable. Add to this the influence of politics, which always intrudes its demand for jobs, even when the work to be done required specialized skills and successful experience, and some of the results are not too difficult to forecast. Politics undoubtedly played other parts in this operation which can hardly be charged to inexperienced appraisers. Because of this combination of circumstances surrounding the very heart of HOLC's operation, it is not to be wondered at that it suffered many losses that could have been avoided had only expert and impartial appraisers been available in sufficient numbers to do the job in the short time allowed.

Even with liberal appraisals intentionally directed by the HOLC, not all distressed homeowners were able to make satisfactory arrangements with their mortgagees to refinance their loans in the manner indicated above. In some cases the mortgagee was induced to accept the bonds offered, provided it was permitted to take back a second mortgage equivalent to the difference between the total amount of its claims and the amount of the loan offered by the HOLC. And in some cases compromises were worked out.

The net effect of the appraisal policy of the HOLC is evident from the fact that, in order to be eligible for a loan from the Corporation, the borrower must be in danger of losing his home through foreclosure action. In other words, the mortgagee presumably felt that the value of the property was not sufficiently greater than the amount of his claims to justify further postponement of demand for payment. Yet the average HOLC loan of $3,027 represented only 69 percent of the value of the property as established by the Corporation's appraisers. This difference of 31 percent may be accounted for as one measure of the hope for recovery of value from a depressed real estate market.

Extent of Operations The period of time within which the HOLC was permitted to make loans to distressed homeowners was limited by Congress to three years, expiring June 13, 1936. Thereafter, some loans were refinanced by the Corporation, but no new loans were granted. Before this date was reached, applications were received from nearly 2 million homeowners, whose aggregate mortgage debt exceeded $6 billion. This was more than one third of the home mortgage debt in the United States at that time. The Corporation accepted more than half of the applications filed—1,017,821—having aggregate mortgage indebtedness of $3,093,451,321. Before it ceased making loans, it found by a careful check of applications that many of those filed should have been taken care of by their mortgagees. As a matter of fact, the announcement that no more loans would be granted was immediately followed by the recasting of a large number of distressed loans in such manner that the mortgagors could carry their obligations. Of the total number of loans granted, less than 1 percent represented direct cash loans. The very great majority represented exchange of HOLC bonds for mortgages. The amount of cash outlay for other purposes was much larger.

HOLC Defaults Of the 1,017,821 loans originally granted by the HOLC, foreclosure authorizations were ordered eventually against 251,863 debtor accounts up to June 30, 1949. Of this number, 53,157 were subsequently reinstated without foreclosure sale, leaving the number of properties foreclosed as 198,706, or slightly less than 20 percent of the number of loans originally made. A more accurate way of stating this would be to say that the Corporation succeeded in salvaging more than 80 percent of the number of foreclosures with which it started, since the borrower had to be a potential foreclosure case before he was eligible for an HOLC loan.

HOLC and Other Agencies In many respects it was indeed fortunate that the HOLC was placed under the control of the Federal Home Loan Bank Board. While it could have been operated as a separate agency, its success depended in part upon the recovery of home-financing institutions which was fostered by the activities of the Federal Home Loan Bank Board. Any advance in the recovery of private agencies which enabled them to take over their normal functions lightened the burden upon the HOLC. Were it not for this recovery by the time the expiration date of the lending activities of the Corporation rolled around, it seems likely that Congress would have extended the life of these activities and granted the Corporation whatever additional resources it needed for the purpose. As pointed out above, the Home Loan Bank Board failed to use all of the resources authorized by the Congress, although it could have done so very easily. Instead, it was concerned with the recovery of private financial institutions. It frequently used some of the resources of the HOLC to that end. In doing so it not only saved money for the HOLC, but furthered the progress of its other activities as well.

Congress recognized the interrelationship of these activities by several bits of legislation. As a part of the original HOLC law, a provision was included to authorize the chartering and supervision of federal savings and loan associations to become, in effect, the national banks of the thrift and home-financing field. In addition it authorized the board of directors to invest in the shares of these federal associations as a recovery measure. It authorized the HOLC to purchase the stock of the Federal Savings and Loan Insurance Corporation, amounting to $100 million. Each of these bits of legislation is discussed elsewhere in this chapter.

Investments by HOLC in Savings and Loan Associations In order to place newly chartered federal savings and loan associations in a position to serve homeowner applicants for loans and to prime the pump for private investments in these institutions, Congress authorized the Home Loan Bank Board to call upon the Secretary of the Treasury to invest in shares of federal savings and loan associations. Such shares were to be preferred as to assets but not as to dividends. Not more than $100,000 could be invested in any one association. In April 1934, the preferred status of the Treasury investments was eliminated by Congress, as was the upper limit of $100,000. The total amount authorized by Congress for this purpose was $100 million, but only $50 million was appropriated. By subsequent legislation, the Congress authorized similar investments by the HOLC in either the accounts of federal savings and loan associations or of state-chartered associations that were members of the Home Loan Bank System or whose accounts were insured. In every case the application for such investment required the approval of the board of directors of the HOLC.

The amount of HOLC funds authorized to be used for this purpose was $300 million. Of the amount authorized, only $224 million was invested in accounts of nearly 1,500 associations. In order to encourage applicant institutions to hustle for private investments, HOLC (and the same limitation applied to the Treasury) would not invest in any association more than three times the amount of investments from private sources. As a matter of practice this limit was seldom reached. HOLC could not demand the withdrawal of any of its investments for a period of five years after the investment and thereafter not more than 10 percent in any one year. Meantime, the institution paid to the HOLC the same rate of return that it paid for the use of private money. It had the privilege of redeeming Treasury and HOLC investments as of any dividend-paying date or within 30 days thereafter.

With returning interest of private investors in the investment opportunities offered by these associations, nearly all of such public investments were prepaid long before they were callable. Meantime the HOLC and the Treasury enjoyed handsome profits from these investments. The dividends received therefrom were, in the aggregate, substantially higher than the cost of the money to them.

The whole investment program was in the nature of a rehabilitation attempt. Therefore the board of directors of the HOLC let it be known that funds would no longer be freely invested for this purpose as soon as it became evident that ample private funds could be had by aggressive managements. Thereafter, the remaining funds authorized by Congress for this purpose were reserved for the use of associations that faced unusual difficulty in effecting their rehabilitation. Applications from that time forward were carefully screened with this objective in mind. All such investments have since been recovered by the Treasury and the HOLC.

Service of HOLC to Lenders and Others While the HOLC was set up primarily to assist distressed homeowners, it was a boon to other groups as well. By exchanging readily marketable bonds for frozen assets, it provided much needed liquidity to the former mortgagees. This ready cash or its equivalent in turn enabled financial institutions to better meet the demands of their investors for the withdrawal of funds. From commercial banks it took 28 percent of their mortgages in return for $525 million in bonds; from mutual savings banks, 17 percent in mortgages in return for $410 million in bonds; from savings and loan associations, 15 percent in mortgages in return for $770 million in bonds; from life insurance companies, 10 percent in mortgages in return for $165 million in bonds; and from all others, 13 percent in mortgages in return for $880 million in bonds.

In addition to providing liquidity for such institutions, it helped them to remain solvent by building floors under the whole real estate market at a time when it appeared that the bottom might drop out of it. The millions of dollars paid by the HOLC to liquidate both delinquent and current taxes aided the plans of local governmental units materially. Other millions advanced for repairs and maintenance costs provided employment for building labor and for factories engaged in producing building materials. Thousands of attorneys, appraisers, and others were employed to conduct the far-flung operations of this agency. Even homeowners whose properties were not directly affected by its operations nevertheless benefited from the lift which this Corporation gave to the idea of homeownership in general and to the stability of real estate values in particular.

Losses of HOLC When the Home Owners Loan Corporation was created by Congress it was generally conceded that it would lose considerable of the taxpayers' money—perhaps $200 million or even as much as $500 million. In its early years its losses mounted to approximately $300 million. Later on, its accumulated earnings absorbed these losses. Its $3.5 billion of bonds were redeemed. Its initial capital stock of $200 million, contributed by purchase by the Reconstruction Finance Corporation and later taken over by the U.S. Treasury, was completely liquidated. The profit of the HOLC was realized not from selling foreclosed real estate above its book value, as has been generally assumed in some quarters, but from the spread in the cost of money to the Corporation and the interest charge it made on its mortgage loans. For most of its life the latter was $4\frac{1}{2}$ percent. The former was originally 4 percent but was successively reduced through refunding operations to less than $1\frac{1}{2}$ percent. The spread between the cost of its money and the interest charged on its mortgage loans enabled the Corporation to meet its direct operating expenses and to accumulate a loss reserve sufficient to wipe out early losses. When the HOLC was liquidated in 1951, the U.S. Treasury received a profit of some $16 million. This "profit" is somewhat misleading, since the HOLC paid no dividends on its stock owned by the RFC.

QUESTIONS AND PROBLEMS

1. What were the circumstances giving rise to the need for federal savings and loan associations?
2. Describe the conditions under which federal savings and loan association may make loans?
3. What important protections is a member of a federal savings and loan association certain to have which he may not have as a member of a state-chartered association?
4. What are the objectives of the Federal Savings and Loan Insurance Corporation? Have these objectives been accomplished?
5. Describe briefly the Federal Savings and Loan Insurance Corporation and how it operates.
6. Do the limitations on the availability of actuarial data in the case of FSLIC insurance cast serious doubts concerning the financial soundness of the program? Discuss.
7. What is the effect of FSLIC insurance on the investor's decision where to place his account? Will a New York investor be willing to place his funds in a California association? What factors would be considered?
8. How are the costs of FSLIC insurance met? Has the loss experience been favorable or unfavorable?
9. What is the Federal Home Loan Mortgage Corporation and why was it created?
10. What was the Home Owners Loan Corporation and why was it created?
11. Describe how the HOLC operated.
12. How did the HOLC assist: (a) distressed homeowners; (b) mortgage lenders; and (c) newly chartered federal savings and loan associations?
13. What is your appraisal of the results of the HOLC operation?

25

Federal Housing Administration

Legislative History of FHA Unlike some of the other legislation discussed in this part of this volume, the law which set up the Federal Housing Administration had many friends and few enemies. Its godfathers included not only several types of financial institutions, but builders, real estate groups, manufacturers of building supplies and equipment, representatives of organized labor, and so forth. Those who did not favor this type of legislation were not very articulate. They held their fire until later. The fact that the bill was passed only on the last day of the session, in June 1934, is no indication that it was railroaded through. It did have relatively little discussion, to be sure. On May 14, 1934, the President sent a special message to Congress requesting the passage of this legislation. Congress acted favorably on the request June 18, and the National Housing Act became law June 27.

One feature of the law that perhaps could not have been anticipated belongs in the category of off-the-record discussion. Since the administration of the law brought the FHA into direct competition with some of the activities of the Home Loan Bank Board, it seemed quite unfortunate that its administration was not assigned to this board at the time the law was passed. Instead, it was set up as a separate agency, administered by a single commissioner. As provided by the President's Reorganization Plan No. 3 of 1947, the FHA became a constituent element of the Housing and Home Finance Agency. In 1965, this agency became a part of the newly created Department of Housing and Urban Development. Since March 1971, the FHA has been officially referred to as "HUD-FHA," but for brevity the discussion in this text has used the shorter "FHA" apellation.

Objectives of the FHA At the outset, the legislation which established the Federal Housing Administration had two broad objectives: First, Titles I and II undertook to entice timid investment money to come out of hiding and start work in the construction field. By shifting much of the risk from private investors to a governmental agency, it was hoped that employment in the building trades would be stimulated and that production schedules in the durable goods industries would be stepped up. By these means it was hoped that the FHA would contribute to recovery from the depression. How well these two titles worked will be discussed later.

The second major objective at the beginning was expressed in Title III. Those who were disappointed that the Home Loan Bank System set up a credit reserve program based upon loans to be repaid by the borrowers, instead of a mortgage discount system that would enable mortgagees to free their capital by the sale of mortgages in order that they could finance new mortgages, looked to Title III to meet their requirements. In other words, it was intended as a means of establishing a secondary market for mortgages. The operation of this title will also be discussed later.

These early objectives gave no consideration to the social direction of real estate credit through the FHA. Recovery rather than reform dominated the thinking of the Congress that passed the law setting up this agency. It was primarily in order to encourage owners and prospective owners of modest homes to undertake construction programs that would hire building labor and purchase building material that the government offered to lift much of the financial risk from the shoulders of the private lenders. It was expected that all financing under Titles I and II would be undertaken on a sound basis.

From time to time during the life of this agency its objectives have shifted substantially—in each case with the expressed approval of Congress. For example, the FHA was drafted to help win World War II. Its part was to encourage private construction to provide housing for workers employed in defense areas. So long as the insured mortgages applied to properties in defense areas which met the appraisal requirements of the FHA at the time of construction, such properties were eligible for mortgage insurance.

When Title VI was added in 1941, the emphasis was placed upon lower cost houses, with an increase in the amount of appraised value to be insured. As the emergency created by the war was prolonged, and as the effects of inflation of prices of real estate and construction costs became more apparent, Congress adjusted the policies of Title VI accordingly. Permissible insurance allowances per unit were increased. The original emphasis upon economically sound projects changed to attention to acceptable risks in view of the emergency. More discretion was given the Administrator to use his best judgment in doing those things necessary to secure priority of housing accommodations for war plant employees. In recent years, the FHA has been enlisted to help provide housing for the elderly, nursing homes, and replacement homes of those displaced by slum clearance programs. With amortization periods extending up to 40 years and a preferential interest rate, such loans are obviously based primarily on social policy rather than conventional economic concepts.

Meantime, the temporary character of Title II has gradually undergone considerable modification. Starting as a depression measure to help lift the real estate market out of the doldrums of the depression in the early 1930s, it responded to one emergency after another under successive amendatory legislation by Congress. Year by year the life of this supposedly temporary agency has been extended, and its authority for insuring mortgages has been increased. Finally, in 1946 the almost annual extensions of life were abandoned, and all restrictions upon its future existence were removed. Likewise, Congress in other ways apparently recognized that mortgage insurance is now firmly fixed as a part of the machinery for financing residential property in this country.

Functions of the FHA Since its organization in 1934, a variety of functions have been added to the FHA program. As expressed by statutory authority, these functions involve the operation of housing loan insurance programs "designed to encourage improvement in housing standards and conditions, to facilitate sound home financing on reasonable terms, and to exert a stabilizing influence in the mortgage market."[1] The FHA is not a direct lender, nor does it plan or build houses. It does markedly affect lending terms and building plans and specifications, as well as selection of housing sites, by the conditions under which it permits insurance to be granted. The various types of loans on which insurance is issued by the FHA are defined by several titles of the National Housing Act of 1934, as amended.

Title I insures lending institutions against loss on loans which finance the alteration, repair, improvement, or conversion of existing structures and the construction of new, small, nonresidential structures. The FHA liability is limited to 90 percent of loss on individual loans and to 10 percent of all such loans made by any institution.

Title II covers those types of loans representing the major function of the FHA. Section 203 of this title provides for insuring mortgages on one- to four-family dwellings. This section has accounted for about 70 percent of all mortgage insurance written by the FHA. Section 207 authorizes the insurance of mortgages, including construction advances,

---

[1] *Thirteenth Annual Report of the Housing and Home Finance Agency* (1959), p. 46.

on rental housing projects of eight or more family units. It also covers projects undertaken by nonprofit corporations for occupancy by elderly persons. A further provision of this section extends the authority to insurance of loans on mobile home courts. The Housing Act of 1959 added a new Section 231 to Title II to replace the authority of Section 207 in regard to insurance of rental housing for persons 62 years old and older. The terms of Section 231 are similar to those under Section 207, except that projects of profit-motivated sponsors were also made eligible for insurance. Mortgage ceilings were established at $12.5 million for a private mortgagor and at $50 million for a public mortgagor. For public mortgagors or nonprofit private mortgagors insurance may be granted up to 100 percent of estimated replacement cost (for proposed construction) or 100 percent of estimated value (for rehabilitated properties). For mortgagors operating for profit, insurance may not exceed 90 percent of these values.

Section 213 of Title II (added in 1950) authorizes the insurance of mortgages on cooperative housing projects of eight or more family units. The section provides for two types of FHA-insured cooperative housing projects—the management type and the sales type. Under the management type, the mortgagor must be a nonprofit ownership housing corporation or trust, with permanent occupancy of the housing facility restricted to members. In a sales-type project each individual member is a stockholder of the cooperative corporation, or a beneficiary of the trust, undertaking the construction of the housing project. Upon completion of the sales-type project, provision is made for the acquisition of title to an individual housing unit by each member and the insurance of an individual mortgage thereon. A corporate investor may qualify for FHA insurance under this section by undertaking construction of a management-type project and certifying his intention of selling the project to a cooperative group within two years after completion. Under this section, the FHA is also authorized to furnish technical advice in the organization of cooperatives and in the planning, development, construction, and operation of the housing projects.

Sections 220 and 221 of Title II (added in 1954) are designed to aid in slum clearance programs. Section 220 permits insurance in connection with financing the rehabilitation of existing salvable housing and the replacement of slums with new housing. Section 221 authorizes mortgage insurance on low-cost housing for relocation of families in connection with urban renewal and slum clearance programs. Under this authority, in a community whose clearance and improvement program is approved by the Secretary of the Department of Housing and Urban Development (HUD), the FHA may insure the number of units certified by HUD as needed to provide housing for the displaced families. By the Housing Act of 1961, the benefits of Section 221 were extended to any family of low or moderate income. Section 221 (d) (3) provides special terms for housing located in approved urban renewal areas and sponsored by public agencies (other than local housing authorities that obtain their funds exclusively for public housing from the federal government), cooperatives, nonprofit corporations or associations, such as labor unions or churches, or limited-dividend corporations. With such sponsorship, the maximum interest rate can be reduced, at the time of completion of construction and final endorsement of the mortgage for insurance, to 3 percent. On mortgages carrying this rate, FHA waives its mortgage insurance premium and the mortgages will be purchased by the Federal National Mortgage Association. Because of the low-interest rate, activity under Section 221 (d) (3) is limited by the amount of FNMA-assistance funds available for purchasing such mortgages since they are not attractive to other investors. The Housing Act of 1964 extended the coverage of Section 221 (d) (3) to any mortgagor (which could include a trust, partnership, or individual) approved by the Federal Housing Commissioner. Approval requires that the mortgagor be regulated by the Commissioner in regard to rents, charges, and methods of operation in a manner that will effectuate the purposes of the program. A mortgagor acting by virtue of Commissioner approval is limited in the amount of mortgage insurance available to him to 90 percent of the amount authorized under Section 221. Under the 1964 law, an individual person 62 years of age or older or a handicapped person is accorded the same treatment as a "family" under this and various other sections defining the FHA program.

Section 221 (d) (2), as amended in 1968, provides for insurance of mortgages up to $15,000 for single homes, permits a mortgagor to contribute the value of his labor to the acquisition cost of his dwelling, and authorizes the Secretary of HUD to reimburse the mortgagee for its expenses in handling the mortgage. The ratio of the loan to property value can be 100 percent for an owner-occupant, except when the home was not constructed under FHA or VA inspection or over a year has passed since its completion. In the latter case, the maximum ratio is 90 percent. The minimum cash investment is $200 for a displaced family and 3 percent of acquisition cost for other families. Normal FHA ceiling interest rates apply, and a ½ percent mortgage insurance premium is charged. In the case of displaced families the term of the mortgage can be up to 40 years. For other families, it is generally 30 years.

Section 221 (h) of the Federal Housing Act was added in 1966 to establish a program to promote homeownership for low-income families with the assistance of FHA mortgage insurance. Under this authority, the FHA insures mortgages of nonprofit organizations to finance the purchase and rehabilitation of deteriorating and substandard housing. Mortgages may also be insured to finance the resale of housing to low-income families or individuals who are eligible for rent supplements under the rent supplement program.

The mortgage to the nonprofit organization may be insured for an amount equal to the appraised value of the property plus estimated rehabilitation costs. Its maturity is set by the FHA. Under the 1966 legislation, the regular FHA ceiling interest rate was prescribed until final endorsement of the mortgage for insurance, then 3 percent. Under the 1968 amendment, the interest rate may be as low as 1 percent for purchasers whose income is low enough to warrant the lower rate. As a result, individual mortgages insured under this section may bear interest between 1 and 3 percent, depending on the individual incomes and needs of the homeowners. The mortgage of the homeowner in any individual case can be an amount equal to the unpaid balance of the mortgage of the nonprofit corporation selling the property that is allocable to the dwelling being sold. The minimum down payment required is $200, but this may be applied to closing costs. The maximum mortgage term is 25 years. The mortgage must contain a provision that the interest rate will increase to the highest rate permitted by FHA if the mortgagor does not continue to occupy the property; however, this provision is not applicable to a case of resale back to the nonprofit organization from whom the property was originally purchased, or a sale to a local housing authority or another low-income purchaser approved by the FHA.

The rent supplement program, previously mentioned, was established by the Housing and Urban Development Act of 1965 in Section 221 (d) (3) of the Federal Housing Act. By this authority, low-income individuals of families who are either elderly, handicapped, displaced by government action, occupants of substandard housing, or occupants or former occupants of homes damaged by acts of God are eligible for admission as tenants to new or rehabilitated housing owned by a nonprofit organization participating in the below market interest rate (BMIR) program. The housing owner contracts with the Secretary of HUD for federal rent supplement payments. The contracts run for terms up to 40 years. The rent supplement payments are limited to the excess of the fair rental value of the unit over one fourth of the tenant's income. When the tenant can afford to pay the whole rent by this standard he may continue to live in the unit without a rent supplement payment.

The Housing and Urban Development Act of 1968 extended the rent supplement program to owners of housing projects financed under a state or local program which provided assistance through loans, loan insurance, or tax abatements, provided the project meets the approval of the Secretary of HUD for rent supplement benefits before completion of construction or rehabilitation. Rent supplement benefits may also be extended to housing financed by direct loans under Section 202 of the Housing Act of 1959.

Section 222 of Title II (also added in 1954) authorizes FHA insurance for mortgages on dwellings owned by members of the Armed Forces or the Coast Guard upon proper certification by the Department of Defense, or the Treasury Department as to Coast Guard personnel. The underlying objectives of such a program in the interests of national security, particularly at the more remote outposts, are apparent.

Section 232 of Title II (added in 1959) authorized FHA insurance of mortgages on urgently needed nursing homes. The insurance is applicable to convalescents who do not require hospitalization but who do need nursing care. To qualify a home for such insurance, the appropriate state agency charged with licensing and regulating such establishments must certify that the home is needed and that minimum operating standards will be enforced in the home. The mortgage amount may not exceed $12.5 million and it must not be over 90 percent of the FHA estimate of value. The property may be new or rehabilitated, but it must have at least 20 beds.

Section 233 of Title II (added in 1961) gave the FHA authority to insure mortgages on experimental housing. This insurance was available for mortgages or home-improvement loans meeting the requirements of any of FHA's Title II programs. The 1968 legislation extended this program to all types of operations. The experimentation may involve the utilization or testing of new design, materials, construction methods, or experimental property standards for neighborhood design. Major effort is directed toward improving low-income housing construction.

Section 234 of Title II (also added in 1961) authorized FHA to insure a mortgage covering a family unit in a multifamily building of five or more units and an undivided interest in common areas and facilities serving the structure. This kind of ownership is known as "condominium." Under the 1961 Housing Act, the insurance was limited to a mortgage on a structure carrying mortgage insurance under one of the FHA multifamily insurance programs other than Section 213. By the Housing Act of 1964, insurance was authorized for blanket mortgages to finance the construction or rehabilitation of multifamily projects to be sold as condominiums, provided the mortgagor certifies that it intends to sell the project as a condominium and will make all reasonable efforts to sell the family units to FHA-approved purchasers.

Section 235 of Title II (added in 1968) was designed to establish a homeownership assistance program for the purchase of new, single-family homes by low and moderate income families. The assistance takes the form of periodic payments to the mortgagee by the Secretary of HUD to make up the difference between 20 percent of the family's monthly income and the required monthly payment under the mortgage for principal, interest, taxes, insurance, and mortgage insurance premium. The amount of the subsidy varies according to the income of the homeowner, and is available to families in the general range of $3,000 to

$8,000. In calculating the gross income of the homeowner on which the 20 percent calculation is made, $200 is deducted for each minor child in the household who is a member of the immediate family. The income of minors is not included in the homeowner's income computation.

The mortgage maxima are generally $15,000 ($17,500 in high-cost areas), but these may be expanded to $17,500 and $20,000, respectively for larger families. The Secretary of HUD will not approve purchases of homes that are extravagantly designed or overpriced in terms of appraised values.

The effect of this section is to expand the function of Section 221 (h), and to incorporate generally its provisions. It is expected that Section 235 will supplant the earlier section. Until the latter section is fully operational, however, Section 221 (h) will still be utilized.

The accompanying Table 25–1 sets forth the probable range of assistance payments for a mortgage under Section 235.

Section 236 of the National Housing Act (added in 1968) was established to provide the counterpart of Section 235 for rental and cooperative housing for low and moderate income families. This section emerged from the below-market interest rate program authorized under Section 221 (d) (3) which has been successful in providing needed rental and cooperative housing for families whose incomes are too high for public housing and too low for standard housing available in the competitive market.

Section 221 (d) (3) has suffered from the limitation of depending on direct federal lending from the special assistance funds of FNMA to support its 3 percent mortgages. The limited availability of these funds greatly restricted the activity. The new subsidy program makes it possible to obtain funds from the private mortgage market. The new Section 236 program is expected to replace the Section 221 (d) (3) BMIR program, and also the program of direct 3 percent loans for the elderly and the handicapped established by Section 202 of the Housing Act of 1959.

Under the Section 236 program the mortgagor-owner of the housing must make a monthly payment for principal and interest under the mortgage as though it bore a 1 percent interest rate. The difference between this amount and the monthly payment due under the mortgage, which bears the market rate of interest, for principal, interest, and mortgage insurance premium is paid to the mortgagee on behalf of the mortgagor by the federal government.

From the standpoint of the tenant, a basic rental charge is established on the basis of a 1 percent mortgage interest rate. The tenant is then required to pay either the basic rental charge or 20 percent of his income, whichever is greater.

TABLE 25-1

Estimated Monthly Assistance Payments under Sec. 235, by Mortgage Amount and Homeowner's Annual Income Based on 6¾ Percent 35-Year Mortgage with ½ Percent Mortgage Insurance Premium

Adjusted Annual Income*	20 Percent of Monthly Income	Mortgage Amount						
		$8,000	$10,000	$12,000	$14,000	$15,000	$17,500	$20,000
$3,000	$ 50	$17.63	$32.84	$45.72	†	†	†	†
$3,600	60	7.63	22.84	39.66	$ 53.34	$ 57.15	‡	†
$4,200	70	—	12.84	29.00	46.52	54.85	$ 66.68	†
$4,800	80	—	‡	19.66	36.52	44.85	66.27	$ 76.20
$5,400	90	—	—	9.66	26.52	34.85	56.27	76.20
$6,000	100	—	—	—	16.52	24.85	46.27	67.52
$6,600	110	—	—	—	6.52	14.85	36.27	57.52
$7,200	120	—	—	—	—	‡	26.27	47.52
$7,800	130	—	—	—	—	—	16.27	37.52
Monthly payment due the mortgagee	—	67.63	82.84	99.66	116.52	124.85	146.27	167.52
Maximum subsidy (based on a 1 percent interest rate)	—	30.48	38.10	45.72	53.34	57.15	66.68	76.20

* Total income of family less $200 for each minor child and any income earned by a minor child.
† Cost to buyer would exceed 25 percent of his monthly income in addition to assistance payments in order to meet payments on this mortgage amount.
‡ Less than $5.
Source: Department of Housing and Urban Development.

Table 25–2 shows estimated rental reductions under a Sec. 236 program.

Section 237 of Title II was added in 1968 to extend FHA mortgage insurance to families of low or moderate income with impaired credit histories or irregular income patterns. Such families may become eligible if the Secretary of HUD finds them to be reasonably satisfactory credit risks and capable of homeownership with proper financial counseling. Mortgages insured under this program must generally meet the requirements of the specific FHA program for financing under which the applicant seeks assistance. The credit and income requirements do not apply, however, and the principal obligation cannot exceed $15,000 ($17,500 in high-cost areas). Insurance will not be authorized under Section 237 unless the monthly mortgage payments for principal and interest, plus real estate taxes, can be paid with 25 percent or less of the mortgagor's monthly income, based on the last year or the past three-year average, whichever is greater.

In addition to the relaxation of credit restrictions, the 1968 legislation has given the FHA more flexible authority to accept insurance on properties in declining urban areas. Insurance may now be accepted in areas that do not meet normal eligibility requirements. Acceptance of these mortgages is permitted when the FHA is able to establish that the area is "reasonably viable," giving consideration to the need to provide adequate housing for families of low or moderate income in the area, and that the property is a reasonably acceptable risk in view of such consideration. This authority enlarges upon the 1966 amendment to Section 203 of the National Housing Act whereby the secretary of HUD was authorized to insure one- to four-family dwellings in areas fraught with riots or other disorders, without regard to economic soundness, in view of the urgent need for adequate housing for low and moderate income families in the areas.

The 1968 Housing and Urban Development Act, in Section 238, has established a "Special Risk Insurance Fund" to receive premiums from and pay claims under programs that are not intended to be actuarially sound. These include mortgages insured under the new Sections 235, 236, and 237, as well as Section 223, as it relates to properties in declining areas that do not pass minimum standard tests for economic soundness, as discussed in the preceding paragraph. Also included in this fund are mortgages issued under Section 233, primarily oriented to the development of new technologies for lower income housing.

Title VI is now inactive except for outstanding mortgage insurance in force. Sections 603 and 608 of this title were originally enacted to encourage war housing through the use of more liberal insurance than was provided in Title II. These sections lapsed at the end of World War II, but were revived in 1946 to assist the housing of veterans.

TABLE 25-2

Estimated Reduction in Monthly Rental under Sec. 236, by Mortgage Amount and Tenants Annual Income Based on 6¾ Percent 40-Year Mortgage with ½ Percent Mortgage Insurance Premium

Annual Income	20 Percent of Monthly Income*	Mortgage Amount					
		$8,000	$10,000	$12,000	$14,000	$15,000	$17,000
$3,000.........	$ 50	$ 31.45	†	†	†	†	†
$3,400.........	57	31.45	$ 39.31	†	†	†	†
$4,000.........	67	31.45	39.31	†	†	†	†
$4,600.........	77	25.27	39.31	$ 47.18	†	†	†
$5,200.........	87	15.27	36.15	47.18	$ 55.04	$ 58.97	$ 66.83
$5,800.........	97	5.27	26.15	47.18	55.04	58.97	66.83
$6,400.........	107	—	16.15	40.79	55.04	58.97	66.83
$7,000.........	117	—	6.15	30.79	55.04	58.97	66.83
$7,600.........	127	—	—	20.79	45.40	53.33	66.83
Basic rental charge based on a							
1 percent interest rate.........	—	70.82	83.84	100.61	117.36	121.36	127.59
Fair market rental charge.........	—	102.27	123.15	147.79	172.40	180.33	194.42

* Rounded.
† Cost to tenant would exceed 30 percent of his monthly income in order to meet basic rental on this mortgage amount.
Source: Department of Housing and Urban Development.

Section 603 provided for insured mortgages on one- to four-family dwellings, and no new commitments were made under it after April 30, 1948. Section 608 provided for insured mortgages on rental housing projects, and no new commitments were made under this section after March 1, 1950. Also in the process of liquidation are obligations under this title providing for insurance of short-term loans on manufactured housing under Section 609; mortgage insurance under Section 610 on specified types of permanent housing sold by the federal government (now handled under Section 223 of Title II); and insurance on projects of 25 or more single-family dwellings under Section 611. This section was enacted to encourage cost reduction by large-scale production methods. The Housing Act of 1954 provided that no new Title VI insurance commitments should be issued after August 3, 1954.

Title VII (added in 1948) authorizes the insurance of a minimum amortization charge and an annual return on outstanding investments in debt-free rental projects. This title has never been used.

Title VIII (added in 1949 as the Wherry Act and rewritten in 1955 as the Capehart Act) authorizes the issuance of mortgage insurance on rental housing projects constructed on or near military reservations for the use of civilian or military personnel of the Armed Forces.

Title IX (added in 1951) provides insurance for housing in critical defense areas. This title is now inactive.

Title X (added in 1965) authorized FHA insurance to finance purchase of raw land and the development of building sites or the development of new communities. The maximum authorized for any one land development project is $25 million, or 75 percent of the value of the developed land, or 50 percent of the bare land value plus 90 percent of estimated development cost. The maximum term of the loan is usually 7 years (extended to 10 years by the 1968 legislation), but it may be longer if the FHA deems a longer payout period reasonable in the case of a privately owned system for water or sewage, or a new community. Development under this title must be consistent with sound land use patterns. New community development must be approved by the local governing bodies concerned and by the governor of the state. Where local governing bodies have home rule, however, approval by the governor is not required.

Title XI (added in 1966) extended FHA insurance of mortgages to group practice facilities to be operated by associations of licensed dentists, doctors, optometrists, or osteopaths engaged in the coordinated practice of their professions if they are unable to obtain uninsured financing for the same purposes on comparable terms. The maximum amount of the mortgage was set at $5 million, or 90 percent of the value of the property on completion, including equipment. A term up to 25 years is allowed.

Activities under the above titles can be classified under the three headings of insurance of home mortgages, rental project mortgages, and property improvement loans. The relative importance of these three classes is shown in Table 25-3.

TABLE 25-3
Distribution of Mortgage Insurance Coverage, 1934-70

	Billions of Dollars	Percent
Home mortgages	$109.4	73
Rental project mortgages	19.3	13
Property improvement loans	20.3	14
Total	149.0	100

Title I, FHA Title I of FHA provided in the beginning free insurance to lenders who made advances for home improvements, alterations, and repairs. The wording was general enough, however, to include some new construction as well. Any lender using this title in 1936 was given originally free insurance up to 20 percent of loans for amounts not to exceed $2,000 each and running for not more than five years. Most of these loans were written for only three years or less. The manner in which this insurance operated was as follows: Suppose that a financial institution granted loans under this title to a total amount of $100,000. This gave it total insurance coverage of $20,000. If it failed to collect any part of one loan, it had full protection so long as its balance of insurance credit was equal to the amount of the loan. In 1936, the 20 percent was reduced to 10 percent.

Since, in the beginning, loans under Title I not only carried free insurance but—on a discount basis—could earn for the lender as much as 9.72 percent, it is little wonder that many lending institutions found it advantageous to make use of it. Even 9.72 percent was substantially less than the rates normally charged on uninsured and unsecured character loans. At the outset the main trouble was to find borrowers willing to make commitments even for needed repairs and improvements to their homes so long as their incomes were reduced or nonexistent and so long as the future remained clouded. One unlooked-for use of Title I soon developed more rapidly than others. Sellers of "packaged goods" such as water heaters, refrigerators, and so on, found this title a fruitful source of business where aggressive salesmanship was employed. Unemployed carpenters, painters, plasterers, and plumbers were not so good as salesmen.

The discussion of the financial arrangements which resulted in the inclusion of Title I in this bill placed great emphasis upon character loans. Up to this time most consumer credit of this type had been supplied by small loan companies, by so-called industrial banks, by credit unions, and occasionally by commercial banks to meet emergencies of their customers. Risks were presumed to be great, and financing costs were correspondingly high. The testimony of two large concerns in the field of home construction and equipment undoubtedly carried considerable weight with Congress in its favorable action on Title I. Previous to 1934 the Johns-Manville Corporation had set up the Johns-Manville Credit Corporation to aid users of Manville products to finance their purchases. The American Radiator Company had formed a subsidiary known as the Heating and Plumbing Finance Corporation to aid in financing the installation of its products. Both of these ventures had had great success in granting consumer loans for periods ranging from 12 to 24 months.

In like manner some of the largest sales finance firms had, just previous to the passage of the FHA law, found installment financing of home appliances a source of satisfactory business. Commercial banks and other financial institutions had never, up to this time, gone into this type of financing.

Since it was anticipated that this title would be needed for only a short period of time, it expired by limitation January 1, 1936. Nevertheless, this title was extended periodically as the process of recovery seemed to indicate its continuing need. Before recovery had advanced sufficiently to warrant the complete abandonment of Title I, defense housing requirements, succeeded by war housing needs, which in turn were followed by postwar needs, resulted not only in the continuation but in the expansion of the purposes of this title.

Under Title I borrowers were not required to give mortgage security for their loans. They were required, however, to have title to the property, whether carried under fee-simple ownership unencumbered, or with mortgage encumbrance; or they had to have possession under a leasehold running for 99 years or more. In several states, enabling legislation was necessary to permit financial institutions to lend money under this act. During the first three years' experience under this title, when it was needed most, the financial institutions which made use of its provisions were as follows: (1) national banks—44 percent; (2) state-chartered banks and trust companies—26 percent; (3) finance companies—22 percent; and (4) savings and loan associations, credit unions, and miscellaneous lending institutions—8 percent.

These percentages are significant from the point of view of accomplishment of one of the indirect purposes of Title I. As noted above, banks and trust companies had never been interested in financing home improvements and home appliances. As a result of Title I, they embarked upon this type of financing "in a big way." For the first time the homeowner had a means of financing in one package various types of repairs, improvements, and equipment items. The lender took little or no risk and was amply compensated for experimenting with a new source of future business.

In addition to the insurance of loans for repair and maintenance of existing structures, Title I has been used from time to time for other purposes. Among these are the financing of construction costs of small homes where the amount of the loan does not exceed the loan limit; the conversion of existing structures into a larger number of housing units to provide for the needs of war workers; the financing of certain farm structures such as barns and silos; and the financing of some structures for uses other than residential or agricultural. Altogether, these minor purposes did not loom large in the whole Title I program, averaging less than 3 percent of the total amount of insurance under Title I.

From 1956 until 1968, Title I loans were limited to a maximum of $3,500 for a five-year term. In order to enable homeowners to cope with increasing costs of home repair and modernization, the 1968 housing legislation raised the loan limit to $5,000 and extended the payment term to seven years and 32 days.

From the initiation of the Title I program in 1934 through the end of 1970, over 29.9 million insured loans have been made under it involving over $20.7 billion in net proceeds to borrowers through private financial institutions. These loans have averaged $681 for each improvement, with the program being active throughout the United States and its possessions. Nearly all such loans were made to owners of single-family residences to provide for the installation and repair of heating systems, for additions and alterations, and for finish and insulation. The average loan made in 1970 was for $1,934; in 1961, it was $999; and in the period 1934–39, it was $353. These figures reflect the marked uptrend in the average size of loans being made under this title.

Types of Institutions Using Title I Since 1950, national and state-chartered banks have accounted for about 80 percent of the proceeds of loans insured. The remaining 20 percent is divided among savings and loans associations, savings banks, and finance companies, with mortgage and insurance companies having less than a 1 percent participation. For the period from 1954 through 1971, the volume of claims in relation to loans insured by type of financial institution varied generally in proportion to the amount of loans financed.

Losses and Expenses under Title I At the outset, no charge was made for insurance under Title I. Since July 1, 1939, however, a premium has been charged for insurance of loans under this title which has been used to apply toward losses and administrative expenses. Before an insurance charge was assessed, administrative expenses were paid from funds obtained from the RFC. Since July 1, 1939, however, all claims and operating expenses have been met out of insurance premiums, and, in addition, a capital and insurance reserve fund has been accumulated. Insurance reserve funds have consistently been in excess of estimated reserve requirements.

From 1934 to 1970, inclusive, 871,107 claims, amounting to over $392 million, were paid. After recoveries, however, admitted losses amounted to about 1 percent of the amount of loans insured.

Absence of Control under Title I Some critics of Title I have been inclined to deplore the absence of control of credit under it. They have expressed the hope that it might be used as a two-edged sword: in times of depression, to stimulate home repairs and improvements; and in times of high prices and great real estate activity, to discourage unnecessary expenditures for these purposes. Such an attitude fails to understand the basic purpose of this legislation. Even the assumption upon which this part of the law was originally conceived failed to produce the desired results for a considerable time. It was expected that, by making financial resources available, borrowers would take advantage of Title I. This did not happen immediately.

One weakness of Title I perhaps could not have been anticipated at the time the regulations governing its operation were drawn up. Also, this weakness probably would not have been easy or economical to correct, since it appeared only occasionally. In the absence of any plan of appraising the value of repairs financed by Title I loans, some contractors took advantage of the inexperience of borrowers who assumed that, since the government was involved in insuring their loans, it would somehow or other protect the borrowers against the results of their own inability to judge the worth of the repairs for which they made commitments. As a result, in some areas borrowers were overcharged for services rendered to them. To be sure, they are expected to protect their own interests in the purchase of any goods which they buy. In the use of Title I, however, the circumstances favored those who rendered the service and who wished to take advantage of those who borrowed the money to pay for such services. More recently, however, the FHA has helped the homeowner avoid incompetent, unreliable, or dishonest contractors by compiling a list of contractors who have conducted their activities improperly. This list is made available to insured lenders. Usually, when a homeowner complains that his work is not done right, the FHA has been successful in getting the contractor to make appropriate amends where the complaint is justified.

As a stimulant, Title I provided both more liberal loans and lower rates of interest, in comparison with alternative forms of repair and improvement financing. Its elimination was sufficient to serve as a check upon this type of financing. It scarcely seems feasible to write a law that would, automatically at least, serve by turns as a stimulant and as a deterrent. Perhaps what is needed is a couple of laws like Title I and Regulation W. As occasion requires, the operation of one could be shut off and the other turned on. As economic conditions change, this process could be reversed.

Title II, FHA Title II of the Federal Housing Administration law set up a system of mutual mortgage insurance which at the outset was intended to encourage the construction of new homes, thus providing a market for building materials and employment for building laborers. Later it was extended to cover rental housing projects as well. In return for insurance of mortgages made by private lenders, an insurance premium was charged which was expected eventually to build reserves sufficiently large to put this title on a self-sustaining basis. The amount of insurance coverage was limited to 80 percent of the appraisal of the property insured, as set by the FHA. This insurance percentage has since been liberalized and applied to different sections of this title according to varying formulas, which usually result in insurance from 85 to 100 percent of the appraisal value. The interest rate was fixed at 5 percent, to which could be added originally 0.5 percent for service charge and 0.5 percent of the original amount of the loan for insurance premium. The net result was a charge of 6.42 percent to the borrower, computed over the life of a 20-year loan. Later the service charge was eliminated, the interest rate was reduced to 4.5 percent, and the insurance premium was reduced to 0.5 percent on the unpaid principal of the loan, producing a charge to the borrower of 5 percent. In the spring of 1950 the interest rate was reduced to $4\frac{1}{4}$ percent, making the total cost to the borrower $4\frac{3}{4}$ percent. In 1953, the interest rate was increased to $4\frac{1}{2}$ percent, and by 1960, the maximum interest rate for most loans had risen to $5\frac{3}{4}$ percent. This rate, combined with an 0.5 percent insurance premium, raised the total loan cost to $6\frac{1}{4}$ percent. By 1964, the maximum interest rate had been reduced to $5\frac{1}{4}$ percent with a total loan costs of $5\frac{3}{4}$ percent. In 1972, the maximum rate stood at 7 percent. There was also an initial service charge equal to the greater of two sums: $20 or 1 percent of the mortgage principal amount for existing property; or $50 or $2\frac{1}{2}$ percent of the loan if the mortgagee made partial disbursements and property inspections of units under construction. Special concession interest rates have been authorized for certain special programs.

The lender must use a monthly payment direct reduction first mortgage, the maturity of which was originally limited to 20 years. This was later increased to 25 years, and then to 30 years or three fourths of the remaining economic life of the property, whichever might be less. Certain loans under sections relating to cooperative housing, slum clearance, or housing for the elderly may have repayment periods extending for as long as 40 years. In case of uncured default, the lender is entitled to receive, from the FHA, debentures equivalent to the amount of the debt then unpaid. These debentures are issued in the name of the mortgage insurance fund but are fully guaranteed as to principal and interest by the government. The interest rate varies around 5 percent, and the maturity is three years after the maturity of the defaulted mortgage.

Use of Title II While Title II, FHA was intended by Congress to encourage new construction, of the original $2 billion of authorized insurance, half was permitted to apply to existing structures in order to facilitate their refinancing and to build volume for the FHA. The administration of this part of the program took some time to become effective, because of the desire to avoid great risks. Likewise, the insurance of mortgages on new properties did not produce desired results immediately. It was cumulative in its effects, however, and, particularly under more aggressive administrators, became a potent factor in real estate finance. With the financial backing of the Reconstruction Finance Corporation, the FHA put on an extensive advertising and publicity campaign, with the result that Americans were made FHA-conscious. For a while, at least, this campaign was so successful that many borrowers were led to believe that they could obtain 5 percent government loans. The added costs of service charges and insurance premiums received less attention in the advertising. Later, this omission was corrected.

On the side of the lending institutions, the acceptance of the FHA insurance program was distinctly spotty. For example, some insurance companies bought FHA mortgages sight unseen. They calculated that, even if half of such mortgages defaulted and were exchanged for government-guaranteed 3 percent debentures (the early rate) and the other half were paid according to contract, the average rate of return on their total investment would still be 4 percent. This they considered to be satisfactory. Some insurance companies have never bought any FHA mortgages. Banks, savings and loan associations, and others have displayed a similar unevenness in making use of mortgage insurance. As a class, savings and loan associations were probably more tardy in adopting its services than were other financial institutions.

At the time the law was passed, many lenders accepted the general idea, prevalent in congressional circles, that mortgage insurance was merely a recovery measure, to be abandoned as soon as lending institutions had acquired sufficient resources and had recovered sufficient courage to be willing to assume normal risks of lending operations. Hence, some felt that it was not worthwhile to embark upon a program that would be in effect for only a short time. Others felt pangs of jealousy because the FHA encouraged mortgage lending by some types of financial institutions that had not been accustomed to engage in such activities. Hence the FHA helped to develop new competition in the home mortgage field.

Typical FHA Home Loan Because of the widespread use of mortgage insurance under Section 203 of Title II, it is interesting to review the types of loans insured. From 1940 to 1970, the average property valuation on existing homes increased from around $5,000 to more than $22,900. Correspondingly, the average insured loan increased from approximately $4,000 to more than $20,900. The average income of borrowers meantime increased from about $2,400 to about $12,200. The ratio of loan to FHA appraisal for new homes ranged from 80 to 91 percent and, for existing homes, from 75 to 92 percent. Currently over 92 percent of all loans on existing homes under this section are single-family dwellings, with less than 8 percent on two- to four-family dwellings. On new properties, the percentages are even more predominantly in favor of single-family dwellings. Total monthly payments for the first year of the loan—including interest principal amortization, FHA insurance premium, hazard insurance, taxes, special assessments, and so on—averaged about one fifth of the estimated income of the borrower. The ratio of property valuation to annual income was about two to one.

Settlement of Claims When a loan has been in default for 60 days, the mortgagee is required to make a report to the FHA. When the arrearages cumulate to as much as 12 months, the mortgagee must start foreclosure proceedings, unless an extension of time is approved by the FHA. By the Housing Act of 1964, some relief is provided home mortgagors whose payments are in default because of circumstances beyond their control. Lenders willing to extend forbearance, rather than proceeding to immediate foreclosure, may recast the mortgage to include delinquent interest and extend the payment period beyond the maximum statutory maturity. The FHA is authorized to agree to include in the debentures issued to pay insurance benefits, if the default finally results in foreclosure, the interest on all of the mortgage payments that had become due and unpaid prior to foreclosure. Should the property sell at foreclosure sale for an amount less than the unpaid balance of the debt against it, the mortgagee is expected to bid it in. Upon taking title to the property, the mortgagee presents his claim to the FHA. If it is found to be in order, he transfers title to the FHA in return for its debentures equal in value to the mortgage. These debentures are guaranteed by the United States. In return for any costs incurred by the mortgagee in foreclosing the mortgage, it receives a certificate of claim. In case the property liquidates for enough to cover any part of this certificate, in addition to the expenses of the FHA and the face value of the debentures, the mortgagee is entitled to the recovery of that part of its expenses. Pursuant to the Housing Act of 1964, certificates of claim will be eliminated in future contracts of insurance, and instead certain compensating increases will be included in the amounts of debentures. The issuance of a certificate of claim may also be discontinued with respect to existing home mortgage insurance unless the mortgagee specifically requests that he receive a certificate. The debentures have a maturity of three years beyond the date of maturity of the mortgage. They pay, meantime, about 5 percent interest.

An extreme case of liberality in loan terms is exemplified in the 40-year loans allowed under the certain sections of Title II. With a period of amortization of that length, the borrower who meets all his obligations without default pays off less than 8 percent of the principal of his mortgage during the first five years of its life. Depreciation may absorb at least 8 percent of the value of the improvements in five years, if not more. Any general price decline might easily affect the mortgage adversely and make it a case to be handled by the FHA.

Mortgage Foreclosures and Losses From 1934 through June 30, 1970, the FHA acquired by foreclosure or the assignment of mortgage notes 393,455 home properties. These acquisitions represented less than 4 percent of the nearly 10 million mortgages insured since 1934. Of the acquired properties, at the end of the 1970 fiscal year all but 27,836 had been sold.

The two principal insurance funds are the General Insurance Fund and the Mutual Mortgage Insurance Fund (largely identified with the original home mortgage insurance program). Through June 30, 1970, losses of $375 million had been sustained through the General Insurance Fund. Losses to the Mutual Mortgage Insurance Fund amounted to $716 million. Income collected from the combined insurance funds through June 30, 1970 was just over $5 billion. Of this amount, about $3.5 billion represented income to the Mutual Mortgage Insurance Fund. Thus, it is apparent that losses to date from that fund, which is responsible for $48.5 billion of the $68.5 billion of mortgage insurance in force, have been only about 20 percent of the premiums and other income. Operating expenses of the combined insurance funds have been about $1.5 billion, leaving a substantial part of the $5 billion of income for loss coverage. To date, FHA operations have reflected a net income.

Types of Institutions Originating and Holding FHA-Insured Mortgages Table 25-4 shows the distribution of home mortgage insurance during 1970, by types of financial institutions, and the distribution of home mortgages held in portfolios at the end of the year. In this table the shift of home mortgages from mortgage companies to insurance companies, savings banks, and federal agencies is notable.

Relative Volume of FHA-Insured Loans One method of showing the relative volume of mortgage insurance on new dwelling units started in this country is to compare the number of insured units with the total volume of construction. The proportion of all new housing units

TABLE 25–4
Percentage Distribution of FHA-Insured Mortgages Originated and Held at End of Year, 1970

	Percent of Mortgages Originated		Percent of Mortgages Held at end of Year	
Type of Institution	Home	Project	Home	Project
National bank	7.6	18.1	10.1	7.7
State bank	3.7	10.2	4.5	7.4
Mortgage company	69.8	50.2	5.1	12.7
Insurance company	1.2	2.1	19.2	14.9
Savings and loan association	12.4	10.6	14.3	3.3
Savings bank	3.7	2.2	23.5	15.7
Federal Agency	0.7	1.0	19.9	17.3
All other	0.9	5.6	3.4	21.0
Total	100.0	100.0	100.0	100.0

constructed in the United States that were insured by the FHA increased from 6.5 percent in 1935 to 35 percent in 1939. The latter proportion held with little change until 1942, when it increased to 55 percent. The peak was reached in 1943, when nearly 80 percent of all new units were financed with FHA loans. This was a year of only 184,000 new units. By 1946, FHA loans financed only about 10 percent of new units. This sharp drop was due in part to the popularity of Section 501 on GI loans, discussed in Chapter 26. During the 1950s about 25 percent of all new units were financed with FHA loans.

Once Title II became really effective, from one fifth to one fourth of all mortgage recordings on one- to four-family homes—including mortgages on both new and existing properties—were insured by FHA from 1934 through 1943. In 1944 the proportion dropped to 15 percent, and in 1946 to only 4 percent. In 1949, it touched a postwar high of 19 percent, and it averaged 10 percent annually for the years 1950 through 1957. The proportion increased from 9 percent in 1957 to 19 percent in 1959. During the 1960s, the proportion declined, dropping to 13 percent for 1968. Institutions became increasingly willing to make conventional loans at higher loan-to-value ratios and for longer periods of time. In a large measure, also, the fluctuation in the volume of FHA-insured loans in relation to conventional loans is determined by the current interest rates in the money market as compared with the maximum rates allowable on FHA loans. It will be remembered, for example, that low-interest rates on FHA loans in 1951 and the years immediately following encouraged the use of conventional loans by many lending institutions, since on conventional loans the lender may charge whatever interest rates the traffic will bear. The higher costs of money during this period led to higher rates charged for its use. A reversal of this pattern occurred for a substantial part of 1958 when a relatively easy money market encouraged extensive use of FHA facilities. In 1959 the trend to higher interest costs resumed. This tendency was substantially offset, however, by an increase in the maximum rates permissible on FHA-insured mortgages in the late 1960s and early 1970s. Higher rate ceilings encouraged FHA financing with the result that in 1969, 16 percent of new starts were FHA-insured and in 1970 the percentage had risen to a significantly higher 29 percent.

National Mortgage Associations The FHA probably did more than any other single agency to create a national mortgage market. As pointed out elsewhere, it transformed a purely local mortgage without a market into a more negotiable instrument that had a ready market throughout the country because purchasers now looked to the insurance for protection rather than to the obligation of the borrower or even the security behind the loan. Anticipating this situation, the sponsors of mortgage insurance undertook to set up, in the law that authorized this insurance, some sort of machinery for providing a national market for mortgages.

Title III of the National Housing Act authorized five or more natural persons to organize a national mortgage association, provided they contributed at least $5 million in cash or government bonds to buy its stock. Such an association could then issue bonds, debentures, or notes to an amount equal to 10 times its capital stock, but not exceeding the face value of insured mortgages to be purchased from the proceeds of the sale of its stock and its other securities, plus its cash and government bonds. Since no capitalists were attracted by this opportunity, the law was amended in 1935 to reduce the required capital stock to $2 million and to increase the amount of bonds, and so forth, that could be issued to 12 times the amount of outstanding stock.

Still no associations were organized. So in 1938, a further amendment permitted such an association to start business with only one fourth of its capital paid in. This payment could consist of cash, government bonds, or insured mortgages. As soon as the minimum capital was paid in, the association was to be authorized to issue bonds, and so on, up to 20 times its outstanding stock. Other changes were also made for the purpose of liberalizing the requirements to the point where private capital might be induced to organize national mortgage associations. No such association has ever been organized, in spite of the fact that a part of the liberal terms included the right of the RFC to invest in the capital stock.

Fear of Insured Mortgages Not all who study insured mortgages have been pleased with the results of their researches. One critic expressed his opinion in these terms:

The insured mortgage is the type of loan which is made without reference to the judgment and prudence of the lender. It is made according to a statutory formula and under the influence and solace of the device of the federal guarantee. The bulk of today's mortgage lending, at present terms, ratios and rates, would not be made by mortgage lenders if they had to assume the full burden of the risks involved. In fact, it is doubtful that government economists themselves would have evolved the present program were it not for the philosophy that housing must be provided for our people at any cost.[2]

The foregoing analysis apparently assumes that there is but one risk to mortgage lending—the risk of loss of a part of the principal amount of the loan—and that it has been shifted to the FHA. If it is true that the bulk of current mortgage lending would not be made except through the help of mortgage insurance, then it must follow that the costs of servicing loans made on today's markets are likely to mount at some time during the life of these loans. Increased servicing costs are not shifted to the FHA. They must be borne by the lender. The FHA steps into the picture only when the borrower is so hopelessly in trouble that foreclosure must follow.

Financial Status of Insurance Reserves The expressed fear of insured mortgages prompts a review of the status of FHA reserves of insurance funds. There is, of course, a major difference between the reserve liabilities of life insurance companies and those of FHA mortgage insurance funds. Human mortality rates are highly predictable, whereas the extent to which claims may arise against the FHA insurance funds are largely dependent upon economic conditions. To deal with this difficult factor of risk, the FHA has predicated its "estimated reserve requirements" on the assumption that "adverse economic conditions of approximately depression magnitude might develop immediately."[3] The FHA's estimated reserve requirements are therefore not a true measure of the solvency of the operation in the ordinary sense. Its estimated liabilities set up for the purpose of meeting claims are contingent rather than actual. Although based on actuarial principles to the extent practicable, the evaluation of underwriting risks in this case involves the additional step that the effect of a sharp economic reversal be taken into account. Reserve requirements are affected by the volume of new insurance written, the aging of insurance contracts in force, and terminations of insurance contracts. Substantial increases in amounts of new insurance written, of course, raise the reserve requirements, while the aging of insurance and any terminations reduce such requirements. Other items considered include a determination of the effect of property acquisitions

---

[2] Frank C. Rathje, "A Present Approach to Mortgage Financing" *Appraisal Journal,* October 1948, p. 467.

[3] *Annual Report,* p. 139.

in exchange for debentures and the later sale of the property and redemption of the debentures, expected future premiums, investment income, and operating expenses.

The outstanding balance of FHA mortgage insurance in force at June 30, 1970, and the insurance reserves and estimated reserve requirements thereon are set forth in Table 25–5.

From this table it appears that under adverse economic conditions of depression magnitude, on $68.5 billion of mortgage insurance outstanding at June 30, 1970, the FHA estimated that its total insurance liability might exceed total funded reserves by about $704.2 million. The Mutual Mortgage Insurance Fund (largely for Sections 203 and 207 loans) showed only a little over 10 percent of the total deficiency. The General Insurance Fund is a consolidation of the other insurance funds. It includes low and moderate income programs and its estimated reserve deficiencies are substantially higher at $490.8 million. The Cooperative Management Housing Insurance Fund was established for management-type cooperative mortgages and loans assigned to one of these funds and future insurance of such mortgages and loans. As previously noted, the Special Risk Insurance Fund was established by the 1968 Housing and Urban Development Act, in Section 238, for programs not intended to be actuarially sound.

It will be observed from Table 25–5 that there has been a substantial increase from 1963 to 1970 in the deficiency of insurance reserves over estimated reserve requirements. From a relatively modest $88.5 million in 1963, the deficiency stood at $704.2 million in mid-1970, an increase of eight times in less than seven years. It should also be pointed out that the relaxation of mortgage insurance programs in certain urban areas not previously insurable, as provided for in the Housing and Urban Development Act of 1968, will place additional burdens on insurance reserves. The possibility of eventual need for congressional appropriations to make up for the reserve deficiencies must, of course, be weighed against the fact that by the end of 1970, this insurance had assisted 10 million families to own homes and had provided housing to another 1.5 million families in multifamily projects across the country.

FHA Valuation Report In the use of mortgage insurance, the FHA deals not with the borrower but with the lender. It is the latter who files the application for the mortgage insurance. Since the FHA takes responsibility for the insured mortgage, it must establish the value of the property. This value is defined as the "price which typical buyers would be warranted in paying for the property for long-term use or investment, if they were well informed, acted intelligently, voluntarily and without necessity."

The valuation report used to make this determination is divided into three parts: (1) the statistical data, covering such subjects as neighbor-

TABLE 25-5
FHA Mortgage Insurance in Force, Insurance Reserves, and Estimated Reserve Requirements, Selected Years, December 31, 1963 to June 30, 1970 ($000,000 omitted)

Insurance Funds	Outstanding Balance of Insurance in Force	Insurance Reserves	Estimated Reserve Requirements	Excess of Insurance Reserves over Estimated Reserve Requirements
As of June 30, 1970				
Mutual mortgage.......	$48,520.7	$1,340.2	$1,414.1	$ −73.9
General insurance.......	16,716.3	208.5	699.3	−490.8
Cooperative management housing.............	802.8	25.7	19.1	6.6
Special risk...........	2,492.2	−3.1	143.0	−146.1
Total, all funds, combined...............	$68,532.0	$1,571.3	$2,275.5	$ −704.2
As of June 30, 1969				
Total, all funds, combined...............	$63,001.3	$1,394.3	$2,041.2	$ −646.9
As of December 31, 1963				
Total, all funds combined...............	$40,913.4	$1,050.6	$1,139.1	$ −88.5

hood influences, site data, and so on; (2) the rating of the location, to determine the degree of mortgage risk resulting from location factors; and (3) the determination of the appraiser's estimate of value and his reasons therefor. Since much emphasis is put upon the location factor, it is worth noting that this includes such items as: land use, attractiveness of the neighborhood, community facilities, transportation and public utility services, local taxes, schools, shopping centers, churches, and recreation facilities.

Appraisal Policies of FHA Concerning appraisals of residential properties, two points of approach characterize the attitude of the FHA. In the first place, this agency is to be credited with greater contributions to the knowledge of appraisal processes than any other agency or influence can claim. Pre-FHA appraisals for lending purposes were not really appraisals at all. The lending institution frequently made no pretense of determining the value of the property which served as the security for its loans. Rather, it was more often interested in finding some sort of answer to the question, "Will this property sell at a price sufficiently high to afford a cushion of safety for our loan?" Particularly if only a low-percentage loan was requested, the property was given in many instances only a "horseback" or "windshield" appraisal. It was looked at from the outside but not always entered.

Because of the liberal loans insured by the FHA—in contrast to lower percentage loans on conventional mortgages—more attention had to be given to the question of value. The HOLC had made a start in the right direction of trying to systematize and formalize appraisal processes. The FHA carried the process much further. It not only collected and collated all existing knowledge on the subject; it added much to our knowledge of the subject through research.

In the second place, the FHA adopted the three-way appraisal formula already made famous by the HOLC—taking into account not only replacement cost, but market price and capitalized rental value as well. This three-way formula is a double-edged instrument. In times of depressed real estate values it refuses to be bound by existing price levels, because they are considered to be too low—to reflect temporary pessimism which will be dispelled when buyers recover their courage and again enter the market to bid prices up. But, in times of inflated real estate prices, it also refuses to be bound by existing price levels, because they are considered to be too high—to reflect temporary optimism (or desperation) which will disappear when a new supply is eventually available to meet sudden increases in demand.

FHA Credit Analysis In insuring mortgages, the FHA gives specific attention to the moral hazard as well as to the appraisal of the property offered as security for a loan. When the lender makes application for mortgage insurance, he submits information about the personal history and the financial responsiblity of the mortgagor. If the FHA is not satisfied with this, it may make its own credit investigation of the borrower. Its effort is directed to a determination of the debt-paying capacity of the borrower and the degree of risk which the financial capacity of the borrower introduces into the mortgage transaction.

In attempting to measure the borrower's financial capacity to meet his obligations, the FHA is interested in the current income of the borrower and its probable continuity. It is interested also in such charges against this income as mortgage payments, insurance taxes, maintenance, and household operating expenses, as well as income taxes, life insurance premiums, payments on installment accounts, and similar payments. In the light of all these factors the borrower is given a rating that may range from "excellent" to "reject."

FHA Mortgage Pattern Rating In rating the mortgage pattern of an application for mortgage insurance, the FHA distinguishes between the mortgage on property to be owner-occupied and that to be used for income. In considering the former, the following relationships are studied: (1) amount of loan to value of property; (2) term of mortgage to remaining economic life of the building; and (3) monthly payment to rental value. All of these ratios are developed from the report of the appraiser. In considering income property, more attention is given to the ratio of debt service to net income. In case the rating of the mortgage pattern is unfavorable, sometimes it is possible to make adjustments that will make the loan eligible for mortgage insurance. For example, if the amount of the loan, or its term, or both, can be reduced, the ratios used above will be more favorable.

Effect of FHA upon Interest Rates The major risk element in mortgage finance is the potential but unpredictable loss ratio that the mortgagee may suffer at the time of foreclosure sale. As we have discussed elsewhere in this volume, the granting of a deficiency judgment is a legal device. It may not have any definite financial value. But making foreclosure unnecessary by permitting the mortgagee to exchange his defaulted mortgage for government-guaranteed FHA debentures does have financial value. In fact, this value very quickly came to be recognized nationally. The effect of mortgage insurance was to transform an unmarketable local real estate mortgage into a more negotiable instrument that commanded a national market. Buyers of mortgages ceased to have any major interest in the mortgagor or the property he offered as security for the loan. The insurance of the mortgage assumed first place in the consideration of the investors.

It is little wonder, therefore, that interest rates on such mortgages reflected the new and more secure status they had attained. A former 5 percent mortgage market in the older section of the country and a 10 percent market in the newer, less well-established markets of the Southwest both acquired the same status so far as insured mortgages were concerned. There can be no doubt of the effect of FHA standard interest rates upon all interest rates charged on real estate mortgages. Since those charged on uninsured mortgages were in direct competition with those where the insurance element was present, the former as well as the latter tended to level off at somewhere near the rates charged on the latter.

QUESTIONS AND PROBLEMS

    1. What are the purposes of Title I of the FHA? What would your appraisal be of the accomplishments under this title?
    2. What institutions make the most common use of Title I provisions? Why?
    3. What are the functions of the FHA provided for in Title II?
    4. Describe the typical FHA home loan.
    5. How are claims settled on an FHA insurance loan in default?
    6. What influence has the FHA program had on the attitudes of the mortgage-lending industry toward home purchasers?
    7. Review the relative importance of FHA-insured mortgages to various types of financial institutions? Where insurance is relatively important, can you suggest reasons why?

8. How have proportions of homes financed with insured loans varied from 1934 to the present? How do you account for these variations?

9. Do you consider the FHA to be on a sound financial basis at the present time? Why or why not?

10. Mention specific ways in which the FHA program has been directly responsible for establishing standards for lending conditions and terms.

26

Financing Homes for Veterans

Early Legislation When World War II ended, the deluge of returning veterans and new family formations created an acute housing shortage. A high level of economic activity provided the veteran with income sufficient to amortize a mortgage in lieu of rent, but he usually did not have the cash down payment required to permit him to buy a home under conventional lending methods. It had been the practice for many years, in compliance with investment restriction laws of the states, for institutional lenders to limit their loans to from 60 to 75 percent of the appraised value of the property. Experience had taught them to require a cushion against depreciation in value that takes place in a forced sale on foreclosure.

It was therefore a revolutionary step when a grateful Congress enacted legislation providing World War II veterans a guarantee by the United States of mortgage debt incurred to acquire a home. This guarantee was intended to be sufficient to substitute, in substantial measure at least, for lack of a cash down payment. The first law, passed in 1944, provided for a 50 percent guarantee up to $2,000 with the interest rate on the loan not to exceed 4 percent. The program was initially placed under the control of the Comptroller General.

As the guardian of governmental expenditures, his construction of the guarantee law was strict. It was soon apparent that the program simply would not work under the Comptroller General's control. Lenders were skeptical and few were willing to make loans except on an experimental basis. The $2,000 maximum was only sufficient to provide a substitute for the 40 percent cash down payment required by many investing institutions on a $5,000 home, and any veteran wanting to buy a home for $6,000, $8,000, or $10,000 would be faced with an increasingly prohibitive problem with the cash down payment required.

In 1945, the law was amended to provide for a 60 percent guarantee, not to exceed $4,000, and the Comptroller General was relieved of his authority. The new provisions permitted a $4,000 substitute for the cash down payment up to 60 percent on a $10,000 home, and a more expensive home could be obtained by an added cash down payment by the veteran; or the lender might satisfy itself with less than a 60 percent guarantee. Now, the program began to function. Furthermore, by regulation of the Veterans Administration, lenders were permitted to recoup advances made for delinquent taxes and insurance and the costs of foreclosure plus attorney fees. Lenders by experience learned that their guarantee claims were quickly honored and that the program was managed by the VA so as to honor just claims and avoid technicalities, thereby encouraging more lenders to enter the program.

By 1950, several things had come to pass which encouraged Congress to liberalize the VA loan law. First, inflation caused the price of housing to increase, and this in turn made the $4,000 guarantee inadequate. Second, experience proved that the veterans were unexpectedly good credit risks and that the cost to the government was far less than had been anticipated—so much so that the loss due to defaulted loans was substantially less than the historical average loss in ordinary commercial lending made by ordinary financing sources to good credit risks. This disposed Congress to increase the maximum guarantee to 60 percent of the loan, not to exceed $7,500. The increase allowed "no down payment loans" in the $12,000 to $13,000 area with larger purchase prices by using a percentage of guarantee of less than 60 percent or by making additional cash down payment, or both. While the inflation of values was going on, there was also a development of a shortage of mortgage loan money at the statutory rate limit for federal guarantee, resulting in a gradual advance of the maximum interest rate to $5\frac{1}{4}$ percent. Incidentally, the VA secured amendments to state and federal laws, permitting VA-guaranteed loans as an exception to other laws imposing restrictions on loan-to-value ratios for institutional investors.

A new loan guarantee program was provided in the Veterans Readjustment Act of 1966 for members of the Armed Forces who have served 180 days or more since January 31, 1955. Guarantee protection follows the terms of the original act, but the borrower under this program is required to pay a fee of $\frac{1}{2}$ of 1 percent of the loan amount at the time of closing. Proceeds derived from the fees are paid into a fund to protect the Veterans Administration from loss through default in mortgage payments.

All termination dates for applying for VA-guaranteed housing were removed by the Veterans Housing Act of 1970. Previously, World War II veterans were no longer eligible after July 25, 1970, and Korean War veterans were to become ineligible after January 31, 1975. The 1970 act also provided that mobile homes are now acceptable security for loan guarantees by the Veterans Administration.

Nature of GI Obligation The legal nature of the VA guarantee is that of an absolute guarantee in which the Administrator becomes liable for the entire amount of the existing guarantee immediately on default. The guarantee has always been a percentage guarantee with a maximum amount fixed by law. Thus, an original loan of $10,000 made today will be guaranteed for 60 percent (or $6,000) and this percentage will adhere to the loan as the debt is decreased by payments or increased by unpaid interest. The practical aspects of the GI loan obligation are set forth by the VA in the foreword to the *Lender's Handbook* in the following terms:

> The execution of a guaranteed or insured loan involves the assumption of a substantial responsibility by all parties concerned. Upon the veteran rests the obligation to repay in full the amount borrowed; the lender assumes the responsibility of servicing the loan adequately and effectually, exerting every reasonable means in default cases to assist the veteran borrower against loss of his home, farm, or business; and the Veterans Administration, on behalf of the Government, must require that both parties fully discharge their responsibilities.

The elements of the above quotation to be emphasized are: the debt obligation of the borrower; the necessity for tempered leniency on the part of the lender; and the determination of the VA to administer the law in a manner to protect the veteran, the lender, and the government. This definition should also be taken seriously by lending institutions. Few veterans have any conception of the responsibilities that go with homeownership. Most of them have had little or no experience as rent-paying tenants—much less as homeowners. Most of them need the financial assistance which the GI law gives them. They need also a great deal of homely advice about homeownership and its responsibilities. In many cases they need to be advised against the purchase of a certain property, even though it will appraise for enough to qualify for a guaranteed loan.

Eligible Lenders Any person, firm, association, corporation, or state or federal agency could be an eligible lender under the GI law. It is expected, however, that most loans will be made by commercial banks—national, state, or private; savings and loan associations; savings banks; insurance companies; credit unions; and other mortgagee institutions which are subject to supervision by a governmental agency. Lenders operating under federal laws, including national banks, federal savings and loan association, and all banks, savings and loan associations, and insurance companies authorized to do business in the District of

Columbia, are permitted to grant GI loans without reference to the limitations or restrictions of any other statute. These restrictions are waived in respect to: ratio of loan to property value; maturity of loan; security requirements; dignity of lien; and percentage of assets which may be invested in loans against real estate as security.

Eligible lenders whose operations are supervised by a governmental agency—state or national—may make loans that are automatically guaranteed so long as they keep within the requirements of the VA. By automatic guarantee is meant that the lender need not secure the prior approval of the VA before making the loan. Approximately one half of all GI home loans have been automatically guaranteed. Some lenders prefer to secure prior approval on all loans granted by them. This is their privilege. By this means they minimize the risk of having the guarantee questioned on technical grounds at a later time. Nonsupervised lenders must secure prior approval, else the loans they make are not guaranteed.

Insured Loans Any loan eligible for a guarantee under this law may be eligible for insurance as well, if made or purchased by a supervised lender. The lender which elects to use the insurance program must notify the VA of its intent at the time the loan is reported. Otherwise it is guaranteed instead of insured. When insurance is elected, the lender's insurance account is credited with 15 percent of each loan insured, provided that it keeps within the maximum amount of the guarantee. In case of default on an insured loan, the lender is entitled to obtain from the VA the full amount of its net loss, regardless of the percentage of loss to value of the property. For example, suppose that the lender has made or purchased $1 million of GI loans. Its insurance credit would be $150,000, which is 15 percent coverage. If the loans are paid down to $600,000, the coverage becomes 25 percent; to $300,000, 50 percent; and so forth. Meantime, any losses suffered by the lender would be charged against its insurance credit. If an $8,000 loan against a property resulted in an $8,000 loss, full recovery could be obtained if the balance to the insurance credit of the lender amounted to that much. Insured home loans are negligible in number and amount. Of over 7 million home loans closed to date less than 0.3 percent were insured.

Gratuity At the time the GI law was passed, Congress apparently intended to have the government pay the first year's interest on the guaranteed part of the loan. The 4 percent gratuity provided for this purpose was afterward interpreted in a manner to let the veteran borrower select the method of application of this gratuity from among the following possibilities: delinquent loan payments; prepayment of installments; reduction of principal; accrued interest; taxes, insurance premiums, and so on. The borrower could recover this gratuity in cash only when he had paid the loan in full without use of the gratuity. If the veteran transferred title to the property before credit for the gratuity had been taken, he was to be given credit for it as a part of the price paid by the vendee. In case the secondary loan was guaranteed under Section 505, the gratuity had to be applied to the second mortgage and could not be applied against the first. This gratuity was abolished in 1953.

Purposes of Home Loan A guaranteed home loan may be used to purchase a residential property to be occupied by the veteran as his home; for financing the construction of his home; or for paying for alterations, repairs, or improvement to the home he already owns. Loans for the purchase of real estate primarily for investment purposes are not eligible for guarantees. Residential properties may consist of not more than four-family units, provided that one is to be occupied by the veteran as his home. Where the property is to be purchased or constructed through joint ownership of two or more veterans, one additional unit may be added for each added veteran. This is being interpreted to mean that two veterans may purchase a six-family unit. In states where home appliances are included as fixtures, they can be included in the guaranteed loan. Where there is doubt, they may not be included, since Title III of the GI law applies only to real estate loans.

Some indication of the measure of cooperation given by the VA in facilitating the plans of the veterans in making applications for guaranteed loans is shown by the very small percentage of loan applications denied. Up to the end of June 1971, only about 5 percent of all home loan applications had been denied or withdrawn. It is interesting to note that, as of the same date, about 51 percent of the dollar volume and more than 47 percent of the number of all guaranteed or insured GI home loans had been repaid.

GI Home Purchase as Hedge The purchase of homes by veterans using the liberal financing terms of the GI law has been looked upon by some of them as a kind of double hedge. In the first place, it has provided a hedge against decisions by landlords. By owning a home being financed by a GI loan, the veteran is assured a place to live at no increase in housing cost so long as he keeps up his payments. He cannot be dispossessed, and his rent cannot be increased. Only taxes, utilities, and repair costs may go higher. Financing costs are fixed for the life of the loan. These are usually no higher than rental payments for comparable accommodations.

In the second place, the ownership of his home affords the veteran a hedge against further inflation in real estate prices. If real estate prices go up substantially, the cost of housing accommodations to tenants sooner or later reflects the increase. Of course, if costs should drop, then the prices of existing properties will follow after a time. Even in such event the homeowner is in a more advantageous position than the real estate speculator or investor. The investor who retains his property after prices decline will probably suffer loss of income. The speculator who buys when prices are high and sells at a lower price will lose a part of his principal. But the owner-occupant of a home still has the use of his property.

Two Lending Plans The home loan features of the original GI law provide two alternative plans. Under Section 501, the VA guaranteed 50 percent of the amount of the loan, or $4,000, whichever was less. Under the amendment passed in 1950 this maximum guarantee was raised to 60 percent, with a ceiling of $7,500. The interest rate of 4 percent was later increased to $5\frac{1}{4}$ percent. In 1968, the mortgage guarantee ceiling was raised to $12,500, to help finance more expensive homes. Pursuant to the 1966 legislation, the Administrator of Veterans Affairs was authorized to establish new maximum interest rates in accord with loan market demands, not to exceed limitations by Section 203 (b) (5) of the National Housing Act. In May 1968, the interest ceiling was raised to $6\frac{3}{4}$ percent, and again in January 1969 to $7\frac{1}{2}$ percent. In 1972, the ceiling rate was 7 percent. The maximum term is now 30 years; it was formerly 25. In 1970, the $12,500 guarantee authority was broadened to include loans to refinance mortgages and other liens of record on homes owned and occupied by eligible veterans. There is no maximum loan, but if a loan exceeds $25,000, it must receive the prior approval of the VA. Although Congress had in mind 100 percent loans to veterans, if necessary, including all costs of making the loan, the amount of any loan is subject to negotiation with the lender selected for financing assistance.

Under Section 505, the VA guaranteed a 100 percent second mortgage up to $4,000, following a first mortgage insured by the FHA. The first mortgage could not exceed 80 percent of the appraised value of the property. The second mortgage could not exceed 20 percent of such value. This means that a veteran was permitted to purchase a $10,000 home with an FHA first mortgage of $8,000, a second GI loan of $2,000, and no down payment. Under an amendment passed in 1950, no Section 505 loans were closed after October 20, 1950.

Maturity of Loans Term loans for five years or less are eligible for guarantee under the GI home-financing plan. Experience has shown, however, that most home loans are monthly payment direct reduction loans. Amortization may follow the standard plan, which provides for a level monthly payment throughout the life of the loan. Under this plan, the same monthly payment will result in a declining interest charge and an increasing proportion of the monthly payments being used to reduce the principal balance. The Springfield plan is also acceptable to the VA. Under it, the same amount must be paid each month to reduce the principal balance, but the interest charge will constantly decline. As a consequence, the total monthly payment will decline month by month. Most of the loans granted follow the standard plan. The maximum maturity allowed is 30 years.

The law provides that payments must be approximately equal; but it also provides that amortization of the indebtedness may follow established procedure in the community where the property is situated. In accordance with this provision, loan plans have been approved which call either for somewhat larger payments in the beginning with reductions later, or for small payments at the start when the borrower's expenses are great, with increases later when income applicable to the loan payments promises to be greater. Extreme variations in payments are not sanctioned by the VA.

Many lenders do not look with favor upon the maximum maturities provided under the GI law. In spite of the loan guarantee, the following reasons are set forth in support of shorter maturities for GI borrowers: (1) The shorter the maturity, the smaller is the amount of interest paid by the borrower. (2) Shorter maturities result in building equities faster at a time when family obligations are not as great as they will be later. (3) The larger the equity, the greater is the probability of forebearance if the borrower needs it.

Down Payment Under the GI law, home loans are guaranteed with or without down payment. The amount of the down payment is subject to negotiation between the borrower and the lender. Some lenders have been willing to make 100 percent loans if other factors have been favorable. Others have insisted upon at least a small down payment in order to make sure that the borrower feels a sense of ownership in the property. Even where the owner's equity is small, he may feel that this can be amortized over a period of a few years as a part of the cost of having an assurance of a place to live. As a general rule, small equities do not give the same sense of ownership that is present when the equity is larger. By the same token, an equity created by a gift is less significant in the mind of the recipient than one created from his own savings.

For the above reasons, some lenders to whom the GI loans are otherwise acceptable have insisted upon substantial down payments of 20 percent or more. Others have considered "sweat" equities as at least a partial substitute for a down payment. If some of the work needed to make the home livable is performed by the veteran, the increase in value—which also means an increase in his equity—is called a "sweat" equity. In some areas where loans are made with uncompleted houses as security, with the assumption that the borrower will complete the structure with his own labor and that of his friends, the name given to such a mortgage is "shell loan."

Prepayments All GI loans on homes must grant the privilege of prepayment of any part or all of the indebtedness at any time. The lender is not required to accept as a prepayment less than one installment or $100, whichever, is smaller. Prepayments may be used to cure defaults, unless they have been once used for this purpose. For example, if prepayments have been applied to reduce the principal balance of the loan and later the borrower defaults, the amounts prepaid may be applied, through a recalculation of the payments, to cure or to prevent a default. The veteran can thus obtain the double advantage of interest reductions and of building a cushion against possible future defaults. In addition, if prepayments are substantial, the veteran may request that the loan be reamortized, reducing future payments; assuming that the reamortization schedule will provide that the entire loan be repaid within the original loan period.

Taxes and Insurance By mutual agreement between the veteran borrower and the lender, the latter may collect with each loan payment a proportion of taxes, assessments, and insurance premiums applicable to the property. The method of collecting and disbursing such payments should be clearly set forth in the mortgage contract. If such added payments are provided for and if the contract so stipulates, failure to meet any such payments may constitute a default just as if the borrower had failed to pay interest or principal installment when due. Custom, rather than the regulations of the VA, generally governs the collection of these added amounts. If the lender is accustomed to collect them on conventional or FHA loans, it will probably collect them on GI loans also. Some lenders have not become acquainted with the advantages of collecting taxes and insurance from their borrowers.

Appraisals Appraisal procedure under the GI law has suffered many pains. As originally written, the law prohibited the application of loan guarantees if the price paid for the property exceeded the "reasonable normal value" of the property, as determined by the appraisers responsible to the VA. Nobody ever knew how to measure "normal" value. Presumably it was intended to provide only for long-term value, from which must be eliminated elements of inflation resulting from temporary scarcity. But the veterans who needed the assistance of the guarantee most urgently were those who were homeless in a period of extreme housing shortages. To bar them from the purchase of homes, even at admittedly inflated prices, meant the practical nullification of the purposes of the GI law.

Subsequently the word "normal" was stricken from the law. Had it been omitted originally, the administrators of this law might have had equally great difficulty in defining "reasonable value." But when "normal" was dropped, its omission was interpreted to mean that reasonable value must take into account current market conditions. This change made it possible for veterans to benefit from the law. By that time, the VA defined reasonable value in its regulations as "that figure which represents the amount a designated appraiser, unaffected by personal interest or prejudice, would recommend as a proper price or cost to a prospective purchaser, whom the appraiser represents in a relationship of trust, as being a fair price or cost in the light of prevailing conditions." This concept abandons the idea of long-term value and places greatest emphasis upon prevailing conditions.

Various methods have been used from time to time to select appraisers to set limits upon real estate values for financing purposes. When combination FHA and GI loans were used under Section 505, it was expected that appraisers approved by FHA would evaluate the properties. They could be used for Section 501 loans, but were not exclusively so used. The VA has had difficulty in deciding whether to approve a list of appraisers for each locality and let the lender make a selection therefrom as each application for a loan was presented, or to select the appraiser to evaluate each property. Both policies have been followed. Each has its limitations.

Red Flags In its handbook issued under date of March 1, 1946, the VA issued a definite warning to veterans on the subject of inflated real estate prices, in the following terms:

> Veterans also should be advised that they will have available to them the loan benefits for a period of ten years after the official end of this World War II. Their attention should be called to the extraordinary lack of supply that exists today and the abnormally high prices that prevail for homes, farms, equipment, and other commodities. Their attention should be directed to the fact that many are trying to buy and very few are anxious to sell; also the possibility of being able to purchase to better advantage in the succeeding years and the probability of loss in resale.

Two years and nine months later, in December, 1948, the new VA Administrator reiterated, "Those caveats are as timely and as true today as they were when written by my predecessor."

On the subject of the appraiser's responsibility to the veteran beyond a proper evaluation of the property, the 1948 edition of the VA handbook says:

> Many new and old properties which a veteran may propose to purchase and which a lender has agreed to finance, have major deficiencies which may jeopardize the veteran's continuing interest in the transaction. In such instances, the appraiser will prepare a letter to the prospective veteran purchaser, calling his attention to evidence of substandard construction or conditions that will require prompt attention or will result in extraordinary operating

expense or maintenance charges, all of which will have been taken into consideration in estimating the reasonable value.

This letter is sent to the VA and, if approved or modified by it, is sent to the veteran with a copy of the certificate of reasonable value.

Interests Covered The GI law on home financing applies to: (1) a fee simple estate, whether legal or equitable; (2) a leasehold estate, running originally for a period not less than 14 years beyond the maturity of the loan, or which is renewable for such a period; and (3) a life estate, if the remainder and reversionary interests are made subject to the lien.

Forbearance The Congress, in passing the GI home loan provisions, sought a means of providing homes for veterans of World War II by the use of a financing program which shifts much of the risk from the shoulders of the lender to the government. It is recognized that some who take advantage of this plan will have at least temporary difficulty in living up to the obligations they assume. In effect, Congress provided an automatic cure for at least one period of default when it included the 4 percent gratuity discussed above. Whenever this gratuity is reserved for such use or whenever it is used to reduce the principal balance, it can be reallocated to cure a default. Also, as has already been discussed, prepayments may be reallocated for this purpose.

In addition, lenders are expected to exercise forbearance whenever borrowers have difficulty in meeting their obligations under their mortgages. This can be accomplished by recasting the loan in such a manner as to extend the term of repayment of the principal balance. This is encouraged by the VA. Forbearance is not interpreted as neglect. The lender is expected to be service-conscious and to keep after delinquent borrowers able but unwilling to meet their obligations. It is only those willing but unable to pay who are entitled to consideration. The VA expects to be kept fully informed of the circumstances surrounding all such cases. Filing of notice of default with the VA still leaves the lender free to exercise patience and leniency with his delinquent borrower. He is not forced to bring foreclosure suit in order to protect his guarantee.

Hopeless cases are dealt with as such when it is determined that there is no probability that the loan will be reinstated and the default cured. When it appears that the borrower can no longer carry the property, all parties concerned are urged to find a buyer for the property. If a new buyer can take over the mortgage and pay the mortgagor something for his equity, if any, well and good. If the real estate market is not favorable; if the condition of the property is such that it does not attract buyers; and if forbearance has been carried to such a point that the sale price of the property is less than the guarantee: then the

VA will consider a proposal for the sale of the property at a price that will require it to make up to the lender the difference between the mortgage indebtedness and the amount assumed by the purchaser, but not in excess of the loan guarantee.

As an alternative, the mortgagee may accept a voluntary conveyance in lieu of foreclosure, with the prior consent of the VA. The policy of the VA is to encourage the acceptance of voluntary conveyances because of the saving of time and money.

Open Mortgages The VA regulations authorize the use of open mortgages in those states that have legislation authorizing their use. Lenders are encouraged to inspect the properties securing VA loans at least once a year for the purpose of determining their physical condition. Such an inspection may disclose evidence of intentional or unintentional waste as well as any unusual conditions that cause the property to depreciate in value more rapidly than usual. Even ordinary wear and tear needs to be offset by maintenance and repair. Mortgages protecting GI loans are permitted to contain clauses allowing the lender to make advances to cover the cost of expenditures for these purposes. As noted above, the lender is still obligated to observe due caution to make sure that, in his locality, such advances may not jeopardize the dignity of his lien. The VA discourages the use of open-end mortgages and although the VA mortgage form affords a lien to the holder for advances made for taxes and insurance, none of its printed forms contains a general provision for any state. But, the view of the VA is that it cannot prevent their use, which might nevertheless be followed by a reduction of a claim on a guarantee.

Filing of Claims In line with a desire for forbearance in case of default by a veteran borrower, the GI home loan program operates as an improved, automatic HOLC. Should a borrower become delinquent for any period of three months, consecutive or not, the lender may file a claim with the VA. The VA may elect to make good the amount of the delinquency, bringing the loan current again. Any payments made by the VA to the lender in this fashion do not reduce the amount of the debtor's obligation. The VA becomes subrogated to the amount of claim against him that is paid to the lender. Subsequently the VA may assert this claim in any manner it sees fit. It may determine that conditions are such as to require the VA to pay off the claim of the lender and take over the mortgage. Meantime it may help the veteran and the lender to dispose of the property, in case it appears clear that the mortgagor can no longer carry it.

As a last resort, it may be necessary to foreclose the mortgage. This step is undesirable, for several reasons. One such reason that may assume greater potency at some future time is that the veterans of World War II and their families constitute the greatest potential political bloc that we have ever experienced. Consequently we are not likely to witness a flood of foreclosures of GI home loans at any future time. Other means will be used to take care of defaults, including new legislation if any is needed.

In isolated cases where for any reason a foreclosure sale is conducted, the VA does not encourage the lender to take a deficiency judgment unless it appears clear that it can probably be collected. In no event is the lender obligated to undertake to collect, by resort to legal proceedings, any debts owed by the veteran borrower to the government on account of a GI home loan.

Custody of Property As soon as the holder of a VA-guaranteed mortgage elects to convey property to the VA after acquiring it through foreclosure or voluntary deed, it must so notify the VA. Thereupon the VA expects to assume custody of the property. By this means the former lender is relieved of any responsibility for loss to the property or damage for personal injuries in connection therewith. Since the VA is a self-insurer, it has no need for any kind of commercial insurance coverage. If the holder of the title sees fit to renew any insurance policy or to place insurance against the property following its acquisition, it does so at its own risk.

In turning over property to the VA, the holder of the title has no responsibility for securing the eviction of any occupant who is a trespasser on the property. But the VA will require a showing that any occupant is not claiming to own the property, because every purchaser of property is charged with notice of all rights of all parties in possession. In case title is obtained by foreclosure action, the occupants should be joined in the suit in order to cut off whatever rights they may attempt to assert.

Title Evidence When the VA takes title to a property from a former lender, it will accept the same quality of title that was required at the time the guaranteed loan was closed. It must be in such form as to be readily acceptable to prudent lending institutions, informed buyers, title companies, and attorneys in the community. As soon as the holder of the title elects to convey it to the VA, he should state the evidence of title to be transferred. The holder must furnish, without cost to the VA, such evidence of title as was obtained at the time the loan was closed. The cost of current title evidence will be paid by the VA. Titles transferred by supervised lenders, or by holders whose financial responsibility is acceptable to the VA, are accepted and filed immediately, without title examination.

In all other cases the holder must warrant the title in such manner as to assume responsibility for his acts and for those claiming under him. The consideration for the property is paid as soon as the transfer of title is accepted by the VA.

Sale of Property A veteran who purchases a home with financial assistance afforded by a GI loan may sell his home without restrictions, so far as the VA is concerned. Because of the low interest rate and small monthly payments, the purchaser will usually want to assume the mortgage rather than refinance and discharge the mortgagee. But there is a pitfall in so doing, for the veteran will remain liable on the debt to the holder of the loan; and when the purchaser defaults, and the VA pays on the guarantee, the veteran will be indebted to the VA for the amount paid on the guarantee. This debt is actively enforced by both the VA and the Department of Justice. On the other hand, if the purchaser not only assumes the mortgage debt, but also the obligation of the veteran to reimburse the VA in case it has to pay on its guarantee, and if the purchaser meets the VA requirements as a good credit risk, the veteran and the purchaser may apply to the VA to have the veteran released from all obligation on the debt, including reimbursement to the VA. When the VA accepts the purchaser fully in lieu of the veteran, the latter will be completely released, even though the originally guaranteed debt remains in force and effect against the purchaser. Some veterans have taken advantage of these circumstances and have sold their homes at a profit. In some cases real estate salesmen have sought out veterans interested in disposing of their homes, because of the appeal of the GI financing plan.

The veteran who sells his GI-financed home may be placing his family at a disadvantage in seeking a new home. Once he has used up his guarantee in the purchase of one home, he no longer has the privilege of GI home financing in the purchase of a second one. The purpose of the home-financing section of the GI law has been served when the home is financed. The law did not intend to give the veteran a method of securing successive profits by the purchase and sale of residential real estate on a speculative basis

Direct Lending At the time the GI bill was first discussed in Congress, there was considerable pressure to provide direct loans by the government to the veterans of World War II. Private lending guaranteed by the VA was finally substituted for direct lending. From time to time since the law was originally enacted, there has been pressure to add direct lending features. Finally, in 1950, the law was amended to provide that:

Upon application by a veteran eligible for the benefit of a home loan guarantee who has not previously availed himself of this privilege, if the VA finds that private capital is not available for the purchase or construction of a home, the VA may make a loan directly under the following conditions:
  (A) That he is a satisfactory credit risk,
  (B) that the monthly payments to be required under the proposed loan

bear a proper relation to the veteran's present and anticipated income and expenses,

(C) that he is unable to obtain from private lending sources in such area at an interest rate not in excess of 4 percentum per annum a loan for such purpose for which he is qualified under Section 501—of this title.

Loans made under this amendment were to bear interest at the rate of 4 percent (increased in subsequent years consistently with the guarantee and insurance programs) and were subject to the following limitations:

(1) The original amount of such loan shall not exceed $10,000 (since increased in steps to $21,000); and

(2) The guaranty entitlement of the veteran shall be charged with the same amount that would be deducted if the loan had been guaranteed to the maxima permitted under Section 500 (a) of this title.

Volume of Direct Lending Subsequently, Congress authorized the investment of the proceeds from the sale of mortgages held by VA, from principal repayments, and from additional advances from the Treasury. By the end of December 1971, a total of over $3 billion had been invested in 313,000 mortgages. Congress authorized the VA to sell mortgages to any private lending institution evidencing ability to service loans with the proviso that it may guarantee any loan thus sold subject to the same conditions, terms, and limitations which would be applicable to privately originated loans with an automatic guarantee. Public Law 92-66, approved August 5, 1971, gave the administrator of VA authority to sell such VA-held direct loans at any price deemed reasonable under conditions prevailing in the mortgage market. Previously, as authorized by Public Law 88-402, approved August 4, 1964, such loans could be sold for no less than 98 percent of par value.

Up to December 31, 1971, a total of almost 58,000 direct loans, representing an original investment of over $619 million, had been sold. In numbers, this represented 18½ percent and in dollars slightly over 20 percent.

As of December 31, 1971, 28 percent of the 313,000 direct loans had been fully repaid. Repayment, sale, foreclosure, and conveyance of direct loans through December 31, 1971 had reduced the original $3,022 million in loans originated to $1,134 million.

Participants in GI Home Loan Program Some interesting trends have become evident in the GI home loan program from the end of World War II to the present. Table 26–1 shows the holdings of the major types of financial institutions for selected years. It is apparent from review of the table that mutual savings banks have become by far the most im-

TABLE 26-1
Holdings of VA Mortgage Debt by Main Types of Financial Institutions for Selected Years, 1950 through 1970 ($000,000 omitted)

Year	Mutual Savings Banks	Commercial Banks	Life Insurance Companies	Savings and Loan Associations
1950	1,457	2,630	2,026	2,973
1955	5,773	3,711	6,074	5,883
1960	8,986	2,859	6,901	7,222
1965	11,408	2,688	6,286	6,389
1970	12,008	2,589	5,390	8,507

Source: *National Fact Book of Mutual Savings Banking*, May 1971, National Association of Mutual Savings Banks, 200 Park Ave., New York, N.Y.

portant source of private credit for GI loans. Next in importance are savings and loan associations and life insurance companies.

Default Experience and Losses Of the nearly 7.7 million GI home loans closed up to the end of December 1971, 1,937,453 had been reported in default. Of the total reported defaults, efforts to restore the loans to good standing had been successful in 84 percent of the cases. The number of defaults and claims declined from fiscal year 1964 through fiscal year 1970; 1971 saw a modest rise. A summary of the operations from initiation of the program through June 30, 1971 follows:

		(In millions)
Total funds expended:		
For payment of claims and acquisition of property		$2,916
For acquisition of loans, property expense, selling expense, etc.		753
Other		226
Total expenditures		$3,895
Less receipts		3,236
Net expenditures to be accounted for		$ 659
Less assets other than cash:		
Equity in properties	$112	
Equity in loans	389	
Other	67	568
Estimated net loss		$ 91

Compared to the total of $85 billion of loans guaranteed or insured by the program, this loss represents less than 0.11 of 1 percent.

This experience compares favorably with that of lenders on conventional loans, which have the advantage of large cash down payments to provide the borrower with greater incentive to avoid default. The record supports the hypothesis that the GI program was never intended to be a "giveaway" and has never been administered as such. A veteran applicant must be a good credit risk to qualify for a loan. By the terms of the law, furthermore, the veteran becomes indebted to the federal government for anything the government has to pay on a guarantee. The VA and the Department of Justice have been diligent in effecting collections, and the VA has recovered a large part of its loss through offsetting payments of compensation, pensions, or insurance dividends.

The program has provided substantial social and economic benefits. As the statistics on loan volume show, the VA program has played an important part in converting this from a nation of predominantly renters to one of predominantly homeowners. Beyond this, the demands for goods and services resultant from home construction induced by this facilitative financing have had a large and continuing effect on the economy.

Management and Capital Funds The actual guarantee and insurance of loans and the making of direct loans are under the supervision of the Loan Guaranty Service, which maintains 55 VA regional offices in addition to its headquarters in Washington, D.C. A loan guarantee revolving fund was set up at the beginning of the 1962 fiscal year to utilize money received from principal reduction and interest payments on certain VA-owned mortgage loans for the payment of claims and costs of acquiring, managing, and selling properties. Prior to the new arrangement, principal and interest receipts went directly to the general fund of the Treasury; and the costs of claims, property acquisitions, and property management were handled by direct appropriation.

There is also a direct loan revolving fund. Sources of money for this fund are: Treasury advances: proceeds from principal reductions on outstanding direct loans; and amounts received from the sale of direct loans to private investors.

QUESTIONS AND PROBLEMS

1. Describe the evolution of the GI home loan program.
2. What part does the Veterans Administration play in the GI home loan program?
3. What financial institutions are eligible lenders under the GI law? What is the relative importance of the participation of each?
4. May a GI loan eligible for a guarantee be eligible for insurance as well? Explain.
5. It has been stated that a GI loan may provide the home buyer with a "double hedge." Explain.
6. Do you favor 100 percent loans? What are the arguments for and against allowing such loans?
7. What is the appraisal procedure and what appraisal standards are applied in connection with GI loans?

8. What are the remedies of a lender against the VA in event of the mortgagor's default on a GI loan?

9. What is the likelihood of extensive foreclosures on GI loans in times of economic stress?

10. Assume that a veteran has bought a home and financed the purchase by a GI loan. He desires to sell his home. May he assign his loan to a nonveteran? What, if any, advantages may the nonveteran gain from such an assignment? What are the disadvantages to the veteran?

11. What is the extent of participation of the Veterans Administration in direct lending to veterans?

12. Review the percentages of GI home loans guaranteed to the total of home loan recordings. What conclusions do you draw as to the importance of the program?

27

Secondary Mortgage Markets

Growth of Mortgage Loans Since World War II, net flows of funds into real estate mortgages have consistently exceeded net flows into any other type of long-term capital investment. In 1965, for example, about 40 percent of the total long-term funds placed in mortgages, corporate securities, and government obligations combined were invested in mortgages. In the years since 1965, this mix has been distorted by the unprecedented demands for government funds to finance domestic and military programs.

During the decade of the 1950s the total mortgage debt more than doubled, expanding about $128 billion. The expansion of loans was 50 percent greater during the last five years of the decade than during the first five years. Outstanding mortgage loans doubled again during the decade of the 1960s, rising from $190.8 billion at the beginning of 1960 to $425.3 billion at January 1, 1970. By the 1970 year-end, the outstanding mortgage debt had risen to $451.1 billion. This remarkable growth took place in spite of periods of extreme credit stringency during the last five years.

The great increase in the demand for mortgage money can be accounted for principally as the result of three major demand factors. First, and perhaps most obvious, is the rapidly increasing national population. This factor, however, has not been as important as two others: (1) the rising unit cost of homes and (2) the higher loan-to-value ratios. For federally underwritten mortgages on single-family homes, the increased average loan between 1950 and 1970 reflected a rise in purchase price of from 4 to 7 percent per year. For the same period the loan-to-value ratio rose from 76 percent to over 90 percent. A similar trend has been confirmed for conventional loans closed by insured savings and loan associations, where the average amount of the loan more than doubled from 1950 to 1970 and average loan-to-value ratios rose from 58 percent to over 70 percent during the period. Another factor, longer maturity dates for loans, has also had an impact on the increased rate of borrowing.

The very policy of increased liberalization of financing terms for homeownership as supported by the federal program has had a contradictory effect. Through stimulated demand for housing and concomitant higher prices, home market values are highly dependent upon a continuation of such liberal policies. With low down payments, conservative interest rates, and long maturities, such loans may quickly become submarginal from the point of view of the private lender. It is at this point that another need arises. That is the need for a reliable secondary market for real estate mortgages to which institutions may resort to release funds for a continuation of a lending program under continually favorable conditions in an expanding real estate construction program.

Changing Character of Real Estate Mortgages Until recent years investment in real estate mortgages was a highly specialized type of money commitment. Few investors were willing to undertake the risks associated with such a commitment except where they had personal knowledge of the security, based upon inspection and appraisal, and there they could keep in touch with the debt-paying habits of the borrower by performing their own servicing operations. While this is still true of conventional loans, even here the urgency of the need for personal knowledge of the security and of direct servicing is not as great as it once was.

The coming of government guarantee and insurance of mortgages, accompanied by the increasing use of title insurance, has changed the above pattern materially. No longer does the ultimate holder of a real estate mortgage think of his commitment as the financing of a real estate project. Instead he gives prime attention to the insured or guaranteed paper which he holds as a receipt for his investment. Knowledge of the security for the mortgage is subordinated to faith in the guarantee or insurance of the mortgage, supported by title insurance. This change in the concept of real estate mortgages adds greatly to their liquidity and thereby points up the need for secondary markets for mortgages.

Supply of versus Demand for Mortgage Funds If the supply of funds available for mortgages were just equal to the demand for such funds in each market area there would be little need for a secondary market for mortgages. Mortgages could be retained by the individuals and the institutions which originated them until they were amortized in an orderly fashion. There would be no occasion either to buy or sell such mortgages.

While this kind of a situation obtains in some sections of the country, in large and growing areas our economy is not simply organized. In some sections we face what amounts to mortgage money surpluses. Here the supply of funds available for investment in real estate mortgages exceeds the demand for mortgage money. In other areas, where the population is growing at rates faster than the average for the entire country, the reverse is true. The demand for mortgage funds far exceeds the local supply. Means must be found to permit money-surplus areas to supplement mortgage funds in money-scarce areas; and conversely to permit money-scarce areas to provide investment outlets for a part of the funds available in money-surplus areas. Secondary markets provide one answer to this problem.

Development of a Secondary Mortgage Market The development of a secondary mortgage market system for all types of sound real estate mortgages has been a slow process, and it is still in an intermediate stage. Since 1913, commercial banks have been able to maintain liquidity through privileges of rediscounting certain paper with the Federal Reserve System or of receiving temporary advances from the Federal Reserve Bank in return for the pledge of acceptable collateral. Although the credit reserve principle prevailed over the mortgage discounting system in the establishment of the Federal Home Loan Bank System in 1932, there was a clearly defined purpose that the Home Loan Banks should provide liquidity to their member institutions. A serious limitation of the Home Loan Banks from a practical aspect, however, lies in the relative concentration of its membership in savings and loan associations. Although eligible, few mutual savings banks and insurance companies have joined the system, largely it may be presumed because of reluctance to become a part of a minority group in the membership. Furthermore, the use of the credit reserve principle of providing liquidity through advances rather than by purchase of mortgages has greatly limited the volume of funds which can be provided by the Home Loan Banks. The concept that the credit is temporary or that any loan with a maturity beyond one year must be amortized over the period of the advance seriously limits the use of the advanced funds in the hands of the borrowing institution.

Institutions without recourse to the Federal Reserve or Home Loan Bank systems have no direct and assured means of achieving liquidity for funds committed to real estate mortgages. Mortgage bankers, in particular, who are not eligible to Home Loan Bank membership and who are typically thinly margined on capital, feel a special need for a strongly supporting secondary mortgage market system. The federal government made gestures toward the establishment of a secondary market for mortgages with the establishment of the federal assistance program for real estate during the 1930s. Only fairly recently, however, has there been a secondary market worthy of the term. The secondary real estate mortgage market has been defined as the aggregate of all purchase and sale transactions in such mortgages. For such a market to be effective and worthy of acceptance, private or governmental funds must be available at all times to permit the purchase of mortgage loans meeting prescribed standards. The investor in mortgages can deal with greater confidence if he can be assured of the existence of a secondary market where he can liquidate his holdings on a reasonable basis under the conditions then current. Often the ability to sell existing mortgages in the secondary market is the only means by which the holder of such mortgages can regain the liquidity necessary to finance new housing or to recover funds for an alternative use.

A purchasing institution may acquire mortgages in the secondary market either for resale or for retention as investments. Thus, to a certain extent, private institutional investors provide a secondary mortgage market to mortgagees, investors, and other holders of mortgage loans. By far the most important factor, however, in the secondary market for residential housing mortgage loans is the Federal National Mortgage Association. One of its charter obligations is to provide a secondary market for federally underwritten mortgages and recently it was empowered to deal in conventional mortgages.

HOLC as a Secondary Market Those who contend that the HOLC constituted a secondary market for mortgages overlook one important feature of its operations. Because it exchanged government-guaranteed bonds which had a ready market for defaulted mortgages, its operations in effect represented a monetization of mortgages rather than a marketing operation.

In a sense, HOLC could have become a secondary market for mortgages. As the managers of investment institutions began to recover their courage after the Great Depression of the thirties, various proposals were made to the HOLC to purchase large blocks of mortgages. Since the interest of such potential purchasers was limited to the best mortgages in the HOLC portfolio, this corporation dared not entertain the proposals. With its far-flung servicing organization, the HOLC needed to retain its strong mortgages to help pay the losses on the weak ones. It was only when the total mortgage holdings were reduced to a point that its servicing organization was no longer economical to operate that bulk sales were made of all remaining mortgage holdings. By this time even the weak mortgages had become fairly well seasoned.

RFC Mortgage Company In 1935, the Congress authorized the organization of the RFC Mortgage Company—to become a subsidiary of the RFC—as one method of providing a secondary market for real estate mortgages. Its broad powers made possible several lines of activity. It could refinance existing loans on a long list of income-producing properties which could not be financed from ordinary private sources. Such properties included apartments, apartment hotels, hotels, office buildings, and so on. Similarly, this company could provide new construction loans for income-producing property where insufficient funds were available for such purposes. A third type of activity was in the field of loans to distressed holders of real estate bonds against income-producing property. Finally, this company was empowered to purchase FHA-insured mortgages against properties containing more than four-family units in order to help provide a secondary market for them.

The success of the HOLC in providing relief to distressed home-owners suggested the possibilities of applying the same principles to the refinancing of distressed owners of income-producing property. Had the RFC board seen fit to use the program outlined above to its fullest extent, the RFC Mortgage Company could easily have developed into another HOLC. The need for refinancing distressed office buildings, apartment houses, and so forth was great. However, the RFC board did not see fit to use its opportunities in this field very liberally.

The standards established by the RFC Mortgage Company were quite rigid. Also it appeared that, at least in the purchase of FHA mortgages, private investors were sufficiently interested to make a secondary market provided by a government agency unnecessary. The RFC Mortgage Company was not an outstanding success. In establishing this subsidiary the RFC purchased its stock for $25 million. Further funds were advanced by the parent corporation in return for its notes. Ten years after it was organized, the assets of the RFC Mortgage Company amounted to $55 million, consisting chiefly of: owned real estate loans, $36 million; real estate, $8 million; and government obligations, $6 million. Its capital stock was $25 million; its loans from the RFC, $26 million; and its surplus, $3 million. Because there was no apparent need for the continuance of this corporation, it was liquidated by order of Congress as of June 30, 1947.

Federal National Mortgage Association Failing in its efforts to induce private capital to form national mortgage associations for the purpose of providing a secondary market for insured mortgages, Congress in 1938 authorized the RFC to form a subsidiary to be known as the Federal National Mortgage Association. This institution is familiarly known as "Fannie Mae," and commonly designated by its initials, FNMA. Its original capital was $10 million, with a paid-in surplus of $1 million, all provided by the RFC. Its original purposes were to purchase insured mortgages and to assist in the financing of large-scale rental projects. In purchasing mortgages from approved mortgagees it permitted them to continue to service the loans, retaining a fee of 0.25 to 1 percent for this purpose, according to the requirements as viewed by the RFC. FNMA was authorized to issue notes when it needed resources greater than its original capital and surplus.

Although established to provide a secondary market for insured mortgages, FNMA was never freely used at the time it was chartered. The restrictions it placed upon purchases tended to discourage mortgagees from selling their mortgages in this market. This was particularly true because a more satisfactory market was provided by banks, insurance companies, and so forth, which made their purchases on terms more liberal to the sellers. As a consequence, FNMA was not a major factor in the insured mortgage market until it was revived in the postwar years.

FNMA after World War II The principal initial objectives of FNMA were:

1. To establish a market for the purchase and sale of first mortgages insured by FHA covering properties upon which were located newly constructed houses or housing projects.
2. To facilitate the construction and financing of economically sound rental housing projects or groups of houses for rent or sale through direct lending on FHA-insured first mortgages.
3. To make FNMA bonds or debentures available to institutional and individual investors.

Since July 1, 1948, FNMA has also been permitted to purchase certain VA mortgages guaranteed under the provisions of the Servicemen's Readjustment Act of 1944, as amended. At the same time, the Association's authority to make direct FHA-insured multifamily housing loans was discontinued.

FNMA was a subsidiary of the RFC until 1950 when it was transferred to the Housing and Home Finance Agency which had been created in 1942. By becoming a part of the federal agency primarily concerned with housing and home finance, FNMA's activities in the secondary market for home mortgages could thereafter be more closely coordinated with the Home Loan Bank Board and its affiliated agencies as well as those of the FHA.

The demand for assistance from FNMA developed after World War II because of the differential between interest rates on FHA-insured and VA-guaranteed loans and yields on government bonds. Originally VA loans were made at 4 percent and, at the same time, FHA loans were made at $4\frac{1}{4}$ percent. For some time, government bonds were selling to yield less than $2\frac{1}{2}$ percent. This differential created a favorable climate for investing in federally underwritten mortgages rather than government bonds, even considering additional risk factors and servicing costs involved with investments in mortgages. As general interest rates began to rise in the late 1940s, lenders became reluctant to make commitments to large builders because of the danger that by the time of completion of projects the current interest rates might be still higher and their mortgages worth less than face value. At this point FNMA rendered an invaluable service to both lenders and builders by entering the secondary market on a commitment basis. By its commitment, FNMA agreed to purchase at an established rate the lender's mortgage paper during the commitment period. This assured a continuing flow of funds from lenders to the mortgage market.

An additional complication has always existed with reference to both FHA and VA mortgage loans. This complication is that they have a ceiling interest rate. As the market rate of interest on government bonds, for example, rose above 3 percent, while FHA and VA loans were at $4\frac{1}{4}$ percent and 4 percent, respectively, most investors considered bonds more desirable than the federally underwritten mortgages, all costs and risks considered. At this time, FHA and VA mortgages had few takers except to the extent that FNMA made advance commitment to lenders to take such loans off their hands. Under such circumstances, FNMA placed itself virtually in the position of a primary supplier of real estate mortgage funds.

1950 FNMA In 1950, Congress authorized an additional $250 million for the purchase of insured mortgages by FNMA. The fee charged for such purposes could not exceed 1 percent. No lender could sell to the FNMA more than half of the amount of insured mortgages originated after April 30, 1948. In order to make sure that this agency should operate as a clearinghouse for insured mortgages instead of a dumping ground, the House and Senate conferees agreed to suggest that FNMA sell its mortgage holdings—present and future—in an orderly fashion. The price to be set at any time was to be fixed only after consultation with the Secretary of the Treasury. Up to the end of 1952, FNMA had purchased nearly half a million mortgages having a dollar volume of nearly $3½ billion. Resale, amounting to about one fourth of purchases, and amortization had reduced the holdings of FNMA to approximately $2¼ billion by the end of 1952. In addition to the low rate of interest as a deterrent to the resale of mortgages purchased by FNMA, most of those retained failed to make a strong appeal to the normal market for mortgages because they had as security government-sponsored housing projects for military personnel, defense workers, and veterans of World War II. Since many of the latter required 100 percent financing of their homes, their mortgages were not readily salable in a market which could command both higher interest rates and lower percentages of loan to value.

FNMA ceased making advance commitments to lenders in March of 1950, and was on an over-the-counter, or noncommitment, basis from that time through 1953. In the face of generally rising interest rates during the period, FHA and VA mortgages went to substantial discounts and lending of funds in this area dwindled. Even with the administrative increase of FHA and VA interest rates to 4½ percent in the spring of 1953, by fall of that year both types of mortgages were selling in the secondary market at 2 to 3 points discount.

Secondary Market Operations to FNMA since 1954 The Charter Act of 1954 authorized FNMA specifically to conduct secondary market operations to provide supplementary assistance to the secondary market for home mortgages by providing a degree of liquidity for mortgage investments, thereby improving the distribution of investment capital available for home financing. Secondary market operations began under this mandate on November 1, 1954. Purchases were limited by the Charter Act to FHA-insured or VA-guaranteed mortgages on residential property originated on or after August 2, 1954.

In the acquisition of its mortgages, FNMA uses an auction market. Its procedures are described in Chapter 28.

Since it began operations under the 1954 charter, FNMA has gone a long way toward providing a high degree of service, with benefits approaching those of a central banking facility. It has continually been in the market for federally underwritten mortgages. Purchases have been heaviest when there otherwise has been little buying in the secondary mortgage market, and lightest when funds have been more available from other mortgage investors. The secondary market operations have closely followed the money market trend for investable funds in real estate. For example, FNMA purchases rose from $86 million in 1955 to $575 million in 1956 and to $1,021 million in 1957, reflecting an increasing tightness in the mortgage market. With easier financing conditions and a decreased need for FNMA to provide liquidity, its purchases declined to $260 million in 1958, and during the same year it sold mortgages in the amount of $455 million. With the tightening of the market for funds in 1959, FNMA purchases rose again to $735 million. For 1960, purchases by FNMA under its secondary operations program exceeded $1.2 billion. Purchases exceeded sales by moderate amounts during 1961 and 1962. In the course of the first half of 1963, the spread between the supply and demand for mortgage funds steadily widened, bringing about a general easing of mortgage credit and creating an overabundance of long-term capital savings, which actively competed in the market for profitable investment outlets. Institutional investors, looking for mortgages to acquire, bought $977 million from FNMA during the first half of 1963. FNMA, during the same period, purchased only $164 million. As supply and demand factors were more nearly equated at midyear, resulting in stabilized mortgage prices and interest rates, FNMA returned to a more neutral operation, with sales of $151 million and purchases of $126 million for the second half of the year.

During the years 1966 through 1970, mortgage holdings of FNMA went up considerably, reflecting the tight credit conditions existing in the mortgage market FHA-insured mortgages increased from $3.4 billion in 1965 to $15.4 billion in 1970, an increase of nearly five times. Even VA-guaranteed mortgages, which had been declining as portfolio holdings since 1959, rose from $1.3 billion in 1965 to $4.4 billion in 1970, for an increase of over three times. It is important to note that with positions in the mortgage market assuming such proportions, the Association has a substantial effect in sustaining an even flow of funds into FHA-insured and VA-guaranteed mortgage credit.

Institutional Commitments in Mortgage Lending[1] In many respects the mortgage banker stands in about the same relationship to the institutions and other investors to whom he sells his mortgages as the investment banker stands to the investing public which buys his corporate securities. He must originate a satisfactory obligation and he must finance it until such time as it is sold to the ultimate investor. Prior to the time that a real estate mortgage is ready for sale, however, there has often been a long gestation period, and many arrangements for interim credits have had to be made—often more complicated and of longer duration than the investment banker must undertake. These interim financing problems arise because of the basic conditions out of which a new mortgage is derived. Often a new property or a new development is being constructed. The builder is ill equipped to provide his own financing, and the mortgage banker with a thin capital equity is not able to give him much help from his own funds. To accomplish their objectives, both need a construction loan. To support the construction loan credit, a commercial bank or other lender which might make such a loan often requires a firm commitment from an institutional investor to take over the mortgage on the property once the building has been completed. In fact, such commitments have proved to be increasingly important to the mortgage-lending operation in recent years. The commitments have been principally of two types: (1) "advance" or "forward" commitments and (2) "standby" commitments.

The first type of commitment, called an "advance" commitment by the Federal Housing Administration and termed a "forward" commitment by the Life Insurance Association of America, is virtually a purchase order for a mortgage on property to be constructed. A firm obligation is undertaken for the period of the commitment to purchase the federally underwritten mortgage on property to be constructed in accordance with acceptable plans and specifications. On the strength of the knowledge that the mortgage has a market once the property is completed, other institutions are willing to provide the necessary interim financing to bring the property to such a state of completion that the mortgage is eligible for sale under the commitment.

The "standby" commitment is an arrangement, usually worked out

---

[1] Mortimer Kaplan, "Recent Institutional Arrangements in Mortgage Lending," *Journal of Finance,* Vol. XIII, No. 2 (May 1958) pp. 188–200.

with a commercial bank, whereby the latter will buy mortgages, generally from a mortgage banker, at a substantial discount in event they cannot be sold more favorably to an institutional or other investor by the end of the commitment period.

The advance, or forward, commitment has been used in greatest volume at those times when credit conditions have eased, and the institutions with large volumes of funds to place have taken this means of providing for ready investment of their cash inflow. As money rates tighten, the institutional lenders find alternative uses for their funds equally attractive, and they are less inclined to enter into such commitments, as they feel overcommitted at lower rates on the obligations that they have already undertaken. Furthermore, rising interest rates with declining bond prices tend to make the sale of bonds for the purpose of obtaining funds for an alternative use an unattractive prospect.

A correlative of a restriction in advance commitments is an increased need for the standby commitment. In the absence of a certain market for the mortgage once construction is complete, the mortgage banker or the builder will accept an alternative avenue for disposition at a substantial discount, on the chance that a more desirable buyer can be found after origination of the permanent mortgage and before expiration of the commitment period. The use of this device tends to exert a stabilizing influence upon the availability of funds at times when a tightening money market tends to dry up the supply. The effect is limited, however, by the fact that as the volume of standby commitments increases the bank issuing the commitments will lower its forfeiture price until the potential financing costs become prohibitive and the plans for more construction are dropped.

Mortgage Inventory Loans, or "Mortgage Warehousing"[2] Interim loans by commercial banks to nonbank lenders are often specifically designated as "mortgage inventory" loans. Bankers commonly identify as inventory loans those made on securities being underwritten by an investment banker while the issues are being prepared for sale and distribution to individuals and financial institutions who buy them for their investment portfolios. Mortgage inventory loans serve exactly the same purpose for the mortgage banker, as he requires financing to expedite the originating, sale, and distribution of his mortgages to permanent investors. The practice of granting such loans has been called "mortgage warehousing." The notion of warehousing arises from the temporary nature of the advance as the mortgage passes from its originator to the ultimate lender.

There are three general types of warehouse loans. Two of these commonly involve mortgage bankers directly. The most common is the "com-

---

[2] Jack Guttentag, "Mortgage Warehousing," *Journal of Finance*, Vol. XII, No. 4 (December 1957), pp. 438–43.

mitted-technical" warehousing loan, which has been made for many years. Under this arrangement, the commercial bank simply lends to the mortgage banker to provide financing between the time of payment for construction and the time when he can deliver perfected mortgages to the permanent investor. This loan is supported by a prior commitment of the investor to purchase the mortgages when completed. Numerous details must be handled before the mortgage is ready for purchase. The loan must be closed; the credit of the owner of the property must be checked; the FHA insurance or the VA guarantee must be obtained; title insurance or a counsel's opinion must afford adequate title protection; other appropriate insurance must be bound; and delivery and recordation of necessary documents must be effected. All of these processes, together with assembling mortgages in the proper amounts, usually take five to six months. The amount of the warehousing loan is usually based upon the commitment of the permanent investor. The lending bank will be limited to the amount of the commitment or to a figure slightly less than that amount.

A second type of warehousing loan is called the "uncommitted-technical" loan. It differs from the first only in that there is no prior commitment of a permanent investor to take up the loan from the mortgage banker. When a commercial bank lends under this arrangement, it may lend either with or without recourse. If the loan is with recourse and a permanent investor has not been found by the end of the interim lending period, the mortgage banker must take up the loan from the commercial bank. He must then either carry the financing himself or arrange it elsewhere until he manages to sell the mortgage. If the warehousing loan from the bank is without recourse, there is a different result. In case the mortgage banker has not placed the mortgage with a permanent investor before the maturity date of the interim loan, the commercial bank retires the loan by purchasing the mortgage given as security at its prearranged forfeiture price, which is normally at a discount. The obligation of the commercial bank in this situation is the previously mentioned standby commitment for which it is paid a fee irrespective of whether a forfeiture is declared.

Still a third type of warehousing loan has come into prominence since the mid-1950s. It has been designated as "committed-institutional" warehousing. This type of loan is made directly to large institutional investors rather than to mortgage bankers, and the credit is designed to give investors more flexibility in arranging for mortgage investments by providing for their unusual requirements for investable funds which will later be met permanently out of the receipts of funds in the ordinary course of business. These loans by the commercial bank are usually of longer duration, ranging from a year to 18 months, with the borrower having a prepayment option. The use of this financing method is largely the result of the decline in the bond markets in recent years, rendering these securities relatively unavailable for sale by institutional investors to provide funds to meet advance commitments to mortgage bankers. Should bond prices rise again, so that capital gains instead of capital losses might result from bond sales, it may be presumed that committed institutional warehousing will become less important for this purpose. The method is available, however, to deal with any situation in which the cash inflow of an institution does not meet its expectations.

Social and Economic Impact of Mortgage Warehousing[3] It becomes apparent from studying the operating methods of mortgage bankers today that mortgage warehousing is essential to the smooth and orderly performance of their present functions. They do not need and are not organized to provide directly the funds necessary to carry the large volume of mortgages which they may originate for institutional investors. Commercial banks can meet this requirement for them on a flexible and economic basis, with credits expanding or contracting consistently with their commitments. In uncommitted warehousing, commercial banks can again be of real assistance in appraisal of the investment demand, the mortgage market, and other significant factors in the process of granting the credit line. Through the establishment of this line, and a forfeiture price, mortgage bankers are afforded a platform from which they can work with some assurance while they proceed during the period of the interim loan to seek out new markets on a national basis. They are thus enabled to originate mortgages beyond the time that they could remain in the market if they were limited to reliance upon prior commitments. Similarly, committed institutional warehousing permits large mortgage investors to anticipate their cash inflows for as long as two years, or more, in advance and to issue forward commitments to their correspondent mortgage originators. Such commitments enable the correspondents to maintain an uninterrupted lending program, without breakdown or cutoffs, and thus support the building industry in a continuous construction program.

Although it may generally be presumed that mortgage warehousing has a stabilizing effect, it has been pointed out that such great dependence upon the commercial banks renders the supply of current funds available for real estate lending directly subject to commercial bank policies. Bankers point out that they may cease lending on this type of credit when they feel they have reached proper and judicious limits. A decision by bankers en masse not to make further warehousing loans, whether for reasons of money market conditions or better alternative uses of funds, could bring about a disturbing result in an otherwise stable market. Of course, if the bankers should decide that a reversal

---

[3] Ibid., pp. 443–50.

in real estate market conditions has made further such loans unwise, the impact would be inevitable.

Economists point out that under certain conditions the provision of warehousing credit may be inflationary. Under conditions of full employment, with productive resources in short supply, any additional credit expansion has this effect. Thus, any new demand for productive resources injected into the housing industry would be competing for resources already in demand and prices would be driven upward. Should this situation develop in critical proportions, a problem in credit control would arise. It has been suggested that for such a special form of credit, with regard to which quantitative and qualitative controls as generally conceived would be too broad and the need for prompt action would be paramount, a program of "moral suasion" would probably be most effective.

Other Developments When the National Housing Act of 1934 was passed, its Title III provided for the organization of privately owned and managed national mortgage associations to afford a secondary market for mortgages. As passed originally, this law provided liberal financial support from the federal government for any association organized under it. Although this government support was further liberalized in subsequent amendments, no such association was ever organized. Apparently, private capital could not find sufficient advantage in making use of this law to give it a test.

For many years the Federal National Mortgage Association stood as the only major secondary market facility, and its assistance was only available for federally underwritten mortgages. Now its scope of operations has expanded to the conventional mortgage markets.

Under the 1968 housing legislation, provision was made for the newly created Government National Mortgage Association to guarantee securities issued by private issuers approved by it for this purpose, so long as the securities are underwritten by the FHA or VA, or by the Farmers Home Administration under Title V of the 1949 Housing Act, and are set aside or placed in trust in a prescribed manner. This permits recourse to the public directly by large private lenders to generate funds for new lending. As these benefits are extended to properly seasoned, qualified conventional mortgages as well, much more will be accomplished.

Members of the Federal Home Loan Bank System have recently been empowered to use the system facilities to provide a warehousing mechanism for those of its members who wish to buy or sell mortgages. As discussed in Chapter 24, the Emergency Home Finance Act of 1970 has established this facility and it is in operation. Over time, it is now reasonable to project that large amounts of pension funds and other institutional holdings will be brought into the real estate mortgage market through the sale of debentures or other securities by the Federal

Home Loan Mortgage Corporation (FHLMC) and the use of the sales proceeds to acquire eligible liens.

Some students of secondary markets profess to see in current improvements not only a solution to the problem of geographical variations in the availability of mortgage funds but a solution to the problems involved in both major and minor seasonal and cyclical variations in the demand for and the supply of mortgage money. If we dare to assume that such mechanisms could have access to unlimited capital at all times and that there would be no controls over interest rates—governmental or otherwise—undoubtedly much could be done to provide a free market for real estate mortgages. But these are large assumptions.

QUESTIONS AND PROBLEMS

1. What have been the major factors leading to the growth in mortgage loans during the last decade?
2. How has the investment character of the real estate mortgage changed in recent years?
3. What is a secondary mortgage market?
4. What is the need for a secondary mortgage market at the present time?
5. Did the HOLC provide a secondary market for mortgages? Explain.
6. Review the history of the RFC Mortgage Company. Why did it not become an important factor in the secondary mortgage market?
7. Distinguish between "advance" or "forward" commitments and "standby" commitments and define each.
8. What is mortgage warehousing?
9. What are the three general types of mortgage warehouse loans? Describe each.
10. Is the practice of mortgage warehousing a favorable influence on economic conditions? Why or why not?
11. Do you favor establishment of a central mortgage bank? Why or why not?
12. What legislation or changes in federal policy would you recommend to improve the functioning of our secondary mortgage markets?

28

The Federal National Mortgage Association and the Government National Mortgage Association

The Federal National Mortgage Association Charter In the previous chapter the origins of the Federal National Mortgage Association (FNMA) were mentioned. It was organized on February 10, 1938, by the Reconstruction Finance Corporation under authority contained in the then Title III of the National Housing Act. It operated as a subsidiary of the RFC until it was transferred by a presidential reorganization plan, on September 7, 1950, to the Housing and Home Finance Agency, now embodied in the U.S. Department of Housing and Urban Development (HUD). In 1954, the Congress rechartered the Association under the terms of the Federal National Mortgage Association Charter Act. Operations commenced under the new charter on November 1, 1954. The terms of the Charter Act will be presented next, and then the changes as effected by the Housing and Urban Development Act of 1968 and the Emergency Home Finance Act of 1970.

Chartered Functions of FNMA The Charter Act assigned to FNMA three separate and distinct activities: (1) secondary market operations in federally insured and guaranteed mortgages, (2) management and liquidating functions, and (3) special assistance functions. Each function was carried out as though it represented the operation of a separate corporation. Each had its own assets, liabilities, and separate borrowing authority.

Secondary Market Operations and Their Financing For several years, organizations such as the National Association of Home Builders, the Mortgage Bankers Association of America, the National Association of Real Estate Boards, and the United States Savings and Loan League had advocated the formation of a new secondary market facility to be expanded from a nucleus of the FNMA mortgage portfolio. Dominant among the recommendations was the position that governmental participation in the operation of the principal secondary market facility should gradually be replaced by private enterprise. A major objective of the FNMA Charter Act was to set up a procedure whereby FNMA would over a period of time be transformed into a privately owned and managed organization. By converting FNMA to a private operation rather than setting up a new one, it was contemplated to take advantage of FNMA's years of experience in the secondary market during the transition period and eventually to concentrate the whole operation in private hands.

The Charter Act authorized issuance of nonvoting $100 par preferred and common stock for the financing of secondary market operations. The preferred stock was issued to the Secretary of the Treasury and the common was issued only to sellers of mortgages or borrowers as they participated in FNMA's secondary market operations.

The first sale of the preferred stock, held exclusively by the U.S. Treasury, was effected at the beginning of operations under the new charter on November 1, 1954. The original purchase by the Secretary of the Treasury amounted to approximately $92.8 million, $20 million of which was equivalent to the Association's prior capitalization and paid-in surplus of $21 million plus about $72 million of reserves for losses and contingencies and undistributed earned surplus as of the close of the operation at October 31, 1954. Additional stock was issued to the Secretary of the Treasury as the mortgage market required more funds. FNMA was permitted to retire the preferred stock out of its capital surplus and general surplus accounts as soon as it deemed such redemption feasible, but it was never able to accomplish more than partial and temporary redemptions until total retirement of the preferred stock on September 30, 1968, pursuant to the provisions of the Housing and Urban Development Act of 1968. A major purpose of this legislation was to achieve this transfer of FNMA to private ownership with government sponsorship, so that its status might become analogous to that of the Federal Home Loan Banks and the Federal Land Banks. Although FNMA is still government-sponsored, its entire equity interest is now privately owned.

The original issuance of FNMA common shares has been limited to sellers of mortgages to the Association who, for the privilege of sale, are required by statute to make nonrefundable capital contributions in prescribed amounts. Between August 2, 1954 and August 7, 1956 the required common stock subscription for mortgage sellers was 3 percent of the original principal amount of mortgages involved in the transaction. Since that time until 1970, pursuant to statutory provision, the subscription rate has moved between 1 and 2 percent of the unpaid principal amount of the mortgages involved. In the later years until 1970, FNMA held the rate at 1 percent. Borrowers from the Association have also been required to make capital contributions—in an amount equal to not more than ½ of 1 percent of amounts borrowed. Although there is no limitation on stock resale, historically, there has also been a stock retention requirement for each servicer of mortgages for FNMA. This requirement is established by FNMA, subject to approval of the Secretary of HUD, at a level not to exceed 2 percent of the aggregate unpaid principal balances of mortgages being serviced. This retention requirement was reduced from 1.0 to 0.7 percent on all commitments made on or after August 10, 1970 and further to 0.5 percent on all commitments made on or after January 27, 1971. Common stock purchase requirements were reduced similarly to 0.5 percent of loans purchased by the Association and on January 26, 1972 were reduced again to 0.25 percent.

The board of directors has generally set the issue price of FNMA common shares at approximately book value. For long periods of time in the past, subscribers to these shares have had to absorb losses should they desire to resell in the open market. More recently, the market has been more favorable. Since 1960, subscribers desiring to resell the shares have been afforded some federal income tax relief. Instead of being forced to take losses from selling such shares as capital losses, and subject to limited deductibility, subscribers have been permitted to claim these losses as ordinary and necessary expenses of operation, fully deductible, to the extent that the subscription price exceeds the fair market value at date of issue. Inversely, profits from such transactions are treated as capital gains.

Under the Charter Act, FNMA will purchase acceptable mortgages from all lenders, including banks, savings and loan associations, mortgage companies, and other organizations that have qualified as eligible sellers and have entered into a selling agreement with the Association. The selling agreement requires that the seller either qualify as an FNMA servicer or proffer the facilities of another servicing institution with respect to each mortgage offered for purchase, excepting multifamily housing mortgages which are serviced directly by the Association.

The subscription requirement imposed upon sellers of mortgages to FNMA raises the question of the acceptability of such shares as stock holdings. Any national bank or state member bank of the Federal Reserve System, any member of the Federal Deposit Insurance Corporation, trust company, or other banking organization organized under any law of the United States, including laws relating to the District of Columbia, is authorized to make capital contributions and to receive, hold, or dispose of the stock of FNMA. Furthermore, the FHA allows an approved FHA mortgagee a credit at face value for FNMA common stock toward establishing the net worth requirements that the mortgagee must meet to qualify for FHA approval. Stock acquired in the open market, however, is normally credited for such purposes at cost or market value, whichever is less. National banks and federal savings and loan associations have been authorized by the Comptroller of the Currency and the Home Loan Bank Board, respectively, to carry at the lower of par or acquisition cost any FNMA common stock acquired in connection with the sale of mortgages by them to FNMA.

As a federally sponsored agency, FNMA is exempt from all state and local taxes, excepting those on real estate. Consistent with its private and proprietary nature, however, it is fully liable for payment of federal corporate income taxes.

In addition to funds provided through the issuance of common stock, FNMA is also authorized to raise funds through the sale of its credit obligations either to the Secretary of the Treasury or to the public. Under Section 304(b) of the Charter Act, FNMA was permitted to have outstanding at any one time obligations in an aggregate amount not to exceed 15 times the sum of its capital, capital surplus, general surplus, reserves, and undistributed earnings. By authority of Section 309(b) of the Charter Act, the Secretary of HUD may approve a ratio of debt to capital of FNMA greater than the 15 to 1 ratio described above. In the more recent period of heavy demands upon FNMA, the Secretary raised the approved maximum borrowing ratio to 25 to 1.

As a backstop to public demand, the Secretary of the Treasury, by authority of Section 304(c) of the Charter Act, is permitted to purchase on a discretionary basis up to $2,250 million of FNMA's secondary market obligations. As an operating practice, the Association has obtained its permanent long-term borrowed funds from the public. Its borrowings from the U.S. Treasury have been for interim requirements to meet unusual needs on a daily basis and for general corporate purposes. Temporary borrowings from the Treasury have been repaid out of the proceeds of debenture offerings when the magnitude of the fund requirements has justified a new resort to the market. Net proceeds from operations and loan reductions have also been used to pay off Treasury borrowings and were invested until they might be used to retire outstanding debentures.

The Housing and Urban Development Act of 1968 The principal effect of Title VII of the 1968 legislation in regard to FNMA was to provide for the transfer of assets and liabilities in connection with, and control and management of, the secondary market operations to a private corporation. The earlier years had indicated that the FNMA operations are economically sound and capable of being financed solely from private sources.

In the reorganization process, FNMA secondary operations were separated from the special assistance and management and liquidating functions. The latter remain with the Department of Housing and Urban Development and are now performed through a new corporation known as the Government National Mortgage Association (GNMA).

The 1968 legislation removed previous restrictions against buying mortgages in excess of par and against mortgages offered by, or covering property held by, state and local authorities. Furthermore, the purchasing authority of FNMA was expanded to include certain mortgage-backed securities guaranteed by GNMA, so that, when desirable, FNMA can act to support the secondary market for such securities.

Besides FNMA debentures and short-term discount notes, two new forms of borrowing were provided for by the 1968 legislation. First, FNMA was permitted to issue subordinated notes, in a manner similar to the "capital notes" permitted banking institutions. These obligations are usually issued for long terms and may include provisions for convertibility to common shares. They may be considered as part of the corporate capital for purposes of the debt-to-equity ratio. These obligations may be issued up to twice the sum of capital, surplus, and retained earnings.

The second new borrowing form authorized issuance and marketing of securities backed by earmarked pools of portfolio mortgages, and this authority is without any ratio limitation. GNMA is authorized to guarantee the payment of principal and interest on any such securities issued by FNMA. Incidentally, GNMA is authorized in a similar manner to guarantee securities issued by private parties approved for this purpose, when the securities are backed by federally underwritten mortgages and subjected to a trust similar to that established by FNMA. The gain sought here is to create a soundly backed security that will attract new money into the mortgage market, particularly from pension and retirement funds.

The Secretary of HUD will continue to have general regulatory powers to assure that the purposes of the Charter Act are served. He must authorize all issues of corporate securities and obligations. He will participate in the decision-making process regarding the levels of mortgage purchases under varying economic conditions. He may also require that a reasonable portion of FNMA mortgage purchases be related to low and moderate income housing, but only under conditions of a reasonable economic return.

Recent Legislation The authority of FNMA to buy, sell, and otherwise deal in mortgages not federally insured or guaranteed (so-called conventional mortgages) was recently conferred by the Emergency

Home Finance Act of 1970. A conventional single-family mortgage purchase program began in February 1972. FNMA continues to recognize that its primary responsibility is to the market for federally underwritten mortgages and expects for the foreseeable future that conventional mortgages will represent a small proportion of its total mortgage portfolio. Strict qualifications will be enforced to assure proper limitations on the additional risk inherent in operating in the conventional mortgage market.

Recent legislation has also extended the powers of FNMA to permit it to deal in loans made for the construction and modernization of hospital facilities. Authority to receive federal subsidies has been further extended to allow FNMA to absorb losses from ownership and disposition of federally insured low- and middle-income mortgages acquired at prices above those warranted by the going rates in the mortgage market.

FNMA Purchasing Procedure Until May 6, 1968, FNMA set prices to be paid for already existing mortgages. In practice, when FNMA purchases increased and credit conditions brought about a reduction in mortgage prices, the private secondary market tended to set its prices below FNMA. Originators came to FNMA first without even testing the market, because they knew that FNMA would be offering the best price available. Instead of FNMA buttressing the private secondary market, quite the opposite took place, particularly in 1966 when FNMA was forced to turn to nonprice restrictions. Buyers who needed low equity financing available through federally backed mortgages had to postpone purchases, and builders and sellers were forced to pay large discounts or take their properties off the market.

To achieve a more competitive market better suited to FNMA's secondary market role, the set pricing technique was replaced by the "Free Market System Auction" under which FNMA announces the total dollar commitments to purchase "single-family mortgages" (mortgages on one- to four-family residences) available at specific auctions. These auctions are held on a weekly or biweekly basis. Approved sellers submit bids indicating the amount of commitments bid for, the prices they wish to be paid, and the terms of the commitments. The term can be one of three: within 3 months, about equivalent to immediate over-the-counter purchase arrangements; 6 months, to give sufficient time to provide for the sale and financing of existing properties; and 12 months, to be used for proposed construction. Successful bidders are notified in the form of a firm commitment to purchase a fixed amount of federally underwritten mortgages at the firm price bid and for the term bid. In the case of oversubscriptions, the total amount offered is allocated to the three maturity options in direct proportion to the amounts bid without regard to price. This achieves differential pricing by the term of the commitment.

Successful bidders may choose among three alternatives during the commitment period. They may: (1) exercise their right to sell to FNMA, (2) decide to retain the mortgages for their own portfolio, or (3) sell the mortgages to another buyer. If option (2) or (3) is elected, FNMA simply receives a commitment fee for its agreement to stand ready to purchase. These fees are ½ of 1 percent of funds committed for 3 months, ¾ of 1 percent for 6 months, and 1 percent for 12 months. For an additional ¼ of 1 percent, a commitment may be extended for 3 months for certain delays in connection with proposed construction.

Purchase prices for mortgages on multifamily housing projects are not set by the auction system. FNMA establishes these prices periodically, using the auction results for guidance. As under the auction system, the fees are adjusted to the type of commitment made. Commitments for multifamily mortgages differ from those under the auction system in that the holder of commitments on multifamily mortgages, unless excused, must deliver the full amount of qualified mortgages to FNMA within the commitment period.

Servicing of Mortgages For every mortgage offered to FNMA for purchase, the seller must provide a satisfactory servicing agreement. If the seller is himself qualified as an eligible servicer by FNMA standards, he will ordinarily be permitted to service the mortgage upon signing a servicing agreement with the Association. If the seller cannot qualify as a servicer, he must proffer the facilities of a servicer with an outstanding servicing agreement with FNMA. In either event, the servicer must have an office with servicing facilities satisfactory to the Association within 100 miles of the mortgaged property. FNMA provides direct servicing of mortgages on multifamily dwellings. The duties of the servicer include collecting the mortgage installments and tax and insurance deposits, paying taxes and insurance premiums when due, and handling assessments and other charges against the property in such a manner as to keep the mortgage security good. The servicer is also required to make inspections of the property, personally service accounts which have become delinquent, maintain appropriate records, make a proper accounting for the funds which he receives, and report what action he has taken on delinquent accounts. After it becomes apparent that a delinquent account cannot be salvaged short of foreclosure, the account may be turned over to the Association for further action. The servicer is not obligated to foreclose mortgages for the Association or to bear any part of the expenses of the foreclosure proceedings. In general, the servicer's objectives are to liquidate mortgage accounts in an orderly manner, to preserve the mortgage security, to keep amortizations on a current basis, and to deal effectively with mortgagors in default. To assure full compliance with these objectives and with the terms of the agreement between FNMA and the servicer, the Association conducts periodic audits at the servicer's place of business. Maintenance of proper accounting records to reflect adequate and accurate information and other precautions essential to the full protection of the Association's interests are verified in this manner.

As compensation for his efforts, the servicer is allowed to retain out of collections an amount equal to $\frac{1}{2}$ of 1 percent per annum on the unpaid balance on any mortgage being serviced under a contract entered into prior to August 10, 1970. Servicing contracts begun on or after that date provide for a $\frac{3}{8}$ of 1 percent fee. The impact of the fee reduction is partially offset, however, by permission to servicers of retention of all collections to cover taxes, insurance, and other costs.

Short-Term Loans by FNMA Since June 30, 1961, FNMA has been authorized, as part of its secondary market activities, to make short-term loans secured by FHA-insured and VA-guaranteed mortgages. Such loans are intended to further home construction by providing additional liquidity for certain mortgage investments. Loans may not exceed 90 percent of the aggregate unpaid principal balances of the mortgages securing the loans or have terms in excess of 12 months. Extensions, not to exceed 12 months, with the consent of FNMA may be negotiated. The volume of lending activities and the establishment of interest rates, loan ratios, maturities, and charges or fees required are determinable by FNMA with the objective of preventing excessive use of the Association's facilities and of assuring that the operations will be fully self-supporting. Borrowers under this authority are required to buy common stock of FNMA as previously indicated.

FNMA Sales Procedure Although the major emphasis in the FNMA programs has been in the areas of mortgage purchases, at times an equally important function may be mortgage sales. Inherent in the performance of secondary market functions is that under certain conditions it is in the best interests of an orderly market that FNMA be a seller as well as a buyer. Sales from the portfolio of the secondary market operations are made at prices based on prevailing prices for similar classes of mortgages in the general secondary market, with due regard for the impact which the contemplated sales will have on future prices. Sales of home mortgages from the special assistance portfolio are not made at less than cost, while multifamily mortgages are sold on a negotiated basis.

Lists of mortgages for sale are available to prospective purchasers in the various Association agency offices. With respect to multifamily dwellings, FNMA will issue sales options under proper circumstances. As to other mortgages, those selected by a potential buyer will be reserved for his consideration and will not be available to any other investor for a period of 15 days. This period is allowed to give the prospective purchaser an opportunity to inspect the mortgage premises and examine the notes, mortgages, and other documents related to the security at the Association agency office. A sales price is quoted in the reservation letter sent by the Association to the prospective purchaser. This price, however, is subject to change without notice during the reservation period. The actual price paid is that in effect at the time of the signing of the FNMA mortgage sales agreement when the investor consummates his purchase. Upon receipt of the sales price, the investor is assigned the mortgage without recourse, subject to the servicing agreement between the Association and the servicer, which may be canceled on 30 days' notice.

FNMA Mortgage Sales The major volume of mortgage sales from the FNMA portfolio has been in particular years. At other times, sales have not been in significant amounts. Fiscal years with high volume were 1943–45, 1950–51, 1954–55, 1958–59, and 1962–63. Sales during the 1943–45 period were consistent with the limited objectives of the Association at that time. In fact, by the end of the fiscal year 1947 the total FNMA portfolio had been reduced to less than $5 million. The selling program during 1950–51 was curtailed as a result of a change in conditions in the mortgage market. Higher interest rates on conventional mortgages, large-scale new construction commitments made by institutional investors during the fall of 1950, a decreased rate of cash inflow to institutional investors, a Treasury revision of the bond support program which resulted in a sharp reduction in the liquidation of bonds in exchange for mortgage investment—these factors shrank the market for FNMA mortgage sales. The heavier volume of sales in 1954–55 was largely the result of the Association's "one-for-one" program, inaugurated in 1953. Under this program, provided for by congressional act, FNMA was authorized to make "advance contracts to purchase" covering the purchase of eligible mortgages within one year of the contract date in a dollar amount equal to the principal amount received by FNMA from mortgages sold to private investors out of the FNMA portfolio. The one-for-one plan expired July 1, 1954. The upturn in sales activity in 1958–59, after the comparative lull during 1956 and 1957, was the result principally of the combination of two favorable circumstances. There was an increased volume of investors funds seeking long-term investment, and over a period of time FNMA had accumulated a substantial volume of well-seasoned mortgages available for immediate delivery. Again, in 1963 and 1964 there was a similar surplus of institutional funds seeking mortgage investment, and FNMA accommodated the market by extensive sales. From 1965 to date, the FNMA program has been predominantly one of acquisitions rather than sales. For example, during the calendar year 1970, the combined FNMA portfolio and outstanding purchase obligations rose from $14.5 billion on January 1 to $20.6 billion on December 31.

Administration of FNMA The board of directors of FNMA consists of 15 members, one third of whom are appointed by the President of the United States and the remainder of whom are elected by the stockholders. All terms are for one year. The presidential appointments are required to include one person each from the homebuilding, real estate, and mortgage lending industries. All directors are removable by the president, but only for good cause shown.

The chief executive officer of FNMA is its president. Other officers include a vice president, general counsel, secretary, treasurer, and controller. Because of the technical nature of the functions performed, employees are usually specialists who must meet high professional standards. The Association by its very nature, in its secondary market and other operations, must be exclusively sensitive to the national need and impervious to the exhortations of special interests if it is to fulfill its highest objectives as a supplement to the existing privately financed institutions. To assist the board of directors in its establishment of sound financial policies, in 1959 the Association established a FNMA General Advisory Committee consisting of eight representatives of the housing and home financing industries. The broad purpose of the committee is to provide advice and counsel directed toward increasing the effectiveness of FNMA in the various phases of its operations. The work is conducted out of five agency offices strategically located across the country.

Record of FNMA Through its many years as the only federal agency with common stock in the hands of private investors, FNMA stood unique. It stood apart from most governmental agencies in other respects. For example, it operated like a business, made a profit, and paid the equivalent of full corporate income taxes. It has taken a position uniformly consistent with the support of private mortgage lending. As a federal agency, it has often had to oppose clamorings for substantially easier credit for home builders on artificial terms that would thrust the U.S. government far deeper into the business of housing. Its activities in buying and selling mortgages have been dedicated to a principle of consistency in the flow of capital funds into the housing market on a free market basis, with purchases in times of credit stringency and sales in times of excess funds in the private financial institutions.

Out of its political background, the present position of respect which FNMA holds in the financial community did not come easily. Originally organized as a facility to which a seller could sell home loans if no other buyer could be found, it became a natural target for the dumping of substandard mortgages. The task was not made easier when, during the early postwar years, large amounts of additional funds were appropriated for purchase of mortgages and FNMA ended up with a portfolio designated by one lender as a $3 billion grab bag of "the worse mortgages bought at the best prices." Largely to provide a liquidation program for this portfolio and to give FNMA a new dignity, the Charter Act of 1954 was passed. This act, however, contained basic contradictions in that it provided for sound concepts of liquidation of the old portfolio and an effective secondary market program, but it also included an inflationary potential in the area of "special assistance functions," which would permit the injection of funds into the real estate market at the will of either the President or the Congress.

As the desire of the government to enter into housing subsidy became more pronounced, the necessity of splitting off the secondary market activities of FNMA from the governmental special assistance subsidy programs became clear. By creating GNMA to administer subsidy-oriented programs and permitting FNMA to maintain its past integrity in supporting the secondary mortgage market, the Housing and Urban Development Act of 1968 eliminated much of the conflict inherent in the three-directional charge imposed upon FNMA in the Charter Act of 1954. Acting in concert, FNMA and GNMA are having ever-increasing impacts on the mortgage markets.

THE GOVERNMENT NATIONAL MORTGAGE ASSOCIATION

The New Corporation When the Housing and Urban Development Act of 1968 privatized FNMA and concentrated its responsibilities on maintenance of a normal secondary market for mortgages, the law relieved the Association of its two other major functions under the 1954 Charter Act. These functions, the management and liquidating of certain previously acquired mortgages and special assistance government lending, were assigned to a newly created corporation, known as the "Government National Mortgage Corporation" (GNMA), also called "Ginnie Mae" in the industry. The new corporation was charged, in addition, with the development of a mortgage-backed securities program to attract investors into the mortgage market who up to that time had not found real estate liens sufficiently attractive. Its operations have continued to be financed in substantially the same manner as they had previously been under FNMA, through funds from the U.S. Treasury.

Management and Liquidating Functions The Charter Act of 1954 authorized FNMA to manage and liquidate the existing mortgage portfolio at the close of its former operation as of October 31, 1954. At that date, the mortgage portfolio of FNMA consisted of insured and guaranteed mortgages amounting to $2,368 million, outstanding commitments to purchase such mortgages in the amount of $603 million, and $42 million of RFC Mortgage Company direct loans and Defense Home mortgages. The aggregate of debt and commitments was $3,013 million. These amounts represented a considerable reduction from the balances owing at the original acquisition by FNMA. In fact, the principal amount of the 618,993 FHA and VA mortgages purchased pursuant to contracts entered into before the effective date of the new Charter Act of 1954 totaled $4,858 million. The balances owing on the RFC Mortgage Company direct loans and Defense Home mortgages were $105.7 million. According to the 1954 act, the total mortgages and commitments under the management and liquidating functions could not exceed those outstanding at October 31, 1954, and in no event could they be greater than $3,350 million. From the beginning of operations under these functions as defined in the 1954 act, obligations were required by law to be progressively reduced by orderly amortization until their complete liquidation. By August 1957, the purchasing phase of the management and liquidating functions had been completed as contemplated by the 1954 act and there had been a loan reduction of $686 million from the November 1, 1954 balances. In September 1959, however, Congress expanded the management and liquidating functions to authorize FNMA to purchase or make commitments to purchase, service, and sell any mortgages offered it by the Housing and Home Finance Agency (now the Department of Housing and Urban Development) where the Administrator deemed their acquisition by FNMA to be in the best interest of efficient management and liquidation. This authorization has been actively used. At December 31, 1970, the Management and Liquidating Functions portfolio, now being administered by GNMA, had a balance of $1,821 million, as compared with the balance of $3,013 million at October 31, 1954. Although it has moved upward from its lowest point, the portfolio has been reduced by 40 percent over the past 16 years. The management and liquidating functions are directed by statute to be carried out in an orderly manner with a minimum of adverse effect upon the residential mortgage market and a minimum loss to the federal government. The operations thus far have been profitable.

Special Assistance Functions In its assumption of responsibility for governmental special assistance functions, GNMA has acceded to the responsibility placed upon FNMA in the Charter Act of 1954. This act charged the Association with the obligation to provide special assistance in connection with certain residential mortgages when, and to the extent that, the president of the United States determines such assistance to be in the public interest. Under this function the Association also supports special housing programs as designated by the Congress. The special assistance program is specifically intended to meet two general needs. The first need relates to housing in underdeveloped areas. GNMA is charged with the responsibility, when the president so directs, of making financing available for selected types of residential mortgages (pending establishment of their marketability) which are originated under special housing programs designed to provide housing in areas where it cannot be provided under established home financing programs. The second great need arises when a decline in mortgage lending and home building threatens the stability of a high-level national economy.

To carry out the purposes of the special assistance functions, GNMA is authorized to purchase or enter into commitments to purchase mortgages or participations therein as directed by the president or as prescribed by law. So far as practicable, mortgages purchased under these functions must meet the purchase standards imposed by private institutional investors. The crucial factor justifying the purchase by GNMA is that, because of other circumstances surrounding the location of the property, the borrower, or economic conditions, the mortgages are not likely to be readily acceptable to private lenders.

By December 31, 1970, GNMA and its predecessor had been authorized by presidential authority to expend $4,002 million for special assistance programs deemed in the public interest. The extent and nature of these programs is shown in Table 28–1.

In addition to the special programs inaugurated by the president, the Congress has authorized GNMA to maintain three additional programs by public law. Two of these programs are extensions of special

TABLE 28–1
Special Assistance Programs under Presidential Authorization through December 31, 1970 ($000 omitted)

Program	Funds Authorized	Contracts Executed	Contracts Cancelled or Withdrawn
Disaster	$ 7,000	$ 5,298	$ 42
Guam	22,000	29,249	2,623
Urban renewal	199,000	1,084,149	337,236
Alaska (terminated)	56,975	62,049	5,074
Military and defense (terminated)	11,072	11,131	59
Consumer cooperative (terminated)	710	710	....
Elderly persons	50,000	292,532	149,196
Low cost (terminated)	1,744	2,294	550
Below-market interest rate	2,490,000	2,745,306	179,868
Experimental housing	7,236	6,884	735
Restricted Indian lands	1,000	913	154
Rent supplement	45,257	78,269	32,360
Section 235(j)	30,000	20,688	2
GNMA/FNMA tandem plan	650,000	292,950	279,161
Section 235	500,000	138,188	138,188
Liquidation recoveries on terminated programs	−69,510	....	....
Total	$4,002,484	$4,770,610	$1,125,248

Source: *1970 HUD Statistical Yearbook*, Table 97.

assistance areas initially designated by the president. The congressional programs relate to assistance in financing of cooperative housing, housing for the Armed Forces, and low- and moderate-priced housing covered by FHA or VA mortgages. A tabular summary of the results of GNMA activities under the congressional program is shown in Table 28-2.

TABLE 28–2
Cumulative Special Assistance Program Activity under Public Law through December 31, 1970 ($000 omitted)

Program	Funds Authorized	Contracts Executed	Cancelled or Withdrawn
Cooperative	$ 225,000	$ 365,691	$ 91,383
Consumer	65,150	83,337	34,987
Other	159,850	282,354	56,396
Armed services	168,342	582,737	94,753
Secs. 803 and 810	109,592	488,046	75,942
Sec. 809	58,750	94,691	18,811
Low and moderate priced (terminated)	92,213	1,000,759	157,720
Low and moderate cost	1,750,000	642,989	123,857
Total*	$2,628,897	$3,540,604	$653,849

* Footings adjusted.
Source: *1970 HUD Statistical Yearbook*, Table 97.

As with the other operations, the special assistance functions are contemplated to be fully self-supporting. Both commitment fees and purchase and marketing fees are charged. Currently, the commitment fee is 1 percent of the unpaid principal balance of the mortgage, payable when the commitment is issued; the purchase and marketing fee is ½ percent, assessed when the mortgage is delivered for purchase. The principal source of income, of course, is interest from mortgages held. Operations of the special assistance functions have resulted in a cumulative net income through June 30, 1971. Income earned is retained as a reserve for losses and contingencies.

The Mortgage-Backed Security Program GNMA is authorized by Section 306(g) of Title III of the National Housing Act to guarantee the timely payment of the principal and interest on securities that are based on or backed by a pool of mortgages insured by the FHA or Farmers Home Administration or guaranteed by the VA. The Department of Justice has rendered an opinion that the GNMA guarantee constitutes a full faith and credit obligation of the United States, and the Secretary of the Treasury has ruled that GNMA may properly borrow from the Treasury to meet its obligations under the guarantee.

The process of pool organization is initiated by a mortgage originator who becomes the issuer of the certificates. An issuer must be an FHA-approved mortgagee and GNMA seller-servicer in good standing; it must further meet a specific net worth test. FNMA and FHLMC are also active as issuers. The issuer applies to GNMA for permission to issue certificates against the mortgage pool that the issuer has assembled or expects to assemble. The aggregate value of the pool must be at least $2 million. The mortgages must meet standards of homogeneity as to type, interest rates, and maturity. For example, single-family mortgages cannot be mixed with multifamily mortgages. Furthermore, the mortgages are required to be insured or guaranteed no more than one year prior to the date on which GNMA issues its commitment to guarantee the certificates.

Upon favorable response to the issuer's application, GNMA issues a commitment to guarantee the issuer's certificates at such time as the issuer can verify that it has good title to an acceptable pool of mortgages. Documents showing proper formation of the pool are then submitted to the bank or fiduciary that is to act as custodian. Upon appropriate acknowledgment of receipt of documents by the custodian, GNMA prepares the certificates for issue.

After the certificates are issued, the issuer assumes responsibility for servicing the loans and passing through to certificate holders their proportional share of monthly interest and amortization payments. The issuers must also provide accounting statements reflecting the results of the certificate holders' participation in the pool.

In addition to the GNMA guarantee, several other features commend these certificates to the whole investment spectrum, including savings and loan associations, savings banks, credit unions, pension funds, commercial banks, insurance companies, corporations, and partnerships, as well as individuals. Although the certificate has many of the characteristics normally associated with direct investment in a first mortgage loan portfolio, it has the advantage of avoiding the management problems of loan origination and servicing. The improved marketability of the GNMA certificate over individual mortgages is a decided plus factor, particularly as the secondary market is expanding through active participation of major financial institutions. The price varies, of course, with current interest rates. Hence, if prevailing interest rates for comparable securities are lower than the face rate on the certificate, the certificate will sell at a premium; if higher, it will sell at a discount. The Internal Revenue Service has ruled that these certificates are "loans secured by an interest in real property." This ruling is of particular interest to savings and loan associations and savings banks, since it means that such certificates do not jeopardize their eligibility for special bad debt reserve deductions permitted under the Internal Revenue Code. For income tax purposes, real estate investment trusts are to treat these certificates as direct mortgage investments. The Internal Revenue Service has further held that the exempt status of employees' pension and profit-sharing funds is not adversely affected by ownership of these certificates.

Many developments of the mortgage-backed security program are taking place. For example, "serial maturities" and pools of FHA-insured mobile home loans are logical extensions. A mortgage-backed security guaranteeing the interim payments on a construction loan can assist substantially in the financing of multifamily projects.

Bond-type securities have been developed, as well, that differ from the pass-through type in that their principal is paid at maturity. These securities create a problem for the issuer when the mortgagor prepays his obligation because such prepayments must be reinvested, since they cannot be passed through. If interest rates have fallen, the issuer may be hard pressed to reinvest at a rate sufficient to keep up coupon payments at the higher rate. Issuers of such bonds must have a large enough net worth to absorb the losses that might result from changes in the money market. On May 19, 1970, regulations were announced setting a minimum net worth requirement for such issuers at $50 million. The minimum amount permitted in a single issue was set at $100 million. So far, the only issuers of the bond-type securities have been FNMA and the Federal Home Loan Mortgage Corporation.

As of the end of 1971, over $2.6 billion of the GNMA mortgage-backed "pass-through" securities had been sold. About three fourths of the sales had gone into thrift institutions. The other 25 percent had been picked up by pension funds, credit unions, and other nonmortgage-oriented investors—those for which the plan was primarily intended. It is to this latter group that GNMA is directing its especial marketing effort, to attract new money into housing rather than merely to divert funds that would already flow into the real estate financing area.

The Tandem Plan GNMA and FNMA recently instituted a new cooperative system of financing known as the "tandem plan." The program combines the GNMA guarantee with the FNMA secondary market operation to maximize the utilization of special assistance funds to aid lower income families.

By this plan, in two steps, financing is afforded nonprofit sponsors of projects providing either rent supplements or interest subsidies for lower income families. In the first step, GNMA issues a commitment to buy at par a mortgage upon completion of the qualified project. By prior arrangement, FNMA has agreed to purchase a certain amount of these mortgages at market prices. As the second step, the long-term mortgage is sold to FNMA at the market price, with GNMA making up the difference of the discount between par and the market price.

The great advantage of this arrangement is its leverage to provide government assistance. Authorities state that the tandem plan can provide as much as 30 times the financing possible if GNMA were to buy and hold the mortgages outright. This is true because the privately derived funds of FNMA actually carry the mortgage with GNMA merely absorbing the discount. A further significant point in this connection is that nonprofit sponsors could ill afford the discount that would have to be absorbed if financing were to come from outside lenders, and the project would often languish or die. As of the 1971 year-end, commitments in excess of $1 billion had been issued by GNMA under this program.

The New Philosophy in Action[1] When President Johnson praised the Housing and Urban Development Act of 1968 as "the most farsighted, the most comprehensive, the most massive housing program in all American history," he was endorsing more distinctly than had ever been done in the past a primary assumption by government of responsibility for direct housing assistance. Prior to this event, the major governmental thrust had been encouragement and reinforcement of the private home mortgage market. The 1968 act greatly expanded the government's previously sharply limited program of submarket interest loans; it liberalized FHA lending standards beyond what might be considered economically feasible by private entrepreneurs in many instances; it also created GNMA subsidy potentials which have since been greatly expanded by increased special assistance authorizations from Congress and by inauguration of the tandem plan. Augmented activities of the Federal Home Loan Bank System and the Farmers Home Administration, combined with all the other efforts, have clearly placed the federal government in a position to dominate the housing market. It is a far cry from 47,000 federally subsidized new homes in 1950 to nearly 500,000 in 1971. In percentage terms, this reflects a growth from 2.4 percent of all new housing starts in 1950 to nearly one third in 1971. The impacts on the lending and servicing institutions of such massive subsidization must not be overlooked. Added controls, higher administrative costs and responsibilities, and less room for self-determination of institutional policies are necessary concomitants. With the irregularity of congressional infusions and the whimsical nature of policies with political implications, new kinds of uncertainty are added to the usual businessman's risks. The benefits of direct subsidy in the achievement of social goals must repeatedly be weighed against the free mortgage market acting to achieve an economic allocation of resources.

QUESTIONS AND PROBLEMS

1. Review the reasons for the formation of FNMA in 1938 and the general history of its operations prior to 1954.

[1] Miles L. Colean, "Quarterly Economic Report," *The Mortgage Banker,* November 1971, pp. 37–39.

2. What were the three principal activities of FNMA under its 1954 charter? How are they now administered? What is GNMA?

3. How are the secondary market operations of FNMA financed?

4. Describe the purchasing procedures whereby FNMA acquires mortgages in connection with its secondary market operations.

5. How are mortgages acquired by FNMA serviced?

6. What has been the FNMA experience as a mortgage seller?

7. How is FNMA administered?

8. How are the GNMA management and liquidating functions financed?

9. What is the composition of the mortgage portfolio which is handled under the management and liquidating activities of GNMA?

10. How are the special assistance functions financed?

11. What type of projects qualify for special assistance from GNMA? Review those programs in which the Association is presently engaged.

12. Describe the federally insured mortgage-backed securities program as administered through GNMA. What is the "tandem plan"?

13. What is your appraisal of the prospective effectiveness of FNMA and GNMA in the federal financial assistance program for homeowners?

29

Government Financing of Real Estate

Meaning of Social Control Whenever the seriousness of any problem that involves a great many people receives general recognition, some group takes the lead in advancing a proposed solution. All such proposals which are adopted may be classified under the head of social control. The term "social control" is much misunderstood. Many people see its manifestations in terms of society acting together in its own interest. A brief glance at the manner in which social controls come into being should cause us to question this approach.

In the first place, social controls almost always undertake to place restrictions upon the practices of one or more groups in our society. In other words, except for the existence of programs that some of us dislike, there would be no need for social control. In the second place, nearly all so-called social controls that are imposed from time to time face bitter initial opposition from those against whom they are aimed. In a democracy we are inclined to ignore natural rights—if indeed there ever were any—and to let the rule of effective majorities determine the policies that govern our actions. Consequently, every attempt to impose a new social control develops into a test of political strength. Not every successful venture of this kind has either justice or logic on its side. It does, however, have enough votes to ensure its success, at least temporarily.

This suggests that, on most issues, society does not think or act as a unit. Instead, it is made up of groups that possess considerable fluidity. These groups take sides as issues that interest their members appear. Some group alignments are hard to understand. Bitter rivals on one important issue fight side by side on the next one to be decided. The reasons why several groups favor or oppose any given issue frequently lack both consistency and ready understandability. Nevertheless, group alignments and realignments account for the success or failure of proposed social controls. Apparent success in one case may be turned into certain failure if one group shifts its strength from support of the issue to opposition to it.

It is clear that social control can best be understood if we think of it as group control. Almost always it involves the repression of the ambitions of one group in the interests of another segment of society. It will be well to keep this point of view in mind throughout this chapter.

Social Control and Land Ownership The group concept of social control developed in the field of land ownership as soon as the growth of cities made necessary the creation of codes for mutual protection against practices that cause much less concern in rural areas. When we speak of "ownership of land," this term is best understood as meaning a bundle of rights. Ordinarily we think of the paramount rights of land ownership as the right of possession, the right of quiet enjoyment, and the right of disposition.

In urban communities particularly, real estate ownership has long since lost any connotation of absolute rights to do with one's own as the titleholder sees fit. Property may not be used in a manner to jeopardize the health and safety of neighbors or to create nuisances. Even the normal rights of possession, quiet enjoyment, and disposition are subject to definite limitations whenever the dominant groups in a community decide that a political unit needs the property for public uses. While compensation is awarded when eminent domain is exercised, it is the dominant groups, rather than the owner of the property, that decide the use to which the property shall be put.

This concept of limitation of rights in real property finds expression in many ways. Building codes, zoning ordinances, control over subdivision activity, use restrictions, fair housing laws, are all imposed for the purpose of protecting some groups against practices of others that the articulate majority consider to be undesirable. Many of the practices against which controls are aimed are not the results of studied efforts to take advantage of anybody. Like Topsy, they "just grew." In more sparsely settled areas they may still be tolerated because they encroach upon the plans of neighbors less seriously. Most of the controls which affect land ownership stem from urbanization and its problems. As greater concentration of population takes place, the tendency will be further to restrict private rights in land ownership.

Urban Redevelopment We sometimes think of city planning as something new. All cities have been planned. They were planned in terms of the anticipation of future needs that was current at each stage of each city's development. The inadequacies of such planning become apparent when the rate of growth exceeds expectations. Because of these inadequacies, not only buildings, but whole districts, become obsolete. The pattern of city streets, the distribution of real estate uses, the character of buildings, and so on, all need replanning. As a consequence, present insistence upon urban redevelopment programs is not limited to the replacement of obsolete individual buildings with bigger and better skyscrapers. Instead, it contemplates the replanning of considerable areas, with abandonment of street patterns and their replacement with more modern means of transportation and communication; greater attention to a proper balance of real estate uses; consideration for public uses; and so forth.

The need for urban redevelopment testifies to the dynamic nature of the problem of American city change. Careful study of this problem must result in a recognition of the paradoxical nature of much of our thinking about city planning. For example, we place great emphasis upon the need for "master" plans. This connotes a finality which is possible only under static conditions. But so long as a city remains dynamic, characterized by fundamental changes which cannot always be anticipated very far in advance, planning must necessarily be a continuous operation. Technological changes combine with social preferences and aggressive salesmanship to confuse and confound those who would establish a "fix" for any urban community pattern. Even international relations intrude their uneasy potentialities upon the otherwise peaceful horizons of city life in ways which may help to dictate future urban patterns.

The above analysis does not negate the need for prompt and continuous attention to the problems of urban redevelopment. It should erase from our minds any lingering hope that what we do now will serve for all time to come as the final answer to the problems which we face. If we can do a reasonable job in meeting the issues of our generation, we can leave to those who follow us the task of changing our results in a manner that will best meet the requirements of their time. We are changing what our forefathers did in their day. What reason is there to expect that similar changes will not be needed after we have done our best to fashion what we consider to be modern cities? What we inherited was once modern. It has become the yesterday of today. Today must inevitably become the yesterday of tomorrow.

Approaches to Redevelopment Programs In general, there are three approaches to urban redevelopment programs:

1. Private enterprise is relied upon to assemble the land necessary for a redevelopment project; demolish existing structures; replan the real estate uses in the area; and construct the buildings needed to supply these uses. In assembling and replanning plats, it may be necessary to endow private corporations with some public powers. For example, in order to acquire all land needed, some owners may refuse to sell

except at holdup prices. What amounts to the power of eminent domain may be needed to induce them to sell their properties at a fair price. If a new street pattern is needed, this must have public sanction.

2. An alternative plan places the responsibility for land assembly upon the shoulders of local public authorities, such as municipalities or local housing authorities created by them. Land so assembled is then made available for redevelopment, under supervision by the local instrumentality, by private interests. Such land may be either sold or leased for this purpose. In either event, its use pattern, the construction standards needed to make it effective, and so on, are all specified by public agencies. This plan may involve a subsidy. The price paid for the land—whether purchased at private sale or under condemnation—may be more than it can be rented or sold for. In such case the difference must be made up from tax moneys.

3. Under the third plan, not only the assembly of the land, but the construction of buildings thereon, is the responsibility of public agencies. This plan necessarily involves subsidies of one kind or another. The two kinds most commonly used are capital grants and annual operating subsidies. Both types of subsidies are discussed later in this chapter.

America's Housing Problems Years ago, Jacob Riis dramatized the evils of slum dwellings in America's largest city. No one disbelieved him. Most of his readers felt no personal affiliations with the conditions described, because they did not live in New York City. It has only been in recent years that America has become really housing conscious. As a result of a variety of circumstances, we have come to appreciate that not only New York City, but our own town as well, has housing problems. Curiously enough there exists a surprising unanimity of opinion on the subject of desirable housing objectives, at least when we talk in general terms. Sound health, safety, good morals, and the promotion of the general welfare of all American families have universal approval. At least opponents—if there be any—are inarticulate and make no outcry against these objectives.

Also, it is quite commonly admitted that there is a relationship between housing and health, safety, morals, and general welfare. Beyond this point, groups and individuals quickly come to the parting of the ways. Just what the relationship is and how it may be improved do not respond to common definitions. Most attempts even at establishing boundaries quickly develop violent oppositions. For example, just what are the limits of "general welfare," and how much of it can be traced to the kind of housing facilities enjoyed by those who are the objects of study?

In the absence of accepted standards on which to base arguments for and against specific housing programs, it is little wonder that the same words used by different groups carry different connotations. Terms like "substandard housing conditions," "high cost of shelter," "slums," "blighted areas," "decent housing environment," and "unstable housing markets" invite endless arguments when they are marshaled for defense or attack. Seldom are they the focus of impartial analysis, because emotions too often rule out logic. One of the greatest obstacles to a meeting of minds, even on definitions of terms to be used in argument, is the presence of fixed and immovable opinions held by those who are most interested in the subject of housing. In addition to such questions as cost, sanitation, environment, and fluctuating markets, one of our biggest housing problems is our failure to agree upon the foundation stones of any verbal structure required to discuss the subject.

Amount of Substandard Housing There is no general agreement on the number of substandard housing units in this country. Published estimates have varied from 2 to 12 million, or more. This wide disparity is a reflection of the lack of agreement on the definition of "substandard." The distribution of substandard units—regardless of the means of identification used—is uneven throughout the country. Some cities suffer from a larger proportion than others. None is free from some poor housing. Rural areas also are afflicted with ill-housed families. Even if we had an accurate census, based upon complete agreement about the kinds of units to include, the resulting number would serve only temporary purposes, because our ideas about what constitutes substandard housing are constantly changing. Few would deny that, whatever the exact number is, it is larger than it should be in a country possessing the wealth and productive capacity of America.

Reliance upon Private Capital For the most part, private capital has, until recent years, been relied upon to provide housing for all American families. It is generally admitted that the provision of new housing facilities for families in the lowest income groups has never attracted adequate private capital. Instead, used houses have filtered down to these groups. Not only houses, but whole neighborhoods, have been afflicted with blight, have lost their appeal for other reasons, or through the mere passage of time have become less desirable to those who formerly occupied them. Successive waves of classes of occupants have taken their turns at living in them. Eventually, absentee ownership becomes more interested in income from such properties than in maintaining their amenities.

It must not be assumed that all slum areas consist of makeshift houses built near city dumps from the remains of packing boxes deposited there as waste. On the contrary, many slum areas once housed the aristocracy of the city. The materials and workmanship which created these structures are frequently far superior to what is being used currently in many new housing projects. Through neglect, waste, and even vandalism these well-built old houses have become almost unlivable in many instances.

One proposal that has been urged from time to time as one means of solving this angle of our housing problems is to establish minimum standards of health and safety and to measure every housing unit by these standards. If the owner of any unit fails to meet decent requirements within a reasonable time, his property should be closed to further use until he sees fit to rehabilitate it as directed. The experience of Baltimore is an outstanding example of what can be done by this means. It is probable that existing authority is already present in most cities to force such structural changes, if it should be applied firmly. Various types of pressures operate to prevent the application of existing police power over unsafe and unsanitary housing conditions. Owners of properties affected are not enthusiastic about expending the money needed for such rehabilitation programs. Had they fully approved such changes, they probably would have effected them voluntarily, thus making compulsion by a public agency unnecessary.

Another source of pressure against the use of existing police power to close housing units which do not measure up to minimum standards is the absence of a surplus of housing accommodations. If any substantial number of units were closed for this reason, their occupants might find it difficult to secure substitute facilities. Had there been an available surplus renting for amounts that the occupants of slum areas could afford to pay, the use of police power might not be needed. The owners of substandard housing units would be under pressure to rehabilitate their properties as the price of securing tenants.

Past Private Subsidies Housing subsidies are not new. They have assumed new characteristics in recent years, but in one form or another we have had them for generations. Of the two forms that have been most common in the past, one has received relatively little recognition. It is properly described as private subsidy. Over the years a great many property owners have tolerated rent delinquencies and have accepted inadequate incomes from their investments from those tenants unable to pay an economic rent for the facilities made available to them. Probably there has been a great deal more of this type of housing subsidy than has ever been publicized.

Cause and effect become confused easily in the discussion of private housing subsidies. The obsolete character of the property limits its use to those who cannot afford to live in better surroundings. This lowers the value of and the income potential from properties in slum areas. The low and uncertain rents in turn provide inadequate funds from which to keep the properties adequately maintained and to leave any return upon the investment in them. Consequently the failure to maintain such properties has resulted in further declines in value and in income potentials. Unconscionably heavy tax burdens have not offered much relief to landlords who own housing units in slum areas. Because such properties are frequently situated on the fringes of business districts, taxes are assessed as if the land devoted to housing low-income families were already being devoted to commercial or industrial uses.

It is easy to point to investments in slum properties that have paid their owners high rates of return. The number of instances of private subsidies in such areas is also undoubtedly large. In some cases, owners have accepted inadequate rents because they hesitate to dispossess families that cannot meet their obligations. In other cases, the owner has been content to accept less than an economic return upon his investment, pending the happening of a hoped-for miracle. He has retained his investment in the housing unit while he waited for the appearance of someone willing to pay enough for the land for a higher and better use to offset the loss of income from the housing facilities. In a discouraging number of cases, such a miracle never happens. To be sure, this is the speculative chance which the owner takes. But his tenants meantime are being subsidized by him.

Another type of private subsidy that has received little attention is the financial assistance given to families in need by friends and relatives. Among certain racial and religious groups in particular, there has long been great pride in programs which have resulted in caring for members of their groups in need of assistance. Family pride has been a powerful source in keeping members from applying for public assistance under any circumstances. Private charities—organized and unorganized—have played major parts in providing housing subsidies.

Past Public Subsidies Whatever the reasons, most communities include a varying number of families who are unable, temporarily or permanently, to pay an economic rent for housing accommodations. Some are unable to pay any rent. Others can pay something but not enough to secure adequate housing facilities. In the past, this problem has been met in part by governmental subsidies at the local level. The public treasury has borne the burden of rent payments. Without any long-range policy on the subject, each case has been considered as it arose, with the rent being one of the items which local authorities provided along with food, fuel, clothing, and so forth.

This type of subsidy was handed out on a charity basis. Only the handicapped sought its benefits. Except for the occasional indigent family headed by a philosopher who had reached the conclusion that the world owed him a living, an appeal to a public agency for financial assistance to pay for housing costs was resorted to only when all other possible sources of assistance had been exhausted. Some families whose handicap consisted of the temporary loss of a job for the breadwinner considered even public assistance to be a loan, to be repaid when good fortune smiled again.

While the burden of local public rent subsidies has been heavy in times past, particularly in periods of economic depression, it has been lightened by the mental attitudes of most people, who looked upon the acceptance of public charity as a form of disgrace and an admission of incompetency. Undoubtedly it would have been much greater if people had been encouraged to believe that their government insisted upon helping all who needed or desired financial assistance.

Public Subsidy Formulas During the depression of the 1930s, construction of public housing was advanced as a relief measure. It was sponsored as a means of public employment of people who had lost private jobs. The formula presented as the prerequisite for securing public moneys for this purpose was quite complicated. Since it involved contributions of one kind or another by local communities which were to gain an advantage from it, these communities must first be authorized to accept proffered assistance. This called for enabling legislation, since none of the states had anticipated the need for joint participation of local and federal governmental agencies in such ventures.

Although two thirds of the states hastened to pass the necessary legislation to enable their communities to obtain a share of federal grants for relief housing projects, fumbling and confusion prevented both the ill-fated NRA and the WPA from accomplishing any significant results in this area. Meantime the sponsors of federal participation in housing construction for low-income groups persisted in pushing their programs in Congress. By 1937 they succeeded in securing the adoption of a new housing formula which shifted the emphasis from relief to reform.

In that year Congress established the U.S. Housing Authority. After a change of name in 1942, and after absorbing several other agencies concerned with public housing, it became the Public Housing Administration of the Federal Housing and Home Finance Agency, established by executive order in 1947. Its chief function has been to administer loans and grants by the federal government to local housing agencies throughout the country. The scope of its operations has been determined by the amount of money Congress has seen fit to appropriate for these purposes.

With respect to the potential operations of the PHA (now the Housing Assistance Administration), there are two schools of thought. One would have all decisions made at the federal level. The timing, the location, and the amount of public housing would be determined in Washington. The other school contends that all policy-making decisions should be made at the local level. If in a given locality those in authority should decide that private construction, using the filtering down process, will reasonably meet the housing needs, well and good. If this should require repressive action against owners of substandard housing units to force their rehabilitation, that too should be decided at the local level, according to this formula. The amount, if any, the location, and the timing of public housing to supplement the results of private construction should also be determined by local housing authorities.

These two alternatives have been before Congress in various forms since 1937. Both require subsidies from both the local and the federal government. The former is required to contribute land, services, money, or its equivalent in the form of tax exemption of some kind. The latter is expected to make both capital grants and annual contributions to absorb operating deficits. In order to provide new housing accommodations for families that cannot pay an economic rent on even used housing units, two things are necessary: (1) Capital must be provided for construction costs. (2) Since by definition the occupants are not expected to pay their own way, someone must absorb deficits. Uncle Sam is the source of funds on both counts.

Change in Emphasis The principles upon which public housing programs are founded cause a complete shift in emphasis on the subject of housing subsidies. Instead of reluctant acceptance of such assistance as a desperation measure when no other alternative is available—as was largely true when announced housing subsidies, both public and private, were looked upon as gestures of charity—many people are coming to consider decent and adequate housing a right of all American families, whether an individual family can afford to pay the bill or not.

Those with an opposing point of view look upon this change of emphasis as a vindication of the philosophy of the exceptional indigent householder who years ago accepted charitable assistance with enthusiasm because he had reached the conclusion that the world owed him a living. During his day the great majority of his fellow citizens believed that they must earn what the world paid them. If the ideas of the indigent philosopher should become commonly accepted by a great segment of the community, will the effect be to chill or even to kill the incentive for individual responsibility for one's own welfare? If Uncle Sam displays an inclination to care for our needs, will we be willing to sit back and enjoy the handouts without expending too much effort to earn them? Questions like these trouble the opponents of housing subsidies on a project basis.

Housing Act of 1949 The present federal housing program of slum clearance and housing for low-income families had a major part of its beginnings in the Housing Act of 1949. This law formalizes a "Declaration of National Housing Policy" which reads, in part, as follows:

> The Congress hereby declares that the general welfare and security of the Nation and the health and living standards of its people require housing production and related community development sufficient to remedy the serious housing shortage, the elimination of substandard and other inadequate

housing through the clearance of slums and blighted areas, and the realization as soon as feasible of the goal of a decent home and a suitable living environment for every American family.

As an expression of a desirable goal, the above declaration would probably be opposed by no one. In working toward the attainment of the objective of "a decent home and a suitable living environment for every American family," the law outlines the steps to be included in the following terms: (1) Private enterprise shall be encouraged to serve as large a part of the total need as it can. (2) The government shall assist private enterprise to serve more of the total need. (3) Local public bodies shall be assisted and encouraged to undertake programs of developing "well-planned, integrated residential neighborhoods, the development and redevelopment of communities, and the production, at lower costs, of housing of sound standards of design, construction, livability, and size for adequate family life." (4) Governmental assistance will be available for the elimination of substandard and other inadequate housing through the clearance of slums and blighted areas. Such assistance will be available also to provide "adequate housing for urban and rural nonfarm families with incomes so low that they are not being decently housed in new or existing housing." (5) Governmental assistance is to be extended to provide farmers with "decent, safe, and sanitary farm dwellings and related facilities" where private financial arrangements are out of the reach of farm owners.

While the above recitation of procedures starts with a reference to the part to be played by private enterprise, it is quite evident that those primarily responsible for drafting this law were most interested in the participation by the federal government. No legislation is required to encourage private enterprise to do what it can to provide housing accommodations for our people. For generations, private enterprise has been busy providing housing facilities for all American families. They have not all been new structures, nor have they always measured up to the standards described in this law. It is necessary to pass laws to implement the remaining features of this act. After stating step number 1 above, the law concerns itself with the other four steps.

Housing Act of 1954 Although the concept of "urban renewal" was incorporated in the 1949 housing act, the program moved slowly in its initial stages. New federal assistance in planning and financing was provided by the Housing Act of 1954, and the urban renewal program stands today as an effective tool whereby individual communities can curtail the spread of blight into good areas, rehabilitate areas where existing properties can be restored, and clear away slum structures and replace them with desirable housing where no other form of reclamation is satisfactory.

Administration of the Federal Housing and Urban Development Program The agency principally responsible for the housing and urban development activities of the federal government is the Department of Housing and Urban Development (HUD). Its head is designated as "Secretary," and he serves as a member of the President's Cabinet. The Department was created in 1965 to extend and intensify the activities and programs of the Housing and Home Finance Agency. The scope of the department activities is indicated by a schematic portrayal of administrative subdivisions:

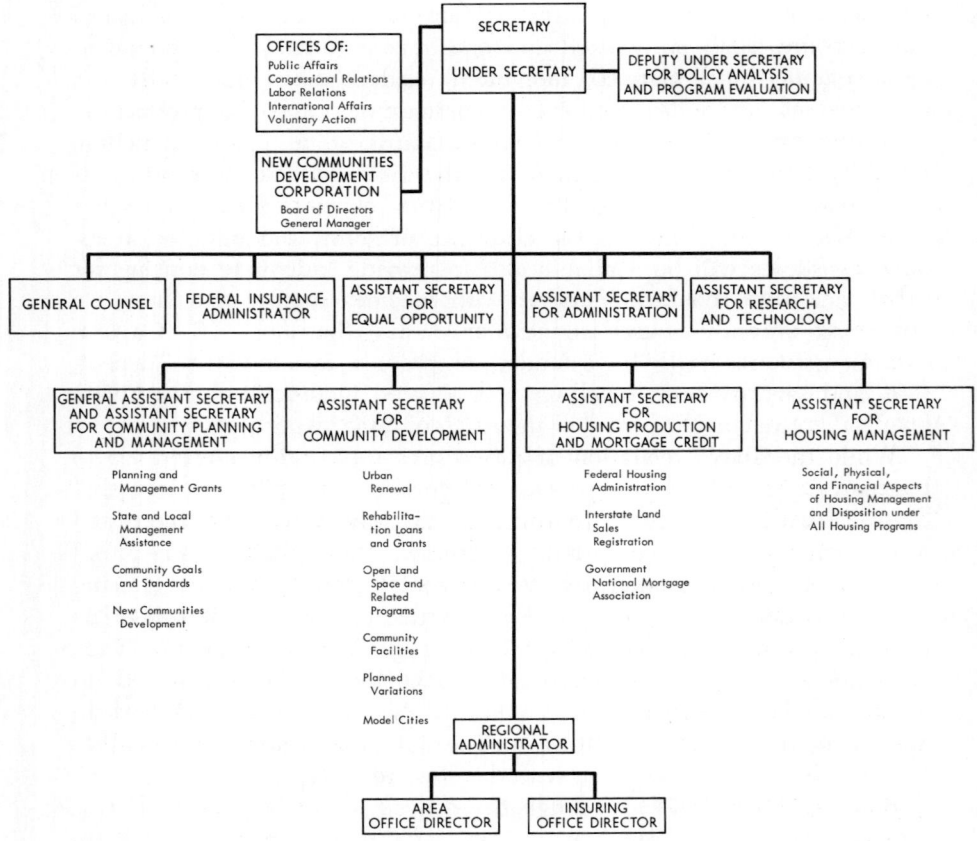

Certain federal housing and home finance activities have been delegated to other departments. The Department of Agriculture operates the farm housing program authorized under Title V of the Housing Act of 1949. The Department of Defense is responsible for certifying the need for military housing financed by mortgages insured under the federal program or for the provision of family housing where necessary in the interests of national defense. The Atomic Energy Commission handles the certification of the need for housing for its personnel at AEC establishments where mortgages financing the housing are to be FHA-insured. The Small Business Administration makes loans to victims of disasters so that they may restore their damaged homes or buy or build new ones. It also assists small businesses in becoming reestablished where they have suffered substantial economic injury as result of displacement by an urban-renewal program or similar governmental project. The Departments of Commerce and Labor are of particular assistance to the national housing program in providing housing and construction statistics and in setting standards for construction materials and labor.

Office of the Assistant Secretary for Community Development Since March 1, 1971, all community development programs have been under the Assistant Secretary for Community Development. These include:

1. Urban renewal—loans and grants
2. General neighborhood renewal plans—grants
3. Community renewal programs—grants
4. Code enforcement projects—grants
5. Rehabilitation—loans and grants
6. Neighborhood facilities—grants
7. Open space land—grants
8. Urban beautification
9. Model or demonstration cities programs—loans or grants

Urban Renewal Urban renewal begins with the community itself. It is based on local plans and resources. The community must survey its total problem and work out in detail a plan for dealing with it. When this plan meets the standards which qualify the community for federal aid, it is known as a "workable program." To have a plan certified as a workable program by HUD, the community must commit itself to the attainment of the following seven objectives:

1. Adequate local codes and ordinances, effectively enforced
2. A comprehensive plan for development of the community
3. Analysis of blighted neighborhoods to determine treatment needed
4. Adequate administrative organization to carry out urban renewal programs
5. Ability to meet financial requirements
6. Responsibility for rehousing adequately families displaced by urban renewal and other governmental activities
7. Citizen participation

A major responsibility of the Assistant Secretary for Community Development is the administration of federal loan and grant aids to communities to further planning and completion of urban renewal projects. His office allocates the funds for local use and establishes policies and procedures to be followed by urban renewal specialists on HUD regional staffs. Under the 1949 housing act, federal aid was virtually limited to clearance of badly blighted and slum areas. Under the 1954 act, eligibility for federal assistance was considerably expanded. Projects may extend to areas that need planned rehabilitation only. Thus, urban renewal programs today may involve either rehabilitation or clearance and redevelopment, or both.

Financial Assistance Although federal assistance is available in the form of advisory service, by far the most important aid is financial. Financial aid is designed to prepare the way for private investment by subsidizing the costs of making urban renewal projects ready for redevelopment. Federal funds may be used only for this purpose. Once the project area is cleared, the land is sold to private investors or to public agencies—anyone who will agree and can demonstrate a capability to redevelop the area in accordance with the urban renewal plan. The principal federal financial aids are of three general types. The aid may be an advance for the purposes of financing surveys and feasibility studies in connection with preliminary planning for urban renewal. Or it may take the form of a temporary loan to the community to finance property acquisitions in the slum areas and to defray the costs of clearance and other preparations for redevelopment or rehabilitation. The third type of financial assistance has been designated as a capital grant. The purpose of this grant has been to aid the local community in making up the difference between the cost of acquiring and preparing the area for redevelopment or rehabilitation and the total amount recovered from the sale of the cleared land to individuals, corporations, or public agencies for new construction under the urban renewal plan. By capital grant, the federal government assumes two thirds of this difference between costs and recoveries. The other one third must be paid by the community in the form of cash, property, or services rendered. If the community, however, elects to pay all costs of planning, surveys, and administration of the plan, it can obtain a three-fourths capital grant from the federal government.

One of the prerequisites of urban renewal is that the local public agency must offer families displaced by the projects decent, safe, and sanitary housing at prices and rents within their means. In addition, grants are made available to communities to reimburse site residents and businesses forced out of urban-renewal areas for their moving expenses and direct losses of property. Payments to families and individuals are made up to $200. For businesses the payment has been limited to $3,000 for moving expenses and loss of property; however, where actual moving expenses alone, incurred after October 1, 1962, are greater than $3,000, the maximum relocation payment to a business concern may be the total actual moving expenses or $25,000, whichever is less, with no allowance for loss of property. The 1964 Housing Act provided for additional payments upon relocation of displaced persons and certain businesses. To displaced families and elderly individuals (62 or over), a relocation adjustment payment was authorized equal to the difference between the average monthly rental required for standard housing and 20 percent of the monthly income of the displaced family or elderly individual. The total payment authorized is the amount of money required to make up the monthly difference for a period of 12 months, but not to exceed $500. Displaced business concerns with average annual earnings of less than $10,000 may receive an additional relocation payment of $1,500. This additional payment is available, however, only for businesses which are not a part of an establishment outside the urban renewal area.

At the end of 1970, there were 2,090 approved renewal projects in 974 communities in 47 states, Guam, Puerto Rico, the Virgin Islands, and the District of Columbia. More than 70 percent of the communities participating were under 50,000 in population.

Urban Renewal under Neighborhood Development Programs Recent experience has taught that it is not always best to deal with blight in terms of complete treatment of small areas one at a time. Large communities often have areas with broadly distributed deterioration. Programs of larger magnitude are often indicated, encompassing several urban renewal areas and over a longer span of years.

In the Housing and Urban Development Act of 1968, a new neighborhood development program was enacted into law to deal with the larger problems on an effective basis. Under the new act, the contract for loan or capital grant for the annual increment of a program can cover activities in several contiguous or noncontiguous urban renewal areas. The funding will be based on the amount of funds needed to carry out the activities planned for a 12-month period in each of the urban renewal areas in the community program. There is no obligation to fund beyond the immediate year for which a contract is effective, but, if funds are available, the community can anticipate receiving continuing financial suport in subsequent years for acceptable programs. Plans governing the physical activities will be flexible, often permitting rehabilitation activities to proceed along with public improvements, and detailed planning may proceed simultaneously with actual development in the area.

The costs of neighborhood development programs are financed like urban renewal projects, except that net project costs may be calculated on the basis of costs incurred and proceeds derived for the account of the program during the specified year period, and may be recalculated for successive annual periods to reflect additional costs and proceeds. If property has been acquired but not disposed of prior to the computation or recomputation of the net project cost, temporary federal loans made to finance these activities may remain outstanding until the property is disposed of and the proceeds from such disposition or from other sources available to the program are sufficient to permit repayment of the loans. If the proceeds from the sale of the land by the public agency and the land retained by it for use in accordance with the urban renewal plan exceed the total project cost for any annual period, the local agency must pay to the Secretary of HUD two thirds of the excess, or three fourths in case the program is on that grant basis.

This new program does not imply the elimination of the earlier approach to urban renewal with more formalized planning and area designation. The earlier approach is still necessary where significant changes in land use require assurance that the project is thoroughly and completely planned and undertaken as a single enterprise.

Long-Term Leasing in Urban Renewal In some instances, cities engaged in urban renewal projects have not sold the land to developers, but have leased it instead. Baltimore; Philadelphia; Washington, D.C.; New Haven, Connecticut; Murfreesboro, Tennessee; and possibly others have employed long-term leases. If granted a tenure at least as long as the economic lives of the structures to be erected, builders will become interested in leasing as well as buying. The terms of such leases run from 30 to 99 years, some with and some without purchase options.

The federal government will make its capital grant under the lease arrangement as well as where there is a sale. When the land is leased, the sale price is determined as the capitalized rental value. From the standpoint of the city, it can gain from a leasing procedure if it can carry the land at a money and administration cost less than the rental paid by a lessee-redeveloper. For example, assume that a redeveloper can afford a rental equal to 6 or 7 percent of the capitalized leasehold value over the life of the proposed improvement. Borrowing costs to the municipality to carry the land will normally range between 3 and 5 percent. Management expenses should not exceed 0.5 percent of the capitalized leasehold value. Thus, under the least profitable projection, the city would make 0.5 percent annually (6 percent minus 5.5 percent) and under the most profitable it might make as much as 3.5 percent (7 percent minus 3.5 percent).

Under appropriate conditions, the redeveloper may also find leasing more desirable than purchase. Leasing enables him to gain control of the land without dissipation of his equity capital. If this advantage is not lost by less favorable terms for construction financing, he may prefer to lease. Most lenders, however, will require higher mortgage amortizations and larger down payments on mortgages on leaseholds, irrespective of the term of the lease.[1]

FHA Assistance in Urban Renewal Provisions of the Housing Acts of 1954 and 1961 broadening FHA functions gave added impetus to the urban renewal program. These provisions (Sections 220 and 221 of Title II) extended mortgage insurance programs to urban renewal conditions where financing of private housing construction or improvement might not otherwise be feasible.

Section 220 provides mortgage insurance on liberal terms to finance rehabilitation or new construction of housing under certified urban renewal plans. It may also be used to assist in financing new sales or rental housing, on single or multifamily structures, in areas certified to the FHA by HUD. Section 220 (h) provides specifically for FHA-insured home improvement loans on properties in urban renewal project areas. These loans may be as low as $1,000 and may not exceed $10,000 per dwelling unit. The maturity may be as long as 20 years, but not more than three fourths of the remaining life of the property.

Section 221 grants similar benefits to private financing of low-cost relocation housing for sale or rent. Under this section, satisfactory housing, either through existing or new construction, can be provided to families who are displaced by urban renewal programs. When a community has been certified for urban renewal, contractors may then apply through mortgage lenders to the FHA for commitments to insure Section 221 loans. These commitments will not be granted in a number greater than the number of units certified for the community. Unlike Section 220 loans, which require some down payment, Section 221 loans may be made in amounts equaling 100 percent of the FHA-appraised value, with maxima ranging from $18,000 to $24,000 per dwelling. These loans are available to mortgagors who become occupants of either new or rehabilitated existing construction. If the mortgagor does not become an occupant, the mortgage may not exceed 85 percent of the appraised value. The maximum mortgage maturity is 40 years. The scope of Section 221 actually extends beyond urban renewal. It also applies where families are displaced by any form of government action, as where the property is taken under eminent domain proceedings or eviction is pursuant to a building code. Under Section 221 (d) (3), a below-market, or low-interest rate, rental housing program is provided not only for displaced families, but also for other low and moderate income families. The effect of this program is discussed in subsequent paragraphs relating to middle-income housing.

---

[1] For a detailed study of this and related problems, see "Long-Term Leasing in Urban Renewal: An Alternative Method of Municipal Land Disposition," *The Yale Law Journal*, June 1959, pp. 1924–58.

Other FHA programs which have proven useful in urban renewal have been financing of management-type cooperative housing under Section 213, assistance in providing housing for the elderly under Section 231, and home improvement loans on homes outside of urban renewal project areas under Section 203 (k), where refinancing of existing mortgages on the property is not required.

The great benefit derived from FHA insurance in connection with urban renewal has been in the creation of a national market for the mortgages arising out of the process. Improved financing conditions have automatically activated the market for the houses, both existing and newly constructed. By virtue of the federal underwriting, these mortgages are eligible for purchase by FNMA. Funds were specifically allocated by the federal government to FNMA for such purchase under "special assistance functions." In the early phases of the urban renewal program, the great bulk of Section 220 and 221 financing was provided by FNMA. It is the chief financial sponsor for the three major programs for "housing for low and moderate income families":

1. The rent supplement program provided for by Section 221 (d) (3)
2. The interest subsidy program provided for in Section 236, under which the government makes monthly payments to the owner of an apartment in -order to keep the rents down to levels which families of modest means can afford
3. A homeownership program provided for in Section 235, under which the government pays part of the monthly interest charge on the mortgage and the buyer pays the rest

Generally speaking, people who qualify for these kinds of programs have low enough incomes to qualify for a "public housing project," but in some instances their income may exceed the public housing level by as much as 35 percent. During the recent period of high interest rates, there has been practically no other source of funds for financing projects of this kind. In 1970, FNMA issued commitments to buy $3.2 billion of mortgages on these projects. This financing provided over 200,000 living units, or more than 90 percent of all the assisted housing initiated or contracted during the year.

During the 1960s, private sponsorship emerged in many localities. In addition to local businessmen, well-known industrial firms provided support in cities where they found special interests—for example, in Pittsburgh and Cleveland, the United States Steel Company; in Newport News, the Chesapeake & Ohio R. R.; in the Philadelphia area, Scott Paper; in Birmingham, Monsanto Chemical; in Chicago, Commonwealth Edison; in Battle Creek, Ralston-Purina; in Fargo, Northwestern Bell Telephone; in Baltimore, Sheraton Corp.; and in Oakland, Safeway Stores. Several insurance companies have assumed important roles, as Prudential, in Chicago and Boston; the Travelers, in Hartford; New

York Life, in New York and Chicago; Metropolitan Life, in New York; and Mutual Benefit Life, in Newark. From 1960 through 1963, Aluminum Company of America invested over $29 million in 18,707 apartments and 562 town houses as part of urban renewal projects in seven cities.[2]

Meeting the requirements of real estate development during the 1970s will require a close working relationship between government and the large corporations. The rise of modular housing, the integration of land development in contrast to previous piecemeal development, and the requirements for mass transit plans and facilities call for a merging of large aggregations of private capital and government and public interests. The National Association of Homebuilders predicts that by 1975 more than 50 percent of all new homes built in the United States will be manufactured types—panelized, sectionalized, and modular. The land requirements, where the new home buyers are now demanding open space, landscaping, and recreational facilities, as well as shopping centers, schools, and churches, become increasingly hard to meet. Expeditious transportation is the key to success of the new town or trade area of whatever sort.

To date, private investors have had to learn much from experience. Lack of local leadership with the necessary stamina to complete the projects has been a serious shortcoming. Some investors have expressed dissatisfaction with limitations imposed to secure the benefits of the FHA insurance, and they recommend that Congress raise the loan-to-value ratio limits for conventional institutional mortgage loans. Construction delays, proximity to slums, and long rent-up periods have all contributed to upsets in long-range plans for many projects.

There have been, however, several outstanding examples of Section 220 and 221 projects financed exclusively or largely with private capital. The 600-acre "Southwest Redevelopment Area" of Washington, D.C.; the multimillion dollar middle-income housing project in Chicago, "Prairie Shores," with five 19-story buildings containing 342 apartments each; the "Capitol Hill Redevelopment Program" in Nashville, Tennessee: extensive projects such as these indicate an appeal to large investors who believe they can benefit from the liberal mortgage insurance provisions.

General Neighborhood Renewal Plans Community planning in preparation for urban renewal activities is of two types—general neighborhood renewal planning and specific project planning. General neighborhood renewal planning is undertaken when an area to be renewed is of such size that renewal activities may have to be spread over a period of up to eight years, and planning for the entire area is desirable

---

[2] J. Richard Elliott, Jr., "Opportunities in Blight," *The Mortgage Banker*, December 1961; Robert J. Beran in *The Mortgage Banker* for July, August, September, and October 1959; and see also Karl G. Pearson, "Real Estate in 1980 Will Be a New Ball Game," *Real Estate Review*, Vol. 1, No. 3 (Fall 1971), pp. 48–53.

in advance of planning and carrying out specific projects. Planning for particular projects is concerned with such matters as eligibility and feasibility, boundaries of the renewal area, proposed new land uses, and preparations for relocation, land acquisition, site clearance and improvement, land disposition, and other necessary operations. Costs of both types of planning are defrayed from funds that become available in the form of federal planning advances when specific projects are undertaken.

To stimulate the interest of private enterprise, and particularly mortgage lenders, in urban renewal the federal assistance program makes available special "demonstration project grants." These grants defray as much as two thirds of the cost of pilot projects designed to improve techniques for the elimination of slums. For example, such a project was designed for Baltimore to test the feasibility of rehabilitation in a one-block zone of the Harlem Park urban renewal area. The testing sought a determination of how property values would be affected by carrying out the urban renewal plan; to what degree obsolescence could be overcome by remodeling; the adequacy of federal and other financing arrangements; and whether property owners and tenants would participate in rehabilitation on a voluntary basis.

Another form of federal assistance has been directed at providing funds for effective urban planning in less populous areas without regard to an urban renewal program. For municipalities of less than 50,000, "grants for urban planning assistance" may be authorized. These grants are available to state planning agencies in such localities, and the funds may be utilized to defray as much as half of the total costs of the projects for which the grants are made. Similar grants are available to state or local planning agencies for planning work in (1) metropolitan or regional areas and (2) areas confronted with the prospect of rapid urbanization because of establishment or expansion of a federal installation, as well as for certain other planning work.

Community Renewal Programs Federal grants are available to pay up to two thirds of the cost incurred in preparing a community renewal program of a scope to meet a full range of local needs. Such a program approaches the problems of blight on a total, rather than piecemeal, basis. All the deteriorated and declining areas of the city can be identified and classified as to the urgency and type of remedy required. Community resources for supporting urban renewal action—for financing, relocating displaced families, utilizing cleared land, and carrying to completion a unitized program—can be determined. The community can develop a long-range program incorporating related public improvements, balancing its needs against its total resources. It can establish priorities and schedule activities over a longer period of time than would otherwise be feasible.

At the end of 1966, grants of $27.3 million to 164 communities had been approved to utilize this method of outlining a staged program for renewal. By early 1971, 271 communities were engaged in this activity with approved grants of over $58.2 million.

Code Enforcement Since 1965, the federal government has subsidized code enforcement activities. Grants are available to cities and counties to defray part of the cost of concentrated code enforcement programs in designated areas. The prerequisites to federal assistance require that:

1. The local agency must have a workable program for community improvement currently in effect and must have adopted a comprehensive system of codes that meets certain minimum standards. These codes must be under current enforcement.
2. The local agency must agree to maintain a level of expenditures for code enforcement, exclusive of any code enforcement expenditures for areas assisted by urban renewal project grants or code enforcement grants, that is at least equal to normal expenditures for code enforcement activities prior to the federal assistance grant.
3. The local agency must make satisfactory provision for all necessary public improvements for the areas assisted by the grant.
4. The local agency must provide appropriate housing and relocation assistance for any individuals or families displaced by code enforcement activities.

To qualify for such assistance, the area must be built up, predominantly residential, and with code violations existing in 20 percent or more of the buildings. Conditions must be favorable for elimination of these code violations and arrest of future decline of the area.

Code enforcement grants may cover up to two thirds (or three fourths in the case of localities with a population of under 50,000) of the cost of a concentrated code enforcement program. Eligible costs may include expenditures for code administration, for related staff services in connection with providing assistance on relocation and on direct federal rehabilitation loans and grants, and for construction and maintenance of streets, curbs, sidewalks, street lighting, and similar improvements.

At the 1970 year-end, code enforcement grants had been approved in 137 cities in an amount of $261.3 million.

Demolition Grants Another program inaugurated in 1965 provides for federal grants to cities, other municipalities, and counties to assist in financing the cost of demolition of structures determined to be structurally unsound or unfit for human habitation where the locality has authority to demolish. Grants may be for up to two thirds of the cost of demolition.

Conditions under which the grants may be made include present operation under a certified workable program of community improvement; the structures to be demolished must constitute a public nuisance or a threat to public health or welfare; other available legal remedies must have been exhausted. As in the case of code enforcement programs, displaced persons must be assured adequate substitute housing and relocation assistance.

By the 1970 year-end, 130 demolition grants had been approved in 105 cities for an amount totaling $21.8 million.

Rehabilitation Loans The Housing Act of 1964 authorized the Housing Administrator to make low-interest loans to owners or tenants of homes or business property in code enforcement or urban renewal areas to finance the rehabilitation required to make the property conform to code requirements or to carry out the objectives of the urban renewal plan for the area, in order to reduce the need for demolition and removal of structures which could be rehabilitated. These loans are authorized only after the borrower finds himself unable to secure the necessary funds from other sources on reasonable terms and conditions and the loan is established as an acceptable risk. The interest rate on any such loan may not exceed 3 percent, and maturity may not be greater than 20 years or three fourths of the remaining economic life of the structure after its rehabilitation, whichever is less.

Under the Housing and Urban Development Act of 1968, this loan program has been expanded in two ways. First, the funds may be used to rehabilitate property in an area, other than an urban renewal or code enforcement area, which the local governing body certifies to the Secretary of HUD contains a substantial number of structures in need of rehabilitation. Qualified owner-occupants may use the funds to improve their dwellings so that they conform to public standards for decent, safe, and sanitary housing, as required by applicable codes.

The second area of expansion of the rehabilitation loan program extends to qualified owners and tenants whose property is uninsurable because of physical hazards. The property must be located in an area that will support long-term values or in which a public or private program gives reasonable assurance of creating a stable environment. Under this provision, loans can be made to owners or tenants of property determined to be uninsurable because of physical hazards disclosed by an inspection carried out pursuant to an approved statewide property insurance plan as provided in the urban property protection and reinsurance program approved under Title X of the 1968 legislation.

Rehabilitation Grants Since 1965, federal grants have been available to qualified low-income owner-occupants of housing in an urban renewal or code enforcement area for the repair and improvement of their homes to achieve required conformity. The maximum grant is $3,500. The grant may not exceed:

1. The actual cost of repairs and improvements, if the applicant's income is $3,000, or less; or
2. If the applicant's annual income exceeds $3,000, an amount not in excess

of that portion of the actual cost of repairs and improvements which cannot be paid for with any available loan that can be amortized as part of the applicant's monthly housing expense without requiring that expense to exceed 25 percent of the applicant's monthly income.

Under the 1968 legislation, the rehabilitation grants program has been extended beyond urban renewal and code enforcement areas and to properties deemed uninsurable because of physical hazard in the same manner as previously discussed in connection with rehabilitation loans. At the end of 1970, grants totaling $63.1 million had been made to 25,509 persons.

Neighborhood Facilities The Housing and Urban Development Act of 1965 authorized the neighborhood facilities grant program. Its purpose has been to assist in financing the development cost of neighborhood facilities for programs of community service. Grants may not exceed two thirds of the development cost of the facilities, or three fourths in areas officially designated for redevelopment. The local community must provide the remainder of the cost and assume responsibility for operating and maintaining the facilities after completion.

The centers will be used to provide a wide range of public services, such as employment and training referrals, family counseling services, information on citizens' rights and legal services, adult and remedial education, day care services, homemakers' services, and physical and mental health consultations. These centers are presently in use in New York, Boston, Chicago, Cincinnati, Detroit, Minneapolis, Washington, St. Louis, Dallas, Oakland, Louisville, Chattanooga, Jacksonville, and Philadelphia.

Open-Space Land Communities may receive federal grants of up to 50 percent for acquisition, preservation, and development of lands having park, recreation, conservation, scenic, and historic uses. Built-up portions of urban areas may be purchased and cleared with grant assistance where adequate open-space land is not otherwise available. Relocation assistance including payments, is allowable for parties displaced by the purchase of land with grant aid. At the 1970 year-end, 2,257 open-space grants had been made in all of the states to assist in acquisition of nearly 324,000 acres. Grants totaled $267.9 million. About 90 percent of these grants were within Standard Metropolitan Statistical Areas.

Urban Beautification Local beautification programs may receive support by federal grants when appropriately directed toward the greater use and enjoyment of open space and other public land in urban areas. The support available may represent up to 50 percent of the applicant's increase in its usual beautification expenditures over those for previous years for comparable activities. At the end of 1970, there had been 443 beautification grants, totaling $51.8 million.

Demonstration Program Administration The Demonstration Cities and Metropolitan Development Act of 1966 established an entirely new program known as the "demonstration cities" program. The genesis of this program was found in the inadequacy of other federal programs for urban aid in dealing with the total problem. Previously established programs have emerged to deal with specific inequities or unfulfilled needs, leaving other problems untouched. The demonstration cities program is designed to help participating cities plan and carry out comprehensive and coordinated physical and social programs to deal with the full requirements for satisfactory living conditions in the urban community. Federal, state, and local governmental agencies and private interests are to be coordinated into an effective effort. Utilization of resources of the neighborhood is to be maximized to achieve housing construction and rehabilitation, in-job training, health facilities, welfare assistance, and educational programs. Federal financial assistance is authorized as follows:

1. Direct aid for planning and development of comprehensive city demonstration programs in selected cities.
2. Supplementary grants, providing funds over and above those available under existing grant-in-aid programs. These grants can be up to 80 percent of the total nonfederal contributions required for projects assisted by other federal programs. Such grants may be used to assist any activity included as part of a demonstration program—even one not assisted by a federal program.

A city may apply for assistance under this program through its own "city demonstration agency," established and approved by its local governing body. Administration at the federal level is through the Demonstration Programs Administration in the Office of Demonstrations and Intergovernmental Relations of HUD.

At the 1970 year-end, 150 cities were participants in this program under planning grants of $22.7 million. Supplementary grants totaling over $617.5 million had been made in support of special projects or activities and to supplement assistance available under other grant-in-aid programs.

Planned Communities The New Communities Act of 1968, Title IV of the Housing and Urban Development Act of 1968, established a new massive program of federal support for private building of new communities with balanced housing, commercial, industrial, and recreational facilities. In administering the program, the Secretary of HUD must be satisfied that the program is a sound and complete plan for the community, meeting state and local requirements and providing satisfactory supporting facilities for the future residents.

This program was established to fulfill a long-standing deficiency in new community development, i.e., the acquisition of substantial acreages of land and readying the area for sale as building sites to private developers and builders. Acquisition and installation of the basic facilities, such as sewer, water, streets, parks, and amenities, can easily cost $50 million for a large community. Beyond the sheer magnitude of the cash requirement for land development by the private entrepreneur, there is a long development period—for planning, land acquisition, and installation of the improvements—before a cash return can be realized through lot sales. Meanwhile, taxes, operating overhead, and interest costs place heavy burdens on the whole operation.

The new program permits the federal government to guarantee cash flow debentures issued by accredited private developers. The federal guarantee would make the debentures attractive to institutions that would not be interested in a straight mortgage to finance such a venture. The program gears the repayment of principal and interest to the internal cash flow of the project. Thus, if repayment is deferred until there is a favorable cash flow, loan retirement may not begin until five or more years after the original borrowing. This takes the financial pressures off the developer during the long period leading up to initial sale of developed sites.

The federal guarantee may cover a loan to a developer up to the lesser of (1) 80 percent of the Secretary's estimate of the value of the property upon completion of the land development, or (2) the sum of 75 percent of his estimate of the value of the land before development and 90 percent of his estimate of the actual cost of the land development.

Not more than $50 million may be guaranteed for a single project. Interest and repayment of principal must be provided for under rates and conditions satisfactory to the Secretary of HUD. Up to $500 million may be guaranteed under this program at any one time. To encourage local communities to support these privately sponsored new cities, the Secretary may also authorize supplemental grants. These grants may cover an additional 20 percent of construction costs. Programs of particular application in this connection are the basic water and sewer grants and the open-space land grants, administered by HUD. The water and waste disposal facilities grant program of the Farmers Home Administration may also be useful.

At the 1970 year-end the new communities program had only five projects under way. One each in Arkansas, Illinois, Maryland, Minnesota, and Texas. Obviously, projects of this magnitude are many months in the planning stage and the effectiveness of the program will have to be evaluated over the longer term.

National Housing Partnerships The 1968 legislation authorized the President of the United States to create one or more private corporations to engage in activities directed at providing more and better housing for low and moderate income families. Each corporation is to be organized by the President, by and with the advice and consent of the Senate, and financed by a public stock offering. The corporation is to have a 15-member board of directors; 3 members to be appointed by the President, with Senate confirmation, and the other 12 to be elected by the stockholders.

The corporation is authorized to enter into and participate in all forms of partnerships and associations, to conduct research and study projects, to provide technical assistance, and to provide financing assistance to other organizations in connection with its activities. The corporation is specifically authorized to form a limited partnership in which the corporation becomes the general partner and each stockholder may become a limited partner. The scope of activities of the limited partnership would be the same as those of the corporation. The partnership investment in any low and moderate income housing undertaking will usually be limited to not more than 25 percent of the initial equity investment.

Federal Housing Administration In addition to the programs discussed in Chapter 25, the Federal Housing Administration is responsible for the administration of the following programs:

Low-rent public housing and related low-rent programs
College housing loan program
Senior citizens' housing loan program
Alaska housing program

Low-Rent Public Housing Under the U.S. Housing Act of 1937, the federal government assumed responsibility for the administration of a public housing program. Under this program, the federal government has provided financial aid for housing owned and operated by local housing authorities for the benefit of low-income families who otherwise would be unable to afford decent housing in the locality. Single elderly persons of 62 years of age or older, or persons who, regardless of age, are under disabilities which entile them to retirement benefits under the Social Security Act, are eligible for admission as "families of low income," except when restrictive state housing laws prevail.

This segment of the federal public housing program has always been in a great measure the responsibility of the local community concerned. The actual construction and operation of housing projects is the responsibility of local housing authorities. These are nonprofit public agencies which own and operate the project. Construction is performed by private contractors under contract to the housing authority. Costs of this construction are met through the public sale of bonds by the local housing authority. Such obligations are exempt from federal income tax. To encourage further the private purchase of local housing authority obligations, the federal government guarantees the repayment of both principal and interest. All such private financing is under the control of the HUD administrator, who determines maximum maturities, interest rates, and so on. The interest rates are fixed in conformity with a formula outlined in the law which relates them to the rates on applicable government bonds.

Federal aid takes the form of (1) loans to help finance the preliminary development and (2) annual contributions to permit operation of the housing development at rents within the means of low-income families. Actually, the local housing authority pays all operating costs from rental income, and the federal contribution goes only toward bond retirement.

As a part of its complementary service, HUD also sets standards and offers technical assistance to the local housing authorities. In the consummation of new construction programs, the local authorities often undertake a simultaneous elimination of a number of substandard dwellings, either by demolition or by rehabilitation, equal to the number of units constructed for public housing.

No annual contribution will be made by the federal government unless the housing project to which it applies is exempt from all real and personal property taxes imposed by state, city, county, or other political subdivision. In lieu of such taxes, the local housing authority may contract to make payments to taxing districts not to exceed 10 percent of the annual shelter rent charged in the housing project.

At the end of 1970, there were nearly 900,000 units of public housing under management. About 50 percent of all public housing was occupied by black families and 38 percent by senior citizens.

Prior to 1965, public housing was geared to new construction, specifically built for the purpose. In 1965, Congress authorized local housing agencies to acquire existing housing or private built new housing for low-rent tenants. Such programs are now known as "instant housing" or "turnkey" acquisitions. They are backed by an annual contribution contract under which HUD provides financial assistance to the local housing authority for acquisition and operation of the projects.

Also in 1965, for the first time Congress authorized the use of federal assistance to permit local housing authorities to lease private dwellings to low-income tenants. This program is initiated by the governing body of the community approving by resolution the application of this plan to the community. Upon HUD approval, listings of available homes and apartments are obtained from private owners and real estate companies. The public housing authority and the property owner usually sign a lease which provides for subleasing to eligible tenants. Other leasing arrangements are possible. The local housing authority pays the federal contribution either to the owner directly or to the tenants. If the latter, the tenant places the contribution with the balance of the rent and makes the total payment to the owner.

Local housing authorities have recently become more interested in housing specially designed to meet the need of the aging and physically handicapped. More liberal cost allowances have been allowed. In addition, in view of the low incomes of a large number of the elderly and handicapped, an additional operating subsidy of up to $120 per year has been authorized for each dwelling where it is necessary to maintain project solvency.

College Housing Loan Program The program for providing loans for college housing had been in existence 20 years at the end of 1970. During this period 3,340 projects had been built or approved for faculty members, interns, and residents, as well as major construction for college students. The HUD supported loan amount exceeded $3.8 billion. Service facilities, such as dining halls, infirmaries, and college unions, may be constructed with the loans. Loans may also be extended to hospitals, but only for housing purposes.

After the application has been approved by HUD, bonds are issued by the institution to cover the cost of the project. They are advertised for public sale and bought by the government only if private buyers do not offer terms at least as favorable as those of HUD. The loans may have terms up to 50 years and bear interest currently at 3 percent.

Under the Housing and Urban Development Act of 1968, HUD is authorized to make loans for the construction or the purchase of existing facilities, or may, as an alternative to all or part of any particular loan, make annual grants to the institution to reduce the cost of its borrowing from other sources to the preferential interest rate established under the provisions of Title IV of the 1950 Housing Act. Currently, this rate is 3 percent. These grants are made under contracts of up to 40 years duration.

Loans for Senior Citizens Housing The senior citizens loan program is administered by the Federal Housing Administration under the authority of Section 202 of the Housing Act of 1959, as amended. The program provides financial assistance in the form of low-interest, long-term loans to nonprofit, private corporations, consumer cooperatives, and public agencies for the construction of rental housing for elderly persons. Such loans may be made for 100 percent of the development cost of the project for periods up to 50 years. The law provides that no loan shall be made unless the applicant shows that it is unable to secure the necessary funds from other sources upon terms and conditions as favorable as those under this program. Occupants are restricted to persons who are 62 years of age or over and whose annual incomes, at the time of admission, do not exceed the official maximum income limits established by the HUD administrator as applicable to the area within which the project is located. Within the national limits of $4,000 a year for single elderly persons and $4,800 for two-person families, specific income limits are established for individual communities. The purpose of these limits is to assure that occupany is restricted to the lower middle-income group in each locality. Currently, the interest rate on senior citizen HUD housing loans is 3 percent.

Alaska Housing Program In 1966, the Secretary of HUD was authorized to make loans and grants to the state of Alaska to assist in provision of housing for Alaska natives and residents who are unable to finance housing otherwise. Terms and conditions are set within the means of the recipients.

The loans and grants are administered under a statewide program set up by the state and approved by the Secretary of HUD. Statutory specifications for the program require that it (1) specify the minimum and maximum standards for the housing and facilities (not to exceed an average of $7,500 per dwelling unit); (2) encourage self-help in construction of the housing and facilites; and (3) provide experience and encourage continued participation in self-government and individual homeownership. Grants can not exceed 75 percent of the total cost of housing and related facilities constructed under an approved program.

The Road Ahead What has been said in this chapter emphasizes growing recognition of the existence of a serious problem—the inadequate housing of many American families. Nothing in this chapter has been posed as the final answer to this problem. With each passing year the magnitude of the problem has grown in size and complexity. The country is forced to face, rather than look beyond, the needs and entitlements of minority groups, particularly at the core of the inner city. The proportions of the national malaise are amorphous and multidimensional. Financial factors are affected by noneconomic illnesses in the ghetto culture—crime in the streets, dope traffic, weak school systems, and undeveloped work habits, to name a few.

There is no mistaking that the American system is sending more and more dollars in the direction of achieving "a decent home and a suitable environment for every American family." Through current legislation, federal subsidy is becoming a greater support to the private housing system. Many now see an approach to our national housing problem like that of the Marshall Plan for European economic recovery as not only appropriate but necessary to achievement of a satisfactory standard of housing for all—to restore personal esteem, pride in family, appreciation of economic opportunity, and respect for the rights of others.

This was much of what was in the minds of Congress as expressed in Title XVI of the Housing and Urban Development Act of 1968 establishing the machinery for the 10-year plan to meet all of the nation's housing needs and eliminate all of its substandard housing by 1978. The 10-year plan set a goal for housing production at 26 million units, of which 20 million would be private financed and 6 million government subsidized. Although in the early period of the 10-year span total production has lagged below the 2.6 million units required annual average, plans calls for creation of new units at the rate of about 3 million annually from 1974 through 1978. This involves estimated federal subsidy for over 700 thousand units and unsubsidized starts of about 2,300 thousand annually.

The high priority for this type of federal assistance is now more formalized than previously. It will work, however, only through combined efforts of private and governmental interests. In this way, job creation, for example, may be coordinated with improvement in education and living facilities. Private and state and local financial resources will become exhausted and it will be to the federal government that the community will look for residual loans and grants in aid.

By simple mathematics, it is apparent that at $10,000 per unit the 10-year cost of 26 million new housing units would require $260 billion of financing. The magnitude of this need is of the order of the cost of waging a military action the size of the one in Vietnam. Such figures, of course, are hypothetical and meaningless unless they are derived with respect to direct applications to real situations. Much of any investment could be recovered through employment of the previously unemployable, increase in the property tax rolls, and decrease in the welfare rolls.

The challenge of housing the population of America lies not only in seeking the best solution to some part of the problem, but more often in learning what the facets of the problem are and how they interrelate.

QUESTIONS AND PROBLEMS

1. How do the problems involved in urban redevelopment differ from those of original city planning?
2. Describe three possible approaches to urban redevelopment programs.
3. What are the shortcomings of complete reliance upon private capital for the elimination of substandard housing and slum areas?
4. What is the present expressed goal of the national housing policy?
5. How is the federal housing program administered?
6. What are the prerequisites to HUD certification of an urban renewal program as "workable"?
7. What forms of federal financial assistance are available for urban renewal or urban renewal planning?
8. How may long-term leasing be used in urban renewal?
9. In what ways has the FHA added impetus to the urban renewal program?
10. What are the arguments for and against public housing?
11. How do the concepts of urban renewal and public housing differ?
12. How does the Federal Housing Administration assist in construction of low-rent public housing?
13. What action has been taken to meet the need for moderate and low income housing? Is it appropriate?

Selected References

SPECIALIZED BOOKS AND BOOKLETS

American Bankers Association. *Farm Real Estate Financing.* New York, 1949.

———. *Government Loan and Credit Programs.* A reprint from *Banking,* the journal of the American Bankers Association, April, 1964.

———. *Mortgage Banker Handbook.* New York, 1963.

American Institute of Real Estate Appraisers. *Real Estate Appraisal Practice.* Chicago, 1958.

American Institute of Real Estate Appraisers. *The Appraisal of Real Estate.* Chicago, 1960.

Atteberry, William. *Modern Real Estate Finance.* Columbus, Ohio: Grid, Inc., 1972.

Banfield, Edward C., and Grodzins, Morton. *Government and Housing in Metropolitan Areas.* New York: McGraw-Hill Book Co., Inc., 1958.

Barbeau, E. A. *The Mortgage Bond Racket.* Philadelphia: R. Swain Co., 1932.

Beaton, William R. *Real Estate Investment.* Englewood Cliffs, N.J.: Prentice-Hall, Inc., 1971.

Bingham, Robert F., and Andrews, Elmore L. *Financing Real Estate.* Cleveland, Ohio: The Stanley McMichael Publishing Organization, 1924.

Brown, Robert K. *Public Housing in Action: The Record of Pittsburgh.* Pittsburgh, Pa.: University of Pittsburgh Press, 1959.

Bryant, Willis R. *Mortgage Lending Fundamentals and Practices.* New York: McGraw-Hill Book Co., Inc., 1962.

Campbell, Kenneth D. *Mortgage Trusts: Lenders with a Plus.* New York, N.Y.: Audit Publications, Inc., 1969.

Candilis, Wray O. *Variable Rate Mortgage Plans.* Washington, D.C.: The American Bankers Association, 1971.

Clurman, David, and Hebard, Edna L. *Condominiums and Cooperatives.* New York: Wiley-Interscience, 1970.

Colean, Miles L., and Saulnier, Richard J. *The Real Estate Lending Activities of the Farmers Home Administration* (A Report to the Mortgage Bankers Association). Chicago, 1963.

Conway, Lawrence V. *Mortgage Lending.* Chicago: American Savings and Loan Institute Press, 1960.

De Huszar, William I. *Mortgage Servicing.* Chicago: Mortgage Bankers Association of America, 1954.

Duggan, I. W., and Battles, R. U. *Financing the Farm Business.* New York: John Wiley & Sons, Inc., 1950.

Financial Institution Monographs
  Prepared for the Commission on Money and Credit
    The Commercial Banking Industry (The American Bankers Association).
    The Consumer Finance Industry (National Consumer Finance Association).
    Life Insurance Companies as Financial Institutions (Life Insurance Institute of America).
    Mortgage Companies: Their Place in the Financial Structure (Miles Colean, for the Mortgage Bankers Association of America).
    Mutual Savings Banking: Basic Characteristics and Role in the National Economy (National Association of Mutual Savings Banks).
    Property and Casualty Insurance Companies: Their Role as Financial Intermediaries (American Insurance Alliance; Association of Casualty and Surety Companies; and National Board of Fire Underwriters).
    The Savings and Loan Business: Its Purposes, Functions, and Economic Justification (Leon T. Kendall, for the United States Savings and Loan League).
  These monographs were published by Prentice-Hall, Inc., Englewood Cliffs, N.J., 1962.

Haar, Charles M. *Federal Credit and Private Housing: The Mass Financing Dilemma.* Action Series in Housing and Community Development. New York: McGraw-Hill Book Co., Inc., 1960.

Jones, Oliver, and Grebler, Leo. *The Secondary Mortgage Market.* Los Angeles: Real Estate Research Program, Institute of Business and Economic Research, University of California, 1961.

Kahn, Sanders A., Case, Frederick E., and Schimmel, Alfred. *Real Estate Appraisal and Investment.* New York: The Ronald Press Co., 1963.

Killbridge, Maurice D., O'Block, Robert P., and Teplitz, Paul V. *Urban Analysis.* Boston, Mass.: Division of Research, Harvard Business School, 1970.

Kinnard, William N., Jr. *Industrial Real Estate.* Washington, D.C.: Society of Industrial Realtors of the National Association of Real Estate Boards, 1967.

Klaman, Saul B. *The Postwar Rise of Mortgage Companies.* New York: National Bureau of Economic Research, Inc., 1959.

Krooss, Herman E., and Martin R. Blyn. *A History of Financial Intermediaries*. New York: Random House, 1971.

Lintner, John. *Mutual Savings Banks in the Savings and Mortgage Markets*. Boston: Division of Research, Graduate School, Harvard University, 1948.

McMichael, Stanley L. *How to Operate a Real Estate Business*. Englewood Cliffs, N.J.: Prentice-Hall, Inc., 1967.

———. *McMichael's Appraising Manual*. Englewood Cliffs, N.J.: Prentice-Hall, Inc., 1951.

———. *Real Estate Subdivision*. Englewood Cliffs, N.J.: Prentice-Hall, Inc., 1949.

———, and O'Keefe, Paul T. *How to Finance Real Estate*. Englewood Cliffs, N.J.: Prentice-Hall, Inc., 1967.

Maisel, Sherman J. *Financing Real Estate*. New York: McGraw-Hill Book Co., Inc., 1966.

Mao, James T. *Residential Mortgage Financing*. Ann Arbor: Bureau of Business Research, University of Michigan, 1960.

May, Arthur A. *The Valuation of Residential Real Estate*. Englewood Cliffs, N.J.: Prentice-Hall, Inc., 1953.

Mortgage Guaranty Insurance Corporation. *MGIC Fact Book*. Milwaukee, Wis., 1964.

Murray, William G. *Farm Appraisal*. Ames, Iowa: The Iowa State Press, 1954.

National Municipal League. *The Businessman's Role in Renewal*. Reprint from *Journal of Housing*, January, 1960.

Nelson, Richard L., and Aschman, Frederick T. *Real Estate and City Planning*. Englewood Cliffs, N.J.: Prentice-Hall, Inc., 1957.

O'Block, Robert P., and Kuehn, Robert H., Jr. *An Economic Analysis of The Housing and Urban Development Act of 1968*. Boston, Mass.: Division of Research, Harvard Business School, 1970.

Pease, Robert H., and Kerwood, Lewis O. *Mortgage Banking*. New York: McGraw-Hill Book Co., Inc., 1965.

Philadelphia Housing Association. *Ends and Means of Urban Renewal*. Philadelphia, 1961.

Ramsey, Charles E. *Condominium: The New Look in Co-ops*. Chicago: Chicago Title and Trust Company, 1961.

Reep, S. N. *Second Mortgages and Land Contracts*. Englewood Cliffs, N.J.: Prentice-Hall, Inc., 1928.

Ring, Alfred A. *The Valuation of Real Estate*. Englewood Cliffs, N.J.: Prentice-Hall, Inc., 1970.

Rossi, Peter H., and Dentler, Robert A. *The Politics of Urban Renewal—The Chicago Findings*. New York: The Free Press of Glencoe, Inc., 1961.

Saulnier, R. J. *Urban Mortgage Lending by Life Insurance Companies*. New York: National Bureau of Economic Research, 1950.

Schultz, Robert E. *Life Insurance Housing Projects*. Homewood, Ill.: Richard D. Irwin, Inc., 1956.

Seldin, Maury, and Swesnik, Richard H. *Real Estate Investment Strategy.* New York: Wiley-Interscience, 1970.

Snider, Harold W. *Life Insurance Investment in Commercial Real Estate.* Homewood, Ill.: Richard D. Irwin, Inc., 1956.

Society of Residential Appraisers. *Appraisal Guide.* Chicago, 1956.

Thomas, Howard E. *The Mortgaging of Long-Term Leases.* Reprint from *Dicta,* Vol. 39 (November-December 1962).

Thompson, Richard G. *A Study of Shopping Centers.* Research Report No. 16. Berkeley, Calif.: Real Estate Research Program, Institute of Business and Economic Research, University of California, 1961.

United States Savings and Loan League. *Anatomy of the Residential Mortgage.* Occasional Paper No. 2. Chicago, 1964.

University of California Extension. *Commercial and Investment Properties.* Berkeley, Calif., 1955.

University of Chicago. *One Hundred Years of Land Values in Chicago.* Chicago: University of Chicago Press, 1933.

Van Huyck, Alfred P., and Hornung, Jack. *The Citizen's Guide to Urban Renewal.* West Trenton, N.J.: Chandler-Davis Publishing Company, 1962.

Wendt, Paul F. *Influence of Transportation Changes on Urban Land Uses and Values.* Reprint No. 21, Berkeley, Calif.: Real Estate Research Program, Institute of Business and Economic Research, University of California, 1960.

———. *Real Estate Appraisal.* New York: Henry Holt and Co., Inc., 1956.

Wendt, Paul F., and Cerf, Alan R. *Real Estate Investment Analysis and Taxation.* New York: McGraw-Hill Book Co., Inc., 1969.

Winnick, Louis. *Rental Housing: Opportunities for Private Investment.* New York: McGraw-Hill Book Co., Inc., 1958.

GENERAL REFERENCE WORKS ON REAL ESTATE LAW

Dykstra, Gerald O., and Lillian G. *The Business Law of Real Estate.* New York: The Macmillan Co., 1956.

Grange, William J. *Real Estate, A Practical Guide to Ownership, Transfer, Mortgaging, and Leasing of Real Property.* New York: The Ronald Press Co., 1940.

Grange, William J., and Woodbury, T. C. *Manual of Real Estate Law and Procedures.* New York: The Ronald Press Co., 1967.

Hebard, Edna L., and Meisel, Gerald S. *Principles of Real Estate Law.* New York: Simmons-Boardman Publishing Corp., 1964.

Kratovil, Robert. *Real Estate Law.* Englewood Cliffs, N.J.: Prentice-Hall, Inc., 1969.

Lusk, Harold F. *Cases in Law of the Real Estate Business.* Homewood, Ill.: Richard D. Irwin, Inc., 1961.

———. *The Law of the Real Estate Business.* Homewood, Ill.: Richard D. Irwin, Inc., 1965.

Thompson, George W. *The Law of Real Property*, Vol. 1-12. Indianapolis, Ind.: The Bobbs-Merrill Co., Inc., 1941.

Tiffany, Herbert Thorndike. *The Law of Real Property*, Vol. 1-6. Chicago: Callaghan & Co., 1939.

GENERAL REFERENCE WORKS ON PRINCIPLES AND PRACTICE

Case, Frederick E. *Modern Real Estate Practice*. New York: Allyn and Bacon, Inc., 1956.

———. *Real Estate*. New York: Allyn and Bacon, Inc., 1962.

Fisher, Ernest M., and Fisher, Robert M. *Urban Real Estate*. New York: Henry Holt and Co., 1954.

Friedman, E. *Real Estate Encyclopedia*. Englewood Cliffs, N.J.: Prentice-Hall, Inc., 1961.

Hoagland, Henry E. *Real Estate Principles*. New York: McGraw-Hill Book Co., Inc., 1955.

Holmes, Lawrence G. *The Real Estate Handbook*. Englewood Cliffs, N.J.: Prentice-Hall, Inc., 1948.

Husband, William H., and Anderson, Frank Ray. *Real Estate*. Homewood, Ill.: Richard D. Irwin, Inc., 1960.

Martin, Preston. *Real Estate Principles and Practices*. New York: The Macmillan Co., 1959.

North, Neilson L., and Ring, Alfred A. *Real Estate Principles and Practices*. Englewood Cliffs, N.J.: Prentice-Hall, Inc., 1967.

Ratcliff, Richard U. *Real Estate Analysis*. New York: McGraw-Hill Book Co., Inc., 1961.

Unger, Maurice A. *Real Estate*. Cincinnati: South-Western Publishing Co., 1969.

Weimer, Arthur M., and Hoyt, Homer. *Principles of Urban Real Estate*. New York: The Ronald Press Co., 1966.

PUBLICATIONS IN PERIODICALS

Aronsohn, Alan J. B. "The Real Estate Limited Partnership and Other Joint Ventures," *Real Estate Review* (Spring 1971), pp. 43–49.

Bailey, E. Norman. "Real Estate Investment Trusts: An Appraisal," *Appraisal Journal* (October, 1966), pp. 487–99; also *Financial Analysts Journal*, May-June 1966, pp. 107–14.

Baxter, Margaret C. "Sources and Factors of Real Estate Financing," *University of Illinois Law Forum* (Fall 1957), pp. 350–59.

Berkowitz, Louis. "How a Builder Puts the 235 Project Together," *California Savings and Loan Journal* (April 1971), pp. 14–15.

Bernard, Frank C., and Perlstadt, Sidney M. "Sale and Leaseback Transactions," *University of Illinois Law Forum* (Winter 1955), pp. 635–54.

Bloomstein, Max, Jr. "Sale of Corporate Real Estate," *University of Illinois Law Forum* (Spring 1956), pp. 1–21.

Breckenfeld, Gurney. "Misleading Myths of Middle-Income Housing," *House & Home* (March 1964), pp. 137–42, 146–47, 161, 178.

———. "The Emerging Giants," *House & Home*, Vol. 18, No. 1 (January 1963), pp. 67–71, 113–15.

Cameron, C. C. "A Hard and Close Look at Mortgage Banking's Future," *The Mortgage Banker* (October 1963), pp. 15–20.

Campbell, Kenneth. "Producers Strengthen Ties to Builders," *House & Home*, Vol. 24, No. 5 (May 1964), pp. 6–7.

———. "The Real Estate Investment Trust—New Wonderchild," *Real Estate Review* (Winter 1972), pp. 25–30.

———. "REITs: New Opportunities for the Mortgage Banker," *The Mortgage Banker* (May 1972), pp. 46 ff.

Cannon, Arthur M. "Danger Signals of Accountants in 'Net Lease' Financing," *Journal of Accountancy* (April 1948), p. 312.

Cary, William L. "Corporate Financing Through the Sale and Leaseback of Property: Business, Tax, and Policy Considerations," *Harvard Law Review* (November 1948), p. 1.

Clark, William Dennison. "Leverage: Magnificent Mover of Real Estate," *Real Estate Review* (Winter 1972), pp. 8–13.

Colean, Miles L. "Mortgage Banking in a New Era," *The Mortgage Banker*, (December 1963), pp. 34–36, 44.

"Condominiums—A Symposium," *The Appraisal Journal*, Vol. 30, No. 4 (October 1962).

Edwards, Edward S. "Changing Character of the Real Estate Mortgage Markets," *The Journal of Finance*, Vol. 19, No. 2, Part 1 (May 1964), pp. 313–20.

Elliott, J. Richard, Jr. "Opportunities in Blight," *The Mortgage Banker* (December 1961), pp. 19–24, 29.

Etka, Donald D. "Shopping Center Leasing," *Journal of Property Management*, Vol. 30, No. 3 (May–June 1965), pp. 136–39.

Everett, William S. "Condominium and Co-operative Apartments—The New Frontier in Housing," *Journal of Property Management*, Vol. 27, No. 1 (Fall 1961), pp. 4–16.

Fass, Peter M. "The Regulated World of the Real Estate Syndicates," *Real Estate Review* (Winter 1972), pp. 52–56.

"Federal Assistance in Financing Middle-Income Cooperative Apartments," *The Yale Law Journal*, Vol. 68, No. 3 (January 1959), pp. 542–613.

Fegan, Thomas H. "Tools of Real Estate Financing," *University of Illinois Law Forum*, (Fall 1957), pp. 335–49.

Fisher, Robert M. "Foreclosures and Delinquencies: Dimensions of a Problem," *The Mortgage Banker* (April 1964), pp. 24–28, 46.

———. "Outlook for Mortgage Markets," *The Journal of Finance*, Vol. 15, No. 2 (May 1960), pp. 280–84.

Fitzhugh, Gilbert W. "The Life Insurance Companies' Urban Investment Program," *The Mortgage Banker* (June 1968), pp. 18–24.

Garrett, William B. "Land Trusts," *University of Illinois Law Forum* (Winter 1955), pp. 655–80.

"Ginnie Mae, New Girl of Mortgage Finance," *HUD Challenge*, (March-April 1970), 1970.

Godfrey, Dudley J., Jr., and Bernstein, Joseph M. "The Real Estate Investment Trust—Past, Present and Future," *Wisconsin Law Review* (July 1962), pp. 637–71.

Graham, D. H. "Shopping Centers: Financing, Appraisal, and Management," *Journal of Property Management*. Vol. 31, No. 3 (May–June 1966), p. 115 ff.

Grebler, Leo. "A Searching Analysis of the Quality of Mortgage Credit," *The Mortgage Banker* (February 1964), pp. 32–36.

Greenwalt, Philip L. "Title VIII and 'Ginnie Mae'," *The Mortgage Banker* (September 1968), pp. 14–15.

Guttentag, Jack. "Mortgage Warehousing," *Journal of Finance*, Vol. 12, No. 4 (December 1957), pp. 438–50.

Haar, Charles M. "The New Communities Act of 1968: New Financing for Planned Communities," *The Mortgage Banker* (September 1968), pp. 9–13.

Harvey, Robert O. "Valuation of Mortgage Security," *University of Illinois Law Forum* (Fall 1957), pp. 412–19.

Higginbottom, Elzie. "Fulfilling Nonprofit Housing Goals with Limited Dividend Partnerships," *The Mortgage Banker* (November 1970), pp. 76–80.

Hunter, Oakley. "Fannie Mae Prepares for a New Role in Conventional Mortgage Market," *Banking* (October 1971), pp. 66–70.

Johnson, Harry E. "Lending Opportunities for the Mortgage Banker in the FHA Cooperative and Condominium Programs," *The Mortgage Banker* (November 1969), pp. 76–78.

Johnstone, Quintin. "Title Insurance," *The Yale Law Journal*, Vol. 66, No. 4 (February 1957), pp. 492–524.

Jones, Oliver. "Private Secondary Market Facilities," *The Journal of Finance*, Vol. XXIII, No. 2 (May 1968), pp. 359–366.

———. "The Revolution in Mortgage Finance: Will It Generate Enough Funds for the Housing Boom of the Seventies?" *The Mortgage Banker* (June 1969), pp. 37–41.

Leverett, E. J., Jr. "Lease Guarantee Program," *Journal of Property Management*, Vol. 33, No. 2 (March–April 1968), pp. 88–91.

Levy, Daniel S. "ABC's of Shopping Center Leases," *Real Estate Review* (Spring 1971), pp. 12–16.

"Long-Term Leasing in Urban Renewal: An Alternative Method of Municipal Land Disposition," *The Yale Law Journal*, Vol. 68, No. 7 (June 1959), pp. 1424–58.

McCarthy, John C. "Restrictive Covenants," *University of Illinois Law Forum* (Winter 1955), pp. 709–39.

McFarland, M. Carter. "Major Developments in the Financing of Residential Construction Since World War II," *The Journal of Finance*, Vol. 21, No. 2 (May 1966), pp. 382–402.

McKillop, Hart. "Title Insurance," *University of Florida Law Review*, Vol. 8, No. 4 (Winter 1955), pp. 447–64.

McMullen, William H., Jr. "Truth in Selling: The Interstate Land Sales Full Disclosure Act of 1968," *Real Estate Review* (Spring 1971), pp. 94–98.

Maisel, Sherman J. "Some Relationships between Assets and Liabilities of Thrift Institutions," *The Journal of Finance*, Vol. 23, No. 2 (May 1968), pp. 367–78.

Morris, Jack S. "Shopping Centers—The Role of the Lawyer," *University of Illinois Law Forum* (Winter 1955), pp. 681–708.

"New Role for Ginnie Mae," *Title News* (December 1969), pp. 4–6.

O'Keefe, Raymond T. "The Why and How of Making Mortgages on Leaseholds," *The Mortgage Banker* (June 1962), pp. 31–33.

Opperman, John C. "Lender-Developer Participation," *The Mortgage Banker* (September 1968), pp. 30–35, 38.

Prather, William C. "Foreclosure of the Security Interest," *University of Illinois Law Forum* (Fall 1957), pp. 420–61.

Proceedings of Shopping Center Workshop presented at the International Appraisal Conference in Chicago, May 1961. *The Appraisal Journal*, Vol. 30, No. 1 (January 1962), pp. 76–108.

Rapkin, Chester. "New Towns for America: From Picture to Process," *The Journal of Finance*, Vol. 22, No. 2 (May 1967), pp. 208–19.

Ratcliff, Richard U. "A Restatement of Appraisal Theory," *The Appraisal Journal*, Vol. 32, Nos. 1 and 2 (January and April 1964).

Reiling, William S. "A Program for Joint Ventures," *The Mortgage Banker* (August 1971), pp. 24, 36–42.

Rose, Cornelius C., Jr. "Equity Participations," *The Mortgage Banker* (June 1968), pp. 44–47.

Rudolph, E. George. "The Installment Land Contract as a Junior Security," *Michigan Law Review*, Vol. 54, No. 7 (May 1956), pp. 929–52.

Schulkin, Peter A. "Construction Lending at Large Commercial Banks," *Real Estate Review* (Spring 1971), pp. 54–60.

Schwind, Robert L. "Land Trusts—A Real Estate Syndication Device," *Trusts and Estates* (July 1962), pp. 650–52.

Shenkel, William O. "Residential Net Ground Leases," *Journal of Property Management*, Vol. 29, No. 4 (March and April 1964), pp. 180–93.

Slayton, William L. "What's in Urban Renewal for Mortgage Bankers?" *The Mortgage Banker* (April 1962), pp. 22–25.

Smith, Halbert C. "Institutional Aspects of Interregional Mortgage Investment," *The Journal of Finance*, Vol. 23, No. 2 (May 1968), pp. 349–58.

Smith, J. W. Brabner. "The Financing of Large-Scale Rental Housing," *Law and Contemporary Problems* (Autumn 1938), pp. 60–81.

Sonnenblick, Jack E. "Shopping Center Financing," *Journal of Property Management,* Vol. 30, No. 6 (November–December 1965), pp. 303–6.

Spiezio, Nicholas J. "The Housing and Urban Development Act of 1970," *The Mortgage Banker* (February 1971), 12–19.

Stefaniak, Norbert J. "Management Policies of Real Estate Investment Trusts," *Journal of Property Management,* Vol. 33, No. 2 (March–April 1968), pp. 63–67.

Stevenson, Eric. "A Commitment Made and Kept: The (Life Insurance Companies') Urban Investment Program," *The Mortgage Banker* (May 1970), pp. 18–27.

Strunk, Norman. "A Federal System of Mutual Savings Banks?" *Savings and Loan News* (May 1963), pp. 36–52.

Sunderland, Lowell E. "Why Columbia Succeeded Where Others Failed," *The Mortgage Banker* (June 1970), pp. 10–20.

"The GNMA Mortgage-Backed Security," a special issue of *The Mortgage Banker* (May 1971) covering this topic.

"The Real Estate and Mortgage Investment Trust," a special issue of *The Mortgage Banker* (September 1970) covering this topic.

"The Two Faces of 221 (d) 3," *Savings and Loan News* (March 1968), pp. 30–35.

"Urban Renewal and Rehabilitation—Its Problems, Objectives, and Opportunities," *Savings and Loan News* (July 1962), pp. 26–35.

Waldron, William D. "Participatory Investment Reviewed," *The Mortgage Banker* (August 1971), pp. 44–49.

Warner, Arthur E., and Becker, Alvin G. "Condominium," *Business Topics,* Vol. 11, No. 4 (Autumn 1963), pp. 17–29.

Weil, S. Douglas "Land Leasebacks Move Up Fast as Financing Technique," *Real Estate Review* (Winter 1972), pp. 65–71.

Wendt, Paul F. "Large-Scale Community Development," *The Journal of Finance,* Vol. 22, No. 2 (May 1967), pp. 220–39.

Williamson, John C. "The Real Estate Investment Trust Act—The Catalyst Which is Making Real Estate 'Go Public'," *Journal of Property Management,* Vol. 27, No. 2 (Winter 1961), pp. 68–79.

SUGGESTED SOURCES FOR CURRENT DEVELOPMENTS

The Appraisal Journal. Published quarterly by the American Institute of Real Estate Appraisers, 36 So. Wabash Ave., Chicago 3.

Banking. Published monthly by the American Bankers Association, 5601 Chestnut Street, Philadelphia.

Casey, William J. *Real Estate Investment Transactions and Ideas.* New York: Institute for Business Planning, Inc. Looseleaf service published with current material. Also see volume titled *Real Estate Investment Forms.*

Federal Reserve Bulletin. Published monthly by the Board of Governors of the Federal Reserve System, Washington, D.C.; and Federal Reserve Bulletins published by the various Federal Reserve district banks.

Life Insurance Fact Book. Published annually by the Institute of Life Insurance, New York.

The Mortgage Banker. Published monthly by the Mortgage Bankers Association of America, Chicago.

Mutual Savings Banking. Published monthly by the National Association of Mutual Savings Banks, New York.

The National League Journal of Insured Savings Associations. Published monthly by the National League of Insured Savings Associations, Washington, D.C.

Proceedings of the annual conferences on savings and residential financing, sponsored by the United States Savings and Loan League, Chicago and Washington, D.C.

Proceedings of the annual conventions of the Mortgage Bankers Association of America, Chicago.

The Real Estate Analyst. Looseleaf statistical service published by Roy Wenzlick Research Corp., St. Louis.

Real Estate Review. Published quarterly by The Real Estate Institute of New York University, 89 Beach Street, Boston, Mass.

The Residential Appraiser. Published monthly by the Society of Real Estate Appraisers, 7 So. Dearborn St., Chicago 3.

Savings and Loan Fact Book. Published annually by the United States Savings and Loan League, Chicago and Washington, D.C.

Savings and Loan News. Published monthly, except semimonthly in August, by the United States Savings and Loan League, Chicago and Washington, D.C.

Title News. Published monthly by the American Title Association, Detroit, Michigan.

Various publications of governmental agencies, including particularly the reports of Congressional hearings, annual and special reports of the Federal Home Loan Bank Board and the Department of Housing and Urban Development, releases of the Veterans Administration, and the statistical abstracts of the United States.

CASE PROBLEMS

David, Philip. *Urban Land Development.* Homewood, Ill.: Richard D. Irwin, Inc., 1970.

Mao, James T. *Cases in Real Estate Finance,* Michigan Business Reports, No. 31. Ann Arbor, Mich., 1959.

Vidger, Leonard P. *Selected Cases and Problems in Real Estate.* Belmont, Calif.: Wadsworth Publishing Company, 1963.

Index

A

Absence of prepayment privilege, 84
Absentee ownership, 203, 364
Absorption of loan fee, 260
Abstract, 350, 354, 355
   companies, 353
   definition of, 355
   versus title insurance, 364
Abstractor's certificate, 356
Acceleration clause, 23
   absence of, 25
Accounting for leases, 166
Added title hazards, 363
Adjustments, 390
Administration of FNMA, 543
Advance commitments, 411, 530
Advance payments, 50
Advances
   to members, 447
   for taxes, 469
Advantages
   of cooperatives, 125
   for lessee, 147, 170
   for lessor, 147, 172
Advisory council, 449
Affiliates of Home Loan Bank system, 456
Alaska housing program, 579
Alternatives to strict foreclosure, 57
American Bankers Association, 279, 429
American housing problems, 555
American Institute of Certified Public Accountants, 167
Amortization
   of land trusts, 158
   plans, 49–51, 426

Amortized mortgage, 49
Amount of mortgages, 1
Annual plan, 307
Annual rest, 65
Applicant information, 317
Application form, 315
Appraisal
   an art, 330
   of conditions, 213
   for farm loans, 428
   by FHA, 211
   for financing, 330
   for GI loans, 510
   policies, 210
      of FHA, 499
   practices, 469
   process, 334
   records, 211
Appraising
   apartments, 344
   retail stores, 345
   single homes, 343
   special-purpose property, 345
   specific-use property, 346
   vacant land, 347
Arbitrary discounts, 333
Armchair appraisals, 340
Assessments, 415
Assignment
   of fee, 153
   of ground rents, 102
   of land contracts, 136
   of mortgage, 80
Assumption agreement, 76
   of mortgage, 76, 132, 316, 385

Index

B

Background
  of FSLIC, 461
  of HOLC, 467
Backstop, 444
Baltimore ground rents, 100
Bank
  lending on real estate, 217
  management, 445
Bases of mortgage decisions, 323
Bauvereine, 178
Below market interest rates, 479, 480, 482
Binder, 326, 360
Bipartisan board, 441
Black sheep, 285
Blank check trusts, 115
Blanket mortgage, 53
  policy, 382
Blind pool syndications, 294
Bond
  covenant, 112
  default, 112
  indenture, 110, 112
  or note, 28
  trustee, 113
Bonds, 109, 410
Book value of real estate, 194
Borrowed capital, 7
Branch offices, 247, 248
Broker as appraiser, 340
Brokerage of leases, 155
Building societies, 178
Business buildings, 408

C

Call privilege on bonds, 110
Cancellation
  of contracts, 276
  of leases, 165, 166
  of lien, 29
Capital
  grant, 564
  of Home Loan Banks, 442
Capitalization
  rates, 336
  of rent, 155
Causes of delinquency, 386
Century-old subdivision, 394
Certificate
  of appraisal, 212
  of investment, 456
  of purchase, 22
  of reasonable value, 510, 514
  of title, 350

Change
  in emphasis, 560
  of ownership, 384
  in savings bank policy, 223
Changing character
  of bank loans, 237
  of mortgages, 521
Chattel mortgage, 52
Chattels, 52
Chronic delinquency, 276
Church loans, 346
City
  growth, 4
  planning, 553
Clashes in personalities, 389
Coapplicants, 320
Code enforcement programs, 571
Cognovit note, 28
Collateralized loans, 447
Collections, 378
Collective
  farms, 2
  mortgages, 34
College housing loans, 578
Commercial
  banks, 217, 229, 431
  loan insurance, 307
  property loans, 273
  real estate, 156, 252
Commitment fee, 540, 547
Committed-institutional warehousing loan, 530
Committed-technical warehousing loan, 530
Common stock of FNMA, 535
Community renewal program, 570
Compensation to solicitors, 259
Complex nature of leases, 145
Condemnation clause, 162
Condition of property, 319
Conditional commitment, 326
Condominiums, 125
  for investment, 128
Conference of Bank Presidents, 449
Conflict of interests, 383
Connecticut plan, 164
Consent of mortgagee, 384
Consolidated bonds, 443
Construction
  financing under ground rents, 101
  loan fees, 41
  loans, 40, 41, 42, 106, 406
    and mechanics' liens, 106
  projects, 398
Contingency factor, 308, 321
Contract for deed, 129
Contradilution in trusts, 122
Contribution by FSLIC, 465

Index   593

Conversion of state-chartered associations, 457
Conveyance, voluntary, 74, 79
Cook County, Torrens system in, 352
Cooperative
 apartments, 122, 123, 125
 banks, 186
 housing, 578
Cooperative Management Housing Insurance Fund, 498
Corporate mortgage, 54
Cosigners, 320
Cost
 accounting, 278
 approach, 334
 of insurance, 463
 of loan origination, 278
 of servicing, 278
Country banks, 266
Covenants in bonds, 112
Creating new cities, 415
Credit, 7 ff.
 agencies, 316
 bureaus, 202
 "Cs" of, 202, 213
 rating of applicant, 316
 report, 261, 311, 316
 reserve system, 454
 unions, 290
Curbstoners, 355
Current
 assets, 112
 liabilities, 112
Cushion of safety, 322
Custody of property, 322

D

Data for appraisals, 335
Dayton plan, 187
Debentures, 297
 of FHA, 493
Debts of decedent, 36
Decline in savings bank mortgages, 223
Decrease in income, 387
Deed
 and money escrow, 368
 of trust, 36, 69, 112
Default, 55
 on bonds, 112
 of GI loans, 517
 by vendee, 138
Defeasance clause, 20
Defects in record, 358
Deficiency judgment, 57, 63, 68, 77
 laws against, 64
Delinquency
 causes of, 386

Delinquency—*Cont.*
 prevention of, 372
 study of, 276
Delinquent taxes, 380
Demand for mortgage funds, 520, 521
Demand mortgages, 47
Demolition grants, 571
Demonstration program administration, 574
Demonstration project grants, 570
Department of Housing and Urban Development, 475, 562 ff.
Departmentalization of mortgage banking, 257
Dependence upon FHA and VA, 263, 280
Deposits
 of members, 444
 of mutual savings bank, 219
 in savings and loans, 192
Depression blues, 388
Description
 of property, 23, 131
 of security, 110
Development construction projects, 398
Development projects, 395
Direct lending, 433, 434, 515, 516
Direct reduction mortgage, 49, 85
Direct sale, 253
Disadvantages of cooperatives, 125
Discharge
 of bond indenture, 112, 113
 of debt, 29
 of mechanics' lien, 107
Discount
 of junior mortgages, 92
 on lots, 402
Distribution of mortgage loans, 215, 244
Dividend policies of savings and loans, 188
Domestic troubles, 388
Double assignments, 80
Dower, 23
Down payment, 509
Drafting of leases, 146
Dual obligations of lenders, 372
Dummy corporations, 320
Durable goods, 8
Duress, 74
Dynamic nature of cities, 554

E

Easements, 368
Economic qualities of land, 6
Educational institutions, tax exempt, 176
Effect of lease on value, 154
Elderly and handicapped, 479, 480

594   Index

Eligible lenders, 505
Eligibility for membership, 448
Emergency statutes, 68, 88
Eminent domain, 113
Enabling acts, 457
Encroachments, 367
Equitable mortgage, 32, 34, 35, 36, 139, 165
Equity
  amount of, 322
  participations, 302
  of redemption, 20
  trusts, 115
    as an investment, 117
Escalator clause, 26
  in event of default, 27
Escrow, 368
  agent, 369
Estate loans, 289
Estoppel certificate, 80
Evolution of title information, 349
Examination of members, 450, 464
Exceptions, 367
Exchange trusts, 116
Exclusive contracts, 271
Exclusive outlets, 271
Existing trusts, 116
Expansion of title insurance coverage, 363
Expense schedule, 344
Experience of savings banks, 221
Experimental housing, 481
Extension agreement, 81
  alternative to, 82
Extra title fees, 362
  hazards of, 363

F

Face-lifting operations, 416
Failure
  to pass title, 137
  to service loans, 386
Fairless Hills, 417
Family
  budgets, 317
  income, 317
  loans, 289
Farm
  family operated, 421
  financing, 420, 421
  meaning of, 420
  mortgages, 235, 245
    purposes, 425
    sources of funds for, 430
    types of, 424
Farmers Home Administration, 433
Fear withdrawals, 220

Federal Deposit Insurance Corporation, 461
Federal Home Loan Bank system, 438
  supervision, 451
Federal Home Loan Mortgage Corporation, 466
Federal Housing Administration, 364, 475, 567
Federal Land Banks, 432
Federal National Mortgage Association, 215, 265, 524 ff., 534 ff., 568
  purchasing procedure, 539
  record, 543
  sales procedure, 541
  servicing of mortgages, 540
Federal Reserve Act, 233
Federal savings and loan associations, 201, 456, 472
Federal Savings and Loan Insurance Corporation, 193, 461
Fee
  mortgage, 153
  ownership certificate, 103
  paid by borrower, 272
  purchase option, 153
Fees, fines, and forfeitures, 181, 183
Filing of claims, 513
Financial irresponsibility, 389
Financing
  of buildings, 153, 406
  deals, 325
  development projects, 404
  farms, 420
  leaseholds, 145, 148
  management and liquidating functions, 544
  resales, 414
  sale of lots, 414
  special assistance functions, 545
  subleases, 151
  surveys, 564
Finder's fees, 248, 260, 285
First default, 378
First impression, 314
Five-man board, 441
Fixtures, 51, 52
Fluctuations in mortgage holdings, 235
Forbearance, 512
Forced savings, 186
Foreclosure
  clause, 80
  of deeds of trust, 69
  by entry, 70
    writ of, 70
  of junior mortgage, 97
  laws, 71
  parties to, 61
  sale, 61, 139

Foreclosure—*Cont.*
  strict, 56
  volume, 70
Foresight versus hindsight, 333
Forfeitures
  in building society, 181
  of equity, 138
Forms of notice, 32
40 percent plan, 123
Forward commitment, 528
Free rent, 139
French plan, 299
Front money, 302, 304
Frugality banks, 218
Full coverage demand, 359
Functions of solicitors, 258
Funding short terms, 425
Future advances, 38, 39, 42
Future of lease-back, 174

G

General neighborhood renewal plans, 569
Geographical distribution of mortgages, 235, 244
GI home loans, 503
Government National Mortgage Association, 269, 532, 544
  management and liquidating functions, 544
  special assistance functions, 545
Government ownership, 2
Grandfather clause, 356
Grants for urban planning assistance, 570, 574
Gratuity, 506
Ground rent assignment, 102
Ground rents, 100, 101, 102
Group control, 553
Growth
  of cities, 4
  of federal associations, 460
  of mortgage loans, 520
  of savings banks, 219
  of savings and loans, 214
Guarantee stock, 188

H

Hawaii-Kai development, 102
Hedge of GI home purchase, 507
Hedge versus rising prices, 119
Hierarchy of mortgages, 99
High percentage loans, 182
Hindsight in appraisals, 333
History
  of commercial banks, 231
  of FHA, 475

History—*Cont.*
  of mortgage lending by insurance companies, 241
  of real estate bonds, 109
Holding companies, 197
Home office operations, 250
Home Owners Loan Corporation, 77, 202, 203, 467
  appraisals, 469
  background, 467
  defaults, 471
  investments, 472
  loans, 468
  losses, 471, 473
  and other agencies, 471
  as secondary market, 473, 523
Homestead associations, 186, 456
Hoover conference, 438
Horseback appraisals, 211, 340
Hot money, 190
Housing Act
  of 1934, 461, 475, 477, 532
  of 1937, 576
  of 1949, 433, 463, 560
  of 1950, 478, 578
  of 1954, 478, 480, 486, 561, 567
  of 1959, 478, 481, 578
  of 1961, 481, 567
  of 1964, 479, 578
  of 1965, 480, 573
  of 1966, 479, 574, 579
  of 1968, 188, 206, 229, 397, 434, 479 ff., 537, 565, 575, 578
  of 1970, 205, 434, 466, 504, 532, 534, 538
Housing and Home Finance Agency, 475, 562
Housing and Urban Development, 475
  administrative subdivisions, 562 ff.

I

Illness, 387
Ills of real estate finance, 13
Improvement bonds, 406
Improvement costs of development project, 405
Improvements directed by vendee, 141
In-and-outers, 238
Income
  approach, 335
  potential of bonds, 111
  property, 312, 380
  shares, 187
  statements, 312
  taxes, 168
Incorporation of building societies, 179
Indemnity policies, 272

Independent appraisals, 341
Individual lenders, 287, 288, 290
Individual owners of farm mortgages, 430
Individual purchasers of mortgages, 265
Industrial property, 346
Inexperience of buyer and seller, 324
Inflation, 4
Inflationary effect of warehousing, 532
Influence of FHA, 412
Informal application, 312
Informal extension agreement, 82
Inspection of security, 275, 374
Instability of real estate values, 439
Installment
  commitment, 318
  sales contract, 129, 303
  thrift shares, 187
Institutional
  buyers, 265
  commitments, 528, 530
  investors, 411
  savings, 254
Institutional Securities Corporation, 228
Insurance, 381, 506
  of accounts, 461
  clause, 79, 132
  commercial mortgage loans, 307
  companies, 240, 431
  lease guaranty, 307
  records, 382
  settlements, 383
  and taxes, 510
Insured loans, 305, 477, 506
Insured mortgages, 305, 434
  fear of, 496
Interest rates, 10, 225
  effect of FHA on, 495 ff.
Interest covered by mortgage, 16
Interim mortgages, 121
Interstate Land Sales Full Disclosure Act, 397
Intervening interests, 21
Intervening liens, 41, 44, 46, 85
Investment
  in farms, 420
  by HOLC, 472
  real estate, 164, 251, 252
  trusts, 115
  by U.S. Treasury, 472, 535 ff., 544

J

Joint venture, 304
Judgment note, 28
Judgments, 32
  and land contracts, 141
Judicial sale, 60

Junior financing, 90
Junior lien, 42, 62, 63, 90
Junior position of leasehold mortgage, 149

K

Kicker, 121
Kinds of mortgages, 34
Klaman, Saul B., 263 n

L

Laissez faire, 17
Land
  acquisition, 394 ff., 400
  assembly, 555
  contracts, 129, 414
  ownership, 553
  planning, 412, 569, 574
  sales disclosure requirements, 397
  trust certificates, 156
  trust as mortgage, 158
Large corporations as developers, 418
Large investors in mortgages, 364
Late payments, 87, 378
Laws against deficiency judgments, 68
Lawyers Title Insurance Corporation, 353
Lease
  guaranty insurance, 307
  meaning of, 145
  and mortgage, 150
  and option contract, 142
  and release, 400
  terms, 158, 161
  in urban renewal, 566
Leaseback, 161
Leasehold
  bonds, 109, 148, 151, 159
  formulas, 155
  meaning of, 149
  title policy, 359
Leases in urban renewal, 566
Leasing of farms, 422
Legal character of lease contract, 165
Legal definition of abstract, 355
Legal nature
  of land trust, 157
  of loan application, 310
Legal opinion of title, 357
Legal theory, 17
Legals, 220
Legislation affecting savings banks, 220, 229
Lending area, 460
Lending operations, 459
Lending plans for veterans, 506, 508

Lending policies of savings and loans, 199
Level payments, 424, 425, 509
Leverage, 118
Levittown, 417
Licensed abstracters, 356
Lien
  cancelled, 29
  theory, 19
Life insurance
  assets, 240
  companies, 240
  with loan applications, 320
Life Insurance Fact Book, 240
Lifting clause, 99
Limitations on land ownership, 553
Limited prepayment, 249, 272
Line of credit, 448
Lintner, John, 218 n, 226
Liquidated damages, 138
Liquidating lease, 161
Liquidation value of bonds, 111
Liquidity
  needs, 190, 191
  requirements, 191, 445
Loan
  acquisition profits, 260
  applications, 212, 310
  collection, 372, 378
  correspondents, 248, 259
  expense, 325
  fees, 249, 259, 260
  by FSLIC, 462, 465
  guarantee, 375
  insurance, 305, 375
  percentages, 204
  plans, 458
  servicing, 86, 284
    costs, 391
  terms, 342
  turnover, 375
Loan Guaranty Service, 518
Loan-to-value ratios, 237
Local sources of funds, 440
Limited partnerships, 294 ff.
Location of Home Loan Banks, 442
Long-term lease, 145
Lookers, 310
Loss reserves
  mortgage insurance, 308
  title insurance, 361
Losses
  of HOLC, 473
  measuring of, 195
  under private mortgage insurance, 308
  under title insurance, 360 ff.
  under Title I, 489
Low and moderate incomes, 481 ff., 567

Low percentage loans, 439
Low-rent public housing, 576
Lower-cost houses, 476

M

Management
  of condominiums, 127
  of cooperatives, 124
  factor, 336, 337
  and liquidating function, 544
Manager-operator, 422
Mandel plan, 300
Market
  for junior mortgages, 94
  for land contracts, 143
Market approach, 335, 336, 343, 348
Mass selling, 393, 396
Massachusetts trust, 125, 157
Master plan, 554
Master policy, 306
Maturity
  of advances, 447
  of loans, 204
    GI, 508
  of mortgages, 47
  of shares, 184
  of Title II loans, 491
Mechanics' liens, 104, 141, 142, 363
  discharge of, 107
  and mortgages, 105
Member Appraisal Institute, 340
Merchandisers of mortgages, 257
Merging of mortgages, 93, 98
Methods of acquiring mortgages, 238
Methods of financing mortgages, 262
Milkers, 65, 78
Minimum standards, 557
Miscellaneous sources of funds, 282, 297
Miscellaneous types of securities, 297
Mixed trusts, 116
Monetization of mortgages, 523
Money and deed escrow, 368
Money-good loan, 321
Money lender's escrow, 368
Money partner, 304
Moral hazard, 25, 201, 423
Moratorium laws, 87
Mortgage
  adjustments, 74
  assignment of, 80
  assumption of, 76
  banking, 257, 263
    problems, 279
    profits, 278
  blanket, 53
  brokers, 282
  chattel, 52

Mortgage—*Cont.*
  clause
    in insurance, 79
    in land contract, 134
  for construction, 40
  contents, 22
  decisions, 323
  default, 55
  definition, 16
  experience of insurance companies, 244
  experience of savings banks, 221
  files, 376
  foreclosure, 56
  forms, 22
  for future advances, 38, 39
  insurance companies, 305
  inventory, 529
  kinds of, 34
  loan brokers, 282
  loan department, 247
  loan servicing, 371
  loans by banks, 231, 232
  maturity date of, 47
  packaged, 51
  recasting of, 85
  record, 31
  release of, 83
  specialists, 285
  title policy, 359
  trusts, 115, 116, 117
    expansion, 121
  turnover, 206
  warehousing, 529, 531
Mortgage-backed security program, 547
Mortgage Bankers Association of America, 154, 257, 263
  Research Committee Trends Reports, 278
Mortgage Insurance Corporation, 306
Mortgagee title insurance, 358
Mutual Mortgage Insurance Fund, 494
Mutual savings banks, 218
Mutuality of savings and loans, 192

N

National Association of Mutual Savings Banks, 221
National Association of Real Estate Boards, 146, 294
National bank law, 233
National banks, 217, 233, 234
National Bureau of Economic Research, 244, 249
National farm loan associations, 432
National Housing Act; *see* Housing Act
National Housing Partnerships, 575
National mortgage associations, 496, 532
National mortgage market, 264
Nationalization of interest rates, 11
Negative nature of regulation, 453
Negotiation for loan, 324
Neighborhood, 130, 203
  development programs, 565
  facilities, 573
Net defined income, 303
New charter of FNMA, 527, 534
New cities, 415, 417, 418
New patterns of financing, 328
Nonbusiness loans, 289
Nonexempt investors, 169
Normal value, 429, 510
Note or bond, 28
Notice
  of payment due, 87, 378
  of sale, 68
  in savings banks, 220
Nuisance lien, 108
Nuisance payments, 138
Nursing homes, 481

O

Objectives
  of credit reserves, 454
  of FHA, 476
  of Torrens system, 352
Office of Interstate Land Sales Registration, 397
Off-standard property loans, 267, 273, 286, 327
100 percent
  loans, 313, 478, 504, 509, 567, 578
  location, 168
  plan, 123
One-night-a-month associations, 197
One-year mortgages, 47
Open-end mortgage, 38, 43, 513
Open-market offer, 254
Open space land, 573
Operating costs of subdivisions, 402, 413
Operating results of FHA, 494
Option, 401
  to purchase, 142
  to repurchase, 35
Optional savings shares, 187
Originating fee, 249
Outlet for savings, 4
Overbuilding, 114
Owner's title policy, 359
Ownership of real estate, 251
Oxford Provident Building Association, 179

P

Packaged mortgage, 51, 53
Parasitical subdivision, 393, 399
Partial amortization, 426
Partial prepayment, 208
Partial release, 83
  of security, 367
Participants in GI loans, 516
Participation mortgage, 45
Parties
  to bond issue, 112
  to foreclosure, 61
Partnership in farms, 421
Party in possession, 33
Pass-through securities, 549
Past-due notices, 87
Patterns of real estate finance, 12
Payments
  under land contract, 134, 139
  on mortgages, 132
Penalty for prepayment, 208
Pennsylvania ground rents, 101
Pension funds, 268
Percentage lease, 155
Peter Cooper Village, 416
Photograph, 451
Physical qualities of land, 6
Planned communities, 574
Plowing back earnings, 411
Police
  power, 557
  protection, 2
Possession
  as notice, 33
  significance of, 64
Power
  of attorney, 86
  of sale, 67
Practical politics, 441
Preferred stock, 299, 410
  of FNMA, 535
Preliminary costs of development, 405
Premiums for loans, 181
Prepaid shares, 187
Prepayment
  clause, 223 ff., 510
  penalties, 84
  privilege, 50, 83, 249, 272, 427
    absence of, 84
Prepayments, 207, 223, 510
  on land contracts, 134
Present value of future rentals, 155
Pressure loans, 327
Prices, determinants of, 9
Pricing of lots, 401, 414
Pride of ownership, 373
Prior approval, 262

Prior lien mortgage, 100
Priority of lease and mortgage, 150
Private
  capital, 556
  enterprise, 1
  mortgage insurance, 307
  offering, 444
  placements, 253, 255
  subsidies, 557
  syndicates, 291
Probate escrow, 370
Profit escrow, 369
Property management, 251
Proposed federal chartering, 229
Proprietary interest in business, 176
Protections to mortgage holder, 149
Provision for deed, 135
Provisions
  of long-term holder, 148, 149
  of long-term leases, 146
Prudent investment theory, 165
Public
  building financing, 409
  facility loans, 573, 578
  housing administration, 559, 576
  subsidies, 558, 559
Purchase
  of assets, 463
  and lease-back, 161, 302
  of mortgage
    by grantee, 75
    by grantor, 78
  option, 149, 159, 166
Purchase-money mortgage, 32, 35, 45, 112, 288, 325
  and mechanics' liens, 105
  second mortgage, 91, 384
Purchasers of mortgages, 265
Purchasing trusts, 116
Purpose
  of appraisal, 342
  of GI loans, 507
  of mortgage loans, 213
  of recording, 32

Q–R

Qualifications of appraisers, 338
Quality of construction, 440
Raiding, 29, 261
Rating sheet
  for borrowers, 202
  for neighborhoods, 203
Real estate
  bonds, 109
  brokers, 325
  contract, 129
  credit, 8

Real estate—*Cont.*
  investment trusts, 114
    management of, 115
  law, 17, 357
  limited partnership syndicates, 294
  ownership, 251
  prices, 9
  syndicates, 291, 292, 294
  taxes, 50
  trusts, 114, 300
Real property, 6
  law, 17
Reappraisal of property, 373
Reasonable value, 510
Reasons for loan applications, 311
Recasting of mortgages, 85
Receivership, 66
Reconstruction Finance Corporation, 468, 523 ff.
Reconstruction Finance Mortgage Company, 523
Recording
  of land contracts, 140
  of leases, 150, 152
  of mortgages, 31
Recovery program of FHA, 476
Red flags, 511
Redemption
  equity of, 20
  statutory, 21
Redemption clause in second mortgage, 99
Redevelopment programs, 554
Refinancing
  of cooperatives, 124
  of farms, 427
Refunding of farm mortgages, 425
Regulation versus management, 453
Rehabilitation financing, 428, 572
Reinsurance of title, 361
Release
  of grantor, 77
  of mortgage, 83
  partial, 83
  of security, 319
Remainder value, 173
Remnant sales of lots, 401
Renewal option, 149, 172
Rent
  capitalization, 155
  clause, 65
  potential, 331
  receipts, 3
  supplements, 482
Rental on long-term leases, 147
Rental trust certificates, 159
Repurchase options, 166
Resale of lots, 414

Research Committee Trends Reports, 278
Reserve ratios, 191, 214
Reserves, use of, 192
Restrictions
  upon assignments, 136
  upon loans by insurance companies, 242, 244
  upon savings bank lending, 220
Restrictive covenants, absence of, 168
RFC; *see* Reconstruction Finance Corporation
Rights of tenants, 133
Riis, Jacob, 555
Ringing doorbells, 261
Risk
  of element in mortgages, 193, 227, 336
  experience of savings banks, 226
  factor, 336
  private mortgage insurance, 308
  rating of loan applications, 321
Riskless investments, 196
Road ahead, 579
Rural housing loans, 433
Rural origins of real property law, 17

S

Safe harbor rules, 295
Safe loan, 371
Sale
  by advertisement, 68
  and buy-back, 303
  of contracts, 402
  of land contract, 143
  and lease-back, 161
  of lots, 130
  of property, 57
    GI, 515
Sales to establish losses, 172
Sandwich lease, 151
Satisfaction piece, 30
Saulnier, R. J., 244 n
Savings
  banks, 218
  in commercial banks, 230
  and loan associations, 178, 199
  members, 185
Second guessing, 324
Second mortgage, 13, 44, 287
  association, 196
  company, 301
  frowned upon by FHA, 96
  as supplemental security, 94, 95
Secondary market for mortgages, 365, 520, 522, 534
  financing under FHLMC, 466
  financing under FNMA, 535

Index 601

Section 220 loans, 478, 567
Securities and Exchange Commission, 13, 95, 167, 254, 293
Security
 for bonds, 111
 map, 203
 regulation, 254
 search for, 3
Seizin and warranty, 23
Selecting sites, 416
Self-imposed restrictions, 244
Self-servicing loans, 371
Sell out and get out, 403
Senior citizens housing loans, 578
Senior mortgage, 96
Senior Real Estate Appraiser, 340
Senior Residential Appraiser, 340
Serial association, 184
Service of HOLC, 473
Servicing
 costs, 278
 department, 275
 Federal Land Bank loans, 432
 fee, 248, 278
 for FNMA, 540
 of mortgages, 540
Settlement of claims, 493
Share-accumulation sinking-fund plan, 182
Share loans, 184
Sharing the blame, 380
Shell loan, 509
Shifting population, 5
Shopping centers, 408
Short check of record, 44
Short-term
 abstract, 356
 financing, 425, 439
 lease, 145
 loans, 410, 425, 541
Side-line business, 260
Signatures on land contract, 131
Single-season subdivisions, 394
Sinking fund, 112, 427
Site selection, 416
Sleeper clause, 24
Slum areas, 344, 555
Slum clearance, 478, 561
Social control, 552
Social impact of warehousing, 531
Society of Real Estate Appraisers, 340
Soliciting business, 258
Sound loans, 371
Sources
 of business, 284
 of credit information, 316
 of farm capital, 421

Sources—*Cont.*
 of funds for Home Loan Banks, 442, 443
 of funds for lease-banks, 163
 of savings, 287
Special assistance functions, 545
Special federal grants, 564, 567 ff., 570, 571, 572, 574
Special-purpose real estate, 273, 345
Special Risk Insurance Fund, 498
Special warranty deed, 135, 136
Specific-use property, 346
Speculation
 in building societies, 180
 in equities, 156
 in ground rents, 102
Splitting the fee, 303
Springfield plan, 49, 426
Stages in loan servicing, 385
Standard amortization plan, 49
Standardization of interest rates, 11
Standby commitments, 305, 528
State supervision, 450
Statute of limitations, 77
Statutory covenants, 22, 23
Statutory redemption, 21, 69, 70
Stock
 of Federal Home Loan Banks, 442
 of Federal Home Loan Mortgage Corporation, 466
 of FNMA, 535 ff.
Stocks, 298, 410
Straight loans, 207, 459
Street improvements, 405
Strict foreclosure, 56, 140
Stuyvesant Town, 416
Subdivisions, 393
Subject to, 78
Subleases, 151
Subordinated debentures, 104, 110
Subordinated notes, 538
Subordination clause, 46
Substandard housing, 556
Summation values, 337
Supervision, 451, 464
 absence of, 278
 of commercial banks, 236
 of mortgage banks, 278
Supplemental security, 319
Supply of mortgage funds, 521
Sureties in extension agreement, 81
Surveys, 367
Sweat equity, 143, 509
Syndicates, 291, 403
 limited partnerships, 294
 private, 291
 for small investors, 292

T

Tail sheets, 364
Take-home pay, 318
Take-out letter, 274, 412
Tandem plan, 549
Tax
   advantages to lessee, 170
   exemption of lessor, 168, 174, 175, 176
   Reform Act of 1969, 296
   sale, 59
   shelters, 119
   title, 59
Taxable business lease income, 169
Taxes, 380, 510
   in default, 58, 380
   under land contract, 132, 134
Tenancy versus ownership, 3
Tenants, rights of, 133
Term mortgages, 48, 207, 425
Terminating association, 180
Termination of leases, 152
Three approaches to appraisal, 334
Three-way appraisals, 469, 500
Thrift, 8
   shares, 187
Tight money, 26
Title
   analysis, 349
   evidence, 349, 514
   examination, 350
   at foreclosure sale, 61
   hazards, 354
   opinion, 349, 351, 357
   plant, 355
   theory, 19
Title insurance, 351
   binder, 360
   commitment, 360
   companies, 365
   losses, 360
   meaning of, 358
   policies, 358
Title I, FHA, 476, 487
   absence of control under, 490
   institutions using, 489
   losses under, 489
Title II, FHA, 476, 491
   use of, 492
Title III, FHA, 496
Topography, 404
Torrens system, 351, 352
Traditions of real estate finance, 10
Transportation, 404
Treasury loan to FSLIC, 465
Treasury-owned stock
   of FNMA, 535

Treasury-owned stock—*Cont.*
   of Home Loan Banks, 442, 443
Treasury support of FNMA, 535, 537
Trustee for real estate, 112, 113
Trusteed funds, 231
Trustees of savings banks, 219
Types
   of accounts, 187
   of farm mortgages, 424
   of institutions using FHA, 494
   of leases, 154
   of loans, 271
   of property, 200
   of real estate loans, 237
   of securities, 297
Typical FHA home loan, 493

U

Uncommitted-technical loan, 530
Underlying fee, 153
Undivided profits, 188, 214
Uniform mortgage law, 18
Uninsured portion of account, 462
Union College, 162
Unique nature of real estate, 13
Unit owners' association, 127
U.S. Housing Authority, 559
Unpaid assessments, 406
Unrecorded liens, 63
Unrelated business taxable income, 169
Unusual uses of loan application, 316
Upset price, 60
Urban
   areas, 5
   beautification, 573
   planning assistance, 570
   redevelopment, 553, 554
   renewal, 563
Uses of land contracts, 130
Usury laws, 92
Utilities in development projects, 406

V

Vacancy allowances, 344
Vacant land, 331, 347
Valuation report, 498
Value, 322
   and price, 332
   trends, 4
Variable interest rates, 26, 196, 209
Vendee in land contract, 131
Vendee's lien, 36
Vendor in land contract, 131
Vendor's lien, 35
Veterans' financing, 503

Volume
 of direct lending, 516
 of farm mortgages, 435
 of FHA loans, 494
 of foreclosures, 70
 of GI loans, 516, 517
 of HOLC loans, 470
 of loans serviced by mortgage companies, 263
 of mortgages in banks, 234
Voluntary conveyance, 74, 79, 97, 513
Voluntary trusts, 179

W

Waiver clause, 407
Waiver of mortgage, 152
Walk-in customer, 258
Warehousing
 in bank system, 531
 of mortgages, 529
Warranty deed, 75
Waste, 67, 81
Weak owners, 440
Weaknesses
 of cooperatives, 125
 of Title I, 490
Wholesale financing of developments, 409
Windshield appraisals, 211, 340
Withdrawal practices, 183
Wraparound mortgage, 304
Wrigley, Edmund, 182, 394 n
Writ of entry, 70
Written leases, 422

DATE DUE